The Legacy of Ronald Dworkin

The Legacy of Ronald Dworkin

Edited by Wil Waluchow
and
Stefan Sciaraffa

OXFORD
UNIVERSITY PRESS

OXFORD
UNIVERSITY PRESS

Oxford University Press is a department of the University of Oxford. It furthers
the University's objective of excellence in research, scholarship, and education
by publishing worldwide. Oxford is a registered trademark of Oxford University
Press in the UK and certain other countries.

Published in the United States of America by Oxford University Press
198 Madison Avenue, New York, NY 10016, United States of America.

Library of Congress Cataloging-in-Publication Data

Names: Waluchow, Wilfrid J., editor. | Sciaraffa, Stefan, editor.
Title: The legacy of Ronald Dworkin / Edited by Wil Waluchow
and Stefan Sciaraffa.
Description: New York : Oxford University Press, 2016. | Includes
bibliographical references and index.
Identifiers: LCCN 2015039298 | ISBN 9780190466411 ((hardback) : alk. paper)
Subjects: LCSH: Dworkin, Ronald. | Law—Philosophy. | Justice.
Classification: LCC K230.D92 L44 2016 | DDC 340/.1—dc23 LC record available at
http://lccn.loc.gov/2015039298

3 5 7 9 8 6 4 2
Printed by Edwards Brothers Malloy, United States of America

Note to Readers

This publication is designed to provide accurate and authoritative information in regard to
the subject matter covered. It is based upon sources believed to be accurate and reliable
and is intended to be current as of the time it was written. It is sold with the understanding
that the publisher is not engaged in rendering legal, accounting, or other professional
services. If legal advice or other expert assistance is required, the services of a competent
professional person should be sought. Also, to confirm that the information has not
been affected or changed by recent developments, traditional legal research techniques
should be used, including checking primary sources where appropriate.

*(Based on the Declaration of Principles jointly adopted by a Committee of the
American Bar Association and a Committee of Publishers and Associations.)*

You may order this or any other Oxford University Press publication
by visiting the Oxford University Press website at www.oup.com.

CONTENTS

CONTRIBUTORS

Lawrence A. Alexander is the Warren Distinguished Professor at the University of San Diego School of Law, Legal Research Center.

Aditi Bagchi is a Professor of Law at Fordham University School of Law.

David O. Brink is a Distinguished Professor in the Philosophy Department of the University of California, San Diego.

Thomas Christiano is a Professor in the Department of Philosophy at the University of Arizona.

Candice Delmas is an Assistant Professor of Philosophy and Political Science at Northeastern University and the Associate Director of the Politics, Philosophy, and Economics Program.

Luís Duarte d'Almeida is Reader in Jurisprudence at the University of Edinburgh.

David Dyzenhaus is Professor of Law and Philosophy at the University of Toronto Faculty of Law.

Christopher Essert is Assistant Professor in the Faculty of Law at Queen's University in Kingston, Ontario.

Michael Giudice is Associate Professor in the Department of Philosophy at York University, Toronto, Ontario.

Daniel Halliday is a Lecturer in Political Philosophy in the School of Historical and Philosophical Studies at the University of Melbourne.

Kenneth Einar Himma is a Professor in the Department of Philosophy at Seattle Pacific University.

Joseph Raz is a Professor at Columbia Law School, and a Professor at King's College London.

Connie S. Rosati is an Associate Professor in the Department of Philosophy at the University of Arizona.

Lawrence G. Sager is the Alice Jane Drysdale Sheffield Regents Chair at The University of Texas School of Law.

Stefan Sciaraffa is an Associate Professor of Philosophy at McMaster University.

Hamish Stewart is a Professor in the Faculty of Law at the University of Toronto.

François Tanguay-Renaud is an Associate Professor at Osgoode Hall Law School and in the Graduate Faculty of the Department of Philosophy at York University in Toronto, Ontario.

Wil Waluchow is a Professor of Philosophy at McMaster University and the Senator William McMaster Chair in Constitutional Studies.

EDITOR'S INTRODUCTION

The Legacy of Ronald Dworkin (collected essays)

Wil Waluchow and Stefan Sciaraffa,* editors.

In June 2014, the McMaster University Program in Legal Philosophy sponsored a conference titled *The Legacy of Ronald Dworkin* (lawconf.mcmaster.ca). The conference featured ten keynote addresses and thirty-one conference presentations culled from a pool of about eighty submissions. These presentations touched upon many aspects of Ronald Dworkin's wide-ranging contributions to philosophy, including his theory of value, political philosophy, philosophy of international law, and legal philosophy. The present volume comprises sixteen of these papers (eight keynotes and eight conference presentations).

The volume's organizing principle and theme reflects Dworkin's self-conception as a builder of a unified theory of value. The broad outlines of Dworkin's system can be found in a number of passages from his work, including the following:

> We all have unstudied moral convictions, almost from the beginning of our lives. These are mainly carried in concepts whose origin and development are issues for anthropologists and intellectual historians. We inherit these concepts from parents and culture and, possibly, to some degree through genetic species disposition. As young children we deploy mainly the idea of fairness, and then we acquire and deploy other, more sophisticated and pointed moral concepts: generosity, kindness, promise keeping, courage, rights, and duties. Sometime later we add political concepts to our moral repertoire: we speak of law, liberty, and democratic ideals. We need much more detailed moral opinions when we actually confront a wide variety of moral challenges in family, social, commercial, and political life. We form these through interpretation of our abstract concepts that is mainly unreflective. We unreflectively interpret each in the light of the others. That is, interpretation knits values together.[1]

We catch a glimpse of Dworkin's hedgehog in the passage's last two sentences. There, Dworkin asserts that in response to practical challenges, we refine our

---

*We would like to thank the Social Sciences and Humanities Research Council of Canada, McMaster University, and Osgoode Hall Law School for their generous support of the 2014 McMaster Legal Philosophy Conference: *The Legacy of Ronald Dworkin* (lawconf.mcmaster.ca).

[1] Dworkin (2011: 101).

initial unstudied moral and political concepts by knitting them together with other value-concepts. That is, we interpret the requirements of each discrete value-concept so that they fit with and support the requirements of our other value-concepts, including not only the sundry moral and political concepts alluded to above, but also value-concepts from other practical domains. For Dworkin, doing moral, political, or legal philosophy is in large part to engage in this value-concept integrating activity, but in a reflective way.

The volume's first section, Part I, "The Unity of Value," addresses the most abstract and general aspect of Dworkin's work—the unity of value thesis that Dworkin broaches in the passage above. Our hope is that by addressing this material in the volume's first section, we will encourage the reader to keep in mind that Dworkin's corpus is informed and integrated by the unity of value thesis. Joseph Raz's contribution is the lone entry in this first section. Despite his status as a leading proponent of exclusive legal positivism and an incisive critic of Dworkin's non-positivist legal theory, Raz offers a highly sympathetic and nuanced exploration of Dworkin's unity of value thesis. As we hope Raz's contribution and our discussion below of his and the other contributions to the volume illustrate, Dworkin's practical philosophy rests on a web of interconnected and mutually supportive theories of truth, the nature of value, the semantics of value-claims, and how such claims can be justified.

The volume's second section, Part II, "Political Values: Legitimacy, Authority, and Collective Responsibility," addresses Dworkin's contributions to political philosophy. Dworkin holds that political concepts, such as the concepts of law, liberty, and democratic governance enumerated in the passage above, comprise a distinct subset of moral concepts. Namely, political concepts are those moral concepts that pertain to the values realized by collective entities, such as states and other associations to which we belong, rather than our individual actions or characters.[2] The contributions to the volume's second section address Dworkin's discussions of a number of such political concepts, including authority, civil disobedience, the legitimacy of states and the international legal system, distributive justice, collective responsibility, and Dworkin's master value of dignity and the associated values of equal concern and respect.

The volume's third section, Part III, "General Jurisprudence: Contesting the Unity of Law and Value," addresses various aspects of Dworkin's general theory of law. As we shall see, Dworkin held that law is a kind of value, located in its distinct place in the web of interdependent and interdefined values described in his unity of value thesis. As Dworkin puts it in his later writings, he defends a one-system view of law, according to which law is not a normative system distinct from other values, particularly moral, but rather law is part of one larger system of value. This section comprises responses to this one-system view—some sympathetic and others highly critical.

The volume's fourth and final section, Part IV, "Value in Law," comprises pieces that offer accounts of the structure and defining values of discrete areas of law.

---

[2] Id. 327-329.

To put it in widely used terms that (as we discuss below) Dworkin might resist, these pieces are contributions to normative jurisprudence rather than general jurisprudence—more specifically, the normative jurisprudence of constitutional law, the law of contract, and procedural law. Given the systematic and unitary nature of Dworkin's theory of value, it should not be surprising that the border between Dworkin's political philosophy and his normative jurisprudence is porous. For example, Daniel Halliday's contribution challenges the justice of a legal regime that would allow unlimited intergenerational transfer of wealth via bequests. Hence, it both addresses the law of wills and estates and Dworkin's theory of distributive justice, yet we have placed it in the volume's political philosophy section. Similarly, Aditi Bagchi's piece defends a theory of contractual interpretation based on Dworkin's account of authority, and Hamish Stewart criticizes and offers an alternative to Dworkin's claim that fairness and accuracy in fact finding are the key defining underlying values of procedural law. Yet, we have placed these pieces in the volume's final section that addresses Dworkin's normative jurisprudence.

No doubt, good arguments could be made that some of the pieces placed in the volume's final section (e.g., Stewart's and Bagchi's) could have been place in its second section, and vice versa (e.g., Halliday's). Our guiding principle in this regard is that the volume's final section should comprise contributions that focus on the fundamental structure and values of discrete bodies of law. Thus, for example, we grouped Halliday's piece with the contributions pertaining to Dworkin's political philosophy rather than the volume's final section on the grounds that although his piece has implications for the justice of tax policy and laws governing intergenerational transfer, its primary objective is not to explicate the fundamental structure or underlying defining values of a discrete body of law.

There are many arguments and insights contained with this volume that we do not discuss in this introduction despite their cogency and importance. In part, this is due to space constraints. Also, this material ably speaks for itself, and, hence, there is no need to rehearse it all here. Rather, our main objective in what follows is to illustrate the systematic nature of Dworkin's practical philosophy by identifying key Dworkinian threads that run through and unify the various arguments that our contributors have advanced. To this end, we sketch only some of the main arguments from the works collected here, with an eye to situating them both with respect to Dworkin's arguments that are directly relevant and his systematic theory of value. Paralleling the structure of our volume, the following discussion comprises four sections that respectively speak to the volume's four parts and their associated themes: the unity of value; political values; value in general jurisprudence; and value in law.

1. The Unity of Value

As noted above, Raz's contributes the lone entry in our volume's first section. In this piece, Raz seeks to clarify Dworkin's unity of value thesis, and he identifies a research agenda comprising questions that Dworkin has left for us. To this end, Raz sets out a general statement of the unity of value thesis and then explores two interpretations of it. As a preface to his statement of the unity of value thesis, Raz notes that Dworkin's term *value* refers to a broad normative category that includes reasons, norms, virtues, and values in the narrower, more common sense of the term. Raz also cites the following two passages from Dworkin:

> [T]he various concepts and departments of value are interconnected and mutually supportive.[3]

> The truth of any true moral judgment consists in the truth of an indefinite number of other moral judgments and its truth provides part of what constitutes the truth of any of those others.[4]

Although the latter statement refers specifically to moral judgments, Raz takes it to be a particular application and elaboration of the relationship between the departments and categories of values described in the first passage cited immediately above.

Raz formulates Dworkin's unity of value thesis as follows:

> Given what values are, each of them and each value proposition or value belief rests on a constitutive case, and the values included in these cases themselves rest on further constitutive cases.(9)[5]

In sum, as Raz reconstructs it, Dworkin's unity of value thesis holds that the truth-conditions of any value claim refer to other true value statements. That is, for any value-claim, it is true only if and because its truth is supported by other true value-claims.

A large part of Raz's discussion is an exploration of the connection that Dworkin draws between the unity of value thesis and his idea of constructive interpretation. As is well known, Dworkin holds that constructive interpretation comprises three elements:

> Interpretation can therefore be understood, analytically, to involve three stages. We interpret social practices, first, when we individuate those practices: when we take ourselves to be engaged in legal rather than literary interpretation. We interpret, second, when we attribute some package of purposes to the genre or subgenre we identify as pertinent, and, third, when

---

[3] Id. 10.

[4] Id. 117.

[5] Compare Raz's statement of Dworkin's unity of value thesis with his claim that practical reasons are facts that constitute the case that the actions for which they are reasons are valuable. Bear in mind that, as Raz notes, Dworkin would characterize assertions of the form "A has a reason to phi" as value-claims. See, e.g., Raz (2011: 13): "A normative practical reason is a fact that actions of a certain kind have properties that can give a point or a purpose to their performance, properties that make it possible for people to perform those actions because they posses them, and where actions so undertaken are intelligible because of that fact." See also Id. 36: "Reasons for action, I will assume, are facts that constitute a case for (or against) the performance of the action."

we try to identify the best realization of that package of purposes on some particular occasion.[6]

The unity of value thesis figures in the second and third stages of constructive interpretation. In the second stage, the interpreter must look to values external to the practice in question to locate the practice's purposes or, as Dworkin sometimes puts the same idea, the practice's values. And, in the third, the interpreter must look to these underlying purposes or values to determine what the practice requires in particular cases. For instance, on this view, to specify the underlying values and requirements of the practice of acting with courtesy, one must look to values other than courtesy (e.g., respect).[7] In sum, for Dworkin, any value-claim is justified in terms of a network of all other value-claims, each component claim of which is justified in the same way. Hence, no set of values plays a foundational justificatory role.

A key question Raz raises is whether the most plausible reconstruction of Dworkin's unity of value thesis assigns a merely epistemic role to constructive interpretation or an epistemic and innovative role. Raz labels the merely epistemic reading as the Object-Dependence Thesis (ODT), which he formulates as follows:

> Truths about value are independent of any single person's view about what values there are; the constitutive case for them consists of values or propositions about values.(16)

On this view, truths about value are mind-independent in the following robust sense: Dworkinian interpretive reasoning with respect to the relevant initial set of unruly and inconsistent beliefs about value (perhaps an agent's beliefs or beliefs widely accepted within her community) provides practical agents with epistemic access to truths about such values, but such reasoning, even if fully informed and idealized, is not constitutive of those truths.

By contrast, according to a perspectival constructivist reading of the unity of value thesis, interpretive reasoning is both epistemic and innovative, for true value statements just are those that reflect the value judgments that would result from the application of Dworkinian interpretive reasoning to the initially unruly set of value propositions comprised by the relevant perspective. Hence, on the constructivist reading of the unity of value thesis, truths about value are objective and mind-independent in a weak sense of the term, for any single person might make mistakes in her interpretive reasoning about values or might so reason on the basis of mistaken empirical facts. However, such truths would not be mind-independent in the more robust sense of the term that, as we read it, the ODT contemplates, for on the constructivist account, truths about value are constituted by

---

[6] Dworkin (1986: 230-231).
[7] See Id. 46-49.

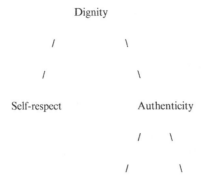

Dignity

Self-respect   Authenticity

Responsibility   Non-Domination

FIGURE 1.1. *Dworkin's Complex Conception of Dignity.*

the deliverances of the method of interpretive reasoning correctly applied to the relevant perspective's set of value judgments.

Note further that, as we understand it, the perspectival constructivist reading is not a response-dependence view. That is, this reading does not hold that a value claim is true if and only if a fully informed and ideal interpretive reasoner would accept it. Rather, the claim is that true-value claims are those that are entailed by the method of interpretive reasoning as applied to the relevant set of initially unruly set of value judgments and the correct empirical facts.

Raz finds evidence for the constructivist reading in Dworkin's discussions of the values of authenticity and responsibility. For Dworkin, the value-concepts of authenticity and responsibility are constituents of a larger complex of value-concepts that Dworkin refers to as dignity, as shown in Figure 1.1.

According to Dworkin, self-respect requires each person to acknowledge that her life matters, and hence the importance of living an authentic life.[8] Dworkin adds that living an authentic life entails acting responsibly, which among other things, involves acting in accordance with the deliverances of interpretive reasoning as applied to one's initially wild and unruly array of value beliefs (as described by Dworkin in the lengthy passage cited in the second paragraph of this introduction).[9]

Raz suspects that Dworkin would accept neither the ODT nor the constructivist interpretation[10] of the unity of value thesis. Nonetheless, he considers these

---

[8] Dworkin (2011: 203-204).

[9] See also Id. 108 & 203-204.

[10] Scattered throughout Dworkin's corpus are a number of discussion that speak to whether he is most charitably read as a kind of metaethical constructivist or could be sympathetically reworked along these lines. See Dworkin (1973: 505-519) for a distinction between two interpretations of Rawls's method of reflective equilibrium: constructive and natural. The latter parallels Raz's Object-Dependence Theory (ODT), and the former parallels the perspectival constructivist

two possibilities in the hopes of clarifying Dworkin's view and the research program that it frames. Raz describes this research programme as follows:

> Given that truths about values are grounded in constitutive cases themselves consisting (in part) of truths about values, each one of which depends on a constitutive case, and so on and so forth, we should research (a) whether, and if so to what degree or in what ways, do the links thus existing between truths about values connect all truths about all values, or only some of them; and (b) how tight are the connections between values so established (do they allow for conflict? Indeterminacies? Etc.)?(22)

Raz recognizes that Dworkin's answers to some of these questions are clear. Namely, Dworkin holds that all values are linked to one another, that there are no incommensurate values, and that there are no fundamental conflicts between values. However, Raz argues that these answers are not required by the unity of value thesis and that Dworkin has provided no argument for them.

Toward the end of his contribution, Raz argues that whether Dworkin realized it or not, the ODT must be the "ultimate foundation of the doctrine of unity."(21) The following passage contains Raz's main argument for this claim.

> [A]t the end of the day Dworkin sees the case for engaging in interpretive reasoning, as he understands that process, that is the case for understanding values through Dworkinian interpretation, as resting on the responsibility project. It is what responsibility requires of us. The case for the responsibility project is that it is valuable, and its value must in the last resort be vindicated by the ODT approach.(21)

One might object that the responsibility project need not in the last resort be vindicated by the ODT approach, for this project could be vindicated by way of a perspectival constructivist approach. That is, at least from some perspectives, engaging in interpretive reasoning with respect to the unruly and wild array of value judgments that constitute those perspectives would lead to endorsement of the responsibility project. In other words, for some, interpretive reasoning might very well be self-affirming.

However, this objection misses Raz's point, which we take to be the following twofold claim. First, the responsibility project is valuable only if the unity of value thesis is true. In other words, engaging in interpretive reasoning with respect to one's value judgments is a valuable project only if, per the unity of value thesis, such reasoning leads to true beliefs about value. Second, if Dworkin's metanormative unity of value thesis is true, its truth is, per the ODT, "independent of any

---

reading of the unity of value thesis. Dworkin endorses the constructive interpretation of reflective equilibrium. See too Dworkin (2011: 63-66). There, he rejects Rawls's constructivism. Note, however, that what he specifically rejects is Rawls's attempt to employ this method in his latter work without relying on moral truths or aspiring to identify such truths. Most vexing for the constructivist reading of Dworkin is his puzzling skirmish with Sharon Street, who is a thoroughgoing constructivist about value. See Dworkin (2011: 446, n. 9). See also Dworkin (1996).

single person's view about what values there are."(16) In sum, we take Raz's claim to be that for the responsibility project to be vindicated, at least one truth about value—namely, the metanormative unity of value thesis itself—must not be a perspectival construction.

Dworkin's sketchy remarks about the concept of truth suggest how one might defend an unalloyed constructivist reading of Dworkin's unity of value thesis:

> We could offer, as our most abstract characterization, that truth is what counts as the uniquely successful solution to a challenge of inquiry. We could then construct more concrete specifications of truth for different domains by finding more concrete accounts of success tailored to each domain. These different accounts would be nested. The value theory would be a candidate account for success across the whole domain of interpretation, and the theory of moral responsibility I described in chapter 6 would be a candidate application of the value theory to the more specific interpretive domain of morality. A different account of success, and hence, truth, would be offered for science.[11]

In keeping with this passage, the Dworkinian constructivist might point out that her theory of value—the unity of value thesis—is itself a candidate account of the success conditions of value judgments. Moreover, she could argue that whether the unity of value thesis is itself correct turns on the set of success conditions that govern such metanormative claims. As we interpret it, Raz's point about the foundational status of the ODT presupposes the robust mind-independence of metaethical truths. However, it is unlikely that Dworkin would have accepted this presupposition.[12]

As the following passage indicates, Dworkin argues that truth is itself an interpretive concept and hence, claims about truth, i.e., claims about the success conditions of claims within any discourse, must be established by way of interpretive reasoning.

> We can rescue philosophical arguments about the nature of truth if we can understand truth as an interpretive concept. We should reformulate the different theories of truth that philosophers have proposed, so far as we can, by treating them as interpretive claims. We share a vast variety of practices in which the pursuit and achievement of truth are treated as values. We do not invariably count it good to speak or even to know the truth, but it is our standard assumption that both are good. The value of truth is interwoven in these practices with a variety of other values that Bernard Williams called, comprehensively, the values of truthfulness.[13]

---

[11] Id. 177.

[12] Dworkin is difficult to parse on this particular issue. See Id. 446, n. 9 and Dworkin (1996) for relevant discussions.

[13] Dworkin (2011: 173).

Thus, in accordance with the tenets of constructive interpretation, Dworkin could argue that to specify the purposes and hence the truth-conditions of any type of discourse, be it scientific or value-discourse, the theorist must engage in first-order argument about the underlying values of engaging in discourse of that kind.[14] That is, one must engage in interpretive reasoning. Accordingly, one committed to a thoroughgoing perspectival constructivist reading of the unity of value thesis might argue that the success conditions of metanormative claims about the success conditions about value (e.g., the unity of value thesis) are not robustly mind-independent. Rather, they too are perspectival constructions of interpretive reasoning.

At this point, it should be clear that Dworkin made many claims and arguments that fall squarely within the domain of inquiry commonly described as metaethics. As we have just discussed, Dworkin defended a theory of the underlying nature of value, the meaning and structure of value concepts and claims, the truth-conditions of value-claims, and how such value-claims might be justified. Moreover, as we hope this volume illustrates, Dworkin's core metaethical claim, the unity of value thesis, is the backbone of all his work.

Readers familiar with Dworkin's work might object to our characterization of the unity of value thesis as a metaethical claim, for Dworkin vigorously expressed his impatience with the distinction between first-order ethics and metaethics. To wit, a section of *Justice for Hedgehogs* bears the title, "Yes, Meta-Ethics Rests on a Mistake."[15] Although we cannot fully unravel this knot here, we think that the discussion of Dworkin's theory of truth puts us in a position to identify a key thread. Namely, Dworkin was not opposed to metaethics broadly construed as inquiry into the semantics, epistemology, and underlying metaphysics of normative discourse. However, he did reject a distinction that he took to be a defining tenet of contemporary metaethics: "the distinction most moral philosophers draw between ordinary ethical or moral questions, which they call first- order substantive questions, and the second- order questions they call 'meta- ethical.'"[16]

As we have just seen, Dworkin rejected this distinction, for he held that truth is itself an interpretive value-concept, and hence, the metaethical project of establishing the success conditions (or the lack thereof) of value claims can proceed only by way of first-order arguments about values. Note further that this view reverberates throughout his work. For instance, as is well known, he similarly holds that no firm line divides general jurisprudence from judging. That is, in his view, there is no firm line that divides establishing the success conditions of first-order legal reasoning (general jurisprudence) from first-order legal reasoning (judging).

---

[14] See Huw Price (2013) and Lynch (2009) for carefully defended and stated theories of truth that in some respects parallel the theory of truth that Dworkin sketches in *Justice for Hedgehogs*.

[15] Dworkin (2011: 67).

[16] Id.

2. Political Values: Legitimacy, Authority, and Collective Responsibility

The volume's second section comprises pieces that address some of Dworkin's key contributions to political philosophy. In their respective pieces, Candice Delmas and Thomas Christiano critically assess a number of Dworkin's claims about the basis and scope of political legitimacy. Delmas and Christiano advance their argument within the framework of Dworkin's account of political legitimacy that holds (1) a state is legitimate only insofar as it possesses the moral liberty to enforce its directives, and (2) such legitimacy is likely fatally undermined if the state does not have the moral power to obligate its subjects by issuing those directives.[17]

Dworkin frames his inquiry into the grounds of political legitimacy in terms of a tension between two kinds of value. On the one hand, he recognizes that a necessary condition for the realization of goods of the very highest moral importance is widespread conformity to and enforcement of networks of putative obligations. For example, the goods of friendship, marriage, and a parent-child relationship can only be realized if the norms that constitute these relationships are followed and enforced. In this same vein, the goods of living in a political community (stability, order, reliable rights protection, and so on) can only be realized if the relevant network of putative obligations that constitute the political community is followed and enforced. Thus, for Dworkin, a key basis of the political obligation to obey a community's laws and the state's moral liberty to enforce those laws is that following and enforcing these norms contributes to the maintenance of the goods of political community.

On the other hand, Dworkin worries that the conformity to and enforcement of such political obligations is a threat to the value of dignity. As Dworkin characterizes this value, dignity requires the moral agent both to stay true to her reasons in the face of irrational contrary impulses and to act in accordance with her own interpretive reasoning rather than the dictates of others. Thus, his worry:

> How can I, given my special responsibility for my own life, accept the dominion of others? How can I, given my respect for the objective importance other people's lives, join in forcing them to do as I wish?[18]

In short, Dworkin's concern is that by conforming to the dictates of others as embodied in the state's laws, the moral agent might fail to manifest appropriate recognition of the fact that her life matters. Similarly, by enforcing those laws, moral agents might fail to respect the importance of other people's lives.

Dworkin holds that this tension can be resolved on the basis of a Kantian principle implicit in the second question of the immediately foregoing passage. This principle holds that self-respect (a component of Dworkin's master value of

---

[17] Dworkin (2011: 321-323) and (1986: 190-192).

[18] Dworkin (2011: 320).

dignity) requires recognition of the objective rather than the subjective ground of the fact that one's life matters—namely, a ground shared by all rational agents. Hence, self-respect requires acknowledgment of the fact that one's life matters as much but not more than the life of other rational agents.[19] Accordingly, he offers the following resolution of the stated worry:

> We find ourselves in associations we need and cannot avoid but whose vulnerabilities are consistent with our self-respect only if they are reciprocal— only if they include the responsibility of each, at least in principle, to accept collective decisions as obligations.[20]

Thus, Dworkin concludes that the conformity to and enforcement of a community's laws is not an affront to one's dignity so long as all members of the community conform and are held to the community's constitutive obligations. To this condition of political legitimacy, Dworkin adds one more. Namely, norms generally accepted as obligations are "genuine obligations... only when they are consistent with an equal appreciation of the importance of all human lives and only when they do not license the kind of harm to others that is forbidden by that assumption."[21]

In sum, in at least two ways, Dworkin's value of dignity plays a crucial role in grounding political legitimacy. First, by conforming to and holding others to the laws of one's community, the moral agent plays her part in a group practice that is a necessary condition for the realization of goods that are integral to the well-being of every member of her political community. In other words, by acting in this way, the moral agent acknowledges that her life and those of her fellow community members matter, thereby according an appropriate measure of respect to each. Second, violating those norms is an affront to the dignity of those who accept and conform to such obligations, for such violations are failures of reciprocity that render others' unrequited conformity to the practice a tacit denial of their equal worth.

In a crucial qualification of the second condition just described, Dworkin allows that political obligations are binding even if they embody an imperfect conception of equal appreciation so long as their deficiencies are not too egregious.[22] However, this qualification introduces yet a further tension. On the one hand, respect for human dignity requires conformity to the extant laws of the community despite their imperfections, yet on the other, it might be that by disobeying those laws one might contribute to efforts that might lead the community to a more perfect appreciation of the equal worth of its citizens. Thus, Dworkin acknowledges that "[i]t is debatable when civil disobedience is an appropriate response to a citizen's more general obligation to help improve his community's

---

[19] See Id. ch. 11.
[20] Id. 320.
[21] Id. 315.
[22] See e.g., Dworkin (1986: 202-206).

sense of what its members' dignity requires."[23] In her contribution, Delmas enters into this debate, and she argues that in addition to the political obligation of obedience to the law, there is a political obligation of civil disobedience. That is, she argues that "resistance to unjust laws, policies, and institutions in overall legitimate communities, as well as resistance to illegitimate governments and are not only compatible with, but required by, the principles of Dworkinian dignity."(26) More pointedly, she argues that contemporary political communities are egregiously unjust, and hence, the predominant duty binding on the members of such communities requires disobedience.

Whereas Delmas responds to Dworkin's account of the basis of state legitimacy, Christiano critically assesses and offers an alternative to his account of the basis of the legitimacy of international law. That is, he assesses and provides an alternative account of the complex of legal norms, such as *jus cogens* norms, the provisions of certain multilateral treaties, and international customs that are commonly recognized as constituting an international legal order with which all states are duty-bound to comply. Christiano criticizes two features of Dworkin's account of the basis of this body of law's legitimacy: its non-cosmopolitanism and its failure to recognize the import of state consent.

As noted above, Dworkin holds that the ability to secure a number of highly important goods is a key basis of a state's political legitimacy. Dworkin enumerates a number of goods that states secure in support of his views concerning the basis of the legitimacy of international law: protection from the depradations of war and human rights abuses; the avoidance of catastrophic collective action failures that can only be cured by international coordination (e.g., climate change or depletion of the oceanic commons); the provision of some say in the enactment and administration of international policies that have significant implications for the well-being of their citizens; and the ability of a state's citizens to acquit their responsibilities to help protect people in other nations from war crimes, genocide, and other violations of human rights.[24] Dworkin argues that international law is constituted by a set of norms practiced by states. More pointedly, they are those norms that constitute an international practice that augments states' capacity to provide their respective citizenries with goods of the sort just enumerated. Dworkin further argues that such norms impose binding obligations for any state insofar as conformity with them augments that state's ability to provide its citizens with those goods.

In sum, Dworkin's account of the legitimacy of international law is non-cosmopolitan, for on this account, international law is binding and hence legitimate only insofar as each respective state's conformity to this body of law mitigates that state's legitimacy deficits with respect to its own citizens. Christiano challenges the non-cosmopolitan structure of Dworkin's account, arguing that the fundamental interests of all persons are the immediate ground of the legitimacy

---

[23] Id. 321.
[24] Dworkin (2013: 17-18).

of international law. His argument is twofold. First, the international community must pursue certain aims, including (1) the realization of international peace and security; (2) protection against human rights abuses; (3) the avoidance of environmental disaster; (4) a decent system of international trade and migration; and (5) the alleviation of severe global poverty. The pursuit of these objectives is required because, as Christiano puts it, "pursuit of anything less would suggest that the fundamental interests of some persons did not matter."(65) Second, a key ground of the legitimacy of the international legal order is that, presently, the best way for states to contribute to the realization of the morally mandatory aims just described entails conforming to and enforcing the network of norms that constitute that order (e.g., *jus cogens*, the doctrine of state consent).

The second main criticism that Christiano marshals against Dworkin's account of the legitimacy of international law pertains to the doctrine of state consent. Christiano argues that by dint of the right of states to say *no,* as set out in this doctrine of state consent, states and, more important, their citizens, enjoy a measure of control over the shape of the international law that sets and implements the international community's objectives (e.g., the five aims enumerated above). Moreover, this doctrine provides citizens with such a say without threatening the integrity of state-level political societies in the way that transnational or global majoritarian voting would. Furthermore, Christiano argues that all persons have a fundamental interest in exercising such control. Thus, allowing for some qualifications, Christiano concludes that a key ground of the doctrine of state consent is the importance of giving all persons control over how the international legal system implements the five fundamental aims listed above. More pointedly, Christiano criticizes Dworkin's account for its failure to recognize that consent is a key ground of the legitimacy of the international order, and he attributes this failing in part to the non-cosmopolitan structure of Dworkin's view. As a notable aside, Christiano and a number of other theorists of democracy marshal similar criticisms of the dismissive account of the intrinsic value of the democratic procedural form that informs Dworkin's defense of the institution of judicial review.[25]

Francois Tanguay-Renaud considers yet another aspect of Dworkin's complex value of dignity, the requirement to hold oneself to account for one's wrongdoing. Dworkin characterizes this requirement as a second aspect of the responsibility project, the first being the requirement (described above) to act in accordance with one's understanding of value.

To see the particular Dworkinian claim that interests Tanguay-Renaud, it helps to consider first a parallel claim that Dworkin advances in the course of his characterization of the first aspect of the responsibility project.

As Dworkin puts this claim:

> Political integrity assumes a particularly deep personification of the community or state. It supposes that the community as a whole can be

---

[25] See, e.g., Christiano (2008) and Waldron (2006).

committed to principles of fairness or justice or procedural due process in some way analogous to the way particular people can be committed to convictions or ideals or projects, and this will strike many people as bad metaphysics.[26]

More generally, Dworkin argues that the members of any number of important forms of community, not just political communities, must personify the relevant community as a necessary prelude to reasoning about their obligations as members of that community—i.e., their associative obligations. That is, any such community member must presuppose that the relevant community as a whole is committed to some fundamental valuable set of points or purposes. This is because the content of her obligations as a member of that community are fixed by the community's mutually recognized and practiced network of obligations, interpreted through the lens of the defining values attributed to the community as a whole rather than any particular member of the community.

Similarly, Dworkin argues that ascertaining responsibility for individual wrongdoing, the second aspect of the responsibility project, requires personifying a collective and identifying a wrong the collective has committed, for in those contexts doing so is a necessary first step in reasoning correctly about individual responsibility.[27] For example, Dworkin would argue that the full range of moral responsibility borne by the individual shareholders or executives of a corporation can only be ascertained by first personifying the corporation and identifying a wrongdoing it has committed (e.g., endangering the public by negligently putting a defective product on the market).

Tanguay-Renaud marshals two main challenges to Dworkin's thesis about collective wrongdoing. First, he questions the coherence of Dworkin's account of collective agents that can bear responsibility for moral wrongdoing in their own right. Second, he cautions against overlooking conceptual resources for characterizing individual responsibility that would obviate the alleged need to identify a collective agent's wrongdoing in order to ascertain the entire range of individuals' wrongdoing.

In the final contribution to the volume's second section, Daniel Halliday critically assesses Dworkin's application of his theory of distributive justice to laws governing inheritance and bequests. Halliday accepts Dworkin's conclusion—namely, that such inheritances should be allowed, but they must be taxed, perhaps, heavily. However, Halliday holds that Dworkin's arguments for this conclusion are not supported by the deeper principles of his theory. As is well-known, Dworkin holds that the values of equal concern and respect imply that the distribution of resources within a society should be ambition-sensitive or, in other words, choice-sensitive yet endowment-insensitive. That is, the distribution of resources within a just society must be sensitive to the social value of one's

---

[26] Dworkin (2011: 167).
[27] See, e.g., Dworkin (1986: 171).

choices of what to do with one's life (e.g., to be an entrepreneur or a person of leisure), but it should only be sensitive to differences in endowments (e.g., intelligence, handicaps, certain kinds of luck) to the extent necessary to preserve the choice sensitivity of redistribution or other important values.

To frame inquiry into the rough contours of polices that would be both choice-sensitive and appropriately endowment-insensitive, Dworkin offers the following famed thought experiment:

> What level of insurance against low income and bad luck would people in our own actual community buy if the community's actual wealth was equally divided among them, if no information was available that would lead anyone or any insurer to judge that he was more or less at risk than others, and if everyone otherwise had state-of-the-art information about the incidence of different kinds of bad luck and the availability, cost, and value of medical or other remedies for the consequences of that bad luck?[28]

Dworkin's hope is that this hypothetical market device supplies a rough and workable frame for reasoning about the levels of taxation and social insurance a just society must implement to mitigate the risk of faring poorly in the endowment lottery.

A point crucial to Halliday's criticisms is that the hypothetical insurance market device is tailored to a very specific set of circumstances—namely, those in which remedying the relevant endowment-sensitive distribution would vitiate the choice-sensitivity of the distribution or some other profoundly important value. For example, Dworkin argues that should any community redress inequalities resulting from severe handicaps up till the point that further expenditures would not bring those so afflicted marginally closer to a position of equality, the bulk of its members "would have nothing left to spend on anything else, and the lives of all other citizens would be miserable in consequence."[29] In a similar vein, he argues that to remedy fully the differentials that result from differences in talent, a community would have to restore "people to a condition of equal wealth, no matter what choices they make about work and consumption."[30] Nonetheless, Dworkin holds that these inequalities should be redressed to some extent, and Dworkin argues that his hypothetical insurance market device is a useful frame for reasoning about the extent to which a just society must redress them.

As Halliday notes, Dworkin marshals his hypothetical insurance market device in support of the conclusion that, as a matter of justice, bequests and inheritances must be taxed, perhaps heavily. Although Halliday reaches a similar conclusion, he argues that the hypothetical insurance market frame is inapposite to this context of inquiry. As we have just seen, Dworkin's hypothetical insurance market device is tailored for contexts in which reasons of great moral

---

[28] Id. 360.
[29] Id. 359.
[30] Id.

weight militate against mitigating endowment-based inequalities beyond a certain point. Halliday argues that it is far from clear that there are reasons of comparable importance relevant to the context of inheritances and bequests. To wit, the only reason Dworkin cites against fully mitigating in this context is that doing so would significantly interfere with the freedom to make interpersonal transfers.

Halliday also disputes Dworkin's characterization of the key worry about an unfettered regime of inheritances and bequests. That is, Halliday argues that, contra Dworkin, the key risk is not that such a regime is likely to produce some endowment-sensitive distributive inequalities. Rather, it is the much graver possibility that such a regime would create and entrench class hierarchies and a whole host of attendant social pathologies, such as failures of social solidarity and mutual understanding as well as the upper class's imposition and maintenance of yet further unjustified distributive inequalities. In sum, Halliday argues that there are powerful reasons to forestall entirely the emergence of such class hierarchies, and, by contrast, very little reason not to heavily regulate inheritances and transfers.

GENERAL JURISPRUDENCE: CONTESTING THE UNITY OF LAW AND VALUE

The volume's third section comprises contributions that respond to Dworkin's theory of law. Dworkin reports that his earliest incursions into legal theory presuppose that law and morality are two distinct normative systems (i.e., the two-system view), for he held that "the law includes not just enacted rules, or rules with pedigree, but justifying principles as well."[31] He also reports that he no longer accepts the two-system view, but rather subscribes to a one-system view according to which the law is a particular branch of political morality.

> Legal rights are political rights, but a special branch because they are properly enforceable on demand through adjudicative and coercive institutions without need for further legislation or other lawmaking activity.[32]

Put in terms of the unity of value thesis (cited above), Dworkin holds that the truth of any proposition of law, i.e., a proposition about legal rights and duties, turns on the truth of an indefinite number of other true value-propositions, particularly those relevant to the question of whether it would be proper for a court to secure the enforcement of the putative law.

In his contribution, Larry Sager accepts Dworkin's one-system view, for he agrees that the law is but a particular branch of political morality. However, he rejects Dworkin's formulation of this one-system view according to which the law comprises only those norms that are judicially enforceable, for Sager argues

---

[31] Id. 402.
[32] Id. 407.

that some norms are law in the sense that they are binding on nonjudicial legal officials, yet it would not be proper for a court to enforce them.

Sager offers the Thirteenth Amendment to the Constitution of the United States (U.S. Constitution or the Constitution) as one of a number of examples that supports his criticism of Dworkin's one-system view. As Sager notes, the United State Supreme Court has recognized that the U.S. Congress has "authority to outlaw private racial discrimination in property transactions, since the abolition of slavery in the Amendment entailed not merely the dissolution of servitude itself but the eradication as well of the badges and incidents of slavery", but "the Court has confined its own enforcement of the 13th Amendment to instances of actual servitude . . . ."(125)

Sager's point, then, is that Dworkin's particular conception of the one-system view problematically implies that if the Court is correct in its view that it must confine its direct enforcement of the Thirteenth amendment to instances of actual servitude, then victims of private racial discrimination would enjoy no more than a "legislative right" requiring the U.S. Congress to outlaw discrimination of this sort. In other words, Dworkin's view would imply that such victims have no "legal right," for according to the Dworkinian variation on the one-system view, if such victims had a legal right, then it would be proper for the court to enforce that right directly. Sager argues that the more plausible view is that the Thirteenth Amendment supplies a legal right not to suffer private racial discrimination that is not judicially enforceable.

Dworkin registers awareness of Sager's counterexample and concomitant claim that some legal rights are not judicially enforceable. Moreover, Dworkin comments that Sager's alternative view "might be tempting if we could sensibly adopt the two-systems view and a positivist theory of how we should decide what the law is."[33] In large part, Sager's contribution is a response to this puzzling passage, for Sager sketches and defends an alternative one-system account of law that is fully moralized but demarcates the realm of legal value in terms of Dworkin's idea of structuring principles rather than judicial enforceability.

As Sager explains at length, Dworkin introduces the notion of structuring principles to accommodate the commonly held thought that there might be a gap between what is legally required and what would be best measured in terms of other values of political morality, such as justice. In a key illustrative example, Dworkin notes that families are loci of a kind of institutional morality, for past familial decisions, actions, and interactions conspire to generate reasons that compete with other moral considerations.[34] We have seen an application of this same idea in our discussion of Dworkin's conception of associative obligations. That is, the value of integrity requires members of a community to conform to the best interpretation of the extant network of putative obligations that constitute the community despite such obligations' significant (but not too egregious) moral

---

[33] Id. 413.
[34] Id.

failings. The key thrust, then, of Sager's response to Dworkin is that the key distinction between law and other categories of value is not that laws are properly enforceable by courts. Rather, as we understand Sager's view, the key distinction is that laws are normative requirements mediated by structuring principles, and, contra Dworkin, they might be so mediated irrespective of the propriety of their judicial enforcement.

David Dyzenhaus discusses at length Dworkin's difficulties characterizing the legal status of deeply unjust putative laws, such as The Fugitive Slave Act of 1850. Enacted by the U.S. Congress, this statute required any authority (including those within non-slave state jurisdictions) to return escaped slaves to their owners. Dworkin argues that, given this statute's profound injustice, the most plausible possibilities regarding its legal status are: (1) it is a law that no judge should enforce save perhaps in exceptional circumstances, or (2) it is not law at all. Dworkin opts for the first possibility.

Dworkin's discussion of the status of the Fugitive Slave Act reveals the full texture of his one-system view of law and morality. On this account, laws are norms that courts are duty-bound to enforce by dint of structuring principles such as integrity and fairness. On his view, the Fugitive Slave Act meets this description, and hence, it is law. However, he adds that other considerations, such as justice, might trump these values and, hence, the duty of enforcement that they ground.

By contrast, Dworkin opts for the second option when characterizing the legal status of Nazi law. This body of putative law, he argues, is not law at all given the pervasive wickedness of the Nazi regime. The thought seems to be that such pervasive wickedness does not merely defeat requirements grounded in structuring principles, such as fairness and integrity that characteristically ground the judicial enforceability of norms; rather, it fully undercuts such values. That is, because of the pervasive wickedness of the Nazi regime, enforcing its laws would neither be fair nor an act of integrity.

Dyzenhaus questions Dworkin's treatment of both the Fugitive Slave Act and Nazi law. With regard to the former, Dyzenhaus notes Dworkin's qualification that legitimacy is a matter of degree. As Dworkin puts it:

> a government is illegitimate in respect to a particular person it claims to govern if it does not recognize, even as an abstract requirement, the equal importance of his fate or his responsibility for his own life.[35]

Accordingly, argues Dyzenhaus, Dworkin must recognize that antebellum American law, a fortiori the Fugitive Slave Act, does not obligate slaves. Reminiscent of Delmas's core claim discussed above, Dyzenhaus also doubts that any law that blatantly denies equal concern and respect is a pro tanto obligation for anyone. More specifically, rather than defeating a requirement to enforce, the injustice of the Fugitive Slave Act undercuts the ground of that requirement. In other words, Dyzenhaus suggests that by dint of the Fugitive Slave Act's

---

[35] Dworkin (2010: 1059).

injustice, no structuring principle, such as fairness or integrity would be realized by enforcing it.

Although Dyzenhaus seems unmoved by the positivist intuition that any adequate theory of law must characterize the Fugitive Slave Act as legally valid, the same cannot be said for Dworkin. Moreover, this intuition is supported by a key aspect of Dworkin's legal theory—namely, the requirement that to be true, any proposition of law must fit and justify extant legal practice. As Dworkin states:

> The judge's decision—his postinterpretive conclusions—must be drawn from an interpretation that both fits and justifies what has gone on before...[36]

Given this view, one might worry that on any plausible characterization of the desideratum of fit, any judicial conclusion that the Fugitive Slave Act was not legally valid would be false, for it would not sufficiently fit the practice. Another way to put this same worry is that there might not have been sufficient resources within antebellum American law to justify an interpretation of that legal practice which casts the enactment and sustained enforcement of the Fugitive Slave Act as mistakes rather than datapoints that had to be accommodated. The latter half of Dyzenhaus's contribution seeks to dispel this worry.

Dyzenhaus's argument rests on the premise that Lon Fuller's inner morality of law is necessarily an element of any extant legal practice. Dyzenhaus notes that even the seminal contemporary positivist, H.L.A. Hart might accept this premise, for Hart at times seems to suggest that a necessary existence condition of any legal system is that its constitutive norms satisfy to a significant degree the eight desiderata that constitute the Fuller's inner morality of law: generality, promulgation, non-retroactivity, clarity, non-contradiction, possibility of compliance, constancy through time, and congruence between official action and declared rule.[37]

With this premise in mind, Dyzenhaus puts what we take to be a key claim of his contributions as follows:

> Dworkin and legal positivists overlook the possibility that if law has to comply with such criteria to a significant degree, it will in fact be the case that an interpretive model of the kind Dworkin advocates will have significant traction in the positive law of any particular legal order.(156)

To clarify this point in terms of the recurrent example, a judgment that the Fugitive Slave Act was not legally valid might well meet Dworkin's dimension of fit, for among the materials that any legal judgment must fit are Fuller's eight formal features of any legal system. Conversely, a strike against characterizing the Fugitive Slave Act as legally valid is that it does not fit well with any legal practice, such as the American antebellum system, that embodies Fuller's eight

---

[36] Dworkin (1986: 239).
[37] See e.g., Hart (1994: 193-200). See also Fuller (1969).

criteria to a significant degree, thereby acknowledging the dignity of the legal subject.

To put the gist of Luis Duarte d'Almeida's contribution in terms of Dworkin's distinction between one-system and two-system legal theories, Duarte d'Almeida contests the assumption held by Dworkin and the majority of legal theorists that H.L.A. Hart was a seminal proponent of a positivistic two-system view, according to which the legally valid norms of any legal system are fundamentally determined by social facts. On the contrary, argues Duarte d'Almeida, Hart had very little to say one way or the other regarding this issue.

Key to Duarte d'Almeida's argument is Hart's distinction between external statements about law and internal legal statements. Key to this distinction is Hart's idea of the rule of recognition. According to this idea, for any legal system, the system's officials converge in the acceptance of certain public standards of validity, and accordingly, they apply this shared standard when identifying the laws of their system.[38] As Hart put it, an internal statement "manifests the internal point of view and is naturally used by one who, accepting the rule of recognition and without stating the fact that it is accepted, applies the rule in recognizing some particular rule of the system as valid."[39] As Hart notes, the simplest kind of internal statement takes the following form: It is the law that . . . (e.g., Oxford University is empowered to amend certain statutes that affect any of its colleges).[40] By contrast, an external statement "is the natural language of an external observer of the system who, without himself accepting its rule of recognition, states the fact that others accept it."[41] For example, an external observer might note that in England, they recognize the enactments of the Queen in Parliament (e.g., the Universities of Oxford and Cambridge Act of 1923) as law.

The key thrust of Duarte d'Almeida's contribution is to contest a commonly held assumption about Hart's theory that informs Dworkin's criticisms of Hart. According to this assumption, Hart offered an analysis of internal statements according to which the legally valid norms of any legal system are those and only those identified as such by the system's rule of recognition, i.e., the standard of legal validity accepted in common by the system's officials. Duarte d'Almeida argues that this was not one of Hart's aims. In his words:

> Hart's core aim, in other words, is to offer an analysis of external statements of the form "there exists a legal system in community *c*." As is well-known, he characterises the relevant social phenomenon as involving "two aspects": general obedience by the bulk of the population to those laws that are valid by the system's tests of validity, and (at least in normal cases) a "unified or shared official acceptance of the rule of recognition containing the system's criteria of validity." As should now be obvious, this analysis

---

[38] Hart (1994: 94, 100 and 116).
[39] Id. 102.
[40] Universities of Oxford and Cambridge Act 1923, section 7(3).
[41] Hart (1994: 102-103).

does not (and is not meant to) give us an analysis of either particular internal statements of legal validity, or internal statements of (or applying) first-order legally valid rules.(185)

In addition to offering a compelling and contrarian exegesis of Hart's legal theory, a further key virtue of Duarte d'Almeida's contribution is twofold. First, it highlights and cogently explicates the underappreciated distinction between "two perspectives (and two corresponding kinds of theories): the external and the internal perspectives of law." Second, it warns against hastily conflating these two kinds of theories. That is, it warns against hastily inferring that if, as a matter of social fact, certain criteria of validity are convergently accepted by the officials of any legal systems, then, from the internal perspective of the officials of any such system, the system's legally valid norms are those and only those that would be identified as such by the convergently accepted criteria. Moreover, in light of the distinctions that Duarte d'Almeida's piece brings to the fore, Dworkin's theory can be readily characterized as focused on a theory of the internal perspective of law, whereas, as Duarte d'Almeida illustrates, Hart's legal theory was at least in part a theory of law's external perspective.

As a lengthy coda to his main argument, Duarte d'Almeida critically assesses the legal theory advanced by Stefan Sciaraffa, one of the editors of the present volume.[42] Duarte d'Almeida worries that Sciaraffa's argument is emblematic of contemporary legal theorists' all too common failure to pay sufficient attention to the important distinction between internal and external legal theories.

In his own behalf, Sciaraffa would argue that rather than posing a challenge to the justificatory view, the very distinction that Duarte d'Almeida carefully articulates and presses is at the foundations of this legal theory. More pointedly, from Sciaraffa's perspective, one of the virtues of Duarte d'Almeida's piece is that its careful articulation of the distinction between the internal and external perspectives of law facilitates a more forceful statement of the justificatory view. That is, put in Duarte d'Almeida's terms, key to the justificatory view is the distinction between Hart's theory of a legal system, a theory of law advanced from the external perspective, from Hart's theory of legal content, an analysis of legal validity as understood from the internal perspective of legal officials.

Whereas Duarte d'Almeida argues that Hart is careful not to conflate the internal and external perspectives of law, Sciaraffa assumes that Hart is no less guilty on this score than many of his followers and critics. Moreover, he argues that any satisfactory theory of legal content (in Duarte d'Almeida's terms, any theory about law's internal perspective) must rest on Hart's theory of law's external perspective. [43] However, Sciaraffa's justificatory view rejects Hart's positivist

---

[42] See Sciaraffa (2012).

[43] The key reason why is that inquiry into the internal perspective of any legal system presupposes that that there is such a system, yet there can be no such system unless there is a body of officials who sufficiently converge with respect to the criteria of validity they accept. Cf. Hart (1994: 122-123).

theory of internal statements partly on the grounds that this aspect of Hart's legal theory is a result of the just described conflation between the internal and external perspectives. In place of this positivist internal theory, the justificatory theory adopts a thoroughgoingly non-positivist one-system theory of law.

To help see the internal aspect of the justificatory view, consider the unoriginal example of a statute enacted by a democratic assembly that places restrictions on the powers of future democratic assemblies. Put in terms of this example, the justificatory view holds that the validity of such an entrenching statute would turn on the particular requirements of the objective political values that justify legal officials in their practice of by and large recognizing the democratic assembly's enactments as law. In sum, the justificatory view holds that the legally valid norms of any legal system are those and only those identified as such by the commonly accepted criteria as modified and extended in accordance with the considerations of political morality that support them.

Ken Himma argues in his contribution that there is an important respect in which Hart's and Dworkin's legal theories are inconsistent, and he sides with Hart with respect to the contested issue. For Himma, the key contrast is that, whereas Dworkin's theory supplies an immodest conceptual analysis (ICA) of the folk concepts relevant to legal practice, Hart's theory offers only a modest conceptual analysis of those concepts.

Himma borrows the distinction between immodest and modest conceptual analysis from Frank Jackson. On Jackson's account, modest conceptual analysis (MCA) seeks to map and rationalize to some degree the folk understanding of a concept, say, law, morality, or belief, as a necessary prelude to determining whether those concepts refer to objects that can be located in the world. Moreover, he holds that this form of MCA is a prelude to determining whether the object of the analyzed concept is entailed by the world's metaphysically basic objects. That is, MCA is a modest first step in what Jackson colorfully describes as serious metaphysics: determining which of our folk concepts we should eliminate by dint of their non-entailment by the world's metaphysically basic features.[44]

By contrast, ICA holds that we can learn and argue about the fundamental nature of the world on the basis of our folk concepts. To borrow one of Jackson's examples, an immodest conceptual analyst might reject the thesis that the world is composed of temporal parts on the grounds that it is inconsistent with our intuition that different things (in this case, different temporal parts) having different properties is not tantamount to change.[45] To help see the contrast between these two modes of conceptual analysis, consider that the modest conceptual analyst who accepted the theory about temporal parts would take the folk concept's inconsistency with it to be a reason to eliminate the folk concept of change.

A key premise of Himma's argument is that MCA as applied to law cannot result in an error theory about law. That is, it cannot result in theory that implies

---

[44] See Jackson (1998: chs. 1-2).
[45] Id. 42-43.

that the folk's beliefs about law are systematically mistaken. One might object to this premise on the ground that one of Jackson's key motivations for engaging in MCA with respect to any folk concept is that it might very well lead to the conclusion that despite its widespread use, the concept has no referent in the world as it is and for that reason should be eliminated from our serious discourse. In other words, one of Jackson's key motivations for engaging in MCA with respect to any folk concept is that it might lead to an error theory.

Though correct as far as it goes, the foregoing objection misses Himma's point, for Himma untethers the methodology of MCA as applied to the folk concept of law from Jackson's larger project of serious metaphysics. Rather, Himma reworks Jackson's distinction in terms of the respective goals of inquiry that he assigns to them. On this account, the goal of MCA is "to understand certain features of the world as they are defined and articulated through our conceptual practices."(207) For Himma, the goal of MCA in the context of jurisprudence is solely to map the conceptual practices that are relevant to legal practice. By contrast, the goal of ICA is "to understand those features as they *actually are* independent of the practices that enable us to describe them."(207) In other words, the goal of ICA as applied to jurisprudence is to ascertain truths about some underlying nature of legal practice that is distinct from our concepts that are relevant to the practice.

The point, then, of Himma's key premise is that the folk cannot be systematically mistaken about the jurisprudential MCA theorist's object of inquiry because that object, the folk concepts relevant to legal practice, is constituted by the folk's beliefs and understanding. As Himma puts it:

> Insofar as our ordinary talk defines the nature of a thing, our conceptual theory of the thing must, at the end of the day, harmonize with ordinary talk; failure to do so is a potentially fatal error for a conceptual theory under MCA.(208)

By contrast, on Himma's view, because the ICA theorist's goal is to ascertain some underlying nature of legal practice that is independent of the relevant folk legal concepts, the ICA theorist must allow that the folk could be systematically mistaken about that nature.

A second key premise of Himma's argument is that Dworkin's theory of law is an error theory, for it comprises a number of theses about law that most legal practitioners would reject. Himma attributes a number of such theses to Dworkin, including the claims that there is almost always a right legal answer even in putatively hard cases, that judges lack a quasi-lawmaking authority and that law includes moral principles that cohere with extant legal practice.

Given that Dworkin is committed to such an error theory, Himma argues that Dworkin faces the following dilemma. Either he is engaged in MCA or ICA. If he accepts MCA, then he must abandon many of the defining theses of his theory, for they amount to an error theory that baldly fails to achieve the goal of MCA— namely, faithfully mapping the folk concepts relevant to law. Alternatively, if Dworkin is engaged in ICA, then he has not given us any reason to think that his jurisprudential conclusions track law's underlying nature better than the folk's beliefs and understandings do. As Himma puts the point:

> The problem is that, for the justification of the imputation of an error theory to some view to succeed, the premises in that justification must be more intuitively plausible than the folk views that the theory seeks to refute. As far as I can see, there is nothing in Dworkin's argument above that jumps out as more plausible . . . .(221)

Read as a perspectival constructivist of the sort described in the first section of this introduction, perhaps Dworkin could respond to this dilemma by embracing its first horn. That is, he could hold that he is engaged in MCA with respect to the interpretive concept of law. On this view, consistent with Himma's version of MCA, the object of inquiry is not law's nature, robustly independent of our beliefs and understandings about the law, for from the constructivist's perspective there is no such robustly mind independent object in the realm of value (which encompasses the law). Nonetheless, the folk might be systematically mistaken about the identity of their system's legally valid norms so long as they have not engaged sufficiently in interpretive reasoning about the law and its requirements. Note that by raising the possibility of this response, we do not purport to adjudicate this issue so much as to identify a potentially important point of contact between Dworkin's legal theory and Himma's criticisms.

Michael Giudice marshals an extended defence of a methodologically pluralistic approach to jurisprudence that stands in contrast to what he characterizes as Dworkin's methodological imperialism. The pluralism Giudice defends comprises three methods: morally or politically evaluative investigation; social-scientific inquiry into the economic, social, and historical influences on the broad array of agents and actions that constitute different aspects of legal practice; and analysis of the concepts that animate the actions and attitudes that constitute this practice. By contrast, Giudice imputes a methodologically imperialistic approach to Dworkin according to which all theories of law must not only be theories of moral evaluation that attribute a fundamental point or purpose to law; they must also be offered from and for the perspective of the judges who participate in legal practice.

A key premise in Giudice's argument is that "each of the three general families of methods" that he defends "is correct and appropriate, and precisely because each responds to different aspects or dimensions of the nature of law itself."(226) As Giudice characterizes this nature: "(i) law is morally (and politically) significant, in that decisions to create, apply, and enforce law affect people's interests and well-being in numerous ways; (ii) law's operation depends at crucial junctures on the decisions and dispositions of humans and human institutions, which are, like all humans and human institutions, products of and influenced by social, economic, psychological, and historical forces of various kinds; and (iii) legal concepts are the creation of shared ideas, notions, and categories, which exist in the form of sets of inter-subjective understandings."(239) In sum, Giudice defends his tripartite pluralistic methodology on the grounds that it is the appropriate approach for inquiry into law given its correspondingly tripartite nature.

Giudice is careful to state that he does not reject Dworkin's methodological approach entirely, for he holds that any fully adequate understanding of law would make use of Dworkinian methodology with respect to those aspects of legal phenomena for which it is appropriate. Rather, he criticizes Dworkin's theory for its methodologically imperialistic claims, and hence its failure to recognize that this methodology is appropriate for inquiry with respect to only one aspect of law—presumably "the part constituted by its moral significance" as described in the following passage.

> Law of course exists at particular moments in time, but it is also part of its nature that it persists through time. It is in turn not outrageous to suppose that to explain law's persistence through time might require different methods, particularly those offered by social scientific theories. From here it is also not hard to see that once we place law back into its temporal context, whereby actual participants (such as judges) have to carry on with their activities in ways responsive to the nature of law, we will also need, again, *because of the very nature of law* (the part constituted by its moral significance), morally and politically evaluative theories of law.(240)

Without pretending to adjudicate Giudice's criticisms of Dworkin's methodological approach, we think it is useful to identify what might be a key point of disagreement between Dworkin and Giudice. Put in terms of Duarte d'Almeida's contribution, the focal concern of Dworkin's theory is the law's internal perspective. There is nothing in this theory that is inconsistent with Giudice's claim that a key aspect of law's nature is the part that is of moral significance; however, from the perspective of Dworkin's theory this aspect of law is not merely of moral significance. Rather, this aspect of law is itself a value—an interpretive value concept that is subject to the unity of value thesis.[46] Accordingly, determining the truth of claims about this value (i.e., claims about its requirements or, in other words, internal legal statements) turns on whether a constitutive case can be made for those statements on the basis of yet other value-claims, particularly (as the discussion above suggests) those relating to justice and the structuring principles of fairness and integrity.

The final contribution to the volume's third section is Chris Essert's piece in which he defends what he refers to as the Simple View of law. Because we think we will be in a better position to situate Essert's arguments with respect to Dworkin's theory after discussing the final section's contributions, we have placed our discussion of Essert's piece in the concluding section of this introduction.

---

[46] See Dworkin (2011: ch. 19).

VALUE IN LAW

The compendium's final section comprises pieces that some would describe as works in normative jurisprudence as opposed to general or analytic jurisprudence. According to this typology, works of the latter sort raise questions about the meaning and referent of claims about law as well as the basis for adjudicating them. So construed, general jurisprudence raises semantic, metaphysical, and epistemic questions about law that are analogous to those posed by metaethicists with respect to morality. By contrast, according to this same typology, normative jurisprudence addresses discrete bodies of law, particularly their structure and the key underlying values that define and animate those areas.

A Dworkinian-minded scholar might resist the foregoing typology on the grounds that the truth conditions of any proposition of law are determined by the requirements of the relevant values, and, hence, metalegal arguments about those truth-conditions must rest on first-order value-claims. Despite this objection, the common distinction is robust. So long as we are careful to acknowledge that on some metalegal views such as Dworkin's, the truth-conditions of legal statements turn on first-order questions of value, it is useful and illuminating to distinguish works that focus on the metaethics of law in general, as it were, from those that focus on the structure and underlying values of discrete bodies of law.

With Hamish Stewart's contribution, we return to a discussion of Dworkin's master value of dignity and the associated values of equal concern and respect. Stewart argues that Dworkin has overlooked an important role that these values play with respect to procedural law, particularly the aspect of procedural law that governs and constitutes courts' fact-finding procedures. Stewart asserts that "the purpose of fact-finding in litigation is not to find facts for their own sake but to use the facts found to grant or deny a legal claim."(376) Accordingly, Stewart holds that accuracy in fact finding is not the only underlying point of procedural law, for there are values other than accuracy in fact finding that should be served by the laws that constitute and regulate courts' fact-finding proceedings. Stewart applauds Dworkin for his recognition of this point and his attempt to provide a more complete account of these underlying values. As Stewart reads him, Dworkin conceives of "procedural entitlements as a way of fixing the level of accuracy in fact-determination, and therefore of distributing the risk of moral harm, in a way that is fair to all potential litigants."(387) Thus, Dworkin holds that in addition to accuracy, fairness to all potential litigants is an animating value of procedural law.

Although Stewart considers Dworkin's account to be a step in the right direction, he argues that procedural law must directly serve the requirements of equal concern and respect. As Stewart puts it, procedural laws should reflect "the more basic demands that the fact of each litigant's personhood places on the process."(387) In support of this claim, Stewart asks the reader to consider the burden of proof that in most any liberal society must be meet in order to convict a defendant of criminal wrongdoing.

Stewart speculates that it very well might be that rules specifying a less demanding burden of proof would serve the values of accuracy and fairness as well or perhaps even better than the beyond-a-reasonable-doubt standard. Thus, for Stewart, the problem with the less demanding standard is not that it is not fair, for it would be so long as all criminal defendants were held to it. Moreover, the problem is not that it would lead to less accuracy in fact finding, for that is a difficult empirical question. Rather, Stewart argues, the key problem is that by subjecting anyone to the harsh dealing of the criminal law on the basis of findings that are not beyond a reasonable doubt, we would thereby fail to accord the respect that her dignity as a person demands. In sum, on the basis of this observation and others along similar lines, Stewart argues that we must include a Kantian principle of respect for personhood in our account of the set of values that animates procedural law.

In their respective pieces, David Brink and Larry Alexander argue that Dworkin defended an originalist theory of constitutional interpretation. Roughly put, theories of constitutional interpretation specify the method of interpretation that judges must employ when interpreting the meaning of constitutional provisions pertinent to their adjudication of the constitutionality of legislative enactments as well as other governmental actions.

As Connie Rosati usefully puts it in her contribution, it is important to distinguish two aspects of any originalist theory.[47] The first specifies the content of the original meaning of constitutional provisions, whereas the second explains the legal effect of such original meanings. Implicit in Rosati's discussion is the plausible thought that to be originalist, a theory of constitutional interpretation must claim not only that constitutional provisions bear a meaning that is recognizably an original meaning but also that this original meaning plays a non-trivial role in determining such provisions' legal effect.

Brink's and Alexander's conclusions are provocative, for Dworkin is typically cast as a leading critic of originalism as well as an exponent of a non-originalist theory. As I shall explain, whereas Brink defends a sympathetic reworking of Dworkin's view (an originalism of principle as he describes it), Alexander explains why, in his view, Dworkin is committed to a highly unappealing form of originalism.

Key to Brink's argument is the distinction between description and referential theories of meaning. On Brink's account, description theories hold that a term's meaning is fixed by an associated nominal definition—roughly, a definition or description conventionally accepted by the competent users of the term. For instance, a description theorist might hold that the term *bachelor* means an unmarried male by dint of the fact that the term's competent users accept and apply this definition when using the term. Accordingly, on this account, the extension of bachelor includes all and only those objects that meet this conventionally

---

[47] See Rosati n. 32 (chapter 14, "The Moral Reading of Constitutions," herein) for a useful typology of forms of originalism and what she takes the key originalist tenet to be.

accepted nominal definition. By contrast, referential theories hold that a term's meaning is fixed by its underlying real definition. For example, a direct reference theorist might hold that the real definition of water is H_2O and, hence the extension of this term includes all and only instances of H_2O.

A key point that Brink cites in support of referentialist versus description theories is that the latter seems implausibly committed to the denial of the intuitively appealing claim that there "can be a fact of the matter about the extension of a term even when there is disagreement about its criteria for application or its extension."(277) The latter, on the other hand, can accommodate this claim. As Brink puts it:

> [W]e don't conclude that the meaning or extension of the word "toxin" is indeterminate just because people disagree about what the criteria for toxicity are or what substances are toxic, and we don't conclude that sense or reference of "justice" is indeterminate because of disagreements between libertarians and egalitarians about the nature of justice.(278)

In sum, for Brink a key point in favor of referentialist theories is that they do not join description theories in this implausible conclusion, for on the referentialist account, meaning is fixed by a real rather than a nominal, and hence conventionally accepted, definition. As an important aside, note that Brink borrows these disagreement-based arguments against description theories from the philosophy of language and that these arguments parallel Dworkin's disagreement-based criticisms of H.L.A. Hart's theory of law.[48]

Brink further distinguishes between a textualist form of originalism "that appeals to the meaning of the words in which the legal provision is expressed and an intentionalist form that appeals to the intentions or purposes of the framers of the provision."(281–82) Brink's textualist originalists divide into two further camps. The first specifies the original meaning of constitutional provisions in terms of their shared public meaning, whereas the second specifies this meaning in terms of the framer's intent (specific according to one version of this view and abstract according to a second). Brink further distinguishes between referentialist and description public meaning textualists. The description public meaning textualist holds that the original meaning of constitutional provisions is fixed by the publicly settled nominal definitions of such provisions' key terms, whereas the referentialist public meaning textualists holds that such meanings are fixed by real definitions.

Brink argues that with respect to those constitutional provisions containing abstract and contentious moral terms, such as equal protection, and cruel and unusual punishment, referentialistic public meaning originalism is much more plausible than descriptive public meaning originalism, for there seems to be no

---

[48] See Brink (this volume), n. 6 for cites to the relevant works from the philosophy of language. See also Dworkin (1986: ch.1) for Dworkin's seminal statement of his disagreement-based criticism of Hart.

settled nominal definition of these terms, yet with very few exceptions those who debate the applicability of such terms to particular cases act as if they mean the same thing by them. Brink argues that Dworkin's theory of constitutional interpretation is a variation of this more plausible referentialistic form of originalism, according to which the meaning of key abstract constitutional terms is fixed by an associated real definition whose content is established by way of interpretive reasoning.

Raz's discussion of Dworkin's unity of value thesis suggests an alternative to Brink's characterization of the semantic theory that informs Dworkin's theory of constitutional interpretation. As discussed above, Raz distinguishes two possible readings of Dworkin's unity of value thesis: the ODT and the perspectival constructivist reading. According to this first claim, true value-claims are robustly mind-independent. Hence, interpretive reasoning provides epistemic access to these truths but it does not constitute them. By contrast, on the second perspectival constructivist reading of Dworkin's unity of value thesis, all truths about value are constituted by the deliverances of interpretive reasoning as applied to the beliefs about value that comprise the relevant perspective.

Brink's referentialistic reading of Dworkin's semantic view complements[49] Raz's ODT, for referentialistic accounts posit real definitions that fix the extension of the relevant terms, in which such real definitions are robustly mind-independent properties by virtue of which the term properly applies.[50] To wit, in Brink's key illustrative example, H_2O is the real definition of water. By contrast, no robustly mind-independent properties figure in the perspectival constructivist account, and hence, strictly speaking, if Dworkin is a perspectival constructivist, then there would be no place in his view for a referentialistic semantic theory. That said, there is a place for some other non-descriptive semantic theory that does not rely on real definitions to explain the sense in which a concept or meaning of a term is shared despite disagreement about its nominal definition. Notably, in the last decade or so, a number of theories (heretofore quasi-referential theories) along these lines have been proposed.[51]

Alexander's contribution seconds Brink's provocative conclusion that Dworkin is an originalist. Key to Alexander's argument is the notion of fit that figures prominently in Dworkin's idea of constructive interpretation. For Dworkin, the constructive interpretation of any object is constrained by dimensions of fit and justification. As he puts it:

> Roughly, constructive interpretation is a matter of imposing purpose on an object or practice in order to make of it the best possible example of the form or genre to which it is taken to belong. It does not follow, even from that rough account, that an interpreter can make of a practice or work of

---

[49] We do not mean to imply that only this semantic theory could serve as a complement to Raz's ODT.

[50] See Boyd (1989) and Brink (1988).

[51] See Sayre-McCord (1997), Van Roojen (2006), and Schroeter and Schroeter (2009).

art anything he would have wanted it to be . . . . For the history or shape of a practice or object constrains the available interpretations of it . . . .[52]

Thus for Dworkin, the correct interpretation of any object or practice must fit the pretheoretical materials that constitute the object or practice to a requisite degree, and it must be justified in the sense that it casts the practice or object as the best possible instance of its genre.

Alexander observes that this account of constructive interpretation commits Dworkin to the existence of a fixed set of pretheoretical materials with which any correct interpretation must fit. Alexander's main claim is that authorial intent is a key element of this fixed set of pretheoretical materials that constrains constitutional interpretation. As Alexander states:

> In order to make the law the best it can be, there has to be a "there" there, something the law is that can be made better. Or, put differently, for the dimension of fit to do any work, there has to be something with which to fit. As Dworkin realizes, at least post-*Law's Empire*, the mere marks of legal texts, when divorced from the intended meanings of the texts' authors, can mean anything. So legal texts must be given their author-intended meanings.(319)

On this basis, Alexander argues that Dworkin must espouse a version of originalism according to which authorial intent informs the meaning of constitutional provisions and constrains judicial constitutional interpretation.

As noted above, Dworkin accepts that a fixed set of preinterpretive materials constrains any act of constructive interpretation. Moreover, he repeatedly states that political decisions as embodied in constitutional provisions belong to the fixed set of pretheoretical materials that constrain legal and, hence, constitutional interpretation. However, Dworkin would likely disagree with Alexander's contention that the authorial intent behind these provisions belong to this fixed set of materials. To help see why, consider Dworkin's comments about the role that speaker intent plays in the context of conversational interpretation.

> Conversational interpretation is dominated by speakers' intentions because the point of interpreting in conversation is almost always the communication of such intentions. Legal interpretation is not dominated by the actual mental states of legislators and other officials because the best understanding of the purpose of interpreting statutes and other legal data makes irrelevant most of what those officials actually think or intend.[53]

In this passage, Dworkin characterizes conversational interpretation as a kind of constructive interpretation. That is, he ascribes the point of communicating

---

[52] Dworkin (1986: 52).
[53] Dworkin (2011: 149-150).

intentions to conversational practice, and given this point, any good interpretation of conversational utterance must adequately fit the speaker's intention. By contrast, as the immediately foregoing passage attests, Dworkin holds that the underlying point of the practice of legal interpretation (which presumably encompasses constitutional interpretation) renders speaker intent irrelevant.

The question that Alexander might press at this point is that if the intent underlying constitutional provisions does not constrain constitutional practice, then what possibly could? The general answer suggested in the immediately foregoing passage is those elements of the pretheoretical passage deemed relevant and hence constraining by the best interpretation of the practice. As applied to the context of constitutional interpretation, these elements might deem authorial intent as irrelevant while at the same time casting some other meaning associated with such provisions (e.g., their referential or, alternatively, quasi-referential meaning) in this constraining role. Note that in at least one passage, Brink seems to employ this approach, for there he points to underlying democratic values of legal practice to support his public-meaning-referentialist account of the meaning of constitutional provisions. To wit:

> There is little to recommend appeal to a speaker-relative, rather than a public, conception of meaning. In fact, as Scalia recognizes, democratic principles argue against both [speakers'-specific-intent and framer's-specific-intent forms of originalism] inasmuch as it is the public meaning and concepts expressed by provisions that are democratically adopted.(287)

In her contribution, Aditi Bagchi amplifies upon the just-described Dworkinian approach to interpretation and employs it to develop a theory of contractual interpretation. As she puts it:

> My aim is not to study [Dworkin's] claim about the nature of political authority but only its relationship to the mode of interpretation he recommends, i.e., reading legal rules in light of normative commitments exogenous to the immediate legal source for the rules. Dworkin inverts the presumptive conceptual chronology by asking how interpretation might serve authority—not yet secured—instead of assuming that we interpret only those texts that are backed by authority.(354)

Bagchi's key observation in this passage is that for Dworkin, content should be ascribed to authoritative utterances in light of the underlying value served by being authoritatively guided by those utterances. To cite an apposite example from Brink's contribution:

> For instance, in identifying the abstract intent of the framers of the equal protection clause of the Fourteenth Amendment with an equality or anti-discrimination constraint on governmental action, we are identifying a value that explains the political purpose that the Fourteenth Amendment was supposed to serve and, hence, rationalizes its adoption. The authority of this moralized reading of fidelity to the intentions of the framers derives

from the fact that our political system is a form of constitutional democracy in which there are substantive moral and political constraints on the
behavior of democratic bodies.(285)

Thus, Brink argues for specifying the meaning of the Fourteenth Amendment in
terms of the abstract intent of the framers because, so construed, the Fourteenth
Amendment is authoritative by dint of the values underlying the practice of constitutional democracy, whereas if construed in terms of the Framers' specific
intent, it is not authoritative.

Along these same lines, Bagchi argues that we should interpret contractual
provisions by way of what she refers to as normative triangulation.

Where authority is content-dependent, the intention of an author is to
that extent displaced. That displacement does not disrespect the author's
authority; it preserves it. For where the authority of the author depends
on how it is exercised, interpreting a text in a way that is faithful to intention but inconsistent with background constraints actually undermines the
author's authority, if not in a single case, then over time.(370)

Bagchi's key claim is that the intent of contracting parties is only one, albeit an
important determinant, of an adequate contractual interpretation. In addition,
background normative constraints are also relevant. Moreover, Bagchi is keen to
emphasize that although these background normative considerations are exogenous to the contracting parties' intent they nonetheless are key determinants of
the content of their contractual obligations.

In a key passage from her contribution, Connie Rosati states:

On one view about the legitimacy of constitutions, a view that I find
appealing, a constitution is legitimate when its content and the processes
of law-making that it specifies are such as to give rise to laws that one has
pro tanto moral obligation to obey; and in order for those law-making processes to give rise to laws that one has pro tanto moral obligation to obey,
the laws to which it gives rise must tend, as a consequence of its content and
law-making processes, to comport with morality, at least over time.(338)

Rosati offers the principle of reading constitutions morally as a corollary to the
view of constitutional legitimacy that she finds appealing. That is, she argues
that judges should interpret constitutions in ways that contribute to their legitimacy, as legitimacy is defined in the cited passage. Thus, Rosati embraces the
core idea that motivates Dworkin's approach to legal interpretation discussed
above. Put it Bagchi's terms, she joins Dworkin in inverting "the presumptive
conceptual chronology by asking how interpretation might serve authority—
not yet secured—instead of assuming that we interpret only those texts that are
backed by authority."(354)

Although Rosati embraces Dworkin's concept of interpretation, she rejects
his conception of the moral reading, for she doubts that interpreting constitutional provisions in the manner that Dworkin proposes (discussed extensively

above) would result in the articulation and enforcement of laws that, over time, would better comport with morality. She offers two lines of argument for this doubt. First, she argues that the interpretive method Dworkin proposes calls on judges to exercise skills for which they have no special training. Second, she fears that the deliverances of Dworkinian interpretive reasoning are likely to be highly indeterminate, thereby leading judges to fill in the gaps with their own particular policy preferences. These criticisms inform her alternative conception of the moral reading, for she aspires to articulate an alternative conception of reading a constitution morally that does not suffer from these defects. In sum, in addition to offering a cogent and carefully defended alternative to Dworkin's moralized conception of constitutional interpretation, Rosati's piece illustrates that a theorist might accept Dworkin's general approach to constitutional interpretation or, for that matter, the constructive interpretation of any number of practices or value-concepts, without accepting his particular conception or interpretation of the object.

Conclusion

We would like to conclude this introduction to our volume with a discussion of Chris Essert's piece, a contribution to the third part of our volume that, as such, responds to Dworkin's general jurisprudence. We have saved this discussion for last not only because, as noted above, doings so better positions us to situate Essert's piece in relation to Dworkin's theory. In addition, we think this discussion serves as a fitting conclusion to our introduction, for we hope here to identify a number of key threads that unify Dworkin's work and the pieces in this volume.

Essert defends what he refers to as the Simple View of law. Essert models the simple view on Niko Kolodny's analysis of the relationship between what we might loosely described as *the ought of rationality* on the one hand and *the ought of reasons on the other*.[54] To see the two relata that Kolodny has in mind, consider that a moral agent might wrongly judge that he has reason to perform some action or course of action—say to drink a quantity of petrol that he mistakes for water or to work long hours in a misguided pursuit of esteem and wealth at all costs. A common thing to say about such an agent is that in one sense he ought not to act in accordance with his mistaken judgment, for whether he knows it or not, the reasons that apply to him require him not to do so. However, a no less common thing to say is that, in another sense, he ought to act in accordance with his mistaken judgments, for it would be irrational not to. Kolodny seeks to explain the relationship between these two seemingly distinct categories of ought—the ought of reason and the ought of rationality.

---

[54] Kolodny (2005).

Kolodny argues for a monistic account of this relationship. According to his view, there is only one category of ought—the ought of reason. Roughly put, he holds that the seemingly distinct ought of rationality is the ought of reason from a point of view—in the examples above, a mistaken point of view. Thus, on his account, to say that the agents described in the example above ought to drink the petrol or work until 10 p.m. every night is to say that from their point of view, they have overall reason to do so.

Essert's key intuition is that the seeming ought-dualism that Kolodny's account unifies parallels a seeming plurality that bedevils philosophers of law— namely, legal and moral obligation. Moreover, Essert argues that this seeming plurality is fundamentally unified in much the same way that Koldony's oughts of rationality and reason are. Namely, on Essert's account, legal obligations are just what agents have the most reason to do from the legal point of view. Thus, for Essert, there is only one kind of normativity—the normativity of practical reason. However, there are many points of view of what such practical reasons require and the legal point of view is one of them.

Although Essert's simple view is monistic in one way, viewed from another perspective it is dualistic. That is, contra Dworkin, the Simple View constitutes a two-system view of law. That is, fundamentally, legal obligation is not continuous with the reasons, moral or otherwise of those to whom they apply. Rather, legal obligations are what those reasons require from the legal point of view—a view that may or may not be mistaken. Hence, Essert holds that there are two systems—the reasons there are, on the one hand, and the legal point of view of the reasons there are, on the other.

Essert ably defends this two-system view, and we have no intent of criticizing it or its supporting argument here. However, we do think it is a useful and a fitting conclusion to our introduction to identify what we take to be two key points of contention between this two-system Simple View and Dworkin's one-system approach.

To see the first point of contention, it helps to consider that whereas Kolodny seems to have in mind a point of view that is constituted by the beliefs and value judgments of a natural person, Essert's legal point of view presumably is constituted in some other way. Essert acknowledges this point, for he holds that "[t]he secondary rules, and in particular the Rule of Recognition, could be understood as picking out the ways in which the legal point of view is formed and so the ways in which legal obligations are determined."(266) In other words, on Essert's account, the legal point of view of any legal system is constituted by norms picked out by the criteria of validity that the officials of that system accept in common.

It is our view that Dworkin is committed to the existence of a legal point of view. More generally, as we have seen, it seems to us that he is committed to the point of view of a wide variety of practices. However, he would reject Essert's account of the legal point of view in favor of his account, according to which the legal point of view, like the point of view of many practices, is constituted by a constructive interpretation of the relevant practice—in this case, legal practice.

As Dworkin puts it, and as we have discussed above, constructive interpretations proceeds via a personification of the community that engages in the relevant practice. Accordingly, Dworkin would hold that, as such an interpretive construction, the legal point of view is partly determined by the best interpretation of the values that animate the relevant practice—in this case, legal practice.

So, for example, in keeping with this account of the construction of the legal point of view, one might embrace Brink's view that the content of constitutional provisions must be specified in accordance with a public meaning referentialist originalism, for attributing this content to this aspect of legal practice would answer to the democratic principles that justify it. Or, we might accept Bagchi's claim that the content we should attribute to the provisions of contracts is a function of the contracting parties' intent delimited by certain constraints of reasonableness, for such an interpretation would best reflect the values that animate the legal enforcement of contracts. In sum, Dworkin would argue that the legal point of view is not a view about the reasons we have; rather, it is a construction of such reasons, and hence, contra the two-system Simple View, the legal point is continuous with rather than distinct from those reasons.

If we read Dworkin as a kind of perspectival constructivist, there is yet a deeper point of contention between Essert's Simple View and Dworkin's theory. Namely, according to this reading of Dworkin, all reasons are constructions of some point of view or other. In other words, per the perspectival constructivist reading of the unity of value thesis, all true value statements (which includes all claims about what reasons there are) just are those that reflect the value judgments that would result from the application of Dworkinian interpretive reasoning to the initially unruly and wild set of value propositions comprised by the relevant perspective. To put this point in terms of Kolodny's dichotomy, read as a constructivist, Dworkin would reverse Kolodny's account of the relationship between the ought of reason and the ought of rationality, for so read, he would hold that the ought of reason is ultimately reducible to the ought of interpretive rationality.

References

Boyd, Richard (1988). "How to Be a Moral Realist." In *Essays on Moral Realism*. Geoffrey Sayre-McCord (ed.). Ithaca: Cornell University Press.

Brink, David (1989). *Moral Realism and the Foundations of Ethics*. Cambridge: Cambridge University Press.

Christiano, Thomas (2008). *The Constitution of Equality: Democratic Authority and Its Limits*. Oxford: Oxford University Press.

Dworkin, Ronald (2013). "A New Philosophy of International Law," *Philosophy and Public Affairs* 41, n. 1:2–30.

Dworkin, Ronald (2011) *Justice for Hedgehogs* Cambridge, MA: Harvard University Press.

Dworkin, Ronald (2010). "Response," *Boston University Law Review* 90:1075–1076.

Dworkin, Ronald (1996). "Objectivity and Truth: You'd Better Believe It," *Philosophy and Public Affairs* 25:87–139.

Dworkin, Ronald (1986). *Law's Empire*. Cambridge, MA: Harvard University Press.

Dworkin, Ronald (1973). "The Original Position," *The University of Chicago Law Review* 40:500–533.

Fuller, Lon (1969). *The Morality of Law*, revised ed. New Haven: Yale University Press.

Hart, H.L.A. (1994). *The Concept of Law*, 2nd ed. Oxford: Oxford University Press.

Jackson, Frank (1998). *From Metaphysics To Ethics: A Defense Of Conceptual Analysis*. Oxford: Oxford University Press.

Kolodny, Niko (2005). "Why Be Rational?" *Mind* 114:509–563.

Lynch, Michael (2009). *Truth as One and Many*. New York: Oxford University Press.

Price, Huw (2013). *Expressivism, Pragmatism, and Representationalism*. Cambridge: Cambridge University Press.

Raz, Joseph (2011). *From Normativity to Responsibility*. Oxford: Oxford University Press.

Sayre-McCord, Geoffrey (1997). "'Good' on Twin Earth," *Philosophical Issues* 8:267–292.

Schroeter, Laura and Schroeter, Francis (2009). "A Third Way in Metaethics," *Noûs* 43(1):1–30.

Sciaraffa, Stefan (2012). "Explaining Theoretical Disagreement and Massive Decisional Agreement: The Justificatory View," *Problema* 4:165–189.

Van Roojen, Mark (2006). "Knowing Enough to Disagree." In *Oxford Studies in Metaethics*, vol. 1, R. Shafer-Landau (ed.). New York: Oxford University Press.

Waldron, Jeremy (2006). "The Core of the Case against Judicial Review," *Yale Law Review* 115, n. 6:1346–1406.

PART I

The Unity of Value

1

A Hedgehog's Unity of Value
by Joseph Raz[*]

Ronald Dworkin was nothing if not an inventive and innovative theorist. Though, like all of us deeply embedded in his time and the ideas of his time, he was carving his views out of his own imaginative resources, to an ever-growing degree free from the need to grapple, in his own contributions, with the conventional paradigms set by others, and at the same time, in his critical commentaries on events and ideas, dissecting the presuppositions, ideas, and writings and exposing the fallacies of opponents.

As is to be expected, some ideas, or perhaps it is better to call them intellectual tendencies, marked, often dominated, the movement of thought in much of his writings. One dominant trend is the striving towards unity. And unity is my topic today, or more specifically the unity of value in Dworkin's *Justice for Hedgehogs*. I will reflect on some of the many things he writes in dealing with that theme. My main aim is to clarify his view about the unity of value. In doing that, I will meander in different directions, trying out some interpretations before turning to others. In other words, I will try to interpret his views in ways that will turn out not to fit them— in part to show that the interpretations do not fit, and in part to see how closely his views resemble them even so. I hope that by the end of this journey, we will better understand his view about the unity of value.

One general caveat before we start: While drawing distinctions between values, virtues, reasons, rights, duties, etc., where appropriate, Dworkin also uses '*value*' in a more indiscriminate, all-encompassing way. Its scope is similar to what other writers regard as the domain of the evaluative or normative, or their combination. The unity of value is about value in that broad sense, and I will use 'value' in that sense in this paper, namely, to refer to reasons, norms, virtues, etc., as well as to values in the narrower sense.

[*]I am grateful to the many participants in the Analytical Legal Philosophy Conference, held in Oxford, 2014, who made many helpful and instructive comments.

1. The Unity of Value: an Introduction

The theme is introduced in the opening sentence: "This book defends a large and old philosophical thesis: the unity of value."[1] The first couple of pages make clear that the one big thing that the hedgehog knows is both how to live well and that value is one. As will emerge below, one lives well if one lives responsibly, namely discharging successfully the responsibility project (a task in which no one can be completely successful). The responsibility project leads one towards the unity of value, and in living well that unity is manifested in one's life.[2]

What does the unity of value mean? You may think that it means that there is but one value, and all the different values we may have in mind are but different names for it (on the paradigm of the view that there is one deity, and that different religions, and sometimes the same religion, have different names for it). But that is not Dworkin's thought. Or, you may think that it means that there is but one value, and the different values we have in mind are but different aspects of it. That may be closer to Dworkin's thought. But that formulation is itself obscure: What makes justice and liberty different aspects of the same value rather than two different values?

History is rife with examples of such views. Perhaps, as utilitarians have it, there is one value, say pleasure, and the different aspects of it are different causes of its instantiations, say poetry and push pin. Or perhaps they are different contexts in which it manifests itself. Perhaps the single value is desire satisfaction (or some subclass of it) and the aspects are its manifestations within family life or in one's professional life (as when one's desire to have supper in the company of one's family, or to complete one's assigned task on time, is satisfied). Or, if the only value is being virtuous, perhaps there is only one virtue, say wisdom, though it can be manifested in different contexts, as when one is courageous, which is being wise when facing danger, or generous, which is being wise regarding the needs of others, etc. But there is no reason to think that Dworkin understands the unity of value in any of these ways.

Some passages may suggest that Dworkin simply means that there is no conflict between different values. But that could be at most part of his meaning;[3] it cannot be all he means. After all, very disparate values may not conflict. For example, some jokes are funny, and that makes them good, at least to a degree or in one way. And sleep can be restful, and that makes that kind of sleep good, at least to a degree or in one way. It may be impossible for the value of restful sleep to conflict with the value of funny jokes[4] (at least I do not know what it could be

---

[1] Dworkin (2011: 1).

[2] I am grateful to Robin Kar for encouraging me to make clear the connection between the unity of value and living well.

[3] Even that is not clear given that Dworkin allows for the possibility of conflict (Dworkin 2011: 120). If he thought that that possibility is sometimes realized then he allowed that the unity of value could co-exist with conflict of values (as I believe that it can).

[4] Though they may be derivatively related to some conflicts (e.g., between buying a book of funny jokes and securing restful sleep).

for them to conflict), yet it does not appear that the two are aspects of one value. Or rather, the fact that they do not conflict does not establish that they are such aspects.

Similarly, that one value cannot be instantiated unless another is (for example, assuming that life and generosity are both values, one cannot be generous unless one is alive), does not in itself establish that they are aspects of one value. And nor does the fact that one value is a constituent part of another establish that they are but aspects of one value. For example, possibly a country is not democratic unless its residents are both free and literate, and possibly these are constituent components of democracy (and I assume that they are all valuable). That does not establish that democracy is an aspect of freedom or of literacy, nor that there is nothing more to the values of freedom or literacy than their contribution to democracy. Therefore, so far as this consideration is concerned, the three are distinct values.[5] Finally, that all values are values does not show that they are aspects of one value. It merely shows that they share something—a common property or properties.

2. The Unity of Value: Consistent with Value Pluralism

I mention these points to distinguish Dworkin's thesis from other familiar theses that are sometimes presented under the same name. Although he does not offer a definitive formulation of his thesis, he says much from which his meaning can be, at least partly, inferred. But before turning to that, it may be worth examining briefly the opposing, or what may be taken to be the opposing, thesis, namely that there are many distinct values.

Needless to say there are different versions of, different views about the nature of value pluralism, not all of them incompatible. I will merely point to some features of pluralism about values that seem to me right. They presuppose a certain understanding of value.

For example, I will be assuming, along with Dworkin,[6] that evaluative properties, namely, features of an activity, object, event, or whatever, that make it valuable in some respect can in principle be understood, meaning that given favorable circumstances (which are metaphysically possible), beings with the capacities that humans commonly have can comprehend what is good about things that are good and why. Again, with Dworkin, I assume that explanations of values are not reductive. They employ other value concepts. Therefore, values do not come in isolation. The value of anything will relate to some other values, which may be constituents or consequences of it, or related to it in some other way that makes it helpful to refer to them in an explanation of the value we are explaining.

---

[5] Things are different if the constituents of one value are not independently valuable. Then they can be thought of as mere aspects of the value to which they contribute.

[6] See Dworkin (2011: 113-115).

Furthermore, our views about the value of things shape our attitudes to ourselves, and the world around us. One aspect of that is that the value of actions, of those actions that are options for us, is a reason for performing them. That connects value to the quality of our life, for at the very least, a major factor that determines its quality is that our life goes well when we engage in activities and have attitudes that we have reason to have. But note that the connection is asymmetric: Our life is good because we engage in activities that are good and that connect us to valuable aspects of the world. It is not the case that these activities are good because they contribute to the goodness of our life.

So far—some observations about features of value in general. Now to value pluralism:

The question is: how are values individuated? That is, what makes one value property distinct, and different from another value property, so that the instantiation of one manifests a different value from that of the other? Think of an example: humour is good and so is camaraderie. But they are different goods, or values, as is manifested by the fact that the explanations of their value will be different. We can, for example, expect that the explanations will refer to different human capacities and dispositions excellence in which these values bring out. Such facts will be part of the explanation of their value. Possibly that will be all that they share, a reference to human capacities and dispositions, and ways, different ways, in which their manifestations can be valuable. The way these capacities or activities excel will be different. We may, metaphorically, say that their *point* is different.

There is no way of avoiding metaphors when discussing the difference between values. When explaining the difference between various derivative values, those properties that are valuable because of their relations to other values (e.g., instrumental values), we proceed by pointing to their dependence on different values. But non-derivative values, precisely because they do not derive from any others, deprive us of a non-metaphorical way of explaining their differences except by engaging in detailed explanations of each value, or value property, and observing their differences.

This understanding of the plurality of value allows for a great inflation in the number of values. For example, there are various kinds of humor: There is satire and irony and broad humor, and sarcasm and so on. In explaining the value of each, we would identify them as species of humor, but will also explain their differences, which make each one good in a different way. One marker of that difference is that they are not interchangeable: what makes a satirical observation suitable to the situation may not make sarcasm suitable. Of course, what makes a remark about Jane suitable on one occasion may not make the same remark about Liz suitable for the same occasion. But with satire and sarcasm, the fact that they are not interchangeable is due to the different excellences they display, whose display is typically appropriate in different contexts.

It is not merely that there are, on this view, many values. There is no end to the possibility of fissure, the possibility that any good kind may develop distinctively good subkinds,[7] though, of course, some values are quite remote from one another, and we normally think of those when referring to value pluralism.

Some people would greet this value inflation with grave suspicion. They may even take it to be an objection to this understanding of value pluralism. I draw a different conclusion from it. It deflates the importance of the difference between one value and another, but without losing sight of their distinct character. In a way, these reflections bring value pluralism, the value pluralism I am discussing, closer to Dworkin's thought. I believe that Dworkin's discussion is not hostile to this view of value pluralism. His idea is not that there is only one value. He is not concerned with criteria for the individuation of values, and does not rely on such criteria to establish the unity of value. His thesis is not that there is only one value but that there are certain relations among values that establish what he calls their unity. When illustrating the unity of value in his first chapter, Dworkin sees it in the fact that the different values mesh together, that they are integrated, or that "the various concepts and departments of value are interconnected and mutually supportive."[8]

3. Exploring the Unity Thesis

This last articulation of the thesis (he describes that statement as "the more general thesis of this book") may strike one as rather distinct from what we would normally understand by the unity of value (e.g., we expect different scientific theories to be mutually supportive and interconnected without being but aspects of one theory). But so long as we are not misled into taking Dworkin to be contending for something he is not in fact arguing for, no harm is done. If one insists we can take him to be arguing for a particular version of value pluralism, one in which the different values are interconnected and mutually supportive.

There is an understanding of such connections that would incline one to speak naturally about the unity of value. Suppose that, while there are various distinct values, one of them is supreme in that (1) all the others contribute to its realization, perhaps by being constituent elements of it, or by their realization being a precondition of its realization, and (2) if it is realized to the highest possible degree, then there is nothing that can improve the way things are. The second condition makes it the supreme value. In combination, all other values, though important in themselves, are fully realized in their contribution to its realization, for no improvement in them matters once it is realized to the highest degree possible. But again, that is not Dworkin's thought, and he says nothing that suggests it.

---

[7] I am presupposing here that the existence of values, at least of some of them, is historically contingent. See Raz (2003).

[8] Dworkin (2011: 10).

His discussion keeps returning to the idea of an "interconnected and interdependent system of principles and ideas."[9] The unity of value seems to consist in that. But it is unlikely that we would find the key to unity in the kind of connections or dependencies that Dworkin has in mind when discussing specific values. He does not advance a view that a specific relationship or a number of such relationships obtains between values generally and constitutes their unity. On the contrary, he is open to the existence of many different types of connections and dependencies, including ones not yet envisaged by anyone: "what can count as an argument for a moral conviction is a substantive matter: we must wait to see what connections among different departments of value seem pertinent and appealing."[10] Rather the unity consists, as this quote illustrates, in the fact that the connections constitute reasons for evaluative beliefs, and in the case for the inescapability of an interconnected system of beliefs of that kind.[11] The argument goes to the conditions of truth about value: a value judgment "can be true only if there is an adequate case...that supports it....[T]hat case must contain further value judgements..... None of those further value judgements can be...true [unless] a further case can be made supporting each of them, and that further case will ramify into a host of other judgements...[that] need yet further cases to show them true."[12]

Dworkin is not discussing here epistemic reasons for believing that value judgments are true. We can reach warranted beliefs about, say, the time of the next train to Brighton, via various routes, each one providing sufficient warrant for a belief about the time, and we can have various different epistemic reasons providing alternative routes to a warranted evaluative belief that, let's say, Eggers's latest novel has important lessons to teach us about the direction of contemporary culture. We may be justified in believing that that is so by the testimony of discerning friends, or by our knowledge of Eggers's work and of his interests, and of the themes explored in the novel (that we did not read), etc. But the "cases" for value beliefs that Dworkin is writing about in the quoted passages are not epistemic cases. They are—in his view—the evaluative analog of truth- conditions, or of truth makers, in relation to non-normative beliefs. Their existence is what makes value beliefs true. Perhaps we could say that we are looking for the

---

[9] Dworkin (2011: 116).

[10] Dworkin (2011: 117).

[11] Nicos Stavropoulos suggested to me that Dworkin took the unity of value to consist in the existence of some specific kind of connections between values, connections whose nature and existence are an open question. According to Stavropoulos, Dworkin is merely asserting that possibly such a unifying connection or connections exist, and that there is some reason to think that they do. Their existence should be explored, and if they are found, then we will know that the unity thesis is true. I believe that that view misconstrues Dworkin's view. He argues that the unity follows from the very nature of values in a way I explain in the text, and therefore can be known even though we do not know which connections between values instantiate it.

[12] Dworkin (2011: 116).

grounds of the truth of value beliefs, and of evaluative propositions more generally, using '*ground*' in the meaning in which it is used in recent writings.[13]

The question Dworkin addresses is not when do reasons to believe some value
judgment warrant belief in it, but what grounds the truth of a true evaluative
belief. His answer begins with the observation, "The truth of any true moral
judgement consists in the truth of an indefinite number of other moral judgements and its truth provides part of what constitutes the truth of any of those
others."[14] So he is not looking for the grounds of the truth of value judgments,
for the relation between the grounds and what they are grounds of is asymmetric, and so generally (though with some exceptions) is the relation between truth
makers and what they make true. As so often, Dworkin's thought defies current
philosophical categories, and is of course none the worse for that. A short way of
referring to what he is after is useful, and I will use the expression 'a constitutive
case'. His thesis is about the constitutive case for the truth of value propositions
and beliefs.

The constitutive case, he explains, is reflexive. It includes the belief for which
it is the case. But there is no question begging or vicious circularity here. A value
belief is not sufficient for its own truth, it is merely a small part of an indefinite
number of propositions that taken together would be the constitutive case for its
truth, if it is true. The quotation above is about moral beliefs. But the constitutive case for the truth of true moral beliefs is not limited to other moral beliefs.
Dworkin explains:

> "Morality is only one department of value . . . Is there any limit to the range
> of convictions to which we might appeal in making a case that some action
> is morally right or morally wrong? Or that someone is virtuous or vicious,
> or that something is beautiful or ugly, or that some life is successful or
> unsuccessful? Could a case for the unfairness of affirmative action include
> an aesthetic judgement as well as a moral one? Could a case for the right
> way to live include claims about the natural evolution of the universe or
> about the biological heritage of animals in human beings? I see no concep-
> tual or a priori reason why not. What can count as an argument for a moral
> conviction is a substantive matter: we must wait to see what connections
> among different departments of value seem pertinent and appealing."[15]

I already remarked on the fact that Dworkin's case for the unity of value does
not include and does not rest on a view of the type of interconnections between
values. The question we examine now is how far the interconnections go. Given
what values are, each of them and each value proposition or value belief rests on
a constitutive case, and the values included in these cases themselves rest on further constitutive cases. These cases, the quotation above explained, may contain

---

[13] E.g. Rosen (2010), Fine in Correia and Shnieder (2012) and other essays in that volume.
[14] Dworkin (2011: 117).
[15] Dworkin (2011: 117).

any other principle or proposition. There is no general argument that excludes any kind of principle, or conviction, evaluative or non-evaluative, from being part of the constitutive case for the truth of any value belief. Dworkin here, and elsewhere in the book, gestures towards the view that all the values are interconnected in a chain of constitutive cases, which possibly include all other true propositions as well.

But anyone who expects Dworkin to provide an argument to that effect may be disappointed. In spite of the repeated reference to the unity of value residing in the "interconnected and interdependent system of principles and ideas," when it comes to providing an argument it seems, as it does reading the quotation above, that after all Dworkin does not know whether values are such a system, whether they are united in that way, unless of course the ignorance is dispelled elsewhere in the book. But it is not. There is nowhere in it a case for taking the totality of true propositions to be the constitutive case for the truth of any single value proposition, nor for the constitutive cases being connected in a chain of justifications that embraces all values, let alone all other propositions.

But perhaps there is, or perhaps Dworkin thinks that there is, such a case in the passage we are discussing. That is, does not the mere *possibility* that any proposition is part of the constitutive case for any value proposition make it part of that constitutive case? Of course, Dworkin does not claim that it is possible that the constitutive case for any true value proposition is the totality of all true propositions, nor does he say that the case for any proposition is chain-linked to the case for any other proposition. All he says is that he sees no reason why that is not so. Possibly he suspends judgment on the issue. But perhaps this is just an understatement. Or, perhaps he believes that not seeing an objection to a possibility shows that it is a possibility. Let that be as it may. The substantive question is worth pondering: If it is possible that a proposition is part of the constitutive case for some true proposition, does it follow that it is part of that constitutive case? So put the answer is clearly "No". It is possible, I take it, that some propositions that are in fact false are true (For some p, p is possibly true and p is false). It seems to follow that if all true propositions are possibly part of the constitutive case for all true value propositions, then so are some false propositions. But no false proposition is, as Dworkin understands matters, part of the constitutive case for any true value proposition. This may be wrong. Whatever Dworkin had in mind, possibly false propositions can be part of the constitutive case for true propositions, for example, if they are part of a *reductio ad absurdum* argument for them. Further thought is required.

If, however, we accept that no false proposition can be part of the constitutive case for any true proposition, then we can rephrase the argument under consideration to avoid the objection above. Perhaps it is the case that for any proposition, if it is true then if possibly it is part of the constitutive case for some proposition, it is part of that constitutive case.[16]

---

[16] I am grateful to Ori Simchen for suggesting this modification of the argument.

The obvious cause for doubting that view is that in denying that the constitutive case for a true proposition discriminates between relevant and irrelevant true propositions, it renders the category unhelpful. But that criticism could be rejected if the set that constitutes the constitutive case includes no redundancy at all, that is, if none of its members can be excluded without undermining the case for the proposition; in other words, without rendering it untrue.

If that is the case for inclusion in a constitutive case, then propositions that merely possibly contribute to establishing its truth cannot be part it. Only those that actually contribute can be. One may doubt that test. It excludes the possibility of over-determination. But that is best dealt with by taking propositions whose truth is over-determined as having two or more constitutive cases, with no redundancy within any single one of them.

Of course, without all true propositions belonging to the constitutive case of each value proposition, we have no reason to think that this account of the truth of value propositions guarantees the unity of value. Perhaps it does. But to see that, we need a better understanding of what makes a proposition belong with the constitutive case for another proposition. So far we avoided that question, for if all of them belong there, possibly the question why they belong there need not be faced, at least not when considering only the unity of value. Now the question is inescapable. And it is difficult to answer because of an important omission in Dworkin's account. I noted earlier the need to distinguish between epistemic reasons to believe in a value proposition and the reasons that constitute the case for its truth. Many, perhaps all, reasons that belong to the constitutive case for the truth of a value proposition are also, or can be depending on circumstances, reasons to believe that the proposition is true. That would be the case at least whenever it is possible to know the constitutive reasons, and know that they are constitutive reasons, independently of knowing the truth of the proposition whose truth they establish.

However, many epistemic reasons are not constitutive reasons. Some are easy to tell apart, for example, testimony. But with others the distinction is less straightforward. I already mentioned the difficulty I encounter as to whether the propositions that figure in a *reductio* argument form a constitutive or an epistemic case for believing its conclusion. Here is just one other example. Often, and to some minds inescapably, we explain the value of something, as well as value properties themselves, by analogy. The excellence of some poetry is similar in some respects to the excellence of some music. The value of patriotism is similar in some ways to dedication to one's family, etc. Such explanations help us to see that whichever side of the analogy we were less clear about is valuable and how it is valuable. They provide reasons, not necessarily conclusive reasons, to believe in propositions about those values. But are they constitutive of the case for the truth of these propositions? Or, are they merely ways of enabling us to "see" that those propositions are true on grounds that do not include the analogy, which is after all merely a gesture to a similarity, one that can also be misleading if taken on its own, etc. etc.?

In my introductory observations about value in general, I endorsed, as does Dworkin, the intelligibility of value, meaning the possibility of making people with ordinary capacities and experience understand what is valuable about possessing value properties, i.e., why they are value properties. Good analogical reasoning is sufficient to secure intelligibility. It is far from clear, however, whether this shows that it is part of the constitutive case for values and evaluative beliefs. The distinction between epistemic and grounding or constituting reasons for a value is important, and without it we lack a proper understanding of what makes a reason part of the constitutive case for a value, or what makes it a ground for the value.

The mere dependence of values on constitutive cases does not secure the unity of value. It is consistent with the constituent cases belonging to disparate, possibly even mutually exclusive domains of value. A substantive argument is required to show that this is not so, that each value depends on all others, and all values are mutually supportive. Dworkin does not offer such an argument, and his failure to provide a distinction between epistemic and constitutive grounds for value beliefs adds to the difficulty in finding in the book any steps towards such an argument.

4. Conflict and Incommensurability

Referring to conflict of values Dworkin remarks: "If I am to sustain my main claims in this book, about the unity of value, I must deny the conflict."[17] The relatively relaxed way that, as I suggested, Dworkin's view about the unity of value is to be understood does not compel that conclusion. Unity, as he sees it, is in interconnections and mutual support, and these are matters of degree. A degree of conflict is compatible with a degree of unity, as (in a different context) is well known to all members of families. Moreover, even Dworkin does not deny all practical conflicts. He denies conflict (though not the appearance of conflict) between different values. Practical conflicts can exist even if there is no conflict of values. The familiar example of a lifeguard on a beach illustrates that. Two people will drown if he does not save them. He can save one but not both. Which one ought he to save? The only values relevant, I will assume, are that of saving or preserving life, and the value of doing his duty as a guard, which he owes both to his employer and to the two people, given that his presence there was publicized, and was the reason bathing there was safe and permissible. Both considerations apply in equal measure to both bathers. He ought to save each of them and he cannot save both. This is a not untypical case of practical conflict, but it does not involve a conflict between different values.[18] However, not being a conflict

---

[17] Dworkin (2011: 118).

[18] See Raz (2011: ch. 9). That is not the only kind of practical conflict that leaves Dworkin unperturbed. He also allows for conflicts between desiderata ("Desiderata almost always conflict.... A community wants the highest level of security, the best educational system.... But its budget is tight." Dworkin (2011: 118).) and between desiderata and values ("Values often conflict

between values these conflicts do not weaken the thesis about the unity of value in the way that conflicts between values do. It is that form of weakening of unity that he resists.

Dworkin is aware that some unity theses are consistent with conflict. He writes:

> "My claim is not just that we can bring our discrete moral judgements into some kind of reflective equilibrium—we could do that even if we conceded that our values conflict .... I want to defend the more ambitious claim that there are no genuine conflicts in value"[19]

Why do values not conflict? Because, as Dworkin sees it, it is never the case that the realization of one of them to a greater degree restricts the degree to which any other value is realized. Dworkin does not deny that some values can be realized to a greater or lesser degree. He does deny that the limited realization of one value can secure the realization of a second value to a greater degree than would have been possible had the realization of the first not been so limited. This, as Dworkin knows, does not strike many people as obvious. Is it not the case that the geography of a region may be awe inspiring, but if it changes in certain ways while losing that character, it may become idyllic as it is not now, or that it may be beautifully colorful, with saturated colors, but if it gets drier it would be less beautiful but more pleasant to live in? All four qualities I mentioned in the two examples are non-instrumental value qualities, or can be so understood. Yet in each example, one value is realized at the expense of another. Are they not examples of cases in which one value is realized at the expense of the other? Perhaps not, perhaps appearances deceive. But first, two differences between these examples and the cases Dworkin discusses.

First, he is often concerned with moral values: honesty and the avoidance of cruelty, and such like. True, but his central thesis, about the unity of value, applies

---

with desiderata.... Some steps we might take to improve safety from terrorists, which we certainly desire, would compromise liberty and honour." Dworkin (2011: 118).) *'Desiderata'* is used by Dworkin not in its common meaning (desirables) but to refer to what is desired ("Desiderata are what we want but do no wrong not to have." Dworkin (2011: 118).). We want what we want for what we take to be reasons. But even so, we often want what we should not want, what is worthless and pointless to have or to want. Needless to say, there may be conflict between what we want and what is of value. But Dworkin's examples, or most of them, are not of this kind. They are of wanting what is worth wanting, indeed in some cases wanting what we ought to want (even on his view, given that he probably believes that a community should strive to protect itself from terrorists). In as much as desiderata are backed by reasons, by values that the wanting or its satisfaction realize, it would seem that the case of such conflict is the same as that of conflict between values. If desiderata can conflict, so can values. However, if persuaded that I am right about these conflicts Dworkin would have denied that desiderata can conflict either.

[19] Dworkin (2011: 119) Scott Hershovitz suggested that as Dworkin writes that the view that values conflict is "conceivable and perhaps someone might make it seem plausible" Dworkin (2011: 120), he does leave the possibility of conflict open. In a sense that is true, it is a "conceivable" possibility. But it is not a matter on which his theory is silent or agnostic. As the quotation above shows, the theory he is advancing denies that that conceivable possibility is ever realized.

to all values. I would be the first to remind us that it does not stand or fall with the absence of conflict. The unity may be greater or smaller, and the presence of some conflicts, or of conflicts in some departments of value, as Dworkin refers to them, is consistent with some kinds or some degree of unity. Dworkin, however, sees a degree of unity, among values in general, that excludes the possibility of conflict.

Second, my examples deal with situations in which the facts that impede or restrict the realization of value may not result from human activity. They certainly need not result from human activity in the pursuit of the values mentioned in the examples. The conflicts that Dworkin is interested in are those that face human agents who have to choose among options that appear to realize one value at the expense of another. True, but the values in my examples can be affected by human actions. Humans have been known to interfere with the landscape to enhance its value in one way even while detracting from the degree to which it manifests another value. It is possible that when people confront such choices, one option is supported by a better reason than all the others. But that in itself does not, as Dworkin reminds us, show that the choice does not manifest a conflict of values.

So why does he deny that the realization of one value may be at the expense of another? Let us look first at cases in which agents are confronted with what appears to be a conflict of values and in which there is a conclusive reason to choose one of the available options over any of the others. Why does Dworkin think that the existence of a conclusive reason results from there being no conflict rather than pointing to the right way of reacting to a conflict? Because, I think the answer is, he cannot think what else it could be. He does not so much offer an argument in support of his view as ask for an explanation of how any alternative makes sense. Here is what he says:

> "A colleague asks you to comment on a draft...and you find it bad. You will be cruel if you are frank but dishonest if you are not....the way to think further is to further refine our conceptions of the two values. We ask whether it is really cruel to tell an author the truth. Or, whether it is really dishonest to tell him what it is in his interests to hear and no one's interest to suppress. However we describe the process of thought through which we decide what to do, these are the questions that, in substance, we face. We reinterpret our concept to resolve our dilemma: the direction of our thought is toward unity, not fragmentation..... What other story might one tell? Consider this one: "Moral conflict is real....not an illusion produced by incomplete moral interpretation; it is a matter of plain fact." But what in the world could that supposed plain fact consist in?"[20]

And he continues to remind us that there are reasons for moral truths, etc. And how could conflict be ultimate if there are such reasons? This is a question that requires an answer. Dworkin is right both that the process he describes here

---

[20] Dworkin (2011: 119).

can make one realize that what one took to be a conflict of values is not one, and that the thesis that values can conflict needs an explanation: How is it that they conflict and why? The need for an explanation applies to all practical conflicts, not only to those that involve a conflict among conflicting values but those that do not, the ones that Dworkin implicitly allows. Of course, quite a number of answers to these questions have been offered. Even my sketchy observations earlier about the nature of value point to a family of such explanations: different values have different points, bring out or enable different excellences, and so on. Given that that is how they are individuated, there are no grounds to doubt that the conditions for their realization may be incompatible, thus yielding a conflict. True to his intention expressed at the beginning of the book, Dworkin does not consider any of the explanations of the possibility of conflict.[21]

Any account that allows for conflicts among values confronts not only the question about the possibility of conflicts, but also the question: What ought one to do when facing a conflict? I share Dworkin's feeling that this task is hard to discharge, even though I am not as pessimistic as he is. I think that often, more often than is sometimes realized, when reasons conflict, no option is backed by a conclusive reason; rather several of them are backed by incommensurable reasons. Dworkin discusses incommensurability at some length.[22] He insists on one important lesson: Do not assume that two values are incommensurable or that conflict between them is indeterminate just because you do not know any better. Do not take incommensurability or indeterminacy to be a default, a view to endorse in the absence of sufficient reasons for either alternative.

There are a good number of different phenomena often described as value or reason indeterminacy or incommensurability. And his advice is sound regarding all of them. I want to make one comment about the one kind of incommensurability that interested me most, namely, when on a particular occasion, an agent confronts several options backed by incommensurate reasons. As Dworkin points out, if this is so, then there are explanations that make it intelligible why it is so, and they operate on two levels. First, they explain how it is that reasons of these kinds can be incommensurate with one another. Second, they explain why the reasons that apply to this particular case are incommensurate. But of course, there are cases in which we have reason to believe that something is the case even though we have no explanation of why or how it is that it is the case. So we may have adequate reasons to believe that the value-based reasons for action in a particular case are incommensurate even when we do not yet have an explanation of why they are incommensurate. In some cases, the nature of the problem and the values that bear on it, coupled with failure to find any grounds for holding that the reasons supporting any option are conclusive even after due investigation,

---

[21] I am not considering the separate question of whether although values conflict in application they cannot conflict in themselves. An intriguing and difficult question, even to understand, it is not one that engages Dworkin in this book.

[22] Dworkin (2011: especially 90-96).

may warrant the conclusion that the reasons are incommensurate. Like many beliefs backed by evidence, the conclusion may turn out to be mistaken. We are fallible even when we form beliefs on rational grounds. Our fallibility does not establish that the beliefs are unwarranted.

5. Constructivist Unity?

It is possible that the preceding discussion seriously misunderstands Dworkin's view.[23] One ground for such a doubt is the absence from my discussion so far of any mention of Dworkin's ideas about personal responsibility. I have approached Dworkin's views about value as expressing an objective stand based on what I will call object-dependent truths (ODT): Truths about value are independent of any single person's view about what values there are; the constitutive case for them consists of values or propositions about values. You may say that it is a form of realism about values, though Dworkin would regard that term as confusing his view with the belief that there are bare facts about values (meaning that there are values that cannot be made intelligible and beliefs in which are not capable of being vindicated by a constitutive case). According to the ODT interpretation of his view, individuals can appreciate what is valuable and why, by engaging in interpretive reasoning. If they do so well they will come to realize truths that are independent of the beliefs about these truths that each one of them holds. Much that Dworkin writes suggests the ODT interpretation of his views. But there are other indications that may point in a different direction. Consider the following early passage:

> "Interpreters have critical responsibilities, and the best interpretation of a law or a poem or an epoch is the interpretation that best realises those responsibilities on that occasion."[24]

Could it be that Dworkin has a constructivist (to use current jargon) understanding of truth about values? Does he mean that the correct or true interpretation will be discovered by an interpreter who lives up to his responsibilities on that occasion? Or, does he mean that the correct or true interpretation is made correct by being the one that an interpreter who acts responsibly will come to endorse? On the first reading, the one I have been following in the previous discussion, the correctness of a belief about values is independent of the way it is arrived at, leaving open the possibility that even a flawless interpretive reasoning

---

[23] I am grateful to Sari Kisilevsky for alerting me to another issue: Is my inquiry inconsistent with Dworkin's rejection of a separate domain of metaethics? I think that I said and implied nothing that offends against Dworkin's views in this regard. But the relevant issue is whether the questions raised here merit an answer. If they do, then if they are inconsistent with his view on metaethics, so much the worse for that view.

[24] Dworkin (2011: 7).

that leads to endorsing it may fail and lead to a mistake. This is how we normally think of truths about, for example, the physical world. But possibly Dworkin has the second view: A correct interpretive reasoning makes a belief true. The truth of any belief consists in the fact that the person who has it reached it, or could have reached it through correct reasoning. If he has it because of such reasoning he cannot be wrong. Which is Dworkin's view? If it is the second, if he is a constructivist about values, then the unity of value is not so much a fact about values as a feature of correct reasoning about values.

In an important passage Dworkin writes:

"We unreflectively interpret each [of our abstract concepts] in the light of the others. That is, interpretation knits values together. We are morally responsible [i.e. act in a morally responsible way, succeed in being responsible] to the degree that our various concrete interpretations achieve an overall integrity so that each supports the others in a network of value that we embrace authentically. To the extent that we fail in that interpretive project—and it seems impossible to wholly succeed—we are not acting fully out of conviction, and so we are not fully responsible."[25]

This pregnant passage is amenable to the second way of understanding Dworkin, and it ties the unity of value not to how values are, independently of what we may discover about them by interpretive reasoning, but to the foundation of interpretation. Interpretation is, among other things, a process of knitting values together. If your conclusion does not show them to be knitted together, you failed to interpret as you should have. It seems that we find unity because we unite values, not because they are united. And of course, we could not unite values unless we made them through our interpretation. This is by no means the only way to understand this passage. But it appears to be supported by its end, which is remarkable in itself.

When our understanding (or aka interpretation) of the various moral values (or aka concepts) does not present them as a network of mutually supportive values (1) we did not succeed in being responsible, and (2) we do not authentically believe, do not believe with conviction what we think we believe (we are not acting fully out of conviction).[26] How can that be? Suppose that the unity of value

---

[25] Dworkin (2011: 101).

[26] Matthew Kramer suggested to me that Dworkin is not saying that, in that case, our beliefs lack conviction, or authenticity. Rather, if our view of value lacks unity, we cannot act on it, and our actions lack conviction and authenticity as they do not match our beliefs. This is an ingenious reading of the text. It attributes to Dworkin the view that evaluative beliefs that are not sufficiently united are not only incomplete, representing only part of the truth, but that they are defective in a more fundamental way, perhaps in ways analogous to the ways in which irrational beliefs cannot be rationally understood. There is no reason I know of to attribute to Dworkin that view. The one possible textual support for Kramer's view is the reference to people not then being fully responsible, but that could be both because their beliefs are not fully theirs as well as because their actions do not match their beliefs. The text is about the interpretations (i.e., interpretive beliefs) not being authentically held and the actions not being done out of beliefs that we hold with conviction.

is an objective feature of value, independent of the view of the person searching for the truth about value. In that case, by failing to realize that they are united, one is ignorant of some truth. One may even have, as a result, some mistaken beliefs. But neither ignorance nor mistakes normally mean that the views one has, even the mistaken views, are not authentically embraced or not held with conviction. If, however, the values and their unity are a product of your interpretation of them, provided it is properly done and follows the correct principles of interpretation, which include the goal of establishing unity among the values, then failure to come up with unity is a mark of not *really* interpreting, and if you did not really interpret, given that beliefs about values are your interpretation of the value concepts, it can perhaps be said that your beliefs are not really, not authentically, your beliefs.

This is strongly supported by much else that Dworkin writes. "Our moral responsibility," he explains, "requires us to try to make our reflective convictions into as dense and effective a filter as we can." The image of a filter indicates the role of our beliefs in containing, reshaping, or blocking, motivations and opinions we have due to the accidents of our history.

> "This requires that we seek a thorough coherence of value among our convictions. It also requires that we seek authenticity in the convictions that cohere: we must find convictions that grip us strongly enough to play the role of filters when we are pressed by competing motives that also flow from our personal histories. . . . We interpret each of . . . [our] convictions, so far as we can, in the light of the others and also in the light of what feels natural to us as a suitable way to live our lives. . . . Much of the rest of this book is an illustration of how we might pursue that responsibility project."[27]

It does look as if the unity of value is a constitutive requirement of the responsibility project. We do not discharge our responsibility properly if we do not find unity in value, or rather if we do not knit value into a unity, which possibly we can do only if what values there are result from our doing so. This passage introduces a further element through its explanation of the authenticity requirement. A responsible interpretation is one that meets two conditions: (1) unity that makes the values intelligible, and (2) being natural for each one of us, given our diverse histories. The second condition has a dual aspect. One is conventional: Our value beliefs, based on our understanding (or aka interpretation) of values, restrain us from acting in some ways that our natural or historically acquired inclinations incline us to behave. The other aspect of that condition is more surprising: Our histories, and the inclination they produce in us, also shape our interpretation. They shape our interpretation of values to ensure that they have a strong grip on us, and that enables them to act as filters, curtailing and shaping our motivations, etc. That grip is what 'authenticity' refers to in Dworkin's discussion. Perhaps the authenticity condition is needed to make beliefs in values have the power to make

---

[27] Dworkin (2011: 108).

us conform to the values that bind us.[28] Absent that kind of authenticity, we can understand why Dworkin might think that our belief in the values we believe in is not complete. But does it also show, as that and other passages suggest, that the values we imperfectly believe in are not the true values, and our (imperfect) belief in them is not a true belief, not being the result of a correct interpretation?

That extra step invites the interpretation that not only do we generate values by correctly reasoning in the interpretive way about values (or value concepts), but that the result of this construction of values, being influenced in each of us by our personal histories, will generate different or differently unified values for each of us. On that understanding, Dworkin's theory of value is one of perspectival constructivism. "Real" values are the products of successful interpretive reasoning guided (possibly along with other considerations) by the aims of unity and authenticity.

At times, it seems clear that Dworkin rejects the constructivist view of value. "Morally responsible people may not achieve truth, but they seek it."[29] But is this a refutation of the constructivist interpretation? The constructivist interpretation relates to successfully responsible people, but often Dworkin uses 'responsible' to refer to nothing more than the people who seek to be completely responsible. He warns us that the term is used for various closely related ideas. It could be that this quotation merely indicates that people who seek the truth, seek to be fully responsible, may fail to construct values by failing to be fully responsible.

6. The Role of Interpretation: Unity Through Division

In much of the paper, I explored the possibility that Dworkin anchors his thesis about the unity of value in the fact that values are intelligible and that each is grounded in a constitutive case for it, a case that relates it to other values in a more or less seamless continuous web. In the previous section, however, I explored the thought that he anchors it elsewhere, namely, in the responsibility project that is identified as the project of integrating values, i.e., establishing their unity, in an authentic way (in the special sense that that term has in the book).

This second way of establishing unity raises, of course, the question of why we are bound by the responsibility project. Dworkin says a fair amount about its value, and though this may strike one as circular, given that on the constructivist reading the responsibility project is the foundation of all value, this circularity

---

[28] Crude Kantian views may stop with the first aspect of the second condition: Value beliefs stop us from acting on some inclinations, but allow us to act on others, so most of our morally permissible actions are not guided by reasons for action, but simply caused by our inclinations. Dworkin is no Kantian. His thought does not rely on any such distinction between value beliefs and inclinations. Rather, as explained in this passage, it takes the interpretation of value to be shaped by our inclinations, making our value beliefs authentic as well as enabling them to filter out other inclinations.

[29] Dworkin (2011: 113).

may not be damaging. What is doubtful is whether what he says about the value of responsibility is sufficient to establish it as the foundation of values, including the duties that are stringently binding on all, including those who have no interest in the responsibility project, or who doubt the cogency of its conception or value. But these doubts do not matter, for Dworkin would reject the allegation that his view is constructivist in the way I explained.

He would also reject the ODT interpretation of his view. He would reject the distinction between the two ways of understanding his view about value and its unity. In Dworkin's view they are one because the fact that being responsible consists in part in finding unity in value connects with the case for unity that derives from the dependence of any value on a constitutive case.[30] The connection is revealed in, and is driven by, his view of interpretation. Dworkin explains:

> "Interpretation is pervasively holistic. An interpretation weaves together hosts of values and assumptions of very different kinds, drawn from very different kinds of judgement or experience, and the network of values that figure in an interpretive case accepts no hierarchy of dominance and subordination. The network faces the challenge of conviction as a whole . . ."[31]

As always, we ask: Is the interpretation in question an epistemic activity, namely, one aimed at discovering what is there, what is the truth, independently of it? Or is it an innovative interpretation that constitutes its object through the activity of interpretation, when correctly done? Only if it is innovative would there be a direct route to attributing characteristics of interpretative activities to the truths that they yield and to the domain those truths are about. Even if interpretation is the only epistemic access to that domain, its features cannot be attributed to that domain just because they are features of interpretations and without additional premises.

But there is an additional premise, one that I share, and in one form or another many writers accept it and its ramifications, at least in part. It is that value truths are intelligible, that people can understand them. That is a crucial and challenging premise. Challenging—for it is as difficult to explain its meaning as it is to establish its truth. However, that is another topic. For our purpose two (possible) implications of the premise are relevant. First, if value truths are intelligible then necessarily the only (non-derivative) way to establish what they are is through interpretive reasoning. Second, it follows that necessary features of sound Dworkinian interpretive reasoning, or more particularly features that sound interpretive reasoning necessarily assigns to its domain, to truths about value, really belong to that domain. Sound interpretive reasoning as Dworkin understands it, is necessarily, according to him, the only non-derivative way to establish truths about values, and to gain understanding about values. Hence features that are necessarily attributed to values by such interpretations are features

---

[30] Dworkin (2011: 112).
[31] Dworkin (2011: 154).

of values: In being necessary features of Dworkinian interpretive reasoning, they are, inescapably, features that any promising attempt to understand values attributes to them. Therefore, if—as we assume—we can gain understanding of what we interpret, essential features of interpretation are also features of the domain we thus understand.[32]

This argument enables us to sidestep the question whether Dworkinian interpretation is epistemic or innovative. Even if it is merely interpretive it can—given the two premises—reveal essential features of values. But perhaps that should warn us that Dworkin might not have accepted this argument as a correct representation of his view. It means that there is no more to the unity of value than what can be established by the epistemic view of Dworkinian interpretation, and that means that there is no more to it than what can be established by ODT.

Dworkin may have taken interpretations as inherently more than merely epistemic.[33] In the end, I do not think that that matters. The features that constitute the ODT approach are, according to Dworkin, essential features of interpretive reasoning, as he understands it. So both when relying on Dworkinian interpretation to provide an account of the unity of value, and when approaching the task independently, the case for unity rests on the ability of the ODT approach to establish what it is.

Furthermore, at the end of the day, Dworkin sees the case for engaging in interpretive reasoning, as he understands that process, that is the case for understanding values through Dworkinian interpretation, as resting on the responsibility project. It is what responsibility requires of us. The case for the responsibility project is that it is valuable, and its value must in the last resort be vindicated by the ODT approach. The ODT approach, on the other hand, does not need the responsibility project to be cogent. It stands and falls by the argument that the dependence of value truths on constitutive cases for them establishes the unity of value.

If the previous observations about Dworkin's way of understanding the unity of value are along the right lines, they show how the different aspects of his theory are integrated. They direct us through various channels to ODT as the ultimate foundation of the doctrine of unity. I see one problem in the case for the unity of the different approaches: Although the authenticity condition can be read into

---

[32] That only features necessarily attributed to its domain by interpretation of values can be attributed to values makes the view consistent with the possibility that even correct interpretive reasoning could yield a mistaken conclusion about values, for the attribution of value to empirical situations usually depends also on ordinary inductive reasoning.

[33] Though Dworkin always allowed that '*interpretation*' designates different kinds of activities. In Dworkin (1986: 52-53) he distinguished scientific interpretation—which is really interpretation only in a metaphorical sense—conversational interpretation and creative, which is constructive, interpretation. In *Justice for Hedgehogs*, the variety of types of interpretations and their dependence on the specific purposes they serve is taken very seriously. Hence, the question about the character of interpretive reasoning about value, and the possibility that there is more than one kind of such interpretive reasoning is consistent with Dworkin's approach to the matter.

some of Dworkin's observations about interpretation (including the passage cited above) in ways that mesh well with its foundation in the responsibility approach, it has no place in the ODT approach. However, it is possible to develop ODT to include a perspectival component that will bring it into line with the responsibility approach.

7. Conclusion

Where do these ruminations lead us? As I see things, Dworkin gave us a research project. Given that truths about values are grounded in constitutive cases themselves consisting (in part) of truths about values, each one of which depends on a constitutive case, and so on and so forth, we should research (1) whether, and if so to what degree or in what ways, do the links thus existing between truths about values connect all truths about all values, or only some of them; and (2) how tight are the connections between values so established (do they allow for conflict? Indeterminacies? Etc.)? Dworkin himself does not provide reasoned answers to these general questions, though on some of them his own beliefs about the results of such inquiries are clear.

References

Correia and Schnieder (2012). *Metaphysical Grounding*, Correia, F. and Schnieder B. (eds.), Cambridge: Cambridge University Press.

Dworkin, R. (1986). *Law's Empire*. Fontana Press.

Dworkin, R. (2011). *Justice for Hedgehogs*. Cambridge: Harvard University Press.

Fine, K. (2012) "Guide to ground." In Correia and Schnieder (2012).

Raz, J. (2003). *The Practice of Value*. Oxford: Oxford University Press.

Raz, J. (2011). *From Normativity to Responsibility*. Oxford: Oxford University Press.

Rosen, G. (2010). "Metaphysical Dependence: Grounding and Reduction." In *Modality: Metaphysics, Logic, and Epistemology*, Bob Hale and Aviv Hoffmann (eds.). Oxford: Oxford University Press.

PART II

Political Values

LEGITIMACY, AUTHORITY, AND COLLECTIVE RESPONSIBILITY

2

Political Resistance for Hedgehogs
by Candice Delmas

We all inhabit numerous social roles such as that of friend, child, colleague, neighbor, and citizen. Each role comes with special, agent-relative obligations, which are called *associative obligations*. For instance, children owe their parents respect and gratitude, and friends ought to support each other. Which obligations accompany the role of citizen? The main political obligation, according to associativist theorists, is to obey the law. There are myriad accounts of what grounds this political obligation to obey the law. For some theorists, the obligation is conceptually entailed by political membership.[1] Others argue that political bonds grow out of the feeling of belonging and sense of identity that members of a polity share.[2] Liberal theorists generally claim that associative political obligation is grounded in the good involved in political membership.[3]

Ronald Dworkin's liberal account of associative political obligation, first exposed in *Law's Empire*, is widely regarded as one of the most influential.[4] Dworkin gave the account a new gloss in *Justice for Hedgehogs*, where he argues that political obligation, like other moral duties, is ultimately grounded in the overarching interpretative value of dignity.[5] Political obligation can be deduced through interpretation from the internal character of political association, the logic of which dictates participants' responsibilities. Life under a government threatens human dignity since obeying the laws of a polity seems akin to surrendering one's dominion over one's life, while coercing other people into doing as the majority wishes—a common feature of democratic politics—appears to violate their dignity. In order to ensure that citizens neither dominate nor unilaterally defer to others, political association must be structured by special and reciprocal concern. Polities structured that way are legitimate and generate an

---

[1] Kelsen (1960); McPherson (1967).
[2] MacIntyre (1984); Tamir (1993).
[3] Horton (2007); Kymlicka (1995); Walzer (1983).
[4] Dworkin (1986: 195-216).
[5] Dworkin (2011: 317-323).

obligation to obey the law, whereas citizens have no such obligation in defective (illegitimate) political communities.

An important, yet oft-neglected question is: What happens in defective polities? Are citizens simply released from any *political* obligation? Champions of political obligation generally assume so, and thereby objectionably ignore, in my view, the possibility of a plurality of political obligations, some of which would arise under unjust political conditions.[6] However, by basing his account of the obligation to obey the law on the principles of dignity, Dworkin provides us with the resources to conceive other kinds of political obligations, which could bind citizens of defective polities.

In this paper, I propose to use Dworkin's own principles to develop an account of citizens' associative obligations—owed to oneself and to others—in the face of threats to, and violations of, dignity within illegitimate as well as basically legitimate polities. I shall argue that resistance to unjust laws, policies, and institutions in overall legitimate communities, as well as resistance to illegitimate governments, are not only compatible with, but also required by, the principles of Dworkinian dignity. In light of the pervasiveness of laws that disregard human dignity, I shall conclude that citizens' main role is not to obey the law, but instead, more commonly, to resist it.

The discussion proceeds as follows. Dworkin's defense of political obligation in *Justice for Hedgehogs* is short and highly condensed, so the first section, of the paper reconstructs his argument. Section 2 defends the existence of associative obligations of resistance, owed oneself and others, for citizens partaking in sociopolitical relationships that threaten or deny human dignity. Part III responds to several objections to the account; and Part IV asks afresh the question: Which obligations accompany the role of citizen? Contra Dworkin's claim that political obligation is usually substantial, and that accepting a reciprocal duty to submit to law is required by respect for dignity, I argue that the obligation to obey the law should be demoted to a lesser rank within citizens' associative obligations. Other responsibilities appear more important to preserve Dworkinian dignity in non-ideal conditions. I sketch a multidimensional account of associative political obligations, which includes, besides the obligation to obey just law, obligations to protest and resist unjust law, to be informed, and to develop empathetic understanding.

1. Dworkin's Liberal Associativism

1.1 OBLIGATIONS AND DIGNITY

Dworkin examines special obligations, i.e., the obligations we have to people who stand in a special relationship with us, in the Chapter 14 of *Hedgehogs*, "Obligations." He identifies two types of special obligations. Those that result

---

[6] Exceptions include Walzer (1983); Parekh (1993); Brownlee (2012); Lyons (2013); and Delmas (2014a; 2014b; 2015).

from discrete, voluntary actions such as promising are *performative*; and those that exist in virtue of some bond, e.g., family, kinship, or partnership in a joint enterprise, are *associational*. If people have a moral duty to obey the law, according to Dworkin, it is a special case of associational, not performative, obligation, since we are usually born into political membership.

The scope, content, and limits of special obligations, according to Dworkin, are determined by contingent conventions, including what is customary in a certain social milieu. Dworkin denies that conventions and social practices are *independent* sources of moral duties, but he argues that they play an important role in clarifying and fixing the obligations of people standing in special relationships. For instance, Western family practices assign the responsibilities of childcare and childrearing to the child's parents (not necessarily the biological parents), while childcare is a collective endeavor in many kibbutzim. Social practices like these are thus parasitic on underlying and independent moral facts such as children's needs.

Special obligations, like other moral requirements, are ultimately grounded in the overarching interpretative value of dignity, according to Dworkin. As he explicates in *Hedgehogs*, dignity requires both self-respect and authenticity. These principles govern and unify both ethics ("living well," centered on the self) and morality ("being good," or what we owe others). From the ethical perspective, the principle of self-respect demands accepting that it is a matter of importance how one's life goes. From the moral perspective, it demands recognizing the objective importance of other people's lives, and showing respect for humanity in all its forms. The principle of authenticity entails what Dworkin calls *ethical responsibility* and *ethical independence*. According to the former, "[e]ach person has a special, personal responsibility for identifying what counts as success in his own life; he has a personal responsibility to create that life through a coherent narrative or style that he himself endorses."[7] The latter forbids us from acting according to decisions and values that are not of our own making. Morally, authenticity demands we recognize and respect the responsibility of other people to design a life for themselves.

1.2 POLITICAL OBLIGATION

Dworkin's defense of political obligation is framed as a solution to what he dubs *the paradox of civil society*.[8] At the heart of this paradox is the following tension: Coercive government seems both essential to, and incompatible with, human dignity. On the one hand, it is essential to dignity because it makes it possible for us to live a meaningful human life. On the other hand, it seems that I cannot properly value my own dignity—i.e., recognize the objective

---

[7] Dworkin (2011: 204).
[8] Dworkin (2011: 320).

importance of my own life, and my special responsibility to make decisions for myself—while submitting to political authority; and that I cannot properly value the dignity of other people while participating in processes and institutions that force them to do as the collectivity wishes (as happens in democracies). Dworkin thus worries that both the exercise of, and the submission to, coercive political power might be incompatible with the basic moral requirements of human dignity.

Dworkin's solution to the paradox of civil society consists in showing that the incompatibility between state force and human dignity is only apparent. He aims not only to reconcile life in political societies with respect for dignity, but also to show that under certain conditions submission to political authority is morally *required* by the principles of dignity. Dworkin deduces political obligation from the internal character of the political relationship, examined in conjunction with the demands of dignity. Although the principle of authenticity forbids subordination, it does not entail a blanket prohibition to defer to the authority of others in decisions that affect us, Dworkin notes. Dignity permits us to share our responsibility for our own lives with others so long as the deference is in some ways reciprocal. Political association is one case of relationship that involves deferring to the interests, opinions, and authority of others. Sexual intimacy is another case: "people who accept that they are lovers place themselves, body and soul, in each other's hands," Dworkin writes.[9]

The internal character of these special relationships dictates the responsibilities of the parties involved. According to Dworkin, the salient features of both political association and sexual intimacy are (1) their great value for us, given their contribution to the success of our lives, and (2) the special kind of harm that they make us vulnerable to, namely, subservience, which is the particular indignity that results from unilateral deference. From these risky relationships thus flows a special responsibility not to dominate the other party or parties. To wit, these relationships must be structured by special and reciprocal concern so as not to compromise dignity.

I think that Dworkin is wrong to treat sexual relationships on par with political association (with respect to the responsibility not to dominate), insofar as there may be nothing wrong with sexual objectification, domination and submission, so long as the partners drew together the shape of their intimate relationship (for instance, they may have consensually entered into a BDSM contract). However, Dworkin should have included other kinds of relationships under the umbrella, or in the vicinity, of the political one. For instance, the family should also express concern and respect for all, even though it may be structured hierarchically, with some members making decisions for others. The important point, for us, is that the responsibility not to dominate is special—though probably not unique—to political associations.

---

[9] Id.

1.3 LEGITIMACY

Is political obligation a justified, i.e., genuine, obligation? According to Dworkin, defective instances of valuable practices (e.g., family) and defective conventions, such as organizations of criminals, impose no genuine obligation on those they purport to oblige. And so, not all political communities impose genuine obligations to obey the law: only those that are legitimate, i.e., respect the dignity of all parties involved, do. State legitimacy thus entails political obligation, for Dworkin: citizens are morally bound to obey the laws of their community when, and to the extent that, these emanate from a legitimate government.[10]

Dworkin distinguishes legitimacy from justice, noting that governments may fall short of justice and still be legitimate, so long as:

> ...their laws and policies can nevertheless be interpreted as recognizing that the fate of each citizen is of equal importance and that each has a responsibility to create his own life. A government may be legitimate, that is, if it strives for its citizens' full dignity even if it follows a defective conception of what that requires.[11]

It is thus a matter of interpretation whether the community cares about its members' dignity and what counts as showing equal concern for them. According to Dworkin, "[t]he interpretive judgment must be sensitive to time and place: it must take into account prevailing ideas within the political community."[12] As a result, it is not impossible to judge that a benevolent monarchy of the past was legitimate. But for contemporary Western political communities to be legitimate, they must recognize their members' political equality by giving them an opportunity to influence collective decisions.

In the manuscript version of *Hedgehogs*, Dworkin went so far as saying that it would be counterintuitive to think that "most of the subjects of most of the political communities over history had no moral duty to obey the laws of their community."[13] Commenting on the manuscript, Susanne Sreedhar and I argued that, well understood, the requirements of Dworkinian dignity would make political obligation the exception, not the norm, in historical and contemporary states, while potentially calling for some form of resistance to dignity-threatening political associations.[14] Dworkin addressed these comments in the published version of the book, noting that legitimacy was a matter of degree, and that it could indeed be "stained" by unjust and exclusionary laws.[15] He also agreed with our suggestion that civil disobedience may sometimes be appropriate to redress injustices. However, Dworkin still affirmed the overall prevalence of political obligation in

---

[10] Other theorists, such as Green (1988) and Greenawalt (1989), deny that legitimacy and political obligation are mutually coextensive.

[11] Dworkin (2011: 321-322).

[12] Id.

[13] Quoted in Sreedhar and Delmas (2010: 746).

[14] Id.

[15] Dworkin (2011: 323).

history, noting that as long as the stain is contained, and political and legal processes of correction are available, the state retains its legitimacy—and political obligation remains substantial. If the stain is dark and widespread, on the other hand, political obligation may lapse entirely, and revolution may be called for.

I remain skeptical that political obligation could prevail, historically and at present. But my goal in the remainder of this paper is to use Dworkin's own principles to develop an account of citizens' associative obligations—owed to oneself and to others—in cases of stains and lapses of legitimacy. Dworkin suggests the possibility of civil disobedience and revolution only in passing. I shall argue that resistance to illegitimate governments, and protest against unjust laws in overall legitimate communities, are not only compatible with, but also required by, the principles of Dworkinian dignity. Before I proceed, let me explain why the account of citizens' associative obligations in the face of injustice which I propose to sketch here is worth developing.

First, it complements Dworkin's defense of the obligation to obey the law, extends his task of showing the unity of all value, and further explores "how we might pursue [the] responsibility project," which demands we find coherence of value among our convictions, and live our life accordingly.[16] This should be particularly appealing to scholars of Dworkin's thought.

Second, proponents of the duty to obey the law in general should also be interested in my account, insofar as it addresses an important and previously neglected question: What happens when political obligation fails or is overridden? Theorists usually assume that citizens are simply released of their obligation to the polity in such cases. This common view is mistaken: while citizens are released of the obligation to obey the law, they take on obligations of a different sort, as I shall show. Because the latter obligations flow from the internal character of the political association, I shall call them political obligations despite theorists' long-standing use of the singular *political obligation* to refer to the duty to obey the law. From this perspective, my project is also to reform the theory, as I shall argue that the duty to obey the law should not be viewed as *the* sole and central political obligation.

Third, skeptics and opponents of the duty to obey the law (among the ranks of whom I find myself) may appreciate the project for the simple reason that it draws out the implications of dignity—a widely embraced value—in contexts of injustice and oppression, and finds it supports engaging in political resistance. So one need not endorse Dworkin's account of political obligation in order to be persuaded by mine; but one does need to accept the validity and force of his principles of dignity, which I shall assume throughout without argument.[17] Systematic treatments of citizens' moral *obligations* in the face of injustice are rare in mainstream political and legal theory, which is generally focused on the *permissibility*

---

[16] Dworkin (2011: 108). On the link between the responsibility project and the unity of all value, see Raz (2016).

[17] For a critique, see Simons (2010).

of resisting or civilly disobeying injustice, while they abound in the feminist literature, in which philosophers have constructed fine-grained frameworks to think about oppression and our duties to resist it.[18] The present paper contributes to this ongoing project of theorizing our responsibilities to end oppression, by proposing to utilize the resources of classical liberal theory.

The basic idea, then, is that by his own lights, Dworkin should have defended associative political obligations of resistance rather than insisting on the obligation to obey the law.[19]

2. Obligations of Resistance

In Dworkin's view, political communities' legitimacy should be assessed on the basis of two criteria: (1) their good-faith efforts to respect the dignity of their members, and (2) their amenability to change through politics. So for instance, Dworkin would consider that the disenfranchisement of women in early twentieth century Western Europe and Northern America stained, but did not rescind, the overall legitimacy of these communities, insofar as they basically met these two criteria. I have no doubt that this would be Dworkin's view, since he proposes to assume at one point that the United States (U.S.) Congress under slavery "was sufficiently legitimate so that its enactments generally created political obligations" (though such obligations to obey and apply the law would often be overridden).[20] The spectrum of legitimacy is thus very broad. Dworkin reserves diagnoses of complete failures of legitimacy to wholly evil legal systems such as Nazi Germany's.[21]

Situating a community on the spectrum of legitimacy involves determining whether it is generally structured in a way that expresses—or strives to express—equal and reciprocal concern, whether it contains particular laws, policies, or practices that threaten (some) members' dignity, and whether there are political channels for reform. Most past and present polities fall somewhere in between the two extremes of the legitimacy spectrum. It seems to me that slavery, colonialism, imperialism, and racial segregation, which characterize an entire system, would generally constitute *lapses* of legitimacy (pace Dworkin's view about US chattel slavery), while particular laws and practices that threaten dignity, such as health insurance policies' exclusion of transgender health care, and police practice of "stop and frisk," which targets young African American men, express lack of concern for members of certain social groups, and thus *stain* legitimacy.

Since legitimacy is both a matter of degree and an interpretive concept, there will be reasonable disagreement with respect to the overall diagnosis and the

---

[18] See e.g., Harvey (1999); Cudd (2006); Young (2011); Hay (2013).

[19] This approach parallels Rae Langton's (1990) as she argues that, "by his own lights," Dworkin should have defended pornography legislation instead of pornographers' free speech.

[20] Dworkin (2011: 411).

[21] For more on Dworkin's treatment of unjust laws and legal systems, see Dyzenhaus (2016).

identification of particular stains on and lapses of legitimacy. Some of these disagreements will be factual. For example, does the government spy on its citizens' electronic and phone communications? Others will be interpretive and possibly intractable, stemming from differing understandings of what counts as respecting or violating dignity. For example, does dignity require we have exclusive control over our metadata? These disagreements are neither avoidable nor always regrettable. They are part and parcel of a community's social, moral, political, and legal practices.

There are various ways in which political associations can threaten their members' self-respect and/or authenticity. Paradigmatic violations include *denial of self-determination*, which consists in depriving an individual or a people of decision-making powers in their life; *humiliation*, that is, demeaning physical or verbal treatment that undermines or denies a person's self-respect[22]; *objectification*, which consists in reducing a person to her body or body parts, or treating a person as a tool for the objectifier's purposes[23]; *discrimination*, i.e., the wrongful imposition of disadvantage on persons based on their (perceived) membership in a salient social group[24]; *exploitation*, or unfairly taking advantage of individuals or groups[25]; *marginalization*, i.e., exclusion from participation in major social activities[26]; and *violence* or the violation of a person's bodily or mental integrity, through, e.g., sexual violence, harassment, and brutalization.[27]

This list—which is by no means exhaustive—points to various types of dignity-threatening political relationships. It also hints at the difficulty of drawing a sharp distinction between self-respect and authenticity, insofar as both principles forbid subservience, and an affront to one tends to be an affront to the other. To deprive someone of the background conditions for living authentically indeed at the same time violates her self-respect, and vice versa. Since the implications of both principles seem practically interchangeable, I shall treat the two principles together.

What does a person owe herself in the face of a polity's failure to treat her as an equal and valuable member? What does a person owe those in her polity who are not treated as equal and valuable members? Dignity demands recognizing one's and others' basic moral worth, taking one's own life seriously, and respecting others' ethical independence: It forbids dominating and unilaterally deferring to others. My contention is that dignity supports a general obligation to *resist* one's and others' violations of dignity. People who are not treated as equal and valuable members of their community—who are socially or politically subservient—have an ethical obligation (owed to themselves) to resist their own mistreatment;

---

[22] Margalit (1996).
[23] Nussbaum (1995); Langton (2009: 228-229).
[24] Altman (2011).
[25] Wood (1995: 150-151).
[26] Young (1990: 53-58).
[27] Young (1990: 61-63).

and members of a polity that violates some of its members' dignity have a moral obligation (owed to others) to resist such mistreatment.

I use the term *resistance* to designate a multidimensional continuum of dissenting acts and practices, which all express, very broadly, a refusal to conform to the dominant system's norms. So in my view, resistance applies to a broad range of activities, from silent protest to verbal opposition, consciousness-raising, petitions, and demonstrations, to strikes, boycotts, civil disobedience, strategic sabotage, and militant armed action. Acts of resistance may thus be legal or illegal, public or covert, violent or nonviolent, addressed to the public (government, citizenry) or a private agent (university, corporation, boss), carried out by agents who are willing to accept punishment or evade it, and who are operating within or without society's public conception of what dignity requires.[28] As we shall see, however, Dworkinian dignity imposes significant constraints on the methods of resistance that can be justified.

The scope and content of the general obligation of resistance—i.e., what it requires in specific circumstances—depends on the kind and magnitude of the indignity threatened, and on the agent's abilities, opportunities, and particular position relative to the indignity. I propose to distinguish four related purposes of resistance, which can all be deduced from the internal logic of dignity-threatening political relationships:

1. *Communication*: communicating condemnation of a law, policy, institution or system;
2. *Rectification*: rectifying the flawed law, policy, institution or system, through reform, abolition, or revolution;
3. *Assertion*: asserting one's dignity; and
4. *Solidarity*: expressing solidarity with the oppressed.

The four goals of resistance are interrelated: Communication is the first step toward rectification, while asserting one's dignity and expressing solidarity are typically communicative acts. So, one should not expect clear lines demarcating each goal. As I shall argue, citizens are bound to engage in resistance in order to communicate opposition to dignity-threatening political conditions and work to rectify these. Asserting one's dignity is an ethical obligation that specifically arises in the face of subordination; and expressing solidarity with the oppressed is a moral obligation that can bind both the oppressed and the privileged members of society. These obligations to resist, which may be deemed semi-general in relation to the general obligation of resistance, are *pro tanto* and imperfect. This means that they may be overridden by countervailing prudential and moral considerations, and that one has broad leeway in deciding how to fulfill them.

---

[28] This picture is much broader than the standard, Rawlsian conception of civil disobedience as a "public, nonviolent, conscientious yet political act contrary to law usually done with the aim of bringing about a change in the law or policies of the government." See Rawls (1999: § 55). For an excellent critique of Rawls's conception of civil disobedience, see Brownlee (2012: 18-24).

2.1 COMMUNICATION

Dworkinian dignity demands establishing laws, policies, or institutions that express equal and reciprocal concern for all. If those that are in place threaten members' dignity, they must be fixed or replaced. Communication often constitutes the first step toward rectification since a community must be aware of the existence of a particular mistreatment in order to rectify it. The mistreatment in question may not be self-evident. In the case of structural oppression, for instance, which tends to hide injustice under the normal workings of the system, resistance should aim at least in part to educate the public.[29] This may involve educational initiatives such as consciousness-raising workshops and teach-ins, whereby the privileged listen to the victims speak about their experiences. According to Jean Harvey, these forms of resistance are essential to expose the hidden mechanisms of oppression and undermine its future occurrences.[30] *Everyday resistance* in the household and the workplace (e.g., challenging put-down humor and stereotypes) also constitutes *educational resistance*.

Civil disobedience, understood as public and nonviolent conscientious law-breaking, can be a particularly appropriate way to draw attention to the community's failure to treat everyone with equal concern. One who engages in civil disobedience, according to John Rawls, "addresses the sense of justice of the majority of the community and declares that in one's considered opinion the principles of social cooperation among free and equal men are not being respected."[31] The conception of civil disobedience as speech act and public address is particularly appropriate to think of the communicative aim of resistance in the context of dignity-threatening political relationships. Civil disobedience movements can expose stains on political legitimacy and highlight the need for reform in a more powerful and spectacular fashion than legal courses of action.[32] For instance, Saudi women have organized defiance days against the ban on women driving, which arguably violates women's dignity and seriously impedes their ethical independence. The defiance campaign urges Saudi women with legal driver's licenses from other countries to run errands in order to mark the fact that it should be normal for women to drive. Since 2011, many women have filmed themselves driving and posted the videos on YouTube.

Resistance is crucial not only to highlight particular dignity-threatening relationships in the polis, but also to improve the community's conception of what dignity requires. This certainly has been part of the goal of Saudi women's defiance movement. For another example, the greatest challenge for prisoner rights activists is not so much people's ignorance about the systematic human rights

---

[29] Oppression is structural when its harms are the unintentional result of an interrelated system of social norms and institutions. Haslanger (2007).

[30] Such initiatives robustly qualify as acts of resistance, even though we are not accustomed to thinking of explaining and learning as such. Harvey (2010: 15-16).

[31] Rawls (1999: 320).

[32] Brownlee (2012: 17-27) and Smith (2013: ch. 2 and 3) offer two excellent discussions of the communicative function of civil disobedience.

violations that plague the prison (from rape to overcrowding to solitary confinement), which by now have been widely documented, as it is people's indifference to prisoners' fate. Successfully resisting the mass incarceration system and its abuses involves not only informing people, but also helping them to recognize prisoners' dignity and see the occurrence of massive rights violations as an affront to the whole polity.

2.2 RECTIFICATION: REFORM AND REVOLUTION

Acts of resistance are critical to start the process of rectification. Nonviolent resistance is a particularly effective way of calling for the elimination or reform of certain dignity-threatening laws or institutions, as history suggests and social scientists recently demonstrated.[33] Some individuals, such as public officials, journalists, and lawyers, may be well situated to contribute to the reform effort through other courses of action than nonviolent resistance. But for most citizens, who lack access to the political arena or to legal processes—and especially for those whose dignity is threatened—civil resistance may be an effective way to reach the political forum.

Resisting domination in illegitimate, unjust, and illiberal regimes, and establishing a legitimate government, may require something more drastic than nonviolent resistance. It did in the South African liberation struggle against apartheid led by the African National Congress (ANC).[34] After fifty years of legal battles and peaceful protests, the ANC formed a military arm, Umkhonto we Sizwe (the Spear of the Nation), that organized sabotage actions and prepared for guerilla warfare. The Manifesto of Umkhonto we Sizwe, issued in 1961 read: "The time comes in the life of any nation where there remain only two choices—submit or fight. That time has now come to South Africa. We shall not submit and we have no choice but to hit back by all means in our power in defense of our people, our future and our freedom."[35]

The principles of dignity impose significant constraints on the justifiable methods of resistance, whether employed for the sake of reform or revolution. Chief among these constraints is the idea that the agent normally cannot violate another person's dignity in order to resist the community's denial of her own. So for instance, Dworkinian dignity cannot support Frantz Fanon's call for violence in the name of self-respect. In *The Wretched of the Earth*, Fanon writes of violence against the colonizers that it is "a cleansing force... It frees the native from his inferiority complex and from his despair and inaction; it makes him fearless and restores his self-respect."[36] It is impossible to construct an interpretation of the

---

[33] Chenoweth and Stephan (2011).

[34] I am here following Nelson Mandela's political narrative as set out in *A Long Walk to Freedom*. But the point is a matter of controversy. David Dyzenhaus (2001) and others argue that the turn to the armed struggle was not a popular decision in the ANC and actually set back the cause.

[35] Command of Umkhonto we Sizwe. Manifesto of Umkhonto we Sizwe (December 16, 1961) http://www.anc.org.za/show.php?id=77

[36] Fanon (1968: 147).

ethical demands of Dworkinian self-respect that would so squarely contradict its moral demands, including the requirement to respect the objective importance of other people's lives.[37] This reveals a strong moral presumption against violence. This presumption, nonetheless, does not yield an absolute prohibition. Resort to violence, if it is deployed in self-defense and/or suitably constrained, can still be justified—as it appeared to have been for the liberation struggle in South Africa during apartheid.

When deliberating about one's course of action, one needs to weigh the potential harm to oneself and others that may come with resistance, against the potential harm the institution, practice, or law is likely to cause if left unchallenged. The right course of action typically depends on the particulars of the situation, the gravity of the injustice, the person's opportunities and capabilities, and the expected consequences of the act. Arguably, legal acts of resistance such as petitions and boycotts should be attempted first, unless it is obvious that they would be pointless. In general, one ought to choose a course of action that appears to (1) have a reasonable chance of success (the success condition), and (2) achieve its goal through the more modest means (the principle of parsimony).[38]

First, the success condition seems hard to satisfy for isolated actions of individuals: No single act can usually be expected to draw the community's attention to the dignity-threatening association, let alone single-handedly lead to its rectification. But correctly interpreted, the success condition simply requires some instrumental, strategic thinking in choosing the method of action. In particular, it weighs in favor of coordinating action in order to maximize chances of success (which does not rule out individual acts of everyday resistance). Indeed, given the systemic nature of political indignities, it is reasonable to think that reform and revolution can only (or most likely) be accomplished through collective action. I return to this point when discussing solidarity below.

Second, the principle of parsimony rules out disproportional methods of resistance (especially resort to terror) without necessarily ruling out acts of protest that are sensational (such as Ukrainian feminist group Femen's topless demonstrations) or even violent (e.g., the English suffragettes' destruction of windows in London's shopping district). Nonviolent acts of resistance can be expected to more readily satisfy the success condition and the principle of parsimony, and align with Dworkinian dignity, but violence cannot be ruled out a priori.

2.3 ASSERTING ONE'S DIGNITY

A Dworkinian account of resistance based on dignity resonates with many liberation movements. Emmeline Pankhurst, suffragist leader, wrote in 1913 that "To be militant [in the suffragist movement] in some way or other is...a moral obligation. It is a duty which every woman will owe to her own conscience and

---

[37] See May (2015) for an account linking nonviolence to dignity.

[38] I follow Brownlee (2011: 186-187) in defending a principle of parsimony rather than a principle of proportionality, the former being stricter than the latter.

self-respect, to other women who are less fortunate than she herself is, and to all those who are to come after her."[39] W. E. B. Du Bois argued that self-respect was incompatible with silent submission to racial subjugation and required protesting against it.[40] The Black Power movement encouraged racial pride and heightened self-esteem, adopting James Brown's "Say It Loud – I'm Black and I'm Proud" as its anthem. As these examples suggest, resistance campaigns often include resounding assertions of dignity—directed at oneself and others.

Dignity-threatening political relationships generate on the part of the subordinated ethical obligations to affirm their dignity. But how can protest be obligatory if there is no hope of righting the situation? Bernard Boxill has argued for the existence of a Kantian duty to oneself to protest one's own subordination.[41] In his view, by protesting her mistreatment, even when she has no hope of rectifying it, a self-respecting person manifests her conviction that she has worth, thereby rendering such conviction more secure. She fends off the fear of losing her self-respect as a result of the illegitimate political conditions she is subjected to. "The self-respecting person wants to know that he is self-respecting," Boxill writes.[42] Protest is thus designed to give the agent this evidence and assurance. It is because unopposed injustice invites its victims to believe that they have no value or rights that the self-respecting person is compelled to protest, over and above the hope that it will bring relief. Boxill's argument can easily be framed in associativist terms, and ground an ethical obligation to assert one's dignity in the face of political relationships that threaten or violate it.

Purely expressive protests—solely meant to assert one's dignity to oneself—may be silent, internal, and thus invisible. This does not necessarily make them failures from the point of view of the assertion. Carol Hay has developed a Kantian account of duties to oneself to resist one's oppression, which is based on the recognition of the fundamental value of our rational nature and of oppression's damaging effects on our rational and agential capacities. Exploring the ways to fulfill these duties, she notes:

> In some cases, there might be nothing an oppressed person can do to resist her oppression other than simply *recognizing that something is wrong* with her situation. This is, in a profound sense, better than nothing. It means she has not acquiesced to the innumerable forces that are conspiring to convince her that she is the sort of person who has no right to expect better. It means she recognizes that her lot in life is neither justified nor inevitable.[43]

Dworkinian dignity has much in common with Kantian rationality: Dworkin dubs the moral dimension of self-respect *Kant's principle*, while his conception

---

[39] Letter to the members of the Women's Social and Political Union, January 10, 1913. http://www.nationalarchives.gov.uk/documents/education/suffragettes.pdf

[40] Du Bois (1999: ch. 6).

[41] Boxill (1976).

[42] Boxill (1976: 67).

[43] Hay (2013: 141).

of authenticity is close to Kantian autonomy. Recent Kantian accounts of duties to oneself to resist oppression like Boxill's and Hay's thus illuminate the present associativist account. Asserting one's dignity, by itself, is one important way to meet the demands of dignity when rectifying the mistreatment seems impossible. And it can play an important role in thwarting some of the corrosive effects of oppression on one's dignity.

2.4 SOLIDARITY

Recall that on Dworkin's account of dignity, the reason you have to care how your life goes is a reason for you to care about other people's lives. The moral requirements of dignity thus mirror its ethical demands. For example, if women are morally obligated to protest their disenfranchisement, or a ban on driving, men too are morally bound to address these injustices. This is important because it means that even if I am not responsible for some of my fellow citizens' mistreatment, I have responsibilities to them in virtue of our co-membership in the polity. I must do what I can to correct the dignity-threatening relationship. (If I am an agent of their mistreatment, then I have other moral duties, besides these associative political obligations, such as a duty to undo wrongs.)

Dworkin's principles thus imply that violations of some members' dignity are everyone's concern and call for everyone's action. This does not mean that anything goes as soon as one citizen's dignity is threatened. Compliance with law may be justified by appeal to other moral and non-moral considerations. However, a citizen cannot be morally bound to abide by rules that systematically violate the dignity of her fellow citizens. For if she were to accept an obligation to obey laws that denigrate certain minorities, she would fail to recognize the objective importance of other people's lives, as authenticity demands. This is a radical implication of Dworkin's account, as it suggests, and provides the rationale for the notion, that the demands of dignity cannot be fulfilled for *anyone* unless the community actually treats *everyone* with equal concern and respect. Solidarity in resistance is a crucial way of expressing proper concern for everyone, and should be viewed as a moral obligation of both subordinated and privileged members of society.

Instrumental and principled reasons support this idea. First, some methods of resistance and protest are inherently collective: One cannot undertake a flash mob or a strike all by oneself, for instance. Beyond the collective nature of certain forms of resistance, there are good empirical reasons to think that for individual acts of resistance to be effective, they must generally be part of a movement. This is not to say that individual acts of resistance are useless: well-situated members of society can by themselves accomplish important things (think of the power of a book like Harriet Beecher Stowe's 1852 *Uncle Tom's Cabin* or Peter Singer's 1975 *Animal Liberation*). But the success condition I presented above favors *organizing* resistance and/or *joining* existing organized movements, insofar as these paths are more likely to achieve publicity and reform. Organizing resistance ensures that volunteers' resources are put to good use rather than risking dissipating them. Alliances and coalitions are also very important (Rawls even makes coordination of activities among organized minority groups one of the conditions for the justi-fication of civil disobedience).[44] Furthermore, once organized movements are in place, joining them may be seen as the default course of action, as it presents the individual with a specific way to discharge her obligations.

Another instrumental argument in favor of joining organized movements of resistance is that numbers matter. For most if not all forms of protest, the more par-ticipants the better: A hundred people rallying for a cause are more impressive than a dozen; and thousands can turn a demonstration into a real event in the public's eye. Erica Chenoweth and Maria Stephan argue, on the basis of their statistical analysis of 323 violent and nonviolent civil resistance campaigns that took place in the last century, that mass participation is a critical source of the success of nonviolent resis-tance: "as membership increases, the probability of success also increases."[45] This is true not only in contexts of concentration, in which large numbers of people gather in public (or private) spaces, as Egyptians did in Tahrir Square in 2011 and 2013, but also in contexts of dispersion, in which acts are coordinated and widespread, as with Saudi women's defiance of the driving ban. So if an organized movement is already in place, joining it may well seem the best method of action. If no organized movement exists, perhaps some individuals with talent (e.g., grassroots organization skills) and influence are able and bound to launch one.

There may also be a direct, dignity-based argument for political solidarity, besides the instrumental argument just laid out, and independently from its causal contribution to rectification. Insofar as Dworkinian dignity both prohibits dominating others and requires resisting others' mistreatment, it can be under-stood to imply a requirement to do one's share in rectifying the system, by joining efforts with those who oppose that scheme and are working to replace it with a just one. From this perspective, political solidarity with the oppressed (conceived as meaningful cooperation and collective action to advance shared goals and values) expresses the commitment of those whose dignity is respected to cease supporting the dignity-threatening political association, and share in the bur-dens involved in the reform.[46] Citizens' passivity and lack of solidarity (conceived broadly as moral support) might then reflect blameworthy indifference to the fate of the oppressed.

3. Objections

As I have tried to show, Dworkinian dignity supports a general obligation to resist one's and others' violations of dignity. People who are not treated as equal and valuable members of their community—who are socially or politically

---

[44] Rawls (1999: 374-375). Coordination of activities is required to regulate the overall level of dissent, according to Rawls.

[45] Chenoweth and Stephan (2011: 39).

[46] Delmas (2014b).

subservient—have an ethical and moral obligation (which they owe themselves and others) to resist their own mistreatment; and members of a polity that violates some of its members' dignity have a moral obligation to resist such mistreatment. This general ethical and moral obligation can entail, depending on the agent and situation, specific obligations to protest in order to communicate opposition to the law or institution that violates people's dignity, to try to rectify the defective law or institution in question, to assert one's dignity, and to express solidarity through collective action. I shall shortly propose to revise our understanding of political obligations, so as to reflect the notion that obeying the law is not the main obligation of citizens—resistance is. But before I do so, I want to examine a series of objections to the foregoing associativist account of political resistance.

3.1 TOO DEMANDING

First, the account may be deemed to require too much sacrifice, since it binds every member of society to resist *any* dignity-threatening political relationship. Given the inevitability and ubiquity of threats to dignity in large political communities like ours, the demands of Dworkinian dignity would constantly pull citizens and seriously impede on their day-to-day activities and life plans. Some readers may consider this problem so serious as to constitute a *reductio ad absurdum* of my argument.

But what exactly is the worry? One way of framing it, in line with Dworkin's thought, consists in saying that political resistance might get in the way of people's authentic self-realization, and thus cannot possibly be required. My response is that this sets up a false dilemma. Authenticity demands that each person exercise independence in—and thus responsibility for—designing one's life. Political resistance could well be part of, or even central to, the values by which one lives and to the pursuit of one's responsibility project. Daniel Silvermint has argued that resisting one's own oppression can be an important component of well-being when living in oppressive circumstances.[47] The same could be said about privileged members of society, given the harmful effects of oppression on privileged and bystanders, not just on the oppressed.[48]

If the worry is simply that obligations to resist are too demanding, my response is that morality *is* demanding and that we have no good reason to expect it not to be. Of course we are naturally motivated to *want* morality to be such that we can easily meet its demands, but nothing follows about morality itself from the fact that we want to be able to discharge our moral duties at reasonable cost.[49]

---

[47] Silvermint (2013).

[48] For instance, the Grimké sisters, who grew up on a slave-owning plantation in South Carolina, suggested that slavery, insofar as it left people morally estranged from one another and thwarted compassion, erodes everyone's moral capacities. Grimké (2003). The point can be generalized to the effects of ideology under oppression. Shelby (2003).

[49] Murphy (2000).

How much sacrifice can Dworkinian dignity demand of us? When grounding the moral duty to obey the law, it is understood to require relinquishing the discretion to act as one wishes, paying taxes to the state, and, in case of military draft, fighting in war. If discharging the duty to obey the law can involve such substantial sacrifices, the same may be presumed about the associative obligations to resist. However, military conscription aside, complying with the law in nearly just societies might be deemed minimally burdensome, compared with political resistance in defective polities. Very heavy costs to oneself, one's family, colleagues, or fellow citizens often attach to resistance. In the United States, 1,300 whites were lynched by white supremacist mobs between 1882 and 1959, many of them for resisting racial segregation (e.g., registering black voters).[50] Even peaceful, nonviolent, and legal acts of resistance could be met with brute force.

This is a real worry. In response, it is reasonable to suggest that grave injustice could require more significant sacrifices than legal compliance under favorable conditions, and that the more serious the injustice or threat to dignity, the heavier associative obligations of resistance might weigh on citizens. Further, not all resistance is going to involve such heavy costs. There often exist movements that call for one's participation and do not appear dangerous. Finally, it is important to reiterate that the obligation to resist is defeasible and imperfect, so that one has discretion over how to fulfill it.

3.2 BURDENING AND BLAMING THE VICTIM

The second objection presses on the very idea that those who are politically subordinated ought to resist their own oppression. Telling people whose dignity is threatened that they ought to engage in resistance, and that they may be blamed for failing to do so, amounts to objectionably burdening the victim as well as blaming her for failing to resist oppression. The complaint expressed here is that, first, the account of associative obligations of resistance inappropriately adds deontic burdens to the burdens of oppression: Not only are people suffering from oppression but they also take on new duties as a result of being oppressed. Let us dub this worry the *burdening the victim* objection. Second, the account tries to hold people accountable for resisting their own mistreatment, insofar as one fails to fulfill one's duties by not resisting. Let us dub this worry the *blaming the victim* objection. The two worries are tightly connected. As Marilyn Frye observed: "Can we hold ourselves, and is it proper to hold each other, *responsible* for resistance? Or is it necessarily both stupid cruelty and a case of 'blaming the victim' to add yet one more pressure in our lives, in each others' lives, by expecting, demanding, requiring, encouraging, inviting acts and patterns of resistance and reconstruction which are not spontaneously forthcoming?"[51]

---

[50] Estimates from the Tukegee Institute; Ginzburg (1988).
[51] Frye (1985).

In response to the burdening the victim objection, I fail to see what it is problematic with the idea that persons whose dignity is violated thereby incur special responsibilities to protect and assert their dignity. Our relations with others make us responsible and vulnerable in all sorts of ways; and part of the appeal of associativist accounts is that they can account for the variety of involuntary and semi-voluntary obligations we come to incur in the course of our lives, as we form bonds with others, voluntarily or not. Further, I noted above that the defense of ethical obligations of resistance accords well with the self-understanding of many liberation struggles, thereby casting doubt on the implausibility, or unpalatability, of the idea of ethical obligations to resist one's mistreatment.

Finally, it is important to note, contra the blaming the victim objection, that the claim that subordinated people could be blamed for passively going along with their own oppression does not entail that it would be appropriate for anyone to blame them.[52] Only people within the subordinated group can appropriately apply social sanctions to those who fail to resist, while privileged people lack the moral authority to do so and would indeed be engaged in an immoral instance of blaming the victim if they were to chastise passivity.

3.3 PATRONIZING THE OPPRESSED

According to the third objection, Dworkinian dignity commands self-sufficiency and weighs against letting other people fight one's struggle. It demands that the oppressed, and no one else, be the ones resisting their oppression. Anything else would amount to "patronizing the oppressed." This idea is consonant with the third goal of resistance—asserting dignity—which is prominent in many liberation movements. For instance, Stokely Carmichael, former chairman of the Student Nonviolent Coordinating Committee (SNCC), who became the Black Panther Party Prime Minister in 1968, refused to allow whites into the movement, and insisted that the organization "should be black-staffed, black-controlled, and black-financed." The latter demand (black financing only) was especially problematic given African Americans' relative lack of resources, but Carmichael insisted: "If we continue to rely upon white financial support we will find ourselves entwined in the tentacles of the white power complex that controls this country."[53] He thought that whites could not relate to the black experience, had an intimidating effect on blacks, and displayed paternalistic attitudes. He further wrote, anticipating the objection considered here: "The charge may be made that we are 'racists,' but whites who are sensitive to our problems will realize that we must determine our own destiny."[54]

Although there is indeed great dignity in the liberation of the oppressed by themselves, I do not think that the objection is ultimately successful. The

---

[52] Hill (1973); Silvermint (2013).
[53] Carmichael (2001).
[54] Id.

existence of ethical obligations to resist one's mistreatment does not cancel the moral obligations of others—oppressors, privileged, or bystanders—to rectify the oppressive arrangements. The slave rebellion led by Spartacus was certainly dignity-affirming and awe-inspiring. But it does not go to show that the abolition of slavery was the slaves' task. On the contrary, it is clear that abolishing an unjust system like slavery was everyone's moral duty. So ethical obligations to resist one's own mistreatment are perfectly compatible with the moral obligations of the privileged to resist oppression, too. From this perspective, Carmichael's point should not be taken to exclude white resistance against racism, but instead it should be understood as highlighting the importance of the composition and organization of the oppressed people's own liberation movement.

3.4 DELINEATING POLITICAL RELATIONSHIPS

A fourth problem concerns the scope of political relationships. The dignity-threatening political relationships I focused on were laws, policies, practices, or institutions (including the government), that express contempt, or fail to express concern, for certain groups in the political community. But political relationships may not always be clearly delineated: there can be disagreements about whether a certain kind of power relations is a political relationship or not. For instance, most people deny that nonhuman animals are members of the moral community, and that considerations of justice apply to our treatment of them. The mistreatment of animals is not usually perceived as violation of their dignity; nor do people see their relations to animals as political. For another example, in spite of the way in which economic decisions made in the United States profoundly affect developing countries where labor is outsourced, we are commonly blind to the political nature of our relationship with, say, Bangladeshi garment workers.

It is appropriate to worry about all the power relationships left out of the Dworkinian associativist account. But I am not convinced that these observations would actually mount an objection against it. Instead, they might suggest extending the account of special responsibilities and associative obligations of resistance beyond political membership and across borders. Although Dworkin explains how the obligation to obey the law flows from political membership, it is in virtue of particular features of the latter that it does, namely, the great value of political association for participants and their vulnerability to subservience. Similar features might be salient to explain how we might have, say, special responsibilities not to dominate or exploit the global poor and associative political obligations to resist the current global scheme (insofar as it favors the wealthy countries and burdens the developing ones). The point is that we could extend Dworkin's principles to construct an account of associative obligations flowing from relationships that do not take place within the boundaries of a political community.

4. Political Obligations Redux

The analysis above, if it is correct, suggests that theorists' heavy focus on the moral duty to obey the law is inappropriate. Given the pervasiveness of injustice, citizens are more often obligated to resist the law, than to obey it. Are the two obligations incompatible? If legitimacy lapses entirely, there is no general obligation to obey the law, and there are weighty obligations to resist the system. But legitimacy being a matter of degree, a stain on legitimacy does not entirely rescind the general obligation to obey the law. Whether one ought to obey or disobey and how to resist in particular instances then depends on both practical and moral considerations (i.e., basically, the advisability and permissibility of a given course of action).

One important point to infer from the foregoing account is that citizens' political obligations are plural. The responsibilities and duties that come with the role of citizen are manifold; and obeying the law is one among many. Under non-ideal conditions, the obligations of resistance that flow from the responsibility neither to dominate nor to unilaterally defer to others are more central to the role of citizen than the obligation to obey the law. The prominence of these obligations of resistance raises a serious issue, since individuals are left to decide for themselves when they are released of their political obligation and have an obligation to resist injustice, and how they ought to discharge it. They might thus, in good faith, come to reject legitimate outcomes of the democratic process and destabilize society by engaging in small or big acts of resistance.[55] Indeed, one may be wrong about one's political obligations, and one may fulfill them more or less well (i.e., more or less fully and responsibly). This is a genuine risk, especially in democratic societies.

But I think that rather than weighing against the account of political obligations of resistance, this risk underscores the need for additional, but prerequisite, second-order duties, which are essential to understand and implement one's first-order moral obligations in the face of injustice. These second-order duties are necessary because of the compound effects of our cognitive limitations (what Rawls calls the burdens of judgment, i.e., the limits on our powers of reason), and the toxic influence of injustice and oppression on our mental world and psychological make-up. Injustices shape our perception of social reality and self-identity; they can erode or bolster our self-respect; they can conceal wrongs behind the cloth of just desert; they can hinder our perception and understanding of injustice by exposing us to a false world-view that seeks to justify the existing arrangements. And so, they can habituate us to grave injustice.

These effects constitute formidable obstacles to the recognition of one's political obligations, including obligations of resistance, and suggest one's responsibility to self-examine and scrutinize the society and world one lives in. More precisely, as I shall now suggest, citizens are morally bound to seek out

---

[55] I thank Stefan Sciaraffa for raising this objection.

information, resist self-deception, and exercise empathetic understanding and care. Such responsibilities are so important to understand and implement one's first-order political obligations in the face of injustice that they should be viewed as parts of our associative political obligations. Someone who does not even try to harbor these attitudes—vigilance, self-scrutiny, and empathy—may be blamed for his or her failure.[56] Let us look briefly at each of these second-order duties.

First, we have an epistemic interest in perceiving reality accurately, which entails a responsibility to do our best to perceive the world and other people accurately. "It is a task to come to see the world as it is," Iris Murdoch wrote.[57] The difficulty may come from states' trying to obfuscate reality through secrecy or deception, or from the disguise of injustice behind the cloth of "business as usual," as it is under conditions of structural injustice. Seeking reliable sources of information, thinking critically, questioning prevalent beliefs, and learning about the experience of the subordinated, are then crucial. However, knowing the basic facts about destitution and oppression does not guarantee the right kind of understanding.

Citizens also have a duty to resist self-deception. According to Tommie Shelby, "We sometimes believe things because to do so would, say, bolster our self-esteem, give us consolation, lessen anxiety, reduce cognitive dissonance, increase our self-confidence, provide cathartic relief, give us hope, or silence a guilty conscience."[58] Avoiding the influence of these noncognitive motives and recognizing oppression requires self-scrutinizing and resisting self-deceit, which itself involves keen perception and courage.[59]

Finally, one has a second-order duty to exercise empathetic understanding, which means that one must do one's best to understand other people. The right kind of understanding involves learning about the experience of one another, with empathy and care. In particular, Laurence Thomas argues that the privileged must listen to the oppressed with a certain attitude he calls *moral deference* and which involves openness and attentiveness.[60] According to Elizabeth Spelman, the privileged must exercise their imaginative capacities to put themselves in the shoes of the oppressed.[61] Imaginative self-projection, empathy, and self-awareness are thus required for proper moral learning.[62]

Fulfilling one's second-order obligations does not necessarily entail the recognition of primary responsibilities; but it does make accurate perception more likely and dogmatism less likely. Conversely, blindness and ignorance may be

---

[56] According to John Draeger, for instance, indifference and failure to care about victims of oppression are morally blameworthy, as they amount to denying the victims' basic moral worth as human beings. See Draeger (2008).

[57] Murdoch (1985: 91).

[58] Shelby (2003: 171).

[59] See also Garrett (2010).

[60] Thomas (1998).

[61] Spelman (1988: 179).

[62] See e.g., Bartky (2002); Harvey (2007).

morally blameworthy if they are rooted in systematic failure to seek to learn about oppression, resist self-deception, and develop empathetic understanding. In conclusion, living in a polity, especially in a democratic society in which one has the power to benefit or harm others, comes with grave responsibilities that have so far been neglected. Dworkin's liberal associativist account provides rich resources for thinking about obligations in the face of injustice. The principles of his theory have indeed radical implications under less-than-ideal political conditions, as they can ground a variety of duties—to oneself and others—in societies that fail to respect the basic requirements of dignity person-by-person.

References

Altman, A. (2011). "Discrimination," *The Stanford Encyclopedia of Philosophy (Spring 2011 Edition)*, ed. E. N. Zalta, http://plato.stanford.edu/archives/spr2011/entries/discrimination/.

Bartky, S. L. (2002). *Sympathy and Solidarity and Other Essays*. Lanham, MD: Rowman & Littlefield.

Boxill, B. (1976). "Self-Respect and Protest," *Philosophy and Public Affairs* 6:58–69.

Brownlee, K. (2012). *Conscience and Conviction: The Case for Civil Disobedience*. Oxford: Oxford University Press.

Carmichael, S. (2001 [unknown]). *The Basis of Black Power*. USA History Archive: marxists.org.

Chenoweth, E. and Stephan, M. J. (2011). *Why Civil Resistance Works: The Strategic Logic of Nonviolent Conflict*. Columbia University Press: New York.

Cudd, A. (2006). *Analyzing Oppression*. Oxford: Oxford University Press.

Delmas, C. (2014a). "Samaritanism and Civil Disobedience," *Res Publica* 20: 295-313.

Delmas, C. (2014b). "Political Resistance: A Matter of Fairness," *Law and Philosophy* 33: 465-488.

Delmas, C. (2015). "Disobedience: Civil and Otherwise," *Criminal Law and Philosophy*. doi: 10.1007/s11572-014-9347-9 (forthcoming in print).

Draeger, J. (2008). "Must We Care About Racial Injustice?" *Journal of Social Philosophy* 39:62–76.

Du Bois, W. E. B. (1999). *Darkwater: Voices from within the Veil*. Mineola, NY: Dover.

Dworkin, R. (2011). *Justice for Hedgehogs*. Cambridge, MA: The Belknap Press of Harvard University.

Dworkin, R. (1986). *Law's Empire*. Cambridge, MA: The Belknap Press of Harvard University.

Dyzenhaus, D. (2001). "'With the Benefit of Hindsight': Dilemmas of Legality." In *Lethe's Law: Justice, Law, and Ethics in Reconciliation*. E Christodoulidis and S Veitch (eds.). Hart Publishing Oxford 65.

Dyzenhaus, D. (2016). "Dworkin and Unjust Law." In *The Legacy of Ronald Dworkin*. W. Waluchow and S. Sciaraffa (eds.). Oxford: Oxford University Press.

Fanon, F. (1968). *The Wretched of the Earth*. New York: Grove Press, Inc.

Frye, M. (1985). "History and responsibility," *Hypatia* 3:215–216.

Frye, M. (1983). *The Politics of Reality.* Freedom, CA: Crossing Press.

Garrett, A. (2010). "Courage, Political Resistance, and Self-Deceit," *Boston University Law Review* 90:1771–1783.

Ginzburg, R. (1988 [1962]). *100 Years of Lynching.* Baltimore: Black Classic Press.

Green, L. (1988). *The Authority of the State.* Oxford: Oxford University Press.

Greenawalt, K. (1989). *Conflicts of Law and Morality.* Oxford: Oxford University Press.

Grimké A. (2003). *Walking by Faith: The Diary of Angelina Grimké 1828-1835.* University of South Carolina.

Harvey, J. (2010). "Victims, Resistance, and Civilized Oppression," *Journal of Social Philosophy* 41: 13–27.

Harvey, J. (2007). "Moral Solidarity and Empathetic Understanding," *Journal of Social Philosophy* 38: 22–37.

Harvey, J. (1999). *Civilized Oppression.* Lanham, MD: Rowman & Littlefield.

Haslanger, S. (2007). "Oppressions: Racial and Other." In *Racism, Philosophy and Mind: Philosophical Explanations of Racism and Its Implications.* M. Levine and T. Pataki (eds.). Ithaca, NY: Cornell University Press.

Hay, C. (2013). *Kantian, Liberalism, and Feminism: Resisting Oppression.* Palgrave Macmillan.

Hill, T. E., Jr. (1973). "Servility and Self-Respect," *The Monist* 57:87–104.

Horton, J. (2007). "In Defense of Associative Political Obligations. Part Two," *Political Studies* 55: 1–19.

Kymlicka, W. (1995). *Multicultural Citizenship.* Oxford: Clarendon Press.

Kelsen, H. (1960). *What is Justice?* Berkeley: University of California Press.

Langton, R. (2009). *Sexual Solipsism: Philosophical Essays on Pornography and Objectification.* Oxford: Oxford University Press.

Langton, R. (1990). "Whose Right? Ronald Dworkin, Pornographers, and Women," *Philosophy and Public Affairs* 19:311–359.

Lyons, D. (2013). *Confronting Injustice: Moral History and Political Theory.* Oxford: Oxford University Press.

MacIntyre, A. (1984). *After Virtue,* 2nd ed. Notre Dame: University of Notre Dame Press.

Margalit, A. (1996). *The Decent Society,* trans. N. Goldblum. Cambridge, MA: Harvard University Press.

May, T. (2015). *Nonviolent Resistance: A Philosophical Introduction.* Polity Press.

McPherson, T. (1967). *Political Obligation.* London: Routledge & Kegan Paul.

Murdoch, I. (1985). *The Sovereignty of the Good.* London: Routledge & Kegan Paul.

Murphy, L. (2000). *Moral Demands in Nonideal Theory.* Oxford Ethics Series: Oxford University Press.

Nussbaum, M. (1995). "Objectification," *Philosophy and Public Affairs* 24:249–291.

Parekh, B. (1993). "A Misconceived Discourse on Political Obligation," *Political Studies* 41:236–251.

Rawls, J. (1999). *A Theory of Justice,* rev. ed. Cambridge, MA: Harvard University Press.

Raz, J. (2016). "A Hedgehog's Unity of Value." In *The Legacy of Ronald Dworkin.* S. W. Waluchow and S. Sciaraffa (eds.). Oxford: Oxford University Press.

Shelby, T. (2003). "Ideology, Racism, and Critical Social Theory," *The Philosophical Forum* 34:153–188.

Silvermint, D. (2013). "Resistance and Well-Being," *Journal of Political Philosophy* 21:405–425.

Simons, K. W. (2010). "Dworkin's Two Principles of Dignity: An Unsatisfactory Nonconsequentialist Account of Interpersonal Moral Duties," *Boston University Law Review* 90:715–735.

Spelman, E. V. (1988). *Inessential Woman: Problems of Exclusion in Feminist Thought.* Boston: Beacon Press.

Smith, W. (2013). *Civil Disobedience and Deliberative Democracy.* London: Routledge.

Sreedhar, S., and Delmas, C. (2010). "State Legitimacy and Political Obligation in *Justice for Hedgehogs*: The Radical Potential of Dworkinian Dignity," *Boston University Law Review* 90: 737–758.

Tamir, Y. (1993). *Liberal Nationalism.* Princeton, NJ: Princeton University Press.

Thomas, L. M. (1998). "Moral Deference." In *Theorizing Multiculturalism*. C. Willet (ed.). Oxford: Blackwell Publishers.

Walzer, M. (1983). *Spheres of Justice: A Defense of Pluralism and Equality.* Basic Books.

Wood, A. (1995). "Exploitation," *Social Philosophy and Policy* 12:136–158.

Young, I. M. (2011). *Responsibility for Justice.* New York: Oxford University Press.

Young, I. M. (1990). *Justice and the Politics of Difference.* Princeton: Princeton University Press.

3

Ronald Dworkin, State Consent, and Progressive Cosmopolitanism

by Thomas Christiano

Ronald Dworkin's moral, political, and legal writings as a whole constitute one of the most impressive achievements of modern philosophy. The works on the nature and basis of equality and the foundations of legal interpretation and institutions remain the most illuminating treatments of these subjects in contemporary thought. In his later work, Dworkin turns briefly to questions of the nature and moral foundations of international society and justice. In "A New Philosophy for International Law," and in sections of *Justice for Hedgehogs*, Dworkin argues, first, against a legal positivist understanding of international law and in favor of his own moralized reading of international law. He argues, second, for a conception of the moral meaning and purpose of the system of international law.[1] This second thesis, or group of theses, is designed to fill out his moralized reading of international law. But it is a separate thesis that can be evaluated on its own. My purpose in this paper is primarily to explore and critique this second thesis or group of theses.

Within Dworkin's conception of the basic moral standards by which the international system is to be evaluated, there are two elements that stand out and that will be the focus of this paper. The first element is the rejection of the doctrine of state consent as the basis of international law. It is directed primarily at the legal positivist idea that state consent, understood in an expansive way that includes both the action of consent to treaties and the attitudes of acceptance of general principles of law, is the basic rule of recognition of the system. But he also argues against the idea that state consent, understood narrowly to include only the actions of signing on to agreements and treaties, can be a morally defensible basis of the international system. We will have to look at the expansive and the narrow understandings of state consent in order to work through these ideas.

---

[1] Dworkin (2011 and 2013).

I agree with Dworkin that state consent in the expansive sense cannot be the sole basis of international law, at least not from a moral point of view. I think there is an important role for state consent in the narrow sense in a morally defensible international system, but Dworkin seems to leave no room for this.

The second element in Dworkin's conception of the morality of international politics is his commitment to a kind of non-cosmopolitan associativism. To put it bluntly, the true moral purpose of the international system, Dworkin thinks, is to enable each state within the system to enhance its legitimacy vis-à-vis its citizens. The basic moral ground of international law derives from the duty of states to enhance their legitimacy. And the legitimacy of a state, on Dworkin's well-known account, is grounded in the state's treatment of its citizens as equals and as responsible for their fates, which in turn generates associative obligations on the part of citizens to their political society. Dworkin does not articulate an independent conception of the legitimacy of the international system itself and he does not give evidence of believing that it constitutes a distinctive political society with its own important aims. To be sure, Dworkin seems ambivalent about this in his work, and I will indicate where that ambivalence is expressed, but this does seem to be his official thesis.

I will contend that the rejection of state consent as a moral ground of international law, whether in the expansive or in the narrow sense, is connected with the non-cosmopolitan approach to the international system. I will argue that we ought to reject both of these theses and that a more satisfactory conception of the moral standards for evaluating the international system emerges once we do these.

I will start by discussing his rejection of state consent and try to get at the fundamental arguments for this. I will then articulate Dworkin's basic principles of international law. I will critique them, suggesting that though they shed a great deal of light on the morality of the international system, they do not support his idea that the enhancement of state legitimacy is the true moral basis of international law. I will then argue that though the premises of the fundamental arguments may imply that state consent in the expansive sense cannot be the moral basis of international law, they do not undermine the importance of state consent in the narrow sense as a ground. Finally, I will suggest how a more satisfactory picture of the international system emerges once we accept the idea that there is an international political community and that state consent has an important role to play in the shaping of that international political community.

1. Dworkin on State Consent

Dworkin's statement of the idea of state consent as the basis of international law is initially focused on the issue of legal positivism, or the question of whether the legality of international law can be said to be based on social facts. But his criticism extends further and can be taken as a moral criticism of the idea of state consent as the basis of international law. The basic thesis he is criticizing is, "Law for nations, is grounded in what nations—or at least the vast bulk of those that others counts as 'civilized'—have consented to treat as law."[2] This suggests that state consent is the basis of all of international law, including the recognition of other states and the most basic principles of law such as *pacta sunt servanda*. But we should note here that the notion of state consent, in the expansive sense that Dworkin uses, covers both (1) the actions of states that constitute consent to treaties and perhaps consent to custom (by not persistently objecting) and (2) the attitudes of states such as the recognition of other states and the acceptance of general principles including the principle of *pacta sunt servanda* and the *jus cogens* norms.

Dworkin gives five main arguments against state consent as the basis of international law. First, he asserts that the different kinds of state actions of consent and attitudes of acceptance are not ordered in terms of moral or legal importance. Thus, he seems to be saying that they cannot serve as the basic rule of recognition because they leave open a great deal of indeterminacy in the law. Second, he states that there are valid international norms to which states have not consented, such as ongoing customary international law, *jus cogens* norms, and the general principles of international law. Here too, aside from appearing to be a counterexample to the thesis of state consent as a ground of all international law, there is a worry about indeterminacy in that it does not answer the question, "Whose consent counts?" Third, he asserts that state consent provides a slim basis for interpretation of international law, here too pointing to indeterminacy in the law. Fourth, he says that state consent is either circular as a ground of customary law because of the centrality of *opinio juris* in customary law or customary law must be grounded in a different principle. Fifth, he says that state consent cannot account for the bindingness of law across generations at least in the case of customary international law (since subsequent generations have not consented to it).[3]

This criticism of state consent is what leads Dworkin to reject state consent as the basis of international law and search for deeper principles, which are his principles of limited sovereignty, mitigation, and salience (understood narrowly in terms of the state legitimacy enhancement thesis). Again, these arguments are meant to give reasons for rejecting the legal positivist approach to international law, which is alleged to be based in the rule of recognition of state consent. I do not want to assess these considerations as they apply to the question of legal positivism in international law.[4] I am interested here in questions of political philosophy. And I am interested in the question of the role of state consent in a morally defensible international legal order.

Dworkin's most fundamental criticisms of state consent are that it makes international law excessively indeterminate such that it cannot be an independent

---

[2] Dworkin (2013: 6).

[3] Dworkin (2013: 6-10).

[4] See Besson (2010) and Lefkowitz (2010) for illuminating discussions of how legal positivists could respond to these worries.

basis of international law. The significance of state consent must be based in distinct and more fundamental principles. It cannot be a free-standing basis of international law. This is a worry about the moral basis of international institutions as much as it is a concern with the possibility of a rule of recognition. All five of the criticisms stated above can be articulated in terms of these two central worries.[5] But the main worry is articulated by Dworkin in earlier work. This worry can be succinctly stated as Dworkin does: "An involuntary obligation lies behind any voluntary one."[6] And he states in the essay that: "If we want to explain why promises do create moral obligations, we must point to different more basic principles that a promise invokes."[7]

Dworkin's basic idea here is one that he attributes to David Hume.[8] He argues that one cannot simply produce new obligations at will and that voluntary obligations are dependent on prior general obligations. He says: "Promising is not an independent source of a distinct kind of moral duty. Rather it plays an important but not exclusive role in fixing the scope of a more general responsibility: not to harm other people by first encouraging them to expect that we will act in a certain way and then not acting that way."[9]

With regard to state consent, Dworkin asks why a society is bound to act in accordance with that to which it has consented. In particular, he is worried about why subsequent generations of a society are bound to consent as some previous generation has. The mere invocation of the general principle of *pacta sunt servanda* does not help the case but simply deepens the question. Dworkin says that we must look for deeper principles.

2. Dworkin on the Fundamental Principles of International Law

Ronald Dworkin elaborates his conception of the meaning and purpose of international law in essentially three stages. The first stage is a discussion of what he calls the Westphalian conception of international law. This conception is not laid

---

[5] I am not convinced by the first two, at least, as articulated by Dworkin. The first says that there must be hierarchy among the basic sources of international law but that state consent is ineluctably plural so there must a basic principle that undergirds its variety. We might think that this plurality is desirable for the international legal system at the moment and that its desirability has to do with the need for negotiation and compromise and flexibility in the system, which concerns are also motivated by the need for consent. The second asserts that there are unconsented to norms but it seems to be invoking a notion of state consent that is less expansive than the one he invokes in the first criticism and in his definition of state consent. The more expansive version, which includes attitudinal acceptance or recognition, would seem to cover at least the *jus cogens* norms and the general principles of international law.

[6] Dworkin (2011: 319).

[7] Dworkin, (2013: 10).

[8] David Hume (1948a: Book III, Part II, Section V, "Of the Obligation of Promises," and 1948b).

[9] Dworkin (2011: 304).

out in much detail except when it is contrasted with the modern conception of international law. But the most important feature of this conception is the adherence to a principle that states are sovereign. In effect, Dworkin seems (though he never quite explicitly states it) to be accepting a defeasible principle of state sovereignty, such that the conditions of defeat are specified by the principles of mitigation and salience. The second stage consists of the elaboration and defense of what he calls the principle of mitigation. This principle asserts that the main purpose of the system of international law since World War II has been to mitigate the dangers that are created by the Westphalian system of sovereign states. The third stage articulates and defends the principle of salience. This is essentially a principle of coordination in efforts to pursue the mitigation of the dangers of the Westphalian system.

3. Mitigation

The principle of mitigation, which asserts a duty to mitigate the dangers that can arise from the system of sovereign states is articulated by describing four challenges that a system of sovereign states faces: threats to peace, widespread violations of human rights, the dangers of economic and environmental disaster, and the requirement that political institutions permit the participation of affected persons in the creation of international law. Dworkin illustrates his conception in the following ways. (1) International law constrains the use of force among states. (2) International law authorizes the criticism, pressure, and sometimes intervention against states that engage in widespread violations of basic human rights. (3) It is designed to mitigate climate change and other global threats that require cooperation to solve. (4) It enables persons to participate in making decisions that affect them but that are outside their state. (5) It enhances the legitimacy of states by establishing the legitimacy of the international system from which states get their legitimacy. By signing treaties designed to mitigate climate change, reduce the danger of war or widespread human rights violations, states enhance their legitimacy because they protect their citizens from these dangers.

Dworkin affirms that "the general obligation of each state to improve its political legitimacy includes an obligation to try to improve the overall international system.... That requirement sets out, in my view, the true moral basis of international law."[10] I will call this the State Legitimacy Enhancement Thesis. The basic idea behind this is that the challenges to the system of sovereign states are in reality challenges to the legitimacy of the states that participate in the system. They meet these challenges by creating international law. Dworkin seems to argue that the principle of mitigation can be derived from the duty of each state to try to enhance its own legitimacy.

---

[10] Dworkin (2013: 17).

It should be noted that the State Legitimacy Enhancement Thesis does not require states to enhance the legitimacy of states generally but only the legitimacy of the state that is acting. It appears to be a kind of agent relative requirement. This is what generates the non-cosmopolitan aspect of Dworkin's approach, though it is mitigated by the principle of salience and by Dworkin's apparent adherence to the thesis that a state's legitimacy may partly depend on it enabling its citizens to fulfill cosmopolitan duties. But the basic picture is that each state's relation to international law is determined by its moral relationship with its citizens. And the duties of international law are generated by the extent to which a state's participation in international law enhances those relationships.

4. Political Legitimacy

We need briefly to review Dworkin's conception of political legitimacy. Dworkin defines legitimacy in terms of the justification of coercion by the state and political obligation, which he conceives to be primarily a function of the state's treatment of its citizens as equal and responsible persons. He states that: "[Governments] can be legitimate if their laws and policies can... be interpreted as recognizing that the fate of each citizen is of equal importance and that each has a responsibility to create his own life.... if it strives for its citizens' full dignity even if it follows a defective conception of what that requires."[11] This conception of legitimacy is an associative conception. Of political obligations, the conditions of which he asserts are sufficient conditions for government legitimacy, he says they are "... a special case of associational obligation. We... have political obligations because we are related to our fellow citizens in some special way that gives each of us special responsibilities to the others independently of any consent."[12]

5. The Principle of Salience

The second main principle that Dworkin defends is what he calls the principle of salience. This principle is meant to give concrete specification to the duties implied by the principle of mitigation. It states that:

> If a significant number of states, encompassing a significant population, has developed an agreed code of practice, either by treaty or by other forms of coordination, then other states have at least a prima facie duty to subscribe to that practice as well, with the important proviso that this duty holds only if a more general practice to that effect, expanded in that way,

---

[11] See Ronald Dworkin (2011: 321-322) and (1986: 195-206) for an earlier elaboration of this conception of legitimacy.

[12] Dworkin (2011: 319).

would improve the legitimacy of the subscribing state and the international order as a whole. Dworkin (2013: 19)

It is worth noting here that Dworkin draws a distinction between international law that is genuinely universal and international law that has a more club-like character. He distinguishes in this way the institutions of the United Nations (UN), the Charter of the UN (Charter) and the UN Security Council (Council), from those of the World Trade Organization (WTO) or the European Union (EU) He says: "The charter and institutions of the United Nations are best understood not as arrangements binding only through contract or on signatories but as an order all nations now have a moral obligation to treat as law. . . . It is therefore important to distinguish the force of such multinational treaties, and the appropriate interpretive strategies for them, from that of agreements creating international organizations, like the European Union and the WTO, that are designed from the start for only a club of signatory nations and members . . . "[13] The former are his subject and are not based on consent but on the principles of limited sovereignty, salience, and mitigation while the latter are based on consent.

The principle of salience seems to me to be a kind of principle of moral coordination. The thought is that states do better by their legitimacy if they join the practice in question than they do if they fail to join the practice. Coordination is suggested also by the fact that Dworkin thinks there are a number of possible and reasonably good ways of improving the legitimacy of states by means of international regimes and so the principle of mitigation does not determine exactly what states ought to do. Salience introduces determinacy because it makes a state's obligation depend on what a lot of other states are already doing. Just as a driver of an automobile does not get determinate guidance merely from the rule of driving to avoid oncoming cars but must choose a side of the road to drive on depending on what side most others are driving on, so a state best advances its legitimacy by choosing to conform to a legitimacy enhancing regime to which other states conform. Dworkin does not spend a lot of time on why this kind of coordination is necessary to legitimacy. But we might think that the example of climate change fits well, since many think that the construction of either some kind of cap and trade market for carbon or a universal carbon tax is necessary to solve the problem. In human rights, the strength of the regime as an enforcer of human rights may increase as it applies the same standards of human rights to which any society can have access. And perhaps international security is advanced by the creation of a reasonably clear and common set of rules that all can abide by and be seen to abide by.

Seen in this way, we can see how the principle of salience can have a kind of moral force for the states in the international system. In effect, the idea is that a state does worse on the moral legitimacy score if the state does not join. And Dworkin has argued that states have duties to increase their legitimacy scores.

[13] Dworkin (2013: 20).

Hence they have duties to go along with international law that serves the principle of salience.

The two basic principles he articulates, the principles of mitigation and salience, along with limited sovereignty, are meant to explain the significance of consent in the international arena. He claims that these principles give a better moral explanation of the three main sources of international law as articulated by the International Court of Justice (ICJ) in 1945 (consent to treaties, customary international law, and the general principles of international law) than the state consent doctrine.

And we can see how salience has a reasonably natural connection with customary international law. Customary international law does seem to establish coordination points for states in their interactions with each other and we can think of these coordination points as, in many cases, enhancing the legitimacy of the states. But this claim seems a stretch in many other cases. International telecommunication conventions, banking conventions, and many other conventions serve as coordination points but it is not clear how they enhance the legitimacy of the states that are parties to them.

Dworkin says that the principle of mitigation explains the *jus cogens* norms. He does not discuss any particular examples but the idea would seem to be that the principle of mitigation imposes certain duties on states that restrict their sovereignty such as the norms against aggressive war, torture, genocide, etc. This seems right but there is also the *jus cogens* norm against slavery and this does not seem to be a norm that mitigates against sovereignty, at least primarily. Still, these are cases in which mitigation and salience shed important light on aspects of international law. They may fit imperfectly, but they do show something.

I want to bring out one last distinction here before I go on. We can distinguish broad and narrow versions of both the mitigation and salience principles. The narrow version connects mitigation and salience to the enhancement of state legitimacy. It says we mitigate the dangers of the sovereign state system to the legitimacy of states, and we cooperate if this enhances the legitimacy of states. The broader version is that we seek to overcome the dangers of sovereign states to any morally important values, and we seek to cooperate whenever there are morally desirable gains to be made from cooperation. It seems clear that Dworkin emphasizes the first concern and not the second, though we will discuss a way in which the broader principle could be folded into the narrower principle later in the paper. This distinction is of some significance because it derives from a distinction between two different conceptions of international society. The first one, which is the one Dworkin articulates, is a thinner conception of an international society that does not have its own distinctive aims. Each participant society merely attempts to advance its own moral relationship with its own citizens. The second suggests that the moral aims of international society are independent aims that all societies have common reasons to pursue. These reasons provide the moral ground of international law and the importance of state consent to that law, or so I will argue.

There is one further point to note here. Though Dworkin has articulated a conception of political legitimacy for states, which is an associative conception, he does not seem to try to apply this conception of legitimacy to the international system as a whole. Dworkin does mention the idea that the international system can have legitimacy as a whole but the standard he applies to states is not applied to it. Here, he seems to say that states are obligated to comply with the international system because that is the way they can enhance their own legitimacy, which they have an obligation to enhance.

6. Problems with Salience, Mitigation, and Universality

But there are a host of problems here. First, it is very unclear why salience and mitigation must go with essentially universal treaties. A question Dworkin does not answer is why the coordination would need to be global in order to serve the principles of mitigation and salience. Perhaps there is a case to be made for this in the case of climate change, though even here, many have argued against the idea that a treaty for mitigating climate change ought to be universal. Many argue that such a treaty is highly unlikely to be effective because it would have to be watered down too much to get global agreement. These people argue that only a select ten or so of the high emitting states, with the EU being one of them, should develop highly demanding and particular treaties with each other.[14]

The human rights of European states are probably better served by the reasonably effective and respected European Convention on Human Rights and the European Court of Human Rights than by international human rights law. The latter is, relatively speaking, watered down and has not proved to be particularly effective. But of course the European Court of Human Rights and the European Convention on Human Rights are created by treaty and are binding only on states that have consented to them. Nevertheless, they have proved to create a very solid coordination point for European states.

Probably the most successful of all modern international agreements is the General Agreement on Trade and Tariffs (GATT) and the treaty founding the WTO. They have made a significant impact increasing the wealth of developed and many developing countries, though the increase has not been spread to all societies. This is a very clear case of a complex coordination point. But Dworkin does not think of it as forming the part of international law he is analyzing. It is based on the consent of states, though some of that consent seems to have been given under unfair circumstances. Do the GATT and the WTO enhance the legitimacy of their members? Dworkin does not tell us but he seems to think not.

Second, here is a related but deeper worry for the view Dworkin is suggesting. International law and its binding character, he says, arise out of the capacity

---

[14] See, for instance, Victor (2011) for an argument of this sort.

of international law to enhance the legitimacy of the states that are part of the system. There is some plausibility to this idea when it comes to the protection of human rights. One might think that a state is more legitimate if it better protects the human rights of its citizens. And it is generally thought that some states do sign on to human rights treaties because that will lock in the state to future protection of human rights.[15] This is a good case for Dworkin's thesis that international law can enhance a state's legitimacy in accordance with a plausible conception of the equality of citizens.[16]

But there are two ways in which Dworkin's basic idea concerning the moral foundations of international law are not satisfying. One, he wants to argue that people have duties to help others avoid invasion and severe human rights violations everywhere.[17] And this seems like the kind of thing one would want to say about the moral grounds of human rights treaties. But this ground does not sit well with Dworkin's official account of the moral basis of international law. It is hard to see how the legitimacy of a state is enhanced by its offering to protect the rights of others from severe human rights violations or invasion, at least on the kind of conception of legitimacy that Dworkin is suggesting. Dworkin's notion of the legitimacy of states is a legitimacy that is based on the quality of association the state supports. And his central principle for assessing legitimacy, as we have seen, is that states treat their citizens as equals according to some minimally plausible conception of equality. But this does not seem to imply anything about how these people treat others outside of the society. For example, this might suggest that, according to the narrow versions of mitigation and salience, European states do not have a duty to subscribe to international human rights treaties outside those of Europe since that adherence does not increase the legitimacy of those states.

One could respond to this by saying that a general rule protecting all people from human rights violations would help a state's legitimacy in the unlikely case that it can be stopped by others from violating the human rights of its members. But though this is not wrong, it just does not get at the main impulse behind these human rights laws for states that are fairly stable human rights protectors. And it also does not respond to the worry that a universal treaty might be rejected in favor of a regional treaty when that regional treaty works best.

So, to limit the moral basis of international law to what states can do to increase their own legitimacy seems to fail to capture much that is important about the moral basis of international law as we actually understand it. But to extend the moral basis of international law to include moral concerns beyond state legitimacy seems to put international law in the service of a different kind

---

[15] See Andrew Moravcsik (1995) for a discussion of the origins of the European Convention on Human Rights in terms of the interests of new democratic states in locking in their democratic rights. See also Beth Simmons (2009) for the beneficial effects of international law on domestic politics.

[16] Ronald Dworkin (2011: 322).

[17] Dworkin (2013: 17).

of community altogether, namely, a cosmopolitan community of people who are divided into states.

A third worry is that there does not seem to be much in the way of reasons for excluding the increase in wealth or the alleviation of global poverty from considerations grounding the moral basis of international law. Yet these do play an important role in international law. Both concerns play a central role in the motivation behind the WTO.[18] And the second plays a central role in the United Nations Millennium Declaration.[19] Of course, it is hard to see how these could play a role in Dworkin's conception of legitimacy enhancement, given what we have said about it. But to the extent that these are important elements in international law, Dworkin's conception seems to fall short.

A fourth worry is that the last two instances of mitigating the failures of the system of sovereign states seem to extend significantly past the domestic legitimacy enhancement thesis. The idea that people ought to be able to participate in the making of international law does not seem to involve enhancing the legitimacy of domestic societies at all. It seems merely to be a possible standard of legitimacy of international law and institutions. They ought to be such that they are created with the participation of the people who are affected. This suggests a new concern with a cosmopolitan political community. The idea that one ought to promote the legitimacy of the international system on the grounds that it is the condition of the legitimacy of the states that are in it does relate to domestic legitimacy but does so in a way that takes the focus off domestic communities. It is hard to see what the thought is here and Dworkin does not say anything more about this. But it seems ill suited to his associationist conception of the political legitimacy of states.

The idea that the enhancement of the legitimacy of domestic societies is the true moral basis of international law, as it is articulated in the principles of mitigation and salience, does not seem to hold up. International law either goes beyond the two principles to the extent that they are focused narrowly on domestic legitimacy or it is undermined by the plausible extensions of these two principles to a lot of different aims and purposes of international law. And furthermore, it is not clear why we need to think of mitigation and salience as connected exclusively or even primarily with universal law, even if we restrict their meaning to legitimacy enhancement.

One might respond to my criticism by formulating a more general reply by Dworkin. He could argue that state legitimacy, which depends on treating people as equals and responsible for their fates, implies that the state helps people conform to their duties to all human beings.[20] The idea is that people generally have duties to help others in need and to protect them from human rights violations as

---

[18] See preamble section of the *Agreement Establishing the World Trade Organization*.

[19] United Nations Millennium Declaration, Resolution Adopted by the General Assembly, "Values and principles" (2000).

[20] Dworkin suggests this at (2013: 18).

well as other harms. And these duties extend to all human beings on the globe. Dworkin can then argue that the state's legitimacy is partly dependent on the state's enabling people to fulfill these duties to all other human beings. In this case, the state legitimacy enhancement thesis would then imply that international law should enable states to enable their citizens to alleviate global poverty and avoid widespread human rights abuses. And so we would be able to explain the normative basis of international law that advances human rights protection and poverty alleviation. This looks like it has some of the missing elements we noted above.

There are two main worries about this possible reply. First, it is hard to see how the associationist approach to political legitimacy can ground the claim that the state's legitimacy is dependent on its enabling citizens to carry out their cosmopolitan duties. This is for the simple reason that it is hard to see how the quality of association among individuals is dependent on how well they are treating those outside the community. To treat persons as equals and as responsible for their fates does not seem to me to suggest this implication. We need a much fuller account of the relevant association and the conditions of association to help us draw this conclusion.

The second worry is that the approach suggests a different account of the moral purposes of international law. If persons have duties to protect others from war and human rights violations and to help them in need, then perhaps these duties on their own are a sufficient ground of much of the morally important parts of international law. In other words, if there are duties that are sufficient to ground the state's duties to participate in international law advancing the basic human rights, why not see the normative underpinning of international law as directly grounded in these duties? The idea would be that states represent collections of persons who have these duties and thus possess a kind of duty to attempt to fulfill the duties of their members in the making of international law. States are uniquely capable of carrying out this function in the light of the fact that they are the main institutions in the modern international system that are capable of making power accountable to persons. This kind of function need not be incompatible with the state legitimacy enhancing feature of international law. One can think that international law can help states achieve greater legitimacy while at the same time enabling persons, through the activities of states, to fulfill their cosmopolitan duties to their fellow human beings.

7. Mitigation, Salience, and State Consent

With these observations in mind, I want to argue that the opposition between the principles of mitigation and salience, on the one hand, and the idea that state consent is an important ground of international law is misconceived. International law can be thought of as in the service of advancing morally important aims. The role for state consent consists in making it possible to experiment with different ways of solving the difficult problems of international society and doing so by means of a process that is accountable to the people subjected to it.

What is most puzzling about Dworkin's discussion is that he does not discuss treaty-made law at all in this context. The norm of state consent, in the narrow sense of a state action voluntarily creating an obligation, and the principle that states are not bound by treaties they have not signed are quite important elements of the making of international law. There are exceptions to these principles but they are rare (though important). In addition, the aspect of customary international law that permits states not to be bound by custom if the state registers persistent objections is also curiously absent.

Failure to explain why state consent is so important to international law seems to me to be a severe lacuna in the picture. If we look at some of the most developed and effective parts of international law, consent and the moral liberty not to consent or to exit play central roles in these institutions. The WTO and the EU are just among the most important consent-based organizations we see. But there are many consent-based regional trade and security arrangements among states throughout the globe. International environmental law is also, at least in an important respect, consent based. The Montreal Protocol for the Protection of the Ozone is based on consent, though there is some qualification to this. And most of international human rights law is based on the consent of the state parties (some human rights have become *jus cogens* norms, though the exact list is controversial).

To be sure, the purposes of many of these treaties is to advance morally essential aims that states cannot pursue on their own or without cooperation, so mitigation and salience are present here in important ways. But the element of consent is also central to these treaties, as it is to most treaties. And, *pace* Dworkin, the vast majority of treaties are ones that one can exit from voluntarily, so subsequent generations do have a say in the treaties.[21] We need to understand why this is so.

8. State Consent, Indeterminacy, and the Accountability of International Law to Persons

Dworkin's two main arguments against state consent, the argument from indeterminacy and the Humean argument, do not undermine the idea that state consent can play a central role in the justification and legitimation of the international system.

The premise that state consent generates a great deal of indeterminacy in the content of international law seems to me to be correct. But it does not support the idea that state consent is not morally very important in the making of

---

[21] Helfer (2005).

international law. It merely shows that international law needs other institutions to fill in the gaps that are left open by the agreement-making processes. And we see that international law does have such institutions and they are usually a mix of judicial and diplomatic elements. The International Court of Justice, the Dispute Settlement Mechanism of the WTO, the Human Rights Council, among other bodies, all have the job of interpretation, construction, and negotiation of differences. They have to fill in many gaps left open by the crafters of the agreements. In some ways, they operate like domestic courts, but they contain much larger components of diplomatic resolution than ordinary domestic courts. This does not undermine the importance of state consent any more than the need for domestic courts to interpret legislation undermines the importance of democratic legislatures; it merely shows that it is not the whole picture.[22]

The Humean premise that the moral significance of agreement making must be grounded in deeper principles also seems to me to be correct. But it does not undermine the importance of state consent. I want to argue that the processes of interstate negotiation and state consent (and refusal of consent) can be parts of a process that respects persons as equals in the process of making decisions for the international community, which decisions are focused on pursuing morally important aims on which there is significant disagreement and conflict of interest. In this respect, the process of state consent, when it is among states that represent their peoples and when negotiation is carried out fairly, is the analog of democracy in the process of making collective decisions for domestic societies.[23] Democracy is a way of making decisions on issues of grave moral concern that treats persons as equals in the context of disagreement and opposing interests. And democratic principles are principles by which we evaluate the political processes of our political systems. In the same way, the idea of fair and representative state consent can be a standard by which we evaluate the processes of making international law.

Democracy's value is not itself grounded in democratic approval but it is based on the idea that it is essential to the realization of treating persons as equals in the process of decision making in domestic societies, if there is significant disagreement and conflict on the right course of action.[24] In the same way, state consent is not itself grounded in consent but it may nevertheless be an essential vehicle to the treatment of persons as equals in the process of making international law, as I will argue below.

I want to say that the making of international law is not merely an aid to states in shoring up their legitimacy. International law involves the creation of a new and distinct cosmopolitan society that is to be evaluated on its own distinct

---

[22] I do not think we need to take a stance here on whether the positivist account of filling the gaps is the right one or whether some version of the Dworkinian approach is superior. Dworkin accepts that there is a kind of special moral importance to democracy even though democratic legislation must be interpreted and filled in by courts. Dworkin (1996: "Introduction").

[23] I develop this further in Christiano (2010).

[24] I develop this further in Christiano (2008).

norms. We create international law ideally because we see ourselves as part of a larger community that is very incompletely structured. International trade, environmental law, human rights law, and the law of collective security are all ways in which we express the fact that we have come to see ourselves as parts of a larger community, and we want to play some role in shaping that community in accordance with our judgments.

This does not mean that we ought to abandon states. States remain and will remain very much necessary to the kinds of core concerns we have in establishing just and stable arrangements with our fellow human beings. International society is not capable of providing much in the way of justice for the world as a whole or fulfilling the core responsibilities that states fulfill, much as we might hope for it. That is still done in a patchy way by states and is done much better in some places than in others.

But, increasingly, we can see ourselves as part of a larger community. And our concerns for this larger community cannot be summarized merely in terms of the effects of that larger community our own society, morally or otherwise. We are concerned with global poverty, clearly expressed in the United Nations Millennium Declaration in 2000, not because we are afraid that we might fall into poverty and we want some institution to be prepared to help. We are concerned with the poor who are far away, for their own sakes as fellow human beings. We are concerned about stopping severe widespread human rights violations abroad not merely because we hope that our own society will be deterred from such violations by a community that protects against such violations. We are concerned with the human rights of other human beings. And we are creating a community of international trade at the global level and at regional levels and we evaluate these not merely in terms of whether they benefit our own society. We are sharply critical of the trade policies of our own society if they are seriously detrimental to the welfares of those in developing countries.

As this international society slowly takes shape, we must be concerned with the question, Who gets to shape it? Who gets to determine the rules of international trade, migration, human rights, the distribution of benefits and burdens of environmental law, and the structure of collective security? There are many disagreements about the appropriate rules and there are many conflicts of interests along a lot of different dimensions. And many states would want to impose their wills on others and have imposed their wills on other societies in the making of international law. State consent, it seems to me, suitably modified by norms of fairness in negotiation, and a requirement that states represent their peoples, supplies a way in which the process of making international law can be shaped by the diverse peoples and societies of the world. It provides some check on the powers of some and it makes the process accountable to the people who are subjected to international law.

To be sure, when we see actual instances of negotiations among powerful and weak states, and between developing and developed societies, there is much to complain about. Developed states often take advantage of their superior capacities for understanding and advancing their own interests when dealing with developing countries, as we saw in the formation of the WTO.[25] Developed states take advantage of superior economic and military strength in negotiating agreements that benefit them much more than developing countries. But these are familiar cases of unfair bargaining and negotiation. And these criticisms of unfairness in the creation of treaties are often pointed to in undermining, to some considerable extent, the legitimacy of the treaties that are designed. These examples suggest not that state consent is unimportant but that we have more refined standards of moral evaluation of the processes of agreement making than merely the absence of force or fraud. These standards of evaluation would be parts of the standards for evaluating the legitimacy of the international system.[26]

9. The Political System of International Society

Here I will need to lay out briefly a picture of the international community as a distinctive political system and I want to explain the moral significance of state consent. What makes the international system a kind of political community are the following: (1) There are certain morally mandatory aims that the international system is meant to pursue and these aims must be pursued by significant cooperation among societies. (2) There is significant disagreement and uncertainty about how best to pursue these aims and a significant conflict of interest over how to pursue them. (3) States remain by far the most important mechanisms by which power is, or can be made, accountable to people and states remain essential for many of the core responsibilities political societies pursue. In a sense, this is the version I want to promote of the principles of mitigation and salience that Dworkin discusses, but without the exclusive focus on the legitimacy of the states. Since there are conflicts of interests and disagreements about the exact specification of the aims and means for pursuing these aims, it makes sense to devise a political process that can be effective at pursuing the aims and that can treat persons as equals in the process.

---

[25] See, for instance, Steinberg (2002) for a discussion of the hard bargaining in the formation of the WTO.

[26] Here it seems that at least one of the instances of mitigation that Dworkin discusses can be supplied by a reasonable system of state consent. The concern that people be able to participate in decisions that affect them even though they are made in other political societies can be met by the idea that states negotiate with each other. Canadians have some say in the environmental policies of the United States through its negotiation of treaties regarding transboundary pollution, such as the acid rain agreements. Mexicans have some say in the economic policies of the United States through their state's negotiations with the United States on the terms of the North American Free Trade Agreement (NAFTA). Developing countries have some say in the migration policies of developed countries in the negotiation of bilateral agreements on migration.

It is not obvious to me how such negotiations enhance the legitimacy of the states in question but they do seem to lend some support to the legitimacy of the international regimes that are constructed by those states.

Let us start with a quick list of some of the main morally mandatory aims. They are the following: (1) the realization of international peace and security and cooperation in a scheme of collective security is necessary for achieving these aims. (2) The protection of persons against human rights violations is another basic aim and this can be pursued in a variety of ways including through the responsibility to protect. (3) The avoidance of environmental disaster is another basic aim and will require major cooperation in a scheme that helps transform the world's energy system. (4) The creation of a decent system of international trade and international migration is essential. (5) The alleviation of severe global poverty is another such aim.

These aims are provisional aims that the international community, as it is currently constituted, can be expected to pursue and has some capacity to pursue. They do not exhaust the complete hopes for human kind regarding the global community in the long run. We must hope and press for a more complete global justice that includes all human beings. But for the time being, the pursuit of these aims reflects the international community's concern with the fundamental interests of all its members. This is why I want to call this view a *progressive cosmopolitanism*.

The pursuit of anything less would suggest that the fundamental interests of some persons do not matter. Hence their pursuit is a basic condition of the justification and legitimacy of the international system. Furthermore, all (or nearly all) of the states of the international community have signed on to these aims in the texts of the United Nations Framework Convention on Climate Change, the Millennium Declaration of the United Nations, the preambles of the GATT and the WTO and Article 1 of the Charter of the United Nations.

These aims need to be pursued through cooperation among states and other entities. This cooperation does and must take the form expressed in international agreements and treaties that states sign. The reasons for this are the centrality of states in making power accountable to persons and the necessity of states in carrying out the basic functions we expect from political societies. This is meant to explain why it is states that must cooperate and why states ought to cooperate primarily by means of agreements among them.

States must be the primary vehicles for the time being because states are the principal resource for making power accountable to persons, and we want the international system to be accountable to persons. No other entity in the international system can have the kind of accountability that states have. International nongovernmental organizations (NGOs) can play a central role in the process of accountability in much the same way that organizations in domestic civil society facilitate the accountability of democratic assemblies to persons. International institutions can also help but they are far too dependent on states to take the primary role.

Furthermore, state consent is essential to the international system as well. This is because the domestic political societies that states are composed of are still the main providers of essential services, public goods, and justice for human beings. And they are still the main sources of accountability to persons regarding those goods. Moreover, these goods are provided by means of highly integrated legal and political systems that have developed over time. The implication of this is that the integrity of the legal and political systems of these societies is essential to the provisions of these goods. The international community can be looked at as a kind of division of labor in which these goods are provided by each state to particular groups of people assembled within the borders of that state. A number of the parts of this division of labor do not function very well, but it is still the best provider we have of many of the most important goods provided by political society. And recognition of this essential function of states is completely compatible with a morally cosmopolitan view of the world.

State majoritarianism and various forms of transnational majoritarianism are in serious tension with the protection of the integrity of political societies and thus can threaten the division of labor that the international system depends on for providing essential goods to persons. This is one main reason why it is important that states consent to international law. Only through consent can they revise their legal systems while preserving the integrity of those systems.[27] And so for the time being, we must expect that the international cooperation necessary for the pursuit of the mandatory aims must be pursued through state consent.

Furthermore, there is a great deal of uncertainty and disagreement about the exact specification of the morally mandatory aims, the best means for pursuing them and the proper distribution of benefits and burdens in the pursuit of the aims. Much of this disagreement is reasonable. Some of it is not. But we can see a significant amount of disagreement and uncertainty as to how to resolve the problems of climate change, how to devise a reasonable system of international trade, how to alleviate global poverty, and how to ensure international peace and security and the avoidance of widespread human rights violations.

A system of state consent involves, first, the moral liberty of states to remain free of obligation in at least some circumstances and even to exit those agreements they have made in some circumstances. Second is the power of states to shape agreements in a way that accords with their judgments about what the best way of pursuing an aim. Third, a set of obligations must be generated through state consent.

The first question that needs to be answered is: What is the basis of the moral liberty of states and is there any limit to this moral liberty? At first, one might think that there cannot be any moral liberty since the aims are mandatory and cooperation is necessary to meet the aims. This seems to be the reason why Dworkin ignores state consent. But I want to argue that there is some significant moral liberty for states to the extent that there is a great deal of reasonable disagreement and uncertainty on how to pursue the aims. In addition, each society has interests in being able to think through how it wants to pursue the aims as well as interests in being able to pursue the aims in a way that it sees fit.

---

[27] I make this argument in greater detail in Christiano (to be published) *NOMOS Migration*.

Furthermore, the international community has an interest in considering diverse solutions to the problems it faces in the light of the uncertainty it faces. In the international arena, this means that there is significant room for experimentation on how to pursue the aims. This experimentation can take place in different regional associations of states as well as competing global associations of states.

This gives us some reason to endorse the moral liberty of states to say *no* and the liberty of states to shape agreements as they see fit. It is important for states to be able to refuse entry into agreements and to exit agreements to the extent that it is important for states to experiment with different ways of solving international problems in the pursuit of the mandatory aims. Hence, the need for cooperation and the need for states to have a moral liberty not to cooperate are grounded in the same need to pursue the mandatory aims.

But I want to say that it also gives some grounds for determining the limits of the moral liberty. I said earlier that the moral liberty is grounded on reasonable, scrupulous disagreement. In cases of unreasonable or unscrupulous disagreement or outright refusal, I think that refusal of consent is not permitted. This is the result of the fact that we are talking about mandatory aims that require cooperation. This does not mean that, in effect, the state has consented, as David Estlund would have it.[28] Nevertheless, it does suggest a basis of a permission on the part of other states to pressure the state that is unreasonably or unscrupulously refusing consent into either cooperating or giving a good reason not to consent. In particular, if a state refuses consent because it wants to free ride on the efforts of other states or refuses to shoulder any burden in the pursuit of the mandatory aim, other states can resort to various forms of pressure to ensure cooperation. Or, if a state refuses consent on irrational grounds, such as the denial of the opinion of the vast majority of scientists, it becomes liable to pressure. Or, and this is much like Dworkin's principle of salience, if a state refuses to cooperate with others on the grounds that there is a superior coordination point to the one most states have chosen, even though insisting on the superior coordination solution is self-defeating, then that state becomes liable to pressure from other states.

In contrast, in all those cases in which the state refuses consent because it does not think the proposed arrangement will solve the problem and because it thinks it can form a superior arrangement, then, as long as this disagreement falls within the area of reasonable disagreement, the state is permitted to refuse consent.

We see something like this already in some aspects of international environmental law in which trade sanctions are sometimes justified as a means to getting states to join particular treaties.[29] So the moral liberty is limited, but it does not disappear because there is a lot of reasonable disagreement and there are interests in each party and in the international society as a whole, in each acting in accord with its judgment.

---

[28] Estlund (2008: ch. 7).
[29] See Barrett (2005) for some examples.

So we see here a system in which state consent (along with the moral liberties to refuse consent and to shape agreements as states see fit) plays an important role in the shaping of the system of international treaties. That role is limited by the considerations of the mandatory aims the states must pursue and the need for cooperation. It is also limited by *jus cogens* norms. But it is a real role nevertheless and it guarantees some of the basic interests that are also prominent in democratic citizenship. A system without state consent would be unresponsive to the fundamental interests of the persons within the distinct states involved.[30]

To be sure, this conception of state consent as enabling the participation of persons in the making of international law must include the requirement that states must be broadly representative of the peoples subject to them. And this account also requires an account of fairness in the process of interstate negotiation in order for it to be a process that treats persons as equals. The development of these further requirements is beyond the scope of this paper.[31]

10. Conclusion

Dworkin rightly rejects consent as the moral basis of all of international law. He correctly points out that the requirement of consent and the obligation generating character of consent must be based on deeper moral principles that are not themselves the products of consent. But it does not follow from this that state consent cannot play a vital role in the justification and legitimation of the international system, as I have tried to argue here. Again, the analogy of the central moral importance of democracy for domestic societies may be instructive here. The moral importance of democracy must derive from deeper moral principles that are not themselves dependent on democratic approval for their binding character. But this does not imply that the equal say that citizens are guaranteed as democratic citizens is not itself an essential part of the justification and legitimation of domestic societies. I claim that the same holds for the processes of interstate negotiation and state consent in the process of the making of international law. Although the moral significance of state negotiation and consent (and its refusal) depend on the need to cooperate in pursuit of the morally mandatory aims, these processes of international law making are themselves essential moral components of a system of international law that treats persons as equals in the making of that law.[32]

---

[30] I develop this more in Christiano (2012).

[31] I have begun to lay out a conception of fair negotiation in Christiano, (to be published) *San Diego L. Rev.*

[32] Thanks to Stefan Sciaraffa, Connie Rosati, and Andrew Williams for discussion and comments on a previous draft.

References

Barrett, Scott (2005). *Environment and Statecraft*. Oxford: Oxford University Press.

Besson, Samantha (2010). "Theorizing the Sources of International Law." In *The Philosophy of International Law*, S. Besson and J. Tasioulas (eds.). Oxford: Oxford University Press: 163–186.

Christiano, Thomas (2008). *The Constitution of Equality: Democratic Authority and Its Limits*. Oxford: Oxford University Press.

Christiano, Thomas (2010). "Democratic Legitimacy and International Institutions." In *The Philosophy of International Law*, S. Besson and J. Tasioulas (eds.). Oxford: Oxford University Press.

Christiano, Thomas (2012)."The Legitimacy of International Institutions." In *The Routledge Companion to the Philosophy of Law*, A. Marmor (ed.). New York: Routledge Publishers.

Christiano, Thomas. "Legitimacy and Fairness in the International Trade Regime," *San Diego Law Review* (to be published).

Christiano, Thomas "Democracy, Migration and International Institutions." In *NOMOS: Migration*, J. Knight (ed.). New York: NYU Press (to be published).

Dworkin, Ronald (1986). *Law's Empire*. Cambridge, MA: Harvard University Press.

Dworkin, Ronald (1997). *Freedom's Law: The Moral Reading of the American Constitution*. Cambridge, MA: Harvard University Press.

Dworkin, Ronald (2011). *Justice for Hedgehogs*. Cambridge, MA: Harvard University Press.

Dworkin, Ronald (2013). "A New Philosophy of International Law," *Philosophy and Public Affairs* 41, n. 1:2–30.

Estlund, David (2008). *Democratic Authority: A Philosophical Framework*. Princeton: Princeton University Press.

Helfer, Lawrence (2005). "Exiting Treaties," *Virginia Law Review* 91:1579–1648.

Hume, David (1948a). *A Treatise of Human Nature* (selections). In *Hume: Moral and Political Philosophy*, H Aiken, (ed.). New York: Hafner Press.

Hume, David (1948b). "Of the Original Contract." In *Hume: Moral and Political Philosophy*, H. Aiken (ed.). New York: Hafner Press.

Lefkowitz, David (2010). "The Sources of International Law: Some Philosophical Reflections." In *The Philosophy of International Law*, S. Besson and J. Tasioulas (eds.). Oxford: Oxford University Press 187–203.

Moravcsik, Andrew (1995). "Explaining International Human Rights Regimes: Liberal Theory and Western Europe," *European Journal of International Relations* 1, n. 2: 157–189.

Simmons, Beth (2009). *Mobilizing for Human Rights: International Law in Domestic Politics*. Princeton: Princeton University Press.

Steinberg, Richard (2002). "In the Shadow of Law or Power? Consensus Based Bargaining and Outcomes at the GATT/WTO," *International Organization* 59: 339–365.

Victor, David (2011). *Global Warming Gridlock: Creating More Effective Strategies for Protecting the Planet*. Cambridge: Cambridge University Press.

4

To Fill or Not to Fill Individual Responsibility Gaps?

by François Tanguay-Renaud*

1. Individual Moral Responsibility Gaps and the Appeal of Group Responsibility

At the end of Chapter 5 of *Law's Empire*, Ronald Dworkin introduces what is now considered to be a major challenge for reductivist theorists who insist that all questions of moral (as opposed to legal) responsibility for bad outcomes, and associated ascriptions of blame, can be distilled to questions of *individual* moral responsibility and blame. Dworkin writes:

> Suppose an automobile manufacturer produces defective cars that cause terrible accidents in which hundreds of people are killed. [. . .] We might find someone to blame. Perhaps some employee neglected an inspection, perhaps some officer approved a design he should have known was faulty. Maybe the chief executive officer or some member of the board of directors had reason to doubt the standing procedures for reviewing design and failed to improve them. But we might not find anyone to blame. Perhaps no one acted in a way we can judge wrong by personal standards of conduct.[1]

The point of Dworkin's hypothetical scenario seems to be, at least in part, to appeal to our intuitions about blame and the proper scope of its application.

*Associate Professor, Osgoode Hall Law School, and member of the Graduate Faculty of the Department of Philosophy, York University, Toronto. Adjunct Associate Professor of Philosophy, McMaster University. I would like to thank Antony Duff, Neha Jain, Sandra Marshall, and the editors of this volume for comments, as well as those who attended presentations of this chapter at McMaster University and SUNY-Binghampton. This research was made possible by a grant from the Social Sciences and Humanities Research Council of Canada.
[1] Dworkin (1986: 169).

Many people died, and they did not die from, say, some freak weather event. They died due to deficiencies that human agents brought about through their considered acts and omissions. Even if these individuals did so in ways that do not warrant individual blame—*ex hypothesi*, they did nothing wrong or, let us assume, they had a full justification or excuse for it if they did—many will still feel that blame ought to fall somewhere. At any rate, the thought that no one can properly be held morally responsible, in the central sense of appropriately being thought responsible at a basic level and then singled out for moral criticism for such human-generated bad outcomes, will likely strike many as distressing.[2]

One suggestion is that, perhaps, blame could appropriately be directed at those who set up the corporation and initially failed to design adequate routines of checking and management. Let us assume, though, that they too did nothing wrong, or otherwise blameworthy, in light of what they knew and the evidence available to them at the time. For many, this further proviso will only accentuate the distress. They will long for an explanation that captures the full extent of organized action that led to the calamity and which, at least in principle, could have been orchestrated otherwise. They will yearn for an account that differentiates the calamity from a freak weather event, and that allows them to judge negatively, call to answer, or channel their heartaches and other relevant moral reactions towards some responsible moral agent. Assuming that invoking acts of God will not provide such a satisfactory explanation, and that at least some basically responsible agency is required for one to be a proper subject of blame in the core sense that interests me here, is their search bound to remain in vain?

In recent years, an increasing number of theorists, motivated at least partly by this intuitive yearning for blame in the context of human-generated bad outcomes when there is a so-called individual responsibility gap (IRG) or shortfall of individual responsibility (referring to situations in which no individual can appropriately be held morally responsible for the outcome), have sought to defend a negative answer.[3] In scenarios like the one presented above, they argue that we should envisage the possibility that blame should be ascribed to a responsible agent constituted by the organized group—that is, a corporate agent constituted and energized by individual members, yet whose actions are in some salient sense distinct from theirs, and which may be held responsible for bad outcomes for which none of them could properly be held responsible. Dworkin's own response to the hypothetical scenario is a version of this proposal. We should suppose, he tells us, "that the corporation must itself be treated as a moral agent." We should

---

[2] On the difference between *basic responsibility* as an agent's ability to respond appropriately to reasons—including moral reasons in the case of moral agents—and a *holding of responsibility*, understood as the singling out of someone to bear adverse consequences for rational, including moral, lapses and their harmful outcomes, see further Gardner (2008). In this chapter, I roughly follow this usage, except where obvious, and focus primarily on holdings of responsibility understood as ascriptions of moral blame for bad outcomes.

[3] See e.g. List and Pettit (2011: 165-167), Copp (2006: 216), French (1984).

personify it, and then "proceed by applying facsimiles of our principles about individual fault and responsibility to *it*."[4]

In this chapter, I take Dworkin at his word that there can be morally unsettling IRGs in cases of collectively generated bad outcomes. I do so, despite various objections to their existence,[5] since I believe that Dworkin's handling of this possibility and other, more robustly realist, corporatist responses—such as that of Christian List and Philip Pettit—are worth exploring in their own right for what they reveal about moral responsibility and blame when groups are involved. To be more precise, the chapter highlights some reasons, related to responsibility and blame, why advocates of such approaches should be especially cautious when developing them.

I organize my discussion around what I take to be two of the more provocative aspects of Dworkin's discussion of the issue—one explicit and one implicit. On the one hand, I seek to problematize and deflate Dworkin's key contention that holdings of group responsibility are indispensable for comprehensive moral evaluations of individuals' predicaments when there is an IRG. First, I challenge this position by arguing that many individual-centric forms of moral evaluation must be exhausted before the existence of a thoroughgoing IRG can be ascertained, and before the indispensability of responding to it with a holding of group responsibility can be soundly defended. Why, I query, should we depart from individual-focused morality to the point of insisting on more controversial non-individual units of evaluation if a sufficiently sophisticated deployment of the former can already provide an adequate moral account of the situation? I further suggest that, in cases involving actual IRGs, group responsibility and blame may still not be necessary for the provision of a morally adequate assessment of the situation. In fact, in some such cases, even individual responsibility and blame may not be necessary at all. I strive to bolster this further suggestion by appraising Dworkin's approach in light of the broader and more discerning lens of moral liability, as developed in the context of some reductivist theories of self-defense and just war. Thus, I aim to put into perspective and temper the sense of inadequate moral explanation that may arise if responsibility and blame cannot easily be ascribed for human-generated bad outcomes. Though it may be true that blame plays an important moral role if the conditions for it obtain, if they do not and pretending that they do is not consequentially justified, individual morality often still has much light to shed on the situation and may, on different grounds, single out individuals to bear various burdens and become the subjects of appropriate moral reactions.

On the other hand, I address the related contention that, when faced with IRGs, conceiving of groups as entities responsible for harmful moral lapses, for which they can be blamed, allows for the realization of significant expressive value. Though this suggestion is only implicit in Dworkin's work, it deserves significant

---

[4] Dworkin (1986: 170).
[5] For example, Braham and van Hess (2010).

attention as having become a dominant rallying cry for contemporary defenders
of group responsibility and blame. I argue that even insofar as expressive value
can be found in practices of group blame, it cannot always be straightforwardly
equated with the expressive value of practices of individual blame. In Dworkin's
case, blaming what may amount to no more than a fiction of responsible agency
risks being no more expressively valuable than blaming any other make-belief,
and risks encouraging pathological responses evidencing a refusal to face the
facts. In the case of more robustly realist corporate theories such as that of List
and Pettit—or Dworkin's own, if reinterpreted along such lines—the blame of
responsible group agents may still not be analogized in all respects to the blame of
individual agents. Key differences between the two kinds of agents may impact the
expressive value of group blame, which should give pause to anyone tempted to
claim that, when apposite, group blame can, without further analysis, expressively
fill IRGs. I also stress the wider limits of such line of argument, emphasizing that
in many IRG cases, no group will meet the conditions of responsible group agency
necessary for it to be a real and appropriate subject of blame.

Overall, I defend the position that, however powerful one may find the intuitive pull of IRGs, there are weighty reasons why moral theorists should take care
not to point too quickly to group responsibility and blame as the best and most
discerning ways of demystifying them. Furthermore, insofar as group blame is
ever an appropriate way of addressing such gaps, theorists defending it must take
care to lay out clearly what such blame entails, the specific facts on which it rests,
as well the moral foundations and limits of their argument.

2. Holdings of Group Responsibility and Moral Evaluation in Individual Responsibility Gaps

Here is one thing Dworkin is *not* arguing. Although he defends holdings of corporate (group, collective—I treat these terms as synonyms) responsibility as resting,
in an important sense, on a fiction, since he insists groups have "no independent
metaphysical existence" [6] of their own and are only to be treated "as if" they did,[7]
this fiction might be justified on sheer consequentialist grounds. For example, if
blaming the group would reduce accidents by incentivizing individual members
to organize themselves better, or if it would help survivors and their kin move on,
then it may be that, all things considered, one should treat the group as if it were
blameworthy. However, Dworkin is explicitly not concerned with the prospects
of such sheer consequentialist, or pragmatic, justification.

His main justification for personifying groups and holding them responsible
for bad outcomes has a more deontological flavor. He argues that when a group
generates a bad outcome yet there is an IRG, holding it responsible *qua* distinct

---

[6] Dworkin (1986: 171).
[7] Dworkin (1986: 168).

collective moral agent is an "indispensable" or "necessary first step," or "plateau," for "judgments about particular people."[8] In other words, such a holding is an essential component of a full moral evaluation of the situation. Why is that? Dworkin gives the example of an individual shareholder of our automobile manufacturer. He writes:

> A shareholder is no part of the causal chain leading to the accidents; he added no capital to the corporation's resources just by buying its stock on the exchange. Some might say: it is a principle of personal morality that if someone shares in the gains of another's action he must also share the responsibility for wrongs that other person does. This suggestion begs the question, however, for we still lack any reason to suppose that any wrong has been done. That is, our problem is not one of vicarious liability, of finding some reason why a shareholder should share some other person's or group's primary responsibility; it is rather that we can find no one else who is primarily responsible and in whose responsibility he might share.[9]

Dworkin argues for a personification of the corporation, and for holding it responsible for the bad outcome, as an entry point for the evaluation of the shareholder's moral position. He continues:

> We might say that anyone who has full control over the manufacture of a defective product has a responsibility to compensate those injured by it. No individual employee or shareholder has had that control, but the corporation has. Then we ask, as a further and subsidiary question, how the various members and agents of the corporation should be seen to share in that fault or responsibility. But we approach that independent question using a different set of principles, among which might be found the principle just mentioned, that any member of the corporation who is entitled to share in its profits must share in its responsibilities as well. That principle would justify paying compensation from the corporate treasury, and thus from the account of shareholders, rather than, for example, deducting it from the wages of employees who actually played a causal part in the unfortunate story.[10]

The general arc of Dworkin's argument is sometimes conveyed as follows. When we consider that an individual is a member or is otherwise relevantly related to a group that, under some reasonable description, is thought and said to have engaged responsibly in some wrongdoing, we can see that there are particular moral standards that apply to that individual that would not otherwise apply. If this interpretation is correct, though, Dworkin's own principle about individuals having to share burdens insofar as they share in gains resulting from another agent's wrongdoing seems like an ill-chosen example. It is true that, according to its own terms, Dworkin's principle only applies if there is another agent in whose

---

[8] Dworkin (1986: 171).
[9] Dworkin (1986: 169-170).
[10] Dworkin (186: 170).

wrongful gains one may share. However, in theory at least, nothing prevents this agent from being yet another individual agent, as opposed to a corporate agent. To wit, Dworkin's principle is plausibly as applicable to shareholding individuals in their capacity as shareholders of a wrongdoing corporation, as it is more generally applicable to them *qua* sharers in the wrongful gains of any other wrongdoer. In principle at least, there seems to be nothing about a corporation that makes this alleged moral tenet more applicable to its members than to others more generally.

It is the fact of the IRG, and the related lack of individual wrongdoers in whose gains others may share, that generates the alleged need for a holding of group responsibility for the bad outcome. That is, if one insists on applying the said principle to shareholders so they can be held accountable and made to bear remedial burdens based on it, and there is no wrongdoer in sight, then one better think and speak as if there were such a wrongdoer and defend this practice as morally legitimate. Otherwise, such a moral explanation for obtaining compensation from shareholders, or saddling them with other burdens, has no argumentative footing.

Yet, should or need one so insist on applying Dworkin's principle? Perhaps there is another way of providing a morally satisfactory account of the normative position of shareholders that is simpler and less dependent on a somewhat enigmatic argumentative invocation of group personification and responsibility. For example, are there no moral principles of unjust enrichment, paralleling the legal ones, that do not rest on wrongdoing and could apply in such cases? Or consider this further suggestion. Even if our shareholder engaged in no wrongdoing that resulted in the accidents and cannot be blamed for them, an argument may still be made that risks of mechanical malfunctions are inherently part of automobile manufacturing. Thus, anyone who buys into the company's ventures may appropriately be thought to assume at least a proportion of such risks. In other words, it is arguable that the shareholder tacitly consented to bear some burdens, including remedial burdens, of the sorts that are inherently tied to the venture he joined (up to some reasonable threshold). If sound, this alternative argument could well do all the moral work needed to satisfy our intuition that shareholders are liable to bear some burdens, as a result of the harms engendered by the company's defective vehicles. Holdings of group responsibility invoked for this purpose may then be superfluous.

Dworkin may reply that, in *Law's Empire*, he is not concerned with providing an exhaustive account of all, or even of the simplest or most elegant, ways in which individuals can justifiedly be saddled with obligations and burdens in the face of IRGs. His ambition, he may retort, is only to focus on one important such way—namely, individual obligations and burdens that flow from holding a group agent responsible for some outcome. Still, by asserting that judgments of group personification and responsibility are indispensable to judgments about particular people in the face of IRGs, and insisting on the inherent limitations of more individualistic forms of evaluation, Dworkin can be criticized for giving too short shrift to the possibilities that individual morality may be sufficient, as in the case of shareholders, and that many alleged such gaps may not be as empty as first appears.

On this last point, consider again the case of the automobile manufacturer in which, *ex hypothesi*, no individual can appropriately be held responsible in full for the accidents. It may still be that various individual acts or omissions, taken either on their own or in some loose combination, amounted to some unjustified wrong or the other, even if it falls short of the wrong of killing. Perhaps the attitudes with which individuals participated in work related to the outcome, or the character they exhibited while so doing, were morally defective in relevant ways. Moreover, it may be that these individuals' ignorance of the risks associated with their activities or the pressures inherent in their work only afforded them partial excuses, due to their roles in the company's organization and the expectations associated with them. In other words, perhaps some individuals could appropriately be blamed at least *to some extent*, however minimal, for the bad outcome. Or, if they are not to blame for the outcome itself, perhaps they are for something relevantly connected to it. No doubt, working out the details of such analysis would require one to know a lot more about the scenario in question. Still, the kind of retort envisaged—i.e., that some holdings of individual responsibility are appropriate in the situation—should be clear enough.

If taken as a point of departure and followed too closely, then, Dworkin's approach may have the pernicious effect of encouraging unsuspecting moral inquirers to curtail, too hastily, their investigation into important, even if subtle, individualistic ways of evaluating such intricate scenarios. It may steer them away from what, in the last analysis, could prove to be intuitively satisfactory moral conclusions that challenge claims of thoroughgoing IRG (leading them, instead, to confront distressing moral voids that can only be filled through question-begging argumentative suppositions). Furthermore, Dworkin's approach threatens to muddy inquiries into alleged IRGs by making it seem appropriate to invoke responsible group agency where doing so would stretch the limits of reason.

To sharpen these last two points, consider these further examples. First:

> **Homophobe Slice and Patch.** Slice and Patch are homophobes. B, a homosexual patient, enters their ward needing an immediate operation that will prevent a very serious illness. Because he is a homophobe, Slice (who is the only one able to slice) will not slice even if Patch will patch. Because he is a homophobe, Patch (who is the only one able to patch) will not patch even if Slice slices. Slice could not persuade nor force Patch to act were Slice so inclined and *vice versa*. B is better off having nothing done to him than either being sliced without being patched or being patched without having been sliced.[11]

Insofar as "ought implies can," Slice does not wrong B by refraining to slice, given Patch's unmovable inaction. She does not violate B's right to receive

---

[11] This case is a revised version, suggested to me by Victor Tadros, of a similar case developed by David Estlund (to be published). Slice-and-Patch-type cases are a more vivid rendering of a set of examples developed by Donald Regan (Whiff and Poof examples) that are structurally the same, but presented more abstractly. See Regan (1982: 18).

treatment nor her correlative duty, as a doctor, to provide it to him, as she simply cannot (and, let us also assume, knows that she cannot) provide B with treatment. She cannot save him, or even make him better off. She can only make him worse off. The same can be said of Patch. Still, in such a case, it does seem that B is wronged, and wronged in a blameworthy way.

Is this puzzle, suggestive of an IRG, most perspicuously addressed by supposing that the group constituted by Slice and Patch is engaged, *qua* distinct agent, in blameworthy wrongdoing? Insofar as such a claim of responsible group agency is sound, under some reasonable description, this response would at least meet part of our intuition that some blameworthy wrongdoing is involved. Thus, it is tempting to focus on it. Yet, doing so threatens to obscure an important dimension of Slice and Patch's individual moral predicaments. Even if ought implies can, and neither Slice nor Patch wrong B by not treating him, both still wrong him by failing to consider him for treatment on an equal basis. They both wrong him in this way assuming, of course, that they would readily slice and patch heterosexual patients who, let us further assume, are equally or less seriously ill. Together, these individual wrongs lead to B not being treated. It is also arguable that, all else being equal, these wrongs make it permissible to blame and impose at least some other burdens on Slice and Patch—be they preventive, compensatory, or even punitive.

When scrutinized from this more individualistic lens, one begins to see better why it may not matter at all, either intuitively or argumentatively, whether the group of Slice and Patch can also be said to have acted in a distinctly wrongful and blameworthy way. We may already have satisfactory moral answers through individualized analysis—thus avoiding reference to group responsibility and any controversies that may be associated with such an additional layer of argument. Still, Dworkin may say, if holding the group responsible allows us to ask *further* questions, say, about Slice and Patch's complicit omissions or contributions to the group's distinct wrong, should these not also be asked for the sake of completeness?

An important problem for this last rejoinder may not be as obvious in the context of a surgical team, such as Slice and Patch's. It may not be, since corporatist theorists may be able to build a plausible case that such a team is a real (as opposed to a mere fictional or personified) morally responsible group agent, given its integrated organization and the collectivized mental states that may be attributed to it as a result.[12] Insofar as such theorists are correct, individual complicity with group wrongdoing is then a live issue. However, consider this other scenario involving a far less organized group for which an account of responsible group agency is much less plausible:

Stranded Ambulance. A random group of adults happens to be standing outside smoking, something that is not allowed inside the bar they happen to have been hanging out in. An ambulance with lights flashing rolls

---

[12] For more on this possibility, see Section 3.

by, slips, and careens into the ditch. It would not be difficult to free the ambulance to continue on its way if all the smokers worked together. As it happens, though, each of them is a slackard—none would be moved (or, indeed, could be forced) to help even if some or all of the others were willing to work together. Furthermore, if any person were to try alone, the risk of serious injury would be high, and so would the risk of tipping the ambulance over the edge of the cliff. Thus, the ambulance sits stranded, as the coronary patient inside expires soon after the accident, for lack of emergency room care. Suppose that the smokers are each aware of all the facts I am describing.[13]

Assuming again that ought implies can, it seems that none of the individual smokers wronged the patient. There is nothing that any of them could have done to free the ambulance. The only way it could have been freed was for all smokers to act together. However, there was no reasonable prospect of this happening. Again, an intuitive reaction may be to think that *the group* of smokers ought to have helped, and that its failure to do so is blameworthy—thus filling what may be perceived as an IRG. However, the collection of individual smokers is not of the kind whose acts or omissions we tend to think of, or refer to, as those of a group agent. The group in question is far too disparate for this. Indeed, any claim that it is *not* too disjointed would face the following strong objection: There is nothing that unifies, or could be said to unify, the individuals present into an agent meaningfully distinct from its parts that could be held responsible as such, like an individual wrongdoer could be. At most, one might be able to speak of individuals involved in a similar scenario—in which a coordinated collective response was a reasonable prospect—as blameworthy for failing to take part in the response, opting instead to privilege themselves in a way that accords with their lazy dispositions. Still, such a judgment would be about individuals and their own moral failings. It would not be about any responsible group agent, the possibility of which is only contemplated prospectively in the argument (insofar as it is contemplated at all and coordinated collective action is thought to be a mark of real responsible collective agency).[14] Thus, embarking on the moral assessment of an alleged IRG case, like *Stranded Ambulance*, by holding the group responsible for the bad outcome would, in addition to steering us away from more refined judgments about individuals, test the limits of intelligibility.

Note that Dworkin's approach has this implication most starkly if we remain faithful to his contention that the personification that must be engaged in is "deep," and consists in taking the group "seriously as a moral agent"[15] that has what it takes to be held responsible, and even "condemned," as "a single distinct

---

[13] Once again, I borrow this example from Estlund (unpublished draft).

[14] This realization is important for answering claims, such as that of Virginia Held (1970: 479), that a random collection of individuals may be held "morally responsible for failing to transform itself into an organized group capable of taking action rather than inaction."

[15] Dworkin (1986: 171).

moral agent."[16] As I suggested, in respect of cases like *Stranded Ambulance*, such a judgment would likely amount to fiction gone wild. To make matters worse, such language even seems to stand in the way of less controversial proposals that, arguably, could supplement the strict individualist paradigm that Dworkin criticizes, in a way that at least advances his argument in spirit. That is, such language seems to rule out holdings, which are less dependent on the actual presence of robust group responsibility, that a collection of individuals could (prospectively) engage in some form of group agency, or that what they did (or did not do) in some more loosely defined joint fashion (short of responsible group agency) was wrong.

My critique of Dworkin may be too rigid. Could his position not be softened in ways that remain compatible with his overall argument? For one thing, in *Law's Empire* itself, Dworkin writes that his idea of personified group agency is "a creature of the practices of thought and language in which it figures."[17] Insofar as there is no practice of thought and language representing the collection of individuals in *Stranded Ambulance* as a responsible group agent, Dworkin may argue that it should not be treated as such in argument. Still, such a concession would leave him vulnerable in cases in which collections of individuals are commonly referred to as morally responsible agents, yet remain fundamentally disparate—think here of various cases of spontaneous destructive mobs.[18]

Then again, perhaps, despite indications to the contrary, Dworkin does have a more realist account of group agency in mind. In later work, he builds on his idea of groups constituted by social practices and attitudes, and argues that they can form "collective units of agency" that are real enough.[19] Their reality arises, he claims, when the acts of individuals constituting them are performed self-consciously, as contributing to collective acts, rather than as isolated acts that happen to coincide in some way. Since such cooperative intentions are clearly absent from individuals' minds in *Stranded Ambulance*, as well as from many cases of destructive mobs, Dworkin could then deny in a principled way that either should be treated as group agents. At the same time, such intentions are often present amongst the individual members of states *qua* political communities and companies, the two kinds of groups that Dworkin is most concerned with in *Law's Empire*.

Still, notice that the reality of collective units of agency so described is limited, and seems to come down to what many have more recently described as joint, or

---

[16] Dworkin (1986: 187).

[17] Dworkin, (1986: 171).

[18] Cf. Tuomela (1989), who argues that mobs can be held collectively responsible for harm if at least some of their members contribute directly to it and others either facilitate these contributions or fail to prevent them. The reason for this, he claims, is that all mob members are implicated in mob action, even if not all of them produced specific harms or organized together to do so. Notice, though, that if responsibility and blameworthiness can be reduced to that of individuals, as this argument implies, it seems fair to wonder what, if anything, an invocation of group responsibility adds beyond serving as shorthand. Arguably, this approach adds nothing, while threatening, not unlike Dworkin's approach, to ride roughshod over important differences of kind and degree in individual participants' responsibility, blameworthiness, etc.

[19] Dworkin (1989: 495).

shared, agency. Consider, for example, how it may be accurate to say that soldiers jointly carry out an attack. Various theorists argue that if soldiers each intend or desire that they together carry out an attack by following a strategy individually acceptable to each, if each intend to do their bit in its execution while playing their part in the strategy, each believe that others intend to play their part and do their bit, each intend to do their bit because of believing this, and each believe in common that the other clauses hold, then these individuals can perform genuinely joint attacks.[20] The possibility of such joint agency can have important moral ramifications. For example, if, by acting jointly rather than independently, soldiers can realize their just objectives in less harmful ways, then it is arguable that they should so act. In other words, the principle of necessity that otherwise applies to individual soldiers' resort to harmful force must be calibrated to account for the possibility of less harmful joint action.[21] It is interesting that this point falls in line with Dworkin's repeated claim that thinking of groups as agents can impact how various moral principles apply to their individual members. Any evaluator omitting to acknowledge the possibility of joint action in a situation involving multiple individual actors would do so at the risk of missing out on an important moral dimension of their predicaments—and, possibly, of exposing IRGs where there are none, by failing to notice joint wrongdoing.

Unfortunately, this interpretation of Dworkin's argument fits awkwardly with its presentation in *Law's Empire.* To see why, note that many defenders of joint agency insist that joint actions are generally explainable, and most transparently evaluated, as individual group members' actions carried out for shared individual intentions and with shared individual beliefs. For many such theorists, then, group *qua* joint agency does not entail a distinct form of group responsibility. Holdings of responsibility in such cases remain most clearly elaborated in individualized terms, allowing for an accounting of different degrees and kinds of individual participation.[22] Now, recall that Dworkin first invokes responsible group agency and holdings of group responsibility in response to an alleged IRG—in which, *ex hypothesi,* no holdings of individual responsibility can appropriately be made. So, for the group *qua* joint agency interpretation to explain his group responsibility approach in *Law's Empire,* Dworkin would, at the very least, need to argue for why such agency leads to some form of *group* responsibility, thus filling the IRG. No such argument is provided. According to Dworkin, irrespective of whether there is actual group responsibility, it is necessary to suppose it, insofar as social practices of thought and language so warrant, to get a full assessment of relevant individuals' moral predicaments. Moreover, whereas a credible defense of genuinely shared intentions giving rise to joint agency would require some discussion of their metaphysical foundations, however modest they may

---

[20] Pettit and Schweikard (2006). Similar versions are developed in Bratman (1992: 338) and Tuomela (1991: 263).

[21] See further Lazar (2012: 29-38).

[22] Bratman (2014: ch. 6), Sylvan (2012), Lepora and Goodin (2014: chs. 3-4).

be, Dworkin is adamant that his analysis is immune from such controversies and elaborates no further. If this is the reasoning of a theorist of real group agency and responsibility, then it is markedly underdeveloped—to the point that one can seriously doubt that Dworkin actually contemplates this position in *Law's Empire*, irrespective of how well it may bolster the spirit of his overall argument.

To recap, so far, I have challenged Dworkin's insistence on holdings of group responsibility as indispensable for adequate moral evaluations in the face of IRGs, by suggesting that one should be careful not to jump too quickly to the conclusion that there is, in fact, such a gap. However, a more radical challenge could also be mounted—namely, that Dworkin's insistence on holdings of group responsibility if there is an actual IRG is a symptom of an overly responsibility-centric view of morality. By *responsibility-centric*, I mean a view of morality according to which basic moral responsibility and responsibility-based criteria, such as wrongdoing and blameworthiness, are central to moral judgments and permissible impositions of burdens. If one holds such a view, then one will feel most acutely the bite of IRGs and the pressure to address them, however creatively. In passages reproduced above, Dworkin seems influenced by this view, given the anxiety with which he presents his search for individual wrongdoing and blame with respect to the deadly automobile accidents and, in their absence, the way he insists on suppositions of corporate responsibility and wrongdoing.

Of course, such a responsibility-driven approach is not the only contender. Theorists of self-defense and revisionist just-war theorists have recently begun to shed light on a broader way of identifying morally salient factors, which Dworkin sidelines without argument. I am referring here to the idea of moral liability. Although *moral liability* is a term of art, it refers to the familiar moral idea that harming or burdening a person, even against her will, need not wrong that person, even *pro tanto*. Consider, for example, the liability to pay taxes, or the liability to be conscripted. Liability claims typically take the following form: X (a person) is liable to have *b* (something burdensome) imposed on her by Y (some agent who has standing), in the pursuit of some goal, if Y does not wrong X by imposing *b* on her for this goal without X's consent.

A general theory of liability aims to provide a general explanation of the fact that we lack certain rights against interference with our valuable independence and interests. Some confine their understanding of liability to cases in which X forfeits her rights through responsible action, including blameworthy action.[23] However, there is nothing in the concept of liability that necessarily grounds it in responsibility or blameworthiness.

No doubt, some specific forms of liability—such as liability to blame, insofar as blame is understood as a kind of burden—may be necessarily grounded in these specific moral facts. But liability to harms and other burdens, more generally understood, may also have other grounds. For example, Victor Tadros argues that a nonresponsible threat, such as a person blown down a well by the

---

[23] Jeff McMahan (2009: 7-15), who introduces the concept, espouses such a view.

wind, may be liable to be harmed to avert the threats that her body poses to those stuck at the bottom of the well, who may be harmed or killed by her fall. This nonresponsible threat has done nothing to forfeit any of her rights, but this does not entail that harming her wrongs her. She may have lost her rights not to be harmed in virtue of, say, the fact that her body poses a threat and, just as she is entitled to be the prime beneficiary of her body, so she must bear greater costs that emanate from it.[24] So, causally contributing to a threat that one is not morally responsible for, and considerations of benefit, may render one liable to bear burdens. To be sure, Tadros argues that causation and benefit, taken on their own, may sometimes ground liability to bear some burdens. So may considerations of beneficence—think of one's liability to suffer some reasonable costs for the sake of rescuing a drowning child that one happens to be passing by.[25] These are only examples and the list of grounds of liability that are not responsibility-based could plausibly also go on.

Some of these grounds will be controversial. However, my point is simply to underscore the wide variety of nonresponsibility-dependent questions that the lens of individual liability allows us to ask, and possibly address, about the appropriate moral distribution of burdens if there is an actual IRG. For example, can the fact that our shareholder benefited, or was entitled to benefit, from the sale of cars built with defects ground his liability to provide at least some compensation for the accidents that resulted from it? As I already suggested, this question need not rest in any way on the existence, real or fictional, of a responsible group agent. Or can the mere fact that employees caused the accidents ground their (strict) liability to incur some burdens? Again, no group agent is required to evaluate our scenario intelligibly in such terms. With such distinctions in hand, it is unclear why, per Dworkin, it would be indispensable for a moral appraiser to go any further, and make any argumentative suppositions of responsibility and blame, for the analysis to be complete. In this case at least, less may be more.

Insofar as Dworkin conceives of liability, he rejects it as a useful concept. Recall his claim that "our problem is not one of vicarious liability, of finding some reason why a shareholder should share some other person's or group's primary responsibility."[26] Dworkin is right that the problem as viewed from the lens of liability is not vicarious in nature. What he fails to acknowledge, though, is that liability may not only be vicarious, but also deeply personal, in the sense expounded earlier.[27] I mention this here to underscore that, were he still with us today, and were this theoretical advance to be brought to his attention, he would have to contend with an important other set of arguments against hasty group personification. A set of arguments that holds the promise of a more discerning

---

[24] Tadros (2011: ch. 11 and 336-338).

[25] Tadros (2012: 271-277).

[26] Dworkin (1986: 170).

[27] As Tadros (2014: esp. 47-54) explains, vicarious liability is itself a more marginal case of liability.

individual morality, able to identify salient distinctions, and suitably demarcate rights and burdens, whether or not moral responsibility and blameworthiness are present. A set of arguments that may allow us, without any supposition of distinctly responsible group agency (especially if there is really none), to address, in a morally satisfactory way, a large part of our intuitive yearning for specific moral targets and the ascription of compensatory, punitive, and preventive duties, as well as other moral intuitions related to IRGs.

I will come back, in conclusion, to how illuminating the lens of individual liability can be for my inquiry when treated as a counterpoint. As I said, I invoke it here merely as yet another reason why one should exercise great circumspection before affirming the argumentative necessity of holdings of group responsibility for addressing IRGs. No doubt, much more could be said about why such methodological caution is imperative, including more detailed scrutiny of other examples suggested by Dworkin. For instance, one could seek to challenge his claim that state officials' duties of political justice can only properly be understood by treating group responsibility as logically prior to, and constitutive of, these individuals' moral predicaments.[28] Indeed, accounts of state officials' duties of justice as ordinary individual duties—which states are often, though merely contingently and instrumentally, best placed to discharge—have already been famously defended by others.[29] Still, doing justice to this question would lead me too far adrift from my focus on IRGs, so I simply choose to invite a similarly healthy dose of suspicion.[30]

Instead, I consider it important to use the rest of this chapter to highlight yet another significant way, implicitly related to Dworkin's line of argument, in which those considering whether to address IRGs with holdings of group responsibility should proceed with special care. I am referring here to the tendency of many theorists to think that holdings of group responsibility can expressively fill IRGs.

3. Group Blame in the Face of Individual Responsibility Gaps

At one point, Dworkin claims that, insofar as group responsibility matters, it does not matter for its own sake.[31] If, by that, he means that holdings of group responsibility are only valuable to the extent that they are valuable for individuals— given the ways in which they may impact and shape their moral lives then the claim is rather uncontroversial. It accords with the widely held principle of value individualism, which most contemporary theorists of group responsibility now endorse.[32] In *Law's Empire*, the claim is mostly developed in terms of how holding

---

[28] Dworkin (1986: 173-175).

[29] See e.g. Tadros (2011: 299-307), grounding his argument in Raz (1986: Part I). See also Caney (2008).

[30] The same could be said of Dworkin's rather brash dismissal, not unlike in the case of the manufacturer's shareholder, that benefits enjoyed by many Americans as a result of past discrimination against blacks account for special duties towards them (1986: 172).

[31] Dworkin (1986: 171).

[32] E.g. Raz (1986: 194), Newman (2011: ch. 5), List and Pettit (2011: 181-182).

groups responsible for outcomes can shed light on their individual members' moral obligations and burdens. However, Dworkin's remarkable anxiousness to ascribe responsibility and blame when assessing collectively generated bad outcomes points to another important reason why one may want to champion holdings of group responsibility—namely, their expressive value (for relevant individuals) in the face of IRGs and, possibly, more generally.

In *Law's Empire*, Dworkin's own discussion of expressive value is only indirectly tied to the prospect of holding groups responsible for bad outcomes.[33] Dworkin frames the issue more broadly in terms of the expressive value that can flow from supposing seriously that certain groups are: entities to which moral principles (e.g., integrity, fairness) can apply directly; entities that can be blamed, or condemned, for their contraventions of such principles; and, thus, entities whose contraventions individuals who constitute them ought to make a special effort to forestall or rectify. This reasoning may suggest that the expressive value that Dworkin associates with treating groups as responsible agents attaches exclusively to the ability of such a practice to capture the special moral predicament of group members. After all, this feature of the practice constitutes Dworkin's explicit focus in *Law's Empire*, culminating in his famous discussion of group members' associative obligations. However, given his insistence that holdings of group responsibility are necessary to unravel IRGs satisfactorily, coupled with his consideration of various emotions—such as shame and outrage—that may be appropriately directed at groups and experienced by their individual members in such situations,[34] it seems only a short leap to the inference that he also thinks that such holdings are expressively valuable. That is, they are valuable in enabling and channeling the expression of key moral reactions, generally subsumed under the rubric of blame (including self-blame). Though Dworkin's emphasis on the internal moral dynamics of groups—as opposed to groups' external duties and nonmembers' reactions to their violations—may conceal this suggestion, it remains implicit in the argument.

Admittedly, insofar as Dworkin conceives of group agents in merely fictional terms, one may wonder how much expressive value there can really be in blaming them. Recall that, for him, a group that is held responsible, as if it were a morally responsible agent in its own right, does not have any metaphysical existence of its own. Nor does it have any "distinct interest or point of view or even welfare of its own," let alone any capacity to understand how to act morally or any freedom to act as such.[35] Thus, according to one interpretation of Dworkin's argument, a group agent's only reality resides in the self-understandings and the social and intellectual practices of group members.[36]

---

[33] Dworkin (1986: 189-190).

[34] Dworkin (1986: 172, 175).

[35] Dworkin (1986: 168).

[36] Such reality is consistent with my use of the term *fiction*, following its definition in the *Oxford English Dictionary* as "A supposition known to be at variance with fact, but conventionally accepted for some reason of practical convenience, conformity with traditional usage, decorum, or the like."

It may be true that blaming a fictional moral agent for a bad outcome resulting from the synergy of its blameless individual parts is expressively valuable,
just as it was valuable to blame hurricanes David and Katrina for the destruction
resulting from the synergy of their constitutive air and water particles. In both
cases, the cause or, as it were, the explanation for the calamity may be usefully
captured by speaking at such a holistic level of generality. However, the kind of
holding of responsibility, *qua* blame, that Dworkin has in mind is explicitly not
such causal blame. It is *moral* blame, which assumes an *interpersonal* evaluation
of the actions, attitudes, and the like, of a given moral agent. This focus may
partly explain why Dworkin insists on personifying groups, and treating such
personification as if it were real and not just shorthand. Yet, insofar as we know
it to be false that the group is a real person with morally responsible agency of its
own, is not the expressive value of blaming *it* for something *it did* at best rooted in
self- or social deception? The point holds true irrespective of whether one understands moral blame in cognitive terms as a negative normative judgment, as a
specific kind of emotional or conative response, as a functional form of protest or
communication, or as a mixture of any or all of these elements. Morally blaming
what we know not to be an appropriate target of moral blame, just because we
yearn to ascribe such blame, verges on blame fetishism. If expressively valuable,
it is only pathologically so: a symptom of a refusal or inability to face the facts.

Notice, however, that this objection would not have the same force if, despite
the doubts I conveyed, Dworkin's position were best understood along narrower
realist lines. One would then have to contend with the following possibility: If
some groups are, in fact, moral agents that can appropriately be held responsible
in their own right, then blaming them in the face of IRGs may be as expressively
valuable as blaming individual agents in other contexts. Citing the intuitive pressure to fill individual responsibility gaps as a key motivation, a variety of contemporary theorists have recently undertaken to defend this line of argument in
more detail. Recognizing explicitly the limits and drawbacks of fictions,[37] they
argue that some adequately constituted groups really are responsible corporate
moral agents that may, as such, be blamed for their harmful moral lapses. Given
various undeveloped traces of this position in Dworkin's own work, as well as the
centrality it has recently come to occupy in debates about group responsibility
and IRGs, it seems important to explore it further here, if only, once again, to
question its suitability to address such gaps.

Let me sketch what I take to be the most plausible and sophisticated such
view currently available.[38] Christian List and Philip Pettit argue that some groups
can be conversable agents in their own right, in the manner of individual human
beings. That is, they can be constituted in ways that make it possible to reason
and do business with them over time *qua* groups—for example, by entering into
agreements (contracts, treaties, etc.) with them, reasonably expecting that these

---

[37] See especially Pettit (2014).
[38] List and Pettit (2011).

will be honored. For such conversability to be possible, the group needs to be responsive to the attitudes and inputs of its individual members. However, it must also be responsive in a way that secures group sensitivity to reason over time, with a reasonable level of consistency and coherence. According to List and Pettit, these features can obtain if the group functions in keeping with an adequate normative framework, or constitution.

A constitution is adequate in this sense when it sets out a decision procedure that ensures that the organized group's judgments, as well as action-directing attitudes and plans are, on the whole, functionally independent, as opposed to a mere reflection, of the corresponding judgments, attitudes, and plans of group members. For the sake of simplicity, consider the following three-person example, in which A, B, and C are deciding whether $X\&(Y\&Z)$. If A believes $X\&(Y\&\neg Z)$, B believes $X\&(\neg Y\&Z)$, and C believes $\neg X\&(Y\&Z)$, then if the group votes on each of X, Y, and Z in turn, the group will hold that $X\&(Y\&Z)$ although no member actually believes this. In a very real sense, the voting procedure makes it so that the final decision is the group's decision and not the decision of any of the individual members.

An additional issue arises at this point. Broadly stated, individual responsiveness—in my example, to the beliefs of A, B, and C—may, over time, compromise the minimal rational consistency that we expect from agents proper. So, for conversable group agency to be possible, a process must also be in place to ensure that the group keeps track of where its accumulating decisions are taking it, and can respond appropriately to that information. In other words, balances and checks must be in place to make sure that, over time, the group can revise its corporate judgments so as to restore reasonable consistency.

One of the strengths of this kind of account is that it genuinely seeks to address Dworkin's metaphysical discomfort with recognizing groups as real responsible moral agents. For List and Pettit, such discomfort is misplaced, since their argument rests on the non-mysterious premise that group agents derive all their matter and energy from their individual members. Although group agents may have a distinct point of view and be able to understand how to act morally, they have, to use Dworkin's own words, no "mind that is more real than flesh-and-blood."[39] It is through their individual members that organized groups can access evidence and gain the understanding required to make evaluative judgments about the reasons for action and normative options they face. The overall contention, though, is that, by jointly committing and adhering to an adequate constitution, group members can generate a single, relatively autonomous, and enduring corporate agent. They can generate an agent that, when faced with normatively significant choices, is capable of reasoning, deliberating, and making irreducible and reasonably consistent judgments about how it should respond—about what is good and bad, right and wrong. This corporate agent, which in an important

---

[39] Dworkin (1986: 168).

yet less metaphysically suspect sense has a mind of its own, may then formulate objectives, make decisions, and develop strategies and plans to implement these over time, all in saliently irreducible ways. It may then relevantly control for the execution of such plans by arranging things so that some individuals are directed, or empowered, to perform relevant tasks, while others are identified as possible back-ups. As List and Pettit argue, a corporate agent that arranges for action in this way is fit to be held responsible, in the sense of being blamed, as the responsible "source of the deed" or the "planner" at its origin.[40] Furthermore, they contend, such corporate agents may even appropriately be described as persons, insofar as a *person* is understood, in the limited sense of an agent capable of appropriately responding to reasons and performing in the space of obligations.[41]

Of course, the individuals who give life to such a moral agent still have to answer for what they do in making corporate agency possible. They remain moral agents in their own right. However, the entity they maintain also has to answer as a whole for what it does at the corporate level. Thus, if individual members are not blameworthy for some bad outcome that originates at that level (and, in fact, even when they are), the group itself may also be an appropriate target for blame.

Insofar as it is successful, this line of argument constitutes a significant advance on Dworkin's equivocal realist tendencies. In cases in which a group meets the conditions of responsible agency, it may develop morally defective dispositions and intentional attitudes of its own, and engage in wrongdoing with, at times, quite harmful results. If it does so in an unjustified and unexcused way, the group may then be a real and appropriate subject of moral blame.

Accounts of this kind are controversial, as some will remain suspicious of the claims of supervenience and irreducibility, however thin, that accompany them. Still, even if we assume their soundness *arguendo*, an important challenge, tied to the suggestion that blaming group agents is expressively valuable, remains for their proponents. Namely, can blaming a corporate agent ever be as expressively valuable as blaming an individual human agent? Or, to put it in terms of our initial puzzle, can addressing a so-called IRG by blaming the group *qua* moral agent ever be an adequate substitute to individual blame? Since, according to List and Pettit, the moral agency of individual members and those of their corporate group are saliently distinct, blaming one does not replace blaming the other. However, does the possibility of blaming the group if no individual member is blameworthy ever a satisfactory answer to our intuitive search for an appropriate subject of blame in such situations?

Arguably, it all depends on what blame involves and what it takes to be an appropriate subject of blame. Moral theorists generally assume that to blame people is to respond in a particular way to something of negative moral significance about them or their behavior. However, the precise nature of this response is contentious. For one prominent school of thought, a blaming response consists,

---

[40] List and Pettit (2011: ch. 7).
[41] List and Pettit (2011: ch. 8).

primarily, in adopting a negative emotional stance towards the person or the behavior—typically resentment, anger, or contempt.[42] If group agents are real responsible moral agents, then it seems that, like other such agents, they may, through their behavior, attitudes, and the like, trigger such emotions in individuals. Furthermore, individuals may deliberately and reasonably channel these emotions toward them in what these theorists deem to be a blaming response. Insofar as the capacity of individual blamers to experience and direct relevant emotions at other agents is not in doubt, there seems to be no special problem with subjecting group agents to blame so conceived.

Still, some such theorists go further and insist that the emotional stance constitutive of blame must also be capable of being experienced as such by its subjects, be it in the form of feelings of guilt, remorse, or plain suffering. For these theorists, it is part and parcel of a blaming response that it be geared at inducing such feelings in those subjected to it. One interesting feature of this more robust account is that it offers an explanation for why we may experience a distressing yearning for blame in the face of IRGs. In such situations, there is simply no one who could appropriately be made to experience the said feelings. *Ex hypothesi*, no individual can properly be blamed, and group agents, whose irreducible existence is allegedly solely cognitive, are not the kind of agents that have conscious, including affective, experiences of their own.

This suggestion is a function of what conscious states are—namely, states that are constitutive of the personal experience of their subject.[43] True, according to List and Pettit, group agents may be able to process individuals' emotions cognitively as morally relevant facts. However, they provide no reason for thinking that any individual in a group can have conscious access to the experience of other group members from a first-person perspective, or that any subjective experience inaccessible to individual members can emerge at the level of the group. List and Pettit even explicitly distance themselves from such possibilities.[44] Once again, their position has the advantage of avoiding the kind of mysterious metaphysical implications of which Dworkin is suspicious. Indeed, the position that references to feelings of group guilt, remorse, or suffering are no more than summative and reductive accords with contemporary common wisdom. If a group of people is suffering, we have many suffering individuals and nothing more.[45] Peter Strawson, the original defender of the emotive understanding of blame described here, himself seemed to endorse this position, arguing that the practice derives its value from what it reveals about relations *between individual human beings*.[46]

---

[42] To cite only two well-known examples of this understanding of blame: Wallace (1994) and Wolf (2011).

[43] The *locus classicus* for this position is Nagel (1974).

[44] List and Pettit (2011: ch. 8).

[45] On this point, see further Tanguay-Renaud (2013: 128-132).

[46] Strawson (1962).

So, if the yearning to find an appropriate subject for the infliction of feelings of guilt, remorse, or suffering is what guides the intuition that blame ought to be ascribed to the group in IRG cases, then blame of group agents is unlikely to assuage it. It is unlikely to do so assuming, of course, that the practice is not abused as a way of indirectly eliciting these feelings in individual group members who, by hypothesis, are not blameworthy. Should one then infer that tendencies to blame groups, *qua* distinct agents, in such situations are categorically inappropriate? Insofar as there are group agents, such an inference seems like an overkill, and the fact that it does suggests either that there is more to blame than the inducement of harsh feelings, or that this subject-centered emotive account rests on a mistake.

There are grounds for thinking that at least one of these possibilities is correct. For example, could a case not be made that such an account conflates blame, understood more basically as an ascription of responsibility for something of negative moral significance, with further retributive responses that build upon it and involve a disposition towards inducing experiences like suffering? Although it is unclear that punishment requires its subjects' suffering, as opposed to the mere imposition of an inconvenient deprivation or burden on them, many retributivists insist that the intent to inflict suffering is a key distinguishing mark of the practice. However, if blame and punishment are to be retained as distinct ideas playing different, though perhaps complementary, moral roles, such theorists should likely resist the conflation. For all others who may be tempted to tether blame to an imposition of suffering, consider the following. On the one hand, if, according to a given conception, blame is only deemed valuable insofar as, or because, it is geared at inducing its subjects' suffering, then one may wonder how valuable its expression really is. On the other hand, if, as I think likely, blame can still play an important moral role when knowingly directed at individual agents who, due to their hardened affective make-ups, will not experience suffering, guilt, or remorse, then equating blame and an inducement of such experiences seems misguided.

Note that a version of the penultimate point could also be leveled at thinner emotive accounts of blame focusing solely on the blamer's, as opposed to the blamee's, affective stance. Insofar as a blamer's stance is understood in terms of retributive emotions like resentment or anger, which, arguably, can be more destructive than facilitative of human relationships, then one may wonder how valuable expressions of blame really are.[47] Here, though, one should be careful not to throw out the baby with the bath water. Recall that the intuition we are working with is that group blame may address a morally meaningful yearning that is experienced when confronting IRGs. Therefore, one may think, short of concluding that the intuition is itself misplaced or insignificant, one needs to hold fast to the idea that a blaming response has what it takes, in terms of its phenomenal content,

---

[47] Gary Watson (2004: 255-259) notably argues that what blame, so understood, "expresses is itself destructive of human community," in the sense that it poisons human relationships with animosity.

to offset this yearning. This commitment leaves open various possibilities, including that some retributive emotions may be intrinsically valuable in ways not considered by those who decry them. It also leaves open the possibility that blame, so conceived, may be valuable in a special way when directed at group agents that cannot experience negative feelings that would otherwise count against it. To be sure, in the face of individual responsibility gaps, blame of a group agent may constitute a welcome pressure valve for victims and their kin, without them having to worry about the affective implications of their response for the blamee. The strength of their blaming, *qua* emotional response, may also provide a powerful reason for the group to ensure that it reorganizes itself in a way that prevents similar bad outcomes in the future. Though such reasoning departs from Dworkin's move away from consequentialist justifications of holdings of group responsibility, they can hardly be ignored at this stage of the analysis. Or perhaps blame is better understood as a threshold, responsibility-ascribing response, which serves as a gateway for the appropriate channeling of a variety of reactive emotional stances. Thus, appropriate stances may not be limited to retributive ones, but also include stances such as compassion, forgiveness, or the sheer relief of finding an imputable interlocutor in an otherwise tragic and senseless situation.

Still, the close association of blame and suffering in much of the literature, coupled with deep suspicions about the expressive value of retributive stances such as those described, have led many theorists to propose radically different understandings of blame. The most recent example is Tim Scanlon, who thinks of blame as fully applicable to group agents. For Scanlon, blame derives its core moral meaning from the relationships in the context of which it is invoked. More specifically, to blame someone is (1) to judge him or her to have acted in a way that "shows something about his or her attitudes towards others that impairs the relations that others can have with him or her", and (2) "to take [one's] relationship with him or her to be modified in a way that this judgment of impaired relations holds to be appropriate."[48] No doubt, insofar as there are any group agents, relationships may be developed with them, and modified in light of their relationship-impairing cognitive attitudes.[49] Assuming that Dworkin's automobile manufacturer is such an agent, it is perfectly conceivable to think of the working relationships it has with its employees, or its commercial relationships with consumers. Relationships of trust and loyalty may even be developed with it. Thus, it is conceivable that, over time, these relationships may be modified by those engaged in them in light of the corporation's attitudes.

Still, if, according to this view, group agents may appropriately be blamed in the context of relationships they actually have, is it not an issue that they are not entities with which we can have the same range of relationships as with other individual agents? For example, it is much harder to conceive of deep and affective relationships, such as friendship and romance, with a manufacturing

---

[48] Scanlon (2008: 129-129).
[49] Scanlon (2008: 162-165).

corporation. Once again, this intuitive distinction seems to flow at least partly from the implausibility of holding that corporate agents have affective experiences of their own.[50] If that is the case, and a relational view of blame like Scanlon's is sound, then it seems that group blame will inevitably be inappropriate in a variety of cases in which individual blame would be appropriate. Even following such a wider understanding, then, group blame remains more narrowly, or differently, applicable than individual blame. Its ability to fill IRGs, even if there is a group agent involved, is correspondingly limited.

Then again, perhaps such a relational theory of blame is also misguided. Not necessarily misguided because of Scanlon's untethering of emotional stances from blame, since the modifications of impaired relationships he has in mind could well have characteristic affective aspects he does not explore. But misguided because it is not so uncommon to think that unrelated strangers may, at least sometimes, appropriately blame each other. It should be no surprise, then, that other theorists, often equally wary of tethering blame to an emotionally loaded ideal of retribution, argue for even wider conceptions of the practice that are less reliant on relationships and, consequently, less vulnerable to charges of disanalogy between group and individual blame. Noteworthy are those who think of a blaming response as solely cognitive, along the lines of a negative judgment that an agent has failed to live up to some relevant moral standard or has shown ill will.[51] Or consider those who contend that the gist of a blaming response is conative, in the sense that it arises from a desire that the agent not have so behaved.[52] Or again, consider those who think of blame primarily in terms of its function, be it to protest an agent's actions or character, or communicate condemnation, disapproval, or a call to answer for alleged moral lapses.[53]

All these conceptions of blame seem quite directly applicable to group agents as List and Pettit understand them. These agents may exhibit attitudes, make judgments and decisions, and program for actions in ways that are morally problematic. As a result, they may be judged negatively. One may desire that they would not have so acted, and respond accordingly. One may also conceivably protest their actions, and seek to communicate various things to them *qua* conversable agents. So, as per these understandings, blaming a corporate agent may be just like blaming an individual human agent, and just as valuable in terms of what it expresses. It is true that some of these conceptions deny, or fail to make clear, that a blaming response must have a phenomenal component. If what I suggested earlier about the importance of affect for assuaging the yearning experienced in the face of IRGs is sound, then group blame so conceived is bound to fall short. Notice, however, that it is also bound to fall short in addressing

---

[50] As Dworkin (1989: 498) provocatively reminds us, there should be no denying here that group agents could in principle engage in the more dispassionate parts of otherwise affective relationships, perhaps even including some of their sexual aspects.

[51] Watson (1996) and Hieronymi (2004).

[52] Sher (2006: ch. 6).

[53] Smith (2013), McGeer (2013), and Duff (1986).

any yearning for moral accountability that we may experience, including outside IRGs when blameworthy individuals are involved. So, insofar as we persist in thinking that blame must at least partly express something affective that tracks this yearning, conceptions that do not allow for it may well have to be rejected. One possible retort is that, despite what I have assumed so far, the yearning triggered by IRGs can be satisfactorily answered by a purely cognitive response. Thus, it would be a mistake to think that only an affective response can assuage it. Perhaps all that matters, or what matters most, is a sense that a negative judgment can be appropriately directed at a responsible agent, or that there is an appropriately responsive target for critical communication or protest.

Still, even assuming that moral psychology would validate either of these rejoinders, it remains unclear whether they have what it takes to extinguish all reasonable concerns about the expressive value of group blame. An additional worry may be that constitutive dissimilarities between group and individual agents, over and above consciousness-related ones, can significantly impact the expressive value of blaming the former. Consider that most accounts of blame surveyed assume that, to be blameworthy, an agent needs to have been responsible at some basic level for a moral contravention. Such basic responsibility tends to be fleshed out in terms of the contravening agent's capacity to understand what is at stake and to reason practically about how to respond. Many also contend that agents can only be worthy of moral blame for aspects of their lives—that is, actions, attitudes, or character—they meaningfully control.[54] Maintaining otherwise, the argument typically goes, would imply that moral blame merely tracks causal relations, as opposed to moral responsibility, such as blaming uncontrolled hurricanes for the devastation they cause. Now, if List, Pettit, and others who defend the possibility of morally responsible corporate agency are correct, are these not all capacities that corporate agents share with individual agents?

This is where the rot may be thought to set in. As List and Pettit themselves concede, corporate action-directing attitudes, decisions, and plans are only ever *relatively* autonomous from those of their individual members, upon which they supervene. This concession should come as no surprise if individuals provide group agents with all their matter and energy. Similarly, the realization of group decisions and plans always has to go through the intercession of individual human agents, even if it is the group that programs for them by ensuring that someone is on hand to implement them. Does not this deep dependence of group agency on individual members' agency impact the value that blaming groups for bad outcomes may have? It is tempting to think that it does since, even if, in some significant sense, group agents' moral understanding, practical reasoning, and control is theirs; it is never *just* theirs. When blaming a group agent, one is always, at a deeper level, also commenting on the behavior of other agents—namely, individual members—whether or not they are themselves blameworthy

---

[54] For Dworkin (1986: 172) himself, "people must not be blamed for acts over which they had no control."

and actually blamed. Thus, unlike the blame of individuals, corporate blame always has an intermediate quality to it, in the sense that it always points to a multi-faceted agency story and comes with the risk of eliding more fundamental moral facts.

Does this constitutional difference really impact the expressive value of group blame? Though I am unsure that it does, some may want to point to this feature as a reason why, when a group like a commercial corporation is blamed for a bad outcome, yet no specific individual is found to be blameworthy for it, popular clamor for blame often fails to subside. After all, List and Pettit's group agents are no more than social arrangements that individuals maintain, through coordinated efforts, to serve social ends. So, blaming them without blaming any of these individuals may fail to address in full the sense of tragedy that can come with collectively-generated bad outcomes if there is an IRG.

A more sustained look at conditions of individual blameworthiness may help take some heat out of this controversy. One may reply that, insofar as autonomous practical reasoning and control are conditions of blameworthiness, only *some degree* of autonomy is sufficient on both counts for individuals to be appropriately blamed. For example, although third-party coercion and manipulation can reduce individuals' responsiveness to reason or diminish their control over relevant aspects of their lives, such exogenous determinants may well not completely eliminate their blameworthiness for harmful deeds. This tends to be a central lesson of accounts of partial excuses and partial denials of responsibility.[55] Moreover, whatever plausible position one adopts in respect of the problem of free will, it is rather uncontroversial that individual agents are never in full control of all mental and physical processes that lead them to deliberate, decide, and act in given ways. Thus, if group agents may meaningfully be said to reason and be in control of their behavior to *some* irreducible degree—it is, after all, corporate attitudes, decisions, and plans that differ from those of their individual members, and which these very individuals may all oppose, that are paradigmatically at issue—could such reasoning and control, however minimal and specific in kind, not be sufficient for blame? And could such blame not be just as expressively valuable as individual blame? My sense is that, according to most conceptions of blame surveyed, it may be so. Unsubsiding popular clamor for corporate blame, in some cases, might then be more accurately attributed to harsher, perhaps misguided, conceptions of blame that require their subject's suffering, or to failures to ascribe individual blame when it would be apposite to do so.

I cannot get to the bottom of this question here. By now, though, I hope to have said enough to build a prima facie case that, based on most conceptions of the practice, blaming a group agent can serve an expressively valuable role, akin to that of individual blame, in the face of IRGs. Whether such blame can satisfactorily fill the yearning that arises in such cases is a separate question, the answer

---

[55] Horder (2004: chs. 2 and 4).

to which depends in large part on what blame is taken to involve, and the extent to which group agents can appropriately be subjected to it. Once again, such a realization should likely give pause to theorists who may be tempted to contend that their accounts of responsible group agency hold the promise of closing, without more in-depth and concept-specific analysis, at least some IRGs. At the same time, it points to the richness and relative infancy of this field of research.

4. Concluding Caveats

I want to conclude with a few caveats aiming to contextualize and round up my discussion in the previous two sections.

The first caveat is that my consideration of responsible group agents in the last section remains a footnote to a larger and obvious point. If and when there are IRGs, there will often be no group that meets the conditions of distinct agency and responsibility that make it an appropriate candidate for blame. If no such group exists, what I have characterized as a yearning for blame will likely remain intact. One might have to resort to blaming a fiction. As I stated, I tend to regard this kind of response with suspicion. At the same time, I am reluctant to hold that this so-called yearning for blame, which we often experience even if there is no one to blame for human-made bad outcomes, is itself completely improper. Could it not simply be that what we yearn for in such cases is not blame per se, or not just blame, but a morally satisfactory explanation, however best developed? That is, may there not be a better way of delineating individuals' moral predicaments in such cases than through the lens of responsibility and blame?

This question brings me back, for my second caveat, to moral liability. Previously, in Section 2, I briefly suggested that acknowledging individual liability as an important perspective from which to assess IRGs holds the promise of taking at least some of the intuitive moral sting out of such scenarios. That is, it holds the promise of providing a more discerning moral picture featuring a broader spectrum of permissible responses, aside from blame, toward individuals involved in bringing about a bad outcome or relevantly related to it. To be sure, liability holds this promise even if it is a moral idea distinct from blame and, thus, no substitute for it. Not only is it a broader concept, it is also essentially instrumental, in that its role is to provide moral organization for various grounds (including, but not limited to blameworthiness) of burdensome actions (possibly including, but not limited to blame), and the parameters of their permissibility for various ends.

As I suggested, a rich and multifaceted notion of individual liability, which may or may not include a notion of joint liability suitably individualized, can put pressure on Dworkin's insistence that holdings of distinctively corporate responsibility are essential to provide a complete moral account of collectively generated bad outcomes. At a more expressive level, the lens of individual liability may also deflate the yearning for group blame that may arise if no individual is blameworthy, by justifying the imposition of other moral labels and burdens on relevant individuals.[56]

Though liability is not my focus in this chapter, I emphasize it again in conclusion as a useful piece of context for my analysis. Its wider lens helps give credence to the contention, underlying the chapter, that irrespective of the intuitive appeal of IRGs, one should take care not to point too quickly to group responsibility and blame as the best and most discerning way of unraveling them. This is not to say that there is no valuable and distinctive moral space for group blame or holdings of group responsibility more broadly understood, be it in terms of their role in moral argumentation, their expressive role, or otherwise. It only means that, in any given situation, one needs to proceed with circumspection before affirming their indispensability.

Overall, then, my discussion has sought to caution against the swiftness with which Ronald Dworkin and others tend to gloss over IRGs and assert ways of handling them morally by focusing on group agency and responsibility. I did not undertake to address any specific claims made by Dworkin about the specific obligations and rights that the members of some groups may have, or the specific kinds of groups that may generate such obligations and rights. Neither did I question the intuitionist approach to moral philosophy that characterizes many discussions of IRGs, nor the deep soundness of more recent accounts of real responsible group agency that currently dominate the debate, like that of List and Pettit. Still, I hope to have highlighted enough fault lines and intricacies in what I take to be an exciting area ripe for further philosophical research to convince others, including Dworkin scholars, that it is so. No doubt, Dworkin may not have foreseen in 1986 that such a fertile and contemporarily relevant discussion could be provoked by the few passages of *Law's Empire* that inspired this chapter. That such a discussion could be generated in reaction to them is a testament to Dworkin's larger-than-life philosophical acumen and timeless legacy—a legacy replete with challenging ideas that it will likely take many other lifetimes and efforts, both individual and collective, to unravel.

References

Braham, M., and van Hess, M. (2010). "Responsibility Voids," *The Philosophical Quarterly* 61(242):6–15.

Bratman, M. (1992). "Shared Cooperative Activity," *The Philosophical Review* 101:327–341.

Bratman, M. (2014). *Shared Agency: A Planning Theory of Acting Together.* Oxford: Oxford University Press.

---

[56] I am not claiming that there are no other ways of channeling our yearning for moral targets in cases of bad human-made outcomes in IRG cases. For one thing, we may call on the law to posit this or that person as legally accountable—that is, as the one who, according to the law, carries the can, or sits at the desk where the buck stops. However, my premise here is that, unless the law reflects morality quite closely, and the understanding of morality it tracks is discerning enough, such legal maneuvering may still leave behind some sense of moral shortfall that we yearn to fill.

Caney, S. (2008). "Global Distributive Justice and the State," Political Studies 56: 447–518.

Copp, D. (2006). "On the Agency of Certain Collective Entities." In *Midwest Studies in Philosophy: Shared Intentions and Collective Responsibility,* vol. 30., P.A. French and H.K. Wettstein (eds.). Oxford: Blackwell Publishing, 194–221.

Duff, R.A. (1986). *Trials and Punishments.* Cambridge: Cambridge University Press.

Dworkin, R. (1986). *Law's Empire.* Cambridge, MA: Harvard University Press.

Dworkin, R. (1989). "Liberal Communities," *California Law Review* 77(3):479–504.

Estlund, D. (unpublished draft). "The Puzzle of Plural Obligation," (April 2013, cited by permission of the author).

Estlund, D. (to be published). "Prime Justice." In Political Utopias, K. Vallier and M. Weber (eds.). Oxford: Oxford University Press.

French, P.A. (1984). *Collective and Corporate Responsibility.* New York: Columbia University Press.

Gardner, J. (2008). "Hart and Feinberg on Responsibility." In *The Legacy of H.L.A. Hart: Legal, Political, and Moral Philosophy,* M.H. Kramer, C. Grant, B. Colburn, and A. Hatzistavrou (eds.). Oxford: Oxford University Press, 121–140.

Held, V. (1970). "Can a Random Collection of Individuals be Responsible?" *Journal of Philosophy* 67:471–481.

Hieronymi, P. (2004). "The Force and Fairness of Blame," *Philosophical Perspectives* 18(1): 115–148.

Horder, J. (2004). *Excusing Crime.* Oxford: Oxford University Press.

Lazar, S. (2012). "Necessity in Self-Defense and War," *Philosophy and Public Affairs* 40(1):3–41.

Lepora, C. and Goodin. R.E. (2013). *On Complicity and Compromise.* Oxford: Oxford University Press.

List, C. and Pettit P. (2011). *Group Agency: The Possibility, Design, and Status of Corporate Agents.* Oxford: Oxford University.

McGeer, V. (2013). "Civilizing Blame." In *Blame: Its Nature and Norms,* D.J. Coates and N.A. Tognazzini (eds.). Oxford: Oxford University Press, 162–188.

McMahan, J. (2009). *Killing in War.* Oxford: Oxford University Press.

Nagel, T. (1974). "What Is It Like to Be a Bat?," *The Philosophical Review* 83(4):435–450.

Newman, D. (2011). *Community and Collective Rights: A Theoretical Framework for Rights Held by Groups.* Oxford: Hart Publishing.

Pettit, P. and Schweikard D. (2006). "Joint Actions and Group Agents," *Philosophy of the Social Sciences* 36:18–39.

Pettit, P. (2014). "Group Agents are Not Expressive, Pragmatic or Theoretical Fictions," *Erkenntnis* 79(9):1641–1662.

Raz, J. (1986). *The Morality of Freedom.* Oxford: Oxford University Press.

Regan, D. (1982). *Utilitarianism and Cooperation.* Oxford: Oxford University Press.

Scanlon, T.M. (2008). *Moral Dimensions: Permissibility, Meaning, Blame.* Cambridge, MA: Harvard University Press.

Sher, G. (2006). *In Praise of Blame.* Oxford: Oxford University Press.

Smith, A.M. (2013). "Moral Blame and Moral Protest." In *Blame: Its Nature and Norms,* D.J. Coates and N.A. Tognazzini (eds.). Oxford: Oxford University Press, 27–48.

Strawson, P.F. (1962). "Freedom and Resentment," *Proceedings of the British Academy.* 48:1–25.

Sylvan, K.L. (2012). "How to Be a Redundant Realist," *Episteme* 9(3): 271–282.

Tadros, V. (2011). *The Ends of Harm: The Moral Foundations of Criminal Law.* Oxford: Oxford University Press.

Tadros, V. (2012). "Duty and Liability," *Utilitas* 24(2): 259–277.

Tadros, V. (2014). "Orwell's Battle with Brittain: Vicarious Liability for Unjust Aggression," *Philosophy and Public Affairs* 42(1):42–77.

Tanguay-Renaud, F. (2013). "Puzzling about State Excuses as an Instance of Group Excuses." In *The Constitution of the Criminal Law,* R.A. Duff, L. Farmer, S.E. Marshall, M. Renzo, and V. Tadros (eds.). Oxford: Oxford University Press, 118–150.

Tuomela, R. (1989). "Actions By Collectives," *Philosophical Perspectives* 3:471–496.

Tuomela, R. (1991). "We Will Do It: An Analysis of Group Intention," *Philosophy and Phenomenological Research* 51:249–277.

Wallace, R.J. (1994). *Responsibility and the Moral Sentiments.* Cambridge, Mass.: Harvard University Press.

Watson, G. (2004). "Responsibility and the Limits of Evil: Variations on a Strawsonian Theme." In *Agency and Answerability: Selected Essays.* Oxford: Oxford University Press, 219–259.

Watson, G. (1996). "Two Faces of Responsibility," *Philosophical Topics* 24(2):227–248.

Wolf, S. (2011). "Blame, Italian Style." In *Reasons and Recognition: Essays on the Philosophy of T. M. Scanlon,* R.J. Wallace, R. Kumar, and S. Freeman (eds.). New York: Oxford University Press, 332–347.

5

Inheritance and Hypothetical Insurance
by Daniel Halliday*

This paper examines Ronald Dworkin's treatment of inherited wealth, which is stated only briefly, but represents a sophisticated stance, to which Dworkin remained committed over multiple writings. Dworkin's contentions are that (1) the goal of restricting bequest is to prevent the formation of hierarchies of social class, and (2) this goal can be pursued through a progressive estate tax that models citizens' hypothetical insurance choices concerning protection against class harm. This paper seeks to support Dworkin's commitment to the diagnostic significance of class injustice, but finds problems with his attempt to use the hypothetical insurance approach. After identifying various difficulties around hypothetical insurance, the paper ends on a more positive note: Dworkin's concern to address class hierarchies can be adapted so that an inheritance tax gains support from the various principles that make up the liberty/constraint system in *Sovereign Virtue,* Chapter 3. This may not result in a completely adequate treatment of inherited wealth, but it promises to draw on principles that supplement, rather than rely on, any ideas about hypothetical insurance.

1. Introduction

The question of how to regulate inheritance and bequest clearly lies within the scope of liberal egalitarian theorizing. Nevertheless, egalitarians rarely hold this topic up for sustained attention. Whatever egalitarians have had to say on this matter has tended to occur in the form of tangential discussions or afterthoughts, usually embedded in larger bodies of work in which the main focus is on some

*I would like to thank Tom Parr, Sagar Sanyal, and Kok-Chor Tan for very helpful comments on earlier drafts of this paper. Parts of the discussion developed here were also included in talks at various philosophy departments, including those at the Universities of Auckland, Melbourne, Otago, Victoria (Wellington), Western Australia, and the Australian National University. Thanks to those who attended these talks for the valuable feedback they provided.

other topic of egalitarian concern.[1] Ronald Dworkin's writings on distributive justice are something of an exception to this trend. True enough, his discussions of inheritance and bequest are small, and lie somewhat in the background, relative to other more prominent themes in his work. Nevertheless, Dworkin's contribution to egalitarian thought includes an interesting and principled stance on bequest, which has stimulated a small secondary literature. In spite of its brevity, Dworkin's discussion of this issue represents what might be the most philosophically elaborate egalitarian treatment of inheritance to have emerged during the second half of the twentieth century. It would therefore be a loss to any future scholarship on inheritance if Dworkin's thoughts on this topic were overshadowed by the attention rightly given to the more prominent and influential themes in his impressive corpus. At any rate, Dworkin's position on the topic deserves further attention, and this paper is an attempt to provide some of that. My aim in what follows is to both arrive at an evaluation of the characteristically sophisticated position Dworkin holds on the problem of inheritance, and to explore some connections with other theoretical commitments that Dworkin held, but whose potential relevance to inheritance he did not see.

As a guide, here is how the paper is organized. Section 2, "Dworkin's Egalitarianism," provides a brief overview of Dworkin's egalitarianism, and is followed by an account of his stance on inheritance and bequest in section 3, "Hypothetical Insurance." Later sections examine Dworkin's important claim that the injustice of unregulated bequest is related to the problem of class stratification, and his attempt to ground a progressive inheritance tax on claims about hypothetical insurance choices. Section 4, "Class, Prejudice, and Independence," makes two points in response. First, the hypothetical insurance approach faces certain difficulties, due to complex relationships linking class hierarchy, brute luck, and inherited wealth, which Dworkin never properly examined. Second, the approach does not retain the theoretical motivations that it enjoys when applied to topics other than inherited wealth, largely because inheritance is not so closely related to markets as are other forms of brute luck. I then suggest, more positively, how a progressive inheritance tax might have been developed as a more direct requirement of the state's equal concern for its citizens, using theoretical resources that Dworkin developed separately from the hypothetical insurance approach, in particularly his liberty/constraint system that he used to supplement his envy test. Section 5 concludes.

2. Dworkin's Egalitarianism

It goes without saying that Dworkin's views on egalitarian justice are elaborate enough to make brief summary quite difficult. I will assume that the most general ideas are already familiar to most readers: The summary I give aims to highlight

---

[1] I am certainly not claiming that the topic of inheritance has received no recent attention *at all*. Some good recent discussions can be found in Murphy and Nagel (2002: Ch.7), O'Neill (2012), and White (2008). These works do not extend their focus to Dworkin's position.

the details that are most relevant for the subsequent discussion of Dworkin's position on inheritance and bequest.

For Dworkin, justice is fundamentally about how the state, or government, should act toward its citizens. Justice is done insofar as government acts in ways that express equal concern and respect for each of its citizens. Dworkin has been criticized for taking this view, but I will set such matters aside.[2] Dworkin's fuller conception of justice is developed in his theory of equality of resources. This theory takes much guidance from the idea that distribution should be "ambition sensitive" rather than "endowment sensitive." A society of equals is one in which persons are permitted to develop their own life plans in ways driven by their own tastes, preferences, and convictions, and unhindered, as far as possible, by unchosen personal circumstances.

A maximally ambition sensitive distribution is one that passes what Dworkin calls the *envy test*. A resource distribution passes this test if no person prefers any other person's bundle of resources to their own bundle. Importantly, a distribution's being envy free in this sense does not entail that everyone is entirely or equally happy with their particular resource bundle. Persons could each prefer their own bundle to others available while still wishing that there had been more or better resources to exchange in the first place, and hence better bundles. Part of the point of the envy test, though, is that it represents a way of coping with scarcity and conflict in a very broad sense: It specifies a rule about how society ought to divide what it can actually produce, in ways that make each person's pursuit of ambitions sensitive to those being pursued by others.

To give a greater sense of what it means for a distribution to be envy-free, Dworkin offers a hypothetical thought experiment in which resources are auctioned off until a certain distribution of resource bundles is reached. The auction begins from a position of *ex ante* equality, with persons holding exactly equal shares of some otherwise worthless currency used for making bids (such as clamshells). Participants in this auction know what sort of things they want to get out of life, but they do not know the market value of their talents. As such, they are ignorant of how much ability they possess to pursue their ambitions while coping with the sort of luck that life will throw at them. This will affect how the bidding goes. In particular, it will lead participants to bid for certain forms of protection against bad luck, which Dworkin believes can be modeled by various egalitarian policies regarding taxation and the allocation of its revenues.

Whatever egalitarian policies might be derived from it, the resource auction and the envy test are supposed to make Dworkin's egalitarianism distinctively liberal as well. Generally speaking, more coveted resources will attract higher

---

[2] Here, I have in mind the worry that Dworkin gives undue prominence to the state as a moral agent, such that any subsequently developed conception of justice will be objectionably administrative as per the criticisms made by Samuel Scheffler (2003). It is possible that the presence of a concern about class hierarchy in Dworkin's treatment of bequest suggests he cared more about oppressive social hierarchies than Scheffler's discussion acknowledges. (See n. 11.)

bids, and thus whoever ends up holding them will have had to forego bidding on whatever less coveted resources can be had for fewer clamshells. The role of the auction in realizing the egalitarian requirement of an envy free distribution shows that market exchanges, properly regulated, act as an instrument of justice rather than an impediment to it.[3] By making a distribution pass the envy test, what gets ensured is that the costs one must pay to secure any resource bundle vary with the value that others place on that bundle (the more people want something, the more any person will have to bid in the auction to get it). In Dworkin's words, the auction is a device for making "aggregate opportunity costs . . . equal."[4] Thus, the whole approach is designed to respect human individuality and the diversity of personal ambition.

Importantly, making a distribution satisfy the envy test does not exhaust the requirements of equality of resources. There are two reasons for this. First, many possible resource distributions might pass the test. This is true just because there are many possible ways of identifying and differentiating resources in the first place. A resource such as land plots, for example, could be traded in units of any size and shape, or instead only in units shaped as perfect triangles. An envy-free distribution of land plots could result in either case, but would almost certainly be different in each case. Dworkin uses this point to motivate a requirement that resources be identified "abstractly," that is, made maximally diverse and differentiated. This favors the more intuitive approach of allowing land plots to be sold in all sorts of shapes and sizes. Second, there is the possibility that persons might seek to use their resources in ways that are morally troubling, in ways that are not prevented merely by making a distribution envy-free. This problem motivates what Dworkin calls a liberty/constraint system, which will specify how resources are to be individuated and how they may be used. Several principles end up supplementing the envy test as part of this system, in ways that, for Dworkin, further reveal how liberty and equality are intertwined rather than at war with each other. As I shall explain in section 4, one of these principles may have interesting implications for the regulation of bequest.

Dworkin is at pains to emphasize that the envy test needs to be applied diachronically. It is not a mere "starting gate." He requires that a post-auction distribution be regulated, over time, in ways specified by what sort of outcomes persons would have sought protection (insurance) against. This fixes the degree and type of compensation that might be provided for victims of bad brute luck, for example persons whose talents lack the market value necessary to secure meaningful employment. Persons who are successful or fortunate in life incur larger premiums, so as to fund the policies aimed at helping those less fortunate. These include a welfare state and free (if limited) healthcare. The degree of redistribution is limited by the amount of protection hypothetical purchasers would wish to secure. Because such purchases are included in the hypothetical resource

---

[3] For a quotation, see the discussion in Section 3, "Hypothetical Insurance."

[4] Dworkin (2000: 149).

auction, they count as part of the process that makes the eventual resource distribution envy-free. The fact that insurance purchases have implications for the subsequent regulation of the resource distribution means that their inclusion gives the envy test its diachronic extension. Dworkin's view is that hypothetical insurance choices would err towards substantial but limited redistributive compensation for those who turn out to be less fortunate. It is plausible, Dworkin says, that protection would be sought against physiological handicap and unemployment. But it is unlikely that protection would be sought up to a level that would provide compensation for missing out on the most lucrative careers, or funding for cosmetic surgery. More generally, the prospect of such extensive schemes can be ruled out by the need for some set of better off individuals to pay the taxes that fund them—no insurance scheme makes any sense unless it specifies some set of favorable conditions under which one pays a premium rather than receive a payout. This sort of moderate regulation of distribution is supposed to represent the insurance choices of the people "on average, acting prudently,"[5] while knowledgeable of their ambitions and tastes in life but ignorant of other aspects of their circumstances. Overall, then, hypothetical insurance choices provide a counterfactual guide for designing redistributive taxation, including the calculation of rates and the selection of which policies should be funded by the revenues.[6]

3. Hypothetical Insurance

Dworkin's application of *equality of resources* to inheritance appears within a short but dense discussion in *Sovereign Virtue*, Chapter 9. The position defended here is reaffirmed in some later replies to critics.[7] Dworkin formulates the problem of inheritance in an intuitive and familiar way, namely, as an apparent dilemma between freedom and equality: The act of bequest seems to make a distribution ambition both sensitive in one respect and endowment-sensitive in another. Many parents want to give something to their children in the form of gifts and bequests. Typically, this counts as an important life goal rather than the sort of arbitrary preference that might be held while not really valued. If ambition sensitivity is to be promoted, it therefore seems problematic to impose special restrictions on bequest. On the other hand, however, unregulated bequest makes it almost certain that some members of subsequent generations will be handicapped by their parents' failure to provide for them, while others will profit from much more generous parental support. This sounds like a way in which distribution becomes increasingly endowment-sensitive. This diagnosis can be extended in a certain way: Importantly, and unlike many other contemporary egalitarian writers,

---

[5] Dworkin (2002: 111).

[6] Dworkin (2000: 77-78).

[7] Dworkin's references to inheritance and bequest can be found in the following bodies of text Dworkin (2000: 346-349, 2002: 125, 2004a: 352-353, 2006: 117-118).

Dworkin recognizes that the long run tendency of unregulated, large bequests is to give rise to economic stratification so that social relations take on the "familiar character of a class system."[8]

Unfortunately, Dworkin fails to expand on the meaning of class system in this context. Evidently, he accepts that class hierarchies involve inequalities of status and power that are caused by the intergenerational replication of inequalities in resources.[9] But, so long as nothing is said about the sort of power and status involved, such claims remain more formal than substantive. I think there are two normatively interesting, broad accounts of class hierarchy that are compatible with Dworkin's position so far as it is stated. The first is that class hierarchy is simply the lack of mobility between income levels, such that resource inequalities have a tendency to replicate themselves with each generation. Somewhat wider accounts of class hierarchy leave room for mobility but stress the normative importance of further factors that are hard to describe in strictly distributive terms. These include a variety of distinctly oppressive aspects or consequences of hierarchies, such as patterns of stereotyping, stigma, and segregation.[10] My own view is that it makes the most normative sense to construe class hierarchies in accordance with the second, wider, conception. I suspect that Dworkin, if forced to choose, would err towards a mobility-based conception. This may be only because the coherence of ambition-sensitivity might be complicated by much work connecting oppression with things like adaptive preference. I will proceed on the assumption that an oppression-based conception is the more plausible, although I think it is possible to reconstruct at least many of my criticisms of Dworkin on a mobility-based conception. I will eventually argue, also, that an oppression-based conception would in fact provide Dworkin with certain theoretical resources, to the extent that he may have been better off explicitly endorsing a conception of this kind.[11]

Whatever class hierarchy might be, Dworkin's proposal for restricting bequest resembles the intuitive compromise that many find attractive when it comes to regulating the flow of inherited wealth: Citizens should have a limited right to bequeath, so as to respect parents' decisions about how to live their lives. But this right needs to be limited, so as to protect against the injustice of class stratification. Societies that fail to regulate the acts of gift and bequest *at all* will

---

[8] Here there is a parallel between Dworkin's thinking and recent work that seeks to expand on the Rawlsian reasons for regarding a property-owning democracy as superior to welfare state capitalism—see O'Neill (2012). The taxing of inheritance features prominently here.

[9] Dworkin (2000: 348).

[10] For a useful discussion of the relation between sociological work on mobility and philosophical ideas about equality, see Swift (2000). Thinking of class hierarchy in terms inclusive of things like stereotype and stigma would be to extend important recent work on status hierarchies of other sorts, particularly race. (See note 26, below.)

[11] Dworkin's appeal to social class apparently injects a certain degree of concern for social or intergroup relations into his egalitarianism, something which criticisms of Dworkin might have overlooked when categorizing Dworkin alongside other "luck egalitarians." Readers of Dworkin (2003) will already be aware of his frustration at this. In recording this observation, I leave it open whether Dworkin is right to wholly dismiss the way in which such critics have understood him.

almost certainly fall afoul of Dworkin's observation that egalitarian requirements must work diachronically. Dworkin's solution is to call on the hypothetical insurance approach that he uses at greater length in *Sovereign Virtue* to justify other broadly redistributive policies. Hypothetical insurance represents a desire to secure protection against bad genetic luck or bad talent luck. For example, citizens would want to secure some protection against ending up with a set of talents that the market fails to reward. At the same time, they would want to retain some freedom to use talents that turn out to be lucrative, while paying tax as a premium. Dworkin believes that much the same can be said about inheritance luck: Insurance purchasers would seek protection against being unlucky enough to get little or no inheritance, while retaining the option of being able to provide benefits for their own offspring. Dworkin's conclusion is that this sort of insurance preference could be modeled by a steeply progressive tax on estates.[12]

Now that it has been summarized, it is possible to raise some doubts about the hypothetical insurance approach. First, we might wonder whether hypothetical insurance choices work well as a counterfactual guide for inheritance taxation, even granting that they can guide other sorts of egalitarian tax policies in the way that Dworkin maintains. This is partly because we can distinguish inheritance luck, i.e., concerning how one fares when it comes to receiving any inheritance, and class luck, i.e. concerning what position in a class hierarchy one happens to occupy. Dworkin only speaks explicitly about inheritance luck, when speaking of insurance choices, but he still refers to class when speaking of the harm that such choices are supposed to protect against. It is worth quoting some of Dworkin's remarks here at length:

> We should begin by asking why people would want [inheritance] insurance and what considerations would affect how much they would be willing to pay for it. The harm such insurance protects against is, we might say, relative rather than absolute...Inheritance insurance would make sense, therefore, to guarantee not a higher standard of living in absolute terms, but against the different and distinct harm of occupying a lower tier in a class system – against that is, life in a community where others have much more money, and consequently more status and power, than they do and their children will.[13]

In effect, these remarks treat inheritance luck and class luck as identical. But Dworkin's own remarks offer some signs that they should be kept distinct: The passage reproduced above is drawn from a larger piece of text in which multiple

---

[12] Dworkin apparently modifies this claim, later, in *Is Democracy Possible Here?* Here, he remarks that "it does seem unprincipled to tax an estate at the same rate without regard to the number or wealth of its beneficiaries...it would be much fairer...to treat substantial gifts of any form, including bequests, as income subject to ordinary taxes" Dworkin (2006: 117-118). Dworkin's suggestion here is to move from a traditional estate tax to a receipts tax. There are indeed strong egalitarian reasons for taxing receipts rather than estates. On this, see White (2008).

[13] Dworkin (2000: 348).

references are made to the prospect of simply having ungenerous, imprudent, or stingy parents. Such possibilities represent bad inheritance luck but not really bad *class* luck: It goes without saying that parental generosity need not vary straightforwardly with class position. Indeed, it is perfectly possible for members of the upper classes to suffer a decline in economic position because of the poor financial choices of their parents or simple parental refusal to provide support. Indeed, some of Dworkin's readers have formulated the problem of insuring against inheritance simply as a trade-off between being seeking to benefit one's own children while seeking protection against one's own parents lacking the ambition or ability to bequeath.[14] The plausibility of such claims does not rely on any sort of claim about class harm.

Generally speaking, the class position of any individual is usually determined prior to their inheriting any wealth. Inheritance is in fact coming increasingly late in life, given increasing longevity among wealthy demographics.[15] This suggests that seeking protection against bad inheritance luck may be neither necessary nor sufficient for seeking protection against class luck. This is certainly not to say that class position and inheritance are unconnected, only that it is far from easy to work out the relation between them. It remains plausible that inheritance does much to drive a class hierarchy. Although class position does not depend on an individual's own inheritance, it may still depend on the prior inheritance flow further back in their family line. Plausibly, then, much of inheritance's significance can be traced to its special role in overcoming the temporal lag between concentrations of wealth and membership of a social class. This lag, which runs in both directions, is evidenced by the way in which sudden increases in wealth lead people to be labeled as nouveau riche while persons with low incomes can still be said to come from good stock. There is actually much to be said for approaches to inheritance and bequest that target the sorts of inherited fortunes that cascade down successive generations.[16] Sensitivity to this sort of iterated inheritance is not part of standardly progressive inheritance taxes, which merely tie liability to

---

[14] This appears to be the reading offered in a recent discussion by Matthew Clayton, who writes: "Individuals will come to the choice they face with different views concerning the importance for them of giving to particular individuals who are close to them and of ensuring that they or their children receive monetary resources, and it is their view of the relative importance of these ambitions that will guide their insurance decisions" Dworkin (2012: 109). Clayton recognizes Dworkin's preoccupation with class harm later in his discussion—my point here is merely to highlight the way in which protection against bad inheritance luck comes apart from protection against class harm.

[15] On this point, which may also undermine some traditional moral defences of the right to bequeath wealth, see Ackerman and Alstott (2000: 36).

[16] Most significant here are the writings on iterated bequest, and how to design ways of restricting it, that were discussed in the early twentieth century. See especially Rignano (1925) and Wedgewood (1929: esp. ch. 11). These works appeared during a sort of heyday in philosophical discussions of inheritance and social justice, but have now been largely forgotten about in philosophical circles. I am currently engaged in writing a book manuscript, which devotes some attention to these views. A philosophically sophisticated summary of the historical context around these works can be found in Erreygers and Di Bartolomeo (2007).

the economic value of a bequest or receipt. Similarly, the fact that inheritance can have a cumulative rather than immediate impact is almost never appreciated in recent political philosophy.

Dworkin's failure to properly separate inheritance luck from class luck remains a weakness in his short discussion. That said, the idea of inheritance luck might be broadened so as to include the presence or absence of inheritance further up one's family tree. This would, at least, be a way of redefining inheritance luck so as to make it correlate more closely with class luck. There is nothing incoherent about insuring against complicated aspects of one's family history alongside more immediate parental poverty or stinginess. And there is nothing theoretically problematic about hypothetical insurance choices being modeled by an inheritance tax that ties the liability of a bequest to facts about earlier inheritance in the family line, rather than just to its sheer size. Dworkin's commitment to the significance of class might require him, ultimately, to favor a tax scheme more complex than a traditionally progressive estate tax. But this may be an interesting, rather than a damaging, result. It remains hard to see how it can be established that an inheritance tax, ultimately aimed at removing class luck (by removing a class hierarchy altogether), is a model of hypothetical insurance choices that aim at individuals' protection against bad inheritance luck.

A second doubt emerges once it is asked whether, when applied to inheritance and bequest, the hypothetical insurance approach retains all the motivations behind its application in other contexts where bad brute luck operates, such as the labor market. I will begin by drawing attention to the difference between the idea of preventing class hierarchy from occurring, and the fact that insurance (hypothetical or otherwise) is basically a nonpreventative device, used to instead mitigate or compensate for the effects of some event that the insurer is unable or unwilling to take steps to prevent.[17] What this means is that though there is nothing wrong with regarding inheritance tax as a device for removing or preventing class hierarchy, there is something strange about treating inheritance tax as a model of insurance purchases. Dworkin apparently acknowledges, at the beginning of his discussion,[18] that an inheritance tax must aim at *preventing* class hierarchies from forming in the first place. This preventative character remains evident in his brief recommendations about how to spend inheritance tax revenues, which aim broadly at promoting equality of opportunity across

---

[17] The idea that the hypothetical insurance approach mitigates rather than removes or neutralizes the effects of brute luck features in some other general interpretations of Dworkin's position. See, for example, Mason (2004: 150-152). My points in this paragraph also resemble a criticism that Colin MacLeod has made about Dworkin's position on disability. As I read him, MacLeod's point is (roughly) that many of the injustices suffered by persons with disabilities are features of their social environment rather than the resource distribution, including patterns of stereotyping and stigma. MacLeod uses this point to suggest that the hypothetical insurance approach misconstrues certain types of disadvantage, partly because of the way it seeks to mitigate or compensate disadvantage rather than directly address underlying factors.

[18] "I must now say something about why equality of resources *would not generate* class distinctions" Dworkin (2000: 346, emphasis added).

demographic groups. But to insist that a preventative use of tax revenues models a hypothetical choice whose function is to compensate or mitigate is to stretch what it means for the proposed actual tax to model what is (merely) a curative rather than preventative strategy.[19]

This point can be strengthened by connecting it with Dworkin's original motivations for the hypothetical insurance approach. These draw on his views about the role of the market in the pursuit of liberal equality. The case for invoking hypothetical insurance relies partly on the claim that markets have some valuable features but also some disturbing ones that call for regulation. For example, some brute luck disadvantage is unavoidable given that some persons lack the sort of talents that can command any sort of job security, let alone decent incomes, in the labor market. One view is to regard the market as a source of injustice. As I have said, a pillar of Dworkin's liberal egalitarianism is his unwillingness to accept anything like this. Dworkin famously tells us that "the idea of an economic market, as a device for setting prices for a vast variety of goods and services, must be at the center of any attractive development of equality of resources."[20] Among other things, markets promote a form of fairness by requiring people to spend more of their resources if they want to acquire something that other people want as well—recall the earlier remark about aggregate opportunity costs. The fact that some people lose out as a result of an unplanned market economy is part of the price we pay for the advantages (moral as well as economic) of some form of market allocation. This allows the welfare state to be defended as, perhaps among other things, a device for mitigating disadvantage wrought by luck in the labor market, without denying the claim that markets are in some way essential for the pursuit of liberal egalitarian justice.

So, Dworkin has well-worked-out, liberal motivations for regarding the market, when properly constrained, as an essential instrument of distributive justice. And this view of the market is compatible with the egalitarian approach he wants to take to other forms of bad brute luck in the world. But this view remains attractive largely because the brute luck in question is of a sort that we have reason to *merely* mitigate, given that it represents an avoidable downside of some otherwise indispensable process. In other words, the hypothetical insurance approach draws much of its appeal from the very idea that the cures for some ills emerge from a source that it would be wrong to wholly remove. Anybody who rejected Dworkin's view that markets are essential tools of justice would, therefore, be able to reject one of Dworkin's main reasons for proposing the hypothetical insurance approach at all.[21] The problem with applying the hypothetical

---

[19] Dworkin repeatedly mentions that redistributive taxation schemes act as models for hypothetical insurance choices. At no point does he offer a theory or theoretical characterization of what a model ultimately is. Given this, I do not take my line of argument here to be uncharitable.

[20] Dworkin (2000: 66). See also (2011: 356-358).

[21] Hypothetical insurance has other theoretical advantages, not least the avoidance of having to find a purely metaphysical way of separating brute luck from option luck. There may also be ways of responding to this metaphysical problem without invoking hypothetical insurance—see Tan (2012: 93-94).

insurance to the problem of inheritance is that class hierarchy is not like the market. Inheritance is a system of asymmetric or gratuitous transfers, rather than a system of exchanges. As such, it is not really a market phenomenon.[22] Class stratification is not some special tool of promoting justice due to special features warranting its preservation under some set of constraints. Instead, the right response to class hierarchy is just to do what we can to get rid of it.[23] Because of this, it becomes less obvious why the defense of a substantial tax on inheritance needs to appeal to hypothetical insurance choices, even granting that whether persons gain any inheritance is largely a matter of brute luck.

None of the concerns raised in this section demonstrate that hypothetical insurance choices *can not* be used as a counterfactual guide for designing the sort of inheritance tax that would protect society against class hierarchy. But they do not enjoy the same sort of support that Dworkin was able to provide for its application in other contexts. There are two good reasons, each compatible with Dworkin's more fundamental commitments, for keeping the treatment of inheritance away from hypothetical insurance. First, it is just difficult, theoretically speaking, to work out a view on which inheritance tax models hypothetical desires to protect against bad inheritance luck, in ways that neatly coincide with the sort of design that would prevent class hierarchies from emerging. Second, a number of the theoretical reasons for adopting the approach at all seem to be absent, or weaker, with respect to inheritance than with respect to the more straightforward problems of market regulation. It may be that invoking the hypothetical insurance approach remains tempting just because inherited wealth is one of those practices that result in some people having better or worse brute luck than others. But the presence of differential brute luck was never supposed to be a fundamental theoretical motivation for employing the hypothetical insurance approach. Readers of Dworkin will already be aware of the vehemence with which he has made this point in response to certain critics.[24] All things considered, there

---

[22] This observation has been more fully developed against Dworkin by Michael Otsuka (2002, 2004), who observes that gifts and bequest have a tendency to introduce envy into the resource distribution in ways that market exchanges need not. Otuska's point raises a very important question about a way in which gratuitous (non-market) transfers of resources are problematic for Dworkin. Transfers of this sort are insensitive to the opportunity costs of third parties, who do not have the opportunity to bid for the transferred themselves. Dworkin remained unmoved by Otsuka's criticism; see Dworkin (2004: 352-353), but did not, to my mind, give an entirely satisfactory explanation of how to solve this problem. Some more discussion of the disagreement between Dworkin in Otsuka can be found in Williams (2004). Lazenby (2010) shows that the general problem of gift-giving (construed in ways inclusive of bequests) is likely to dog any sort of egalitarianism in which Dworkin's distinction between brute and option luck has direct implications for whether a distribution is just.

[23] I admit that this claim may be easier to accept with the view that class injustice involves oppression as well as low mobility, but I think it is correct for either view.

[24] Dworkin (2004b) stresses that ideas about equal concern, the envy test, and hypothetical insurance do the fundamental theoretical work in *equality of resources*. He denies the "much more extreme" claim that egalitarian justice aims at eliminating inequalities deriving from differential brute luck. At most, he concedes that "the distinction between people's choices and their circumstances is of central importance to justice,"

is no really strong case for extending the idea of hypothetical insurance to the problem of inherited wealth apart from the fact that it is merely one convenient way of refining the idea that something needs to be done about differential levels of brute luck. Apart from the fact that this is not obviously what is unjust about the failure to restrict inheritance in the first place, the difficulties with invoking the hypothetical insurance at least motivate the search for some other source of theoretical guidance when seeking to design a way of regulating bequest.

4. Class, Prejudice, and Independence

Sovereign Virtue, Chapter 3, addresses a variety of principles that are designed to supplement equality of resources, so as to provide the right sort of bridge between equality of resources and the more fundamental requirement of equal concern. Dworkin derives various liberties and constraints on the use of personal resources, which help resolve the indeterminacy of the envy test. This responds to the fact, noted earlier, that the envy test does not select a unique resource distribution, and does not rule out certain uses of resources that Dworkin plausibly identifies as being the sort of thing that a state should prohibit if it is to show equal concern for all its citizens. There is insufficient space for me to work through each of these principles or comment fully on the general objectives of the chapter. But one principle that deserves special mention is Dworkin's principle of independence. This principle is motivated by the need to prevent people from using their resources in ways connected with prejudice.

Dworkin motivates the independence principle partly by noting one important limit of the hypothetical insurance approach:

> Compensation schemes based on hypothetical insurance markets, useful though they may be in ameliorating other forms of handicap, are plainly inappropriate in combating the effects of prejudice. We must find some other way, compatible with the other goals and constraints of equality of resources, to place victims in a position as close as possible to that which they would occupy if prejudice did not exist.[25]

An example accompanying this quoted passage portrays a coordinated group of racists who attempt to buy housing land for the purposes of excluding black residents. Since this use of resources is motivated by prejudice, it ought to be prevented by the state, who can pass laws that combat it. Dworkin's point here, which seems absolutely correct, is that compensation (when understood as grounded in hypothetical insurance purchases) is simply the wrong way of trying to help victims of prejudice. This is not to deny that *some* sort of compensation might be appropriate in these cases—for example, requiring wrongdoers to pay

---

[25] Dworkin (2000: 162).

their victims as part of being punished. The inappropriateness lies with treating things like racism as a "fixed and given threats," in the manner that we treat bad genetic luck. Instead, racism is just something that ought to be stamped out as part of the pursuit of equal concern.

Dworkin's discussion of racism indicates his awareness of the limits of the envy test and, therefore, the hypothetical insurance approach. Now, it is not obvious why the impact of racism on the resource distribution should differ from the impact of social class. This is especially true if social class, like racism, involves prejudice of a sort that impacts resource distribution. Very likely it does, particularly if class hierarchy involves oppression as well as low mobility. One plausible way of further filling out an account of class injustice is to appeal to the antagonistic relationships that form between segregated demographic groups. The relevant sense of segregation here is a broad one: In addition to strict or legally enforced geographic segregation, it covers the more subtle segregation that occurs when members of different groups are educated in different schools, occupy different professional roles, and socialize apart from each other. Any combination of these varieties of segregation can help maintain, and sometimes constitute, oppressive hierarchies of social class. One of the simpler causal mechanisms operates if segregation leads members of different social classes to become ignorant of the basic features of each other's lives. This leads members of groups to stereotype each other as the lack of understanding necessitates a greater reliance on heuristics. Since the stereotyping of disadvantaged groups tends to be negative, it can lead to demonization that expresses profound disrespect for members of lower class group, and compounds the disadvantage that gave rise to it in the first place (often perpetuating a cycle of yet more stereotyping).[26]

What this means is that the injustice of class hierarchies is, in part, constituted or unavoidably correlated with the operation of prejudice. This is evident in a host of examples. Certain politicians and parts of the media demonize the poor (which we may treat roughly as a class group) as being lazy welfare cheats who prefer to live off the state than to find work. A plausible sociological explanation is that such demonization succeeds only because the poor *appear* to be lazy *from the perspective* of the better off. This is because better off members of society are ignorant about the incompetency of the institutions tasked with implementing welfare policy. Someone who has never been unemployed, or formed friendships with unemployed persons, will likely fail to appreciate why it can be rational to turn down an offer of short-term paid work, on grounds that the benefits system is so fallible that it is a safer option to stay on it, rather than risk a long delay in getting benefits reinstated after the short period of paid work is over.[27]

---

[26] This paragraph has been guided by Anderson's (2010) discussion of the mechanisms behind oppressive social hierarchies. Anderson's work focuses on racial segregation in the United States, but much of the conceptual framework does not exclude other sorts of hierarchy.

[27] Some similar concerns to these are raised in Wolff's (1998) discussion of why conditional welfare benefits require the badly off to undergo scrutiny and shameful revelations about their private affairs.

Class hierarchy is not, of course, wholly like racial hierarchy.[28] Often, people do not realize that they are participating in the relevant form of stereotyping: Government elites who think the poor must be given incentives to take paid
work are often benevolent but simply very ignorant, with often disastrous effects.
Dworkin's example of the racist landowners suggests that he has in mind prejudice as a very conscious phenomenon. But to insist on prejudice being conscious
lacks motivation, and is not in any case suggested by anything Dworkin says.
Plenty of racial prejudice is unconscious, to the extent that persons exercising
it are distressed and mortified when it is revealed to them. More important, it
is hard to believe that by letting a prejudice be exercised, the state succeeds in
treating its citizens with equal concern, just because this prejudice is unconscious. After all, prejudice does not need to be conscious in order to "destroy
some people's lives." This sort of outcome is a very real possibility in cases in
which class prejudice leads people to use resources in ways that are very bad for
others. To treat such profound consequences as detached from the resource distribution is implausible and under motivated, and certainly not ever insisted on
by Dworkin. If such detachment could succeed, it would probably only show that
there is something wrong with conceiving of requirements of justice as things that
regulate the resource distribution in the first place.

I have been critical of Dworkin's attempt to address the problem of inheritance
within the scope of his hypothetical insurance approach. But my criticisms help
lead to the suggestion that Dworkin may have done better to locate the treatment
of gift and bequest in the same place that he located the racially prejudiced use of
resources. Dworkin's response to the racism example is to propose what he calls
the independence principle. As Dworkin formulates this principle, it imposes on
the use of resources a set of "constraints necessary to protect people who are the
objects of systematic prejudice from suffering any serious or pervasive disadvantage from that prejudice."[29] Given the very general formulation that Dworkin

---

[28] In earlier work, Dworkin drew a distinction between external and personal preferences
(1977: 234-238). Roughly speaking, *external preferences* concern the resources or opportunities
assigned to others whereas *personal preferences* concern only those held by oneself. Dworkin makes
it explicit that, if external preferences have racist content, their accommodation by the state will
be incompatible with equal concern for citizens. This view remains present in *Sovereign Virtue*
(298: n.12). It is not entirely clear that *all* external preferences are incompatible with equal concern, although some of Dworkin's formulations imply the weaker claim that it is always unfair
for external preferences to influence the resource distribution. A preference to bequeath meets the
broad, formal definition of an external preference since it concerns the assignment of goods and
opportunities to another person. But it is also a preference about how to use one's own resources,
e.g., not to spend them down prior to one's death. What's more, preferences to bequeath lack the
overtly contemptuous content of a racist preference to avoid having black neighbors. My reasoning
in the above paragraph is guided by the view that accommodating external preferences violates
equal concern so long as such accommodations are causally related to the emergence of prejudice
or similarly objectionable elements of oppressive hierarchy. This allows that such preferences do
not aim at oppression so far as their content is concerned. It also allows that some other external
preferences do not violate equal concern at all.

[29] Dworkin (2000: 161).

uses here, it remains plausible that bequest could be fitted into its scope, particularly if the reason to restrict bequest is derived in some way by requirements to combat class hierarchy, *and* class hierarchy is understood as a phenomenon involving oppression, and not just lack of mobility between income levels.

This relocating of gifts and bequest retains the spirit of Dworkin's liberal egalitarianism, which seeks a compromise between restricting the tendency of bequest to make distribution sensitive to brute luck, while allowing parents the freedom to devote their lives to supporting their children's future. There is every reason to believe that *some* amount of bequeathing wealth is compatible with reining in the growth of class hierarchy and the prejudices to which it gives rise (construed as involving stereotyping, demonization, and so on). Given this, there is reason to believe that the case for a substantial inheritance tax could be just as strong under the independence principle as Dworkin took it to be under the hypothetical insurance approach.

5. Conclusion

Dworkin's position on inheritance rests on an important diagnostic insight, but he is led to his preferred solution due to a certain amount of naïveté about what the diagnosis really contains, and perhaps a failure to have seen the further advantages of other aspects of his theory of justice. But Dworkin's work on inheritance is driven by precisely the right sort of concern, which is that unregulated bequest leads to a socially stratified society, in which class distinctions corrode social life and make people's fortunes all the more dictated by arbitrary facts about their ancestry. Further progress in the search for a compelling egalitarian treatment of bequest needs to proceed by way of an intensified focus on exactly how the practice of inheritance perpetuates social hierarchies of class. Dworkin's own reflections on inheritance take some important steps in this direction, perhaps more so than any other egalitarian philosopher of his generation. Although it is not the most substantial or perhaps successful piece of his enormous contribution to legal and political theory, it would be a genuine loss to scholarship on inherited wealth and social justice if it were entirely overshadowed by the more major themes in his rightly celebrated contributions to legal and political philosophy.

References

Ackerman, B., and A. Alstott. (2000). *The Stakeholder Society.* New Haven, CN: Yale University Press.

Anderson, E. (2010). *The Imperative of Integration.* Princeton, NJ: Princeton University Press.

Clayton, M. (2012). "Equal Inheritance: An Anti-Perfectionist View." In *Inherited Wealth, Justice and Equality*, J. Cunliffe & G. Erreygers (eds.). London: Routledge.

Dworkin, R. (1977). *Taking Rights Seriously.* London: Duckworth.

Dworkin, R. (2000). *Sovereign Virtue: The Theory and Practice of Equality.* Cambridge, MA: Harvard University Press.

Dworkin, R. (2002). "Sovereign Virtue Revisited," *Ethics* 113(1):106–143.

Dworkin, R. (2004a). "Ronald Dworkin Replies." In *Dworkin and His Critics,* J. Burley, ed. Malden, MA: Blackwell Press.

Dworkin, R. (2004b). "Equality, Luck and Hierarchy," *Philosophy & Public Affairs* 31(2):190–198.

Dworkin, R. (2006). *Is Democracy Possible Here?* Princeton, NJ: Princeton University Press.

Dworkin, R. (2011). *Justice for Hedgehogs.* Cambridge, MA: Harvard University Press.

Erreygers, G., and G. Di Bartolomeo. (2007). "The Debates on Eugenio Rignano's Inheritance Tax Proposals," *History of Political Economy* 39(4):605–638.

Lazenby, H. (2010). "One Kiss Too Many? Giving, Luck-Egalitarianism, and Other-affecting Choice," *Journal of Political Philosophy* 18(3):271–286.

MacLeod, C. (1998). *Liberalism, Justice and Markets: A Critique of Liberal Equality.* New York, NY: Oxford University Press.

Mason, A. (2006). *Levelling the Playing Field: The Idea of Equal Opportunity and its Place in Egalitarian Thought.* Oxford, NY: Oxford University Press.

Murphy, L., and T. Nagel. (2002). *The Myth of Ownership: Taxes and Justice.* New York: Oxford University Press.

O'Neill, M. (2012). "Free (and Fair) Markets Without Capitalism: Political Values, Principles of Justice, and Property-Owning Democracy." In *Property-Owning Democracy: Rawls and Beyond,* M. O'Neill & T. Williamson (eds.). New York, NY: Oxford University Press.

Otsuka, M. (2002). "Luck, Insurance, and Hierarchy." *Ethics* 113(1):40–54.

Otsuka, M. (2004). "Liberty, Equality, Envy and Abstraction." In *Dworkin and His Critics,* J. Burley, ed. Malden, MA: Blackwell Press.

Rignano, E. (1925). *The Social Significance of Death Duties,* trans. J. Stamp. London: Noel Douglas.

Scheffler, S. (2003). "Equality as the Virtue of Sovereigns," *Philosophy & Public Affairs* 31(2):199–206.

Swift, A. (2000). "Class Analysis from a Normative Perspective," *British Journal of Sociology* 51(4):663–679.

Tan, K. (2012). *Justice, Luck and Institutions.* New York: Oxford University Press.

Wedgwood, J. (1929). *The Economics of Inheritance.* London: Pelican Books.

White, S. (2008). "What (if Anything) is Wrong with Inheritance Tax?" *The Political Quarterly* 79(2):162–171.

Williams, A. (2004). "Equality, Ambition, and Insurance," *Proceedings of the Aristotelian Society: Supplementary Volume* 78:131–150.

Wolff, J. (1998). "Fairness, Respect, and the Egalitarian Ethos," *Philosophy & Public Affairs* 27(2):97–122.

PART III

General Jurisprudence

CONTESTING THE UNITY OF LAW AND VALUE

6

Putting Law in Its Place
by Lawrence G. Sager[*]

1. Introduction

I think that it is altogether possible, indeed likely, that Ronald Dworkin will be best remembered for his legal philosophy. But in *Justice for Hedgehogs*[1]— Dworkin's last major work—law comes late and very little is said. To a large extent, Dworkin incorporates his earlier work—most notably in *Law's Empire*[2]— by reference. But he does focus at some length on what he calls the "one-system" approach to the question of the relationship between law and morality. In the one-system approach, law *is* morality . . . more exactly, law is a branch of political morality.

The one-system view is more radical sounding in prospect than it is in conceptual detail. But it is far from uncontroversial. I have a special interest in Dworkin's claim, because he sees it as a virtue of the one system view that it undermines the idea that there can be valid propositions of law that are not properly enforceable by courts. I have long insisted that there are such propositions and that their *underenforcement* by the judiciary does not undo their status as law. Dworkin and I have gone back and forth about this; I am deeply sorry that I will have the last word in our exchange.

2. The One-System View and the Impasse in Jurisprudence

Dworkin offers a strange account of what motivates the one-system view. He begins with a conceptual conundrum that gets in way of progress in the debate between positivism and moralized views of the law like his own interpretivism.

[*]Alice Jane Drysdale Sheffield Regents Chair in Law, University of Texas, Austin.
[1]Dworkin (2011).
[2]Dworkin (1986).

In the two-systems structure, we have two sources of authority, law and morality, and we have to decide at the outset which to consult in choosing between positivism and interpretivism. If we consult law, we quickly discover that we have merely deferred the question. We have to decide whether, in reading legal materials, we pursue interpretive protocols that involve moral precepts, or regard legal content as a matter of pedigree and non-moralized social facts. If the former, then morality is at the table from the outset; if the latter, a strong version of positivism is built in from the beginning. If we try to avoid this impasse by consulting morality rather than law as to the nature of law, then we have built in morality from the outset, and positivist theorists have a legitimate complaint that the rabbit was put in the hat at the moment we chose to consult morality.

In a two-systems world, argues Dworkin, arguments for either positivism or interpretivism, are thus unhappily circular. And we cannot avoid this circularity by looking to convergent linguistic practices, because those practices reflect the entrenched disagreement we are hoping to resolve.

But, argues Dworkin, we can surmount this impasse if we adopt the one-system view, and conceive of law as a branch of political morality. The disagreement between interpretivism and positivism may well remain, but now we understand that debate as turning on an issue within morality. We will understand interpretivism and positivism as rival interpretive claims about the nature of law, and there will in principle be a right answer to the question they address. To be sure, that answer may regard law as heavily positivistic; but the grounds for that conclusion will be normative propositions of political morality. Positivism and interpretivism thus emerge as rival theories of political morality.

I began by saying that Dworkin offers an odd case for the one-system-law-is-a-branch-of-political-morality view. To see why, think about how a positivist might respond to this reframing of the disagreement. There are two reasons why a positivist might strongly object.

The first is this: Conceiving of law as a branch of morality is a least as loaded a beginning as it would be to embrace the two-system view and elect to treat the question of positivism versus interpretivism as situated in the domain of morality. It is an entailment of the one-system view that the dispute is commended to moral analysis—at least if the one system turns out to be morality.

The second positivist objection is more a matter of an unspoken conceptual predilection. If we start with the idea that law is a branch of political morality, we do more than merely give morality conceptual priority as the starting point. We are saying that law as an ongoing matter is a practice underwritten by morality. And there will be a strong tendency, if not a formal conceptual presumption, to make morality immanent in our legal analysis. Think about the widely shared view that past legal outcomes can and should deflect judgments about what the law is, away from the outcome that political morality would otherwise treat as best. If law is a branch of political morality, then this departure from the direct moral outcome needs a justification, and presumably that justification will be moral. Or think about the regard of legislation in the one-system world. It will be natural to invoke the democratic normativity of the legislature, as well as the conventional authority of its pronouncements.

One way to put this is to note that there are two questions to ask with regard to the debate between positivists and interpretivists: First, what kind of question is at stake? Second, What role does morality play in the best answer to the question? The one-system view stipulates that what is at stake is a moral question. And as to the ultimate question of what role morality has to play in the ongoing content of law, the one-system view stacks the deck in favor of a moralized view like interpretivism.

The claim that we need to evaluate concepts of law and the law itself from a moral perspective is appealing; indeed, it is hard to understand what other perspective is available that ultimately would not owe its bona fides to a foundational moral claim. But the one-system view as proffered by Dworkin defends that outcome on the implausible ground that it is a neutral way of resolving the debate between positivism and interpretivism.

3. How Law Is Distinct and Why It Is Suboptimal

Dworkin does, however, undertake to dispel two worries that he thinks flow from the idea that law is a part of morality: First, how if at all are legal rights distinct from other moral rights? And second, how can law be a part of morality and yet be morally suboptimal—even unjust—in its stipulations?

Legal rights are distinct, on Dworkin's account, because they are properly enforceable on demand through adjudicative institutions and the coercive institutions they direct—for example, sheriffs or the police. Only those political rights that are enforceable in courts without any further official decisions are legal rights, and in turn only those propositions that could properly be enforced by a court compose the law. A claim that an official or an official body is obliged to do something or to refrain from doing something cannot be a legal claim if there are reasons that a court should not involve itself in enforcing that outcome. This is true even if the obligation or right in question is based on a command of the relevant constitution, or for that matter, an applicable statute. In such cases, Dworkin would say that the rights at stake are *legislative* rights, not legal rights, and that as such they are essentially of a piece with the general run of claims grounded in political morality. I have a lot of trouble with this, which forms the basis of my long-standing disagreement with Dworkin over judicial under-enforcement. But I will postpone this until we see this concept of the limited domain of law in action.

Dworkin acknowledges that it is essential that there be a distinction between what the law is and what it ought to be. It follows that the possibility of moral suboptimality is wrought into the law. To explain how the law can be a branch of political morality and yet be morally suboptimal, he offers the analogy of a family with two children. As the parents make decisions over time concerning their children, they confront a myriad of questions about when they should intervene in the choices each child makes, what the substance of their intervention should be, how strong are the demands of consistency between the treatment of the two children, and the processes by which changes and the announcement of changes will take place. The best answers to these questions will shape a special family code; and the reasons for the distinct shape of that code are moral, involving "principles of fairness that condition coercion," which Dworkin calls *structuring principles*.

Dworkin's responses to these two opposing worries about the one-system view—how is law distinct from the ordinary run of political morality, and how can law be a part of morality and yet be morally suboptimal—may on first blush seem complementary. Law on this account is limited to judicially directed official coercion; and law, for this very reason, is morally suboptimal in its first-order substance, because that substance is deflected by principles of fairness over time and across cases, principles that temper legitimate coercion.

But the family code analogy that drives the explanation for law's first-order moral suboptimality is in considerable tension with the stipulation that only those precepts enforceable by courts constitute law. The fairness that motivates Dworkin's structuring principles applies not just to institutions of the state but to families on this account. Parents are—or struggle to be—in positions of authority with regard to their children. Their ability to influence their children's behavior includes formal acts of enforcing that influence—the refusal to grant necessary approval for activities, the refusal to fund opportunities, the with-holding of allowance, the formal entailments of "grounding" for periods of time, and so forth. But most parental authority, most of the time, rests on respect and regard, on the realized expectation that an appropriate relationship of authority will prevail. There are powerful reasons for parental authority, including moral reasons. But parental authority is not dependent on brute coercive force; and the obligation of parents to behave fairly with regard to their children is not con-fined to those judgments that are enforced or enforceable by brute coercive force. In the family code analogy, slightly mysterious qualities of law like structuring principles (and from Dworkin's familiar earlier work, *integrity*), become more recognizable and convincing as principles of fairness over cases and over time, in recognition of the equal stature of the governed. But the idea that law is ineluctability tied to courts and brute coercive authority suffers as a result.

When we move from the family code analogy to the domain of political rights, the same doubts hold: Accepting for the moment the distinction between legislative and legal rights, how can legislative rights escape the demands of fairness that motivate structuring principles? Beyond the brute coercion of judicially ordered police activity, constitutional and legislative provisions speak with distinct moral authority to the officials they address; distinct precisely because of the processes of their enactment, promulgation, and interpretive meaning.

I am not suggesting that constitutional and legislative provisions speak without the normative mediation of interpretation, or that they claim authority over their addressees without the involvement of moral precepts. To the contrary, I think that the relationship of authority between constitutions, legislation, and public officials—like the relationship of authority between courts and public officials— is thoroughly moralized. For present purposes, my point is narrow: Among the moral precepts alive in that relationship are the structuring principles of political justice that Dworkin regards as critical to the identity of law; and that is true whether or not any given provision is appropriately enforceable by the judiciary and the forces of brute coercion it arguably[3] commands. The apparent complementarity between the view that the availability of judicially authorized coercion is what distinguishes law and the view that structuring principles account for law's first-order moral suboptimality unravels on close consideration.

4. Evil Law

Dworkin offers two examples of how legal philosophy and practice will shift if the one-system model is accepted. The first is the long-standing problem of evil law. Dworkin offers a genuinely evil example, the Fugitive Slave Act of 1850, which required officials in free states in the United States to capture and return slaves to the slave-holding states from which they had escaped. Per Dworkin, asked to enforce the Act, a judge under the influence of the two-system view would think that she had to choose among three bad choices: enforce an evil law; resign, or lie about what the law was. This unhappy choice would be forced by the understanding that the law demanded one thing and morality another. In the one-system view, says Dworkin, the question would instead be whether the slave-holders' moral claims to a judicial decision enabling them to reclaim their slaves were outweighed, or trumped, by the grotesque immorality of slavery. There is still a moral clash, a dilemma, but now we recognize that it is moral claim versus moral claim and we side with "the morality of freedom." We can express this two ways: The Fugitive Slave Act is law, but too unjust to enforce; or the Act is too unjust to count as law. The first way is preferable, suggests Dworkin, in part because it clarifies the distinction between an evil law in a legitimate legal system like the Fugitive Slave Act and a law in a pervasively evil system like that of Nazi Germany. As to the latter, we can say that there is no moral reason to enforce the law at all. But the choice, in the end, is "sadly close to a verbal dispute."

It is a little unclear what Dworkin hopes to establish here. The most modest possibility is defensive. A standard claim on behalf of keeping law and morality distinct is that the separation lends conceptual clarity to claims that individual laws and whole legal systems are deeply immoral. His more ambitious claims aside, Dworkin may be most concerned with showing that the analysis of evil law

---

[3] Arguably, because prosecutors, sheriffs, the police, and other officials make numerous decisions that intervene between judicial pronouncements and the application of collective physical force.

and evil legal systems can proceed intelligibly under the one-system view. By the example of his analysis, he makes *that* case persuasively.

Much more doubtful is the proposition that the one-system approach *improves* our capacity to analyze evil law and evil legal systems. In this regard, Dworkin implies an advantage that he cannot defend. He begins, you will remember, by describing the plight of the two-system judge faced with an evil law, who has to choose between enforcing the law, resigning, or lying about the law. The one-system judge, seeing the question as one of conflicting moral claims, chooses "the morality of freedom", and apparently finds a fourth way: she refuses to enforce the law, but she stays in office and describes the situation truthfully. But the one-system view is neither necessary nor sufficient to this improved resolution of the problem of the judge called upon to enforce an evil law. The important moral question, under both a two-system and a one-system view, is whether a judge's role permits her to stay in office and yet decline to enforce the law. That fourth possibility is what the evil law example cries out for, and it is hard to see either how that possibility is excluded by the two-system/positivist view or painlessly facilitated by the one-system/law-is-a-branch-of-morality view.

5. Underenforcement

The second example of how our understanding about law is improved by the one-system approach is the underenforcement problem, the issue over which Dworkin and I wrestled in recent years. The question can be put simply: Can there be valid and binding propositions of law that are not properly enforced by courts? I say *yes*; Dworkin says *no*, because he has defined legal rights as claims that be satisfied on demand by adjudicative institutions that respond to entitlements on demand and direct the action of agents with coercive authority, like the police. Our disagreement has both conceptual and practical consequences, and is worth pursuing as a free-standing matter. In *Justice for Hedgehogs*, Dworkin gives our disagreement importance local to his one-system approach by arguing that the idea of legitimate judicial underenforcement of law only makes sense to positivists still under the influence of the view that law and morality are separate systems.

In support of this, Dworkin begins by invoking an example dear to the hearts of underenforcement theorists: a national constitution that is best understood as conferring on citizens the right to minimally adequate healthcare, but which courts with good reason would decline to enforce in a direct and full-blooded manner. I would see this situation as creating a legal obligation on the part of the relevant governmental actors to make best efforts to secure these constitutional minima for their citizens, who in turn, have a legal, constitutional, right to such efforts. Dworkin would deny that we are operating in the legal branch of political morality. The legislature may bear a moral obligation and the citizens may enjoy moral claims, but this obligation and these claims are best assimilated with other, nonlegal, moral claims that citizens may have against their government. He contrasts this situation with that posed by the Fugitive Slave Act. There, a judge is caught between two moral claims, one of which is distinctly legal. The structuring principles of law combine with past legal events—most notably the enactment of the Act—to give judges a moral reason to enforce its terms, but the grotesque immorality of slavery supervenes on that obligation. In the underenforced, minimum healthcare constitution case, by hypothesis, there is no moral reason for *a judge* to fully enforce the adequate healthcare provision of constitution, and therefore, under the one-system view, no law is involved.

The italicized *a judge* is crucial to understand what is otherwise a puzzling argument by Dworkin. There are vivid structuring principles—principles endemic to the regime of law—at play in the case of the underenforced constitution. The constitution was drafted, debated and ratified. Its background, text, and associated understandings and actions by courts, legislators, and citizens all combine to support the view that the constitution is best understood as conferring a right to adequate healthcare. These facts provide robust structuring principles, but these principles are most fully and directly apt to legislators and other, nonjudicial, officials. Everything law-like is present, not merely on a positivist, social fact account, but on a fully moralized, one-system account—except for one thing: the authority and obligation of judges to act. At bottom, what is doing the work for Dworkin at this point is the stipulation with which he began, namely, that only propositions that are properly enforceable by courts are law. But that is the premise that is at issue, and it cannot find support in its own iteration.

The comparison of the Fugitive Slave Act and the constitutional right to minimally adequate healthcare is instructive, but not in the way Dworkin argues. In the Fugitive Slave Act case, there is a prima facie moral obligation to enforce what would be the law were it not outweighed by the immoral substance of what the law stipulates. Indeed, somewhat surprisingly, Dworkin prefers that the judge recognize the Act as law, and then decline to enforce it on grounds of the supervening injustice of slavery. The weight of the prima facie obligation to enforce the law is substantial . . . substantial enough to lead Dworkin to characterize the situation as one in which that obligation is overborne by a "moral emergency." In the case of an underenforced constitutional provision for minimum healthcare, the same sorts of structuring principles are apt, and they ought to be understood as giving on to a similarly robust prima facie obligation to enforce the law. The only difference between the two cases is the identity of the officials upon whom the obligation falls; in case of the underenforced constitution, the obligation falls on nonjudicial officials, including legislators, administrators, and executive leaders. To be sure, there is no grievous moral conflict; here, the moral obligation to enforce the law is reinforced by general principles of political justice. But that is hardly a reason to deny the force of the structuring principles that surround the enactment and interpretation of the constitution. Dworkin finds clarity in treating the Fugitive Slave Act case as an instance of moral claim versus moral claim, rather than as law versus morality. In the healthcare case, he inexplicably wants to introduce the confusion of distinguishing between the *legal* obligation of judges to enforce the law, and the *nonlegal* obligation of legislatures and other nonjudicial leaders to respond to provisions that are underwritten by exactly the same structuring-principle-generating circumstances.

6. Why It Matters

But is there anything important at stake? Is our disagreement "dangerously close to a verbal dispute?" Here, there is a great deal at stake. Legal obligations claim an urgency and a priority over other concerns that might be morally competitive were structuring principles set aside. They place distinct demands on their addressees and make those addressees vulnerable to distinct criticism if they fail to meet those demands. Legislators, administrators, and executive leaders have a special moral obligation to respond to legal sources just as judges have a special legal obligation to respond to the same legal sources. Failing to treat judicially underforced provisions as law denies that important truth.

In this respect, Dworkin has things backwards in *Justice for Hedgehogs*. He thinks that judicially unenforced premises can only look like law from the vantage of a positivist who assigns a normatively detached, legal provenance to constitutional and legislative provisions. Moreover, he believes that calling judicially unenforced premises law obscures the absence of the moral structuring principles that give law its special role within political morality. The reverse is true: On a thoroughly moralized account of underenforcement, it is important to acknowledge that constitutional and legislative premises that are outside the scope of judicial enforcement are nonetheless law precisely because the structuring principles of law place distinct moral obligations on nonjudicial governmental actors.

Beyond the importance to nonjudicial actors in properly identifying judicially underenforced provisions as law, there are a number of situations in which adjudicated law and non-adjudicated law connect and interact, and treating judicially underenforced commands as law is deeply clarifying, if not conceptually essential. I will set out three, two of which are suggested by the jurisprudence of the United States Constitution.

The enforcement provisions of the Thirteenth, Fourteenth, and Fifteenth Amendments to the Constitution compose one such example. Very roughly: the Thirteenth Amendment abolishes slavery; the Fourteenth Amendment demands equal protection and due process of state and local governments and their officials; and the Fifteenth Amendment insists that the right to vote not be abridged on account of "race, color, or previous condition of servitude." Each amendment includes a concluding section, which grants the Congress of the United State the authority to enforce it by "appropriate legislation." The scope of congressional authority under these provisions is a matter of considerable controversy, but this much is reasonably clear: Congress is not limited to merely restating the text of the relevant amendment in statutory form and attaching penalties and enforcement procedures; nor is it limited to addressing conduct that the Supreme Court of the United States would make illegal in the course of spontaneously interpreting the amendment. Congress can go further than would the Court in enforcing these provisions. The most extreme example of this is provided by the Thirteenth Amendment. In *Jones v. Alfred Mayer*,[4] the Court held that Congress had authority to outlaw private racial discrimination in property transactions, since the abolition of slavery in the amendment entailed not merely the dissolution of servitude itself but the eradication as well of the badges and incidents of slavery—what we can identify in a different vocabulary as the enduring and tentacular elements of caste. But the Court has confined its own enforcement of the Thirteenth Amendment to instances of actual servitude; it has never held that private racial discrimination violates the amendment as judicially enforced. How should we think about this very broad gap between the authority of Congress to enforce the Thirteenth Amendment and far more restricted authority the Court treats itself as having with regard to the same enterprise? The most direct and illuminating characterization of the gap is this: The Thirteenth Amendment is best understood as calling for the abolition of institution of slavery *and* the eradication of the structural injustice it has left behind. For reasons of institutional competence, there is a division of labor between the Court and Congress, with everything other than slavery itself the responsibility of Congress. The Thirteenth Amendment, accordingly, is judicially underenforced, but remains legally valid and binding to its full margins. Congress's power to enforce the amendment is straightforward—it is the power to enforce the amendment fully and is not limited to the Court's institutionally inflected self-restraint.

The second example of the intersection of judicial enforcement and underenforced constitutional provisions involves the secondary enforcement of constitutional entitlements to minimum welfare. In the United States, there are a dozen or more decisions by the Supreme Court that share these characteristics: They involve claims to material benefits that could quite plausibly be considered to be elements of minimum welfare; they involve situations in which these benefits have been denied to the claimants without a formal hearing, or on the basis of principles of distribution that are arguably unfair; the Court rules in favor of those claimants, holding either that they are entitled to a hearing or to the benefits themselves; and the Court justifies that result by straining against its extant doctrine in puzzling ways. Two samples: In one of the cases, the Court held that due process requires a hearing before minimum welfare benefits can be denied, notwithstanding its general reluctance to insist on hearings in other non-rights- bearing contexts;[5] in another, the Court ruled that Texas violated the Equal Protection Clause when it refused to let the children of undocumented

---

[4] *Jones v. Alfred H. Mayer Co.*, 392 U.S. 409 (U.S. 1968).

[5] *Mathews v. Eldridge*, 424 U.S. 319 (U.S. 1976). In *Goss v. Lopez*, the Court took this principle to the extreme of holding that a public school must conduct a hearing before subjecting a student to a short-term suspension from school. *Goss v. Lopez*, 419 U.S. 565 (U.S. 1975).

immigrants attend public schools, despite the claim's poor fit with the structure of equal protection doctrine.[6] Included in this singular group of cases are anomalies such as the Court drawing on a constitutional provision that had lain dormant for over a century in order to protect newly arrived welfare claimants in California.[7]

There is a way to make attractive sense of these cases. On this understanding, the United States Constitution confers rights to minimum welfare; but entwined with the realization of those rights are issues of minimum thresholds, priorities, strategy, and responsibility that are beyond the appropriate role of courts, at least within the tradition and experience of American constitutional law. But courts do have a significant, secondary enforcement role with regard to these rights. Once the legislative branches have provided basic welfare programs, courts can patrol those programs to assure that their constitutional entitlements are fairly distributed. The Constitution, on this account, confers legal rights to minimum welfare, notwithstanding the inability of courts to enforce those rights in the first instance. In turn, judicial insistence on robust procedural and substantive fairness is required to protect the enjoyment of the implicated entitlements.[8]

A third example is the more explicit and complex variation on this theme provided by a number of modern constitutions, which make express commitments to material entitlements in areas like health, education, and housing. Under the prevailing circumstances of scarce resources, there are numerous trade-offs to be made in even beginning to approach the satisfaction of these entitlements: trade-offs, for example, between similarly situated claimants for the same entitlements, claimants for different entitlements, and present entitlement satisfaction as opposed to increased entitlement satisfaction in the future. There are other questions as well, including whether to address broad, low-level needs or targeted, high-resource-demand needs; the appropriate mechanisms to deliver and fund entitlements; the strategic charting of future progress; and the location of authority and responsibility. This list is only suggestive of the politically sensitive, value-charged, institutionally demanding undertakings involved in responding to material constitutional commands. For all of this, a few national constitutional courts have briefly ventured into the direct and full enforcement of their constitutions' material commitments. The results have not been encouraging. Most courts, in contrast, have adopted a posture of limited enforcement. On the

---

[6] *Plyler v. Doe,* 457 U.S. 202 (U.S. 1982).

[7] *Saenz v. Roe,* 526 U.S. 489 (U.S. 1999). The dormant and presumed dead clause was the Privileges and Immunities Clause of the Fourteenth Amendment.

[8] Sager (2004). This is by no means the only way to read these cases. Mine is an interpretation without a clamorous following. Our earlier discussion of Congress's civil rights enforcement authority is also open to dissent. But the point is not that these readings of constitutional jurisprudence in the United States are irresistible and somehow insist on an enlargement of what we consider to be law. Rather, what is important is that they are plausible and attractive accounts of the institutional division of labor in a regime of constitutional law, accounts that depend on the idea that underenforced constitutional precepts are nonetheless law.

robust side, this has included demands of equal treatment under extant national healthcare programs, thereby sidestepping many of the difficult questions that lie outside the boundaries of existing programs. On the restrained side, this has involved only the insistence that government demonstrate that it is committed to the eventual satisfaction of the constitutional requirements, has long-term plans to achieve this, and is not turning its back on small steps that are immediately at hand.[9]

I have gone on too long. The important point is that these modern constitutions have engendered a division of labor between courts and other governmental actors, a division conducted under a conceptual umbrella of legal obligation. The idea of a division of labor driven by institutional capacity and propriety, unified by legal obligation, is the common theme in our three examples—civil rights enforcement and secondary welfare rights enforcement in the United States, and the judicial response to explicit welfare rights commitments in modern constitutions. Let me make clear what these examples are meant to show. The question is whether it matters that we understand traditional legal materials like constitutions to create law when their provisions are not fully enforceable by courts. In these examples, judicial behavior and explanation go best when this natural understanding of what is law is available.

7. Brute Coercion

Still elusive is what motivates Dworkin's insistence that a legal claim must be entitled to immediate recognition by the judiciary. In the end, Dworkin never really defends this. But his demand that judicial enforcement be involved if a proviso is to be law has two parts. The first is that there an adjudicative body which will respond to entitlements on demand; the second is that the body in question have authority over the police or other coercive entities. It is possible that coercion is at the bottom of all this. The point of law, for Dworkin, is that it delineates the appropriate and necessary occasions for the collective use of force, that it directs and legitimates the coercive authority of the state. Courts, in Dworkin's view, direct or command collective force; legislatures and other nonjudicial bodies and officials—including citizens in their sovereign constitution-making roles—do not. Hence judicial enforceability as the *sine qua non* of law.

The purpose of law is to shape the behavior of officials and citizens of a state, to direct and coordinate behavior. Coercion is undoubtedly important to this function. But, as our discussion of Dworkin's family analogy shows, the ability of rules uttered by authoritative entities to direct behavior is by no means limited to occasions of brute coercion, or necessarily dependent in each instance on the possibility of such force. In the complex social and political environment of the

---

[9] Sager (2013).

modern state, coercion comes in many forms: social regard, professional regard and advancement, electability, and so on.

Even if we focus on the brute application of collective physical force by the state, the behavior of legislators and other nonjudicial officials in response to judicially unforced constitutional or legislative commands will directly shape the coercive profile of the state. Think again about the judicial underenforcement of modern constitutional requirements that create rights to minimum welfare. And assume that the legislative and executive branches of the state in question respond to their constitutional obligations, and give the constitutional demands for minimum welfare attention and priority that the implicated policies would not otherwise enjoy. Programmatic differences follow: Taxation is different; governance structures are different, and the delivery of healthcare, education, and opportunities for housing are all different by virtue of official responses to the obligations that the constitutional provisions are understood to entail. The result of all this will change the collective coercion of the state in all these ways going forward. It seems a conceptual confusion to insist that law's overall connection to the legitimate use of collective force demands that the stipulations of traditional legal sources like constitutions and legislation cannot qualify as law unless—on a retail, proviso-by-proviso basis—those stipulations can be judicially enforced.

If, as Dworkin suggests, the one-system view sets itself against the idea of judicially underenforced law, that would count against the one-system view. But what I hope to have shown is that in a moralized understanding of law like the one-system view, acknowledging the legal bona fides of underenforced norms is not only intelligible but important both conceptually and practically.

8. Dworkin's Legacy

My remarks here have been largely critical. But I want to close on a different note.

Dworkin's astute and creative approach to everything that came under his gaze, his ability to draw sharp and vivid conceptual lines and—to borrow the term used by Joseph Raz in a presentation at the conference that saw the birth of this essay—his *fearlessness*, meant that many of us learned from him when he was wrong . . . perhaps especially when he was wrong. And much of what he taught us was so persuasive that we have taken it on board almost unconsciously.

This is true, I think, of the idea of interpretation, the conceptual river which runs through *Law's Empire*. Dworkin not only saw law as at its heart interpretive, he saw the role of philosophers and legal scholars as one of interpreting law; and, of course, he offered an interpretation of the conceptual act of interpretation. He did not so much instruct us as explain to us what we were doing. The extent of our intellectual debt is great, and easy to overlook.

The one-system view of *Justice for Hedgehogs* may itself prove to be an anchor tenant in a major turn in the philosophy of law. There are a number of interesting and provocative theories emerging which share with the one-system view the insight that we do best by abandoning the idea that law lies in a distinct conceptual domain[10]. The authors of these theories have all come of age in an environment heavily influenced by Dworkin's work and by Dworkin himself. Their work—partly sympathetic and partly oppositional—will help secure this aspect of his legacy.[11]

References

Dworkin, R. (1986). *Law's Empire*. Cambridge, MA: Harvard University Press.

Dworkin, R. (2011). *Justice For Hedgehogs*. Cambridge, MA: Harvard University Press.

Greenberg, M. (2014). "The Moral Impact Theory of Law," *Yale Law Journal* 123: 1288–342.

Hershovitz, S. (2015). "The End of Jurisprudence," *Yale Law Journal* 124: 1160–204.

Kornhauser, L. (2015). "Doing Without The Concept of Law," Publication Forthcoming.

Sager, L. (2004). *Justice in Plainclothes*. New Haven: Yale University Press.

Sager, L. (2013). "*Cortes constitucionales, derechos sociales y el 'spacio de colaboracion' entro el significado y la doctrina*" (Constitutional Courts, Social Rights, and the Collaborative Space Between Meaning and Doctrine), in *Diálogos constitucionales de Constitution con le Mundo*. Bogatá: Universidad Externado de Columbia. Translation on file with author.

Waldron, J. (2013). "Jurisprudence for Hedgehogs," (to be published).

---

[10] Greenburg (2014); Kornhauser (2015); Hershovitz (2014); and Waldron (2013).

[11] Ronald Dworkin and I were on the New York University law faculty together for decades. Nominally, we were colleagues. But I regarded myself as his student. I will always be deeply grateful for all that I learned from him, and for the inspiration of his ferocious intellect and relentless insistence on getting to the bottom of things.

7

Dworkin and Unjust Law
by David Dyzenhaus[*]

1. Is There a Puzzle Regarding Unjust Law?

In the short chapter 19, "Law," in *Justice for Hedgehogs*, Ronald Dworkin says that "the puzzle of evil law" has had a "prominent place in seminars on legal theory" despite the fact that it is of "almost no practical importance."[1] In his view, the puzzle is primarily about cases in which judges find themselves faced with the problem of enforcing such a law. Should we say that the judges should not enforce it because it is unjust, or that they should not enforce it because it is not law? Since we are agreed on the practical outcome—judges should not enforce it—Dworkin claims that the "ancient jurisprudential problem is close to a verbal dispute."[2]

Dworkin was driven to confront the dispute in earlier work because his position is a natural law one in that he denies the Separation Thesis of legal positivism that there is no necessary connection between law and morality.[3] Since natural

[*] Professor of Law and Philosophy, University of Toronto. I thank members of my Introduction to Legal Philosophy class in the Fall semester of 2013 at New York University for the barrage of challenges and questions that have shaped much of its analysis; and Steve Coyne, Candice Delmas, Cheryl Misak, Hillary Nye, Hamish Stewart, and Kenneth Winston for many helpful suggestions about how to clarify its argument. In addition, I am thankful for the discussions with audiences at *The Legacy of Ronald Dworkin* (lawconf.mcmaster.ca), the McMaster University conference on the legacy of Ronald Dworkin, which was sponsored by the Ontario Legal Philosophy Partnership; at the Law Faculties of Amsterdam, Birmingham, Fordham, Genoa, Michigan, and New York Universities; a seminar at Vanderbilt Philosophy; as well as Steven Ascheim, Moshe Halbertal, Stephen Holmes, Mattias Kumm, Liam Murphy, and Bernhard Schlink. My greatest thanks are due to Ronald Dworkin for his patient and generous supervision of my doctoral thesis between 1984 and 1988, and for the questions he posed for me then that I am still struggling to answer, to this day. Earlier versions of Sections 1 and 2 of this chapter, as well as portions of Sections 4 and 5 were published as Dyzenhaus (2014).

[1] Dworkin (2011: 410).
[2] Dworkin (2011: 412).
[3] Hart (1958). Prominent legal positivists these days deny that Hart proposed this thesis or that legal positivism is committed to it, for example, Green (2008). I shall come back to this issue in Section 5.

law positions seem committed to the proposition that a law that violates the connection between law and morality is likely invalid, at the least legally suspect, the
existence of unjust law confronts them with a stark problem. To use the classical
formula, Dworkin has to be committed in some important sense to the proposition, *lex injusta non est lex*—an unjust law is not law—which means he has to face
the predicament for his theory created by the sheer facticity of unjust laws and
illegitimate legal systems.

Indeed, in *Justice for Hedgehogs*, Dworkin seemed to strengthen his natural
law commitments by deeming it a pervasive mistake for legal theory, one which
he himself had made, to suppose that the issue is whether there is a connection
between "two different intellectual domains" or systems: (1) law, which "belongs
to a particular community," and (2) morality, which does not, because "it consists
of a set of standards that have imperative force for everyone." Law, on this mistaken view, is "made by human beings" and it is a contingent fact what its content
is, whereas morality is "not made by anyone . . . and it is not contingent on any
human decision or practice."[4]

Dworkin suggested that we should replace the two-system picture of legal
theory with a one-system picture.[5] "Legal rights are political rights, but a special branch because they are properly enforceable on demand through adjudicative and coercive institutions without need for further legislation or lawmaking
activity."[6] Moreover, in the manuscript version of *Justice for Hedgehogs*, though
not in the book, Dworkin said that it would be counterintuitive to think that
"most of the subjects of most of the political communities over history had no
moral duty to obey the laws of their community."[7]

The puzzle of unjust law faces natural lawyers because they accept that among
the most important determinants of law are social facts—facts about the criteria
in a particular legal order for the validity of law, whether legislation, judge-made
law, administrative rule-making, even customary law. When, as a matter of fact,
individuals or groups with the authority to do so act in accordance with these
criteria, law comes into existence. Only this aspect of law can explain why, for
example, we distinguish between the law of the United States of America and
the law of Canada and why we do not suppose that we can find out the law of
either by asking what kind of law would it be morally best for either jurisdiction
to have made.

Natural lawyers, however, can be understood as supposing that in addition
to social facts, morality necessarily plays a role as a legal determinant, indeed,
that ultimately the authority of law is grounded in moral facts.[8] Consider that

---

⁴Dworkin (2011: 412).
⁵Dworkin (2011: 402).
⁶Dworkin (2011: 407).
⁷Quoted in Sreedhar and Delmas (2010: 746).
⁸I borrow the language of "determinants" from Coleman (2011). I say "can be seen as" because,
as I shall suggest in Section 5 the idea of moral facts acting as determinants is in itself rather
positivistic.

Dworkin's interpretivism holds that in a "hard case", the ideal judge decides the case by extracting a theory from the relevant positive law that shows the law, and the legal order as whole, in its best moral light. Whatever answer the theory gives to the legal question posed by the case is the "right answer", the answer that the judge is under a legal and moral duty to give. Dworkin's position is thus plausibly understood as claiming that the authority of law (as he would put it, law's ability to justify coercion) is grounded by that moral theory.

We shall see below that Dworkin came to reject this understanding of law's authority because it leaves him vulnerable to the following kind of objection. In an illegitimate legal system, one dedicated overall to extreme injustice, the best explanation of the law will surely be that it is the product of a morally repugnant ideology. Dworkin must thus suppose that a judge is under a legal duty to apply the repugnant ideology in hard cases since that ideology grounds the authority of the law in that order. It was on this basis that, in 1984, a South African law professor, and adherent of Dworkin's interpretivism, urged the liberal judges on the South African bench to resign. He argued that, at that stage in apartheid, a judge had no choice but to see that the best theory of the law was a white supremacist ideology that the judge was under a legal duty to use to resolve questions about what the law required.[9] And critics of Dworkin's position used the apartheid legal order as an example that showed why Dworkin's interpretivism had to be rejected.[10]

We shall also see below that Dworkin's response to this objection landed him in a dilemma between the natural law position that very unjust laws are invalid and the legal positivist position that if they are valid we should say that the laws are so unjust that they should be disobeyed. I have indicated that he sought to draw the sting from this dilemma by saying that it did not matter which limb one embraces because all will agree on the practical outcome—the judge should not apply such laws. But the obvious positivist response is that the limb that requires the judge to deny that a valid law is law replicates the mysteries of the natural law tradition, one that ultimately precludes "the possibility of morally illegitimate legal systems."[11] In contrast, legal positivism, with its focus on law as a matter of social facts, can support the limb that permits the judge unmysteriously to say, "This law is valid but too unjust to apply." Moreover, since positivism denies, in its Separation Thesis, that there is any necessary connection between law and morality,[12] it does not face any puzzle.

If this conclusion were so easily reached, there would be no puzzle about unjust law for philosophy of law, and philosophers of law would all be positivists.

---

[9] Wacks (1984).

[10] As Joseph Raz wrote in 1985, Dworkin's position would seem to "require a South African judge to use his power to extend Apartheid;" Raz (1994: 194, 208). For extended discussion of this claim, see Dyzenhaus (2010), the revised version of my Oxford thesis with Dworkin.

[11] Shapiro (2011: 49).

[12] Hart (1958: 620).

Seminars in legal theory would not have to discuss the merits of natural law positions, unless the seminars were focused on the history of legal thought. In that case, natural law could be brought out briefly from the dustbin of debunked theories, in much the same way as the command theory of H. L. A. Hart's utilitarian predecessors Jeremy Bentham and John Austin gets a cursory glance in such seminars, usually through the lens of Hart's summaries of their position. And just as Dworkin suggested that the problem of unjust law is an unproductive distraction, at times legal positivists suggest that legal theory is needlessly distracted by natural law positions, since these are not general theories of law, but projects for legal reform or (the charge against Dworkin) parochial theories of adjudication suited to one jurisdiction.

But even if one accepts that there is no puzzle of unjust law for legal positivism, positivists have been much preoccupied with unjust law. Hart, in *The Concept of Law,* devoted considerable space to explaining just why legal positivism's "wider concept of law," one which includes the study of valid legal rules with an unjust content, is to be preferred to the narrower concept of the natural law tradition, which he thought must deem such rules not to be law and thus not fit for jurisprudential analysis.[13] And positivism's facility with dealing with unjust law, exemplified in the Nazi legal system, is the motif of much of Hart's 1958 article "Positivism and the Separation of Law and Morals," that set the stage both for *The Concept of Law* and debates in legal philosophy in the latter half of the last century. Hart is best understood as arguing that positivism should be accepted because it has the correct theory of the nature of law and that an additional distinct advantage of the theory is its facility with clarifying the moral issues raised by unjust law.[14] But his preoccupation with unjust law could lead one to suppose that one should adopt legal positivism because of that facility.[15] Indeed, Scott Shapiro complains in his impressive attempt to redirect legal positivism that,

> Whether trying to debunk the law's pretensions to authority, or constructing a general theory of law, legal positivists have spent an excessive amount of time focusing on morally inadequate systems and tailoring their theories to fit those regimes. Their obsession with the Nazis and the Problem of Evil, however, has blinded them to a basic jurisprudential truth; a wicked regime is a botched legal system, much as 'the Earth is flat' is a failed scientific theory.[16]

Shapiro is not admitting here that legal positivism has a problem responding to unjust law. Rather, his point is that we should take as our paradigm for understanding law not law as the instrument of injustice, but law when it is doing what we think law in its nature does; in Shapiro's view, establishing plans that make it

---

[13] Hart (1994: 209-212).
[14] I agree on this point with Green (2013: 177; 203-207).
[15] Murphy (2008).
[16] Shapiro (2011: 391).

possible to solve pressing moral problems in complex societies that only the institution of law can solve. Like Dworkin, Shapiro regards unjust law as a distraction from what should be the main project of philosophy of law, though unlike Dworkin, he regards the existence of unjust law as a refutation of any natural law position, because the content of the legal plan can just as well be apartheid ideology as, say, liberal democracy.[17]

However, as I shall argue below, and as Shapiro acknowledges, a different problem does arise for legal positivism.[18] Recall that the problem of unjust law seems to arise directly for natural law positions because for them morality is a determinant of law. On the other side of the ledger, their claim about morality makes it easier for them to explain that law is not only a matter of social facts, but also something that has authority over its subjects. Legal authorities have or at least claim the right, we might say, to tell subjects what to do.[19] And we can plausibly suppose, as I suggested in my sketch of Dworkin's interpretive theory, that if law had the moral basis to it that a natural law position claimed, that basis would ground law's claim to authority.

Legal positivists accept that philosophy of law must explain law's authority. Consider that, in *The Concept of Law*, Hart identified as one of the three "recurrent issues" of legal philosophy the fact that both moral and legal rules share a vocabulary of obligation—"they withdraw certain areas of conduct from the free option of the individual to do as he likes." Moreover, Hart said that "one idea," "that of justice ... seems to unite both fields" and that justice "is both a virtue specially appropriate to law and the most legal of virtues. We think and talk of "justice *according* to law" and yet also of the justice or injustice *of* the laws.[20]

These facts alone, Hart said, "suggest the view that law is best understood as a "branch of morality or justice" which leads to the assertion that "an unjust law is not a law." But that assertion, he continued, has the "same ring of exaggeration and paradox if not falsity, as 'statutes are not laws' or 'constitutional law is not law'." And it has that ring because of the important differences between legal and moral rules.[21] Not least among these differences, he noted later in the book, is that moral rules and principles are immune "from deliberate change"; hence, "the idea of a moral legislature with competence to make and change morals, as legal enactments make and change law, is repugnant to the whole notion of morality."[22] In other words, Hart argued for a two-system picture, according to which law is contingent and subject to deliberate change by the body empowered to make that change, whereas morality is not.

---

[17] See Dyzenhaus (2012) for a discussion of Shapiro's claims in this regard.

[18] Shapiro (2011: 49).

[19] There is an important difference between saying that law has authority and that it claims authority, as I shall explain below.

[20] Hart (1994: 6-7). His emphasis.

[21] Hart (1994: 8).

[22] Hart (1994: 175, 177).

Yet Hart also warned against overreacting to natural law in a way that reduces law to facts that require no explanation of the vocabulary of obligation that law and morality share.[23] He rejected the command model of law—law is comprised of the commands of a legally unlimited sovereign backed by threats—in part because, as he famously put it, "Law is surely not the gunman situation writ large, and legal order is surely not to be thus simply identified with compulsion."[24] And such acknowledgment faces legal positivism with its own puzzle—how to generate the *ought* of legal authority from the *is* of social facts. Positivism sets itself the task of showing that the social facts of law are somehow also normative facts, but in a way that does not make the mistake of supposing that the obligations that arise from these facts are moral in nature.

I shall argue in Section 2 that one puzzle does lead to the other, that Hart's incorporation of a specifically legal idea of authority into philosophy of law raises very starkly for legal positivism the kinds of problems that we shall in Section 3 see also plague Dworkin's position. Indeed, the problem of unjust law, whether it manifests itself in the relation between legal subject and law or judge and law, serves mainly to point to a deeper problem about how to reconcile our intuitions that law is both a matter of fact and a matter of authority. That deeper problem manifests itself when a judge has to apply such a law to an individual. Sections 4 and 5 sketch how a modified version of Dworkin's theory, one that is enhanced with Lon L. Fuller's account of legality, might respond to the problems, thus illuminating the path forward for legal philosophy.

Three preliminary points help to frame the overall argument. The first is methodological. In my own work, I adopt a method of "integrative jurisprudence" that combines inquiry into politics, morality, and history.[25] As I understand it, this method takes seriously the pragmatist claim that all inquiry must be answerable to experience. Philosophy of law's answerability requires a mix of painstaking attention to actual legal experience, as well as painstaking attention to the minutiae of debates within legal philosophical positions that attend to the relevant aspects of the experience. This chapter is an exercise in the latter mode of analysis with the former side relied on in a summary of past work towards the end.

The second point is terminological. I shall use the term "unjust" rather than "evil" to describe the kind of law that creates the problem that is my focus. No natural law position argues for the anarchist claim that law is not law merely because it seems unjust to me. Rather, law is not law only when it is extremely unjust by some objective standard, and I shall use "unjust" in this sense. Moreover, as I shall argue below, that standard has to be internal to law. Law ceases to be law only when it fails by its own moral standards, which have to do with maintaining

---

[23] Hart (1994: 8). Hart mentions here Holmes's dictum that "The prophecies of what the courts will do in fact, and nothing more pretentious, are what I mean by the law," but he clearly has in mind, as well, Bentham's and Austin's command model of law.

[24] Hart (1958: 603).

[25] Berman (1988). Berman attributes coinage of the term to Jerome Hall.

the equal status as persons of the individuals law addresses. In other words, a natural law position holds that there is a moral order immanent in the law as we find it, in social facts about the law as it is, and this moral order responds to the problem of extremely unjust laws. The legal positivist tradition that Joseph Raz describes as "realist and unromantic"[26] in its outlook on the law would be part of an opposing tradition that does not think that the legal world as we find it has the resources to respond to such injustice, so it consigns the problem elsewhere; we might say, from the legal to the moral system. The difference between using "unjust" (and therefore manageable by law) and "evil" (and therefore unmanageable by law) as the description of such laws should therefore indicate which tradition one belongs to, though as we have seen with Dworkin, actual debate is not precise in this way.[27]

The final point is about the implications of the debate about unjust law, which often seems to those observing it strange because it is a debate about law in distant places or times.[28] However, as I shall argue below, the debate does matter to those who think that their legal orders are more or less just, or at any rate not unjust, because it helps to alert them to problems of injustice that might be otherwise hard to detect. Indeed, law itself helps in this regard in that the commitment

---

[26] Raz (1994: 194).

[27] In making such claims, natural law positions join what Susan Neiman in her illuminating work on evil in modern thought calls the theodistic tradition, which holds that God's works in the world as we find it are for the best, according to some intrinsic moral order; Neiman (2002). Neiman suggests that an atheistic position can also fit within this tradition. Consider, first, that in the debate I am about to describe Hart rejected natural law positions because they share a "romantic optimism that all the values that we cherish ultimately will fit into a single system, that not one of them has to be sacrificed or compromised to accommodate another." And he quoted the following lines as an expression of the optimism he rejected:

All Discord Harmony not understood
All partial evil Universal Good.

These lines are from Alexander Pope's philosophical poem, *Essay on Man*, as Neiman shows, a central text in the theodistic tradition. See Hart (1958: 620); Neiman (2002: 31-6). Consider, second, that Lon Fuller in his response to Hart thought that the fundamental difference between them boiled down to Hart's assumption that "evil aims may have as much coherence and inner logic as good ones," whereas Fuller expressed a belief he recognized might seem naïve that goodness and coherence were more likely to go together because

when men are compelled to explain and justify their decisions, the effect will generally be to pull those decisions towards goodness, by whatever ultimate standards of goodness there are. Accepting these beliefs, I find a considerable incongruity in any conception that envisages a possible future in which the common law would "work itself pure from case to case" toward a more perfect realization of iniquity. Fuller (1958: 636).

See further, Shapiro (2011: 49): "Just as theologians have struggled to explain how evil is possible given the necessary existence of God, the natural lawyer must account for the possibility of evil legal systems given that law is necessarily grounded in moral facts. Positivists, on the other hand, have no such difficulties."

[28] See Dworkin's comment in note 79 below.

to governing through law helps to bring injustice to the surface as a problem that the legal order needs to solve in order to maintain itself in good legal shape.

2. The Puzzle for Legal Positivism

In Part IV of his 1958 essay "Positivism and the Separation of Law and Morals," Hart addresses the topic of unjust law in an engagement with Gustav Radbruch, the German philosopher of law. After the war, Radbruch, in reaction to the horrors of Nazism and what he regarded as German lawyers' complicity, advanced what became known as the "Radbruch Formula": "Extreme injustice is no law."[29] Hart vehemently rejects Radbruch's claim that law's role as an instrument of Nazi evil should undermine the positivist commitment to the Separation Thesis. In particular, he was affronted by Radbruch's suggestion that the German legal profession's commitment to a positivist view of law had contributed to the horrors because the positivist slogan, "Law is law," caused their failure to "protest against the enormities they were required to perpetrate in the name of the law."[30] Hart accuses Radbruch of naïveté because he had only "half digested the spiritual message of liberalism," the message in fact delivered by legal positivism: "Law is law" tells us that law "is not morality," hence, should not be thought to "supplant morality."[31]

Hart seems to think that the point is sufficiently made by quoting a paragraph in which Austin imagines a law that makes punishable by death an "act innocuous, or positively beneficial." I am tried and condemned for committing this act and object that it is "contrary to the law of God," that is, to natural law. Austin says that "the court of justice will demonstrate the inconclusiveness of my reasoning by hanging me up, in pursuance of the law of which I have impugned the validity."[32] Hart appears to endorse Austin's claim that this example shows that those who say that human laws cease to be law if they conflict with "the fundamental principles of morality" are talking "stark nonsense."[33] Rather, they should "speak plainly" and say "that laws may be law but too evil to be obeyed."[34]

But Hart suggests that he can add support for his position by going beyond a "mere academic discussion" to a problem of legal practice, the issue raised by the Grudge Informer Case. In this case, as he understood things, a postwar German court found that a woman was guilty of the crime of illegal deprivation of liberty for turning in her husband for making derogatory remarks about Hitler. Such remarks were considered a crime under two Nazi statutes, and so the woman

---

[29] Radbruch (2006).
[30] Hart (1958: 617).
[31] Hart (1958: 618). See Cottrell (2013) for a nuanced treatment of Radbruch.
[32] Hart (1958: 616).
[33] Hart (1958: 616).
[34] Hart (1958: 620).

claimed that what she did was not illegal. Thus the court had to rely on the Radbruch Formula in order to claim that the Nazi statutes were not really law.[35]

Hart's argument is that the Radbruch Formula obscures the moral dilemma raised by the case: Should one leave the woman unpunished or should one "sacrifice a very precious moral principle endorsed by most legal systems," the principle against retroactive punishment?[36] The formula does so because it requires the judges to pretend that valid law was not really law. The only way for the dilemma to be candidly faced if one thinks that the woman should be punished is, Hart asserts, for the legislature, fully conscious of the moral sacrifice involved, to "enact a frankly retroactive law."[37]

Hence, Hart supposes that a correct moral appreciation of this difficult practical problem is facilitated by the Separation Thesis, which is an important corrective to the reaction in Germany that the decisions of the postwar courts that deployed the formula signaled the triumph of natural law over legal positivism, a reaction that Hart describes as "hysteria."[38] Legal positivism, in contrast to natural law, permits us to "speak plainly" by using "a moral condemnation which everybody can understand" and "makes an immediate and obvious claim to moral attention." In contrast, an assertion that "these evil things are not law" is one "many people do not believe" and it raises "a whole host of philosophical issues before it can be accepted."[39]

Most participants in the debate that followed Fuller's response to Hart failed to notice that Hart implicitly relied on a difference between two perspectives in play in Part IV of "Positivism and the Separation of Law and Morals." There is the perspective of a citizen confronted by an unjust law and thus with the question of the moral evaluation of law's claim that he is under a duty to *obey* the law. And there is the perspective of a judge confronted by the same unjust law, but with a question that must be framed differently, even if we suppose that the answer is no different. For the judge's question is whether she is under a duty to *apply* the law to whomever it affects, thus facing the affected subjects with the first question.

It might seem that Hart should suppose that his own formula—"Disobey unjust law, but don't deny its validity"—needs only a slight adaptation for the situation of judges—"Do not apply unjust law, but don't deny its validity." But both Austin in the paragraph Hart quoted and Hart himself in his analysis of the

---

[35] Both Hart and Fuller relied on a flawed report of the case, as H. O. Pappe pointed out in Pappe (1960). The court did not invalidate the laws but came to the conclusion that the woman was guilty because she was the "indirect perpetrator" of the crime of illegal deprivation of liberty. For my own discussion as well as my translation of the case, see Dyzenhaus (2008). Hart (1994: 304) said that Pappe's analysis should be "studied," but did not himself take the time to confront it, in my view, because of the assumption I discuss in the text that the law can have any content.

[36] Hart (1958: 619-620).

[37] Hart (1958: 619-620).

[38] Hart (1958: 619).

[39] Hart (1958: 620).

Grudge Informer Case reject this adaptation. Notice Austin's deliberate use of the phrase "court of *justice*." His point is that the justice the law demands might be something we should morally condemn; as Hart put it in the next section of the essay, the "justice in the administration of the law" is "not justice of the law."[40] But it seems that the judge *qua* judge is not entitled to refuse to apply the law and Hart commits himself to the same view in reserving the authority to retroactively invalidate the Nazi statutes to the legislature. For although Hart's main point is that something goes wrong if one pretends that a valid law is not law, in 1958, he did not appear to think it permissible for a judge to engage in an exercise of frank retroactive invalidation of unjust law or to refuse to apply it.

Now we might think that the question of whether judges have the authority to invalidate retroactively is to be resolved by looking at facts about the jurisdiction, and Hart is making the likely unproblematic assumption that postwar German judges did not have such authority. But why does he deny to judges the option of refusing to *apply* unjust law if "law is law" in the way that the Separation Thesis insists we understand that slogan?

One possible answer is that the judge *qua* judge is under both a moral and a legal duty to apply the law as she finds it. She is thus precluded from considering the moral considerations external to law that the citizen should rely on when it comes to the question of obedience, or from confronting the kind of moral dilemma that Hart thought was at stake in the Grudge Informer Case. It would follow that unjust law does confront judges with a moral dilemma, since (to use Fuller's terminology) judges subscribe to an "ideal of fidelity to law" that requires them to uphold the law, whatever its content. In other words, the standing legal and moral duty for judges anywhere to apply the law, whatever its content, does face them with moral problems if the content is unjust, but the legal and moral duty side always overrides the purely moral duty side. Alternatively, one might say that judges are under a moral and legal duty to apply the law whatever its content, but that in the case of unjust law, they may weigh the moral costs of not doing their legal and moral duty against the moral costs of doing it.

Indeed, the dilemma becomes even more complex if one characterizes, as might seem more intuitive, the "very precious principle" against retroactivity as a principle of *legality* endorsed by all legal orders. Such a characterization is not meant to contrast legality with morality, but, as Fuller argued, in order to point out that there are some moral principles that are intrinsic to legality. That Hart chose to describe the principle against retroactivity as moral rather than legal is significant, a point I shall come back to below. For the moment, I want to note that Hart, in my view, would have rejected both the alternatives set out in the last paragraph with the attendant moral complexity they raise. But that rejection is problematic in light of the elaboration of and changes in his position with the publication in 1961 of *The Concept of Law*.

---

[40] Hart (1958: 624).

Hart argues there that "obedience" misleadingly describes what judges do when they apply the law since one can obey the law without supposing that this is the "right thing" to do; for example, because one fears punishment. In contrast, courts have to adopt the "internal point of view" according to which the "rule of recognition"—the ultimate rule of the legal order that certifies the validity of particular rules—provides "a public, common standard of correct judicial decision."[41] Indeed, if judges do not adopt that internal point of view, one of the "two minimum conditions necessary and sufficient for the existence of a legal system" no longer obtains.[42] Hence, it seems that judges are indeed under a standing obligation of some sort to apply the law of their jurisdiction whatever its content, which distinguishes their normative situation from that of the citizen.[43] For the law does create a legal obligation for the citizen, and thus faces him, in certain situations, with a clash between legal and moral duty. But since the legal duty seems morally inert in Hart's view, we could say that the citizen is in a purely prudential dilemma—obey an unjust law or be punished. In contrast, the judge's legal duty to apply the law seems normatively different from the morally inert, legal obligation of the citizen to obey, yet Hart remained anxious to insist that there is no moral component to it.

However, one has also to take into account that in *The Concept of Law*, Hart seems to have changed his mind about the situation of the judge faced by unjust law. When he returns to the issues of Radbruch and the Grudge Informer Case, he revises his own formula to read: "This is law; but it is too iniquitous to be applied or obeyed."[44] And Hart emphasizes that though he still thinks that the Separation Thesis helps to clarify the moral issues to which the existence of unjust law gives rise, one has to appreciate that the problem of morality and justice for a person who had to decide whether to obey an unjust law is "very different" from the problem that the postwar courts faced.[45] Thus, in 1961, Hart clearly has in mind that the dilemma the courts faced was the moral dilemma he described in 1958, between letting the woman go unpunished and sacrificing the principle of *nulla poena sine lege*. But matters have to be more complicated, as I indicated, if only because the court that decides to punish the Grudge Informer has to say: "As a judge it is my duty to apply the law; the law requires that you not be punished; but I am going to punish you, because that is what my moral duty requires." The question remains how we give content to the idea of a duty to apply the law

---

[41] Hart (1958: 116-117).

[42] Hart (1958: 116-117). See Mertens (2002: 202-4) for a careful discussion of these issues, although I disagree with him on the question of whether Hart failed to see that the judicial perspective requires a different analysis.

[43] Joseph Raz suggested to me at the McMaster Conference that Hart might have supposed that judges are under such a duty because of their oath of office. But my argument is that Hart thought there was such a duty even if the absence of an oath.

[44] Hart (1994: 208).

[45] Hart (1994: 211).

as found, if the law is morally inert as Hart seems to suggest in advocating the Separation Thesis.[46]

Notice that if the Separation Thesis does not help to respond to such complexity, one of the reasons Hart advances for adopting the "wider" or positivist concept of law that regards unjust law as morally but not legally problematic, is undermined, because the wider concept fails to assist "our moral deliberations."[47] Does that leave intact the other reason—that positivism is superior to natural law theories because of the way it assists "our theoretical inquiries"? Hart thinks that it does. Natural law's narrower concept of law excludes from legal philosophy rules that are legally valid, but beyond the moral pale; and it is the task of legal philosophy to "group and consider together as 'law' all rules which are valid by the formal tests of a [legal] system . . ., even though some of them offend against a society's own morality or against what we may hold to be an enlightened or true morality."[48]

The natural lawyer can respond to Hart's claims about both moral deliberation and theoretical inquiry in the following way. Hart's concept of law fails to bring to light the moral complexity caused by the existence of unjust law because that concept cannot explain why a judge faced with such law is troubled in a way not reducible to the clash between two moral values that Hart detected in the Grudge Informer Case. And Hart cannot do so because his commitment to the Separation Thesis precludes him from supposing that the legal duty of the judge has any necessary moral quality to it.

Indeed, as we saw, Hart declines to call even the moral principle against retroactivity a legal principle, which is odd because the principle is not a free-standing moral principle, but one which has a place only within the institutional structure of a legal order. If he had said it was both legal and moral that would go some way to explaining why the postwar judges had both a moral and legal duty to apply the law, as found, that was not dependent on a contingent fact about their legal order. Rather, the judges would have a duty to uphold principles of legality, including the principle against retroactivity, because the internal point of view of judges anywhere requires a commitment to such principles. They are among the "conditions necessary and sufficient for the existence of a legal system."

Notice that this point suffices to make the issue more than a failure to account for moral complexity. Hart's theory of law might be seen as narrower than that of natural law because it does not include whatever feature of law gives law the moral quality that gives rise to such complexity, for example, a legal and moral principle such as the principle against retroactivity, or whatever might ground a

---

[46] Fuller (1958: 656). It does not help to put the matter into a kind of *oratio obliqua*. Raz, for example, offers the suggestion that we might consider the judge's duty here as in the same light as we consider such statements as, "As a Catholic, my duty is . . ." But he also argues that judges must consider their legal duty to apply the law as a duty from the moral perspective. See Raz (2004).

[47] Hart (1994: 209).

[48] Hart (1994: 209).

standing obligation for judges to apply the law. Of course, Hart could respond, as he did in Part V of his 1958 essay, and was to do more elaborately in his later critiques of Fuller, that even if such principles are necessary features of law, compliance with them is "unfortunately compatible with very great iniquity."[49]

Hart was, however, rather and perhaps deliberately ambiguous about this response. He might have meant that no important connection between law and morality emerges out of the fact that law has to conform to principles of legality to be law, because even though the principles of legality are moral, the moral quality they give to law is so weak that it is easily outweighed by other moral considerations. But, as he sometimes indicated, and as Raz was to argue in an important essay on the rule of law,[50] on the positivist view, such principles are not moral. They serve only to make law into a more effective instrument of the goals enacted into law, so that one's moral focus can be that of the citizen on the moral merits of the content of the law. But if that argument is correct, we are still left with the question of what feature of law makes it authoritative.

Perhaps more importantly, Hart's objection to natural law theory that it narrows the scope of philosophy of law by consigning the study of unjust laws to some discipline other than philosophy of law has to be matched with an objection that positivism consigns all moral questions that arise about unjust law to other disciplines, thus impoverishing philosophy of law. To say with Austin that "[t]he existence of law is one thing, its merit or demerit another,"[51] is to assert that the other thing—the question of obedience to law—is a matter for moral, not legal philosophy.

Similarly, Hart argued in 1958 that in cases in which it is controversial what the law requires, judges have to legislate by deciding the matter in accordance with their view of what law ought to be. He offered two reasons why one should not infer from the necessity of such judicial reliance on "oughts" that there is a necessary connection between law and morality. First, this kind of decision takes place in the penumbra of uncertainty about what the law requires, in contrast to the determinate core of settled law.[52] Hence, all philosophy of law can say about such decision-making is that it amounts to an act of discretion or judicial legislation based, at least ultimately, on extra-legal considerations. Second, the judicial sense of the appropriate ought will be contingent not only on the judge but also on the legal order, so we should see that the oughts operative in the penumbra might be highly immoral.

Hart offered as an example an ought that he thinks might have informed the interpretation of the Nazi judges who convicted and sentenced to death the husband of the Grudge Informer: "What sentence would both terrorize the public at large and keep the friends and family of the prisoner in suspense so that both

---

[49] Hart (1994: 207).

[50] Raz (1983: 210). For discussion of Hart's changing position, see Waldron (2008).

[51] Hart (1958: 596).

[52] Hart (1958: 607-615).

hope and fear would cooperate as factors making for subservience?"[53] Hart notes that the "prisoner of such a system would be regarded simply as an object to be used in pursuit of these aims," but, he says, this would "still be an intelligent and purposive" decision and "from one point of view the decision would be as it ought to be."[54]

The first reason is the more important one for Hart. The second is offered as a kind of *ad hominem* refutation of those who might "invite" us to accept a different description, one offered by a Dworkinian account of adjudication whose main features Hart succinctly and presciently outlined in 1958.[55] In other words, the first reason is that "legislation" accurately describes what judges do in such cases, whereas the other reason points out that those who suggest that there are values inherent in the law that determine morally and legally right answers are committed to supposing absurdly that the immoral point of view Hart sketches in his example can tell the judge what he morally speaking ought to do.

Hart appears to think that the kind of ought in his example is legally unproblematic. Consider, however, the point of view of the prisoner who has to regard himself as, in Hart's own words, "an object to be used in pursuit of these aims." Why may the prisoner not draw on the resources of Hart's legal positivism and say that he is the victim of a gunman situation writ large, not a legal order that purports to exercise authority over him? Put differently, it is one thing for Austin to say that the execution of the condemned man, in the example Hart quotes in refutation of Radbruch, proves the man's mistake in saying that the law was no law, since Austin's theory of law *is* that law is the commands of an uncommanded commander backed by threats. But it is altogether another thing for Hart, who rejects that theory, to say of the person objectified in this way that he should regard as authoritative the directive that consigns him to prison and execution— that he should regard the directive as having changed his normative situation, however undeniably it changed his physical situation.

Moreover, a law that told judges to impose the harshest sentence possible in a bid to intimidate the population, no matter what the criminal law of their land directed them to do, would be a very odd law, legally speaking. It would tell judges to act arbitrarily in violation of part of the law directly relevant to their decision. As H. O. Pappe pointed out, the law did not in fact tell judges to act so, since large parts of pre-Nazi German law survived into the Nazi period, including the law under which the Grudge Informer was prosecuted.[56] That point is subject to a challenge that the presence of such resources for judges was entirely contingent, and I shall come back to this issue in Section 4. But we should note that Pappe also argued that one should be a little slower than Hart in getting to the conclusion that such an ought—one from a point of view that made the

---

[53] Hart (1958: 613-614).
[54] Hart (1958: 614).
[55] Hart (1958: 612).
[56] Pappe (1960: 271).

wishes of party officials the standard—could be made into a legal standard, another issue I shall return to.[57]

Hence, the question of the role of legal oughts in the interpretive process, which Hart thinks he can put aside when he deals with Radbruch and the Grudge Informer Case, potentially complicates his assumption that the problem is how to respond to law that is clearly law and clearly unjust. For there is a prior question in the situation of unjust law about both whether there is law at all and if there is, what its content is. But even to see that question requires a concept of law that does not suppose that law can have any content whatsoever, and it is only because Hart makes that supposition that he can compartmentalize the different criticisms of the Separation Thesis and pick them off one by one.

Consider that in Part V of the 1958 essay, Hart mentions "the normally fulfilled assumption that a legal system aims at some form of justice colours the whole way in which we interpret specific rules in particular cases, and if this normally fulfilled assumption were not fulfilled no one would have any reason to obey except fear (and probably not that) and still less, of course, any moral obligation to obey."[58] He goes on to say that if there were not some group that received the benefit of protection from the law, the system would "sink to the status of a set of meaningless taboos" and "no one denied those benefits would have any reason to obey except fear and would have every moral reason to revolt."[59]

Now Hart, in Part V, is anticipating a Fullerian position that law has to comply with principles of legality to be law and that such compliance imparts a moral quality to the law. He concedes that legal orders do all overlap with morality in that they afford morally valuable protections to individuals, for example, in criminal law and property law. He also concedes that there is "in the very notion of law consisting of general rules, something which prevents us from treating it as if morally it is utterly neutral, ... " Generality, Hart says, requires "[n]atural procedural justice" which consists of "principles of objectivity and impartiality in the administration of the law" and "which are designed to ensure that rules are applied to only to what are genuine cases of the rule or at least to minimize the risks of inequalities in this sense."[60] But such concessions do not, Hart claims, undermine the Separation Thesis. The protections do not have to be afforded to everyone, and laws "that are hideously oppressive" can be applied with "pedantic impartiality."[61]

However, this claim leaves in place and indeed sharpens the question raised by Part II of his 1958 essay. Why should we think that law, on the assumption that it more than the gunman writ large, governs the lives of those in the group that get no protection and who are deprived of it by hideously oppressive commands

---

[57] Pappe (1960: 271-272).
[58] Hart (1958: 622).
[59] Hart (1958: 624).
[60] Hart (1958: 624).
[61] Hart (1958: 624).

backed by force? And the concessions complicate Parts III and IV of the essay because, if there are legal reasons for thinking that in the normal case "some form of justice colours the whole way in which we interpret specific rules in particular cases," it seems to follow that judges confronted by an unjust law face a legal problem, not merely a clash between legal and moral duty. Such a problem requires them to ask, "Does the law really have that content despite the fact that the legislature seems in fact to have stipulated exactly it?" And if their answer to the question is "Yes," they are driven by legal duty to confront the Radbruch Formula, since if they apply that content to the oppressed group, they are carrying out the gunman's commands, not implementing law.

The deep issue here is the question of the role of authority in Hart's conception of law. If a central feature of law that any philosophy of law has to explain is law's authority, legal positivism is faced with the puzzle of unjust law. If the commands of the powerful are incapable of sustaining a claim to be exercised with right on those subject to their power, the commands lack authority, and therefore lose any claim to legal status.

Hart would, of course, think that this argument merely reproduces Radbruch's "naïveté." And in *The Concept of Law*, he describes "an extreme case" in which "the internal point of view with its characteristic use of normative legal language (This is a valid rule) might be confined to the official world." Such a society, he goes, on, might be deplorably sheeplike; the sheep might end in the slaughterhouse." But, he adds, "there is little reason for thinking that it could not exist or for denying it the title of legal system."[62] Hart's point is that if there is a rule of recognition and that rule certifies other rules as valid, the other rules have authority, whatever their content. But if the only reason those outside the official group follow the rules is that they are sheeplike, that is, they think that the fact that a rule has been validly made is reason enough to obey it, they are making the rather large mistake, in Hart's own argument, of only "half digesting" the message of legal positivism. Moreover, the source of their mistake is in thinking that a secondary rule of recognition imparts full legal authority to primary rules, whatever their content, whereas in a "primitive society" in which there are only primary rules, recognition as authoritative is content-dependent: "the rules must be widely accepted as setting critical standards for the behaviour of the group."[63]

From a natural law perspective, the mistake is to suppose that rules have full legal authority, whatever full legal authority means, as long as the rules have been certified as valid. In contrast, a natural law position that argues that law's authority is grounded on some moral basis beyond such certification will not make it so easy for individuals to become sheep. Nor, despite positivists' claims to the contrary, need such a position lead to "obsequious quietism"[64] because individuals are asked to accept that law has a moral quality. Rather, the individuals have

---

[62] Hart (1994: 117).

[63] Hart (1994: 117).

[64] Bentham's phrase, see Hart (1958: 598).

to weigh their legal/moral duty to obey the law against the dictates of conscience. This is a morally complex situation, the complexity of which can only be appreciated by a natural law position that explains why law has some moral quality to it that makes plausible law's authority.

When Hart's position is viewed through the lens of his responses to the issue of unjust law, we can appreciate not only why unjust law presents a puzzle for his version of legal positivism, but also why important developments within his tradition of legal philosophy make the puzzle more acute. I have in mind here primarily Raz's argument that it is in the nature of law that law must claim legitimate authority and that judges are committed to endorsing that claim.[65]

---

[65] Although Raz took the features of authority that he identified to be exemplified in legal practice, the direction of the argument is from the nature of authority to the nature and limits of law. See Raz (1994). On that account, an entity that is capable of claiming authority, which satisfies the "non-moral conditions" for being an authority, is one that can communicate a judgment to others on what the balance of reasons that applies to them requires; Raz (1994: 199-202). The entity thus not only claims authority but also justified authority. But whether or not it has such authority will depend both on whether its judgment is right and whether those subject to it would in fact better serve their own interests by following the authority's judgment than by following their own. The entity has to satisfy the conditions set by the "normal justification thesis," Raz (1994: 198). On this account, judges in telling parties what the law is that applies to them are committed to endorsing law's claim to legitimate authority.

The implications of this account are not that easy to settle. Here are some candidates:

1. If law does not live up to the normal justification thesis, one possibility is that since the law is illegitimate, it lacks authority, and therefore is not law. That is, if the moral conditions for having authority are set by the normal justification thesis, and if satisfying those conditions is necessary for law to have authority, then satisfying the non-moral conditions does not suffice for an artifact to be law.

2. Another possibility is that the de facto authority of the law is one thing, established by satisfying the non-moral conditions, but legitimate authority is another, since it requires satisfying the moral conditions. But then Raz's account would be no different from Hart's, with his claim about a moral component to judicial duty no more than, as Hart said of Dworkin's theory, an "idle decoration," Hart's charge against Dworkin in Hart (1982: 127, 152).

3. Yet another possibility is that, somewhat like Robert Alexy, Raz thinks that among the non-moral conditions that have to be satisfied is that the law must claim to have legitimate authority and officials must endorse that claim. See Alexy (1989: 176-177). Thus the Nazis had law as long as Nazi officials made such claims, and despite the fact that Nazi law was wholly illegitimate. But that seems to make a legal order's existence turn not on the rule of recognition, various institutions, etc. Instead, it turns on a very formal claim that will always be satisfied—that at least the officials will claim and likely think that the order they serve is legitimate. See further Raz (1979: 8-9).

Note that Hart, unlike Raz, can say that the law *has* authority, not merely that it *claims* authority. And Hart can say this because, in his view, the authority law has is morally inert. Hence, for Hart, the legitimacy of law depends on some source external to law, for example, liberal morality. (Though in an interview in 1988, Hart distinguishes between legal legitimacy and moral legitimacy and seems to suggest that the law always has the former. See Hart (1988: 283-284).) He disagrees with the command theorists in that, as he understands them, they do without a theory of law's authority. The command theory is compatible with a claim that *the* law has authority, for example, when the gunman is a democratic legislature. But then the authority of the law comes from a source external to law, which requires an argument about the legitimacy of making decisions about the public good democratically. But law as such has no claim to either authority or legitimacy and we do not need

On this kind of argument, which seems to build moral aspirations into the concept of law, it is even more difficult to see how X could be law if it were unjust. It also becomes difficult to see how these are not developments in legal positivism that begin to blur the divide between it and natural law. It is for such reasons that, in my view, Hart in an essay followed an attack on Dworkin, which I shall sketch in the next section, with vigorous resistance to Raz's early thoughts along these lines.[66] But my argument in this section has been that Hart himself blurred that divide and confronted legal positivism with the puzzle of unjust law the moment he made the idea of authority central to the positivist account of the nature of law.

3. The Puzzle for Dworkin

When Dworkin put judge Hercules at center stage of his interpretivism, he both reconfigured the debate about unjust law and made himself vulnerable. On the one hand, he reconfigured the debate because the issue of unjust law had traditionally been seen as one about the appropriate stance of the individual—the legal subject—faced with such a law. On the other hand, because the moral quality seemed to come from the fact that correct answers to hard cases were those constructed in light of the best theory of the positive law, it also seemed that Dworkin made interpretivism hostage to facts about the positive law.

Consider that, on Dworkin's view, interpretation has two dimensions. The first is "fit"—What range of answers is plausibly consistent with as much as possible of the relevant positive law? The second is "justification"—What answer is given by the theory that best justifies that law? Dworkin was clear that justification is the more important dimension. A more sound justification should be preferred to a less sound one that fits more of the relevant positive law. But it seemed that if, on the dimension of fit, the social facts about the law of a jurisdiction overwhelmingly pointed to an underpinning immoral ideology of which the positive law was the instrument, then on the other dimension, the theory that best justified the law would be one that showed it in a very bad moral light.

In his first response to this kind of challenge, Dworkin contemplated that a situation might arise in which the "institutional right is clearly settled by established legal materials...and clearly conflicts with background moral rights."[67] The institutional right, he said, "provides a genuine reason, the importance of which will vary with the general justice or wickedness of the system as a whole, for a decision one way, but certain considerations of morality present an important reason against it." In this situation, he concluded, the only options open to the

---

the idea of authority to explain the nature of law. Notice that if one adopts this option, there is no problem in saying that if the law has authority, the authority it has is justified, because these two judgments are one and the same and purely external.

[66] Hart (1982: 153-161).

[67] Dworkin (1978L 326-327), responding to Greenawalt (1977).

judge are to lie, by saying that "the legal rights are different from what he believes they are," or to resign, which will "ordinarily be of little help," or to stay in office and hope "against odds, that his appeal based on moral grounds will have the same practical effect as a lie would." Dworkin also said that he agreed with Hart's argument for candor in the 1958 essay that it would be "unwise to make this lie a matter of jurisprudential theory." Hence, the "accurate description" is "that legal and moral rights here conflict." And that description, Dworkin went on, applies to both easy and hard cases, so that "in spite of the influence that morality must have on the answer in a hard case," "jurisprudence must report the conflict accurately, leaving to the judge both the difficult moral decision he must make and the lie he may be forced to tell."[68]

Hart seized on this set of remarks, as well as a passage in which he reports Dworkin's concession, that in a wicked legal system the '"soundest theory of the law"' would include morally repugnant principles sanctioning an absolutist dictatorship or morally odious policies like "blacks are less worthy of concern than whites."[69] In Hart's view, these concessions "surrender the idea that legal rights and duties are a species of moral right and duties," leaving Dworkin's theory with the truism that there will be a moral justification for good law but not for evil law, i.e., with a position "indistinguishable from legal positivism."[70]

The only answer Dworkin could have to this criticism, Hart thought, is the "last-ditch" and "hopeless" defense that individuals in a wicked legal system have a moral right that judges treat like cases alike, whether this is a matter of deciding a case by reference to settled law or by reference to the least bad principles underpinning unsettled law when the law is indeterminate. Since there can be no moral reason for repeating "past evil," Hart concluded that this defense failed when it came to settled law. Dworkin's moral terminology here amounted "an idle but confusing decoration to the positivist simple conclusion." And he added that when the law is unsettled, there can be no moral reason for extending principles merely because they are the least morally odious available.[71]

Dworkin gave a two-part answer to what he regarded as the "uncharacteristic vehemence" of Hart's criticism,[72] and the structure of that answer remained constant through to *Justice for Hedgehogs*. The first part was an *ad hominem* criticism which I will not spend much time on here, both because Dworkin did not elaborate it, and because my detailed account of Hart in the last section was intended in part to explain why the criticism is on the mark. It is that if positivists wish to claim that legal philosophy clarifies how law makes the situation of a judge faced with applying an unjust law morally complex, they must suppose that the fact that

---

[68] Dworkin (1978: 326-327).

[69] Hart (1982: 127, 150), quoting from Dworkin (1978: 343).

[70] Hart (1982: 150-151). Hart adds that there cannot in any case be any individual expectations when the law is indeterminate, that is, because (at least on the positivist account) the law supplies no answer in such cases.

[71] Hart (1982: 152-153).

[72] Dworkin (1984: 257).

there is law supplies a moral reason of some kind to the judge to apply the law. The fact that there is law either affects the moral situation, something Dworkin's theory seeks to explain, or it is morally inert, as Hart seemed to insist, in which case the judge is not in a moral dilemma.[73] The contribution of the last section is thus in part to show that Dworkin was right to claim that legal positivism finds itself in a dilemma on this issue. But, as I now explain, that contribution also prepares the way for seeing why Dworkin cannot on his own escape a similar dilemma.

Dworkin's new argument confronts the situation of a judge starkly faced with a clearly unjust law, though he did, we should note, express doubts that such situations will easily arise.[74] It supports a different set of options for the judge, replacing the previous three—lie, resign, apply the law and make a moral protest—with two. The judge declares the law invalid because it so unjust, not merely because of the injustice of the particular law, but because the law partakes of the pervasive injustice of a wholly illegitimate system. Alternatively, the particular law is unjust but the system is on the whole legitimate, or at least not altogether illegitimate, in which case the judge should recognize the law as valid, but refuse to apply it.

Dworkin's argument uses the analogy of an ill-advised and vague promise. For example, I promise a friend who is also my employee to fire another employee.[75] Suppose that the best interpretation of the promise is that it was made out of a flawed conception of friendship that required the employee be fired even if she had done nothing wrong. If one thinks there is any kind of moral reason to keep such a promise, that reason cannot depend on the principles that figured in working out its content; rather, it must have its source in the "morality of promise-keeping."[76]

On this analogy, one should see that it is a mistake to suppose with Hart that Dworkin's account of "how legal rights are identified in hard cases" supplies the reasons for supposing that those rights, "once identified, have some claim to be enforced in court."[77] In terms Dworkin coined later, Hart had mistaken the question that is the legal philosopher's focus, the question of the "grounds of law"— the circumstances in which particular propositions of law should be taken to be sound or true"—with the political philosopher's question about the "force of law"—"the relative power of any true proposition of law to justify coercion in different sorts of exceptional circumstance."[78]

At least two questions arise from this set of claims. First, what could make it the case that an unjust legal system creates moral reasons? Second, does the answer to that question tell us why morally decent legal systems create moral

---

[73] Dworkin (1978: 327); (1984: 259). Fuller (1958: 656) made exactly this criticism.

[74] Dworkin (1984: 299, note 4).

[75] Dworkin (1984: 257-258).

[76] Dworkin (1984: 258). For the most elaborate account of this point, see Dworkin (2011: 407-409).

[77] Dworkin, (1984: 257).

[78] Dworkin (1986: 110).

reasons or does it apply only in the "exceptional circumstances" of an unjust legal system?[79]

Dworkin argues that if an unjust legal system is a source of moral reasons for judges to apply its laws that arises from the fact that there is a "general political situation" such that "the central power of the community has been administered through an articulate constitutional structure the citizens have been encouraged to obey and treat as a source of rights and duties, and that the citizens have in fact done so."[80] But his point is only that if there were such reasons, the situation would be the source of the reasons, not that the fact that there was such a situation supplied reasons. Indeed, in *Justice for Hedgehogs*, he says that since the Nazi order was wholly illegitimate, it faced judges with a "prudential" rather than a moral dilemma, because there was no force to Nazi edicts. In contrast, in the antebellum situation of American judges from northern states faced with a duty by constitutionally authorized Fugitive Slave Acts to return escaped slaves to their situation of slavery, there was a moral reason. The American legal order, Dworkin thinks we may assume, "was sufficiently legitimate so that its enactments generally created political obligations."[81]

> The structuring fairness principles that make law a distinct part of political morality—principles about political authority, precedent, and reliance— gave the slaveholders' claims more moral force than they otherwise would have had. But their moral claims were nevertheless and undoubtedly undermined by a stronger moral argument of human rights. So the law should not have been enforced.[82]

Hence, it is better to say in this situation "what most lawyers would say that the Act was valid law but too unjust to enforce." For that "expresses nuances" that the claim that there was no law there "smothers." "It explains why the judges confronted with the Act faced, as they said, a moral dilemma and not simply a prudential one."[83]

---

[79] An additional reason for not taking the puzzle of unjust law seriously Dworkin once advanced is that it is "not very important...from the practical point of view, because the judgments we make about foreign wicked legal systems are rarely hinged to decisions we have to take"; Dworkin (1984: 260). Indeed, in the line preceding the claim about the "practical point of view" he said that wicked legal systems "should be treated...like hard cases that turn on which conception of law is best rather than easy cases whose proper resolution we already know and can therefore use to test for any particular conception for adequacy"; Id. (See also Dworkin (1986: 108), "The question of wicked legal systems...is not one but many questions, and they all arise, for legal theory, at the level where conceptions compete.") But that claim despite the qualification that followed seems to make wicked legal systems quite important. After all, for Dworkin hard cases—cases in which lawyers reasonably disagree about what the law requires—provide the resource for working out both the content of rival conceptions of law and for adjudicating between their substantive merits. One might say that the "hard case" of legitimacy in a wicked legal system provides us with an insight into the "easy case" of the legitimacy of a morally decent system.

[80] Dworkin (1984: 258).

[81] Dworkin (2011: 411).

[82] Dworkin (2011: 411).

[83] Dworkin (2011: 411).

But there is something else that helps to explain why judges in both the Nazi era and in the antebellum American order faced a dilemma, however described, as long as they had moral convictions that condemned the injustice of the content of the *artifact* that confronted them. I use this term for the moment in an attempt not to prejudge whether the Fugitive Slave statutes were law and whether there were legal rights, because for one side in the debate to call something *law* implies that it supplies a special kind of moral reason to judges to enforce it, while for the other side nothing of the sort is implied, since law is morally inert.

The artifact confronts the judges because it is produced in accordance with whatever formal procedures their political order recognizes to mark the distinction between, on the one hand, the rights people think they should have, and, on the other, whatever it is they have by virtue of the artifacts that have in fact been produced. As Dworkin says, such a distinction can only be made "in a community that has developed some version of what Hart called secondary rules: rules establishing legislative, executive, and adjudicative authority and jurisdiction."[84] And it is rights of the latter sort—institutional rights—that "people are entitled to enforce on demand, without further legislative intervention, in adjudicative institutions that direct the executive power of sheriff or police."[85]

Now despite my attempt to keep the description clean of talk of rights, it has crept in, as it does for Dworkin in the passage quoted above in which he talks about the slaveholders' "weak moral claims." The problem is that he has at times insisted that there is law in these situations only in the "preinterpretive sense."[86] But there is then law in this sense across a political continuum of legal orders. These orders range from liberal democratic, to liberal but not democratic, to democratic but not liberal, to thoroughly illegitimate. But there is a continuum because they all have secondary rules that make the distinction possible between law in this sense and the rights people should have. Of course, not all political orders have such rules, in which case they have no claim to be legal orders. But since Dworkin concedes that the presence of secondary rules gives rise to the distinction, he appears to concede everything to positivism, as Hart had argued. Dworkin seems then stuck with the truism that in good legal systems, those in which principles of enlightened morality have contingently been incorporated, legal duties are also moral duties.

Note that in response to a paper in a symposium on the manuscript of *Justice for Hedgehogs*, Dworkin said that the legitimacy of a legal order is "a matter of degree" and that though it is possible to say in the abstract what a perfectly legitimate government would be, one that treats all citizens in accordance with the best moral conception of equal concern and respect, it is "harder to state a floor beneath which any purported government is wholly illegitimate." He suggested that "a government is illegitimate in respect to a particular person it claims

---

[84] Dworkin (2011: 405).
[85] Dworkin (2011: 405).
[86] Dworkin (1986: ch. 3).

to govern if it does not recognize, even as an abstract requirement, the equal importance of his fate or his responsibility for his own life."[87] In an illegitimate legal system, it follows that the government has "no legitimacy" for those in the oppressed group—"they have no political obligation at all." But the rest are in a "morally complex and difficult situation." They might consider disobedience. But they still have an obligation to their fellow citizens to obey "those laws, fair in themselves, that maintain civil society…"[88]

It thus follows from Dworkin's concession that he is faced with the kind of theoretical dilemma he diagnosed for Hart: the dilemma between saying that there is law for the oppressed group despite the fact that law supplies them with no moral reasons and saying that there is no law for that group because it fails to give them such reasons.[89] That theoretical dilemma becomes a practical dilemma for judges who have to consider applying an artifact that they must see as legal to individuals who the judges know should not consider the artifact as legal. And given that, unlike both Hart and Raz, Dworkin supposes that law generally does supply moral reasons, as well as his embrace in *Justice for Hedgehogs* of the one-system picture of law and morality, the problem of unjust law might seem even sharper for his position than it is for theirs.

Moreover, his responses to that problem at times seem to place him on the wrong side of the positivist–natural law divide in that he consigns the problem of the injustice of unjust law to morality, thus presupposing the two-system picture of the relationship between law and morality that he wished to reject. I shall now sketch a way forward for Dworkin, one whose outline he had seen. However, he did not take it, in my view, because it requires combining his position with one that he thought he had good reason to reject—Fuller's position that there is an internal morality of law.

4. Fuller Revisited

Recall that Dworkin expressed some doubt that the situation of a judge starkly faced with a clearly unjust law would easily arise. In a long footnote to that claim, Dworkin said that he needed to distinguish more sharply than he had in his

---

[87] Dworkin (2010: 1075-1076), responding to Sreedhar and Delmas (2010).

[88] Dworkin adds "while they work to improve the state's legitimacy," Dworkin (2010: 1076). This addition might seem to be a rider that builds democracy into Dworkin's account of when this situation prevails, since he seems to presuppose that the law accords the people in the privileged group the space to work against the system's injustice. But it is clear that he considers that an undemocratic society can be legitimate as long as its laws are not too substantively unjust, so that illegitimacy is measured across two dimensions, corresponding to fit and soundness, the lack or absence of democracy, and the substantive content of the law. These two dimensions are united by the principle of equal concern and respect, or as Dworkin was to term it in Dworkin (2011: 264-267), the "Kantian principle of dignity."

[89] Allan (2009).

earlier work between "explanation" and "justification".[90] In his view, an explanation does not "provide a justification of a series of political decisions if it presents,
as justificatory principles, propositions that offend our ideas of what even a bad
moral principle must be like."[91] He also said that he has more confidence than
he had in earlier work in what he called the "screening power of the concept
of a moral principle." He claimed that the requirement his theory imposes on
judges—that they provide an argument that shows the legal record in its best
moral light—will tend to screen out or exclude morally unacceptable principles.[92]

However, Dworkin did not pursue this line of inquiry, other than by offering
hypotheticals in an illegitimate system like the Nazi one in which a judge could
and should resist reasoning by analogy from an explicitly unjust law. For example, in a private law dispute, an Aryan claims that in tort law Jews are subject to
strict liability while Aryans are not, because in contract law a statute stipulates
that only Aryans have remedies available to them in disputes with Jews. In such
examples, it seems clear that the case is hard because a discriminatory ideology
evidently explains or fits one area of private law, and perhaps much of the law of
the system, but in the area in which the dispute occurs, it is still possible to claim
that individuals are entitled to equal concern and respect.[93]

However, the resource of a screening principle in tort law seems removable by
a stroke of a legal pen, whether by a discriminatory statute or by a Dworkinian
judgment that finds that Aryan ideology overwhelmingly explains the rest of
Nazi private law, not to mention public law, and hence requires that, in a hard
case, a judge should extend that ideology. At that point, or before, as we have
seen Dworkin advise of a system that is arguably wholly illegitimate, one should
decide that the artifacts of the political system supply no moral reasons and are
therefore not law.

We are thus returned to the positivist point from Section 2 that the existence of
moral resources in the law that make genuine justification possible is contingent.
However, neither the positivists nor Dworkin inquire into what happens to *legal
order* when particular laws are used to consign a whole group to second-class
status, since they assume that the dispute is, as Dworkin liked to say, about law
in the doctrinal sense: what makes claims true or false about what the law of a
particular place requires.[94]

---

[90] Dworkin (1984: 299, n. 4).

[91] Dworkin (1984: 299, n. 4).

[92] Dworkin (1984: 299, n. 4).

[93] Dworkin (1984: 299, n. 4). Compare Dworkin (1986: 105-108).

[94] Dworkin (2006: 2). Dworkin identified a second, "sociological concept", which he took to be
Fuller's. Such a concept seeks to set out precisely "what kind of social structure count as a legal
system" but he says that it would be "silly" to ask whether a system that had a lot of ex post facto
law *"really"* is a legal system; Dworkin (2006: 3), [emphasis in the original]. He identifies, in addition, a "taxonomic concept", which asks questions such as whether moral principles can count as
principles of law, which he attributes to Raz and rejects as a "scholastic fiction." He does endorse a
third conception of law, the "aspirational conception", "which we often refer to as the ideal of legality or the rule of law." This is a politically contested concept, with the lines drawn between more

But, as we have seen, it is the combination of the assumption that the debate is doctrinal with the assumption that philosophy of law must explain law's authoritative nature that leads to the puzzle of unjust law. To move forward, we should return to a modified version of one of the alternatives for a judge faced with an unjust law that Dworkin discarded under fire from Hart: The judge who stays in office, applies the law under explicit protest, hoping, "against odds, that his appeal based on moral grounds will have the same practical effect as a lie would." But we must substitute "legal grounds" for "moral grounds" and to do this we need to see that there were more differences between Nazi law and, say, American law than that the Nazis used their laws to achieve ends that are odious to an American.[95]

Fuller identified eight desiderata of the rule of law: generality, promulgation, non-retroactivity, clarity, non-contradiction, possibility of compliance, constancy through time, and congruence between official action and declared rule (which he took to be most complex).[96] A system that fails completely to meet one of these requirements, or fails substantially to meet several, would not, in his view, be a legal system. It would not qualify as government under law—as government subject to the rule of law. Fuller's claim is that compliance with the principles imbues law with an "inner" or "internal" morality that makes a positive moral difference to all legal systems. Even a tyrant who wanted to govern through the medium of law would have to comply and this would preclude rule by arbitrary decree and secret terror, which, Fuller says, is the most effective medium for tyranny.[97] However, Dworkin and the positivists argued both that only prudential reasons prevent a tyrant from making his unjust aims altogether explicit in the law at his command and that compliance only serves to make those commands more effective, not, as Fuller argued, to exert a moral discipline on law that provides a *legal* obstacle to such aims.[98]

Notice, however, that Fuller's legal theory presents a kind of one-system picture since the morality in question is internal, or already immanent in the law. In addition, Fuller's morality is not at the level of positive law, but at the level of formal criteria of legality. Indeed, Fuller could be taken to agree with Hart against Dworkin that a general philosophy of law has to address this formal level.[99] There are "minimum conditions necessary and sufficient for the existence of a legal system."[100] And we should recall that Hart at times seemed to suggest

---

substantive rights-based conception and more positivist, formal conceptions; Dworkin (2006: 13). Notice that Fuller's "sociological" conception seems excluded from this contest, despite the fact that Fuller presented his theory as one about the rule of law and legality and dubbed it "aspirational." Fuller (1969: 41). In my view, Dworkin's division of conceptions has the same effect as Hart's positivism— both unhelpfully separate problems that need to be addressed together.

[95] To adapt Fuller's acute charge against Hart in Fuller, Fuller (1958: 650).

[96] These are set out in detail in Fuller (1969: ch. 2).

[97] Fuller (1969: 157-159).

[98] Dworkin (1965); Hart (1994: 206-7). See further, Raz (1983: 223-226).

[99] See Hart's remark in *Concept of Law*, vii, that the book is an exercise in "descriptive sociology."

[100] Hart (1994: 116-117).

that Fuller's criteria were among such conditions, though he then hastened to add that they exert no moral discipline on the content of the law.

Dworkin and legal positivists overlook the possibility that if law has to comply with such criteria to a significant degree, it will in fact be the case that an interpretive model of the kind Dworkin advocates will have significant traction in the positive law of any particular legal order. Moreover, that model will not produce the perverse results that Hart thought undermined Dworkin's position, because, as Dworkin himself suggested, one should have more confidence in the "screening power" of moral principles. The basis for that confidence is that the principles are not merely moral, but also legal: They are the principles of legality with which law must comply. Hence, if legislators follow the ethos of law-making set out by the principles, the law that they make will be interpretable by judges in a way that treats the individual subject to the law as someone with "dignity as a responsible agent."[101]

These are theoretical claims, but I have elsewhere marshaled considerable evidence in favor of them: studies of the apartheid legal order,[102] the legal order of Weimar,[103] and legal responses to the threat of terrorism is the post 9/11 era.[104] These studies of legal experience show that legislators who wish to address the individuals subject to their power as lacking "dignity as a responsible agent" have to adopt one of two strategies. Either they can explicitly state that aim, or they can delegate power to officials that permit the officials to achieve the same end, not because this end is explicitly stated in the empowering statute, but because official implementation of the statute is explicitly stated to be unreviewable by judges.

Both strategies use law to place individuals or groups of individuals beyond the reach of the law. But they do so in a way that does not comply with law's form, in the first case by negating generality and its implicit commitment to formal equality before the law; in the second case by ensuring that there is no law with which official action has to be congruent. If the legislators adopt one or both of the strategies in a not altogether explicit fashion, judges are under a duty to treat the law the legislators make to the extent possible as if it were intended to comply with their legislative ethos. As a result, if the form of law is to some extent

---

[101] Fuller (1969: 162). Rundle (2013) especially at 771, where Rundle sets out two dimensions of Fuller's argument, the "distinctive ethos of legislation" that requires law to take a particular form and the way in which that form "presupposes the legal subject's status as a responsible agent." My argument adds a third dimension, implicit in the combination of the first two, that the law has to be interpretable in a way that vindicates that presupposition. (Rundle also provides an illuminating analysis of a tension between Raz's account of authority, which has the rational agent at its heart, and his account of the rule of law that argues that the rule of law serves only to make law into a more effective instrument of policy, including policies that deny agency, for example, by enslaving people.)

[102] Dyzenhaus (2010).

[103] Dyzenhaus (1997).

[104] Dyzenhaus (2006).

respected, to that extent it will be interpretable in a way that respects the "dignity as a responsible agent" of those subject to the law.

This conclusion shows why the principle of publicity exercises a moral discipline on the content of the law, and thus, as Fuller argued, why a tyrant who wishes to govern through law will find himself both legally and morally constrained. In addition, it helps to show why it is not merely a contingent fact that if law is present, so there will be interpretive resources available to judges of the sort Pappe found to exist in the Nazi era.

I also show in these studies that even in a legal order in which there is no entrenched bill of rights, such defects in form can provide the legal basis for a judicial conclusion that the law is void[105] or support treating an explicit provision in a statute as a legal nullity.[106] Finally, the studies show that even if it is not the case that a judge has the legal resources available to declare invalid a statute that offends principles of legality, or to interpret the statute in such a way that the offense is either mitigated or removed, this does not mean that the statute is legally speaking unproblematic. Such a statute might be, formally speaking, valid in that it complies with rule-of-recognition type tests. But it will offend against legal form in another sense—the sense of the principles of legality, observance of which gives law a particular form. If the judge finds that she has to uphold this statute, she can stay in office and take up Dworkin's third option from his initial response to the challenge of a judge faced with applying an unjust law. She can make an explicit protest, but not only on moral grounds, since it is on grounds that are legal as well as moral.

Such a protest is quite powerful. Consider that an analog of it is effective under the United Kingdom's Human Rights Act (1998), which in section 3 requires that judges strain to interpret statutes to make them compatible with the human rights commitments of the statute; and, in section 4, requires judges to make a declaration of incompatibility of the statute with the human rights commitments, if they cannot find an interpretation under section 3. If a section 4 declaration is made, a Minister of the Crown may, in terms of section 10 of the Act, amend the statute. And of course the legislature may amend it, or do nothing, though doing nothing puts the state in violation of its international legal commitment to the European Convention on Human Rights, a matter on which the European Court of Human Rights will eventually pronounce. But though I think it significant that in one jurisdiction such declarations have received positive responses from the legislature, more significant is why there have been such responses. In my view, the responses have much to do with the message otherwise sent to those affected by the offending statute that they are not fully within the moral community constituted by the legal commitments of the political and legal order to which they are subject.

---

[105] Consider the common law view that a bill of attainder is void.

[106] Consider how judges in the common law world have sidestepped or read down privative clauses that strip them of review power of official action.

To be both within the community for some purposes and without for others is to occupy a highly problematic legal status, that of second-class subject or citizen.[107] Second-class status is much more legally problematic in one sense than the status of slavery, as long as slaves are relentlessly consigned to the status of objects or things.[108] For if one is legally recognized as having status as a responsible agent for some purposes but not for others, the parts of the law that seem to relegate one to second-class status are thrown into doubt by those that do not in any case in which a challenge is brought to the former. It was on precisely this basis that human rights lawyers during the apartheid era put their challenges to the laws of apartheid. It is worth remarking that such lawyers claimed Dworkin's theory as a source of inspiration for their work in the standard example of the legal order that was often claimed by legal positivists to refute interpretivism.[109] But my argument in this section has been that we need Fuller to understand how Dworkin's theory could so serve.

Of course, the parts of the law that seem to relegate one to second-class status can be used to throw into doubt those parts that do not, to the point that second-class status for a group is so entrenched that the group is put beyond law's reach. But then we need Fuller too, in order to understand that an illegitimate legal system is a "botched legal order"[110] for two reasons. First, it will fail to solve the moral problems that only law can solve. But, second, it is also botched

---

[107] See Ebbinghaus (1953).

[108] "As long as the class of people is relentlessly consigned . . ." is, it must be emphasized, a big proviso. For slave-owning societies, societies in which the institution of slavery is constituted by law, usually experience immense difficulty in maintaining the enslaved group in a status beyond morality and law and therefore beyond dignity. See, for example, Buckland (1932: 62-66). Consider also the difficulties our society experiences with maintaining nonhuman animals—cows, dogs, pigs, etc.—in the status of things, while giving them some legal protection against various kinds of bad treatment because we recognize that they share certain attributes with us human animals, including the capacity to suffer. In contrast to a society that manages relentlessly to consign a group of people to the status of things, apartheid-era South Africa was a legal nightmare from the perspective of the rule of law, concerned with what it takes to maintain a society "in good shape," legally speaking (See Finnis (1980: 270). And it was so because the ideal that all South Africans were equal before the law—the specifically legal ideal of human dignity—was maintained as an abstract ideal of the legal order throughout the period, even as the particular apartheid laws made it ever clearer that the animating political ideology of the ruling party was one of white supremacy. The reality of that nightmare was lived on a daily basis by black South Africans, as well as the other non-white groups who were accorded privileges that put them somewhere in between black and white South Africans. The nightmare played out in the law in the following: the convoluted attempts in statute law to ensure that the statutes would be interpreted in a fashion more consistent with the political ideal of white supremacy than with the legal ideal of human dignity; the actual administration of the law by officials; and the efforts by judges who took seriously the legal ideal of dignity to interpret the law in light of that ideal. But that the nightmare was played out within the law had the occasional advantage for those who used the law to challenge the law that sought to embed the political ideology of white supremacy.

[109] Du Bois (2004: xi). This collection contains the proceedings of a conference held in Cape Town to honor Dworkin's contribution to human rights lawyering during the apartheid era. Dworkin's "Keynote" in that volume is an early statement of the one-system account.

[110] Shapiro (2011: 391).

legally speaking because it is on the path to becoming something other than a legal order, namely, the order of a "prerogative state"[111] in which arbitrary power reigns. Fuller was not, then, so naïve when he suggested that there is "a considerable incongruity in any conception that envisages a possible future in which the common law would 'work itself pure from case to case' toward a more perfect realization of iniquity."[112]

Fuller might, however, seem naïve or simply wrong-headed in another respect, since his one-system picture of law and morality seems to presuppose a view that we work out what our morals are at the same time as we work out what the law is. But, as I shall now briefly suggest, that view has much to commend it.

5. Law's Laboratory

I have argued that the puzzle of unjust law complicates the division in legal theory between natural law and legal positivism. The central figure here is the judge because of the obligation of judges to apply law that is based on facts that are contingent and may not be morally good. How can we square what seems like a standing judicial obligation to apply the law with the idea that that law has no guarantee to be something that ought to be applied? Hart tries to get out of the problem by minimizing the account of law's authority so that there is no moral requirement to apply it, and Dworkin tries to get out of it by subordinating the factual dimension of law to the moral one and arguing that the criteria in the moral dimension determine the law. But the difficulties each encounters have the result that both are tempted to stray to the other side of the positivism–natural law divide.

In the last section, I suggested that the solution to the puzzle has to do with how principles of legality condition the content of law in a way that makes more plausible Dworkin's claim that an argument that shows the legal record in its best moral light will not include morally unacceptable principles. But this suggestion seems to entail that what gets left in after the screening process is done is moral. It would follow that there is such a thing as "a moral legislature with competence to make and change morals, as legal enactments make and change law," an idea which Hart said is "repugnant to the whole notion of morality."[113]

I am not so sure that a version of this idea is at all repugnant, as long as we are prepared to adopt a certain kind of pragmatist view of moral inquiry, and in *Justice for Hedgehogs,* Dworkin endorsed the Peircean pragmatist view of inquiry as aimed at getting right answers.[114] True or rational beliefs in any field of inquiry

---

[111] See Fraenkel (1969).

[112] Fuller (1958: 636).

[113] Hart (1994: 175, 177).

[114] In *Justice for Hedgehogs*, Dworkin describes his account of truth as pragmatist since he argues with Charles Sanders Peirce, that "truth is the intrinsic goal of inquiry"; Dworkin (2011: 177). And in his work on moral inquiry, he seems to argue, with the pragmatists, that the test for the objectivity

are those that survive the tribunal of experience, against the background of our current beliefs and principles. The settled beliefs that arise from this process of inquiry or deliberation are always provisional since they must be left vulnerable to revision in light of further experience.

I suspect, though, that Dworkin was not willing to embrace fully the implications of his endorsement of the idea that morals are an appropriate subject matter for inquiry.[115] He rejects, in my view, the important pragmatist idea that our compulsory public morality—the morality that we feel is settled and important enough that it be put into law—is simply a subset of the set of judgments that have survived the tribunal of experience and inquiry. My claim here is that philosophy of law can help to show why that idea is plausible, as it shows us how fundamental principles of legality shape our inquiry. That is, our confidence in these compulsory moral judgments is in part built upon the principles contained in the institutional make-up of law.

I have in mind two principles. First is the principle that requires that individuals have the right to ask an independent official for reasons why the law applies to them in a way that addresses them as beings with dignity as responsible agents. Second are the principles that underpin legal mechanisms for changing law in a way that makes the judgments embedded in the law revisable in light of further experience. It is these kinds of principles that make it both possible for those who find themselves relegated by the law to second-class status to ask a judge, "But how can that be law for me?," and for an internal legal imperative to kick in that requires reform.[116]

Fuller is again helpful at this point in his emphasis on the importance of impartial adjudicators in a rule-of-law order, in which the issues submitted to the adjudicators "[tend] to be *converted* into a claim of right or an accusation of guilt. This conversion is effected by the institutional framework within which both the litigant and the adjudicator function."[117] The process of reasoned argument

---

of our judgments is that they are the best we can achieve for the time being in light of our experience, at the same time that we insist that the inquiry be kept open in case we should revise those judgments. See, for example, Dworkin (2013: 54).

[115] Dworkin qualifies his endorsement of pragmatism by saying that pragmatism as an abstract account of truth can recommend "not pragmatic," less abstract modes of inquiry for particular domains; Dworkin (2011: 178); and I do not suppose that he would agree with the claims in this section as they might seem to make morality hostage to facts in the same way as we have seen his legal theory can seem hostage. Fuller preferred to think of himself as a pragmatist rather than a natural lawyer. See Winston (1988). But there is no need to accept this dichotomy—see Selznick (1961).

[116] For exploration of similar ideas, with reliance on Fuller, see Waldron (2012). On my account, the judge is under a standing legal and moral obligation to apply the law; and the citizen should recognize that she has a legal moral and duty to obey, but one that may be outweighed by the moral pull of considerations that make her contemplate civil disobedience. This account might well help to understand the legal and moral complexity of the Civil Rights Movement in the United States, the Suffragettes in the United Kingdom, and that stage in the struggle against apartheid during which the liberation movements engaged in massive "Defiance" campaigns.

[117] Fuller (2001: 101, 111 emphasis added). Hart presented very much the same picture in chapter 9, "Law and Morals," in *The Concept of Law*. As I suggested in note 65 above, it is significant that

requires the person making the argument to present it as more than a "naked demand." It has to be presented as a "claim of right," that is, as "supported by a principle." And that has the consequence that "issues tried before an adjudicator tend to become claims of rights or accusations of fault."[118] Thus Fuller regards courts and other adjudicative institutions as "essential to the rule of law." The "object of the rule of law is to substitute for violence peaceful ways of settling disputes. Obviously, peace cannot be assured simply by treaties, agreements, and legislative enactment. There must be some agency capable of determining the rights of the parties in concrete situations of controversy."[119]

But notice that for this adjudicative conversion process to take place, the law has to be convertible and that requires a prior conversion process. Legislation requires the reduction of a political program to the explicit terms of a statute and thus a conversion of policy into public standards, which produces a kind of legal surplus value. By this I mean that the legitimacy of official action in compliance with the statute is not simply that of compliance with a political policy that the demos or polis has determined to be appropriate. It is also the case that this conversion process adds value because it brings into being a particular type of *public* standard, one that permits the operation of the principles identified by Fuller as the desiderata of the inner morality of law, and which enables claims of right based on legal principle to be adjudicated. If the law is not convertible in this way, a problem is raised that is internal to the legal order and requires that those charged with maintaining the legal order in good shape consider reform.

Once law and legal order are understood in this way, an interesting relationship between law and background culture—the culture of what Hart called "positive morality"[120]—comes into view. Consider that in nineteenth-century Britain, women were not wholly consigned by the law to second-class status. Those bits of the law that recognized their formal equality made problematic those bits that did not. It was just this kind of issue that led to debate and legislation in Britain, I think, about whether "he" in statutory language was gender-neutral. The issue resurfaced in Canada and in the Privy Council in the *Persons* case, with regard to whether women counted as "persons" appointable to the Senate.[121] Looking back at the history of the subordination of women should make us more aware

---

Hart's position is that philosophy of law has to explain the authority law has, not (as Joseph Raz has suggested) the authority that law claims. Hart does not allow, in other words, that law can fail to have authority. In this respect, Hart is more like Fuller and Dworkin than like Raz and differs from Fuller and Dworkin only in that he holds that the reasons that legal authority gives to both officials and subjects need not be moral reasons. The nature of reasons is itself a matter of philosophical controversy, as is the nature of morality; and Hart expressed at times a desire to keep philosophy of law away from such matters. But I think it is safe to say that it is he thought that legal reasons have a normative force that goes beyond the force of prudence—the kind of reason offered by "Your money or your life."

[118] Fuller (2001: 111).
[119] Fuller (2001: 114).
[120] Hart (1981: 17).
[121] *Edwards v. Canada (Attorney General)* [1930] A.C. 124.

of the possibility of injustice in our present situation that we find difficult to see. And here legality can be useful against law, as it were. We might be able to detect moral problems that we should address because of inconsistencies and tensions in our legal treatment of groups.

These ideas require moving away both from a Dworkinian philosophical idiom in which law contains (or does not contain) moral principles that screen out repugnant ideologies and from a positivistic one that sees law as a mechanism that can, but need not, be used to transmit moral facts to legal subjects. It requires a move to an idiom that describes law as a process that in part constitutes our inquiry about what moral judgments we should make. One reason to make this move is that the new idiom accurately describes the way that we mostly talk about the law. The law is a part of our moral fabric. It may require revision, even overthrow, as experience dictates. But this does not distinguish it from other beliefs and theories interwoven into that moral fabric. Moreover, it seems to me that it is only within that idiom that we can describe, perspicuously, what otherwise seem to be two intuitions that are at war with each other in situations of legalized injustice—that law is both a matter of fact and of authority.

Dworkin should therefore have retained, in the final version of *Justice for Hedgehogs,* the thought in the manuscript that it is counterintuitive to suppose that "most of the subjects of most of the political communities over history had no moral duty to obey the laws of their community."[122] The pulling apart of moral duty from legal duty is only apt when massive revision or revolution is being undertaken. In the absence of the need for such revolution, our moral and legal lives are completely and utterly intertwined. It is in that intertwinement that the redemptive power of the law—its capacity to reform itself from within—resides.

References

Alexy, R. (1989). "On Necessary Relations Between Law and Morality," *Ratio Juris* 2: 167.

Allan, T. R. S. (2009). "Law, 'Justice and Integrity: The Paradox of Wicked Laws'," *Oxford Journal of Legal Studies* 29: 705.

Berman, H. J. (1988). "Towards an Integrative Jurisprudence: Politics, Morality, History," *California Law Review* 76: 779.

Buckland, W. W. (1932). *A Text-Book of Roman Law From Augustus to Justinian.* Cambridge: Cambridge University Press.

Coleman, J. (2011). "The Architecture of Jurisprudence," *Yale Law Journal* 121: 2.

Cottrell, R. (2013). "The Role of the Jurist: Reflections Around Radbruch," *Ratio Juris* 24: 510.

---

[122] Quoted in Sreedhar and Delmas (2010: 746).

Du Bois, F. (2004). "Preface." In *The Practice of Integrity: Reflections on Ronald Dworkin & South African Law*, DuBois, (ed.). Cape Town: Juta.

Dworkin, R. (1965). "Philosophy, Morality, and Law: Observations Prompted by Professor Fuller's Novel Claim," *University of Pennsylvania Law Review* 113: 672.

Dworkin, R. (1978). *Taking Rights Seriously*, 2nd ed. Cambridge, MA: Harvard University Press.

Dworkin, R. (1984). "A Reply by Ronald Dworkin." In *Ronald Dworkin and Contemporary Jurisprudence*, Mashall Cohen (ed.). London: Duckworth.

Dworkin, R. (1986). *Law's Empire*. London: Fontana.

Dworkin, R. (2006). *Justice In Robes.* Harvard: Harvard University Press.

Dworkin, R. (2010). "Response," *Boston University Law Review* 90: 1059.

Dworkin, R. (2011). *Justice for Hedgehogs.* Harvard: Harvard University Press.

Dworkin, R. (2013). "Law from the Inside Out," *New York Review of Books* 60, no. 17, November 7: 54.

Dyzenhaus, D. (2014). "Unjust Law in Legal Theory." In *Festschrift für Bernhard Schlink zum 70. Geburtstag,* Ralf Poscher, Henner Wolter and Jakob Nolte (eds.). Heidelberg: C.F. Müller Verlagsgruppe Hüthig Jehle Rehm GmbH.

Dyzenhaus, D. (1997). *Legality and Legitimacy: Carl Schmitt, Hans Kelsen and Hermann Heller in Weimar.* Oxford: Oxford University Press.

Dyzenhaus, D. (2006). *The Constitution of Law: Legality in a Time of Emergency.* Cambridge: Cambridge University Press.

Dyzenhaus, D. (2008). "The Grudge Informer Case Revisited," *New York University Law Review* 23:1000.

Dyzenhaus, D. (2010). *Hard Cases in Wicked Legal Systems: Pathologies of Legality*, 2nd ed. Oxford: Oxford University Press.

Dyzenhaus, D. (2012). "Legality Without the Rule of Law? Scott Shapiro on Wicked Legal Systems," *Canadian Journal of Law & Jurisprudence* 25:183.

Ebbinghaus, J. (1953). "The Law of Humanity and the Limits of State Power," *The Philosophical Quarterly* 3: 14.

Finnis, J. (1980). *Natural Law and Natural Rights.* Oxford: Clarendon Press.

Fuller, L. L. (1958). "Positivism and Fidelity to Law: A Reply to Professor Hart," *Harvard Law Review* 71:630.

Fuller, L. L. (1969). *The Morality of Law,* rev. ed. New Haven: Yale University Press.

Fraenkel, E. (1969). *The Dual State: A Contribution to the Theory of Dictatorship.* New York: Octagon Books.

Fuller, L. L. (2001). "The Forms and Limits of Adjudication," in K. I. Winston (ed.), *The Principles of Social Order: Selected Essays of Lon L. Fuller.* Oxford: Hart Publishing.

Green, L. (2008). "Positivism and the Inseparability of Law and Morals," *New York University Law Review*, 23: 1035.

Green, L. (2013). "The Morality in Law," in L. D. D'Almeida, J. Edwards and A. Dolcetti (eds.), *Reading HLA Hart's The Concept of Law.* Oxford: Hart Publishing.

Greenawalt, K (1977). "Policy, Rights and Judicial Decisions," *Georgia Law* Review, 11: 991.

Hart, H. L. A. (1958). "Positivism and the Separation of Law and Morals," *Harvard Law Review*, 71: 593.

Hart, H. L. A. (1981). *Law, Liberty and Morality.* Oxford: Oxford University Press.

Hart, H. L. A. (1982). *Essays on Bentham: Jurisprudence and Political Theory.* Oxford: Oxford University Press.

Hart, H. L. A. (1988). "Answers to Eight Questions," in D'Almeida, Edwards, and Dolcetti, (eds.), *Reading HLA Hart's The Concept of Law*: 279.

Hart, H. L. A. (1994). *The Concept of Law.* 2nd ed. Oxford: Clarendon Press.

Mertens, T. (2002). "Radbruch and Hart on the Grudge Informer: A Reconsideration," *Ratio Juris*, 15: 186.

Murphy, L. (2008). "Better to see Law this Way," *New York University Law Review*, 23: 1088.

Neiman, S. (2002). *Evil in Modern Thought: An Alternative History of Philosophy.* Princeton: Princeton University Press.

Pappe, H. O. (1960). "On The Validity Of Judicial Decisions In The Nazi Era," *The Modern Law Review*, 23: 260.

Radbruch, G. (2006). "Statutory Lawlessness and Supra-Statutory Law," *Oxford Journal of Legal Studies*, 26: 1.

Rundle, K. (2013). "Form and Agency in Raz's Legal Positivism," *Law and Philosophy*, 32: 767.

Selznick, P. (1961). "Sociology and Natural Law," *Natural Law Forum*, 6: 84.

Shapiro, S. (2011). *Legality.* Harvard: Harvard University Press.

Sreedhar, S. and Delmas, S. (2010). "State Legitimacy and Political Obligation in *Justice for Hedgehogs*: The Radical Potential of Dworkinian Dignity," *Boston University Law Review*, 90: 737.

Raz, J. (1983). "The Rule of Law and its Virtue," in J. Raz, *The Authority of Law: Essays on Law and Morality.* Oxford: Oxford University Press.

Raz, J. (1979). *The Authority of Law: Essays on Law and Morality.* Oxford: Oxford University Press.

Raz, J. (1994). "Authority, Law, and Morality," in J. Raz, *Ethics in the Public Domain: Essays in the Morality of Law and Politics.* Oxford: Oxford University Press.

Raz, J. (2004). "Incorporation by Law," *Legal Theory*, 10: 1.

Wacks, R. (1984). "Judges and Injustice," 101 *South African Law Journal*, 101: 266.

Waldron, J. (2008). "Positivism and Legality: Hart's Equivocal Response to Fuller," *New York University Law Review*, 83: 1135.

Waldron, J. (2012). "How Law Protects Dignity," *Cambridge Law Journal*, 71: 200.

Winston, K. (1988). "Is/Ought Redux: the Pragmatist Context of Lon Fuller's Conception of Law," *Oxford Journal of Legal Studies*, 8: 329.

8

The Grounds of Law
by Luís Duarte d'Almeida*

In this chapter, I discuss two versions of Ronald Dworkin's objection from theoretical disagreement. I start with Dworkin's argument, in *Law's Empire*, against what he calls "the 'plain fact' view of the grounds of law." Dworkin's argument is sound; but the plain-fact view, which he misattributes to H. L. A. Hart, is a straw man. Indeed, Dworkin's argument relies on a distinction that Hart pioneered and the plain-fact view denies: the distinction between "internal," normative statements of law, and "external," factual statements about law. That is my claim in Section 1. In Sections 2 and 3, I turn to a more familiar version of Dworkin's objection—a version that has been revived in recent literature—and to some attempts to answer it. I argue that this version, too, derives its strength from charging legal positivists with the failure to distinguish between external and internal statements. Unfortunately, many theorists are guilty as charged.

1. The "Plain-Fact" Straw Man

1.1. DWORKIN ON THE "PLAIN-FACT" VIEW

In Chapter One of *Law's Empire*, at the beginning of his discussion of "disagreement about law," Ronald Dworkin introduces a distinction between "propositions of law" and "propositions [that] furnish...the 'grounds' of law."[1] Propositions of law are "the various statements and claims people make

---

*For helpful comments and discussion, I am grateful to Barbara Baum Levenbook, Cláudio Michelon, David Plunkett, Euan MacDonald, Fábio Shecaira, James Edwards, Katharina Stevens, Kevin Toh, Martin Kelly, Neil Walker, Pedro Múrias, Stefan Sciaraffa, Thomas Adams, and audiences in Edinburgh, Lisbon, Porto Alegre, and Burlington, Ontario.
[1] Dworkin (1986: 4).

about what the law allows or prohibits or entitles them to have;" here is one of Dworkin's examples:

(P1) [According to law,] no one may drive over 55 miles an hour in California.

Dworkin says that "lawyers and judges and ordinary people generally assume that some propositions of law, at least, can be true or false," or at any rate "sound" or "unsound."[2] This certainly rings true of a proposition like (P1). We assume not only that such propositions can be assessed as true or false—as correctly or incorrectly stating what the law is—but also that if a question arises about the truth or correctness of a proposition like (P1), there will be ways of putting our doubts to rest. If we need to be sure, we may consult a lawyer. Is it really the case, we ask, that no one may drive over 55 miles an hour in California? We would be surprised if she were to answer "I have *no* idea—and there is just no way of finding out." But suppose she replies instead that yes, it is true that the speed limit is 55 miles an hour. "Look," she says, "here it is, in the official statute book: a provision precisely to that effect." That would not strike us as an odd answer. Here the proposition that

(P2) The official California statute book contains a provision to the effect that no one may drive over 55 miles an hour

is being put forth as a proposition that, in Dworkin's terminology, provides the "grounds" of (P1):

> Everyone thinks that propositions of law are true or false (or neither) in virtue of other, more familiar kinds of propositions on which these propositions of law are (as we might put it) parasitic. These more familiar propositions furnish what I shall call the "grounds" of law. The proposition that no one may drive over 55 miles an hour in California is true, most people think, because a majority of that state's legislators said "aye" or raised their hands when a text to that effect lay on their desks. It could not be true if nothing of that sort had ever happened.[3]

The notion of the "grounds" of law is therefore a relational notion. For any particular proposition of law *P*, the grounds of *P* will be given by whatever proposition or group of propositions "make [that] particular proposition of law [*P*] true" or correct.

Familiar as this picture may look, this "grounding" relation that supposedly obtains between (P2) and (P1) raises several questions. In what sense, exactly, does the truth of (P1) depend on—is "parasitic" on—the truth of (P2)? Does (P2) by itself *make* (P1) true? It certainly does not entail it on its own. Or is Dworkin's just a poorly chosen example?

Dworkin points out that there are two importantly different ways in which people may disagree about the truth-value of a proposition like (P1). One

---

[2] Dworkin (1986: 4, 417).
[3] Dworkin (1986: 4).

possibility is that they agree that the following conditional is true, but disagree that its antecedent is satisfied:[4]

> (P3) If the official California statute book contains a provision to the effect that no one may drive over 55 miles an hour, then [according to law] no one may drive over 55 miles an hour in California.

In other words, people may agree that (P2) would, if true, make (P1) true—they may agree that (P2) would, if true, give us the grounds of (P1)—but disagree about whether (P1) itself is true, because they disagree about whether (P2) is true. Another possibility is that they agree that (P2) is true, but disagree about whether (P3) is true. In that case, they disagree that (P2), though true, gives us the grounds of (P1).

Dworkin refers to disagreements of the first kind as "empirical," and to disagreements of the second kind as "theoretical."[5] These labels actually obscure his main thesis regarding the grounds of law. Dworkin wants to argue against what he calls "the 'plain fact' view of the grounds of law."[6] This is the view that, for any true proposition of law, its grounds will consist only of facts of the *sort* indicated in (P2): facts concerning "past institutional decisions,"[7] such as facts about "what statute books and past judicial decisions have to say."[8] According to the plain-fact view, as Dworkin states it,

> [t]he law is only a matter of what legal institutions, like legislatures and city councils and courts, have decided in the past. If somebody of that sort has decided that workmen can recover compensation for injuries by fellow workmen, then that is the law. If it has decided the other way, then that is the law. So questions of law can always be answered by looking in the books where the record of institutional decisions are kept...[According to the plain-fact view] [e]very question about what the law is...has a flat historical answer.[9]

Yet if Dworkin is right that the plain-fact view is false, it follows that the grounds of any given proposition of law will not (or not necessarily) be exhausted by such "plain facts." That means that disagreements about whether the grounds of law are satisfied in any particular case are not necessarily empirical. This is one reason Dworkin's labels are misleading.

Another reason is that it is also far from clear that disagreements about the truth-value of propositions like (P2) are exclusively empirical disagreements, to be settled "in the empirical way."[10] We can plausibly say that whether some document we refer to as "the official California statute book" contains a provision

---

[4] Dworkin (1986: 4-5).
[5] Dworkin (1986: 5).
[6] Dworkin (1986: 7).
[7] Dworkin (1986: 9).
[8] Dworkin (1986: 5).
[9] Dworkin (1986: 7, 9).
[10] Dworkin (1986: 5).

reading "No one may drive over 55 miles an hour" is an empirical matter (in the same sense in which it is an empirical matter whether *Law's Empire* contains a sentence reading "empirical disagreement about law is hardly mysterious"). Yet the truth of (P2) does not turn solely on the fact that some book we call "the official California statute book" contains such a provision. It turns also on the fact that the book containing that provision actually *is* the official California statute book, rather than some other book lacking such force. (P2) is true only if the statute book it refers to is the *valid* statute book in California; but to say that some statute book is valid is not—not clearly, at least—to make an empirical statement.

Here is a different way of making the same point. Consider, for example, (P4) and how it relates to (P2):

(P4) The California State Legislature voted, and the governor signed, a provision to the effect that no one may drive over 55 miles an hour.

(P2) The official California statute book contains a provision to the effect that no one may drive over 55 miles an hour.

The facts reported in (P4) are the sort of facts Dworkin calls empirical; they are Dworkinian "plain facts." Does (P2) follow from (P4) alone? It seems that the answer is "No." In order to get from (P4) to (P2) it must also be true that the California State Legislature is legally empowered to legislate on the matter, and the governor legally empowered to sign the voted provision into law. It must be true, that is, that *if* the California State Legislature votes a provision to the effect that no one may drive over 55 miles an hour (and if the relevant procedures are complied with), and the governor signs it, then that text will become part of the official statute book. So to get from (P4) to (P2) we need something like

(P5) The California State Legislature is legally empowered to pass legislation imposing driving speed limits.

But (P5) is not a Dworkinian empirical proposition. Rather, (P5) is itself a proposition of law—and Dworkin does not think that propositions of law are empirical. So he cannot really maintain that disagreement about whether (P2) is true is necessarily empirical. The truth of (P2) depends in part on the truth of some further, higher-order proposition(s) *of law* (such as those concerning the law-making powers of the relevant bodies, or the procedures on which the validity of legislative enactments depends); two people who agree that (P4) is true may still disagree over (P2) if they disagree that (P5) really is true.

It is therefore misleading for Dworkin to present his two kinds of disagreements the way he does. For any proposition of law *P*, as he suggests, we can ask both (a) "What are the grounds of *P*?" and (b) "Are the grounds of *P* satisfied?" But he is wrong to imply that disagreements about question (b) must be empirical disagreements—disagreements about "plain facts"—"to be settled in the empirical way."

In fact, Dworkin seems to equivocate over the meaning of the expression "plain fact." Sometimes he speaks as if the notion of a plain fact is a function of the kind of disagreement two people have when they have different views on whether a given fact obtains: if disagreement over whether a given fact f is the case is empirical disagreement, f is a plain fact. This is one use of "plain fact." But he also says that facts about "what legal institutions, like legislatures and city councils and courts, have decided in the past"—facts about "past institutional decisions"[11]—are plain facts. This is a different use of "plain fact": we have just seen that disagreements over whether facts like these are the case are not—at least not obviously—empirical.

The view Dworkin means to attack is concerned with "plain facts" in this second sense. Dworkin denies that it is only by reference to past institutional decisions that questions of law can be truthfully answered. What the law is on any given matter is not, he says, merely a question of what "the statute books and past judicial decisions have to say."[12] He thinks judicial practice supports this thesis. For judges can and very often do disagree about *what the law is* even when they agree about what the applicable statutes have to "say" on the matter. For example, judges may disagree over how an applicable statutory provision should be interpreted or construed even when the case falls unequivocally under the letter of the provision.[13] The plain-fact view of the grounds of law cannot explain this phenomenon. It has "no good answer to the question how theoretical disagreement is possible."[14] It fails to account for judicial practice. Therefore, argues Dworkin, the plain-fact view cannot be right.

1.2. SO WHAT?

Dworkin says that many legal philosophers disagree with him on this. Most legal philosophers, he says, endorse the plain-fact view of the grounds of law; they think that "questions of law can always be answered by looking in the books where the records of institutional decisions are kept."[15] But one does not need to be acquainted with the literature to be suspicious of this attribution. Indeed, the plain-fact view seems so obviously false that it would be surprising if many philosophers had adopted it.

Dworkin himself offers an analogy—with poetry—that suggests that the plain-fact view cannot be right:

> Consider the difference between a poem conceived as a series of words that can be spoken or written and a poem conceived as the expression of a particular metaphysical theory or point of view. Literary critics all agree about

---

[11] Dworkin (1986: 7).

[12] Dworkin (1986: 6).

[13] Dworkin (1986: 15-20).

[14] Dworkin (1986: 11).

[15] Dworkin (1986: 6-7).

what the poem "Sailing to Byzantium" is in the first sense. They agree it is the series of words designated as that poem by W. B. Yeats. But they nevertheless disagree about what the poem really says or means. They disagree about how to construe the "real" poem, the poem in the second sense, from the text, the poem in the first sense.

In much the same way, judges before whom a statute is laid need to construct the "real" statute—a statement of what difference the statute makes to the legal rights of various people—from the text in the statute book. Just as literary critics need a working theory, or at least a style of interpretation, in order to construct the poem behind the text, so judges need something like a theory of legislation to do this for statutes.[16]

We can develop Dworkin's analogy. Suppose that I, a literary critic, put forth the following claim:

> (Y) "Sailing to Byzantium" is really a lament about growing old and the proximity of death.

I put forth (Y) as the correct interpretation of Yeats's poem. Suppose you disagree. But I am prepared to defend (Y), with claims or arguments of different sorts. Those are the claims I would give as "grounds" of (Y): propositions which, if true or correct, make (Y) true or correct. Now suppose some philosopher of literary criticism claims that the grounds of (Y) can only include propositions describing plain, historical facts, such as facts, say, about Yeats's age or his actual intentions when he wrote the poem, or his own statements about what he took his poem to mean. Call this the "plain-fact view" of the grounds of propositions like (Y).

Could this view be right? It seems not. It seems, in fact, that the opposite view must be true: among the grounds of (Y), there must be at least one proposition which is not a description of any plain fact. That is because (Y) itself is not a proposition of plain fact. (Y) is a proposition about what the poem "Sailing to Byzantium" means when interpreted *correctly*. I could just as well have phrased it by saying that

> (Y') "Sailing to Byzantium," properly interpreted, is really a lament about growing old and the proximity of death.

In other words, there is a normative aspect to (Y). But if that is the case, then it seems that no set of propositions about plain, non-normative facts could ever suffice to establish the truth of (Y'). The grounds of (Y') must include some normative claim about how the poem *ought* to be interpreted if it is to be interpreted correctly. And any defense of that normative claim would itself have to rely on further normative claims; indeed, there seems to be no point at which a claim of that sort could be defended or justified solely on the basis of plain facts. For

---

[16] Dworkin (1986: 17).

anyone not prepared to reject the "is"/"ought" gap, it seems to follow that the plain-fact view of the grounds of (Y') is false.

A similar argument can be made in the legal case. Texts in statute books can be interpreted in all sorts of ways. But judges have to form their views about what statutory texts "say" or "mean" when interpreted correctly. Dworkin cites well-known examples of cases in which—as he construes them—judges disagreed about the outcome because they disagreed about what the pertinent statutory provision required "when properly read."[17] They disagreed, in other words, about how the "'real' statute" *ought* to be constructed from the relevant "text in the statute book."[18] As a consequence, they disagreed about which of several competing propositions of law correctly stated the law on the matter. They were thus disagreeing about the "grounds" of these propositions of law. Yet their disagreement was not about "any historical matters of fact."[19] The plain-fact view of the grounds of law must therefore be false.

So Dworkin's point is sound. But can it really be that most legal philosophers ignored it before they read *Law's Empire*? I already quoted a passage in which Dworkin characterizes the plain-fact view.[20] Other sentences he uses to describe this view—a "popular" view, he says[21]—include the following:

Law is a matter of plain fact.[22]
Law is always a matter of historical fact.[23]
The law depends only on matters of plain historical fact.[24]

These are familiar-sounding claims about law. They are recognizable as claims associated with the tradition of legal positivism. And it is true that many theorists before and since *Law's Empire* have endorsed some version of legal positivism. Dworkin has H. L. A. Hart's theory principally in mind.[25] But what does legal positivism—or Hart's theory at any rate—have to do with the plain-fact view of the grounds of law as Dworkin characterizes it? The answer, I should think, is "Nothing." To see why, let us return to Dworkin's analogy. Suppose I put to you that

(1) Poetry is always a matter of historical fact,

or even that

(2) Poetry depends only on matters of plain historical fact.

---

[17] Dworkin (1986: 16).
[18] Dworkin (1986: 18).
[19] Dworkin (1986: 23).
[20] See the quotation accompanying n. 9 above.
[21] Dworkin (1986: 10).
[22] Dworkin (1986: 8).
[23] Dworkin (1986: 9).
[24] Dworkin (1986: 31).
[25] Dworkin (1986: 34).

Are these statements true? If we understand them, as would seem natural, as statements about poetry as a kind of activity or practice of both poets and their readers and interpreters—then yes, it would appear that these statements are true. We saw that the truth of a statement like (Y)—the sort of statement a reader of Yeats's poem might make *qua* reader of poetry—does not depend only on matters of plain historical fact. But the activities of both readers and poets are themselves plain facts. That Yeats wrote "Sailing to Byzantium" is a plain fact. That some or even all readers subscribe to (Y) would be plain facts. Poetry exists as a practice because poets write poems and readers and critics read them and ask themselves questions like "What does this poem mean when properly interpreted?" and have certain feelings and dispositions towards poetry. Those are the kinds of facts that make up the activity or set of activities or practices that constitute poetry. So it seems plausible to think that statements (1) and (2) are true, indeed trivially true. But that tells us nothing about the grounds of propositions like (Y). That people *do* ask themselves what poems mean, and that they come up with answers to such questions—these are plain historical facts; but it does not follow that answers *to* such questions must themselves be given in terms of historical facts only. Statements (1) and (2) certainly do not entail anything like the plain-fact view of the grounds of propositions like (Y)—that is, the view that the grounds of any statement of the form "poem *p*, properly interpreted, means *m*" can only include plain facts.

Again, the same can be said of law. There would be no statutes without legislators, and no adjudication according to law without judges asking themselves questions of the form "What does this statutory provision, properly interpreted, mean?" Answers to such questions will characteristically feature as grounds of propositions of law, which are statements made, as Dworkin puts it, from the "internal point of view" of a participant in legal practice.[26] Dworkin contrasts such a participant, whose interest is "practical," with "the sociologist or the historian," who from an "external point of view" are concerned with describing historical facts about the past and present actions and beliefs and dispositions of the members of that community. But why should we think that claims like (3), (4), or (5) below—which as we saw Dworkin attributes to "most legal philosophers"—are claims about the grounds of propositions of law, rather than claims about what law looks like from the external point of view?

(3) Law is a matter of plain fact.[27]
(4) Law is always a matter of historical fact.[28]
(5) Law depends only on matters of plain historical fact.[29]

---

[26] Dworkin (1986: 13).
[27] See the quotation accompanying n. 22 above.
[28] See the quotation accompanying n. 23 above.
[29] See the quotation accompanying n. 24 above.

Let me try to bring out my point more clearly. Consider, for example, the claim made in (3). It is not as transparent as it might be. Let us unpack it slightly as the claim that

(3b) The existence of law is a matter of plain fact.

We can make it clearer. Rephrase (3b) as the claim that

(3c) Sentences of the form "There is [or "there exists"] law in community
        c", if true, are true solely in virtue of plain facts.

or, better yet,

(3d) Sentences of the form "There is [or "there exists"] a legal system in
        community *c*", if true, are true solely in virtue of plain facts.

Is (3d) true? Perhaps it is still equivocal. But what does seem to be true is that one characteristic use of sentences of the form "There is [or "there exists"] a legal system in community *c*" is to refer to a particular social arrangement, the obtaining of which in a community is a solely a matter of plain facts. This is the sense in which a sociologist or an historian would use a sentence like that. In that sense, "There exists a legal system in community *c*" is an external statement that refers to plain facts. If we take it to refer to such external statements, then, (3d) is true.

Statements like (3), (4), and (5) can be naturally understood in this way. They can be understood as statements of the same sort of statements (1) and (2) above. They are statements about what law looks like from the external perspective of an observer; and the claim is that from that perspective, law is indeed a matter of historical fact; it is a social phenomenon, a matter of social fact. That then is what the majority of legal philosophers would seem to accept if Dworkin is right that the majority of legal philosophers accept (3), (4), or (5). But in that case Dworkin has no case against the majority of legal philosophers, for (3d) does not entail anything like the plain-fact view of the grounds of law. In fact, (3d) entails no view whatsoever regarding the grounds of law. (Nor is (3d) in itself a particularly interesting claim. The interesting challenge is to give an account of *what* social or historical facts do have to be in place for an external statement of the form "There is a legal system in community *c*" to be true. Different theorists may give different accounts.) Nor does Dworkin seem to believe that it does. He would agree that the claim that the sociologist's or the historian's external statements about law are statements of plain social fact does not imply that participants' propositions of law—internal statements of what the law actually is on some given matter in some legal system—are themselves statements of plain social fact, or that their truth or correctness is solely a matter of plain social fact.

Why then should Dworkin think that other philosophers who endorse (3), (4), or (5) are thereby committed to the plain-fact view? I see two possible answers. Either Dworkin believes that those philosophers have misunderstood the implications of (3), (4), or (5); or he has himself misconstrued their views. The latter appears to be the case. Dworkin names H. L. A. Hart's 1961 book *The Concept of Law* as "the most important restatement" of the idea that "law is a matter of historical fact." Here is how he reports Hart's take on this idea:

> [Hart] said that the true grounds of law lie in the acceptance by the community as a whole of a fundamental master rule (he called this a "rule of recognition") that assigns to particular people or groups the authority to make law. So propositions of law are true not just in virtue of the commands of people who are habitually obeyed, but more fundamentally in virtue of social conventions that represent the community's acceptance of a scheme of rules empowering such people or groups to create valid law . . . [F]or Hart [the proposition that the speed limit in California is 55 miles an hour] is true because the people in California have accepted, and continued to accept, the scheme of authority deployed in the state and national constitutions.[30]

Consider this last statement, the statement that "the people in California have accepted, and continued to accept" a certain "scheme of authority." This is what Dworkin would call an "external" statement. It describes or reports actions and attitudes of the people in California and what they happen to accept or recognize as law. It is a statement of plain fact.

By contrast, the statement that the speed limit in California is 55 miles an hour is an internal statement. It is a statement or proposition *of* Californian law. Now Dworkin claims that for Hart, this latter proposition is true because of the former. "Because" is ambiguous, but Dworkin's charge here is that Hart thought that internal statements of law are grounded solely—or at any rate "fundamentally"—in statements of plain fact. But the charge is unwarranted. Indeed, the point that Dworkin wants to press against Hart seems actually to be *taken* from Hart's own work; as is, of course, the very distinction between "internal," normative statements of law, and "external," factual statements about law, which Hart introduced and defended.[31] Hart does think that, generally speaking, there is no legal system in a community unless (to put it in Dworkin's somewhat coarse terms) the "community as a whole" accepts a "rule of recognition" that "assigns to particular people or groups the authority to make law;" and this acceptance is taken to be a matter of historical fact. But that does not mean, and Hart did not think, that *that this fact is the case* is what "grounds" propositions of law, what makes propositions of law true or correct.

Am I misreading Hart? It is true that my reading is not entirely uncontroversial. But that is because Hart's distinction between internal and external statements— a distinction that is central in his work—has too often been either misunderstood or just plainly overlooked, not least of all by authors who take themselves to endorse Hartian views.[32] So let me say more about the topic, and try to offer my own reconstruction of the contrast between the two kinds of statements.

---

[30] Dworkin (1986: 34).

[31] See Hart (1955a: 247-249); Hart (2012/1961: 88-91, 102-106).

[32] Kevin Toh has done a great deal to set these matters straight over the past decade—see Toh (2005: 76-78, 110-114); (2007: 404-409); (2008: 451-461, 482-493); (2010: 1287-128); (2013: 459-463);

1.3. INTERNAL AND EXTERNAL STATEMENTS

1.3.1. Particular Internal Statements

It is by reference to the notion of a rule that Hart's distinction between internal and external statements can best be understood. Put legal rules to one side for a moment, and think instead of the rules of a game like football or cricket. Consider a statement that a player in the game is out. Hart says that the function of a statement like this is to assess a particular situation by reference to the rules of the game. A statement that a goal took place ("Goal!") is another example; another would be a statement that the score right now is 2-2.[33] In making statements like these, we are using a rule that we accept (and take others to accept) as appropriate for assessing the game: we are applying the rule to the ongoing game.

Statements of this sort are the paradigmatic instance of what Hart calls an internal statement.[34] When we make them, we are concerned with rules in a particular way: we *make use* of rules to assess particular cases by reference to them. I will call these statements "particular internal statements." Particular internal statements are one of two main species of internal statements, but before introducing the other species it will be helpful to draw the contrast with external statements.

1.3.2. External Statements

There are other ways of being concerned with the rules of a game. We may be interested in the history of the game. We may want to find out how its rules have changed over time, or what specific rules were in fact accepted and applied (and how) in different periods by players and referees and sports fans and commentators. In that case, we will be engaging with rules from the outside, as it were. Our questions will not be about *how to assess* any given situation in a game by reference to any set of rules that we accept as appropriate for that purpose. Rather, they will be questions about *what rules are (or have been) in fact accepted and used by those who do engage (or have engaged) in rule-based assessments of actual games.* To make this clearer, compare these two questions:

(Q1) Is player *p* out?
(Q2) What rule or rules do those engaged in assessing ongoing games accept as appropriate for determining whether a player is out?

Question (Q1) is an internal question. In answering it, one would be applying one of the rules of the game. An answer to (Q1) is an internal statement, a

---

(2015: 696-703)—but although his work is well-known, the relevant points have not been taken up in the literature as much as they should. Similar points have also been made in forceful terms by Pedro Múrias in a couple of pieces that are not as easily accessible (because they are written in Portuguese): see Múrias (2006); (2010). I have found Múrias's and Toh's discussions very helpful, even if there are several aspects of their analyses that I find unpersuasive.

[33] See Hart (2012/1961: 102-103, 142-143).
[34] See Hart (2012/1961: 102-103).

particular internal statement. By contrast, (Q2) is an external question. It is a question about the way in which those who engage with question (Q1) go about answering it: it is a question about how certain people actually go about answering internal questions. An answer to (Q2) is an external statement.

Hart's view is that (Q1) and (Q2) are questions of very different kinds. Question (Q2) is unequivocally an empirical question, a question of empirical social fact. *That* those who concern themselves with internal questions like (Q1) do engage with and apply certain rules when they go about answering those questions, is an empirical fact. So answers to (Q2)—external statements—are descriptive statements of fact. (Of course, (Q2) is only one among the numerous questions of fact that could be asked about how people answer questions like (Q1). What answers have they given on what occasions? Do they always agree? How often do they disagree? And so on. These are all external questions, and their answers would all be external statements of empirical fact.[35])

Answers to (Q1), in turn, are not empirical statements. They are, Hart says, "normative statements." He also says that in answering internal questions we use language "normatively."[36] In what sense are internal statements normative? There is no exegetically clear answer to this question, but the thought seems to be that questions like (Q1) are themselves normative questions; arguments offered in support of answers to such questions will characteristically include normative considerations: no such answer can be completely justified on the basis of empirical premises alone.[37] I say a bit more about this further below (in Section 1.3.11).

1.3.3. General Internal Statements

So suppose I am playing football or some other game, and that I want to answer question (Q1) with regard to a player in the other team. In answering question (Q1), I will be using and applying to a particular case a rule that I accept as being appropriate for that very purpose. My answer to (Q1) is not a statement *of* that rule. The rule that I use is *applied* in my answer, which is a particular internal statement ("Yes, player *p* is out", "No, player *p* is not out"); the rule itself is left unstated. But I *could* give a statement of the rule that I accept as an appropriate rule to use in answering questions like (Q1) in the context of the game. I would then say something along the lines of "A player is out when . . ."

Statements like these—statements *of* rules made by those who accept them as appropriate standards for the assessment of particular cases—are internal statements, too. I will call them "general internal statements."

General internal statements have to be carefully differentiated from external statements reporting that *the rule is accepted* by a certain person or persons. In Hart's words: "it is important to distinguish the *external statement of fact*

---

[35] See Hart (2012/1961: 89).
[36] See Hart (2012/1961: 117).
[37] See Hart (2012/1961: 140).

asserting that members of society accept a given rule from the *internal statement of the rule* made by one who himself accepts it."[38]

1.3.4. The Normal Context of Internal Statements

I said that in the example of a player stating that another player in the game is "out," the speaker is applying a rule that she accepts as appropriate for the purpose of assessing what counts as being out. That is indeed the normal context in which such statements are made: a context in which the speaker not only (a) herself accepts that the rule she is applying is the appropriate rule to use for that purpose, but moreover (b) takes her addressees to also accept that it is the appropriate rule to use.[39] These two facts—(a) and (b)—are also left unstated by the speaker; but if she utters the internal statement "He is out", adding no caveat or qualification, then unless the context is abnormal her listener will be warranted in supposing that both (a) and (b) are true; for what would be the "point" of making such an unqualified statement if either (a) or (b) were false?[40]

Notice that (a) and (b) are straightforwardly factual propositions. *That* the speaker accepts, or takes others to accept, that a given rule is an appropriate to use for the purpose of assessing a given particular situation, is a matter of empirical fact. Notice also that the content of the presupposition mentioned in (b) amounts to an answer to the external question (Q2):

(Q2) What rule or rules do those engaged in assessing ongoing games accept as appropriate to determine whether a player is out?

We saw that an answer to (Q2) is an external statement. So in normal contexts, whoever makes an internal statement applying a given rule to some particular case can be said to presuppose the truth of the external statement that that rule is actually generally accepted as appropriate for that purpose.

What this means, however, is *not* that unless (a) and (b) are true, one cannot sincerely make a particular internal statement. One does not have to accept that a given rule R_1 is the appropriate rule to apply, or to believe that others accept it, in order to sincerely put forth an internal statement applying R_1 to a particular case. If I believe, or believe that others believe, that we should be using a different rule, R_2, to assess whether or not a player is out, I am not thereby prevented from asking and answering the question whether player p is out *when the situation is assessed in terms of R_1*. My answer will be a particular internal statement all the same. I should only take care to *make it known* to my listener—if context does not already make it clear—that either (a) or (b) or both are actually false in this instant case. Unless I actually wish to deceive my listener, I should cancel the implicatures that attach to the utterance of unqualified internal statements of this sort.[41]

---

[38] Hart (2012/1961: 291, emphasis added).

[39] See Hart (2012/1961: 84-85, 142).

[40] See Hart (2012/1961: 103-104).

[41] Things appear to be different, though, with general internal statements, statements *of* rules. It seems that the sincere utterance of an unqualified general internal statement ("A player is out

1.3.5. Internal Statements of Legal Validity

What about the law? Here, too, we can distinguish between external and internal statements, and, with regard to the latter, between particular and general internal statements.

One prominent class of internal statements in the legal domain is the class of statements that some rule is legally valid: "internal statements about the validity of rules," as Hart calls them.[42] These are particular internal statements, not general ones. They are statements applying a general rule governing what rules are valid (a "rule of recognition," in Hart's terminology), to a *particular* rule, which is declared to be valid (or invalid).[43] Such statements, in other words, give answers to questions like the following:

(Q3) Is rule R a legally valid rule?

In answering (Q3), a speaker will apply a rule of recognition RR which is itself "left unstated"[44] when the speaker utters her conclusion—her particular internal statement—that rule R is indeed a legally valid rule. But a speaker who thus applies a given rule RR that she accepts as appropriate for the purpose of answering a question like (Q3) can also, if needed, offer a statement *of* that rule RR. With regard to the issue of legal validity, then, a speaker can (a) offer a general internal statement of RR (which statement might take the form "A rule is legally valid when...") as well as (b) particular internal statements applying RR (which statements would take the form "Rule R_1 is legally valid," "Rule R_2 is not legally valid," and so on). (Hart sometimes gives "What the Queen in Parliament enacts is [valid] law" as an abbreviated formulation of a general internal statement of the rule of recognition of the British legal system.[45])

1.3.6. The Variety of Internal Legal Statements

Internal statements of legal validity are one class of internal statements that can be made with regard to the law. Another class that Hart highlights is the class of statements applying legally *valid rules* to particular cases: for example, statements that a certain person p has a certain legal obligation or right, or statements that a particular transaction is legally valid.[46] Such statements are therefore particular internal statements. They apply a particular legal rule— a "primary," legally valid rule—to a particular case. The corresponding *general* statement—a statement *of* the valid rule that the speaker is applying—is of course possible as well.

---

when...") involves the speaker's own acceptance that *that* is indeed how things are to be done in the context of the game.

[42] Hart (2012/1961: 235).

[43] Hart (2012/1961: 101-103); see also Hart (1959: 167).

[44] Hart (2012/1961: 108, 293).

[45] Hart (2012/1961: 107, 111, 148).

[46] Hart (2012/1961: 103-104).

This means that for any actual instance of a decision applying a first-order, legally valid rule R to a particular case, we can discern four kinds or strands of internal statements:

(1) A general statement of a rule of recognition RR accepted as appropriate to assess legal validity ("A rule is legally valid when...");

(2) A particular statement applying RR to a particular case ("R is a legally valid rule");

(3) A general statement of rule R (for example, "Whoever... is under the legal obligation to φ"; "A will is legally valid when...");

(4) A particular statement applying R to a particular case ("Person p is under the legal obligation to φ"; "This will is legally valid").

It is perhaps worth pointing out that there seems to be no implication from a *particular* internal statement of legal validity regarding some first-order rule R (that is, a statement like (2)) to the *general* internal statement *of* that rule R (that is, a statement like (3)). One can accept the rule that is *applied* in (2) while not accepting the rule that is *stated in* (3); and vice versa.[47]

In what follows, I will concentrate on internal statements of (second-order) legal validity—that is statements like (1) and (2)—but some of the points I will make apply *mutatis mutandis* to first-order internal statements.

1.3.7. The Normal Context of Internal Statements of Legal Validity

The normal background or context in which someone makes an unqualified statement of the form "R is a legally valid rule" is the context in which the speaker is seeking to answer a question like (Q3) *understood as a question relative to the legal system that is actually in force* in the community to which both the speaker and her listeners belong.[48] Characteristically, the speaker (a) herself accepts the relevant rule of recognition RR, and (b) takes that rule to also be generally accepted by other members of the community as appropriate for the purpose of assessing the legal validity of particular rules. (The rule that she and others accept is the rule of recognition that she is applying—*not* the rule R *to which* she is applying it.)[49] So, again, (a) and (b) can be left unstated, and they will be taken by listeners to be true. Of course, these implicatures too can be canceled, for example if the speaker is concerned with assessing the validity of rules of systems which are in force elsewhere (systems of which the speaker or her listeners are not actually participants or subjects in any way) or of systems which are no longer (or have never been) in force anywhere.[50]

---

[47] This point raises further issues that I cannot explore in this chapter. (It is unclear, for example, whether the sense in which one "accepts" a constitutive rule like the rule of recognition or a rule laying down the conditions for a valid will is the same sense in which one "accepts" a rule requiring that a certain action be performed or omitted.)

[48] See Hart (2012/1961: 104-105, 295).

[49] See Hart (2012/1961: 108, 117-118).

[50] See Hart (2012/1961: 104): "[T]hough it is normally pointless or idle to talk about the validity of a rule of a system which has never established itself or has been discarded, none the less it is not

Here, too, (a) and (b) are factual propositions. *That* the members of the community do actually accept the rule the speaker is applying as being the appropriate rule to employ in assessing whether certain rules are legally valid, is a matter of social fact. Indeed (b) involves an answer to the following, external question:

(Q4) What rule or rules do the members of our community in fact accept as appropriate for the purpose of determining which rules are legally valid?

In normal contexts, then, a speaker who, applying a given rule of recognition RR to a particular case, asserts that a certain rule R is (or is not) legally valid, assumes the truth of the *external* statement that RR is in fact accepted as appropriate for the purpose of determining which rules are legally valid.[51]

1.3.8. The Relation Between External Statements About the Rule of Recognition and General Internal Statements of Legal Validity

One of Hart's main claims is that we should not confuse a general internal statement of a rule of recognition RR with an external statement that RR is the rule that in a given community people actually do accept as the appropriate rule to assess whether particular rules are legally valid.[52] We should thus take care not to confuse (A4) and (A1):

(A4) In community c, the rule that is accepted as appropriate for the purpose of determining which rules are legally valid is the rule that whatever the Queen in Parliament enacts is valid law.

(A1) In community c, whatever the Queen in Parliament enacts is valid law.

(A4) is a factual statement. It reports the empirical fact that people in a certain community accept a certain rule for a certain purpose. It is an external statement. What makes it external is *not* the fact that it explicitly refers to a certain community c, as though the speaker is considering it—the community—"from the outside", as it were. What makes (A4) an external statement is that the speaker

---

meaningless nor is it always pointless. One vivid way of teaching Roman law is to speak *as if* the system were efficacious still and to discuss the validity of particular rules and solve problems in their terms." It might also be worth noting that my proposed taxonomy is not meant to be exhaustive; and that the "general"/"particular" contrast does not map onto Joseph Raz's well-known distinction between pure and applied (or applicative) legal statements: see Raz (1980/1970: 48, 217); (2009/ 1979: 62).

[51] See Hart (2012/1961: 108).

[52] See Hart (2012/1961: 103): the "use of an accepted rule of recognition in making internal statements" is to be "carefully distinguished from an external statement of the fact that the rule is accepted"; or (2012/1961: 112): "[t]he ultimate rule of recognition may be regarded from two points of view: one is expressed in the *external statement of fact that the rule exists in the actual practice of the system*; the other is expressed in the *internal statements of validity* made by those who use it in identifying the law."

is concerned with *the rule* "from the outside;" the following statement would also be an external statement:

(A4b) In *our* community, the rule that is accepted as appropriate for the purpose of determining which rules are legally valid is the rule that whatever the Queen in Parliament enacts is valid law.

Both (A4) and (A4b) are statements of fact. They are the sort of statements that could adequately be given as answers to questions like (Q4).

By contrast, (A1) is not a report of social facts at all. It has a very different meaning from (A4). (A1) is a statement that whatever the Queen in Parliament enacts *is* valid law in community *c*. It is or amounts to a statement that *that* is how validity *really is to be assessed* in community *c*. It is a general internal statement *of* the rule (and again, no less internal for the fact that it may be relative to a community other than the speaker's own).

To say that (A1) and (A4) have different meanings is not to say that they are unrelated. Indeed, it seems to have been Hart's view that *if* an external statement like (A4)—a statement that a certain rule of recognition *RR* is accepted—is true of a given community, then an internal statement like (A1)—a statement *of RR*—must also be true relative to the same community. But this thesis should not be misunderstood. The claim is *not* that no internal statement like (A1) can be true unless a corresponding statement like (A4) is true as well: Hart is clear that a legal system can exist even if as a matter of fact there is no convergence on any actual rule of recognition.[53] The claim, rather, is that *when* there is such convergence around a rule of recognition, then that *is* the rule of recognition of the community; and no statement *of* a different basic rule can then be correct.

1.3.9. The Relation Between External Statements About the Rule of Recognition and Particular Internal Statements of Legal Validity

Things are different, however, when it comes to the relation between (A4) and any *particular* internal statement applying the rule—the rule of recognition—stated in (A1) to some particular rule. That there is general agreement among the members of a community that *RR* is the appropriate rule to use in assessing what rules are legally valid does *not* imply that there is general agreement about particular internal statements applying *RR* to particular rules. That may seem obvious. What may not be so obvious is that disputed or controversial particular internal statements of legal validity are still *internal statements of legal validity*.

It is well known that Hart held that for any given rule, there will always be particular cases in which it is uncertain whether the rule applies. In such cases, the application of the rule involves what he called a "fresh choice" on the

---

[53] See Hart (2012/1961: 117-118, 122-123).

decision-maker's part.[54] The decision-maker's is a discretionary judgment; nevertheless it is *still* a judgment aimed at determining whether the rule applies to the case in hand. In other words, the decision-maker's answer to that question will still be a particular internal statement *applying the rule* to the particular case.

This important point is easy to overlook, in large part, no doubt, because in *The Concept of Law* Hart was not as clear about it as he might have been. It is often assumed that Hart's view was that a case in which the relevant rule does not clearly apply—for example, a case in which the language of a statutory rule proves indeterminate—is a legally unregulated case to be decided by making new law rather than by applying any pre-existing legal rule. But that was not Hart's view. He did hold that law is always partially indeterminate: that in any legal system there will be legally unregulated cases to which law provides no answer. But he did not think that "hard cases"—controversial cases in which no clear answer can be given on the basis of pre-existing rules—are *ipso facto* legally unregulated cases. On the contrary, he points out that when a judge is faced with a hard case, very often there are considerations that can be relied upon (and which judges do characteristically rely upon) to warrant the conclusion that the legal rule does apply to the particular case. Arguments by analogy appealing to "many complex factors running through the legal system and [to] the aims or purpose which may be attributed to a rule,"[55] the use of "canons of interpretation,"[56] and appeals to legal principles, are examples of considerations characteristically relied upon by judges as a "reasoned basis for decision" in hard cases.[57] To say that when the judge applies a legal rule to the case at hand on the basis of considerations of this kind, "the conclusion... is in effect a choice,"[58] is not to say that the judge is making law *rather than applying* pre-existing law. The exercise of discretion is required not because the rule does not apply, but because "there are reasons both for and against" holding that it applies;[59] the judge's conclusion, which may well be controversial, will still amount to a particular internal statement *applying* the rule ("Rule *R* is valid," "Person *p* has an obligation to φ"). Controversial "hard cases," then, are *not* the sort of cases that Hart has in mind when he says that law is always indeterminate, that law always leaves some cases unregulated.

Hart came to acknowledge that the point could have been more plainly made in *The Concept of Law* and in some earlier essays; but he took the opportunity to clarify his views. Thus in the "Introduction" to his *Essays in Jurisprudence and Philosophy* he says that

> [I]t may seem from what I wrote... that I thought that judges, when they reach a point at which the existing settled law fails to determine a decision

---

[54] Hart (2012/1961: 128).
[55] Hart (2012/1961: 127).
[56] Hart (2012/1961: 126).
[57] Hart (2012/1961: 204-205).
[58] Hart (2012/1961: 127).
[59] Hart (2012/1961: 123, 127).

either way, simply push aside their law-books and start to legislate de novo for the case in hand without further reference to the law. In fact this has never been my view...[A]mong the features which distinguish the judicial from legislative law-making is the importance characteristically attached by courts, when deciding cases left unregulated by the existing law, to proceeding by analogy so as to ensure that the new law they make is in accordance with principles or underpinning reasons which can be recognized *as already having a footing in existing law.* Very often in deciding such cases courts cite some general principle or general aim or purpose which a considerable area of the existing law can be understood as exemplifying or advancing, and *which points towards a determinate answer for the instant case*...[T]he search for and use of principles underlying the law *defers the moment,* [though] it cannot eliminate the need for judicial law-making.[60]

And also:

[T]he question whether a rule applies or does not apply to some particular situation of fact is not the same as the question whether according to the settled conventions of language this is determined or left open by the words of that rule. For a legal system often has other resources besides the words used in the formulations of its rules *which serve to determine their content or meaning in particular cases.* Thus...the obvious or agreed purpose of a rule may be used to render determinate a rule whose application may be left open by the conventions of language.[61]

In the "Postscript" to *The Concept of Law,* Hart is also quite clear that legally unregulated cases "are *not merely hard cases, controversial in the sense that reasonable and informed lawyers may disagree about which answer is legally correct;*"[62] and again he makes the point that

when particular statutes or precedents prove indeterminate, or when the explicit law is silent, judges do not just push away their law books and start to legislate without further guidance from the law. Very often, in deciding such cases, they cite some general principle or some general aim or purpose which some considerable relevant area of the existing law can be understood as exemplifying or advancing and which points towards a determinate answer for the instant hard case. This indeed is the very nucleus of the "constructive interpretation" which is so prominent a feature of Dworkin's theory of adjudication. [T]his *procedure certainly defers,* [though] it does not eliminate *the moment for judicial law-making.*[63]

---

[60] Hart (1983: 6-7, emphasis added).

[61] Hart (1983: 7-8, emphasis added); see also Hart (1967: 107).

[62] Hart (2012/1961: 252).

[63] Hart (2012/1961: 274-275, emphasis added). The publication of Hart's recently discovered 1956 essay "Discretion" confirms that that had indeed always been his view even before 1961. In this essay, Hart distinguishes "discretion" from mere "choice"; he characterizes the exercise of

This point holds with regard to *any* rules: not merely with regard to the application of *valid* legal rules to particular cases, but equally with regard to the application of rules of recognition to particular rules. Doubts can arise as to the "meaning or scope" of a rule of recognition;[64] there will always be particular cases—particular candidate rules—relative to which the application of the rule of recognition does not yield a clear result. Different decision-makers may then diverge on their assessments of the validity of such rules, and each will be ready to offer reasons in support of their conclusion. The fact that they do diverge—and more generally the fact that there is no widespread agreement on how to treat those particular cases—does not mean that a statement applying the rule of recognition to the hard case ("This is a valid rule") cannot be true or correct.

The lesson to draw is this. We saw that a speaker who applies a rule of recognition and makes a particular internal statement of legal validity can normally be taken to assume that the rule *being applied* is generally accepted by others in the group or community. But as we now see, there is no further assumption that others agree (or are disposed to agree) with the speaker's actual application of the rule as conveyed by particular internal statement. Agreement at the level of the rule being applied does not translate into agreement at the level of the particular statement of validity (and *a fortiori* it does also not translate into agreement at the level of any first-order conclusion applying the *valid* rule to any particular case).

1.3.10. The "Existence" of Legal Rules and Legal Systems

A statement that a given rule "exists" in a given community is ambiguous, according to Hart: it can be understood either as an external or as an internal statement.[65] One thing a speaker might mean by it is that in a given community a certain mode of behavior is in fact accepted as a standard and generally used by its members. That is the sense in which one might interpret the assertion (made at the time of Hart's writing) that "in England a rule exists that we must bare our head on entering a church."[66] This is an external statement (and again, what makes it external is not the fact that it explicitly mentions the community—England—to which it refers, but rather the fact that what is meant by the statement is that certain social facts obtain).[67]

---

discretion in terms of a reasoned or principled attempt to ascertain whether the legal rule does apply despite the fact that it does not clearly "yield a unique answer;" and he specifically includes "disputable questions of interpretation of statutes or written rules"—the sort of questions that give rise to Dworkinian "theoretical disagreements"—within the domain of questions that call for discretion in this sense: see Hart (2013/1956: 656). He had also pointed out in Hart (1959: 168-169) that (a) there is no reason to suppose that "normative internal statements"—*including* "legal statements of rights and duties or validity"—are all deducible from clear determinate rules [in combination with statements of fact]", and that (b) such statements—*internal* statements—are made in clear cases *as well as* in "the more debatable area of penumbra."

[64] Hart (2012/1961: 148).
[65] See Hart (2012/1961: 109-110).
[66] Hart (2012/1961: 109).
[67] See also Hart (2012/1961: 145-146).

But we can also say that a rule exists to mean that a (legal) rule is *valid*—and to say that a rule is valid is to make an *internal* statement applying a rule of recognition *to* that particular rule.[68] We should therefore distinguish, for any given legal rule, between two questions: the *internal* question about whether the rule is valid, and the *external* question about whether the rule is in fact accepted and complied with by the members of the community in general. Some rules, however, cannot by their very nature be said to be either valid or invalid. The rule of recognition of a legal system is one of them. It can therefore be said to "exist" only in the external sense; "the assertion that it exists can only be an external statement of fact . . . [It] exists only as a complex, but normally concordant, practice of the courts, officials, and private persons in identifying the law by reference to certain criteria."[69]

A similar ambiguity affects statements that a *legal system* "exists". These statements, too, can have both external and internal readings. In the external sense, such a statement is a *factual assertion* that refers to "a number of heterogeneous social facts" which are said to be in place "in a given country or among a social group."[70] But the assertion that a legal system "exists" can also be an *internal* statement of law "made from the point of view of one legal system about another, accepting the other system as 'valid'."[71]

Now Hart's core aim in *The Concept of Law* is to offer an account of the "complex social situation"[72] that has to be in place for an external statement that a legal system exists to be true.[73] Hart's core aim, in other words, is to offer an analysis of external statements of the form "there exists a legal system in community *c*." As is well known, he characterizes the relevant social phenomenon as involving two "aspects": general obedience by the bulk of the population to those laws that are valid by the system's tests of validity,[74] and (at least in normal cases) a "unified or shared official acceptance of the rule of recognition containing the system's criteria of validity."[75] As should now be obvious, this analysis does not (and is not meant to) give us an analysis of either particular internal statements of legal validity, or internal statements of (or applying) first-order legally valid rules.

1.3.11. The Normative Character of Internal Statements

As I said, what Hart means by the "normative" character of internal statements of law is not fully clear. But there is no doubt that he took internal statements to be normative in a sense that contrasts sharply with the purely factual character of external statements about law.

---

[68] Hart (2012/1961: 110).
[69] Hart (2012/1961: 110).
[70] Hart (2012/1961: 112).
[71] Hart (2012/1961: 296-297; see also 121-122).
[72] Hart (2012/1961: 100).
[73] See Hart (2012/1961: v, 112-115, 117-118, 201)
[74] Hart (2012/1961: 114).
[75] Hart (2012/1961: 114-115).

Indeed he explicitly contrasts statements *of law* with statements *of fact*,[76] and asserts that there are *"radical* differences between statements of law which operate within a system of rules and a statement of fact."[77] He speaks of the "internal non-factual, non predictive uses of language inseparable from the use of rules,"[78] and says that internal statements involve the "normative use" of language.[79] He denounces the "constant pull" towards an analysis of legal discourse in terms of "fact-stating" discourse,[80] and rejects any reductionist analyses that suppress the "normative aspect" of propositions of law.[81] He says that propositions of law have "normative force," and that "a central task of legal philosophy" is to explain this "normative force of propositions of law."[82] He says that "ought-propositions" cannot "be dispensed with in the analysis of legal thinking," indeed in the "elucidation of the internal aspect of any normative discourse."[83] And he suggests that there is a logical divide between the two kinds, preventing the very possibility of "conflict" between external and internal statements.[84]

1.4. FINAL REMARKS ON THE PLAIN-FACT VIEW

Can I rest my case? Dworkin is right that the plain-fact view is false. It is not true that internal statements of law can all be shown to be true or correct on the basis of factual, external statements alone. So what? He is wrong that legal positivists—or at least positivists who hold something like Hart's views—have endorsed it. On the contrary, it seems that Hart rejected (or would have rejected) the plain-fact view for very much the same reasons that Dworkin tries to use against him.

---

[76] Hart (2012/1961: 58-59, 118-119).

[77] Hart (1955b: 372, emphasis added). See also Hart (1959: 166) for the similar claim that external and internal statements are "two *radically different* types of statement for which an opportunity is afforded whenever a social group conducts its affairs by rules" (emphasis added).

[78] Hart (1959: 167).

[79] This point should not be confused with the further claim that "normative language" is used in *some* first-order internal legal statements: see Hart (2012/1961: 57, 85). Normative language is *not* the distinctive sign of the normative character of internal statements. Consider, for example, that statements of legal validity ("This is a valid rule") are explicitly offered by Hart (2012/1961: 117) as illustrations of the "characteristic use of normative language." Or note, for another example, that Hart clearly takes statements like "He is out" in cricket to be just as normative, even though no normative terminology is used. Besides, normative terminology can feature in external statements as well ("In community *c*, they accept the rule that they *must* φ", etc.).

[80] Hart (2012/1961: 98-99).

[81] Hart (1983: 13).

[82] Hart (1983: 18).

[83] Hart (1959: 166).

[84] Hart (2012/1961: 122).

2. Theoretical Disagreement and the Social Fact Thesis

2.1. DWORKIN ON "NORMATIVE" RULES

But hold on. Even if I am right about Hart, am I not being too quick to dismiss Dworkin's claim that legal positivists are unable to make sense of the phenomenon of "theoretical disagreement?" Is Dworkin's challenge not supposed to constitute a powerful objection against positivism? Have legal positivists not taken it seriously themselves?

Some have. They would accuse me of missing Dworkin's point. In fact, Scott Shapiro thinks *most* people missed it. Here is how—in a relatively recent and well-known essay that succeeded in rekindling legal theorists' interest in the topic—Shapiro articulates Dworkin's "objection from theoretical disagreements":

> The plain-fact view [of the grounds of law], according to Dworkin, consists of two basic tenets. First, it maintains that the grounds of law in any community are fixed by consensus among legal officials. If officials agree that facts of type *f* are grounds of law in their system, then facts of type *f* are grounds of law in their system. Second, it holds that the only types of facts that may be grounds of law are those of *plain historical fact*. As Dworkin convincingly argues, the plain-fact view cannot countenance the possibility of theoretical disagreements. For if, according to the first tenet, legal participants must always agree on the grounds of law, then it follows that they cannot disagree on the grounds of law.[85]

"According to [the plain-fact view's] first tenet," Shapiro says elsewhere, "a fact *f* is a ground of law only if there is agreement among legal officials that it is a ground of law":

> Disagreements among legal officials about whether *f* is a ground of law, therefore, are incoherent: without consensus on whether *f* is a ground of law, *it is not a ground of law*.[86]

Shapiro says this was Dworkin's objection in Chapter One of *Law's Empire*. I do not see much textual evidence to support this attribution. What Shapiro calls the "first tenet" of the plain-fact view is not something Dworkin explicitly articulates as such, as far as I can tell.[87] But it is true that something like this

---

[85] Shapiro (2007: 37).

[86] See Shapiro (2011: 286).

[87] Shapiro gives no page references. Perhaps something like Shapiro's "first tenet" might be reconstructed from Dworkin's discussion of "semantic theories of law" which "suppose that lawyers use mainly the same criteria...in deciding when propositions of law are true or false:" see Dworkin (1986: 33); but that is already part of Dworkin's "semantic sting" discussion, and Shapiro thinks that Dworkin makes his objection from theoretical disagreement *before* he advances the "semantic sting" argument: see Shapiro (2007: 54 n. 57). On the relation between the two arguments, see Smith (2010: 644-648).

objection had already been pressed by Dworkin in his essay "The Model of Rules II," which discusses Hart's characterization of a legal system's rule of recognition as a "social rule." Dworkin claims in that 1972 essay that a social "practice" of the sort that Hart describes as amounting to the existence of a "social rule" in a community is consistent with widespread controversy among the members of the group about what it is that the rule really requires:

> [Hart's] social rule theory...cannot explain the fact that even when people count a social practice as a necessary part of the grounds for asserting some duty, they may still disagree about the scope of that duty.
>
> Suppose, for example, that the members of the community which "has the rule" that men must not wear hats in church are in fact divided on the question of whether "that" rule applies to the case of male babies wearing bonnets. Each side believes that its view of the duties of the babies or their parents is the sounder, but neither view can be pictured as based on a social rule, because there is no social rule on the issue at all.[88]

Dworkin's point is not that this controversy regarding babies ought to prevent a sociologist from saying of this community that they have the rule—the social rule—that men must not wear hats in church. Dworkin's point is that the "content" of the social practice that might warrant this external statement—namely, that men do normally remove their hats in church, and recognize that they ought to do so, and are criticized (and recognize this criticism as justified) when they happen not to remove their hats in church[89]—does not necessarily coincide with the content of the rule—the "normative rule"—that each member of the group might assert "in the name" of the practice:[90]

> If a community has a particular practice...like the no-hat-in-church practice, then it will be likely, rather than surprising, that members will assert different normative rules, each allegedly justified by the practice...It is true that they will frame this dispute, even in this trivial case [regarding whether male babies may wear bonnets in church], as a dispute over what "the rule" about hats in church requires. But the reference is not to the rule that is constituted by common behaviour, that is, a social rule, but to the rule that is justified by common behaviour, that is, a normative rule. They dispute precisely about what *that* rule is.[91]

Disagreement, then, does not prevent each participant from offering statements of what they take the rule to require. Indeed, disagreement *manifests itself* in the form of competing statements of what the rule requires. But it does

---

[88] Dworkin (1977: 54).
[89] Dworkin (1977: 50).
[90] Dworkin (1977: 58).
[91] Dworkin (1977: 58).

prevent the sociologist from asserting the existence of a social rule on the disputed issue:

> [I]f half the churchgoers claim that babies are required to take off their bonnets and the other half denies any such requirement, what social rule does this behaviour constitute? We cannot say either that it constitutes a social rule that babies must take off their bonnets, or a social rule that provides that they do not have that duty.[92]

The same holds for law: disagreement among participants, Dworkin says, is inconsistent with "the concept of a social rule, as Hart uses that concept":

> If judges are in fact divided about what they must do if a subsequent Parliament tries to repeal [by a simple majority] an entrenched rule [itself enacted by a simple majority], then it is not uncertain whether any social rule governs that decision; on the contrary, it is certain that none does.[93]

But why does Dworkin press this point against Hart? The answer is again that Dworkin misrepresents Hart's views on the difference between external and internal statements when he claims that for Hart an internal statement of a normative rule cannot be true or correct unless an external statement of a social rule *with the same content* is true. Dworkin actually depicts Hart as *denying* that external and internal statements differ semantically. In Hart's view, Dworkin asserts, *both* kinds of statement assert that the factual "practice-conditions" are met, and the only difference between the sociologist and the participant or member is that the latter also "displays" his "acceptance of the [social] rule as a standard for guiding his own conduct and for judging the conduct of others."[94]

But this, as we saw, is not Hart's view at all. Observe, first, that for Hart particular internal statements—statements applying general rules to particular cases—are emphatically *not* statements *that* the relevant rule is in fact accepted by the speaker or anyone else in the group. Nor does the truth or correctness of any particular internal statement depend for Hart on the fact that anyone else in the group (let alone the group as a whole) agrees that the internal statement is true or correct. Internal statements are statements of what the speaker thinks *is* right,[95] not of what she thinks everyone else thinks is right. Particular internal statements can be true or correct even if they *are* widely disputed; and indeed no rule is such that its application to particular cases can leave no room for reasonable controversy.[96]

Second, Hart does say that two participants who disagree about what some rule requires in a particular case are still disagreeing about applications of "the" same

---

[92] Dworkin (1977: 54).

[93] Dworkin (1977: 62); the example is Hart's: see Hart (2012/1961: 149-150).

[94] Dworkin (1977: 51).

[95] Hart (2012/1961: 116).

[96] Hart (2012/1961: 123).

rule, and one could think, with Dworkin, that this misdescribes what is going on. If participants disagree about what is required, then they do not really converge on the "same" rule. But that is beside the point. The point is that if Hart refers to conflicting particular internal statements as statements applying the same rule, then it cannot be his view that what each participant takes to be the content of the rule (as Dworkin understands it) is exclusively "fixed"—Shapiro's verb—by agreement or convergent practice. Put differently: it is neither necessary nor likely that the content of what each participant would give as *her* considered internal statement of the group's rule coincides exactly with the content of what a sociologist would describe, on the basis of the group's convergent practice, as the rule that the group "has".[97] This is Dworkin's point—but Hart's view is consistent with it.[98]

So Dworkin's argument that legal positivists must think that theoretical disagreements are incoherent, as Shapiro puts it, is predicated on the same false assumption that underpinned the argument from *Law's Empire* that I discussed in Section 1. Both objections hinge on the false claim that positivists—or Hart at any rate—fail to adequately differentiate between external and internal statements. Both objections can therefore be dismissed for the very same reason.

2.2. WHY A DEBUNKING STRATEGY WILL NOT WORK

Yet Shapiro does not dismiss Dworkin's objection. On the contrary, he thinks it is a "vastly...effective" objection against legal positivism.[99] Others have agreed. That raises the suspicion that these theorists may themselves be unwittingly flouting the distinction between external and internal statements. If that is true, they are making the very mistake that Dworkin had falsely attributed to Hart, and which Hart himself had originally denounced. What is more, it is a mistake that these theorists are making *in the name* of Hartian positivism. Some of their arguments confirm this suspicion. Brian Leiter, for example, takes Shapiro's statement of Dworkin's objection seriously:

> [A Dworkinian] theoretical disagreement is a disagreement about criteria of legal validity, that is, about the *content* of what Hart calls the rule of

---

[97] Notice that this is *not* to say that collective practices are normatively irrelevant from the participant's point of view: see Waluchow (2011: esp. 373-379).

[98] Hart also observes that in the case of rules for which there is no authoritative linguistic formulation, there is no clear line between the uncertainty of a particular rule vis-à-vis some hard case, and the uncertainty of the criterion used to identify the rule itself: see Hart (2012/1961: 148). Notice that Dworkin seems to be assuming that any adequate internal statement, by a participant, of the relevant rule would either clearly include, or clearly exclude, the controversial case. But why should that be? Hart's view seems to be instead that even after a participant has made up her mind about some controversial case, her general statement *of* the corresponding rule could (and probably would) still be articulated in such a way as to leave the controversial case unsettled. Why should we think that a participant's general statement of what she takes to be a rule of her community will *change* every time she reaches a conclusion about the applicability of the rule to some hard case?

[99] Shapiro (2011: 288).

recognition. But the rule of recognition, on Hart's view, is a social rule, meaning its content—that is, the criteria of legal validity—is fixed by a complex empirical fact, namely the *actual practice* of officials (and the attitude they evince towards the practice). So it looks like the only dispute about the criteria of legal validity that is possible, on Hart's view, is an empirical or "head count" dispute: namely, a dispute about what judges are doing, and how many of them are doing it, since it is *the actual practice of officials and their attitudes towards that practice* that fixes the criteria of legal validity.[100]

Since Leiter agrees that judges "engaged in Dworkinian theoretical disagreements... are *not* engaged in an empirical dispute about how their colleagues on the bench typically or generally resolve disputes,"[101] he thinks legal positivists need to be able to explain *away* such disagreements. Leiter acknowledges that judges who disagree, for example, on how to construe a statutory provision do write "*as if* there is a fact of the matter about what the law is, even though they disagree about the criteria that fix what the law is."[102] Legal positivism is therefore unable to "vindicate what it *appears* [judges] are disagreeing about."[103] But Leiter bites the bullet. He thinks that legal positivists can still refuse to take the character of these disagreements at face value. There are two candidate explanations positivists can offer. They can say that parties to these disagreements are being disingenuous. Or they can say that if judges do "honestly think there is a fact of the matter about what the grounds of law are," then judges are simply *wrong* about that: "in truth there is no fact of the matter about the grounds of law in this instance *precisely because* there is no convergent practice of behavior among officials constituting a Rule of Recognition on this point."[104]

This move is unsatisfactory. To see why, consider first this other claim of Leiter's:

> Why should a theory of law be organised around the phenomenon of theoretical disagreements about law, absent some showing—nowhere to be found in Dworkin's corpus—that it is somehow *the* central (or even *a* central) feature of law and legal systems?... Even if we agreed with Dworkin that legal positivism provided an unsatisfactory account of theoretical disagreement in law, this would be of no significance unless we thought that this phenomenon was somehow central to an understanding of the nature of law and legal systems.[105]

---

[100] Leiter (2009: 1222).
[101] Leiter (2009: 1222-1223).
[102] Leiter (2009: 1223).
[103] Leiter (2009: 1223).
[104] Leiter (2009: 1224, my emphasis).
[105] Leiter (2009: 1220).

The truth, Leiter says, is that "there is *massive* and *pervasive* agreement about the law throughout the system:"[106]

> Theoretical disagreements about law represent only a miniscule fraction of all *judgments* rendered about law, since most judgments about law involve *agreement*, not disagreement.[107]

That, he says, is "the most striking feature about legal systems,"[108] and it tells in favor of positivism:

> One of the great theoretical virtues of legal positivism as a theory of law is that it...explains the pervasive phenomenon of *legal agreement*. Legal professionals agree about what the law requires so often because, in a functioning legal system, *what the law is* is fixed by a discernible practice of officials who decide questions of legal validity by reference to criteria of legal validity on which they recognizably converge...legal positivism makes happy sense of the *overwhelming majority of legal phenomena*.[109]

This is an odd claim for Leiter to make against Dworkin. We can of course agree with Leiter that "massive agreement about law—not disagreement—is the norm in modern legal systems."[110] Others have drawn attention to that fact in discussions of Dworkin's views. Matthew Kramer, for example, points out that no legal system is viable without a substantial measure of regularity and predictability regarding the legal consequences of people's actions:

> If serious controversy is typical rather than exceptional—that is, if the legal consequences of people's multitudinous actions are ordinarily (rather than occasionally) "up in the air" and truly murky—then "lawlessness" is the correct designation for such a state of affairs.[111]

Notice, however, that the statement in this passage is an external statement. Or rather, it is a general second-order statement about what as a matter of fact must (not) be the case in any community for the external statement that *that community has a legal system* to be true. Now it would seem that Kramer is right that an external claim that some given community has a legal system is perfectly compatible with the fact that participants sometimes or even often disagree about what the law requires, provided that disagreement does not pervasively extend to every ordinary legal question or outcome. But is that a good point to press against Dworkin's objection? Not for someone who, like Leiter (but unlike Kramer), thinks that Dworkin's objection should be understood as Shapiro suggests.[112] In

---

[106] Leiter (2009: 1227).

[107] Leiter (2009: 1226).

[108] Leiter (2009: 1247).

[109] Leiter (2009: 1228).

[110] Leiter (2009: 1228).

[111] Kramer (1999: 142); see also (2013: 47-49).

[112] For another example of an attempt to rely on the allegedly low frequency of disagreements in support of a debunking strategy, see Shecaira (2012: esp. 137-142).

Shapiro's formulation, after all, Dworkin's objection is not that disagreement in modern legal systems is in fact rampant, pervasively affecting the vast majority of legal issues that arise. (Nor is the objection that positivists make the false empirical claim that disagreements just happen, as a matter of contingent fact, not to occur.) Dworkin's objection, as Shapiro casts it, is that positivists are committed to denying the very possibility of theoretical disagreements. Theoretical disagreements, remember, are supposed to be an incoherent phenomenon.[113] So the empirical frequency of disagreements is neither here nor there. A single instance of theoretical disagreement can be used a counter-example to the positivist claim understood as Shapiro and Leiter understand it.[114]

In fact, the very emphasis on frequency is misguided. The phenomenon of theoretical disagreements itself is not what supposedly needs to be explained and legal positivism fails to explain. What needs to be explained is what the phenomenon of theoretical disagreements is *evidence of*—namely, that judges do not think that the truth or correctness of their statements of law depends on everyone else or even a majority agreeing with them. And of course if that is true, it is true across the board: it is true not merely of statements that happen in fact to be controversial, but equally of statements of law with which everyone else agrees.[115] Think of a judge who quickly disposes of a case she finds clear because, for example, it falls squarely within the "plain meaning" of some statutory provision and no other considerations arise. Is she not committed to the claim that that outcome is indeed what the statute requires when *properly* interpreted? Perhaps everyone agrees with her; but again *that everyone agrees* is neither what the judge's internal statement asserts, nor what makes her statement true or correct.[116] So if Dworkinian theoretical disagreements do exist, then Leiter's legal positivist—far from making "happy sense of the overwhelming majority of legal phenomena"— will in fact fail to explain cases of massive agreement *as well as* cases of theoretical disagreement, regardless of their relative frequencies.

---

[113] See the quotation accompanying n. 86 above.

[114] Tim Dare (2010: 6) makes this point as well.

[115] This is not to say that underlying what appears to be massive agreement about the outcomes of most cases there is a "deeper" theoretical disagreement: compare Leiter (2009: 1228-1229). The explanation of any given instance of outcome-agreement may be that it is the reflection of widespread theoretical *agreement* among judges: that judges do agree on what they take to be the "grounds" of most propositions of law, though they do not hold those views because (or at any rate only because) others do or would agree with them. For a recent discussion (focusing on Leiter's views) of what explanations of agreement in law involve, see Smith (2015).

[116] Dworkin phrases this point vividly if somewhat misleadingly: "[I]t is implausible to think that any judge's convictions that he ought to decide cases in a 'proper' way depend on the convergent behavior of other judges. A judge would think he should decide in a proper way whatever other judges do or think. What is the alternative? Deciding improperly?" See Dworkin (2002: 1661). Dworkin's phrase is misleading because the question is not whether a judge thinks she should *decide in a proper way* whatever other judges do or think *about that* (that is, about whether she should *decide in a proper way*). The question is whether the reason she thinks her decision is *the* proper decision is the fact that other judges agree that it is indeed the proper decision to make.

This means that Leiter's debunking attempt to explain away theoretical disagreements as instances of either disingenuity or error is much weaker than he supposes, since it does imply—differently from what he claims[117]—that legal discourse is systematically mistaken. Leiter himself would agree that this is reason to think that an *error-theory* account of disagreements must be false; and given that the truth of the error-theory account is presupposed by the disingenuity account,[118] the latter must be false as well.

2.3. THE SOCIAL FACT THESIS

The motivation behind debunking strategies like Leiter's is to defend what Shapiro refers to, as we saw, as the "first tenet" of the legal positivist's plain-fact view—the claim that "the grounds of law in any community are fixed by consensus among legal officials."[119] This claim, in turn, is one version of what Shapiro calls the "Social Fact Thesis," which says that

> the existence and content of the law are ultimately determined by certain facts about social groups. Legal facts are grounded, in the final analysis, on social, not moral, facts.[120]

But a moment's reflection reveals that this thesis is unhelpfully equivocal.[121] It can be understood in two very different ways, and the preceding discussion can now help us to see why.

One way of reading the Social Fact Thesis is to understand it as a thesis of the same *kind* as, say, Hart's thesis that "the foundation of a legal system is an accepted rule of recognition specifying the criteria of legal validity."[122] This is a general thesis about legal systems, not a thesis about any particular system. It is true if and only if, for every legal system L (or for every normal or central case of a legal system), a certain subset of the participants of L accept a rule of recognition specifying the criteria of legal validity; and Hart is clear that to say *this* of any legal system is to make an "external statement of fact."[123]

Many people would indicate this thesis as distinctive of Hart's legal positivism: as his own version of the Social Fact Thesis. But notice the precise role that this thesis plays in Hart's theory. It gives us an account of the sort of facts—social facts—that have to be in place for any *external* statement that in some given community "there is" or "there exists" a legal system (or that they "have" a legal system) to be true. It gives us, in short, an account of the

---

[117] See Leiter (2009: 1226, 1232).
[118] Leiter (2009: 1224).
[119] Shapiro (2007: 37).
[120] Shapiro (2007: 33). See also Coleman (2002: 75).
[121] See also Toh (2008: 451-456, 479-493).
[122] Hart (2012/1961: 148).
[123] Hart (2012/1961: 111-112).

truth-conditions of statements about the "existence" of a legal system in some community, where "existence" is understood from the external perspective of an observer or sociologist. These truth-conditions are indeed a matter of plain, historical, social fact. This would suggest that legal positivism and the Social Fact Thesis in particular can be plausibly understood as claims of this sort—as claims about the truth-conditions of external statements about the existence of law or a legal system.[124]

But does it follow that the grounds of internal statements of legal validity— or, more generally, the grounds of statements of what the law actually *is* on any matter in any actual system—are exhausted by considerations of social fact? The answer, of course, is "No." The external statement "In England they recognize as law whatever the Queen in Parliament enacts" does not entail that the truth or correctness of internal statements of English law "depends" or is any way nec- essarily "grounded" in or "fixed" by social facts only. As we saw in Section 1, in fact, Hart would *deny*—and I think rightly—that the truth or correctness of *internal* statements of law could ever be solely a matter of social facts.

Shapiro's formulation of the Social Fact thesis equivocates between these two senses in which one could claim that the "existence and content of the law" are "ultimately determined" by (or "grounded, in the final analysis," in) "social facts." It could simply be read as a thesis about the truth-conditions of exter- nal statements about law, in which case one might agree that the Social Fact Thesis has a strong claim to being true. But if the reference to what "grounds" or "determines" the "existence and content of the law" is understood as a refer- ence to the truth- (or correctness-) conditions of *internal* statements of law as made by participants in a legal system—if it is understood as a reference to what *Dworkin* called the "grounds" of law—then the Social Fact Thesis seems false. Shapiro and Leiter, among others, fail to avert this difference. They fail to heed Hart's distinction between external and internal statements. They think that positivists should be able to defend the "internal" version of the Social Fact Thesis. They are wrong about that. It is no surprise then that they take Dworkin's argument from disagreement as an objection, and a forceful one at that.

---

[124] Would this mean that some version or formulation of legal positivism is true, indeed trivi- ally true? Not necessarily. We should distinguish between two claims: (a) the claim that whether or not the facts that need to be in place for there to be a legal system in some community *actually are in place* is purely a matter of historical fact; and (b) the claim that those facts are *themselves* purely social facts. The former claim is trivially true; but the latter—to which positivists would subscribe—is not: critics of positivism could hold that the relevant facts—the facts that need to be in place for there to be a legal system in a community—cannot be understood or described in purely non-normative or non-evaluative terms. For suggestions that Hart's positivism, or legal positivism more generally, either can or should be understood or at least reconstructed as an external, socio- logical view, see Simmonds (1979: esp. 364-368); Greenawalt (1987: 39-46); Alexy (2002/1992: 27-35); Toh (2008: 451-456, but see also 482-486); Greenawalt (2009: 158).

3. The Justificatory View

To conclude, I want to discuss a hybrid view—a view purporting to combine positivistic and non-positivistic elements—that has recently been put forth as an attempt to account for both interpretive theoretical disagreements *and* massive decisional agreements in modern legal systems: Stefan Sciaraffa's "Justificatory View."

We should differentiate, Sciaraffa says, between Hart's *positivistic theory of a legal system* and his *positivistic theory of legal content*.[125] A theory of a legal system is an account of the "existence conditions" of a legal system.[126] Hart's theory of a legal system was a positivistic theory, Sciaraffa says, because Hart held that "a legal system exists only if its officials converge sufficiently in the criteria of validity that they accept."[127] By contrast, a theory of legal content "is an account of what determines the norms that count as valid law in a legal system"; it is an account of "the foundational determinants of law."[128] Hart's theory of legal content, Sciaraffa says, was also a positivistic theory: he held the view that the "the foundational determinants of law in all legal systems" are social facts.[129]

This distinction is supposed to help us to address Dworkin's objection from theoretical disagreements. Sciaraffa thinks that a "plausible response" to Dworkin is to "abandon the positivistic theory of legal content while remaining faithful to the Hartian theory of a legal system."[130] And interestingly, Sciaraffa's "response" to Dworkin is Dworkinian through and through.

Like Dworkin, Sciaraffa looks at cases in which judges disagree "with respect to theories of interpretation."[131] In such cases, even though judges may all agree on how to identify the relevant valid sources—the valid statutory texts—they disagree over how those valid texts ought to be interpreted. As a consequence, says Sciaraffa, they disagree on what the law actually *is* on the relevant matter. That is because the "source-identifying criteria of legal validity" that enable judges to identify the relevant valid statutes "do not fully determine the legal content, the laws, of a legal system." Rather, the legal content of any particular text "will differ depending on which interpretive approach one takes."[132]

Interpretive disagreements of this sort are quite common, Sciaraffa says:

> [I]nterpretive approaches often remain unsettled. For example, intentionalist originalism, plain-meaning originalism and an analogue of the living

---

[125] Sciaraffa (2012: 167).
[126] Sciaraffa (2012: 170).
[127] Sciaraffa (2012: 171).
[128] Sciaraffa (2012: 170).
[129] Sciaraffa (2012: 170).
[130] Sciaraffa (2012: 167).
[131] Sciaraffa (2012: 174).
[132] Sciaraffa (2012: 176).

tree approach each have a formidable contingent of defenders in American courts and legal scholars.[133]

And he thinks that theorists who adopt a *positivistic theory of legal content* cannot make sense of this phenomenon. After all, these theorists hold that "what fixes a legal system's theory of interpretation" is a *convergent* interpretive practice. "[O]n this view," then, "insofar as there is no convergent interpretive practice, there is no way to fix the theory of interpretation that couples with the legal system's" source-identifying criteria "to determine fully" what the law is.[134] However, judges who disagree over interpretive matters typically "assume a rhetorical stance of discerning rather than constructing the law in those cases;" and Sciaraffa like Dworkin is rightly wary of debunking strategies, like the one discussed above in Section 2, that insist that these judges are either confused or hypocrites.[135]

How then should we account for such disagreements? We should recognize that "fixing the proper interpretive approach... does not turn on the convergence of an interpretive practice amongst legal officials;"[136] we should abandon a positivist account of legal content. Instead, we should adopt the justificatory view, which holds that "the proper interpretive approach is determined by political and moral considerations."[137]

Thus far, as Sciaraffa remarks,[138] he and Dworkin are on the same page. What is the difference between their views? The difference, says Sciaraffa, is that unlike Dworkin's theory, the justificatory view is capable of "explaining massive decisional agreement among [a] legal system's officials."[139] That is because the justificatory view, although it rejects a positivistic theory of legal content, does not reject a positivistic theory of a legal system. Indeed, the justificatory view "accepts and rests upon" what Sciaraffa takes to be "the Hartian [positivistic] theory of a legal system":

> The justificatory view agrees that a legal system exists only if there is sufficient convergence among its officials with respect to the rule of recognition. However, the justificatory view emphasizes that this convergence need not be full convergence. Rather, it need only be sufficient to sustain the massive decisional convergence characteristic of a system of rules rather than a cacophony of conflicting directives. That is compatible with a great deal of disagreement about the proper theory of interpretation to apply to legal

[133] Sciaraffa (2012: 177-178).

[134] Sciaraffa (2012: 177).

[135] Sciaraffa (2012: 181).

[136] Sciaraffa (2012: 184).

[137] Sciaraffa (2012: 184): in "the constitutional-democratic context", for example, the "proper interpretive approach" according to the justificatory view "is the one implied by the best or correct account... of the underlying value of the constitutional-democratic rule of recognition."

[138] Sciaraffa (2012: 184).

[139] Sciaraffa (2012: 186).

sources, and even some disagreement at the margins with respect to source-identifying elements of the rule of recognition, so long as the decisions from these somewhat varying perspectives about the system's rule of recognition generally overlap.[140]

But Sciaraffa's justificatory view is problematic. Notice first that although the non-positivistic element of the justificatory view is supposed to be a non-positivistic theory of legal content, Sciaraffa's argument seems to warrant only a non-positivistic theory of *one aspect* of legal content. Namely, it seems to warrant only a non-positivistic theory of "what fixes a legal system's theory of interpretation."[141] Yet legal content is also a matter of what the valid sources are. Sciaraffa may be right to point out that "source-identifying criteria of legal validity . . . do not *fully* determine legal content;" but surely they do *partly* determine legal content. So does the justificatory view call for a non-positivistic theory of source-identifying criteria of legal validity? This is unclear. One reason to think it does not, though, is that the justificatory view is meant to be committed to what Sciaraffa sees as Hart's positivist theory of a legal system, and this theory as Sciaraffa presents it seems to include a claim precisely about the criteria of legal validity. Here is Sciaraffa's own statement of the "account of the existence conditions of a legal system," which the justificatory view is supposed to accept (and which he takes to be Hart's):

> [A] legal system exists only if (1) its officials converge in accepting from the internal point of view more or less the same criteria of legal validity (as well as the system's related rules of change and rule of adjudication), and (2) the system's citizens generally comply with the norms that the system's officials recognize and apply as law.[142]

Now if the justificatory view adopts a positivist theory of source-identifying criteria of legal validity, then by Sciaraffa's own lights the justificatory view is committed to something like the "social fact" thesis of source-identifying criteria of legal validity. That means that the justificatory view is unable to account for theoretical disagreements among judges regarding what the source-identifying criteria of legal validity actually are. In fact—whether or not the justificatory view is formally committed to a positivistic account of source-identifying criteria of legal validity—Sciaraffa explicitly says, as we saw, that regarding "the source-identifying elements of the rule of recognition," the justificatory view tolerates only "some disagreement at the margins."[143] But then the justificatory view does fall prey after all to Dworkin's objection from theoretical disagreement. Sciaraffa writes as if Dworkin's objection applies only to theories of interpretation.[144] But

---

[140] Sciaraffa (2012: 187-188).

[141] Sciaraffa (2012: 177).

[142] Sciaraffa (2012: 169).

[143] See the quotation accompanying n. 140 above.

[144] "The specific disagreement that Dworkin and others have raised," he says, "is with respect to theories of interpretation": see Sciaraffa (2012: 174).

that of course is not true. As the discussion in the previous sections shows—and as clearly emerges from the variety of cases Dworkin uses to illustrate his point—Dworkin's objection concerns theoretical disagreements about what the valid sources are *as well as* theoretical disagreements about how the valid sources ought to be interpreted.[145] Given that Sciaraffa agrees that Dworkin's objection from theoretical disagreement is sound, it follows that his own justificatory view is wrong.

What could Sciaraffa reply? That as a matter of fact source-identifying disagreements are not as common as interpretative disagreements? That in any viable legal system disagreement about the sources occurs only "at the margins"? But as we saw in Section 2, this reply is a non-starter for anyone who thinks that Dworkin's objection from theoretical disagreements does constitute a forceful challenge to social fact theories. Unless, of course, Sciaraffa insists that the justificatory view is serious about being a non-positivistic theory of legal *content* and is accordingly committed to a non-positivistic theory of source-identifying criteria. But then why should the justificatory view insist on widespread convergence with regard to such criteria? For a non-positivistic theory of legal content, after all, that there actually *is* widespread agreement among officials is a contingent matter; it is not something that a non-positivist theory of legal content sets out to "explain."

These worries are symptomatic of a deeper problem, which is that Sciaraffa too is insufficiently alert to the distinction between the internal statements of law made from the perspective of a participant, and external statements about law made from the perspective of an observer. The following passage, on an example given by Hart in *The Concept of Law*, is revealing:

> Consider a case in which two groups of legal officials fully converge in their understanding of every detail of their system's criteria of legal validity save for one difference. One group holds that legislative enactments are law, including entrenched provisions of such enactments that impose supermajority requirements on future legislatures who might seek to amend or strike the entrenched enactment, whereas a second group holds that legislative enactments generally are law but that any provision putatively entrenching such a law is not legally valid. Thus, these two groups disagree about the legal validity of provisions that purport to entrench a law. What should we say about the legal status of such provisions in the legal system? Are they valid or not?[146]

But this is the wrong question to ask. Whether the entrenched provisions *are* valid law is an internal question—a question about what actually *is* valid law in that system. Any answer to that question will therefore take the form of an internal statement of law, and will commit us to side with one of the two

---

[145] This point is helpfully highlighted in Smith (2010: 641).
[146] Sciaraffa (2012: 171-172).

groups of officials. Sciaraffa says that "the Hartian answer to this question is not obvious."[147] I think, on the contrary, that it *is* obvious that Hart was not at all concerned with questions of this sort to begin with. It is also obvious what Hart would say about the example. He would simply say that *the officials are divided on this point*, even though they converge on all other issues concerning their system's criteria of legal validity; and this of course is an external statement about *what the officials think about the validity of entrenched provisions*, not an internal statement *that* entrenched provisions are (or are not) valid. Hart would also say that if this is the sole extent of official disagreement, then such a community would certainly still have a legal system. In fact, that is what Hart *does* say about examples of this kind:

> The normal conditions of official, and especially of judicial, harmony, under which alone it is possible to identify the system's rule of recognition, would have been suspended. Yet the great mass of legal operations not touching on this constitutional issue would go on as before. Till the population became divided and "law and order" broke down it would be misleading to say that the original legal system had ceased to exist: for the expression "the same legal system" is too broad and elastic to permit unified official consensus on all the original criteria of legal validity to be a necessary condition of the legal system remaining "the same." All we could do would be to describe the situation as we have done and note it as a sub-standard, abnormal case containing within it the threat that the legal system will dissolve.[148]

And this—that in this legal system there is quite simply *no unified consensus* on all of the criteria of legal validity—does seem to be the natural thing for Hart to say. The reason is that it seems plausible to think that from an observer's perspective, a statement that some given community has law—that is, an external statement that *there is* a legal system in a given community—would still be true even in the absence of such a unified consensus, provided that there were a substantial degree of convergence.

This will only be surprising for someone who mistakes Hart's view on what makes such an external statement about the "existence" of a legal system true, for a view on what actually makes a particular internal statement of legal validity—for example a statement of the form "*x* is a valid law" or "*y* is a validly enacted statute"—true or correct. And Sciaraffa seems to me to make this mistake. Like Dworkin, he seems to think that Hart was of the view that, for any particular internal statement *S* of the form "*x* is a valid law," *S* is true or correct relative to some legal system if and only if the officials in this system converge in accepting that *S* is true or correct.[149]

---

[147] Sciaraffa (2012: 172).

[148] Hart (2012/1961: 122-123).

[149] See Sciaraffa (2012: 172).

I have suggested in the previous sections that this could not have been Hart's view. More importantly, however, I suggested that such a view is actually wrong. It is true, as I noted, that many contemporary theorists *have* sought to articulate "social fact" theories of what Sciaraffa calls the "foundational determinants" and Dworkin calls the "grounds" of internal statements of law. Sciaraffa, following Dworkin's lead, does move one step in the right direction. He agrees that "social fact" accounts of what he calls "legal content" must fail. But he should recognize that the relevant contrast to draw is not between positivistic accounts of the existence of a legal system and non-positivistic accounts of legal content. The relevant contrast to draw is between two perspectives (and two corresponding kinds of theories): the external and the internal perspectives of law.

References

Alexy, R. (2002/1992). *The Argument from Injustice: A Reply to Legal Positivism*, trans. S. L. Paulson and B. L. Paulson. Oxford: Oxford University Press.

Coleman, J. (2002). *The Practice of Principle: In Defence of a Pragmatist Approach to Legal Theory*. Oxford: Oxford University Press.

Dare, T. (2010) "Disagreeing about Disagreement in Law: The Argument from Theoretical Disagreement," *Philosophical Topics* 38:1–15.

Dworkin, R. (1977). *Taking Rights Seriously.* Cambridge, MA: Harvard University Press.

Dworkin, R. (1986). *Law's Empire.* Cambridge, MA: Harvard University Press.

Dworkin, R. (2002). "Thirty Years On," *Harvard Law Review* 115:1655–87.

Greenawalt, K. (1987). "The Rule of Recognition and the Constitution." Reprinted in *The Rule of Recognition and the US Constitution*, M. D. Adler and K. H. Himma (eds.). New York: Oxford University Press.

Greenawalt, K. (2009). "How to Understand the Rule of Recognition and the American Constitution." In *The Rule of Recognition and the US Constitution*, M. D. Adler and K. H. Himma (eds.). New York: Oxford University Press.

Hart, H. L. A. (1955a). "Theory and Definition in Jurisprudence," *Proceedings of the Aristotelian Society: Supplementary Volumes* 29:239–64.

Hart, H. L. A. (1955b). "Review of Axel Hägerström's *Inquiries into the Nature of Law and Morals*," *Philosophy* 30:369–373.

Hart, H. L. A. (1959). "Scandinavian Realism." Reprinted in Hart (1983).

Hart, H. L. A. (1967). "Problems of the Philosophy of Law." Reprinted in Hart (1983).

Hart, H. L. A. (1983). *Essays in Jurisprudence and Philosophy*. Oxford: Clarendon Press.

Hart, H. L. A. (2012/1961). *The Concept of Law*. Third edition. Oxford: Oxford University Press.

Hart, H. L. A. (2013/1956). "Discretion," *Harvard Law Review* 127:652–665.

Kramer, M. H. *In Defense of Legal Positivism: Law Without Trimmings.* Oxford: Oxford University Press.

Kramer, M. H. (2013). "In Defense of Hart." In *Philosophical Foundations of the Nature of Law*, W. Waluchow and S. Sciaraffa (eds.). Oxford: Oxford University Press.

Leiter, B. (2009). "Explaining Theoretical Disagreement," *The University of Chicago Law Review* 76:1215–1250.

Múrias, P. (2006). "As Perspectivas Interna e Externa da Normatividade," available at url: <http://muriasjuridico.no.sapo.pt/Interna-externa-normativ.pdf>

Múrias, P. (2010). "Weber e Hart sobre as Perspectivas Externa e Interna: Uma Releitura." In *Estudos em Homenagem ao Prof. Doutor Sérvulo Correia*, vol. 1., J. Miranda (ed.). Coimbra: Almedina.

Raz, J. (1980/1970). *The Concept of a Legal System.* Second edition. Oxford: Clarendon Press.

Raz, J. (2009/1979). *The Authority of Law.* Second edition. Oxford: Oxford University Press.

Sciaraffa, S. (2012). "Explaining Theoretical Disagreement and Massive Decisional Agreement: The Justificatory View," *Problema* 4:165–189.

Shapiro, S. J. (2007). "The 'Hart-Dworkin' Debate: A Short Guide for the Perplexed." In *Ronald Dworkin*, A. Ripstein (ed.). Cambridge: Cambridge University Press.

Shapiro, S. J. (2011). *Legality.* Cambridge, MA: Harvard University Press.

Shecaira, F. P. (2012). "Dealing with Judicial Rhetoric: A Defence of Hartian Positivism," *Australian Journal of Legal Philosophy* 37:131–158.

Simmonds, N. E. (1979). "Practice and Validity," *Cambridge Law Journal* 38:361–372.

Smith, D. (2010). "Theoretical Disagreement and the Semantic Sting," *Oxford Journal of Legal Studies* 30:635–661.

Smith, D. (2015). "Agreement and Disagreement in Law," *Canadian Journal of Law & Jurisprudence* XXVIII:183–208.

Toh, K. (2005). "Hart's Expressivism and his Benthamite Project," *Legal Theory* 11:75–123.

Toh, K. (2007). "Raz on Detachment, Acceptance and Describability," *Oxford Journal of Legal Studies* 27:403–27.

Toh, K. (2008). "An Argument Against the Social Fact Thesis (and Some Additional Preliminary Steps Towards a New Conception of Legal Positivism)," *Law and Philosophy* 27:445–504.

Toh, K. (2010). "Some Moving Parts of Jurisprudence," *Texas Law Review* 88:1283–1321.

Toh, K. (2012). "La Falacia del Doble Deber y los 'Desacuerdos Teóricos' en el Derecho." In *Acordes y Desacuerdos: Cómo y por qué los Juristas Discrepan*, P. L. Sánchez and G. B. Ratti (eds.). Madrid: Marcial Pons.

Toh, K. (2013). "Jurisprudential Theories and First-Order Legal Judgments," *Philosophy Compass* 8/5:457–471.

Toh, K. (2015). "Four Neglected Prescriptions of Hartian Legal Philosophy," *Law and Philosophy* 34:333–368.

Waluchow, W. J. (2011). "Lessons from Hart," *Problema* 5:363–383.

9

Immodesty in Dworkin's Theory: The Lines Dividing Different Kinds of Conceptual Theory of Law

by Kenneth Einar Himma[*]

1. Introduction

Although Ronald Dworkin routinely characterizes his third theory as a rival to positivism, his theory can plausibly be thought of as being about something other than the specific concept of law that positivism seeks to explicate. For example, one might think that the positivist attempts to explicate the content of a descriptive *preinterpretive* notion of law, while Dworkin attempts to explicate the content of a normative *interpretive* concept of law.[1]

Normative and descriptive conceptual explications do not necessarily engage directly. Consider that the concept of law has a normative, as well as a descriptive, sense. The descriptive sense is roughly captured by the claim that laws are, by nature, norms enacted appropriately and properly enforced by the state. The normative sense is usually deployed in evaluating judicial decisions from the standpoint of legitimacy; for example, one might argue that *Roe v. Wade* "is not really law" in the United States. The only way to understand this usage is to understand it as normative: The idea here is that *Roe* and its descendants were incorrectly decided because there is no right to reproductive privacy in the Constitution of the United States (U.S. Constitution or Constitution), properly interpreted. But it should be clear that the normative sense I describe does not engage the descriptive sense I described as a rival; indeed, the normative sense seems, among other things, to be picking out the norms that the law should

---

[*]This study was supported by The Tomsk State University Academic D.I. Mendeleev Fund Program in 2015. The author is a Visiting Professor at Tomsk State University; and a Part-time Lecturer at the University of Washington School of Law.
[1]Dworkin (1987).

contain, whereas the descriptive sense seems to be picking out the norms that were manufactured according to the procedures defined by the criteria for promulgating law.

Indeed, Dworkin's interpretive views about law do a better job of raising puzzlies about core judicial and executive practices, as we normally understand them than challenging positivism, as a rival theory of law. In particular, Dworkin's theory calls attention to a number of philosophical problems involving certain judicial and executive mistakes. How should judicial mistakes be regarded on Dworkin's interpretive conception? On a purely pre-interpretive conception like positivism, judicial mistakes establish the content of the law; however, on an interpretive conception, judicial mistakes do not establish the content of the law. As Dworkin puts this point clearly:

> [W]e should first notice a different, more discriminating claim some legal philosophers have made: that in some nations or circumstances there is no law in spite of the existence of familiar legal institutions like legislatures and courts, because the practices of these institutions are too wicked to deserve that title. We have little trouble making sense of that claim once we understand that theories of law are interpretive.[2]

The pre-interpretive use is, on Dworkin's view, a degenerate use that validates such systems as those of law, while the interpretive use correctly vitiates the status of those systems as systems of law.

These different kinds of conceptual inquiry do not seem to engage directly; as Hart puts the point: 'It is not obvious why there should be or indeed could be any significant conflict between enterprises so different as my own [descriptive] and Dworkin's [normative] conception of legal theory.'[3] Nevertheless, Dworkin, like strong natural law theorists, consistently insists (1) that he is doing the same kind of theory as legal positivism, and (2) that his theory is, as a matter of logic, a rival to positivism, and (3) is better supported by the relevant reasons than positivism.

In this essay, I wish to dispute all three claims. The argument has a number of pieces. First, utilizing Frank Jackson's meta-methodological distinction between modest and immodest approaches to conceptual analysis, I argue that Dworkin, as well as strong natural law theorists, is deploying an immodest conceptual analysis (ICA) approach while positivism deploys a modest conceptual analysis (MCA) approach.[4] Second, I argue that the two approaches make presuppositions about *the nature of the concept* of law—as opposed to the nature of law itself—that are sufficiently different as to justify the claim that Dworkin and positivism are *best construed* as engaging in different theoretical

---

[2] Dworkin (1987: 101-102).
[3] Hart (1994: 241).
[4] Jackson (1998).

enterprises. Third, I will argue that an ICA approach, unlike a modest one, is consistent with our *all* being systematically mistaken about the concept to which the concept-term refers; thus, I infer, an ICA approach can result in an error theory of law, while a modest approach cannot. Fourth, I argue that Dworkin's theory implies an error theory of law, and that he has failed to meet the justificatory burden that must be met to justify abandoning a folk theory of law.

2. The Project of Conceptual Analysis and Its Traditional Connection to Metaphysics

Fundamental to the project of explicating a concept is the task of identifying certain properties that (1) are jointly instantiated by all and only things picked out by the corresponding concept-term and (2) *constitute* anything that instantiates these properties as being a referent of the concept-term. For example, if the nature of a bachelor is to be an unmarried adult male, then being an unmarried adult male might have many causal effects—e.g., loneliness. But it does not *cause* the person to be a bachelor; rather, being an unmarried adult male *constitutes* a person as a bachelor. Likewise, being a mass of floating water vapor does not cause that mass to be a cloud; it constitutes it as a cloud. Conceptual analysis, as traditionally conceived, is therefore concerned with explicating the *nature* of a thing, and it is the instantiation of the properties that exhaust the nature of some thing *L* which *constitute* it as an *L*.

As traditionally conceived, the *nature* of a thing is explained by giving a list of those properties that are *essential* to things of that kind, a notion that can be defined as follows:

> A property *p* is *essential* to being a *C* if and only if it is not possible for a thing to be a *C* without also having *p*.

For example, the property of being unmarried is an essential property of being a bachelor because it is not possible to be a married bachelor. Thus, *p* is essential to being a *C* if and only if it is a *necessary* truth that every *C* has *p*.

The field of metaphysics has traditionally been regarded as concerned with claims that can be justified without more empirical observation than needed to learn the relevant terms expressing the claims. Insofar as no further empirical observation (i.e., beyond understanding the terms) is needed to determine the truth or falsity of a claim, the considerations that confirm or disconfirm the truth of such a claim would seem to obtain in every logically possible world. Claims about the nature of a thing are, thus, metaphysical and expressed in terms of necessary truths. Metaphysical claims can also be (logically) possible, since empirical observation is not needed to discern whether something is possible. Indeed, every metaphysical claim is, on this traditional view, either necessarily true/false or possibly true/false.

3. The Modest and Immodest Approaches
to Conceptual Analysis

Frank Jackson distinguishes two meta-methodological approaches to conceptual analysis: MCA and ICA. Jackson believes that, although metaphysics is about what the world is like, the relevant questions must be framed in a language, and this gives rise to an important methodological constraint:

> [T]hus we need to attend to what the users of the language mean by the words they employ to ask their question. When bounty hunters go searching, they are searching for a person and not a handbill. But they will not get very far if they fail to attend to the representational properties of the handbill on the wanted person. Those properties give them their target, or, if you like, define the subject of their search. Likewise, metaphysicians will not get very far with questions like: Are there *Ks?* Are *Ks* nothing over and above *Js?* and, Is the K way the world is fully determined by the *J* way the world is? in the *absence of some conception of what counts as a K, and what counts as a J.*[5]

Accordingly, the subject of a modest approach is "the elucidation of the possible situations covered by the *words* we use to ask our questions."[6] On a modest approach, it would be appropriate to begin from "serious opinion polls on people's responses to various cases."[7] Conceptual analysis, on this approach, gives us insight into what the world is like *as we structure it according to the ordinary understandings that underlie our linguistic and other relevant social practices.*

Jackson says little by way of defining the ICA approach, but it is fairly expressed as just the negation of the MCA approach. In describing Peter Geach's attack on the four-dimensionalist approach to change, Jackson observes:

> [Geach] is not making any claim, one way or the other, about what the world is like; his claim is simply that if four-dimensionalism is true, it is right to say that nothing changes in the folk sense of change. But, of course, many have taken this kind of consideration to show that four-dimensionalism *qua* thesis about what our world is like is false.... We now have an example of conceptual analysis in what I call its immodest role. For it is being given a major role in an argument concerning what the world is like.[8]

On the immodest approach, then, the character of the features of the world purportedly described by four-dimensionalism is determined independently of any mental states we have. That is, the character of these features is determined independently of what we think about it and independently of how what we think

---

[5] Jackson (1998: 30-31).
[6] Jackson (1998: 33).
[7] Jackson (1998: 36-37).
[8] Jackson (1998: 42-43).

about it gets incorporated into the conceptual framework we adopt to talk about it. According to ICA, then, conceptual analysis gives us insight into what the world is like *independent of our linguistic practices and conceptual frameworks.*

4. Error Theories, ICA, and MCA

The principles that describe the MCA and ICA approaches are meta-methodological insofar as they involve assertions about the nature of the relevant concept, and what that nature entails by way of constraints on methodological principles. They are not fully defined methodologies or methodological theories that have a fully fleshed out epistemology. One could, for example, do what has come to be known as traditional conceptual analysis under a methodology that assumes either an MCA approach or an ICA approach. The MCA and ICA approaches, as Jackson describes them, articulate no more than a goal of a particular kind of theorizing: That goal is either to understand certain features of the world as they are defined and articulated through our conceptual practices or to understand those features as they *actually are* independent of the practices that enable us to describe them.

But even if they do not fully define a conceptual methodology, the principles that distinguish the two approaches have some methodological implications worth noting. To begin, the MCA and ICA approaches entails a methodology that is partly empirical in character insofar as each takes our ordinary intuitions about something as the starting point of conceptual analysis; what intuitions are *ordinary* is, after all, a matter of what intuitions are *commonly shared*—and that is an empirical property.

If the two approaches agree on starting from ordinary intuitions, they disagree on *why* we should start there. Insofar as the MCA seeks to reconcile conceptual theories with ordinary talk, it requires that we consider ordinary talk as a touchstone for evaluating theories about the nature of the relevant thing—and ordinary talk reflects the ordinary intuitions that underlie and ground that talk. In contrast, there is nothing in the articulation of ICA that entails that we take ordinary talk or intuition as a starting point. Indeed, there is nothing in the idea that conceptual analysis seeks to articulate the nature of things as they are independent of our thoughts and practices that would even gesture, as a logical matter, in the direction of starting from ordinary intuitions. Perhaps, the best reason for adopting such a starting point is that it is not clear, as a practical matter, what other viable resource we have for guiding these theoretical inquiries. Every inquiry has to have a standard to guide it, and it is not at all clear where we would start to do something like conceptual analysis if not from undefended assumptions of some kind—and that is how ordinary intuitions function in both approaches.

Not surprisingly, the two approaches differ according to how much epistemic weight should be assigned to the corresponding intuitions. MCA takes these intuitions as providing the ultimate standard for evaluating the relevant conceptual theory because MCA assumes that the object of conceptual analysis is to uncover the nature of the world as we define it through *our* conceptual frameworks and other associated social practices we use to describe it. ICA, in contrast, takes ordinary intuition to be nothing more than a guide to understanding the nature of a thing; our intuitions or ordinary talk are not conceived, under ICA, as defining the nature of the thing. For this reason, ordinary talk enjoys a privileged epistemic status on ICA, as well as on MCA, but that status, in the case of ICA, does not rise to the level of furnishing the ultimate touchstone for evaluating the relevant conceptual theory.

Accordingly, MCA can result in errors but only of a limited kind, whereas ICA can result in errors of a more potentially problematic kind. Insofar as our ordinary talk defines the nature of a thing, our conceptual theory of the thing must, at the end of the day, harmonize with ordinary talk; failure to do so is a potentially fatal error for a conceptual theory under MCA. Although ordinary talk is epistemically privileged under ICA, such talk falls well short of providing the ultimate touchstone it provides under MCA for evaluating conceptual theories of the relevant kind of thing. It is obviously not true, as a general rule, that what we think necessarily shapes what the world is *really* like (i.e., as it is independently of our minds); what we think is limited by our abilities while what the world is really like is not. Only in the case in which what we think, as is true of subjective preferences, defines the relevant aspect of reality—e.g., whether something is experienced as pleasant—is it true that our ordinary thoughts or intuitions about it necessarily provide an accurate picture of the aspect. Insofar as ICA presupposes that our practices do not define the nature of some thing T, any or all of our intuitions about T can be false.

This is the distinguishing feature of objectivity, in general. To say that a claim is objective is to say that its truth-value is determined entirely by considerations that are mind-independent and hence that its truth-value does not turn, even partly, on any person's or group's doxastic or intentional states. Indeed, it is the hallmark of objectivity that every person can be mistaken about an objective matter simultaneously. The earth is and has always been round, for example, even if there were times at which every person believed it is flat.

Further, the objectivity of a claim's truth-makers implies that everyone can simultaneously be systematically mistaken about the truth-value of that claim. It is the mind-independent character of the truth-makers of an objective claim that leaves open the possibility of everyone's being mistaken about its truth-value. Given this, there is no limit on just how deeply mistaken we can be about the content of the concept. Indeed, ICA is consistent with everyone being *systematically mistaken* at the same time about the truth-value of objective claims fleshing out the content of a concept or theory of some thing.

To describe this difference using a term coined by J.L. Mackie, MCA cannot, while ICA can, result in an *error theory*—i.e., a theory that purports to show that everyday thought, or what has the status of being the "folk theory" in some area, is so deeply and widely in error as to warrant its rejection on the relevant matter.

As Mackie puts the point in connection with moral objectivism, "the denial of objective values will have to be put forward not as the result of an analytic approach, but as an error theory, a theory that although most people in making moral judgements implicitly claim, among other things, to be pointing to something objectively prescriptive, these claims are all false." Mackie's error theory, then, asserts that widespread views about the objectivity of morality are *systematically* in error, and should be rejected.

5. Legal Positivism as Assuming MCA

Positivism purports to explain the nature of law *as such*—and this requires an account of the existence conditions for legal systems, as well as laws, since the existence of a legal norm presupposes the existence of a legal system.[9] Since positivism is an account of the nature of law, it is metaphysical in character inasmuch as it purports to provide existence conditions that (1) define essential properties of law which (2) constitute a norm as law. Since the notion of law presupposes the notion of a legal system, positivism must explain both elements. Accordingly, positivism must define the existence conditions for individual legal norms and for legal systems.

H.L.A. Hart provides such an account of the existence conditions for law and legal systems. First, there is a *legal system* in a society L if and only if (1) there is a conventional rule of recognition, defining the criteria of validity, that is accepted and practiced by those who serve as officials in L; and (2) people in L generally abide by the norms that are validated by the rule of recognition. Second, a norm n is a law in a legal system L if and only if there exists a legal system L in which either (1) n *is* one of the recognition norms practiced in L or (2) n has been promulgated in accordance with the rule of recognition in L.

All this is well known; for our purposes, the important point is that legal positivists are explicit in adopting MCA as the meta-methodological principle governing theorizing about the nature of law. As Hart describes his project, it is to identify the most general characterizing features of law (i.e., its essential properties) *as we ordinarily understand it*, which would be the appropriate project under MCA. As he puts it, "The starting-point for this clarificatory task is the widespread common knowledge of the salient features of a modern municipal legal system which . . . I attribute to any educated man."[10]

It is true that ICA would require adopting something like the widespread views of a common educated person as the starting point, but it is clear from

---

[9] The term *law* is ambiguous as between two meanings. Law can refer to an individual valid norm usually, if not necessarily, enforced by some governmental municipality. But law can also refer to the legal system in which such properly promulgated norms count as law that validly binds subjects.

[10] Hart (1994: 239). This is a point first made by Veronica Blanco Rodriguez.

Hart's methodology, if not from explicit remarks, that he assigns these views the kind of epistemic weight that would be warranted only under MCA. Consider, as one example among many of Hart's that could be adduced here, his rejection of Austin's account of obligation on the ground that one cannot derive an obligation to comply with a command from the state's ability and willingness to back the law with coercive enforcement mechanisms. Given the tension between Austin's account of legal obligation and our ordinary views about how the notion of *obligation* per se functions, it is clear that Hart is assigning the special weight to ordinary views and talk that MCA does, and ICA does not.

Joseph Raz is more explicit that it is the concept *that our practices construct* that *is the concept we should explicate*. Raz concedes, for example, that officials can sometimes be confused about the nature of authority, but denies that they can be systematically confused about it:

> Why cannot legal officials and institutions be conceptually confused? One answer is while they can be occasionally they cannot be systematically confused. For given the centrality of legal institutions in our structures of authority, their claims and conceptions are formed by and contribute to our concept of authority. It is what it is in part as a result of the claims and conceptions of legal institutions (Joseph Raz, Ethics in the public Domain (OUP, 1994), at 217).

On Raz's view, the concept of authority that should be the focus of our interest is *our* concept of authority—the one that is constructed by *our* social practices. Raz clearly adopts, although he does not use this language, MCA as the meta-methodological principle.

What this means, given the arguments of the last section, is that legal positivism cannot result in an error theory since it presupposes MCA. Since our ordinary practices construct *our* concepts, we cannot—absent somewhat extraordinary confusion about what our core legal practices are—be systematically mistaken in understanding law. Thus, the adoption of MCA by legal positivists assures that positivism, to succeed in its own implicit and explicit objectives, coheres tightly with ordinary linguistic and legal practices. As we will see in the next section, the strongest version of classical law theory adopts ICA and seems to result in an error theory of law.

6. Strong Classical Natural Law Theory as Assuming ICA

Strong classical natural law theory, like legal positivism, attempts to explicate the existence conditions for law and hence seeks to explicate law's nature. The distinguishing thesis of strong classical natural law theory, roughly put, is that unjust laws are not possible. As William Blackstone put the point:

> This law of nature, being co-eval with mankind and dictated by God himself, is of course superior in obligation to any other. It is binding over all the

globe, in all countries, and at all times: *no human laws are of any validity, if contrary to this*; and such of them as are valid derive all their force, and all their authority, mediately or immediately, from this original.[11]

According to this strongest version of classical natural law theory, it is a necessary truth that the criteria of validity contain a set of moral norms (i.e., the natural law) that must be satisfied by any posited norm to be valid. This entails that it is not conceptually possible to have a wicked law or wicked legal system.[12]

This latter is inconsistent with ordinary intuitions, lay and professional, about core (or paradigm) instances of what counts as law. To begin, it is taken for granted that there can be unjust laws and legal systems. Consider, for example, Austin's famous Hangman argument against Blackstone:

Now, to say that human laws which conflict with the Divine law are not binding, that is to say, are not laws, is to talk stark nonsense. The most pernicious laws, and therefore those which are most opposed to the will of God, have been and are continually enforced as laws by judicial tribunals. Suppose an act innocuous, or positively beneficial, be prohibited by the sovereign under the penalty of death; if I commit this act, I shall be tried and condemned, and if I object to the sentence, that it is contrary to the law of God, who has commanded that human lawgivers shall not prohibit acts which have no evil consequences, the Court of Justice will demonstrate the inconclusiveness of my reasoning by hanging me up, in pursuance of the law of which I have impugned the validity. An exception, demurrer, or plea, founded on the law of God was never heard in a Court of Justice, from the creation of the world down to the present moment.[13]

Further, ordinary legal practice presupposes that every mandatory norm properly promulgated according to the relevant social norms counts as a law that defines a legal obligation. This simply reports clear paradigmatic legal talk and practice: Losing defendants have violated a legal obligation and are subject to either criminal penalties or civil liability. But the uncontroversial ground, on the common view, is that liability of either kind is *legally* justified by the violation of a distinctively *legal* obligation. Violations of purely moral obligations are not actionable in legal systems resembling those of the United States.

Indeed, the idea that there are necessary moral constraints on the content of law is inconsistent with the very pedagogy of legal education in legal cultures resembling that of the United States. This legal pedagogy presupposes that everything in a statute book or a casebook that has not been invalidated in the legally appropriate way by a judicial or legislative act is a law! A law student who seeks to

---

[11] Blackstone (1979: 41).

[12] It is not clear how many natural law theorists have taken this very strong view, but it seems clear that William Blackstone did. In any event, I use this version merely for illustrative purposes as a preface to considering Dworkin's view.

[13] Austin (1995: 157).

refute the reasoning in an opinion by recourse to objections that have their entire ground in moral principles that are not positively implicated or adopted by the law will be quickly—and firmly—disabused of the idea that moral norms function this way in U.S. legal practice.

If this is correct, then this strongest version of classical natural law theory is inconsistent with the ordinary intuitions that (1) a legal system exists wherever the appropriate institutions and practices can be found without regard to the moral quality of these institutions or practices (or their outputs); (2) a norm is a law whenever it is properly promulgated; and (3) mandatory legal norms give rise to legal obligations. Given the foundational character of these intuitions, classical natural law theory implies that we are systematically mistaken about the nature of law. Classical natural law theory, thus, implies an error theory of law.

7. Dworkin's Third Theory as Assuming ICA

Dworkin has always construed his view as an account of the nature and "grounds" of law that is inconsistent with positivism. As he expresses his view, "the law of a community consists not simply in the discrete statutes and rules that its officials enact but in the general principles of justice and fairness that these statutes and rules, taken together, presuppose by way of implicit justification." In essence, then, Dworkin's view of the content of the criteria of validity can be expressed as follows:

Interpretivist Criteria of Validity (ICoV): A norm *n* is a law in *L* if and only if *n* is duly promulgated by a court or legislature *or n* can be rationally derived from the general moral principles of justice and fairness that show the law in *L* in its best moral light.

Construed as a rival to positivism, Dworkin's account of the criteria of validity (or grounds of law, as he characteristically puts it) identifies the properties essential to law and possession of which constitute a norm as law.

Dworkin's theory seems to clash with ordinary views regarding what seem to be two sets of core legal practice. First, Dworkin explicitly denies that judges have a quasi-lawmaking authority that binds other officials, but this is clearly incorrect—at least as far as ordinary legal talk and practice are concerned. For all the emphasis Dworkin places on common-law adjudication, he fails to notice that the common law is left by the legislature to judges to develop or construct. It might be true that legislatures have the authority to take control over any area of the law left to judges to develop; however, the content of the law in those areas subject to the common law authority of judges seems most plausibly characterized as manufactured by judges. Judges paradigmatically, *contrary to Dworkin's view*, have such a quasi-lawmaking authority.

Second, Dworkin's theory appears to commit him to denying the status of law of what, on the modest approach adopted by positivism, appear to be (core or paradigm) cases of law. For example, construed as doing conceptual jurisprudence according to a normative methodology, Dworkin is committed to claiming, and does claim, that the law *necessarily* includes the moral principles that cohere with the existing legal history which show that history in its best moral light. Here, it is worth observing that every conceptual methodology, with the exception of naturalized jurisprudence (and it is not at all clear whether anything properly characterized as "conceptual analysis" is even possible utilizing a naturalized approach), presupposes that the explication of the concept of law will result in either necessary truths or the denial of necessary truths.[14] The claim that law includes some set of moral principles in the grounds of law or criteria of validity must be a necessary truth if it is to count as a rival to positivism in the sense of being inconsistent with it.

Thus, on Dworkin's view, either *Plessy v. Ferguson*, which held that public school race-based discrimination did not violate the Equal Protection Clause of the Fourteenth Amendment, or *Brown v. Ferguson*, which declared such discrimination unconstitutional as violating equal protection, must be mistaken in the sense that it is inconsistent with the principles showing existing legal theory in its best moral light. Accordingly, one of those holdings—presumably *Plessy*, decided nearly 100 years before *Brown*—is mistaken in this sense: Only one of them could be derived from the general moral principles showing the legal history in the best light; the other is logically inconsistent with those principles and hence *cannot count as law*.

The problem this creates for Dworkin's theory can be seen more perspicuously from what he has to say about what it would take to defend or criticize the claim that there is usually one *legally* right answer in hard cases:

> The question, therefore, of whether there are no-right-answer cases in a particular jurisdiction—and whether such cases are rare or numerous—is not an ordinary empirical question. I believe that such cases, if they exist at all, must be extremely rare in the United States and Great Britain. Someone who disputes this cannot ... establish his case by relying on the demonstrability thesis or the other *a priori* arguments considered earlier. But nor is he likely to succeed by attempting to find actual examples of no-right-answer cases in a case-by-case search of the law reports. Each case report carries an opinion arguing that one side has, on balance, the better of the legal argument. Some cases carry a dissenting opinion as well, but this is also an argument that one side has the better case. Perhaps both the majority and minority opinions are wrong.[15]

Although Dworkin does not notice or discuss it, the last sentence of the quoted text calls attention to the problem. If there is one right answer in a particular

---

[14] Inclusive positivism denies the exclusivist claim, for example, that it is a necessary truth that the content of law is fully determined by its sources.

[15] Dworkin (1985: 144).

hard case, then the law itself already, and I mean this loosely, *dictates* a particular result. That result, expressed in the form of normative holding, is *already a
true proposition of law* on Dworkin's theory of law. If, however, the court goes in
the other direction in deciding a case, the court's decision is inconsistent with the
holding derived from the moral principles that show the existing legal history in
the best light. But it seems that such a holding could not establish the content of
the law, on Dworkin's theory.

This poses a dilemma for Dworkin's theory, construed as a rival to positivism.
Either the mistaken holding counts as law or it does not. If it counts as law, then
it seems to be a counterexample to Dworkin's view that "the law of a community
consists not simply in the discrete [enacted] statutes and rules but in the general
principles of justice and fairness that these statutes and rules, taken together,
presuppose by way of implicit justification" insofar as it is inconsistent with the
general principles of justice and fairness that show the existing history in its best
moral light. If it does not count as law, then it would seem inconsistent with core
legal practices in legal systems like those of the United States and the United
Kingdom that presumptively treat mistaken judicial decisions as establishing the
content of the law. Either way, the possibility of judicial mistakes creates problems for Dworkin's theory construed as a conceptual theory of the nature of law.

Consider, for example, the Fugitive Slave Act of 1850, which required, among
other things, citizens and officials to assist in the capture and return of escaped
slaves to their supposed owners. The Fugitive Slave Act was enforced as law
and upheld by a court decision that Dworkin regards as mistaken; as Dworkin
describes the problem:

> The general structure of the American Constitution presupposed as con-
> ception of individual freedom antagonistic to slavery, a conception of pro-
> cedural justice that condemned the procedures established by the Fugitive
> Slave Acts, and a conception of federalism inconsistent with the idea that
> the State of Massachusetts had no power to supervise the capture of men
> and women within its territory. These principles were not simply the per-
> sonal morality of a few judges, which they set aside in the interests of
> objectivity. They were rather, on this theory of what law is, more central
> to the law than were the particular and transitory policies of the slavery
> compromise.[16]

Insofar as the moral principles showing existing legal history in its best light
are inconsistent with the Fugitive Slave Act, Dworkin seems committed to
claiming that it was not valid law. If, as Dworkin claims, that—*as a conceptual
matter*—"the law of a community *consists* not simply in the discrete statutes and
rules that its officials enact but *in the general principles of justice and fairness
that these statutes and rules, taken together, presuppose by way of implicit justification*," then it is hard to see how the Fugitive Slave Act could count as law, given

---

[16] Dworkin (1975: 1437).

Dworkin's statement of his view. If the law cannot be morally justified as a piece of the existing legal history that is law in virtue of being derivable (in the relevant sense) from principles that justify enforcing that history, then it would seem to be conceptually excluded as law. Dworkin and the strong natural classical law theorist seem to converge on having to reject Fugitive Slave Act as being valid law.

One might think that the analysis above rests on a misinterpretation of Dworkin. Strictly speaking, he does not say that *every individual* law must cohere with the general principles of morality and justice that show the existing legal history in its best light. One might think that it is enough for a norm to count as law, on Dworkin's view, that it belongs to *a set of norms that include* the principles of morality and justice presupposed as justification by the properly promulgated norms, *taken together*. On this view, then, it is not that every norm in the law set coheres to the requisite extent with such principles; it is rather that the set of law norms, taken as a whole, coheres to the requisite extent with such principles.

The problem with this response is that it is inconsistent with the way in which judges should, on Dworkin's view, decide cases. In assessing the Fugitive Slave Act, for example, Dworkin does not consider whether the entire body of law coheres with the relevant principles. Rather, he considers the law in isolation in an attempt to determine whether those norms cohere with the relevant principles.[17] Although Dworkin's statement of his position consistently allows for two interpretations, only one makes sense given his core views about how judges decide cases.

Taken together, then, Dworkin's views about what counts as law are inconsistent with at least some core legal practices in the United States. To begin, officials, as a matter of standard practice, regard judicial holdings that result in new common law rules as being legally binding. Additionally, judges, lawyers, and officials, as a matter of standard practice, regard statutes upheld as constitutional as law and treat them as such—indeed, they are required to do so by the Constitution, which is considered "the supreme law of land"—regardless of whether they are consistent with the moral norms showing existing legal history in its best moral light.

These results seem to entail an error theory of law. Dworkin's view that judges lack something like a quasi-lawmaking authority might reasonably be asserted with respect to statutory interpretation; at the very least, the denial of that claim is contentious. But nothing like this seems plausibly asserted of core common law practices; it is commonly understood that judges have the authority to make new rules subject to certain guidelines.

Further, the idea that a mistaken court holding about the content of a properly promulgated norm does not count as law is deeply problematic. We saw this in connection with decisions about the constitutionality of properly promulgated norms. It seems clear that mistaken (on anyone's theory of constitutional mistakes) court decisions about the constitutionality of a properly promulgated law establish the content of the law. But the same problem arises in connection with

---

[17] The same can be said for Dworkin's examples involving Hercules.

any court decision that results in an interpretation of a legal norm that is inconsistent with the moral principles that show existing legal history in its best light. This is problematic because *every* court decision in a hard case is ultimately concerned with a problem of interpretation that the court can get wrong.

In response, one might concede that Dworkin's theory seems inconsistent with certain core practices insofar as it lacks an adequate explanation of the status of what would count as legal mistakes according to his theory, but argue that the mistakes are not sufficiently systematic enough to rise to the level of an error theory. Whether that is true depends on just how prevalent these cases are; if mistakes are sufficiently sporadic, they would not be deep and widespread enough to justify the claim that we are systematically mistaken about our core legal practices.

The problem with this argument is that, for all we know, those mistakes could be sufficiently widespread, numerous, and deep that they entail we are systematically mistaken about what counts as law. Since Dworkin's view presupposes moral objectivism and since no one has infallible or privileged access to the objective moral facts about the content of the law, it is possible that judicial and legislative mistakes (in the sense of producing output that satisfies the procedural grounds of law but not the moral grounds) sufficiently common as to result in our being systematically mistaken. In other words, it is possible for Dworkin's theory to entail an error theory of law.

That is good enough. To justify rejecting a theory of law from the standpoint of a view that takes our concepts as socially constructed, it is enough that it be possible for the theory to entail an error theory of law. Dworkin's theory might, or might not, entail an error theory with respect to legal practice in the United States. But, unlike legal positivism, it is possible for us to be systematically mistaken about these legal practices under Dworkin's articulated theory. For all we know, under Dworkin's theory, we might be systematically confused about our core legal practices—a result that is unacceptable from any conceptual methodology that is concerned to identify the content of *our* concepts.

In closing, it is also worth noting that, as was true of strong natural law theory, legal pedagogy is inconsistent with Dworkin's view. As noted above, the very pedagogy of legal education in legal cultures resembling those of the United States presupposes that everything in a statute book or a casebook that has not been invalidated in the legally appropriate way by a judicial or legislative act is a law! Given that law schools characteristically teach that purely moral arguments regarding the content of properly promulgated norms has no legal force, Dworkin's view is in tension with core ordinary legal practices. Taken together, these problems permeate our understanding of law at the most basic levels and, if Dworkin's view is correct, entail that we could very well be systematically mistaken about the nature of law. Dworkin's theory, thus, implies, at the very least, the possibility of an error theory of law. Accordingly, Dworkin's theory, like the classical natural law theory and unlike positivism, is best construed as adopting ICA as the operative meta-methodological principle.

8. The Justificatory Burden for Error Theories

The fact that ICA can, while MCA cannot, result in an error theory can have some important implications with respect to evaluating a conceptual theory. Error theories attribute a special kind of mistake to commonly held views about the nature of something that are quite stubborn because they come to seem self-evident. From an ordinary point of view, the law consists of those rules that the state promulgates in some official way and (typically, if not necessarily) enforces with its police power. An error theory of law entails that these seemingly obvious views are systematically in error and thus attributes potentially fatal mistakes to the folk view and, thus, requires a strong showing to justify its acceptance.

Consider, for example, the eliminative materialist's contentious ontological view that the furniture of the world contains no substances, properties, functions, or states that have the properties usually thought to distinguish the mental from the physical (i.e., the mental, as a conceptual matter, lacks extension, public observability, etc.). As Paul Churchland describes our folk psychology: "[O]ur common-sense psychological framework is a false and radically misleading conception of the causes of human behavior and the nature of cognitive activity." Thus, the eliminative materialist holds that our shared folk psychology, which is grounded in the idea that people have beliefs, thoughts, desires, and other mental states, is *systematically* in error and should be rejected. Like the term *phlogiston*, the terms "belief," "thoughts," "desires," etc., refer to nothing that, strictly speaking, really exists.

The intuitive implausibility of eliminative materialism calls attention to the issue of what must be shown to justify the acceptance of an error theory. What, exactly, is needed to justify accepting such a theory is unclear, but the burden is high. One could show that an error theory succeeds by showing that the view in question is systematically incoherent. At the very least, however, justifying an error theory requires a showing that is sufficient to overcome the intuitive confidence we have in the views challenged by the theory.

This is the point at which eliminative materialism seems to fall short. Eliminative materialists point, for example, to what they take to be failures on the part of our folk psychology to explain phenomena that a psychology must explain to be justifiably accepted (why, for example, we must sleep), but a few failures of this kind are not, without more, enough to warrant rejecting the folk psychology according to which there exist distinctively mental states that we instantiate. Likewise, the Churchlands point out that folk theories of other phenomena have been replaced by more scientific theories because those folk theories were systematically in error; but that is surely not enough to justify giving up a favored folk theory. The difficulties associated with justifying eliminative materialism arise because most people have far more confidence in the intuition that there are mental states (which, of course, is stubbornly grounded in the immediate experiences of what seem to be such states!) than in any claims that the eliminative materialist could possibly marshal in support of any claim to the contrary.

Dworkin has never expressed his rejection of positivism in terms of its being an error theory, but he has given arguments that would show, if successful, positivism is an error theory of law. Certainly, if Dworkin were correct that (1) the law of a community *necessarily* includes moral grounds of law concerned with justifying the exercise of coercive enforcement mechanisms; (2) judges lack any quasi-lawmaking authority; and (3) there is no conventional rule of recognition, then positivism would fairly be characterized as systematically mistaken about law and hence as an error theory. Although these arguments are not generally thought to have succeeded against positivism, the numerous considerations that Dworkin adduces against positivism would, if correct and taken together, plausibly support the characterization of legal positivism as an error theory—which is one more reason to think that Dworkin's view implies an error theory of law and thus presupposes ICA.

Either way, then, it should be clear that the burden for justifying an error theory is quite demanding precisely because an error theory challenges intuitions in which we have a great deal of confidence and which figure centrally into standardly accepted explications of other important phenomena. Indeed, I would surmise that a theory that implies an error theory to common views should be regarded as presumptively problematic.

9. A Discursive Disconnect Between Positivism and Anti-Positivism?

The idea that one theory X entails that another theory Y entails an error theory presupposes that the two theories are attempting to explain exactly the same phenomenon. It is reasonable to think that only a conceptual theory of law can entail that another conceptual theory of law or legal concepts is an error theory. Construed as rival accounts, positivism and anti-positivism would be candidates for error theories.

But there is another way to construe the disagreement between positivism and anti-positivism—namely, as failing to fully engage one another. Anti-positivists (which include natural law theorists and Dworkin's third theory) and positivists disagree on meta-methodology, and this gives rise to a question as to how to characterize the disagreement between the two theories. First, one might think that anti-positivists and positivists are simply talking past each other. One way of doing so is to think of positivism as being the explication of a purely descriptive concept of law, while Dworkin provides an explication of a normative concept of law.

By way of illustration, consider that there are two concepts of art, one descriptive and the other normative. The prevailing descriptive theory of art views art as being a purely social artifact: according to the institutional theory of art, something counts as a piece of art if it is an artifact created for the purpose of presentation to an audience and designated *art* by a member of the *art world*. According to the normative theory, something that counts as art from a purely descriptive standpoint might fail to be art if it does not meet certain standards of aesthetic excellence. It is the normative concept used in the familiar complaint about modern and post-modern art, "That's not art; my three-year-old could do that."

Dworkin provides a distinction that could be deployed as a starting point for an analysis of a normative concept of law. Dworkin, for example, allows that a wicked institutional normative system, like Nazi Germany's, counts as a legal system in one purely descriptive sense but not in a more important sense from the standpoint of legal theory:

> We need not deny that the Nazi system was an example of law ... because there is an available sense in which it plainly was law. But we have no diffi- culty in understanding someone who does say that Nazi law was not really law, or was law in a degenerate sense, or was less than fully law. For he is not then using 'law' in that sense; he is not making that sort of preinterpre- tive judgment but a skeptical interpretive judgment that Nazi law lacked features crucial to flourishing legal systems whose rules and procedures do justify coercion.[18]

At first glance, Dworkin's answer to the question of whether, "the Nazi system was an example of law," seems to be no more enlightening than the rejoinder, "Well, it depends on what you mean by 'law.'" For what Dworkin is claiming here is that whether the Nazis had law depends on whether the speaker is using *law* in a purely preinterpretive sense or in an interpretive sense.

But this would suggest that Dworkin and positivists are concerned to explicate different legal phenomena. On this construction of the dispute, one could argue that Dworkin's interpretive concept of law is a normative concept in the same sense that the normative concept of art is normative: whether something that counts as law in the descriptive sense also counts as law in the normative sense depends on whether it satisfies certain normative standards. Dworkin's interpre- tive concept is a normative concept, while the positivists are concerned to expli- cate the descriptive (or preinterpretive) concept.

This, of course, is inconsistent with Dworkin's own characterization of what he is doing. From the very beginning, Dworkin has conceived his theory as a rival to positivism—long after many theorists called attention to the possibility that Dworkin's theory did not engage legal positivism or, for that matter, strong classical natural law theory. Nevertheless, as we have seen in this discussion, the claim that positivism and Dworkin are explaining the same concept of law is problematic.

---

[18] Dworkin (1987: 103-104).

10. A Disagreement About the Real Nature
of the Concept of Law

Another way of characterizing the disagreement here is to view it as resting on differences about the proper meta-methodological approach and hence as involving a disagreement about the *real* nature of the concept of law—although it is true that neither anti-positivists nor positivists seem to have thought much in terms of their methodological commitments, and certainly not in terms of the distinction between MCA and ICA. The difference in this construction of the dialogue is that the positivist and anti-positivist are both engaged in attempting to explicate the content of the concept of law; the disagreement is, however, on the real nature of the content of the concept of law.

This can be seen by considering an argument available to the strong natural law theorist as a response to Austin's hangman objection. As Brian Bix has pointed out, the strong natural law theorist can argue that Austin's hangman argument begs the question against classical natural law theory. The strong natural law theorist would deny what Austin is claiming—namely, that the wicked norm enforced against the defendant counts as law.

At first glance, the counterargument to the hangman's argument might seem weak; after all, most people share the intuition that it was *law* that was enforced against the unfortunate defendant in the hangman case. If the game is to compare whose account best coheres with the most common intuitions, positivism probably wins the exchange, despite the fact that at the end of the day, positivism, strictly speaking, begs the question against natural law theory by assuming what strong natural law theory denies—namely, that wicked norms can count as law. But the question-begging character of the argument here is comparatively benign because *every argument has to start somewhere from premises that are assumed without argument.* Insofar as most people accept the premises, the argument is successful—even though a dissenter can argue that one or more of the premises beg the question.

But there is a more powerful, potentially less benign, sense in which the hangman argument begs the question, raising an important conceptual issue about law. One can argue that Austin's hangman argument makes certain meta-methodological assumptions not shared by the strong natural law theorist. If core ordinary legal practices are not decisive, as the question-begging charge presupposes, it would have to be because those core practices do not define the nature of the relevant legal phenomena in the way presupposed by the meta-methodological assumptions of MCA. Thus, the question-begging charge seems to assume that positivists are mistaken in thinking ordinary practices are decisive because they adopt MCA, a false meta-methodology that leads them astray.

What might initially appear, then, as a disagreement about how to characterize an ordinary core legal practice seems to presuppose a much deeper disagreement—and not just about meta-methodology. The two theories disagree, of course, with respect to the content of that concept, but they seem to be disagreeing about what kind of concept the concept of law is. The difference is akin to the difference between the view that X is a *social* concept and the view that X is a *natural* concept. Someone who grounds a rejection of the view that X is a natural kind of concept wholly on the strength of the assumption that certain practices define the nature of X is begging the question against that view, as the distinguishing characteristic of social kinds is, to put it roughly, that they are constructed by social practices—and the circularity here is an obviously vicious one.

Of course, I suppose one could take the position here that positivists and natural law theorists are talking past each other insofar as the positivist attempts to flesh out the concept defined by our practices, while the strong natural law theorist attempts to flesh out the *real* concept of law, defined independently of our practices and understanding. The problem is that there seems to be a real disagreement here, even if it is not one that has been explicitly exposed up until now. It is reasonable to think that most positivists would deny that there is a real concept of law of the sort that seems to be presupposed by natural law theory— and that seems to be a real disagreement, one with important theoretical implications. In consequence, the most plausible way to characterize the disagreement here would be as a disagreement about the *nature* of the concept of law.

11. Resolving Disagreements about the Real Nature of the Concept of Law

It is not entirely clear where Dworkin's argument for the interpretive nature of the concept of law would fit in the classificatory scheme developed here, but he gives an argument that distinguishes a preinterpretive from an interpretive concept of law and argues that the interpretive concept of law is the proper object of conceptual theory. Dworkin's argument attempts to show law is similar to courtesy, but begins with a sustained argument for the conclusion that courtesy is an interpretive concept:

> Imagine the following history of an invented community. Its members follow a set of rules, which they call 'rules of courtesy,' on a certain range of social occasions . . . . For a time this practice has the character of taboo: the rules are just there and are neither questioned nor varied. But, then, perhaps slowly, all this changes. Everyone develops a complex 'interpretative' attitude toward the rules of courtesy, an attitude that has two components. The first is the assumption that the practice of courtesy does not simply exist but has value, that it serves some interest or purpose or enforces some principle—in short, that it has some point—that can be stated independently of just describing the rules that make up the practice. The second is the further assumption that the requirements of courtesy—the behavior it calls for or judgments it warrants—are not necessarily or exclusively what they have always been, so that the strict rules must be understood or applied or extended or modified or qualified by that point. Once this interpretive

attitude takes hold, the institution of courtesy ceases to be mechanical; it is no longer unstudied deference to a runic order. People now try to impose *meaning* on the institution—to see it.[19]

Dworkin goes on to analogize the norms of law to the norms of courtesy to support his view that the concept of law is interpretive—i.e., that the real nature of the concept of law is interpretive and not preinterpretive as the positivist supposes.

There are at least three different conclusions Dworkin might be attempting to justify here. First, he might be trying to justify the adoption of ICA by arguing that the real nature of the concept of law is mind-independent. The idea is that there is some mind-independent point to courtesy to which we strive through our interpretive practices to conform our social practices and norms regarding courtesy. The problem is that there is nothing in the argument that would justify the attribution of anything that is mind-independent to the content of the concept of courtesy. The assumption that 'courtesy doesn't exist but has...some point...that can be stated independently of just describing the rules that make up the practice' does not tell us anything about what that point is. For all Dworkin has said, the point of courtesy could simply be imposed by what people come to commonly believe about courtesy. Nor does the fact that "the strict rules must be understood or qualified by that point" tell us anything interesting about whether the concept of courtesy is defined by our practices or is, instead, mind-independent. If the courtesy argument is deployed as an argument to justify a Dworkinian conclusion about the *real nature of the concept of law*, it falls well short of doing the work.

Second, he could be trying to meet the justificatory burden that an error theory has to meet, but this is very unlikely. Dworkin's target is positivism, but it is reasonable to hypothesize (and this is an empirical thesis) that Dworkin did not see positivism as expressing the folk theory or as expressing the ordinary views of legal practice. His own references to legal practice (especially, judicial practice) are sufficiently prominent to suggest that Dworkin believes that these features of practice are reflected in the folk theory (or ordinary views). He does, of course, believe that positivism is mistaken in a number of particulars, but (1) there is never any indication that he thinks the mistakes rise to the level of implying an error theory; and (2) his many arguments against positivism (e.g., the semantic sting, the existence of legal principles, and arguments against the idea that the rule of recognition is conventional) fall short of being persuasive.

Assuming Dworkin's argument can be deployed to this end, it is problematic. Even if it is true that (1) Dworkin's premises *validly* (though not necessarily soundly) imply that law is interpretive and (2) treating law as an interpretive concept is inconsistent with many claims positivism makes about what is central to legal practice, his argument would still not succeed. The problem is that, for the justification of the imputation of an error theory to some view to succeed,

---

[19] Dworkin (1987: 47).

the premises in that justification must be more intuitively plausible than the folk views that the theory seeks to refute. As far as I can see, there is nothing in Dworkin's argument above that jumps out as more plausible than the claims that (1) judges have authority to create law; (2) every mandatory legal norm creates a legal obligation; and (3) there can be wicked laws and legal systems in a sense that is highly relevant from a theoretical point of view.

Third, one might argue that Dworkin is not actually arguing for something that would entail that the nature of the real concept of law requires the adoption of ICA. Indeed, he grounds his argument for the idea that courtesy is an interpretive concept in various empirical observations about the *core social practices* of courtesy. Thus, for example, he points out that norms of courtesy may change over time, as the purposes that courtesy is supposed to serve are reconceptualized over time. Accordingly, one might argue Dworkin is arguing that law is a social construct, albeit an interpretive concept, that requires the adoption of MCA.

There is a serious, and potentially fatal, problem for this line of argument. If the foregoing analysis is correct, Dworkin's theory seems to entail an error theory in that we are systematically mistaken about the content of a concept that our views and understandings about core legal practices *construct*. But, as we have seen, it is an evaluative constraint on theories of concepts that adoption of MCA cannot result in an error theory. It would appear that, contrary to Dworkin's heavy reliance on what he takes to be ordinary understandings of the core practices of courtesy, he cannot consistently adopt MCA as a meta-methodological approach. Accordingly, his argument that courtesy and hence law are *really* interpretive concepts fails to justify his theory as an error theory and fails to justify the claim that the real nature of the relevant concepts warrant the adoption of ICA (if the latter, as appears *must be the* case, is his intention).

12. Conclusion

Dworkin's third theory of law and strong natural law theory seem to imply an error theory of law that presupposes the adoption of ICA. This raises a number of serious concerns that apply to both theories. First, insofar as each presupposes the adoption of ICA while positivism adopts MCA, anti-positivism and positivism seem to be talking past each other in the sense that they are not explicating the same concept of law, despite the traditional characterization of them as rival theories of the concept of law. Second, insofar as each anti-positivist theory implies an error theory, each must satisfy a comparatively high argumentative burden to fully support accepting that theory, and there is nothing in Dworkin's theory or classical natural law theory that would meet that burden. Further, and most important, there appears to be nothing in either anti-positivist theory or in what is commonly taken to be core legal practices that would support rejecting positivism in favor of anti-positivism. From the standpoint of the meta-methodological distinction between ICA and MCA, positivism seems to have the much stronger justification.

References

Austin, J. (1995). *The Province of Jurisprudence Determined.* In W. E. Rumble (ed.). Cambridge: Cambridge University Press.

Blackstone, W. (1979). Commentaries on the Law of England. Chicago, IL: University of Chicago Press.

Dworkin, R. (1975). "The Law of the Slave Catchers," *The Times Literary Supplement.* December 5, 1975.

Dworkin, R. (1985). "Is There Really No Right Answer in Hard Cases?" *A Matter of Principle.* Cambridge, MA: Harvard University Press.

Dworkin, R. (1987). *Law's Empire.* Cambridge: Harvard University Press.

Hart, H. L. A. (1994). *The Concept of Law,* Rev. ed. Oxford: Clarendon Press.

Jackson, F. (1998). *From Metaphysics to Ethics: A Defense of Conceptual Analysis.* Oxford: Oxford University Press.

10

Imperialism and Importance
in Dworkin's Jurisprudence
by Michael Giudice*

Questions about the nature of law in contemporary jurisprudence tend to occur at two levels. At one level, what we might call an object level, there are questions about the nature of law itself, which invite answers in the form of propositions about what law is and what it is not. At a second, meta level, there are questions about how to investigate and explain the nature of law: What is the correct or appropriate method to study law? There is of course a connection between the two levels. Those who advocate for a particular method for explaining and understanding law typically do so on the basis of argument about what law is actually like: The phenomenon of law demands, so to speak, a particular method for its explanation. In this chapter, I will defend a pluralist view at the meta level: There is more than one correct, appropriate method—three general methods, in fact—and each's correctness or appropriateness is tied directly to the nature of law itself (tied, we might say, to basic, deep facts about law). The first method is what we can call morally or politically evaluative investigation. The practice of law is constituted in large part by legal decisions, and legal decisions to create, apply, or enforce law are decisions of moral or political significance, since they affect people's well-being and interests. If this is true, as I think it is, then understanding law properly must involve moral or political assessment to understand under what conditions legal decisions are morally or politically justifiable (or not). The second method is social scientific: Law as we know it depends at crucial moments on the actions, choices, and decisions of humans and human institutions, from legislatures to juries to individual judges. Such human actors and institutions are, like all human actors and institutions, subject to economic, social, and historical influences

---

* For helpful comments and discussion, I would like to thank Leslie Green, Matthew Grellette, Max Leonov, Stefan Sciaraffa, Sam Steadman, and Wil Waluchow.

of various kinds, and so social-scientific study of law is also both appropriate and essential. The third method is conceptual: Law is constituted in significant ways by the use of concepts that exist as sets or clusters of abstract ideas, notions, expectations, and understandings, such as rights, obligations, contracts, and constitutions. To understand the concepts involved in law, as well as the concept of law itself, requires investigation of how these concepts of law are used and understood in practice, which is to engage in conceptual theory.

My objective in this paper is to argue against the view (which might even be characterized as an attitude) which supposes that the proper response to this diversity in methodology is to choose or argue for the superiority of one method over all others. As I shall maintain, each of the three general families of methods is correct and appropriate, and precisely because each responds to different aspects or dimensions of the nature of law itself. This is a rather tall order, and I can only hope to take a few initial steps here. My strategy is therefore limited in the following way. To show the shortcomings of the superiority or imperialism view of methodology, I will engage in sustained examination of the combination of object level and meta level claims in Ronald Dworkin's theory of law as integrity. To be precise, imperialism is the attempt to find and demonstrate the truth of a single methodological approach to understanding law. Any theory which does not adopt the method claimed to be the correct one is deemed to be inadequate. I believe imperialism has done much to obscure debates about particular legal theories, because it has tended to privilege one incomplete theoretical approach over complementary or competitive approaches that have independent merits. In focusing on Dworkin's work (particularly *Law's Empire*, which I believe still provides the fullest statement of Dworkin's general theory of law), I will identify three interconnected imperialist themes, and show how each, *if taken in isolation from and to the exclusion of other approaches*, contributes to an incomplete and often misleading explanation of the nature of law. The three imperialist themes are (1) all theories of law, to be true to the nature of law, must be theories of moral evaluation; (2) all theories of law must attribute a fundamental point or purpose to law; and (3) all theories of law must be offered from and for the participant's perspective, and in particular, the perspective of the judge.

After assessing each of these commitments, I then turn to a second view of diversity in legal theory, what I call the difference view, which can be understood largely as a reaction to imperialism in general, and Dworkin's imperialism in particular. The difference view maintains that theories should be distinguished and understood in light of their avowed purposes, such that theories of different types cannot be viewed as competitive if their principal aims are fundamentally different. I argue that although the difference view can be considered an improvement over imperialism, it is still to be rejected.

1. Moral Evaluation and Legal Theory

The first and most familiar metatheoretical commitment in Dworkin's philosophy of law is that theoretical accounts of law must be morally evaluative.[1] Julie Dickson terms this commitment the "moral evaluation thesis": "... in order to understand law adequately, a legal theorist must morally evaluate the law."[2] According to Dworkin, to attempt to describe and explain law in a morally neutral or detached way is to misunderstand both the nature of law and its proper method of analysis. One way of understanding the motivation of this commitment is to recall the opening passages of two of Dworkin's most influential works. In "The Model of Rules I," Dworkin highlights the moral significance of judicial decisions:[3]

> Day in and day out we send people to jail, or take money away from them, or make them do things they do not want to do, under coercion of force, and we justify all of this as speaking of such persons as having broken the law or having failed to meet their legal obligations, or having interfered with other people's legal rights.[4]

In *Law's Empire* Dworkin again writes:

> There is inevitably a moral dimension to an action at law, and so a standing risk of a distinct form of public injustice. A judge must decide not just who shall have what, but who has behaved well, who has met the responsibilities of citizenship, and who by design or greed or insensitivity has ignored his own responsibilities to others or exaggerated theirs to him.[5]

What Dworkin observes, as others[6] have also observed, is that all judicial decisions are decisions of moral significance. This follows from the observation

---

[1] Here we can quickly deal with a possible misunderstanding that ought not detain us. Although I identify *three* imperialist themes in Dworkin's work, which may seem contradictory, each of the following three themes to be discussed are to be understood as supporting his central, antipositivist thesis: Law must be understood from a perspective of moral evaluation.

[2] Dickson (2001: 9). Dickson also usefully distinguishes the moral evaluation thesis from the *moral justification thesis* and the *beneficial moral consequences thesis*. The moral justification thesis holds that "in order to understand law adequately, a legal theorist must hold the law to be a morally justified phenomenon." The beneficial moral consequences thesis states that "value judgements concerning the beneficial moral consequences of espousing a certain theory of law may legitimately feature in the criteria of success of legal theories." Dickson (2001: 9). Dworkin, we should note, is also committed to the moral justification thesis.

[3] Although Dworkin intends his account to apply to all types of legal decision-making (legislative, prosecutorial, etc.), I shall focus, as he does, on the process of judicial decision-making. As I shall argue below, Dworkin's account actually fails when applied to contexts outside judicial decision-making.

[4] Dworkin (1978: 15).

[5] Dworkin (1986: 1).

[6] For example, Joseph Raz notes explicitly: "[c]learly courts' decisions affect both defendants or accused and plaintiffs in substantial ways, and every decision by one person which significantly affects the fortunes of others, is, whatever else it may be, a moral decision." Raz (1995: 327-328).

that any human decision made by a rational person that affects, or can be reason-ably expected to affect, the lives or interests of another human being gives that decision moral significance, regardless of whether the person treats it as such. Thus, all judicial decisions that have effects such as protecting a right to equality, not allowing a murdering heir to inherit from his victim, or forcing a business to honor its obligations to customers, are also decisions of moral significance since they play a role in shaping and affecting people's lives. Dworkin reasons that if judicial decisions are in fact moral decisions, and judicial decision-making is a central feature of legal practice, then we ought to have some sort of understand-ing of the process which can make these morally justified decisions. Only such an understanding will provide an adequate answer to the central question, "What is law?" This understanding is best supplied, according to Dworkin, by his familiar theory of "law as integrity."[7]

Dworkin also argues that the process of judicial decision-making is inher-ently a morally committed task by a similar route, grounded more in empirical observation than in examination of the nature of legal decisions. In the "Model of Rules of I," he observes that judges frequently resort to arguments of principle in their decisions, to supplement (and sometimes change) the direction provided by statutes and previously decided cases.[8] Dworkin maintains that such resort to moral principles indicates that what the law is does not hinge solely on applying pedigreed rules to particular cases, but rather the actual criteria or grounds of law are fundamentally a matter of moral argument.[9] Further, Dworkin contends that when judges appeal to arguments of political morality and attempt to dis-cover the true force of past political decisions, they view their answers not as what the law should be or how it should be extended, but rather they believe they have discovered what the law really requires.[10] Dworkin concludes that any answer to the question, "What is law?" must acknowledge the fact that law is an *interpretive* concept; what law is depends on offering an account of the complex arguments of political morality that attempt to make judicial decisions morally justified decisions. He turns these observations into the following methodological commitment:

A full political theory of law, then, includes at least two main parts: it speaks both to the *grounds* of law—circumstances in which particular

---

[7] "Law as integrity" explains the process of judicial decision-making as follows: A judge con-structs a political theory that best fits and justifies current legal and political practices in their entirety (or as speaking in "one voice"), such as precedent-following and legislating, as well as the actual precedents and statutes that have been decided under those practices. The judge then constructs her decision to the case at bar which follows from her political theory. Dworkin (1986: chs 6-7).

[8] See again n. 4.

[9] To explain this alleged fact about law, Dworkin draws a distinction between two different types of disagreement about law: empirical disagreements about the application of particular laws and theoretical disagreements about what makes a proposition of law true. Dworkin (1986: 3-6).

[10] Dworkin (1986: chs 1, 4-5).

propositions of law should be taken to be sound or true—and to the *force* of law—the relative power of any true proposition of law to justify coercion in different sorts of exceptional circumstance.[11]

So according to Dworkin, any serious or adequate theory of law must be morally committed: To understand law properly, a moral evaluation or construction must be produced that shows when the coercive force of the state is justified. From this brief account of Dworkin's commitment to a morally engaged approach to understanding law, the other two metatheoretical commitments can be introduced.

2. An Essential Point or Purpose

The second metatheoretical thesis is that general theories of law "...aim to interpret the main point of and structure of legal practice..."[12] As Dworkin writes, such interpretation is "essentially concerned with purposes rather than mere causes."[13] In the context of his analogy of legal practice with the practice of courtesy, Dworkin continues that "[t]he citizens of courtesy do not aim to find, when they interpret their practice, the various economic or psychological or physiological determinants of their convergent behavior."[14] This contention is clearly meant to disvalue—in the theoretical illumination of law and its practice—causal explanations of law and legal phenomena such as those offered by the social sciences, namely, economics, sociology, psychology, and history, as well as the conventionalist approaches to law usually offered by legal positivists. For example, Dworkin assesses the sort of "sociological jurisprudence" made popular in the United States as follows: "...this emphasis on fact and strategy ended by distorting jurisprudential issues in much the same way as the English doctrinal approach distorted them, that is, by eliminating just those issues of moral principle that form their core."[15] A couple of pages later he concludes "...if jurisprudence is to succeed, it must expose these issues [of moral principle] and attack them as issues of moral theory."[16] Similarly, John Finnis, a prominent contemporary natural law theorist, argues that "actions, practices, etc., [e.g., law] can be fully understood only by understanding their point, that is to say their objective, their value, their significance or importance, as conceived by the people who performed them, engaged in them, etc."[17] So Dworkin's second

---

[11] Dworkin (1986: 110). We may also note that on Dworkin's account the answers to both parts of a theory of law, the grounds of law and the force of law, involve moral argument.

[12] Dworkin (1986: 14).

[13] Dworkin (1986: 51).

[14] Dworkin (1986: 51).

[15] Dworkin (1978: 4).

[16] Dworkin (1978: 7).

[17] Finnis (1980: 3).

metatheoretical commitment, which he shares with Finnis's natural law theory, is the claim that any adequate theory of law must attribute a fundamental point or purpose to law or legal practice. As he maintains, because of the coercive nature of judicial decisions which he observes at the beginning of both "The Model of Rules I" and *Law's Empire*, the fundamental point or purpose of law must be to justify state coercion: "[a] conception of law must explain how what it takes to be law provides a general justification for the exercise of coercive power by the state..."[18]

3. A Participant's Perspective

Dworkin also explains that to understand law fully or adequately, an internal or participant's perspective of law must be adopted; any external, non-engaged account of law will either fail to appreciate law and its features satisfactorily, or is not theoretically meaningful. In the following passage Dworkin explains why he thinks legal philosophers offer competing accounts of law with judges, to support his commitment that theoretical accounts must be from and for the participant's perspective:

> General theories of law... are constructive interpretations: they try to show legal practice as a whole in its best light, to achieve equilibrium between legal practice as they find it and the best justification of that practice. So no firm line divides jurisprudence from adjudication or any other aspect of legal practice. Legal philosophers debate about the general part, the inter-pretive foundation any legal argument must have. We may turn that coin over. Any practical legal argument, no matter how detailed and limited, assumes the kind of abstract foundation jurisprudence offers, and when rival foundations compete, a legal argument assumes one and rejects oth-ers. So any judge's opinion is itself a piece of legal philosophy, even when the philosophy is hidden and the visible argument is dominated by citation and lists of facts. *Jurisprudence is the general part of adjudication, silent pro-logue to any decision at law.*[19]

On this view, legal philosophers are in essentially the same business as legal practitioners: Any theoretical account must explain the actual structure or nature of legal argument, which in turn requires or amounts to participation in the prac-tice (even if only hypothetical). Put in different terms, both legal philosophers and judges attempt to answer the question, "What is law?" Their answers will be

---

[18] Dworkin (1986: 190). Commenting on this quotation, Julie Dickson observes that "[Dworkin's] position, in effect, is that there is no alternative to the approach which he adopts: all legal theories which are worth considering seriously presuppose or depend upon arguments about law's function which are broadly similar to those advocated in his own theory." Dickson (2001: 113).

[19] Dworkin (1986: 90).

qualitatively indistinguishable, and so in competition, and differ only in scale of application or level of abstraction. As Dworkin maintains

> Theories which ignore the structure of legal argument for supposedly larger questions of history and society are...perverse. They ignore questions about the internal character of legal argument, so their explanations are impoverished and defective...It was Oliver Wendell Holmes who argued most influentially, I think, for this kind of "external" legal theory; the depressing history of social-theoretic jurisprudence in our century warns us how wrong he was.[20]

We may also explain the imperialist commitment that theoretical accounts of law must be from and for the participant's perspective in terms of its relation to the first metatheoretical commitment identified above, that theoretical accounts of law must be morally engaged or employ moral evaluation. If legal reasoning and theorizing about law are really species of moral reasoning or evaluation, then a proper understanding must come from the perspective of legal practitioners, i.e., the central participants in the practice of law who must engage in such moral reasoning. If one really wants to know what law is, one has to know what it is like to be a legal official.

But it is not just any legal official that matters. There can be little doubt that Dworkin has the significant and important role of judges in the practice of law as his central and exclusive object of theoretical interest. Indeed, as I will argue below, I believe a more direct way of responding to Dworkin's metatheoretical claims is to focus on the importance he places on adjudication as *the* key feature of law and legal practice, rather than his general anti-positivist thesis that theories of law must offer constructions of political morality.

It is important to note that I do not wish to contest that Dworkin offers a coherent and compelling theory, in terms of both its contribution to our understanding of legal practice, and its commitment to a particular methodological approach. It is certainly true that understanding when law is morally justified in its application, consideration of a fundamental point or purpose to law, and provision of a participant's understanding of legal practice in the form of close attention to judicial decision-making, all *contribute* to a broad and rich understanding of the nature of law, in ways that are responsive to the nature of law itself. The trouble is that, at each of these turns, Dworkin's approach deliberately excludes alternative, and quite possibly very fruitful and illuminating accounts of law. I believe, therefore, that there are two dimensions to Dworkin's account of law and legal theory that must be distinguished and evaluated. The first is the commitment that his theory offers a particularly illuminating account of law or legal practice. This theoretical commitment is unobjectionable, and is in fact

---

[20] Dworkin (1986: 14). [author's notes omitted] For an excellent critique of this aspect of Dworkin's imperialism, see Tamanaha (1997: 183-187).

necessarily shared by any theory of law in the business of explanation, clarification, interpretation, etc. The second, metatheoretical dimension is that Dworkin believes that his particular account or approach, whether successful or not, *is of the type or kind of account or approach that must be adopted*. So, for example, regardless of whether his particular theory of moral evaluation is successful, or that he has attributed the correct essential point or purpose to law or legal practice, or that he has accurately portrayed the role of the judge, alternative theories must still attempt moral evaluation and adopt a purposive approach to law from the perspective of the judge. It is the imperialist nature of Dworkin's metatheoretical commitments that I argue is misguided.

4. Morally Detached, Non-Participant Descriptive Explanations of Law

There is a relatively straightforward argument to make against imperialism in legal theory: It makes the characteristically unphilosophical move of closing-off or ending discussion. As John Stuart Mill said in a different but still relevant context, "[a]ll silencing of discussion is an [unjustifiable] assumption of infallibility."[21] In effect, Dworkin's methodological commitments foreclose discussion about morally detached, non-participant or observer, conventionalist, social scientific, and non-adjudication-focused accounts of law. Unfortunately, however, the cry for philosophical foul play is insufficient here, because Dworkin's imperialist commitments are also claims; they are not simply tools arbitrarily chosen at the outset, but are positions defended with arguments. Dworkin's metatheoretical commitments are supported by what he sees as distinctive and key features of law and legal practice. So, the required method to challenge Dworkin's *particular* imperialist claims must be to show them to be false or misguided, and to do so on the basis of competing observations about law.[22]

However, I do not want to try to counter each of Dworkin's imperialist claims here. There are many replies offered by others that I find convincing, particularly those that defend the possibility and value of descriptive explanatory, morally detached accounts of law. For example, I agree with Wil Waluchow and H.L.A. Hart that a theorist may descriptively explain morally relevant issues in law, without also taking a particular moral stance on those issues.[23] I might simply add that among the assumptions of any general theory of law must be the belief that clear thinking about the social choice and reality of law will yield substantial

---

[21] Mill (1996: 20).

[22] I should make clear that the arguments in the sections that follow in this chapter are not intended to be conclusive, but rather indicative of the existing literature and prospects for alternative approaches to understanding law.

[23] Waluchow (1994: 22-23). Hart (2012: 244).

insight into our nature as social beings. No doubt, law's complex academic, professional, and popular interest demonstrates that it can be *in many ways* a highly revealing social institution. For this reason, the reconstruction of law as a broad and illuminating social phenomenon may permit an approach that attempts to leave its object as it is, without an attempt to show officials (or citizens) how they can do what they do better or better justify existing practices. I also agree with Julie Dickson and others that law might not have any particular purpose beyond guiding conduct at some level, and more importantly, that if law has the particular and distinctive purpose of justifying state coercion, then this ought to emerge at the conclusion of theoretical investigation and not act as a methodological constraint from the outset.[24]

Instead, I wish to focus on Dworkin's metatheoretical commitment of taking adjudication, or the perspective of the judge, to be the central focus of a general theory of law, from which general conclusions about the nature of law can be inferred. I believe that Dworkin's sustained attention to the role of judges as exemplars of legal officials leads to misleading accounts of other officials and participants in legal systems. This is the idea I now wish to explore.

Dworkin certainly enriches our understanding of adjudication by offering an illuminating, and morally and politically appealing account of the role and function of judges. Yet, when applied to lawyers, for example, his account plainly seems to fail as a matter of descriptive accuracy, and perhaps even as a matter of political morality. Though it might be true that to decide cases judges must determine the law that would best follow from a constructive interpretation of law and legal practice as a whole, lawyers characteristically seek to determine the best picture of the law that finds for those they represent. As John Eekelaar observes, "it would be optimistic to believe that the lawyer advising a client will be looking to interpret the law according to the law's 'best light' rather than in the way most favourable to the client..."[25] From the perspective of lawyers, then, law might best be viewed as a collection of sources or materials for use in dynamic argumentative competition. This is quite different from thinking of law as a coherent and unified whole. As well, this oppositional task for lawyers is perhaps even morally justifiable depending on how much value is placed on the belief that an adversarial system is the best guarantor of justice and fairness. Similarly, the role of judges Dworkin constructs would also seem to obscure the role of legislators in a representative democracy, whose concerns may not be primarily a coherent picture of law and legal practice in its entirety, but rather the interests of their constituents. Checkerboard legislation might be undesirable, yet might nonetheless constitute part of the reality of law as legislators see it. Yet another illustration of the myopic focus on judges would be consideration of the function of police officers or border officials, whose job demands understandably leave little room or time for careful reflection on underlying principles of

---

[24] Dickson (2001: 128-131).
[25] Eekelaar (2002: 510).

moral justification at each application of law. From their perspective, law might simply be a set of ready-made rules to guide their actions. So it seems quite possible that Dworkin's focus on the role of judges at least distorts understanding of the actual role of lawyers, legislators, and other legal officials, and hence figures against a more complete picture of the nature of law and legal officials in general. No simple or straightforward inference can be drawn from the perspective of judges to the nature of law.

Matters are only made worse when we look outside the world of officialdom. From the perspective of citizens, law as integrity may often be entirely out of place. Not only do citizens' interpretations of law carry no authority, they live in the consequences of authoritative decisions (which may or may not be consistent, coherent, etc.) made by judges and other official institutions. Yet citizens' experiences of law would seem to be no less important and no less real than that of judges, and so no less worthy of addressing in an investigation into the nature of law. It is also doubtful whether citizens necessarily have reason to try to put the law in its best moral light. Alan Turing, for example, was found guilty of homosexuality under the English criminal law of the 1950s, and given the choice of either prison or chemical castration. He was, of course, only one of over a thousand found guilty under this criminal law, and clearly millions around the world have had different but similarly negative experiences with law. To capture the experiences of those such as Turing and others, and prevent them from being hidden from view, an approach that puts law in its worst moral light might be more illuminating. Indeed, to try to put the law, in these instances, in its best moral light might be nothing short of horrendous. If anything, observations such as these ought to sharpen our alertness to the dangers of theories of law, or imperialisms, which elevate in the overall understanding of law a key but singular feature or perspective of law and legal practice.

Earlier, I argued that emphasis on Dworkin's exclusionary attention to adjudication provides the main support for the general argument against his imperialism. This argument can now be given a further touch. In addition to the argument that Dworkin's account of the role of judges does not explain very well and even obscures the role of other officials in a legal system, as well as the perspective of citizens, there is still yet another reason for not elevating adjudication as the (only) key to understanding law and legal practice. This reason lies in the observation that adjudication, whether carried out successfully or unsuccessfully, legitimately or illegitimately, can also be understood as a central feature of the state of affairs when law fails. Adjudication, after all, is dispute resolution, the resolution of disputes that arose when legal obligations, rights, and rules were not sufficient for their purpose or were simply not observed. Hence there is a certain oddity in focusing exclusively on adjudication, which at the same time is both a salient feature of law and legal practice *and* a means of dealing with the pathologies of legal systems and communities.

5. Difference in Legal Theory

Up to this point I have attempted to confront Dworkin's imperialism head on, albeit in a limited way by showing that his exclusive focus on adjudication overlooks important and significantly different views about law.[26] However, I should again note that I have not objected to Dworkin's methodological approaches taken on their own. Although I shall not pursue it in any detail here, morally committed, purposive, and adjudication focused accounts of legal phenomena are necessary and valuable in their own right and ought not to be discounted in a complete understanding of law. It is only their supposed status as *exclusively* necessary approaches to law that I argue is mistaken. In other words, I am only arguing against the *metatheoretical* approach of imperialism in legal theory, but not against the increased understanding to be gained with any particular *theoretical* alternative to approaching or understanding law. What I want to evaluate now, however, is a common alternative to imperialism, what I will call the difference view of diversity.

The difference view maintains that we must be careful to distinguish different types of theories, because theories can and do differ in their aims and purposes. Failure to distinguish, or insensitivity to differences in aim or purpose, may often lead us to see and think in terms of conflicts where none actually exist. Indeed, it is not difficult to find the difference or cross-purposes view of diversity in legal theory. For example, after identifying five different types of theories of law James Harris asks

> Where, in this welter of meta-theoretical comparisons, is 'the law' itself? The answer is that the law is not something one can lay hold of independently of a focus of interest. Is one engaged in descriptive or critical legal science, or in political philosophy, social psychology, sociology, or anthropology? Answer that, and then one can say which conception of 'rule' or 'system' will be the primary point of reference, the 'law', so far as that discipline is concerned.[27]

In "What is Jurisprudence About? Theories, Definitions, Concepts, or Conceptions of Law?" Michael Bayles writes

> The argument of this paper is that philosophy of law or jurisprudence (the terms are used synonymously here) seeks to provide theories. However, different purposes generate different kinds of theories which it is important to keep distinct. Much of the dispute between positivism and natural law stems from their proponents seeking different types of theories. Moreover, confusion has resulted from scholars implausibly interpreting one type of theory as another type.[28]

---

[26] This section draws on material found in Giudice (2005).

[27] Harris (1979: 166).

[28] Bayles (1990). In a related article, Bayles also writes that "[t]hese different viewpoints even generate different standards for a theory. An external observer wants to make the descriptive theory the best it can be; the participant wants to make the law the best it can be." Bayles (1991: 380).

Even Hart suggests, at one point, that his theory of law and Dworkin's conception of legal theory are sufficiently different so as not to admit of any general conflict: "It is not obvious why there should be or indeed could be any significant conflict between enterprises so different as my own and Dworkin's conceptions of legal theory."[29]

Although it is certainly true that there are different types of theories of law that, because of their difference, may not admit of general conflict, this view can mislead. Specifically, the difference view may encourage the belief that identification of difference in approach or purpose amounts to compatibility among theories of law. For example, commenting on Hart's claim quoted above Joseph Raz writes: "[h]aving decided to restrict the Postscript to deflecting or refuting Dworkin's criticisms of his own views, [Hart] is content to point out that Dworkin's theoretical aims are different from his, as if that makes them compatible."[30] The problem the difference view faces is that not only does it threaten to leave us with a fragmented understanding of law, composed simply of diverse theories of law, but more importantly it also runs the danger of masking or obscuring remaining conflicts. We can return to Eekelaar's interesting article to see an example of how the difference view in legal theory works, but more importantly why we ought to reject it as well.

According to Eekelaar, the apparent incompatibility between the legal positivist Social Thesis and Dworkin's Coherence Thesis can be resolved by distinguishing between a citizen's conception of law and a judicial conception of law.[31] Eekelaar begins with the sensible observation that ". . . there is no reason to suppose that all participants share the same point of view, or that that of participants in the legal process, especially judges, is the only relevant one."[32] He continues "[a]n observer might discern, within the observed phenomenon, various types of participant, on whom the phenomenon acts differently, and for whom the phenomenon holds a variety of meanings."[33] With these observations in place he arrives at his central argument:

> [m]y argument is that the Social Thesis well represents the function of the law in its relationship between citizen and the state, but that, while it may partly account for the role of law in adjudication, it does not *necessarily* apply in that context, and the Coherence Thesis provides a better explanation of the institutional role fulfilled by the law for adjudicators.[34]

---

[29] Hart (2012: 241).

[30] Raz (2009: 76).

[31] Eekelaar (2002). Briefly, the Social Thesis, which Eekelaar associates with Raz's exclusive legal positivism, maintains that all law is source-based. The Coherence Thesis maintains that all law consists of source-based law together with the morally soundest justification for source-based law. Eekelaar (2002: 497).

[32] Eekelaar (2002: 498).

[33] Eekelaar (2002: 498).

[34] Eekelaar (2002: 498).

In explanation, Eekelaar notes, for example, that from a citizen's perspective sometimes the law is best explained as having run out, because there may arise fact situations that are not covered by source-based law. However, from the judge's point of view, the law never runs out, because the distinction between application and creation of law does not apply in the context of adjudication. In reaction to a distinction upon which Raz relies, Eekelaar explains

> The sharp conceptual distinction drawn by Raz between judicial *application* of law (identified by relevant sources) and the creation of new law (governed by 'ultimate rules of discretion'), both of which impose duties on the courts, though he recognizes they may be difficult to separate in practice, has no place in the judicial conception of law, for two reasons. First, the interpretive power permits 'new' law to arise in applying source-based provisions. Second, the conclusions generated by the 'laws of discretion' indicate that apparent 'new' law could be seen as *applying* existing legal principle. In fact, the best characterization of judicial decision is one of *reconstitution* of existing law.[35]

There are two problems with Eekelaar's argument about the compatibility of the Social and Coherence Theses. First, although Eekelaar has attempted to preserve the insights to be had by not restricting explanation of law to the perspective of only one type of participant, he seems to have turned a practical constraint faced by judges into a conceptual feature of adjudication. Even though there may be strong pressure for judges not to alter or create new law, and so they may be forced to present their activities in ways which respect this pressure, as a matter of accurate theoretical explanation they may still be acting as quasi-legislators.[36] Second, Eekelaar's distinction between a citizen's conception of law and a judicial conception of law leaves us with a contradiction about the nature of law. For the citizen, sometimes, law may be uncertain or indeterminate. For the judge, law might be uncertain (though they can never present it as such) but is never indeterminate. This is precisely the sort of problem which can arise for the difference view: We are left not only with different views about the nature of law with no explanation of how they are theoretically connected, but also with the possibility of conflicting propositions about law which are not identified as such. The problem for Eekelaar is only compounded when he admits that in practice the judicial conception can override or be overridden by the citizen's conception of law.[37] How is this possible, and from whose perspective or conception of law

---

[35] Eekelaar (2002: 510-511).

[36] For example John Mackie observes that "...there is a distinction—and there may be a divergence—between what judges say they are doing, what they think they are doing, and the most accurate objective description of what they actually are doing. They may say and even believe that they are discovering and applying an already existing law, they may be following procedures which assume this as their aim, yet they may in fact be making new law." Mackie (1977: 7). See also Hart (2012) 274-275.

[37] Eekelaar (2002: 515).

is such a statement being made?[38] The limits of Eekelaar's account, namely, to go beyond a difference view of participant perspectives, supports the following general conclusion. Although it is important to consider how law appears to a diversity of participants or from a diversity of perspectives, we must take seriously the further question: *What is it about law such that it appears in the ways that it does to various participants?* To get beyond the difference view, we need an account that recognizes distinctions *yet also pursues* connections; otherwise, we may be left with highly unstable differences that in fact conceal remaining conflicts. So, although Eekelaar is correct to observe that law's appearance varies across different kinds of participant, and so is a contingent matter, it is still important to address resulting inconsistent or contradictory claims about law and its practice.

6. Beyond Imperialism and Difference

There is and should be a common goal among different approaches to law: a complete or broad understanding of law. In reaction to imperialism, the difference view of diversity rightly suggests that some theoretical accounts fail to acknowledge that their contribution to this goal is only partial. However, against the difference view we ought to notice that although there are many viable approaches to law and objects of theoretical explanation, identification of differences is not enough, and for two reasons. First, mere identification of differences in aims or objects results in fragmented understanding, in that we are left with a collection of disparate arguments and observations with no account of how they are connected. Second, identification of differences in aims or objects may encourage the belief that different theories are compatible (or composed of compatible sets of claims). The danger of this belief is that it risks concealing remaining conflicts between different theories or conceptions.

Instead of imperialism and difference, I suggest we ought to adopt a metatheoretical view (we might even say attitude) of continuity towards the diversity of theoretical approaches to understanding law. Although I cannot fully develop the view here,[39] I will sketch in broad outline, together with an illustration, its central commitments. First, the continuity view accepts the three basic facts about the nature of law identified at the beginning of the chapter. To recall, these are: (1) law is morally (and politically) significant, in that decisions to create, apply, and enforce law affect people's interests and well-being in numerous ways; (2) law's operation depends at crucial junctures on the decisions and dispositions of humans and human institutions, which are, like all humans and human

---

[38] Eekelaar's argument that the conception of law to be adopted in practice depends on the best practical consequences is theoretically unsatisfactory. Eekelaar (2002: 513-516). For an argument that the practical consequences of a theory of law have no bearing on its truth or explanatory power, see Waluchow (1994: 88-90).

[39] For a more sustained explanation of the continuity view, see Giudice (2005).

institutions, products of and influenced by social, economic, psychological, and historical forces of various kinds; and (3) legal concepts are the creation of shared ideas, notions, and categories, which exist in the form of sets of inter-subjective understandings. It should be emphasized that my characterization of such basic facts as facts about the nature of law is deliberate: Such facts are facts about law wherever and whenever it exists. I shall consider an objection to this way of understanding the idea of the nature of law below, but before doing so, it will be helpful to lay out two more features of the continuity view. The second core commitment of the continuity view follows from the first: Because the basic facts about law are plural, the appropriate methodological approach to understanding law must be plural as well. The basic motivations behind morally and politically evaluative, social scientific, and conceptual theories are all sound, as each responds in their respective ways to different basic facts about law. For this reason, each type of theoretical approach is appropriate, necessary, and important. Simply put, we sell law's interest short if we fail to recognize that it is interesting in more than one way; it stands to reason, therefore, that our metatheoretical understanding of law must be sufficiently broad and inclusive. The third commitment of the continuity view represents its improvement on the difference view: Although different theories must be distinguished in terms of their general motivations and interests, there still remains work to be done to investigate and assess remaining conflicts between different types of theories at the level of particular propositions about law and legal phenomena. Hart and Dworkin, for example, may have been engaged in significantly different but equally valuable enterprises, making a winner-take-all assessment of their debate misguided; but nothing follows from this about whether conflicts might remain between their views. Whether judges do or do not make law in a certain range of cases is one such issue that cannot be resolved by distinguishing between different general types of theories of law.

So, against imperialism, the task for legal theory is to include necessary or important theoretical contributions, rather than argue for the most important theoretical approach that will command exclusive attention. As a reconceptualization of the difference view, we ought to think not of *different* theories or theoretical purposes, but rather *partial* or *incomplete* theories or theoretical purposes that subsequently need to be connected. In general terms, these are the goals and commitments of the continuity view. Some may object, however, to the claim that each of the three types of approaches that I identified are properly understood as theories about the nature of law, and insist instead that, in particular, only conceptual theories of law can identify the properties or features of law which constitute its nature. Typically, those who advance this sort of objection defend positivist views about law, which hold that only a morally neutral, descriptive explanatory account of law can explain law's nature—what it is for law to exist and how it is different from other related social phenomena. On such views, while morally evaluative and social scientific theories might be interesting and important, they are not theories about the nature of law, but merely provide additional, and so nonessential, knowledge about law, for example, under what conditions it morally binds its subjects, and under what conditions it might persist or cease to exist. This is an important objection, and deserves a fuller response than I can provide here, but I should nonetheless at least register my belief that it is relatively misguided. I do believe that conceptual theories occupy something of a primary role in the order of investigation of law, as one first needs to settle on a subject matter or field of inquiry, even if only in a provisional and revisable way, before exploring moral and political assessments of law and social scientific explanations of law's operation in society. But to admit this is not to suppose that evaluative theories and social scientific theories are somehow not about the nature of law, but only about what moral attitudes we should have towards the law or what causal explanations might be available. Both morally evaluative and social scientific theories are about and respond to facts about the nature of law, namely, that law is morally significant and is susceptible to social influence. One way to see these as facts about the nature of law is to notice that the facts about the nature of law upon which positivists tend to focus are facts about law's *social existence*, as if explanation of law's nature is exhausted by explanation of the conditions under which law actually exists in a certain time and place. Such accounts are, as is well known, typically also accounts of the *momentary* existence of law or legal systems, explaining as they do what it means for law to exist at a particular moment in time.[40] Yet momentary accounts of law's existence only provide a partial explanation of its nature. Law, of course, exists at particular moments in time, but it is also part of its nature that it persists through time. It is in turn not outrageous to suppose that to explain law's persistence through time might require different methods, particularly those offered by social scientific theories.[41] From here, it is also not hard to see that once we place law back into its temporal context,[42] whereby actual participants (such as judges) have to carry on with their activities in ways responsive to the nature of law, we will also need, again, *because of the very nature of law* (the part constituted by its moral significance), morally and politically evaluative theories of law.

Continuity, therefore, seems the best way to understand the diversity among theories of law. Although there is always the possibility of partial conflict, each *type* of theory is necessary for a broad and complete understanding of law. For example, someone who had general, morally neutral understanding of the existence conditions of law, but no idea about how, in general or in particular circumstances, law's claims or effects are to be morally assessed, would certainly have a deficient understanding of law (and not just a deficient understanding

---

[40] See Raz (1980: 34-35, 189-197).

[41] On the issue of explaining the continuity of legal systems Raz offers the following intriguing view: "The identity of legal systems depends on the identity of the social forms to which they belong. The criterion of identity of legal systems is therefore determined not only by jurisprudential or legal considerations but by other considerations as well, considerations belonging to other social sciences.... Not wishing to trespass on other fields, I shall confine myself henceforth to the problem of the identity of momentary systems." Raz (1980: 189).

[42] For an interesting and underappreciated article on law's temporality, see Postema (2004).

of this or that law or legal system). And someone who had both existential and moral knowledge of law, but no idea of the general or special conditions under which law comes into existence, persists, or disintegrates, would also lack a general understanding of law. It is indeed difficult to make sense of the claim that one part of a multi-part general explanation or understanding is most important, because this simply misses the fact that *each* is required or necessary for a general understanding of a multi-faceted social phenomenon.

Admittedly, the above account of continuity and the elements of the nature of law is woefully underdeveloped, suggestive, and promissory. But as the main aim of this chapter is to challenge imperialist and difference views of metatheoretical disputes in contemporary jurisprudence, which is no small task, I believe it is excusable to leave development for subsequent work. I do, however, want to conclude this section by sketching an example of where and how a commitment to continuity can be found and pursued.

Consider, for example, a small but not insignificant part of Hart's discussion of the internal point of view. As he explains, though all officials of a legal system must take a critical reflective attitude to the norms they follow, we cannot assume a necessary, unique, or uniform explanation of the precise reasons upon which officials act. Hart maintains instead that the reasons why officials follow any particular norm, or what sort of substantive reasons they suppose a norm demands, can and do vary. On the allegiance of legal officials, Hart writes ". . . [i]n fact their allegiance to the system may be based on many different considerations: calculations of long-term interest; disinterested interest in others; an unreflecting inherited or traditional attitude, or the mere wish to do as others do."[43] One important consideration in support of the any-reasons thesis is Hart's concern to respect the diversity of participant perspectives in life under law. In this respect, the any-reasons thesis represents an important part of Hart's reluctance to make a conceptual claim that is not warranted. However, although Hart did not go further, someone committed to pursuing continuity in legal theory might do so, for the any-reasons thesis presents a point of intersection between a conceptual claim about law, morally evaluative assessment, and social scientific investigation. The intersection works like this. Although officials might base their allegiance to law and legal norms on any number of considerations, because of law's moral significance, we can ask which reasons or considerations ought to count as morally sound reasons or considerations for allegiance to law. Such an account of the moral reasons and considerations that justify allegiance would go some distance toward helping officials carry on with their practices in a morally sound way. Similarly, the intersection works for social scientific investigation as well: Whereas Hart did not encourage or invite social scientific investigation of the reasons or considerations that actually explain the allegiance of officials—he merely offered some possible reasons—there is nothing to stop social scientific

---

[43] Hart (2012: 203).

theorists from exploring what the actual reasons and considerations are, and furthermore, whether these form any uniform patterns. Indeed, we might even say that many branches (though not all of them) of the American legal realist movement are motivated by a hypothesis that such patterns can be discerned with proper study.

There is, then, an important way in which Hart's any-reasons thesis serves to mark an important space for continuity. The thesis is, of course, part of Hart's conceptual account of the nature of social rules, but where Hart is unwilling to generalize about the reasons why officials might follow law, his account leaves room for empirical investigation, and where he does not evaluate the quality of reasons upon which officials might rest their allegiance, he leaves it open for morally and politically evaluative theories to go to work. Each type of account, however, is tied to and properly motivated by features about the nature of law and social rules. Such perspectives are not, therefore, additive or optional, but essential.

So where, exactly, does this leave Dworkin's theory of law? The conclusion I wish to draw from assessment of imperialism and difference views has implications for general debates in the methodology of legal theory, which have grown in significance in the last twenty years or so, but it also has particular relevance for understanding Dworkin's legal theory. Many of the specific objections I raised against Dworkin's account of law are not particularly novel; however, because of the methodological commitments with which Dworkin characteristically makes his claims about law, objections to his theory run the risk of giving the impression that because his imperialism fails, his particular methodological approach must fail as well. This is a mistake. The imperialist, metatheoretical claims of Dworkin's theory can be separated from the soundness and importance of morally evaluative theorizing of law. Dworkin has identified a necessary, and necessarily important approach to theorizing law. This, I argue, ought to be among the lasting legacy of Dworkin's contributions to legal theory, not his imperialism.

References

Bayles, M. (1990). "What is Jurisprudence About? Theories, Definitions, Concepts, or Conceptions of Law?" *Philosophical Topics* 18: 23–40.

Bayles, M. (1991). "Hart vs Dworkin," *Law and Philosophy* 10: 349–381.

Dickson, J. (2001). *Evaluation and Legal Theory.* Oxford: Hart Publishing.

Dworkin, R. (1978). "The Model of Rules I." Reprinted in *Taking Rights Seriously.* Cambridge, MA: Harvard University Press.

Dworkin, R. (1986) *Law's Empire.* Cambridge, MA: Harvard University Press.

Eekelaar, J. (2002). "Judges and Citizens: Two Conceptions of Law," *Oxford Journal of Legal Studies* 22: 497–516.

Finnis, J. (1980). *Natural Law and Natural Rights.* Oxford: Clarendon Press.

Giudice, M. (2005). "Ways of Understanding Diversity Among Theories of Law," *Law and Philosophy* 24: 509–545.

Harris, J. (1979). *Law and Legal Science*. Oxford: Clarendon Press.

Hart, H.L.A. (2012). *The Concept of Law*. 3rd edn, intro by L. Green. Oxford: Oxford University Press.

Mackie, J.L. (1977). "The Third Theory of Law," *Philosophy and Public Affairs* 7: 3–16.

Mill, J.S. (1996). *On Liberty and the Subjection of Women*. Intro by J. O'Grady. Hertfordshire: Wordsworth.

Postema, G. (2004). "Melody and Law's Mindfulness of Time," *Ratio Juris* 17: 203–224.

Raz, J. (1980). *The Concept of a Legal System*. 2nd edn. Oxford: Clarendon Press.

Raz, J. (1995). *Ethics in the Public Domain*. Rev edn. Oxford: Clarendon Press.

Raz, J. (2009). *Between Authority and Interpretation*. Oxford: Oxford University Press.

Tamanaha, B. (1997). *Realistic Socio-Legal Theory*. Oxford: Clarendon Press.

Waluchow, W. (1994). *Inclusive Legal Positivism*. Oxford: Clarendon Press.

11

A Theory of Legal Obligation
by Christopher Essert[*]

I could say that in what follows I plan to do five things. Instead, in the spirit of Ronald Dworkin, I'll say that I plan to do one big thing, and that the five things I'll do are aspects of that one big thing. The one big thing that I plan to do is propose a theory of legal obligation, which I call the *Simple Theory* of legal obligation. According to the Simple Theory, for me to be legally obligated not to φ is just for it to be the case that, from the legal point of view, the reasons for me not to φ defeat any reasons for me to φ. The theory is simple because it explains legal obligation in terms of two simple ideas—reasons and the legal point of view.

As I said, I'll do five things: The principle part of what follows will be an attempt to show that the Simple Theory can explain the sorts of intuitions that lead others to posit more elaborate accounts of legal obligation in terms of, for example, protected reasons. In addition, I'll show how the Simple Theory coheres nicely with some recent work about the nature of precedential reasoning. Then I'll turn to Dworkin twice. I'll show that the Simple Theory makes quick work of the argument from legal principles Dworkin offered in *Model of Rules I*; here my argument will be quite similar to HLA Hart's reply to Dworkin in the "Postscript" to the *Concept of Law*. I'll also consider the relations between the Simple Theory and the kind of one-system view of law that Dworkin came to endorse in *Justice for Hedgehogs*. And this will lead me to close with some thoughts about normative powers and the value of law. So that opening is not, I hope, too much of a stretch: I take the presentation of the Simple Theory to consist, in part, of illustrating how it helps us to understand some of the central problems in jurisprudence in new and interesting ways.

[*] Faculty of Law, Queen's University. Thanks to Leslie Green, Scott Hershovitz, Jennifer Nadler, David Plunkett, Joseph Raz, Stefan Sciaraffa, Scott Shapiro, Wil Waluchow, Grégoire Webber, and Daniel Wodak for comments and helpful discussions. An earlier version was presented at the 2014 OLPP Graduate Conference for Legal Theory; I am grateful for the participants' comments there and to Maggie O'Brian, Katharina von Radziewsky, and Wil Waluchow for that opportunity.

1. The Standard Account of Legal Obligation: Protected Reasons

According to the what I'll call the *standard account* of legal obligation, when I have a legal obligation not to φ that is because there is some legal rule or directive ("do not φ!") and the fact that this rule or directive applies to me is a protected reason for me not to φ, or in other words, a first-order reason for me not to φ protected by a second-order exclusionary reason not to act on some other reasons.[1] The theory is attractive in that it explains two major elements of legal obligation: (1) it explains the *normativity* of legal obligation (the idea that when I am obligated not to φ I have a reason not to φ); and (2) it explains the *peremptoriness* of legal obligation (the idea that when I am obligated not to φ the decision about whether to φ is out of my hands).[2]

Let me say a bit more about these two ideas. To say that legal obligation is normative is to say that it is *about* reasons.[3] In general, it appears that legal obligation is related to reasons: We have reason to perform our legal obligations and (perhaps this is just the same idea again) reason to refrain from breaching them. If we followed the usual (although not universal) characterization of reasons and said that when p is a reason for A to φ, p counts in favor of A's φing, we might say that when I am legally obligated not to φ there is a reason (or reasons) that counts in favor of actions that would constitute not-φing and against actions that would constitute φing. Again, if we followed the usual (although not universal) practice of associating reasons with rational appraisal and criticism of action, we might go further and say that if A is legally obligated not to φ and A φs, A is subject to criticism for φing. This is consistent with the common thought, emphasized by Hart, that failing to perform one's legal obligations subjects one to some kind of criticism.

We often have different reasons to perform different, incompatible actions. What is usually said about this is that, in normal circumstances, what we have reason to do (or perhaps what we ought to do) is that action that is supported by the stronger reasons. If p is a reason for me to φ and q is a reason for me to ψ (and I can't both φ and ψ) then normally I should φ rather than ψ if p is a stronger reason than q, and I would be open to rational criticism were I to ψ rather than φ. With legal obligation, things may not work in this normal way. It seems that

---

[1] The standard account is largely based on the work of Joseph Raz, and constructed most prominently in *Practical Reason and Norms* and *The Morality of Freedom,* with important qualifications and amendments in *Ethics in the Public Domain* and *Between Authority and Interpretation.* But I prefer the generic name, primarily because (1) Raz's own understanding of legal obligation and legal reasons is rich and complex, and as he reminded me it is not limited to protected reasons; and (2) many other prominent legal philosophers can be said, to a greater or lesser extent, to endorse the view: see, e.g., Finnis (2011: ch. ix); Marmor (2011: 125); Gardner (2011: 31 n. 52).

[2] Perhaps a full account of obligation needs to explain the difference between obligation and rules: It is wrong to do what you are obligated not to do but merely impermissible or perhaps irrational to do what a rule tells you not to do. I discuss this point in Section 5, below.

[3] I endorse the view that to explain the normativity of some phenomenon is to explain how it is related to reasons, following, e.g., Raz (2011: 6); and Scanlon (2014: 2).

when we are legally obligated not to φ we are not supposed to deliberate (practically) on our various reasons to φ and not to φ; instead the fact that we are legally obligated not to φ seems to cut off or exclude deliberation about the reasons to φ. It is not up to us to make the decision about φing: We are just not supposed to φ. Legal obligation is peremptory.[4]

These two aspects of legal obligation—normativity and peremptoriness— need to be explained (or explained away) by any theory of legal obligation. As I said above, the standard account does a good job of explaining them: The fact that A is legally obligated not to φ is a protected *reason* not to φ whose first-order element counts against φing. And the fact that A is legally obligated not to φ is a *protected* reason not to φ, whose second-order exclusionary element excludes other reasons to φ, such that A should not deliberate on them and so the matter is closed. It will become clear in what follows that the Simple Theory is, at a certain level of generality, very similar to the standard account and owes a great deal to Raz's pioneering work on the nature of legal obligation. I think Raz's core thought that understanding legal obligation requires an account of the way that law can be normative and peremptory is powerful and important, and it motivates much of the Simple Theory. But although the standard account does a very good job of accounting for these core intuitions about legal obligation, I worry, as argued elsewhere, that it runs into trouble in the details.[5] Those arguments are not repeated here, because I think the Simple Theory can stand alone and that we can motivate it by reference to its simplicity. As Raz himself has noted, the complexity brought on by positing the existence of second-order reasons is unwelcome.[6] So, if I am right to claim that the Simple Theory can account for everything that the standard account does without its complexity,[7] it might be at least more welcome in this respect.[8]

---

[4] The classic statement of the idea is found in Hart (1982: 253-254): "[T]he commander characteristically intends the hearer to take the commander's will instead of his own as a guide to action and so to take it in place of any deliberation or reasoning of his own: The expression of a commander's will that an act be done is intended to preclude or cut off any independent deliberation by the hearer of the merits pro and con of doing the act. The commander's expression of will therefore is not intended to function within the hearer's deliberations as a reason for doing the act, not even as the strongest or most dominant reason, for that would presuppose that independent deliberation was to go on, whereas the commander intends to cut off or exclude it."

[5] I have said that the idea of a protected reason does not work, in Essert (2012a); that the fact that one is obligated not to φ cannot be a reason not to φ, in Essert (2013); and that exclusionary reasons are not reasons, in Essert (2012b).

[6] Raz (2009: 216).

[7] A point about how the Simple Theory accounts for everything the standard account does. The Simple Theory does not quite explain these apparent features of obligation so much as it explains them away: It says that the fact that A is legally obligated not to φ appears to be related to reasons because it obtains in virtue of what the law claims A's reasons (to φ or not) are, and it says that the apparent peremptoriness of legal obligation obtains in virtue of the way that the legal point of view works.

[8] A point of scope to keep in mind: Protected reasons are also taken by some to explain other sorts of obligation, such as promissory obligation and (perhaps) moral obligation. The Simple Theory is officially limited to explaining legal obligation.

2. Points of View in Practical Reasoning

Many others have noted that intentions, decisions, rules, plans, and other practical phenomena seem to be normative and in some sense peremptory in the same way (roughly) as legal obligation. This sometimes leads to a thought that these phenomena can be explained in similar terms. For example, Raz suggests that decisions are to be explained in terms of protected reasons.[9] To similar effect, Shapiro's Planning Theory of Law explicitly builds on Michael Bratman's theory of intentions.[10]

The Simple Theory shares this approach. It draws on Niko Kolodny's work on the (apparent) normativity of intentions.[11] Kolodny's thought might be put in the following way: The apparent normativity of intentions—that there seems to be some irrationality in, e.g., intending an end and not intending its necessary means—can be explained by keeping separate two different points of view from which an agent or her action can be evaluated. The normative pressure to carry out the intention stems from the fact that, from the agent's own internal or first-person point of view, she takes herself to have good reasons to perform the intended action. But this can contrast with what from the external or third-person evaluative point of view she actually has reason to do. This contrast between internal and external points of view, should be familiar to any student of jurisprudence; as we willl see, this is not a coincidence.

Here is a way of putting Kolodny's idea. Imagine that I intend to perform some action φ. We can distinguish two different sorts of advice you can give me about what I ought to do.[12] One the one hand, you can tell me that I am wrong to intend to φ and that I ought to ψ instead. On the other hand, you can tell me that, since I intend to φ, I ought to ξ, where ξ is a means to φing. Suppose you are right that I am wrong to intend to φ. Then that first sort of advice you can offer is straightforwardly advice about what I have reason to do: I am wrong to take myself to have reason to φ and in fact I have reason to ψ and this is what you are telling me. The crucial idea in the account is its explanation of the second sort of advice: If I have reason to ψ rather than φ, why say that I ought to ξ? Kolodny's disarmingly simple insight is that you are giving me advice *from my own internal point of view.* I intend to φ because I take myself to have good reasons to φ;[13] in other words, from my own internal point of view I am correct in intending to φ. Given what I take myself to have reason to do, your advice that I ought to ξ if I want to φ is just advice about what I take myself to have reason to do. (In particular, it is advice about how the reasons for the ends I take myself to have transmit to the means to those ends in the normal way.)

---

[9] Raz (1999: 65-72).

[10] Bratman (1987).

[11] Kolodny (2005).

[12] This contrast is not unique to advice, of course. It also exists in (real or hypothetical) evaluation of actions. But I use advice here for simplicity of exposition.

[13] On *taking,* see Hieronymi (2013: 117, n. 9); Essert (2012b; n. 5).

As the reader will have noted, on Kolodny's account, when you offer the second sort of advice—when you tell me what I ought to do given my intention—you are in fact not making a normative claim at all. Instead you are making a "descriptive, psychological claim" about my attitudes.[14] But this descriptive claim *seems* normative to me. That's because the reasons that I take myself to have are, so far as I am concerned, the reasons that I do have:

> More generally, why does being subject to a rational requirement such as C+ ['If one believes that one has conclusive reason to have A, then one is rationally required to have A.'] feel normative 'from the inside'? Because a reason that someone believes he has is, from his point of view, a reason *simpliciter*. In other words, given what the antecedent of C+ is, it will always seem to someone to whom C+ applies that he has reason to comply with it. This reason is not that given that he satisfies the antecedent of C+, it will be irrational of him not to have A, and irrationality is something to avoid. The reason is instead the reason for A that, in virtue of satisfying the antecedent of C+, he already believes he has. From the first-person standpoint, the 'ought' of rationality is transparent. It looks just like the 'ought' of reasons. It is only from the second- or third-person standpoint that the 'ought' of rationality and the 'ought' of reasons come apart.[15]

So the apparent normativity of my intention is explained (or explained away) just by noting this contrast. Consistent with this, note that from my own first-person internal point of view, my intention does not have normative significance.[16] I do not take myself to have reason to ξ because I intend to φ; rather I take myself to have reason to ξ because of the reasons I (take myself to) have to φ.[17]

---

[14] Kolodny (2005: 557). In fact, this might be too fast: It seems as though you are making what Raz would call a *detached claim*, and detached claims are not straightforwardly descriptive. These semantic issues are outside of my scope here.

[15] Kolodny (2005: 558).

[16] Kolodny's account here is synchronic. This might suggest a worry, to the effect that it cannot explain the normative impact of *forming* an intention. Sometimes the formation of an intention has a normative impact because it changes the non-normative features of the world (and so this impact is explained derivatively, in the way described in the next note). But the point can be pressed further: Put differently, it claims that Kolodny's account ignores a distinction between judging that one has reason to φ and intending to φ. Here, I think Pamela Hieronymi's account of intention formation, according to which to form an intention is to *settle* the question of whether or not to φ can supply the missing piece: Sometimes we can judge that we ought to φ and when we do so in fact we are, in a way, advising ourselves about our reasons without settling the matter; but (when things go well) the settling need not have any distinctive normative effect. See Hieronymi (2009: 214).

[17] A point long ago made by Thomas Nagel with respect to desires: Of course, sometimes the fact that I intend to φ can affect what I have reason to do from the third-person external point of view (as when, e.g., I choose one of two equally rational options and incur some costs as a result of the choice). This is true, but it seems beside the point because the way that my intention affects what I have reason to do here is *derivative*, that is, its normative effect can be explained by reference to the same kinds of explanations that account for the normative effect of any other fact. For discussion, see Kolodny (2011). The general point applies in the legal case: see Enoch (2011).

Kolodny's account is framed in terms of single intentions held by single agents. Although I do not have the space to do this explicitly here, it seems clear to me that the simplicity of the account would easily accommodate an expansion to allow for explanation of the normativity of jointly held policies (as Michael Bratman calls them) about the strength of reasons in certain contexts. Suppose your department adopts a policy to value publications over teaching experience in hiring decisions. Then, when the time comes to make a hire, from the department's point of view, the fact that candidate A has more publications than candidate B is taken to be a stronger reason than candidate B's superior teaching experience.[18] There may be some tricky questions concerning what it is (in general) for a group to take a reason to have a certain strength (and how we could know what strength they take it to have). But in the legal context, as we shall see, these questions are more easily answered.

Note how Kolodny's explanation is metaphysically modest. It does not rely on anything like a protected reason to explain the apparent normativity of intentions. Instead, it explains it just in terms of the normativity of reasons and normal descriptive psychological facts about how people take themselves to have reasons. Thus, an account of legal obligation that explains its apparent normativity in the same modest way would be, in this way, welcome. So now I want to return to the law and construct an account of legal obligation that parallels Kolodny's account of the (apparent) normativity of intentions.

3. The Legal Point of View

As I noted above, the suggestion that our understanding of some normative phenomenon can be furthered by separating distinct points of view from which it can be evaluated is hardly news to legal philosophy. Hart's distinction between the internal and external points of view is central to his jurisprudential project. I will get to Hart below, but now I want to focus on Joseph Raz's notion of the legal point of view, because I think it is the key to the Simple Theory and to the understanding of legal obligation.

In *Practical Reason and Norms,* Raz brings our attention to what he calls the "mixed reaction" appropriate when a person justifiably disregards a legal obligation and we think both praise and (something like) blame are appropriate. Later on in the book, Raz introduces the idea of the legal point of view, but he denies that the legal point of view is, on its own, sufficient to explain what is happening in these cases:

We often express our realization of [the complexity associated with conflicting judgments in mixed reaction cases] by referring to different points

---

[18] Bratman's expansion of his planning account of intentions to joint policies concerning strength of reasons in his Bratman (2004) seems to me straightforwardly adaptable to the Simple Theory.

of view according to which there are different and incompatible things which ought to be done. But the expression 'different points of view' and related expressions are loosely used to indicate a great variety of practical phenomena and such expressions betray little more than an awareness of complexity.[19]

Raz thinks that the notion of an exclusionary reason is required in order to render more rigorous this loose talk:

> The judge [who judges a man from the legal point of view] both regards...himself as justified in acting on some reasons to the exclusion of others. Hence, though it is true that judgment from the legal point of view is a partial and incomplete judgment it serves as a basis for action because this point of view includes an exclusionary reason requiring one not to act on reasons which do not belong to it.[20]

On the standard view, then, we need the idea an exclusionary reason to understand the legal point of view (and the associated phenomenon of the mixed reaction). Only in this way can we render talk of the legal point of view sufficiently rigorous.

Well, maybe. After all, "our discussion will be adequate if it has as much clearness as the subject matter admits of."[21] So what clearness can be found in the idea of the legal point of view? Begin with the thought that the legal point of view is the point of view from which the law is legitimate or just in some way.[22] In some sense, it seems to be a necessary truth about law that, from the legal point of view, the law is legitimate; and, although talk of the legal point of view is not generally part of it, the (Razian) discourse about the law's claim to authority seems to be at least in part about this same idea.[23] Scott Shapiro aims to capture this idea in terms of the legal point of view when he writes that "The legal point of view of a certain system, in other words, is a theory that holds that the norms of that system are morally legitimate and obligating."[24] The validity of the legal point of view in this sense is a question about the justification of legal obligation or the legitimacy of the legal system. I will touch on this point later on.

To fully understand the legal point of view, we need to understand what it is a point of view *on*. Raz's thought, mentioned above, is that the legal point of view is a point of view about some protected reasons. He says that the legal point of view "consists of the norms" of a legal system—which of course he understands in terms of protected reasons—as well as any reasons which those norms require

---

[19] Raz (1999: 44).
[20] Raz (1999: 144).
[21] Aristotle, *Nichomachean Ethics*, I.3, 1094b13.
[22] Coleman (2011: 22).
[23] On law's claiming, see Gardner (2012).
[24] Shapiro (2011: 186).

subjects to act.[25] Shapiro too thinks that the legal point of view is to be understood in terms of norms, but understands norms as plans, not protected reasons.

By contrast, the Simple Theory's explanation is, in its way, simple: It says that the legal point of view is a point of view on the reasons that apply to its subjects (and their strength).[26] Here, the Simple Theory draws on the kinds of considerations that come up in discussions about the law's making claims or representations, which is to say that the law's having a point of view on its subjects reasons is a matter of what is explicitly or implicitly claimed by statements of legal officials, the best explanation of the actions of the organs of the legal system and the actions that the legal system requires of its subjects, and so on. (In the next section, I will say more about how we can know what reasons we have from the legal point of view.)

The Simple Theory's suggestion is that, in fact, this is all that is needed to explain legal obligation. Here, once more, is its central claim: When A is legally obligated not to φ, that is because, from the legal point of view, the reasons for A not to φ defeat any reasons for A to φ.[27] Note the parallels to Kolodny's account. Just as in that case, we can understand claims about legal obligation to be straightforwardly descriptive, in that they are claims about what the law takes or believes its subjects' reasons to be. In other words, there is a sense in which the Simple Theory welcomes the Holmesian thought that the bad man wants to know what sanctions he will be subject to for breaking the law, in the same way that you might want to know about my foolhardy intention in order to predict my behavior. But the thought is that from the law's own internal point of view, those reasons *really are* the reasons that its subjects have, and so from the law's point of view legal obligation is normative.

Recently, Wil Waluchow has offered a defense of Hart in quite similar terms. As Waluchow reminds us, Hart said that obligation-imposing rules "are thought important because they are believed to be necessary to the maintenance of social life or some highly prized feature of it."[28] But, Waluchow asks, rhetorically, will a subject adopting the internal point of view cite, in support of his performing an obligatory action, the *belief* that the rule supports important values?

> Of course he won't. He'll cite the important values. *From his internal perspective*, it's not the serious social pressure that produces the chain that

---

[25] Raz (1999: 171).

[26] In Raz (1999: 171), Raz comes close to the Simple Theory when he says that "people who believe in the validity of the legal point of view [make] normative statements to <u>assert what valid reasons for action there are</u>" (my underlining). Perhaps to the same effect is one part of the discussion in Raz (2011: 188): "We can thus treat the law as a normative point of view in the way in which we might treat Muslim morality as a distinct normative point of view, that is if it is legitimate or valid, then we have the reasons that, according to it, we have."

[27] That is a *"because"* of constitutive, rather than causal, explanation: The fact that A is legally obligated not to φ obtains in virtue of / is grounded in the fact that, from the legal point of view, the reasons for A not to φ defeat any reasons for A to φ.

[28] Hart (2012: 87).

binds... Instead it's the values in light of which such pressure and criticism are believed to be warranted or justified. That the shared social rule is, in his estimation, *actually necessary to social life*, or some highly prized feature of it, is a good part of the reason why it counts among those rules that actually impose obligations on him.[29]

The parallels with Kolodny's discussion of intention are striking. In both cases, we can understand something that seems to be constituted by non-normative facts (intentions or legal obligations) that can be understood purely descriptively (in terms of ordinary social or psychological facts about what someone or some set of people believe to be the case), as normative from a certain perspective. From the internal or first-personal deliberative point of view of a person or a legal system which believes *p* to be a reason to φ, *p* really is a reason to φ. And the Simple Theory accounts for the mixed reaction that Raz noticed: Sometimes what we have reason to do from the legal point of view (that is, what we are legally obligated to do) differs from what we (actually) have reason to do (from outside the legal point of view). And in such cases, choosing one action or the other will result in the possibility of a mixed reaction, as one will have acted rightly from one point of view and wrongly from the other.

Now, there is one way in which the idea of a normative point of view works quite differently in the two cases: Kolodny's story relies on a phenomenological claim about practical reasoning and intentions, the claim that, "from the inside," the normativity of rational requirements is just the normativity of reasons. But the legal point of view, as Shapiro says, is "not necessarily the perspective of any particular legal official." Instead it is "the perspective of a certain normative theory."[30] So what we need is not anything about the phenomenology of the legal point of view but instead some way to know what reasons the law takes its subjects to have. As Ronald Dworkin saw, and luckily for the Simple Theory, the law is very much in the business of providing us with this very information.

4. Precedential Reasoning and the Strength of Reasons

One striking feature of Dworkin's work in legal philosophy is its attendance to and reliance on judicial decisions. Although much analytic legal philosophy might seem to approach law through a statutory paradigm, Dworkin's detailed discussions of *Riggs v. Palmer, Henningsen v. Bloomfield Motors Inc., TVA v. Hill,* and *McLoughlin v. O'Brian* form a core component of his arguments. And, like

---

[29] Waluchow (2011: 382 [the italics are Waluchow's, the underlining is mine]). Perhaps there is some question here about the internal point of view (compare the discussion in Shapiro (2007: 1161-1163). We can sidestep the question by thinking instead about the Razian "ideal law-abiding citizen... who acts from the legal point of view": Raz (1999: 171).

[30] Shapiro (2011: 186).

many others, I find myself drawn to Dworkin's discussions here in the way that they cohere with roughly what I tell my students about legal reasoning.

At times, though, it seems as if the difference between the statutory paradigm that many legal philosophers work in and Dworkin's own approach were never fully grasped. Dworkin complained about this in "Model of Rules II:"

> My point [in 'Model of Rules I'] was not that 'the law' contains a fixed num-
> ber of standards, some of which are rules and others principles. Indeed,
> I want to oppose the idea that 'the law' is a fixed set of standards of any
> sort. My point was rather that an accurate summary of the considerations
> lawyers must take into account, in deciding a particular issue of legal rights
> and duties, would include propositions having the form and force of princi-
> ples, and that judges and lawyers themselves, when justifying their conclu-
> sions, often use propositions which must be understood in this way.[31]

Dworkin is onto something here. The phenomenology of legal decision mak-
ing seems, at least on its face, difficult to square with the standard account of legal obligation. However, I think the Simple Theory can easily explain the facts that motive Dworkin's critique. To defend that claim, begin with Mark Greenberg's posing of Dworkin's point: "the familiar practice of deriving the law from judicial decisions looks…like trying to work out the impact of these decisions [on the applicable reasons]."[32]

Think about ordinary reasoning. Philosophers often talk about reasons as hav-
ing what Raz once called a "dimension of strength" but more recent writing has suggested that this can be a misleading way to talking. He now says that the met-
aphor of a balance of reasons can mislead, and "worse still is the suggestion that reasons come with weights attached."[33] A better suggestion is made by Scanlon, who has recently and helpfully suggested that "the idea of the strength of a rea-
son has no significance for us apart from consideration of [conflicts]."[34] What it is for one reason p to be stronger than another reason q, says Scanlon, *just is* for it to be the case that if p counts in favor of some action φ and q counts in favor of some action ψ that is incompatible with φ, then A would not be "open to rational criticism" were she to φ rather than Y, but she would be open to such criticism were she to ψ rather than φ.[35] In other words, Scanlon thinks that the relative strength of reasons is determined by "general principles about the roles properly given to certain considerations in deciding what to do and in justifying one's

---

[31] Dworkin (1977: 76).

[32] Greenberg (2011a: 75).

[33] Compare Raz (1999: 25) with Raz (2009: 7).

[34] Scanlon (2014: 112).

[35] Scanlon (2014: 106-108). In his review of Scanlon's book (Schroeder (2014)) Mark Schroeder raises some worries about the precise implementation of Scanlon's program in cases involving more than two reasons. These worries are important, but a careful consideration of the way that legal reasoning works—such as that offered by Lamond or Horty, and discussed in the next few paragraphs—can, I think, address them at least in the legal context.

actions."[36] So on Scanlon's view we do not deliberate with a set of reasons, each of which has a property called *strength* independent of any role in practical reasoning; instead reasons have the strength that they have in virtue of the process of reasoning itself. Exactly how this works in morality, that is, how we determine how strong our reasons are, is a difficult question. (I take it Scanlon thinks a process of reflective equilibrium is involved.) But in law, things are easier. This is because the "the familiar practice of deriving the law from judicial decisions" is the practice of the law's determining the strength of reasons from the legal point of view.

What does this practice look like? It has two basic aspects: first, "the fundamental requirement of the common-law doctrine of precedent . . . is that earlier decisions must be treated as correctly decided on their facts," and second, "the *ratio* points to those features of the case that provide sufficient reason(s) for the result, given that context."[37] These two ideas add up to the thought that a later court must treat an earlier court's binding decision as *determinative* of the strength of the reasons given by the facts of the earlier case. The court, in holding for plaintiff (say), is demonstrating that it takes the reasons for plaintiff to be stronger than the reasons for defendant. And its *ratio* is the court's description of what it takes those reasons to be. Subsequent courts, then, must either follow the precedent (if there are no new reasons counting against the subsequent plaintiff's case) or distinguish it (if there are).

The crucial idea is that the strengths of the various reasons themselves are "derived from the decisions reached in precedent cases."[38] Just as on Scanlon's account the fact that one ought to φ rather than ψ explains the fact that p is stronger than $q,$ the fact that a court has decided that plaintiff wins determines that the reasons supporting plaintiff's case are, taken as a whole, stronger than the reasons supporting defendant's case. As Horty and Lamond illustrate, the genius of the common law method lies in the way that the variety of cases to be followed and distinguished makes it possible to state with some specificity what the law takes to be the strength of various considerations in various circumstances. If a court decides that A can enjoin B from playing cricket on B's land if sometimes cricket balls fly onto A's land, then subsequent courts must treat the safety of future plaintiffs in A's position as a stronger reason than the freedom to play cricket of future defendants in B's position, because the earlier court's decision means that, from the legal point of view, the safety is a stronger reason than the freedom in such cases.[39] Note that this way of seeing things supports a much more

---

[36] Scanlon (2014: 112).

[37] Lamond (2005: 3, 16). To the same effect, see Raz (1979: 184); there Raz also presents his own account of precedential reasoning. For an example of the first aspect see *Baird v. British Columbia* (1992), 17 BCAC 315 at para. 20: "Although, no doubt, each of the nine cases reached the correct result on the facts there present. . ."

[38] Horty (2011: 3). Again, here the *deriving* should be read in a metaphysical rather than epistemological register.

[39] *Miller v. Jackson*, [1977] QB 966 (CA). Here I am assuming that these are the only two reasons at play in the case. More accurately, we should say that A's winning the case means that all the reasons for A's position, taken together, are stronger than all the reasons for B's position, taken together.

holistic understanding of legal obligation than the rather atomistic understanding given by the standard account: Previous decisions determine the strength of reasons from the legal point of view, and the class of such decisions may, at least in principle, include any previously decided case on any issue, although of course cases whose facts are more similar tend to be seen as more relevant.[40]

According to the Simple Theory, A is legally obligated not to φ when from the legal point of view, the reasons for A not to φ defeat any reasons for A to φ. The above is meant as a partial cashing out of the idea and a vindication of it in the sense that it is a demonstration that a precedent (A has an obligation not to allow cricket balls onto B's land) can fruitfully and plausibly be understood in terms of the court's (i.e., the law's) assessment of the strengths of the reasons for and against a given action (A's playing cricket in a certain fashion). And remember also that part of the purported virtues of the Simple Theory is its *simplicity*. And indeed, it is helpful that the account of precedential reasoning can be fruitfully linked to the way that we understand reasons and their strength in ordinary morality. In other words, the thought is that precedential reasoning just is the same as moral reasoning (or at least Scanlon's account of it), and this counts in favor of the idea that legal obligation is just a matter of the balance of reasons (from the legal point of view).[41]

5. The Simple Theory

According to the Simple Theory, A is legally obligated not to φ when from the legal point of view, the reasons for A not to φ defeat any reasons for A to φ. We should separate out three cases. First there are cases in which, from the legal point of view, there are no reasons for or against φing: These are cases in which

---

[40] Ideas in this neighborhood can accommodate worries about apparent conflict in legal obligation, as in Fuller (1969: 66): "At one time in canonical law there was a principle according to which any promise made under oath was binding and another principle according to which certain kinds of promises, such as those extorted or usurious, imposed no obligation. What should the courts do then in the case of a usurious promise under oath?" Well, we often think that, in ordinary moral reasoning, two apparently conflicting moral principles ought to understandable in a way that removes the conflict. (On some views, all such conflicts must be resolvable; on others some conflicts cannot be.) The way to resolve such conflicts is by considering the underlying reasons for each principle and determining how they apply to the case at hand: notably in light of what I will argue below, this is the view defended by Dworkin in Dworkin (2011: 119). So in Fuller's example, the court's task is to determine the underlying reasons (from the legal point of view) for and against each principle as applied to the facts at hand and determine what ought to be done in this case, according to the legal point of view.

[41] What about statutes? It seems to me that a theory of statutory interpretation is needed in order to answer that question. And I am not about to provide one of those. But I will register my sympathy with the view offered in Greenberg (2011b). This sympathy is driven by a rather parochial consideration: I am Canadian. Canadian federal legislation is issued in equally authoritative French and English versions, which suggests that knowing what legal obligations are created by those statutes requires more than the sort of textualism that Greenberg argues is required on the standard theory of legal obligation. On the interpretation of such legislation, see Bastarache, Essert, Metallic, and Morris (2008: ch. 2).

the law does not care, so to speak, about how a subject acts, so subjects are not legally obligated one way or the other. Next are those cases in which there are reasons for A to φ that are defeated by reasons for A not to φ. And then there are those in which there are reasons for A not to φ but no reasons at all for A to φ. These latter cases are, I think, comparatively rarer.[42] More common are cases in which the law contemplates the existence of reasons to φ but determines that these reasons in general defeated by the reasons not to. In these reasons not to, φ can be seen as falling into roughly two classes (although perhaps the two classes are better thought of as poles of a continuum): Some reasons would count against φing regardless of the existence of law even though others depend for their force on what we can think of as the nonlegal effects of the law. Let me explain.

The first class of reasons is made up of just the normal reasons (moral, prudential, perhaps aesthetic) that count for and against φ. In the cricket case above, these would probably include the following: In summer time, village cricket is the delight of everyone counts in favor of playing, but that cricket balls might sometimes damage adjacent homes or even harm people counts against.[43] The second class of reasons is different. Quite apart from whatever normative power or authority they claim or have, legal systems are large-scale institutions whose actions, at least sometimes, can change the non-normative circumstances of the world. And sometimes, when changes like this are brought about by the law, they cause a change in the way that some nonlegal reasons or norms or principles apply to legal subjects. The paradigmatic cases of this class are those in which the law solves coordination problems by making one solution salient. By telling Canadians to drive on the right side of the road, the law makes the right side the salient solution to the problem of picking a side of the road to drive on. But there is nothing distinctively legal about this. A really effective advertising campaign would work just as well. This reason-giving here is derivative, in that the law is just triggering (to use Enoch's helpful term) preexisting reasons that apply to its subjects (and which could just as well be triggered by other nonlegal events).[44]

According to the Simple Theory, A's legal obligation is explained by the way that both classes of reasons count against the relevant act.[45] And, crucially, from

---

[42] Which (and how many) reasons are defeated and which are not reasons at all seems to me to be a substantive (legal) question to be addressed from a particular legal point of view of a particular legal system. The Simple Theory can accommodate different views on this question. The difference between exclusion and reweighing has of course been a theme of Stephen Perry's work: see, e.g., Perry (1989: 932-933).

[43] Sometimes these reasons might be correlatively structured or second-personal. Sometimes— but, notably, not always—legal obligation is so structured. The Simple Theory is fine with either possibility.

[44] Enoch (2011). Another well-trodden example of this idea is the Rawlsian duty of fairness: when the law creates a reason by triggering such a duty is not doing so in any distinctively legal case. For discussion of further possibilities of this sort of reason-giving, see Greenberg (2014: 1310-1318).

[45] It seems to me that both types of reasons are present in the intention cases that Kolodny considers, too, although he treats them separately. In "Why Be Rational?" the focus is on the first class of reasons, the reasons on the basis of which an agent forms her intention. Kolodny (2005). In "Aims

the legal point of view, these reasons (of both classes) always come down on the side of legal obligation. That is, it might turn out to be the case that, as a matter of actual fact (i.e., outside the legal point of view), A might have better reasons not to perform her legal obligation not to φ, even taking into account the way that the legal system's actions have caused changes to the reasons that agent has in that second class of cases. But *from the legal point of view,* it is necessarily the case that the reasons A has not to φ outweigh the reasons to φ. That is just what the legal point of view *is*: It is the practical point of view from which we always have conclusive reason to perform our legal obligations. That is just what it is for A to be legally obligated not to φ. Or, at least, so the Simple Theory claims.

Note that the fact that A is legally obligated not to φ is not itself a reason for A on this account. So the Simple Theory explains the normativity of legal obligation (from the legal point of view) in quite a different way than the standard account. It is true, of course, that when A is legally obligated not to φ then (from the legal point of view at least) A has reasons not to φ. But the fact of the obligation itself is not among those reasons. Instead, the fact that A is legally obligated not to φ is verdictive or conclusory: A is legally obligated *because of* all the reasons (of the sort canvassed above) not to φ.[46] So if one is legally obligated not to φ, it is true that one has (at least) a reason not to φ (again, from the legal point of view); it is just that the fact that one is obligated is not itself a reason.

The Simple Theory does make more obvious something that is true also of the standard account, which is that the normativity of legal obligation is only apparent or, as Shapiro would say, perspectival. As I said above, although from the legal point of view, it is necessarily true that the reasons not to φ defeat the reasons to φ (when A is legally obligated not to φ), from outside the legal point of view (that is, in reality), the reasons to φ might win.[47] Were one to perform the obligatory act in such a case, we would see, as Raz suggested, the possibility of a mixed reaction. On the Simple Theory, the mixed reaction arises because of the conflict at the level of points of view: From the legal point of view, the reasons not to φ defeated the reasons to φ and so it was praiseworthy not to φ, and outside the legal point of view things were different and so criticism is appropriate.[48]

---

as Reason," Kolodny shows how the formation of an intention's effect on an agent's reasons is not distinctive of the intention *qua* intention but rather because the formation of an intention is a fact about the world which can trigger reasons just as any other fact can. Kolodny (2011).

[46] Essert (2013).

[47] For the most part, for ease of exposition, I assume that morality is sufficiently determinate that it makes sense to talk about what we have reason to do outside of the law. But it might be the case that morality is not determinate in that way, and that, in a wide and important set of cases, there is no fact of the matter about what we have reason to do. If that were the case, then the kind of Kantian case for adopting the legal point of view that I mention briefly below would make the most sense, in that we would need law (and its accompanying point of view) in order to settle questions about how we ought to act that need settling but which morality (or reasons alone) does not settle. On this kind of thought, see Stone (2011); and for perhaps a similar idea, see Dworkin (1986: 238).

[48] Here, I am interested in the metaphysics of legal obligation rather than its semantics. But a brief note on semantics might be helpful: Putting aside some worries about the precise differences

Note how we are, from the legal point of view, perfectly entitled to perform our legal obligations for any of the various reasons that, according to the law, count in favor of the action in question. Return to the cricket case: Defendants cannot play cricket because they think nuisance law is part of a fair system of cooperation, or because they want to be good neighbors, or because it is raining. So far as the law is concerned, it does not matter which they choose. As long as they do not play cricket, they are not doing what, from the legal point of view, they have no reason to do so from the legal point of view they are not subject to any criticism. (That is, they have not committed a legal wrong.) This is good, because this makes sense of the intuitively attractive idea that the law does not demand compliance of us but only conformity.[49]

What about the peremptoriness of legal obligation? As I noted above, part of the overarching idea of the legal point of view is the idea (sometimes put in terms of what the law claims) that from the legal point of view the law is legitimate. The

---

between the legal point of view and the Hartian internal point of view, we might think that so-called internal legal statements (A has a legal obligation not to φ) are statements made by someone who adopts the legal point of view, which is to say someone who takes the relevant reasons and their weight to be determined by the legal point of view. *Cf.* Coleman (2011: 23). And detached statements are made when the speaker assumes the legal point of view for the sake of argument, so to speak, without actually endorsing it. However, the two types of statements have the same semantic content but appear to have different meaning in that the first includes a form of normative endorsement absent in the second. One proposal (in development by Stephen Finlay and David Plunkett) is that this difference is explained by the pragmatics of the two statements. Precisely how the semantics and metaphysics of legal obligation relate is outside my scope here, but it seems to me that the Simple Theory's point-of-view structure might be suggestive of a semantics that has a similar structure.

[49] Two things to note: First, while the Simple Theory explains legal obligation in terms of the (normative) reasons legal subjects actually have, here and elsewhere I have made reference to the deliberations of legal subjects. This is because I accept the thought, made famous by Bernard Williams and dubbed by Raz, the *normative/explanatory nexus*, that a reason is only a reason if you can be guided by it in action: For discussion, see Essert (2012b). So a theory of legal obligation in terms of reasons needs to be able to make sense of the practical deliberations of the (rational) legal subject. One implication of this idea allows the Simple Theory to account for cases—antidiscrimination laws and fiduciary duties being two prominent examples—in which it seems to matter what reasons a legal subject acts on. The theory claims that, to act as one is legally obligated to, one must act on (i.e., be motivated by) some subset of the reasons for the action in question according to the legal point of view. Normally, there are lots of reasons to choose from and any one is as good as another. But, in some cases, the choice of reasons to act on is more constrained: It is, in general, ok to fire one's employees, which is to say that the reasons to do so can defeat the reasons not to do so, from the legal point of view; but an employee's race or gender or sexual orientation are not among the reasons for which one can fire an employee, and so acting on one of those considerations can amount to violating a legal obligation. Second, and relatedly, I have not said much about sanctions. One way to understand the Hartian point about the sanction theory is that the sanction needs to come (conceptually) after the law has determined what is legally obligatory. That means that the role of sanctions on the Simple Theory is in fact outside the legal point of view: The presence of a sanction is a reason to deliberate from the legal point of view rather than a reason (inside the legal point of view) to perform any given action. (Waluchow's interpretation, cited above, seems to be to the same effect.) The point is not limited to sanctions: It goes for any sort of external motivation to follow the law (like that you promised that you would).

Simple Theory understands this idea in the following terms: it says that part of the idea of legal obligation is that the law claims that we have reason to deliberate according to the legal point of view. And If we deliberate from the legal point of view, we *do not* deliberate from outside the legal point of view. In other words, in adopting the legal point of view as a practical standpoint from which to deliberate upon our practical reasons, we exclude, in a sense, other points of view on the strength of our reasons. So the preemption of legal obligation arises at a holistic or systemic level, rather than at the level of individual legal obligations.[50] Here it is worth noting how, the Simple Theory is, as advertised, *simple*. Recall that Raz characterizes the complexity that protected reasons introduce into our understanding of legal obligation as unwelcome. I take it that the idea, however, is that this unwelcome complexity is justified by what Raz takes to be its unique power to solve the problem of how to understand legal obligation. My suggestion is that we do not need to posit the existence of protected reasons to explain legal obligation, because the idea of legal point of view (along with a pretty plain notion of reasons and their strength) can accomplish all that protected reasons can accomplish.

6. Why Be Legal?

Here a potential objection presents itself: Is there not a real disanalogy between intentions and legal obligation? Intentions are optional: If I intend to φ, then I can be rational by taking the means to φing (that is, by ξing) or I can be rational by abandoning my intention to φ and forming an intention to ψ instead. Obligation is not like this. It is categorical, which is to say that we cannot abandon the goal of complying with the law and thereby solve the problem of noncompliance. Of course this is correct. But I agree with those who think it can be easily accommodated.[51]

Consistent with the Simple Theory, we can understand the law's claim to authority as in part the claim that we have a categorical—that is, not optional, not depending on our personal goals or projects—reason to deliberate according to the legal point of view, that is, to take up or adopt the legal point of view and to judge our actions according to the what the law claims our reasons (and their strength) are. The thought underlying the law's claim here is that the directives of a legitimate authority are binding, which is to say that they apply categorically, and we cannot abandon the goal, so to speak, of following the law in the way that we can abandon a personal project. So the law says that if we fail to perform a legally obligatory act, we are subject not just to the sort of rational criticism that is appropriate when we fail to carry out an intention but that we have acted *wrongly*. This is, I think, consistent with Hart's thought that the difference

---

[50] See also Raz (2009: 8): "it is the law, the legal system as a whole, which pre-empts those background considerations, not any of the legal rules taken singly."

[51] Marmor (2011: 126-127, 138).

between a rule and an obligation lies in part in the fact that the performance of obligations is thought to be "necessary to the maintenance of social life or some highly prized feature of it."[52] Looking at the literature, we see different sorts of stories about when and why law could actually be a legitimate authority, about why (in my terms) we ought to deliberate according to the legal point of view.

One is the sort of explanation that Hart offered according to which some contingent features of our circumstances give us reason to create a legal system and so (on the Simple Theory) to deliberate according to its legal point of view. These circumstances are those discussed by Hart in chapter 5 of *The Concept of Law*. As a group moves from "a small community knit by ties of kinship" to a larger and more complex society, it faces a series of problems giving rise to the need for (or equal the reason to have) the various forms of secondary rules. It is a contingent matter that the group will have enough primary rules to have the need for a rule of recognition, or that its circumstances will change often enough to have the need for a rule of change, or that inefficiencies in the enforcement and application of the rules will give rise to the need for a rule of adjudication. In other words, on Hart's view, it is a matter of the contingent features of the society whether or not there will be reason to create a legal system. Scott Shapiro makes this point quite explicitly. He claims that only societies in what he calls the *circumstances of legality*, which obtain "whenever a community has numerous and serious moral problems whose solutions are complex, contentious, or arbitrary" have reason to create a legal system. By contrast, "[S]imple hunter-gatherer groups usually do not need law because they do not typically face the circumstances of legality and, hence, have no compensatory need for sophisticated technologies of social planning," which Shapiro claims (partially) constitute the existence of a legal system.[53] However, once the relevant features are in place the problems they give rise to are serious enough, on Hart's and Shapiro's views, to warrant our thinking that the reasons we have to create a legal system and so the reasons we have to deliberate according to its legal point of view, are categorical.

A different sort of explanation sees the need for law as arising not out of our contingent circumstances but rather out of some more fundamental features of ourselves as moral agents, such as the fact that we have rights. Kant's theory of law is like this: On Kant's view, the nature of rights and the nature of morality are such that morality requires of us that we create a legal system to resolve disputes about rights in a morally acceptable way. Thus, we necessarily have, just in virtue of our status as moral agents, a categorical reason to create a legal system and, thus, a categorical reason to deliberate according to its moral point of view.[54] This is quite a different explanation of the way in which the legal point of view generates not just judgments of rational criticizability but legal obligation.[55]

---

[52] Hart (2012: 87).

[53] See Shapiro (2011: 170-173).

[54] Kant (1996: 6:306-308).

[55] For discussion of the Kantian account in similar terms see Ripstein (2012); Stone (2012).

The Simple Theory is not tied to a particular story about the reasons to deliberate from the legal point of view. But it suggests some ways that might help to clarify why and how such a story is needed. That and also its catholicism about what story in particular would work seem to me to count in its favor. Later on, I will say a bit more about these sorts of considerations. For now, though, this concludes the presentation of the Simple Theory. Let us turn to Dworkin.

7. The Model of Principles

In this and the next section, I want to hold the Simple Theory up to some of Dworkin's thinking on legal obligation. If you have made it this far into the paper, I assume you know, roughly, the shape of the arguments that Dworkin made against Hart's positivism in "Model of Rules I," and so I will not go through them here. Instead, I want to suggest, briefly, that the purported challenge posed by the existence of legal principles is easily explained by the Simple Theory and, indeed, that this explanation is the one that Hart himself gave in the "Postscript," to *The Concept of Law.* By contrast, Dworkin's argument in the former work does cause at least consternation for the standard account of legal obligation, in that it again makes this more complicated: as I noted above, the standard account is best suited to explaining legal obligation arising out of *directives* and has a harder time with common-law reasoning. How are legal principles, assuming they have the features Dworkin takes them to have, meant to fit into what really can seem at times like a model of rules? At least in part as a result of this consternation, the arguments in "Model of Rules I" can be seen to have lead to the positivism's debate about inclusive-versus-exclusive, and all the fun that was. However, as we will see, the specter of legal principles does not pose a threat to the Simple Theory and to the extent that the theory is friendly to legal positivism, they therefore do not pose a threat to positivism.

Dworkinian principles, like "No man may profit from his own wrongdoing" do not function like rules, which is to say (I think) that they do not have peremptory force, but instead state "a reason that argues in one direction, but does not necessitate a particular result."[56] They have a *dimension of weight or importance* and when two or more principles 'intersect' the conflict must be resolved by "tak[ing] into account the relative weight of each."[57] Even just reading these passages should make clear how the Simple Theory accommodates Dworkin's (I think correct) insight that sometimes courts rely on principles like these in making their decisions. Principles are just statements about the strength of reasons. Statements about reasons come at different levels of generality: We say that you have a reason to spend your time pleasantly, or that you have a reason to watch entertaining movies, or that tonight you should watch *Ghostbusters* again, and each of these statements can be seen as a reason for the same action, posed

---

[56] Dworkin (1977: 26).
[57] Dworkin (1977: 26).

at different levels of generality. Dworkinian principles are just like that: They are statements at a relatively high level of generality about the strength of various reasons. So "No man may profit..." just means that to the extent that an action counts as someone's profiting from their wrongdoing, that is a reason against allowing it.

But wait, you say, surely there is more to the argument than this? Well, I am not sure. The other important advertised feature of Dworkinian principles is meant to be that they are valid in virtue of their content rather than their pedigree. And yet right when Dworkin introduces this idea, he seems to me to take it back in precisely the way that the Simple Theory would require:

> The origin of [these] legal principles lies not in a particular decision of some legislature or court, but in a sense of appropriateness developed in the profession and the public over time... True, if we were challenged to back up our claim that some principle is a principle of law, we would mention any prior cases in which that principle was cited, or figured in the argument. We would also mention any statute that seemed to exemplify the principle... Unless we could find some such institutional support, we would probably fail to make out our case.[58]

If we asked Dworkin to depict principles in a way that demonstrated that they described not just reasons at a particular level of generality but, indeed, reasons from the legal point of view, it would be hard for him to have done better than that.

When common law courts decide the cases they determine, as we saw above, the strength of various reasons according to the legal point of view. Principles just put various cases into groups, as we say that such-and-such a case or set of cases stands for some principle. Surely Dworkin is right that principles are not (usually) determined by any single case. But the relatively high level of generality at which principles are framed is indicative of their application to (and so their derivation from or determination by) many different cases, just as the fact that you ought to spend your time pleasurably means not only that you should spend your evening watching *Ghostbusters,* but also that you should read *Anna Karenina,* visit Paris, eat at Sally's Apizza, and on and on. The difference is just that legal principles are determined over time by various decisions of the courts and by various enactments of legislatures.

This all seems obvious to me. And I am not the first one to have noticed it. Here is Hart, in the "Postscript," discussing Dworkin's argument:

> Some legal principles, including some basic principles of the Common Law, such as that no man may profit from his own wrongdoing, are identified as law by the 'pedigree' test in that they have been consistently invoked by courts in ranges of different cases as providing reasons for decision, which

---

[58] Dworkin (1977: 40).

must be taken into account, though liable to be overridden in some cases by reasons pointing the other way.[59]

Here Hart makes the point that the form of legal principles—their weight, essentially—does not itself constitute a challenge to legal positivism. (I take no stand here on whether other positivist responses to Dworkin on this point are successful.) That said, I do think Dworkin raises an important point in "Model of Rules I" (and especially towards its end), a point already noted about the at-least-partially holistic way that courts reason about legal obligation.[60] The directive-based model of legal obligation that the standard account insists upon always seemed to me hard to square with the method of common-law reasoning. The Simple Theory provides, well, a simple way to accept Dworkin's point here without having to buy into any of the rest of his jurisprudence.

8. One System or Two?

Having talked about Dworkin's earliest work, I now want to skip straight his latest, *Justice for Hedgehogs*. In the brief discussion of law that comes at the end of that book, Dworkin argues for a view about law which is really quite different than the sort of view that seems to be presupposed by the main thread of debate in the field of legal philosophy. As Dworkin depicts things, while most philosophers understand law and morality as two normative systems whose relationship it is the role of jurisprudence to discern, a better view is one according to which there is only one system—morality—of which law is a branch.

Dworkin motivates this thought with a nonlegal example (albeit one that seems straightforwardly extendable to the legal case). He asks us to imagine ourselves as a parent trying to decide whether or not to enforce a promise made by one child to another. This decision, he tells us, will turn on a variety of questions about the family's history and practice in similar situations. But although this history and practice are important,

> It would be wrong to think that the special family history has created a distinct nonmoral code, like traditions of dress, that have some form of authority within the family that is not moral authority. That would be a mistake because the reasons you and other members of the family have for deferring to this history are themselves moral reasons. They draw on principles of fairness that condition coercion—principles about fair play, fair notice, and a fair distribution of authority, for instance, that make your family's distinct history morally pertinent.[61]

---

[59] Hart (2012: 265).

[60] And to the same effect see Dworkin (1986: 245).

[61] Dworkin (2011: 408-409). Similar one-system views have lately been defended in Greenberg (2014); Waldron (2013); and Hershovitz (2015).

The key idea to understand here, I think, is found in the last sentence: Dworkin's claim is that past actions have moral upshots just to the extent that they draw on or implicate moral principles which exist independently of those actions.

We have seen this idea already. In the context of a coordination problem, I said that, sometimes, legal systems have an impact on what reason requires of their subjects not because they are doing anything distinctively legal, but rather because sometimes actions of legal systems cause non-normative changes in the world that trigger preexisting and independent moral principles. On the sort of one-system view that Dworkin offers in *Hedgehogs*, this is the *only* way in which legal systems can affect the reasons of their subjects.[62] That is, on the one-system view, it is not up to the law to decide what legal obligations it creates; rather, legal institutions do things in the world and sometimes the effect of this is that some action becomes legally obligatory. But these effects are quite obviously outside the control of those institutions, and as Greenberg notes, it is quite possible that a legal institution could intend to create an obligation not to φ and somehow create an obligation to φ.[63]

This view is—as Dworkin says—really quite a departure from the dominant way of thinking in jurisprudence. Perhaps this is not in itself a bad thing, but before we depart, we should check to see what we will leave behind when we go. One strange thing about the view is how on its face it makes it very hard to understand the law as a normative enterprise. Remember Hart, Austin, and the gunman. One feature of the gunman situation that Hart seems to me to dance around but never quite reach is this: The gunman's threat—or the Austinian sovereign's command—gets whatever normativity it has from the teller's pre-existing reason to avoid being shot. The normativity of law on a view like Hart's lies, in part, in the ability of law to make a normative or practical difference *directly*, rather than just by triggering pre-existing reasons. (Hart gets closest to this in saying that on the Austinian story, it would be a contradiction to say that an offender had bribed the police and that he had an obligation: by (re)rearranging the non-normative circumstances of the world to make it the case that the law no longer triggers his pre-existing reason not to be punished the offender eliminates the Austinian obligation.) A one-system view like the one Dworkin offers in *Justice*

---

[62] See also Greenberg (2014: 1310). So here I disagree with David Dyzenhaus' claim, in note 115 to chapter 7, "Dworkin and Unjust Law," of this volume that Dworkin's account in *Judgment for Hedgehogs* runs counter to Hart's assertion that "the idea of a moral legislature with competence to make and change morals, as legal enactments make and change law, is repugnant to the whole notion of morality." As his discussion and emphasis on notions of deliberate and direct change make clear, Hart does not mean to rule out the possibility that we change what we are moral required to do by changing the non-normative circumstances of the world; indeed, in his discussion of the ways in which legal changes might cause moral changes, he gives several examples of these types of moral change. His concern is rather with the possibility that we can make such changes without changing the non-normative circumstances. See Hart (2012: 175-178). Dworkin's one-system view in *Hedgehogs,* I am arguing, allows for moral change *only* through changing the non-normative circumstances of the world and thus precisely rules out the kind of changes that Hart is concerned with.

[63] Greenberg (2014: 1322).

for Hedgehogs is on the Austinian side of this distinction. And in being on that side of this distinction, the view requires us, I think, to give up on the possibility of legal authority in the sense of a normative power to change others' obligations. Let me explain.

Consider, for example, Hart's discussion in chapter 5 of *The Concept of Law*. As a group moves from "a small community knit by ties of kinship" to a larger and more complex society, it faces a series of problems giving rise to the need for (that equals the reason to have) the various forms of secondary rules. The secondary rules, and in particular the Rule of Recognition, could be understood as picking out the ways in which the legal point of view is formed and so the ways in which legal obligations are determined. In some circumstances—perhaps what Shapiro has called the circumstances of legality[64]—the only way legal subjects will be able to get anywhere close to doing what they have reason to do is by performing their legal obligations. In these circumstances, there is a sense in which, the Dworkinian one-system account is what the law claims to be the case: The law claims that the moral upshot of the actions of legal institutions is such as to make the relevant actions obligatory. But the Simple Theory insists that this is true *only from the legal point of view*. What happens in reality is outside the control of the law, as I just mentioned.[65]

But in other, perhaps better, circumstances, things might be different. As the law approaches legitimacy, subjects' legal obligations—what they have reason to do from the legal point of view—should get closer and closer to what they actually have reason to do, keeping in mind the ways in which actions of (legitimate) legal institutions will cause changes in those reasons. As this happens, the need for the legal point of view might start to subside and a one-system view will start to look more plausible. But, once again, on this picture there isn't much room for legal authority. To close, I will see if we can find some.

9. Normative Powers and the Value of Law

The way to do so is by noticing that some normative phenomena, most obviously promising, seem to be resistant to an explanation like Kolodny's: When I promise you to φ this seems (in normal circumstances) automatically to create

---

[64] Shapiro (2011: 171).

[65] Something like this might be suggested by a remark of Mark Greenberg's. In Greenberg (2011a: 86-87), Greenberg depicts the basic idea of a one-system view like Dworkin's—that our legal obligations are those moral obligations created by the actions of legal institutions (in the morally proper way)—as a hypothesis about "how the law is *supposed* to operate." He goes on to entertain the possibility that the law purports to operate in this way. And many have linked the idea of the legal point of view to the idea of the law's making a certain kind of normative claim—consider, e.g., Shapiro (2011: 187): "the legal point of view always *purports* to represent the moral point of view"—such that we might understand the Simple Theory's thought "from the legal point of view the reasons not to φ defeat the reasons to φ" as equivalent to the thought "the law purports or claims that the reasons not to φ defeat the reasons to φ." This brings the Simple Theory and one-system views quite close indeed.

an obligation to φ distinct from the obligations created by the non-normative upshots of the promise. This apparently bizarre possibility was what worried Hume promises. Some accounts of promising explain the problem away, by showing (or attempting to show) how my promise obligates me just by triggering some independent moral principle, along the lines of Scanlon's Principle F. By contrast, a powers-based explanation of promising claims that we have moral powers to obligate ourselves through our promises.[66] According to such accounts, promising has a distinctive value that grounds these moral powers, such that when we promise, we change the normative situation directly or normatively, without having to change any non-normative facts of the world (and thereby causing a change in the application of an independent moral principle as in the conventionalist account).

The possibility of such an explanation of promising in terms of normative powers poses a choice for jurisprudence of the following sort. If we think the law has authority, or more generally that it has moral power—the ability, again, to make normative changes directly without manipulating non-normative facts— then the obvious explanation of this fact would be parallel to the explanation in the case of promising. So we would need to posit a distinctive value of law that could ground such normative power. The problem is that, as we have just seen, the Simple Theory suggests that if this value is something like the value that intentions have—something that arises in the circumstances of legality, for example— then it is not the right kind of value to explain normative power, since in the case of intentions their entire normative effect and associated value is explained absent normative powers. In this case, a one-system view like Dworkin's seems more plausible. The obvious alternative is to posit a distinct moral value for law: If law is an institution uniquely able to help us solve certain moral problems which are not best understood in those terms, then this value might be able to explain the possibility of law's possessing genuine normative power. What would such a distinct moral value look like? Above I mentioned Kant's view, which provides us with a possible answer, according to which law is necessary to render our rights consistent. Seana Shiffrin provides a tantalizing suggestion of a somewhat different sort:

> we individuals who share social relations have a duty to create legal systems in order to maintain proper relations to one another, to establish the social conditions that embody and facilitate justice, and, perhaps, to establish a common voice and identity. These duties to one another provide the moral impetus to create legal institutions.[67]

And Raz, at times, says things that I think can be permissibly taken as making a similar point, as when he tells us that "the principles establishing the legitimacy of man-made laws...are themselves, whatever else they are, moral

---

[66] Shiffrin (2008); Owens (2012).
[67] Shiffrin (2008: 522-23).

principles... They are principles that allow, perhaps even require, some people to interfere in important ways in the lives of others."[68] This suggests that a commitment to genuine normative power in the legal case might entail a commitment to law's having a distinctive moral value. I leave discussion of the questions this raises to another day.

References

Aristotle, *Nichomachean Ethics.*

Bastarache, M., Essert, C., Metallic, N., and Morris, R. (2008). *The Law of Bilingual Interpretation.* LexisNexis.

Bratman, M. (1987). *Intention, Plans, and Practical Reason.* Harvard.

Bratman, M. (2004). "Shared Valuing and Frameworks for Practical Reasoning." In *Reason and Value: Themes from the Moral Philosophy of Joseph Raz,* R. Jay Wallace, P. Pettit, S. Scheffler, and M. Smith (eds.). Oxford University Press.

Coleman, J. (2011). "The Architecture of Jurisprudence," *Yale Law Journal* 121: 2.

Dworkin, R. (1977). *Taking Rights Seriously.* Cambridge, MA: Harvard University Press.

Dworkin, R. (1986). *Law's Empire.* Cambridge, MA: Harvard University Press.

Dworkin, R. (2011). *Justice for Hedgehogs.* Cambridge, MA: Harvard University Press.

Enoch, D. (2011). "Reason-Giving and the Law," *Oxford Studies in Philosophy of Law* 1: 1.

Essert, C. (2012a). "A Dilemma For Protected Reasons," *Law and Philosophy* 31: 49.

Essert, C. (2012b). "From Raz's *Nexus* to Legal Normativity," *Canadian Journal of Law and Jurisprudence* 25: 465.

Essert, C. (2013). "Legal Obligation and Reasons," *Legal Theory* 19: 63.

Finnis, J. (2011). *Natural Law and Natural Rights,* 2nd ed. Oxford University Press.

Fuller, L. L. (1969). *The Morality of Law.* Yale.

Gardner, J. (2011). "What is Tort Law For? Part I. The Place of Corrective Justice," *Law and Philosophy* 30: 1.

Gardner, J. (2012). "How Law Claims, What Law Claims." In *Institutionalized Reason: The Jurisprudence of Robert Alexy,* M. Klatt (ed.). Oxford University Press.

Greenberg, M. (2011a). "The Standard Picture and Its Discontents," *Oxford Studies in Philosophy of Law* 1: 39.

Greenberg, M. (2011b). "Legislation and Communication? Legal Interpretation and the Study of Linguistic Communication." In *Philosophical Foundations of Language in the Law,* A. Marmor and S. Soames (eds.). Oxford University Press.

Greenberg, M. (2014). "The Moral Impact Theory of Law," *Yale Law Journal* 123: 1289.

Hart, H. L. A. (1982). *Essays on Bentham.* Oxford University Press.

Hart, H. L. A. (2012). *The Concept of Law.* 3rd ed. Oxford University Press.

Hershovitz, S, (2015). "The End of Jurisprudence," *Yale Law Journal* 124: 882.

Hieronymi, P. (2009). "The Will as Reason," *Philosophical Perspectives* 23: 201.

Hieronymi, P. (2013). "The Use of Reasons in Thought," *Ethics* 124: 114.

Horty, J. F. (2011). "Rules and Reasons in the Theory of Precedent," *Legal Theory* 17: 1.

---

[68] Raz (2009: 188 (my underlining)).

Kant, I. (1996). *The Metaphysics of Morals.* Trans. Mary Gregor. Cambridge University Press.

Kolodny, N. (2005). "Why Be Rational?," *Mind* 114: 509.

Kolodny, N. (2011). "Aims as Reasons," in S. Freeman, R. Kumar, and R. Jay Wallace (eds.), *Reasons and Recognition: Essays on the Philosophy of T.M. Scanlon.* Oxford University Press.

Lamond, G. (2005). "Do Precedents Create Rules?," *Legal Theory* 11: 1.

Marmor, A. (2011). "The Dilemma of Authority," *Jurisprudence* 2: 121.

Perry, S. (1989). "Second-Order Reasons, Uncertainty, and Legal Theory," *Southern California Law Review* 62: 913.

Raz, J. (1979). *The Authority of Law.* Oxford University Press.

Raz, J. (1999). *Practical Reason and Norms,* 2nd ed. Oxford University Press.

Raz, J. (2009). *Between Authority and Interpretation.* Oxford University Press.

Raz, J. (2011). *From Normativity to Responsibility.* Oxford University Press.

Ripstein, A. (2012). "Self-Certification and the Moral Aims of the Law," *Canadian Journal of Law and Jurisprudence* 25: 201.

Scanlon, T. M. (2014). *Being Realistic About Reasons.* Oxford University Press.

Schroeder, M. (2014). "Being Realistic About Reasons," *Australasian Journal of Philosophy* 93: 195.

Shapiro, S. J. (2007). "What is the Internal Point of View?," *Fordham Law Review* 75: 1157.

Shapiro, S. J. (2011). *Legality.* Harvard.

Stone, M. (2011). "Legal Positivism as an Idea about Morality," *University of Toronto Law Journal* 61: 313.

Stone, M. J. (2012). "Planning Positivism and Planning Natural Law," *Canadian Journal of Law and Jurisprudence* 25: 219.

Waldron, J. (2013). "Jurisprudence for Hedgehogs," NYU School of Law, Public Law Research Paper No. 13-45, <http://ssrn.com/abstract_id=2290309> accessed 4 June 2014

Waluchow, W. J. (2011). "Lessons From Hart," *Problema* 5: 363.

PART IV

Value in Law

12

Originalism and Constructive Interpretation
by David O. Brink*

Ronald Dworkin's main legacy in analytical jurisprudence consists in his interpretive approach to the law, his insistence on the moral dimensions of legal interpretation, and his defense of legal determinacy in hard cases. As someone sympathetic with many of Dworkin's ideas about law and legal interpretation,[1] I would like to use the occasion of exploring his legacy to focus on the development of his conception of legal interpretation and explore the connections between some apparently disparate commitments that he made about the nature of legal interpretation over the course of his career. In particular, I would like to focus on five different commitments.

1. The critique of H.L.A. Hart's model of rules and judicial discretion and the defense of the determinacy of the law in hard cases.
2. The distinction between concepts and conceptions and the claim that constitutional adjudication should conform to the best conception of the framers' concepts and values, rather than reproduce their specific conceptions of those values.
3. The critique of interpretive appeals to the intentions of the framers.
4. The defense of constructive interpretation and its appeal to fit and acceptability as the fundamental dimensions for assessing rival interpretations.
5. The defense of a normative conception of legal interpretation, despite the existence of significant normative disagreement.

---

*An earlier version of this material was presented at *The Legacy of Ronald Dworkin* (lawconf. mcmaster.ca), the McMaster University conference on the legacy of Ronald Dworkin, which was sponsored by the Ontario Legal Philosophy Partnership. I would like to thank members of the audience and especially Larry Alexander, Dick Arneson, Tom Christiano, Les Green, Michael Green, Ken Himma, Violetta Igneski, Connie Rosati, Stefan Sciaraffa, Cynthia Stark, Natalie Stoljar, and Will Waluchow for helpful feedback on that version.

[1] See, Brink (1985, 1988, 1989, 2001).

These interpretive claims can be defended and shown to cohere around a conception of interpretation that emphasizes the role of substantive moral and political commitments in defending claims about the meaning of legal provisions and fidelity of principle to the intentions of the framers of those provisions. In this way, I think that Dworkinian interpretive claims can be defended as a version of originalism about legal interpretation.

This may seem surprising inasmuch as originalist insistence on fidelity to the original meaning of constitutional language or the intentions of the framers is often seen as the antithesis of the sort of moralized interpretation that Dworkin defends.[2] But there are different ways of understanding meaning and intention and fidelity to either. Dworkin believes that legal provisions often express and are intended to express moral or political principles. Enforcing the best conception of those principles is what fidelity to original meaning and intention requires. This is a progressive form of originalism, committed to an originalism of principle or concept, rather than conception.

This sort of originalism of principle is reflected in Dworkin's conception of constructive interpretation in its insistence on assessing rival interpretations by the acceptability of their conceptions of a provision's underlying concept. However, Dworkin's insistence on institutional fit as an independent dimension of constructive interpretation qualifies his commitment to originalism in certain ways. However, both originalism of principle and constructive interpretation insist on the normative dimensions of interpretation, especially constitutional interpretation. I conclude by exploring concerns about the viability of a normative conception of interpretation in the face of significant normative disagreement.

1. The Model of Rules, Legal Determinacy, and Judicial Discretion

In *The Concept of Law,* Hart defended a common view about the nature of the law, the limited determinacy of the law, and the need for judicial discretion in the adjudication of hard cases.[3] Hart viewed a legal system as a body of primary rules for the guidance of citizens and the regulation of their behavior that are valid law by virtue of having the sort of institutional pedigree set out in a rule of recognition that regulates the behavior of the officials of the system by identifying certain sources of legal norms as authoritative. At least in morally decent legal systems, Hart believed that courts should interpret and apply the law by applying these primary rules. Hart thought that there were often good reasons for law-makers to enact laws that employed general terms—such as "anti-competitive practices," "due process," and "unreasonable search and

---

[2] For one statement of this common contrast, see Waluchow (2007: 52-69).
[3] H.L.A Hart (1961; 1994).

seizure"—rather than trying to give an exhaustive specification of all the actions and activities that the law should regulate. But, Hart claimed, general terms are essentially "open textured," with the result that cases could be divided into easy cases, to which the legal rules clearly apply, and hard cases, in which it was controversial whether the rule applies (Hart,1961; 119-120). Hart believed that hard cases are legally indeterminate (Hart, 1961; 124, 252). Judges cannot decide such cases by applying the law but only by exercising a quasi-legislative capacity that he called *judicial discretion.* He makes clear that this sort of judicial legislation need not and should not be arbitrary; it should reflect characteristic judicial virtues of impartiality, neutrality, and principled decision-making (Hart, 1961; 124, 200, 273). But such resolution must *ex hypothesi* be based on extra-legal considerations. Hart's argument for judicial discretion in hard cases has something like this form.

1. The law consists of legal rules formulated in general terms.
2. All general terms are open-textured: Though they contain a core of settled meaning, they also have a periphery in which their meaning is not determinate.
3. Controversial or hard cases, about which reasonable people with legal training disagree, fall within the open texture of legal terms within existing legal rules.
4. Hence, hard cases are legally indeterminate.
5. Hence, courts could decide hard cases only on extra-legal (e.g., moral and political) grounds.
6. Hence, in hard cases courts must exercise judicial discretion and make, rather than apply, law.

Consider Hart's example of a municipal ordinance prohibiting vehicles in the park. The core meaning of the term "vehicle" applies to my SUV and my motorcycle. So, if I am caught in the park doing doughnuts in my SUV or wheelies on my motorcycle, my case is an easy case, determinately prohibited by the legal rules. But "vehicle" is an open-textured concept. It is unclear whether it applies to bicycles, skateboards, Segways, and roller blades. Cases involving the use of these devices in the park would be hard cases and, according to Hart, legally indeterminate. Courts could decide such cases, he thinks, only by exercising the quasi-legislative capacity of judicial discretion. The law is gappy, but these gaps are gradually filled in over time by the exercise of judicial discretion.

2. Rules and Principles

Dworkin rejects Hart's arguments for judicial discretion and defends the near-maximal determinacy of the law, claiming that there is a uniquely correct right answer to nearly any case that might arise in the law. One litigant is almost always entitled to a decision in her favor as a matter of pre-existing legal right. Dworkin defends strong determinacy by disputing Hart's model of rules.[4] Dworkin claims that the law is richer than a body of black-letter rules with explicit institutional pedigree, because it contains a variety of legal principles. This leads him to reject premise (1) in Hart's argument. In "The Model of Rules," Dworkin appeals to our practices of legal argument and interpretation to defend this claim, as illustrated in two cases: *Riggs v. Palmer* and *Henningsen v. Bloomfield Motors, Inc.* (Dworkin 1977: 23-24).[5] In *Riggs,* the New York probate court claimed that Elmer Palmer could not inherit under the provisions of an otherwise valid will by murdering his grandfather so as to inherit his fortune. The court apparently ignored the plain meaning of the relevant probate statutes, which made no exceptions for disinheriting those who murdered the testator, and ruled against Elmer by appealing to the principle that no one should be able to profit from his own wrong. In *Henningsen,* a New Jersey court found Bloomfield Motors liable for compensatory damages (e.g., medical expenses for Henningsen's injured wife) caused as the result of defective parts and workmanship in their automobile, despite express limitations in the purchase agreement Henningsen signed, limiting the manufacturer's liability to making good (i.e., replacing) defective parts. Though the court recognized the importance of enforcing voluntary contracts, it justified its decision by appeal to principles requiring the court to make sure that contracts involving potentially dangerous products were fair to consumer and public interests, that contracts did not take unfair advantage of the economic circumstances of the purchaser, and that courts could not be "used as instruments of inequity and injustice."

Dworkin sees courts interpreting the law in light of background principles, as well as black-letter rules. In these cases, principles do not just supplement the interpretation of rules that are agreed on all sides to be uncertain. Rather, they actually counter decisions that seem rather clearly supported by the rules. *Riggs* turns on an unwritten exception to otherwise clearly formulated probate statutes; Henningsen turns on unwritten exceptions to a clearly written voluntary contract. These cases show the interpretive practice of invoking background legal principles that not only supplement but also modify black-letter rules. If there are legal principles as well as rules, Dworkin argues, then indeterminacy and discretion do not follow from the open texture of the rules.

3. The Semantics of Legal Interpretation

Even if Dworkin is right that the law consists of principles as well as rules, this does not much affect Hart's basic argument from open texture to indeterminacy. There is no reason to assume that the meaning of principles will always be determinate if the meaning of rules is not. Principles, as well as rules, are open-textured.

---

[4] See, especially, Dworkin (1977a) and (1977b).
[5] *Riggs v. Palmer* 115 N.Y. 506 (1889) and *Henningsen v. Bloomfield Motors, Inc.* 32 N.J. 358, 161 A.2d 69 (1960).

For instance, even if *Riggs* is an easy case under the principle that no one should profit from his own wrong, *Henningsen* is not an easy case under its principles. It is contested whether the purchase agreement exploited Henningsen's economic necessity and whether enforcing the contract would turn the court into an instrument of inequity and injustice. If Hart's semantic assumptions are true, then it is likely indeterminate whether these principles require finding for Henningsen. We must confront Hart's semantic assumptions directly if we are to resist his thesis about the indeterminacy of hard cases.

Hart makes the semantic assumption that the meaning of language in legal norms (whether rules or principles) is determinate so long as the meaning and range of application (extension) of that language is uncontroversial. This semantic assumption might be plausible if the meaning of a word or phrase consisted in the descriptions conventionally associated with it and the extension of the word or phrase was whatever satisfied these descriptions. For instance, we might say that the meaning of the word "bachelor" is given by the description "man who has never been married" that speakers associate with the word and that the reference or extension of the word is all and only those things that satisfy the description, that is, all and only men who have never been married. On such a view, when speakers associate different criteria of application with a term or disagree about its extension, we might conclude that the meaning of term is indeterminate.

Notice that for a given word or phrase, there are three possibilities about the determinacy of meaning.

(1) descriptions that almost everyone associates with the word,
(2) descriptions that almost no one associates with the word, and
(3) descriptions that some do associate with the word and that some do not.

Something that satisfies (1) is determinately part of the extension of the term; something that satisfies (2) is determinately not part of the extension of the term; and it is indeterminate whether something that satisfies (3) is part of the extension of the word. So, a legal rule using this word or phrase determinately applies in the first case; it determinately does not apply in the second; and it is indeterminate whether it applies in the third. The first two kinds of case are easy cases, whereas the third is a hard case. In hard and only in hard cases, the law is indeterminate.

If Hart is right about these semantic assumptions, then he has a ready reply to Dworkin. As long as cases arising under principles are hard cases in which people disagree about the semantic criteria for the application of a legal word or phrase or its extension, those cases must be semantically and, hence, legally indeterminate. If Dworkin is to block Hart's argument for the indeterminacy of hard cases, he must reject the semantic assumptions on which that argument rests.

Hart's semantic assumptions imply that disagreement in our criteria for applying words or disagreement about the extension of those words implies indeterminacy in their meaning or extension. But this is a problematic assumption. Disagreement does not imply indeterminacy. There can be a fact of the matter about the extension of a term even if there is disagreement about its criteria for application or its extension. For instance, we do not conclude that the meaning or extension of the word "toxin" is indeterminate just because people disagree about what the criteria for toxicity are or what substances are toxic, and we do not conclude that sense or reference of "justice" is indeterminate because of disagreements between libertarians and egalitarians about the nature of justice.

Indeed, if Hart's semantic assumptions were true, then we would have to say that when people have different criteria of application for a term and different ideas about its extension, they mean different things. But this would be a problem, because we could not then represent their disagreement. Disagreement and progress presuppose *univocity*—that is, that speakers are using words with the same sense and extension and are not talking past each other. Otherwise, we equivocate. For instance, we do not disagree if I say, "The bank is a good place to put your money," and you say, "No, the bank is a bad place to put your money," if we use the word "bank" in different senses (me to refer to a savings institution, you to refer to the side of a river). To recognize disagreement or progress requires us to distinguish between the meaning and extension of terms, on the one hand, and the beliefs of speakers about the criteria of application and extension of their terms, on the other. Disagreement is typically disagreement in belief about the extension of terms, which presupposes invariant meaning and extension.[6]

Consider the interpretation of a somewhat dated environmental protection regulation, enacted several decades earlier, which requires special procedures for the handling of toxic substances. No doubt, the statute was drafted under certain beliefs about what makes something toxic and which substances are toxic, beliefs that might well have been revised in the intervening years as the result of advances in the relevant sciences. To see how earlier and later courts might disagree about the correct interpretation of the statute, the word "toxin" has to have an invariant meaning not tied to the beliefs of speakers about the extension of the term. The correct interpretation of the statute depends upon biological and chemical facts about what things are toxic, not on conventional beliefs (then or now) about toxins, though, of course, at any given time one can only rely on the best available evidence about what those biological and chemical facts are.

Or consider the interpretation of the equal protection clause and the disagreement between *Plessy v. Ferguson* (1896) and *Brown v. Board of Education* (1954).[7] The *Plessy* Court relies on a conception of equal protection requiring comparable provision of facilities or services that might nonetheless be separate, whereas the *Brown* Court relies on a conception of equal protection that treats a separate provision as inherently unequal insofar as the separate provision is an expression of disrespect. We want to say that the *Plessy* and *Brown* Courts disagree about the meaning and extension of "equal protection" and that the *Brown* Court has a better understanding of equal protection. But this requires "equal protection" to have an invariant sense and extension, despite this diachronic disagreement.

---

[6] This is a sometimes underappreciated virtue of theories of direct reference and associated referential theories of meaning. See Kripke (1980); Putnam (1975).

[7] *Plessy v. Ferguson* 163 U.S. 537 (1896) and *Brown v. Board of Education* 347 U.S. 483 (1954).

We might say that the correct interpretation of equal protection is a matter of the right conception of the requirement that the government treat its citizens with equal concern and respect, rather than conventional beliefs (then or now) about what that conception is, though, of course, at any given time one can only rely on the best available evidence of what that conception is.

This suggests that the meaning and extension of general terms that occur in legal rules and principles are determined by substantive facts about the nature of the institutions, processes, properties, and relations that these norms concern, rather than conventional beliefs of speakers about the criteria of application or extension of their terms. This means that the semantic assumption underlying Hart's argument for the indeterminacy of hard cases is mistaken. Just because the legal norms at stake in hard cases are controversial does not mean that they are indeterminate in their application to those cases. That does not automatically vindicate Dworkin's belief in maximal determinacy, but it does undermine Hart's argument for moderate indeterminacy that claims that hard cases are ipso facto indeterminate.

I have framed this semantic response to Hart's claims about open-texture in terms of a contrast between descriptional and referential conceptions of meaning and the way in which disagreement presupposes univocity and, hence, invariant meaning despite differences among speakers in their semantic criteria and their beliefs about the extensions of their words. The same idea is sometimes expressed in slightly different philosophical idioms.

It is common to contrast the nominal and real definitions of terms for kinds and properties, where a nominal definition is a sort of dictionary definition that would be available to all speakers competent with the term and a real definition states a substantive and potentially revisionary claim about the essence of the kind or property in question. The nominal definition of the term "water" would be given by a conventional description, something like "colorless, odorless liquid found in lakes and rivers and suitable for drinking and bathing," whereas the real definition would be the property in virtue of which the predicate correctly applies, presumably H_2O. To explain criterial disagreement and disagreement about the extension of term, we need to resort to real, rather than nominal, definitions. Determination of the content of a legal provision using general terms to pick out kinds and properties requires appeal to the real, rather than nominal, definitions of those terms.

This idea is also sometimes expressed in the contrast between concepts and properties. The nominal definition expresses the ordinary or conventional concept of water, available to speakers competent with the term, whereas the real definition of "water" expresses the property of substances in the world that explains why they fall within the extension of the term. In this idiom, the content of a legal provision depends on the property, rather than the concept, associated with the general terms in which the provision is formulated.

Dworkin does not make this semantic argument against Hart in "The Model of Rules." But he needs something like it in order to resist Hart's semantic argument for the indeterminacy of hard cases. Dworkin should find this semantic response to Hart congenial insofar as it coheres with his later critical discussion of conventionalism in *Law's Empire*.[8] Conventionalism (like the view Dworkin calls the plain fact view) is clearly supposed to be a theoretical construct based on Hart's model of rules. Conventionalism understands legal interpretation to be constrained by the plain or conventional meaning of the language in which legal rules are formulated, with the result that what the law is or requires cannot be controversial, except insofar as it depends upon controversial empirical facts. If the law cannot be (legally) controversial, then hard cases are ipso facto indeterminate. Dworkin criticizes conventionalism for its inability to explain legal disagreement in hard cases, how there can be something interpreters are disagreeing about if the law is indeterminate. Though Dworkin sometimes writes as if it is the conventionalist who appeals to semantic constraints on interpretation (Dworkin 1986: 31-46), it seems clear that he must be making his own alternative semantic assumptions—in particular, that the meaning of legal language is a matter of the best interpretation of that language (about which more below), rather than conventional beliefs about the institutions, practices, properties, and relations referred to in that language.

4. Concepts and Conceptions in Constitutional Adjudication

Though Dworkin does not explicitly defend this picture of the semantics of legal interpretation, it also fits with some early claims he made about the nature of constitutional adjudication. In the chapter of *Taking Rights Seriously* entitled "Constitutional Cases," Dworkin defends the method, if not all the details, of the Warren Court's decisions in due process and equal protection cases. To do so, he invokes the distinction between *concepts* and *conceptions* (Dworkin 1977a: 134-36). People share a moral or political concept when there is value, which could perhaps be described in general or abstract terms, that they both accept and when they agree about a number of examples or cases that illustrate this value. For instance, people might share a concept of distributive justice as an appropriate distribution of the benefits and burdens of social interaction and cooperation and might agree about some paradigm cases of justice and injustice. But people also have different views about the requirements and extension of such concepts. These different views about the nature and demands of a concept are different conceptions of that concept. For instance, we could contrast utilitarian, libertarian, and liberal egalitarian conceptions of distributive justice. Indeed, we can only understand different conceptions of a concept as disagreeing with each other by seeing them as rival conceptions of a common concept. Common concepts are what make disagreement in conception possible.

---

[8] Dworkin (1986).

Dworkin believes that the due process and equal protection clauses introduce moral and political concepts, roughly fairness and equality, as constraints on democratic action. Though the framers of those provisions had their own conception of these concepts, the constraints are determined by the correct conception of those concepts. Indeed, it is these shared concepts that explain what different conceptions, such as the different conceptions of equal protection held by the *Plessy* and *Brown* Courts, are disagreeing about. The fact that the framers chose general language is further evidence that these constitutional provisions introduce moral or political concepts to constrain democratic action.

To enforce constitutional constraints on democratic action, it is necessary to identify the correct conception of the underlying concepts, and this cannot be done without the interpreter making substantive normative commitments about the nature and extension of the moral and political concepts at stake.

> Our constitutional system rests on a particular moral theory, namely, that men [persons] have moral rights against the state. The difficult clauses of the Bill of Rights, like the due process and equal protection clauses, must be understood as appealing to moral concepts rather than laying down particular conceptions; therefore a court that undertakes the burden of applying these clauses fully as law must be an activist court, in the sense that it must be prepared to frame and answer questions of political morality [Dworkin 1977a: 147].

Courts and other interpreters have the interpretive responsibility to identify the best conception of the underlying concepts, rather than reproduce the conceptions of the framers.

5. Framers' Intent

We might compare this claim about the importance of constitutional concepts with Dworkin's criticism of interpretive appeal to the intentions of the framers in "The Forum of Principle."[9] There, he addresses and criticizes two different ways of eschewing substantive moral and political argument in constitutional adjudication—an originalist idea that judicial review should be constrained by the intentions of the framers and John Hart Ely's idea that judicial review should reinforce democratic processes, rather than defending substantive moral and political values.[10] Here, I want to focus on Dworkin's critical discussion of originalism.

Originalism has had two waves or phases. Initially, originalism came in two forms: a textualist form that appeals to the meaning of the words in which the legal provision is expressed, and an intentionalist form that appeals to the

---

[9] Dworkin (1985).
[10] Ely (1980).

intentions or purposes of the framers of the provision.[11] More recently, a second wave of originalism appears to take an exclusively textualist form, claiming that interpretation must be faithful to the original meaning of the language of legal provisions.[12] However, this may overstate the differences between new and old originalism, inasmuch as at least some new originalists think that the intentions of the framers provide evidence about original meaning.[13]

In "The Forum of Principle," Dworkin is especially concerned with intentionalist forms of originalism. Why should interpretation be constrained by the intentions of the framers? Why is interpretation not exhausted by ascertaining the semantic content of the provision in question? Sometimes, language may seem to provide uncertain guidance, as when we wonder whether skateboards should count as vehicles in Hart's municipal ordinance forbidding vehicles in the public park. However, in other cases, textual literalism may seem to lead to absurd interpretive results. Ambulances are clearly vehicles, yet it is not clear that the ordinance should be read so as to exclude them from entering the park in order to administer emergency medical treatment to park users in medical crisis. Nor is it clear that the ordinance forbids the installation of an army jeep as part of a war memorial in the park. We might address both sorts of interpretive problems by appeal to the intentions of the framers of the ordinance. For instance, if park safety is the primary purpose of the ordinance, we could frame either interpretive issue by asking which resolution of the matter better promotes the purpose of park safety.

Dworkin is critical of originalist appeals to the intentions of the framers that would constrain interpretation by appeal to historical inquiry into the psychological states of individuals who played an important role in drafting or adopting the provisions in question, in particular, concerning which activities those individuals wanted or expected the provisions to regulate. There are a number of familiar worries about this form of originalism, some of which Dworkin discusses (Dworkin 1985: 34-55; cf. Dworkin 1986: 317-327). Who are the framers of a legal provision? Is it those who drafted the provision? Is it the provision's intellectual spokespersons? Or is it those elected representatives who voted on the provision? If so, just those who voted in favor? Or is it perhaps those constituents whom the elected representatives supposedly represent? Also, we need to ask what an individual intended. Should we attend to the activities she wanted the provision to regulate or the activities she expected them to regulate? Should we focus on the specific activities the framers sought to regulate or the abstract goals and values they sought to implement? Insofar as there can be multiple framers, it seems there could be conflicting purposes or intentions associated with a particular provision. How are we supposed to aggregate conflicting intentions

---

[11] See Bork (1971, 1990); Berger (1977); Scalia (1997). For discussion, see Brest (1980).
[12] See Barnett (1999); Whittington (2004); McGinnis and Rappaport (2009); and Solum (2013). For critical discussion, see Berman (2009); Berman and Toh (2013).
[13] See Alexander (1995).

so as to produce a unitary purpose or intention? In addition to these questions about how to formulate the originalist constraint that appeals to the intentions of the framers, there is also an important question concerning the *authority* of this constraint. Why should interpretation observe this constraint? We cannot answer that that is what the framers intended. It is not clear that that is true,[14] and, in any case, that would be circular reasoning. Dworkin's answer is that we could only defend the originalist constraint on constitutional interpretation as a claim about what approach to interpretation makes constitutional interpretation and judicial review defensible as a matter of political morality (Dworkin 1985: 52-57). He is not only dubious about the merits of this substantive conception of judicial review, presumably because he thinks it will provide an underinclusive conception of individual constitutional rights but also is keen to point out that this would commit originalists to just the sort of substantive argument that they sought to avoid.

It would be easy to infer that Dworkin is and ought to be equally critical of all forms of originalism. But there is a form of originalism about constitutional interpretation with which Dworkin has reason to be sympathetic. We can see this form of originalism by attending to the distinction, which Dworkin recognizes, between *abstract* and *specific* intent (Dworkin contrasts abstract and concrete intent). The interpretive constraint of fidelity to the intentions of the framers tells us very little until we know how to characterize the intentions of the framers. The interpreter can look only to the specific activities that the framers sought to regulate through enactment of the provision—specific intent—or she can look to the provision-specific abstract values and principles that the framers had in mind—abstract intent—and then rely on her own views about the extension of these values and principles. These two conceptions of the intentions of the framers assign quite different roles to judges and other legal interpreters. Fidelity to specific intent appears to be primarily a historical-psychological task that might avoid substantive moral and political commitments. However, fidelity to abstract intent involves the interpreter in making substantive normative judgments about the nature and extension of the values and principles that the framers introduced.

Dworkin correctly observes that the question is not which kind of intention the framers had, because they evidently had both kinds of intentions. Instead, we might ask which kind of intention was dominant or should be controlling. The answer, he notes, depends on the answer to the counterfactual question of what a framer would have supported if he thought he had to choose between his abstract and specific intent.

Suppose that I have the aim of subjecting the manufacture and disposal of toxic substances to stringent standards of care and that I recognize only x as toxic. As a result, my specific intention is that the manufacture and disposal of x but not y be regulated. Suppose I were to come to believe that y as well as x is

---

[14] Cf. Powell (1985).

toxic (perhaps even that y is more toxic than x). Would I (1) come to believe that y, as well as x, ought to be handled with due care or (2) cease to want to regulate the manufacture and disposal of toxic substances?

Or suppose that I have the abstract aim of prohibiting cruel and unusual punishment, that I think drawing-and-quartering is cruel and unusual punishment, but that I do not think hanging is cruel and unusual punishment (for capital crimes). My specific intentions are to prohibit drawing-and-quartering but not to prohibit hanging. Suppose I were to come to think that hanging is morally inhumane. Would I (1) come to believe that hanging is cruel and unusual punishment and ought to be prohibited or (2) cease to want to prohibit cruel and unusual punishment?

Somewhat surprisingly, Dworkin seems to think that the answer to these sorts of counterfactual questions is often indeterminate (Dworkin 1985: 50-51). By contrast, I think that the counterfactual test typically has a determinate answer that supports the dominance of abstract intent. In both examples, the answer seems clear: (1). My dominant aim is to regulate the manufacture and disposal of substances that are in fact toxic, not just those that I now believe to be toxic. My dominant aim is to prohibit those forms of punishment that are in fact cruel and unusual, not just those that I now believe to be cruel and unusual.

This should not be surprising. We might come to accept more specific normative claims as the result of applying more general normative factors or principles in conjunction with our collateral beliefs about the extension of these factors or principles. And even if we did not come originally to accept specific normative claims in this principled or intellectualist manner, it is probably true that our continued commitment to them depends on the belief that they can be subsumed by plausible general principles and collateral beliefs. We might say that specific intent is just abstract intent plus the right collateral beliefs. If so, specific intent is *downstream*, so to speak, from abstract intent and collateral beliefs. So if one were to change one's collateral beliefs in relevant ways, this would normally mean that one would change one's specific intent, not one's abstract intent.[15]

Indeed, one would have expected Dworkin to combine his critique of specific intent with a defense of abstract intent. For an originalism of abstract intent is very similar to Dworkin's own claim that constitutional adjudication should be faithful to the normative concepts of the framers, rather than reproducing their normative conceptions. For the abstract intent of the framers is just the kind of normative constraint they sought to introduce, specified at the level of abstract concept, principle, or value, and their specific intentions are just their beliefs

---

[15] Of course, in some cases, one might be much more certain of the particular judgment than any general theory and principle, and in such cases one might respond to the conflict between abstract intent and specific intent by holding on to one's specific intent and modifying one's abstract values or principles. For example, I might be much more sure that genocide is wrong than I would be about any moral principle that might condone it. But though this is a logical possibility, most of our specific normative convictions do not enjoy this sort of incorrigibility. Instead, they seem defensible just insofar as they can be squared with plausible principles and plausible collateral claims.

about the extension of that concept, which reflects a conception, whether explicit or implicit, about the nature and demands of that concept. But then Dworkin's own conception of constitutional adjudication can be formulated as a form of originalism that insists on fidelity to abstract intent, rather than specific intent. This would be an originalism of principle.

But how would an originalism that appeals to fidelity to the abstract intentions of the framers answer the familiar worries about whose intentions count, how to aggregate conflicting intentions, and the authority of the intent of the framers? These were all reasonable questions about the intentions of the framers conceived of as the potentially conflicting psychological states of individuals, that is, their specific intentions. But the version of fidelity to the intentions of the framers with which Dworkin has reason to be sympathetic understands this constraint as fidelity to their abstract intent. But abstract intent is the normative concept that they share, which is common to their different conceptions. Moreover, though individual framers have abstract intentions, we can understand the interpretive identification of an abstract intent, not as the psychological state of an individual, but as a corporate intention that underlies and explains the institutional adoption of the provision in question (Dworkin 1986: 335-337).[16] For instance, in identifying the abstract intent of the framers of the equal protection clause of the Fourteenth Amendment of the US Constitution with an equality or anti-discrimination constraint on governmental action, we are identifying a value that explains the political purpose that the Fourteenth Amendment was supposed to serve and, hence, rationalizes its adoption. The authority of this moralized reading of fidelity to the intentions of the framers derives from the fact that our political system is a form of constitutional democracy in which there are substantive moral and political constraints on the behavior of democratic bodies. Because these constraints take the form of constitutionally guaranteed rights, it is the institutional role of the judiciary to interpret and apply them to democratic legislation.

6. Originalism of Principle

Dworkin comes closest to formulating his own conception of interpretation in originalist terms in his response to Scalia's textualist or semantic form of originalism.[17] Scalia's central contention is that the rule of law in a constitutional democracy requires that the interpretation of democratically enacted law be constrained by the original meaning of legal texts, as applied to present circumstances, rather than by extratextual sources, such as the intentions of the framers or past or present political ideals. It is the language of the provisions that is democratically enacted, so that a textualism that recovers the semantic content of the

---

[16] Brink (2001: 30-33).

[17] Scalia (1997). This is the revised text of Scalia's Tanner Lecture. Dworkin's response is published in the same volume.

provision is the only method of interpretation that is consistent with democracy. Scalia thinks that ascertaining the meaning of statutory and constitutional language is typically clear and does not require potentially controversial normative commitments on the part of the interpreter.[18] This might be reasonable if meaning was a matter of the descriptions that speakers conventionally associate with terms and original meaning was the descriptions conventionally associated with the language of legal provisions at the time of enactment.

Scalia is a fairly traditional textualist or semantic originalist. If one took this to be the essence of originalism, one might well reject originalism outright. That conception of meaning makes meaning hostage to the beliefs of speakers in a way that ties meaning to the conventional beliefs of speakers, makes meaning fragile, and prevents us from representing serious disagreement among speakers with different criteria for applying their terms and different beliefs about the extension of their terms. This makes it difficult for us to understand interpretive disagreement and progress.

Though Dworkin might have been sympathetic to these concerns about Scalia's brand of originalism, his response is to defend a different form of originalism—an originalism of principle. The meaning of some statutory and constitutional provisions is reasonably uncontroversial. For instance, the meaning of the constitutional requirement that the president be at least 35 years old and have been a resident of the United States for at least 14 years (Article II, §5) is clear and uncontroversial. But many statutory and constitutional provisions use general or abstract normative language, such as "anti-competitive practices," "unreasonable search and seizure," "due process," "just compensation," "cruel and unusual punishment," and "equal protection" of the laws. The meaning and extension of such language is inherently controversial inasmuch as any claim about the meaning and extension of those provisions must endorse some substantive normative conception of the extension of those concepts. No doubt the framers had specific conceptions of those concepts in mind, which shaped how they wanted and expected that language to be understood. But because they chose the abstract language expressing the concept, rather than language expressing their particular conception, what they enacted was the concept. Fidelity to democratically enacted law, Dworkin claims, requires fidelity to the best conception of that abstract concept, rather than to the framers' specific conceptions.

For instance, the Eighth Amendment prohibits cruel and unusual punishments. The framers may have understood that to cover various forms of punishment in the Stuart period, such as (let us assume) torture on the rack, burning the offender at the stake, and drawing-and-quartering. But they chose language that reflects the general concept of inhumane or disproportionate punishment, rather than their specific conception of that concept. So fidelity to the meaning of the language of the Eighth Amendment requires making normative claims about the

---

[18] Scalia (1997: 45).

nature of humane and proportionate punishment, not reproducing the specific conceptions of the framers.

Dworkin distinguishes between forms of originalism that focus on the meaning of constitutional texts and those that appeal to fidelity to the intentions of the framers. But he also suggests that a sensible originalism must appeal to the semantic intentions of the framers.[19] But these semantic intentions of the framers do not substitute some speaker-relative conception of meaning for public meaning. Assumptions about the semantic intentions of the authors of a legal provision are needed to resolve potential ambiguity about the meaning we are trying to recover. We need to know if the relevant meaning of the word "bank" is "financial institution" or "side of the river." This use of speaker's intention is a way of disambiguating public meaning, not a form of private or speaker-relative conception of meaning. Dworkin may also think that a speaker's abstract intent can be relevant to the public meaning of her words, indicating the kind of public meaning we should look for. But it is quite clear that Dworkin does not think that the specific intentions about how the speaker expected or wanted the provision to be applied are relevant to the meaning of the provision. That would be exactly the sort of speaker-relative conception of meaning that he eschews. Interpretation aims to recover the stable public meaning of the language of the enacted provision, which requires the interpreter to make substantive commitments about the meaning and extension of that language and the underlying concepts.

This is a kind of originalism, but an originalism of principle.[20] If we keep in mind various possible choice points about how to understand original meaning and the intentions of the framers, we can see more than one way that Dworkin could be regarded as an originalist. (See Figure 12.1.)

Scalia accepts something like I.A.1. Dworkin's response to Scalia is an alternative form of textualist originalism, specifically I.A.2. But it might equally well be described as a conception of framers' intent originalism, specifically II.B. This would be an equally natural reading of his earlier claims about constitutional adjudication. Indeed, either might be thought to be equivalent to I.B.2, as well, though I don't see any reason to suppose that textualism should be interpreted in terms of speaker's meaning, rather than public meaning. There is little to recommend appeal to a speaker-relative, rather than a public, conception of meaning. In fact, as Scalia recognizes, democratic principles argue against both I.B.1 and II.A, inasmuch as it is the public meaning and concepts expressed by provisions that are democratically adopted.

This suggests that the many forms of originalism cluster around one of two poles, which we might refer to as the poles of concept and conception. Traditional

---

[19] Dworkin (1985: 116-120).

[20] This sort of originalism of principle also fits the interpretive framework of Dworkin's moral reading of the Constitution on display in several essays reprinted in Dworkin (1996). I would note that Alexander, "Was Dworkin an Originalist?" and I agree that Dworkin was an originalist of principle, but disagree about the merits of this form of originalism.

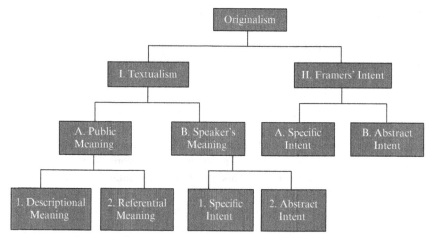

FIGURE 12.1 *Varieties of Originalism.*

conservative forms of originalism appeal to an originalism of conception, which might be defended alternately as a form of I.A.1 or II.A (or, less plausibly, I.B.1). However, originalism might instead be understood as an originalism of concept or principle, which might defended either as I.A.2 or II.B (or, less plausibly, I.B.2). This is the kind of originalism that Dworkin defends.[21] It has the virtue of reflecting a more plausible semantics of disagreement, continuity, and progress, and it makes much interpretation ineliminably normative.

7. Constructive Interpretation

Dworkin develops and refines this sort of originalism of principle in his theory of *constructive interpretation* in *Law's Empire.*[22] There, he motivates his conception of legal interpretation as part of a more general approach to interpretation of various kinds. Constructive interpretation requires the interpreter to represent the object of interpretation in its best light. This interpretive task involves the now familiar distinction between concept and conception. Rival interpretations of a common interpretive object share a common concept of its point or value but

---

[21] Balkin might also be viewed as an originalist of principle. See, Balkin (2011). Although that may be true, Balkin endorses a division of labor between interpretation and construction, and treats much of what Dworkin or I would regard as interpretation as construction. It is unclear to me how Balkin thinks construction is related to interpretation or what constraints he recognizes on construction.

[22] Dworkin's final word about law and legal interpretation is a brief but suggestive final chapter in Dworkin (2011: ch. 19). There, he leaves the details of constructive interpretation largely unchanged but embeds that theory in a view of law as one branch of political morality, which deals with the rights of individuals and the duties of courts within a constitutional democracy.

disagree in their conceptions of that concept. How should we assess conceptions of a concept? Dworkin distinguishes two dimensions for the assessment of interpretive conceptions.

A conception of a concept *fits* well insofar as it accounts for and explains various features of the interpretive data. In the case of interpreting legal provisions, such as statutes or constitutional provisions, that have been institutionally enacted, this will presumably involve accounting for the context of the provision, the language of the provision, and subsequent interpretations of that provision. The best fit need not account for all the interpretive data; it may show some assumptions about the law to be inconsistent, incomplete, or in some other way mistaken. In effect, one conception fits the data better than another insofar as it posits fewer mistakes in the data.

A conception of a concept is *acceptable* insofar as its account of the nature and extension of the underlying concept is attractive and defensible. One interpretation of an object might show it to be more important or attractive than another. If so, the first interpretation is to be preferred, at least along this second dimension. Different metrics of acceptability are possible, including justice, fairness, utility, and efficiency. Acceptability is a matter of which metric is appropriate to the interpretive context and which conception fares best along that metric.

Both dimensions are important if, as Dworkin claims, an interpretation is supposed to show the object of interpretation in its best light. He applies this account of constructive interpretation to the law and legal interpretation. The fundamental concept underlying the rule of law, Dworkin thinks, is that legal decisions that distribute rights and responsibilities ought to be *consistent* with prior distributions of rights and responsibilities. Different conceptions of law provide different accounts of the value and requirements of this sort of consistency. Dworkin's own conception of law—*law as integrity*—understands consistency as consistency of principle. Integrity is the demand that government act on coherent principle, and it is a distinct political virtue, Dworkin claims, alongside justice and fairness. Integrity in adjudication is the demand to decide legal controversies in light of the best conception of the concepts or principles that are reflected in previous decisions. Integrity in adjudication, Dworkin claims, is analogous to the position of a contributor to a *chain novel* that is already well underway. She is constrained by the prior history of the novel—its plot, characters, and themes—but she seeks to add to the novel in ways that make it, as a whole, the best work that it can be.

Insofar as constructive interpretation and law as integrity incorporate Dworkin's earlier idea that interpretation of a legal provision should aim to articulate and apply the best conception of the concepts underlying the legal provision, they can reasonably claim to embody an originalism of principle of the sort I have argued that he elsewhere embraces. But there are two respects in which constructive interpretation arguably departs from this sort of originalism. Both involve attention to legal history and the role of fit in constructive interpretation.

8. Acceptability, Fit, and Precedent

Constructive interpretation says that conceptions of legal concepts should be assessed by both fit and acceptability. Fit seems to be a *backward-looking* dimension requiring consistency with past assignments of rights and responsibilities, whereas acceptability is a *forward-looking* dimension of morally justifiable assignments of rights and responsibilities, however that is best conceived. Presumably, the two dimensions of assessment can pull in different directions, especially in cases in which there is an original provision that has a uniquely acceptable interpretation (let us suppose), but in which there is also a body of case law that fails to interpret this provision in light of the most acceptable conception of the underlying concept. Suppose that we have an initial provision P and six prior decisions D1-D6 that have interpreted that provision but not in the most acceptable way. Now suppose that we have a new case to decide under P and the previous case law. Suppose that there are two possible principles P1 and P2 that might be used to decide the present case, that P1 provides a significantly better fit with D1-D6 than P2 does, but that P2 is significantly more acceptable than P1, such that P2 projects to other possible controversies with more acceptable results than P1. (See Figure 12.2.)

Perhaps we could think of this as a fair description of the choice between the *Plessy* and *Brown* conceptions of equal protection at the time of the *Brown* decision (t7) in which P1 represents *Plessy*'s conception of equal protection as requiring no more than comparable separate provision and P2 represents *Brown*'s conception of equal protection as requiring equal respect that is inconsistent with separate provision on account of race.

Dworkin is not very clear about how the dimensions of fit and acceptability should be aggregated and how they may be traded off with each other. Sometimes, he suggests that fit and acceptability are equal partners in constructive interpretation. At other times, he suggests that fit sets a threshold that any eligible interpretation must meet but above which we should consider only acceptability (Dworkin 1986: 231, 248). However, exactly this issue is resolved, I assume that he thinks that in such a case constructive interpretation might favor deciding the new case (D7) according to P2, rather than P1, despite P1's greater fit with prior decisions than P2.

It seems that this should be the obvious and straightforward result according to an originalism of principle. For that conception of interpretation requires us

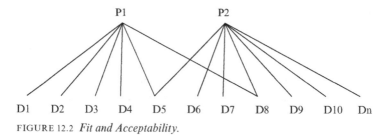

FIGURE 12.2 *Fit and Acceptability.*

to interpret law and decide cases by appeal to the principle that provides the best conception of the underlying concept, in which best conception seems to be the most defensible conception of the nature and extension of the concept. That conception, by hypothesis, is P2. Although constructive interpretation may agree in interpretive result—that the present case should be decided by appeal to P2—it seems to disagree in the analysis. Constructive interpretation is not indifferent to P1's superior fit, as originalism of principle might be. P2's inferior fit counts against its interpretive credentials, even if this interpretive defect does not ultimately carry the day. If this is right, interpretive history exercises an independent interpretive constraint that originalism of principle does not appear to recognize.

This brings out a way in which originalism of principle is selective in its attention to the historical context of provisions under interpretation. Some aspects of the historical context of a provision will be relevant to the originalist task of fixing the relevant abstract concepts and values underlying the provision, which must be performed before the interpreter can identify the best conception of those concepts and values. This use of history is part of originalism of principle. But some aspects of institutional history and fit—in particular, mistaken conceptions of those concepts and values that have played a role in the provision's interpretive history—represent a non-originalist element of interpretation.

Some writers might represent this dualism within constructive interpretation in terms of the distinction between *interpretation* and *construction*.[23] They treat interpretation as aiming to recover the semantic content of a particular provision but allow that more might go into the construction of the provision's legal significance. For instance, we might distinguish between what a particular constitutional provision means and what the law on a given constitutional issue requires if we think that deciding what the US Constitution requires on a given issue requires harmonizing that provision with related provisions and structural principles, such as the separation of powers. We might then claim that originalism of principle is a conception of interpretation and that constructive interpretation is really a conception of construction.

Though we can accept this division of labor between the semantic content of a provision and its legal force or significance, it is less clear whether it is necessary or helpful to mark this division of labor in terms of the distinction between interpretation and construction. That strikes me as a matter of linguistic stipulation. For it is common to distinguish semantic and non-semantic dimensions of interpretation. For instance, if we reject textualism because we believe that a legal provision should not be interpreted literally when doing so would produce absurd results and when appeal to the purposes of the framers would avoid this result, we recognize non-semantic aspects of interpretation. Moreover, Dworkin clearly conceives of constructive interpretation as a theory of interpretation despite its combining both semantic and non-semantic aspects.

---

[23] See Solum (2010).

Constructive interpretation and originalism of principle differ over what makes a conception of an underlying concept best. Originalism of principle focuses on acceptability, whereas constructive interpretation recognizes fit, as well as acceptability. In this respect, at least, Dworkin's conception of constructive interpretation departs from or at least refines the sort of originalism of principle that he elsewhere espouses. Insofar as we think interpretive history ought to make a difference to new interpretations, we have reason to prefer constructive interpretation to originalism of principle.

Interpretive history matters to new interpretation if only because of the relevance of *precedent* to interpretation. The doctrine of precedent implies that, other things being equal, future interpretations should conform to past interpretations. What seems clear is that the doctrine of precedent understands sameness of interpretation in terms of sameness of conception. For instance, prior to the decision in *Brown*, precedent favored the *Plessy* conception of equal protection. Different views are possible about the significance of the interpretive constraint that precedent imposes. All reasonable views treat precedent as a *pro tanto* interpretive constraint that can be overridden in the interest of a significantly more compelling or acceptable conception of the underlying interpretive concept. A strong doctrine of precedent would treat it as creating a very strong presumption in favor of sameness of conception that was very difficult to overcome. By contrast, a more moderate doctrine of precedent would see it as creating a more modest and more easily rebutted presumption for sameness of conception. Arguably, the stringency of precedent should not be invariant across different substantive areas of the law. In certain areas of transactional law in which coordination is especially important, it is arguably more important to have a clear and consistent rule than to have any particular rule. By contrast, in certain areas of criminal, tort, and constitutional law involving individual rights, it is arguably more important to get the rule right than to adhere to the same rule as in the past. This contrast might be reason to have a stronger doctrine of precedent for certain areas of transactional law than for certain areas of tort, criminal, and constitutional law. However, as long as the interpretation of some areas of law should employ some doctrine of precedent, however weak or strong, interpretive history, in particular, past interpretive conception should play an independent role in new interpretation.

9. Constraint and Innovation in Legal Interpretation

The chain novel analogy invites us to view legal interpreters as contributors to a chain novel in which different authors contribute different chapters. Any author contributing after the novel has been started is constrained by the prior course— characters, themes, and plot—of the novel but within those constraints has the task of introducing new characters, themes, and plot that make the novel the best novel that it can be.

However, this analogy is potentially problematic. Legal interpreters seem to have *less freedom* than chain novelists. The chain novelist is free to introduce any new theme that is not inconsistent with the prior course of the novel if that will make the novel better. It is not clear that legal interpreters have this freedom. They seem constrained to interpret existing concepts and principles. They are not free to introduce new legal concepts and principles, not anchored in existing ones.

We should not overstate this contrast between legal interpretation and the chain novel. Legal interpretation can introduce previously inexplicit principles provided these principles are latent in explicit legal materials and part of the best constructive interpretation of those materials. In this context, consider the recognition of the non-enumerated constitutional right of privacy in *Griswold v. Connecticut*.[24] *Griswold* invalidated Connecticut legislation that prohibited the sale and use of birth control devices on the round that it violated a married couple's right to privacy. Douglas wrote the plurality opinion. He conceded that privacy is nowhere explicitly mentioned in the Constitution but claimed that a right to privacy could be found in the penumbras and emanations of various disparate rights in the Constitution's Bill of Rights.

Critics of a constitutional right to privacy have pilloried Douglas's opinion for creating new constitutional rights. But Douglas's argument is a good instance of constructive interpretation. He argues that a value of privacy or personal autonomy is one of the values that provide a plausible rationale for the otherwise diverse cluster of personal liberties explicitly recognized in the Bill of Rights— especially the First Amendment guarantee of freedom of speech, religion, and association; the Third Amendment guarantee of a home owner's right not to have his house invaded during peace time without his consent; the Fourth Amendment guarantee against unreasonable search and seizure; the Fifth Amendment guarantee of due process; and the Ninth Amendment guarantee of non-enumerated rights retained by the people. (See Figure 12.3.)

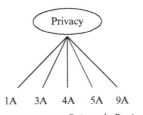

FIGURE 12.3 *Privacy's Rationale.*

Here, privacy or personal autonomy provides a rationale for otherwise diverse enumerated rights. It is an interesting and important question, which Douglas does not directly address, what the *scope* of such a right to privacy should be. The scope of the right will determine what sort of other privacy cases *Griswold* is a good precedent for. But whatever its exact scope, it is not implausible to suppose

[24] *Griswold v. Connecticut*, 381 U.S. 479 (1965).

that a principle of privacy or personal autonomy broad enough to rationalize these otherwise disparate personal liberties in the Bill of Rights would extend to decisions about intimate association and reproduction by competent adults.

It is the structure of this justification for recognizing a constitutional right to privacy that is important for present purposes. It shows how novel legal concepts and rights can emerge in constructive interpretation provided they are anchored in previous legal materials in the right way—as principled extensions of the enumerated values in the provisions and precedents. The chain novel analogy is problematic not because it permits the introduction of novel concepts but because it does not require that these novel concepts be anchored in the prior course of the novel. It appears to allow the introduction of any new plot element, theme, or character that is not ruled out by the prior course of the novel. It does not condition the introduction of new elements on being implicit in existing elements the way that both originalism of principle and constructive interpretation do. For this reason, constructive interpretation is best understood independently of the chain novel analogy.

10. Interpretation and Disagreement

Both originalism of principle and constructive interpretation insist that an important part of legal interpretation is identifying the best conception of the concepts underlying the legal provision in question and what that requires in the case at hand. Originalism of principle says that is all there is to legal interpretation, whereas constructive interpretation says that is an important ingredient in interpretation, to be balanced against considerations of fit, including considerations of precedent. Identifying and defending the best conception of principles and values underlying legal provisions is or at least can often be a philosophical enterprise requiring the interpreter to make substantive and potentially controversial normative commitments. Just as many theories of legal interpretation and judicial review can be understood as involving an attempt to avoid normative commitment within interpretation, Dworkin's signature jurisprudential idea is the recognition and embrace of the normative dimensions of interpretation.

The embrace of contested normative commitments by political and legal officials may appear problematic to those who believe that state action in a liberal democracy should be morally and politically ecumenical. This is an important strand in recent discussions of public reason liberalism that thinks that state actors in a liberal democracy must prescind from sectarian moral and political commitments about which citizens reasonably disagree and make decisions that reflect principles that would be acceptable to an overlapping consensus of divergent moral and political conceptions. This sort of liberal neutrality is most readily associated with John Rawls's later work, especially *Political Liberalism*.[25]

---

[25] Rawls (1993).

Though Dworkin was an early adopter of this kind of liberal neutrality, he later rethought this commitment.[26] A similar worry about the exercise of judicial review in ways that reflect normative commitments about which there is reasonable disagreement is a theme in some recent jurisprudential work. For instance, it is reflected in Cass Sunstein's defense of *judicial minimalism* and reliance on *incompletely theorized agreements*, which constrain appeals to principle to mid-level normative precepts that are common to and can be derived from different comprehensive normative systems.[27] A similar worry about the normative commitments of judges can be seen in Jeremy Waldron's concerns about disagreement over how to interpret and enforce constitutional rights and his skepticism about strong judicial review in which a politically unaccountable judiciary enforces its own conception of constitutional rights.[28] Whereas Sunstein seeks to accommodate disagreement by making interpretation itself ecumenical, Waldron seeks to accommodate disagreement institutionally by defending a democratic conception of judicial review.

Though I am not sure Dworkin ever squarely addressed these worries about normative disagreement and the resulting demand to make legal interpretation more ecumenical, I suspect that he would have rejected any conception of interpretation that sought to avoid normative commitment by arguing that proposals to make interpretation more ecumenical are themselves normative proposals that have to be assessed on substantive normative grounds. Since more ecumenical conceptions of interpretation tend to make judicial review more deferential to majoritarian thinking, they tend to underenforce individual constitutional rights whose role is to constrain majoritarian decisions.

Of course, if the judiciary enforces radically mistaken conceptions of constitutional rights often enough, then we might prefer ecumenical or democratic judicial review to principled judicial review. But Dworkin might think that there already are various institutional safeguards in place to guard against the worst-case outcomes of principled judicial review. Federal judicial appointments require US Senate approval, and the attrition and replacement of judges and justices ensures that there is a steady, if slow, influx of new perspectives into the judiciary. The most consequential federal courts—US Courts of Appeal and Supreme Court—decide cases by groups of judges and justices, and this fact exposes individual interpreters to rival interpretations and imposes some discipline to decide cases by appeal to principles that can survive principled debate and attract coalitions. Moreover, courts are concerned to decide cases in ways that will prove enforceable, and so imperatives to preserve the institutional capital of the courts will also exercise some constraint for courts not to decide cases in ways that get too far ahead of (or behind) recognizable conceptions of individual rights. Of course, these constraints do not preclude reactionary and regressive decisions and periods

---

[26] Compare, for instance, Dworkin (1990: 1-119; 2000: ch. 6).

[27] Sunstein (1996, 2005).

[28] Waldron (1999, 2006).

in constitutional history, but they provide some reason to think that there may already be institutional constraints in place to discipline principled judicial review in ways that limit the specter of abuse that fuels calls for more ecumenical modes of judicial review. The best antidote to mistaken principled interpretation is likely to be better principled interpretation, not a retreat from principle.[29]

There is also a Millian argument to be made that identifying the best conception of our constitutional principles and properly appreciating them requires that we subject rival conceptions, including our own, to critical assessment and debate. Only by engaging in debates about first principles, rather than prescinding from them, are we likely to understand the basis of our common commitments and learn how to extend them to cover new and difficult cases. This is what Dworkin valued about the judiciary as the forum of principle. Sunstein's jurisprudence of incompletely theorized agreements, which appeals to common mid-level principles and eschews appeal to contested first principles, must forego this process of public deliberation about constitutional first principles. By contrast, Waldron's defense of democratic judicial review, performed by democratically elected representatives, preserves and perhaps broadens the public debate about constitutional first principles. But it ignores the fact that in systems with a separation of powers doctrine, such as our own, it is the institutional function of a politically independent judiciary to interpret and apply the law, including the constitutional rights that constrain democratic decision-making.

These are large, complicated, and partly empirical issues about the comparative merits of different conceptions of judicial review. But Dworkin's normative vision of legal interpretation remains a viable approach to the enforcement of individual rights, even if we recognize, as Dworkin himself insisted, that the nature of legal interpretation is contestable.

11. Conclusion

Dworkin consistently opposed conceptions of interpretation that would constrain the meaning of legal provisions by conventional beliefs about the extension of the language in which those provisions are formulated or by the framers' conceptions of the normative concepts underlying those provisions. That opposition reflects a plausible view about the semantics of legal disagreement. If we associated originalism with these discredited semantic assumptions, then Dworkin should be a critic of originalism. But once we are clear about the semantic mistake such interpretive conceptions make, we can understand why Dworkin was attracted to a different form of originalism—an originalism of principle according to which interpreters must ascertain the best conception of the normative concepts that the framers of the provision intended to introduce. This kind of

---

[29] However, this defense of principled judicial review might be improved by the adoption of *term limits* of some kind for federal judicial appointments.

originalism of principle can be understood either as fidelity to the correct public meaning of legal provisions or as fidelity to the abstract intentions of the framers of those provisions. Either way, it implies that the interpretation of legal provisions employing normative concepts cannot be done without making and defending substantive normative commitments about the extension of those concepts. Originalism of principle is an important part of constructive interpretation, but it does not exhaust constructive interpretation, because constructive interpretation includes in its account of fit a role for precedent and continuity of interpretive conception. But within constructive interpretation interpretive history and sameness of conception have only pro tanto significance that can be overridden when a rival conception is a sufficiently normatively superior conception. This commitment to the normative dimensions of legal interpretation is not undermined by the recognition of significant normative disagreement.

References

Alexander, L. (1995) "All or Nothing at All? The Intentions of Authorities and the Authority of Intentions," in A. Marmor (ed.). *Law and Interpretation.* Oxford: Clarendon Press, 1995.

Alexander, L., Chapter 12, "Was Dworkin an Originalist?" herein.

Balkin, J. (2011) *Living Originalism.* Cambridge: Harvard University Press.

Barnett, R. (1999) "An Originalism for Nonoriginalists," *Loyola Law Review* 45: 611–54.

Berman, M. (2009) "Originalism is Bunk," *New York University Law Review* 84: 1–96.

Berman, M and Toh, K. (2013) "On What Distinguishes New Originalism from Old: A Jurisprudential Take," *Fordham Law Review* 82: 545–76.

Berger, R. (1977) *Government By the Judiciary.* Cambridge: Harvard University Press.

Bork, R. (1971) "Neutral Principles and First Amendment Problems," *Indiana Law Journal* 47: 1–35.

Bork, R. (1990) *The Tempting of America.* New York: Simon and Schuster.

Brest, P. (1980) "The Misconceived Quest for the Original Understanding," *Boston University Law Review* 60: 204–38.

Brink, D.O. (1985) "Legal Positivism and Natural Law Reconsidered," *The Monist* 68: 364–87.

Brink, D.O. (1988) "Legal Theory, Legal Interpretation, and Judicial Review," *Philosophy & Public Affairs* 17: 105–48.

Brink, D.O. (1989) "Semantics and Legal Interpretation (Further Thoughts)," *Canadian Journal of Law and Jurisprudence* 2: 181–91.

Brink, D.O. (2001) "Legal Interpretation, Objectivity, and Morality," in B. Leiter (ed.). *Objectivity in Law and Morals.* New York: Cambridge University Press.

Hart, H.L.A., (1961/1994) *The Concept of Law.* Oxford: Clarendon Press.

Dworkin, R. (1977a) "The Model of Rules," in *Taking Rights Seriously.* Cambridge: Harvard University Press.

Dworkin, R. (1977b) "Hard Cases," in *Taking Rights Seriously.* Cambridge: Harvard University Press.

Dworkin, R. (1985) "The Forum of Principle" reprinted in *A Matter of Principle*. Cambridge: Harvard University Press.

Dworkin, R. (1986) *Law's Empire*. Cambridge: Harvard University Press.

Dworkin, R. (1990) "Liberalism," reprinted in *A Matter of Principle*, with "Foundations of Liberal Equality" *Tanner Lectures on Human Values* 11: 1–119.

Dworkin, R. comment in *A Matter of Interpretation*, 116–20.

Dworkin, R. (1996) *Freedom's Law*. Cambridge: Harvard University Press.

Dworkin, R. (2000) *Sovereign Virtue*. Cambridge: Harvard University Press, ch. 6.

Dworkin, R. (2011) *Justice for Hedgehogs*. Cambridge: Harvard University Press, ch. 19.

Ely, J.H. (1980) *Democracy & Distrust*. Cambridge: Harvard University Press.

Kripke, S. (1980) *Naming and Necessity*. Cambridge: Harvard University Press.

McGinnis, J. and Rappaport, M. (2009) "Original Methods Originalism," *Northwestern University Law Review* 103: 751–802.

Powell, H.J. (1985) "The Original Understanding of Original Intent," *Harvard Law Review* 98: 885–948.

Putnam, H. (1975) "The Meaning of 'Meaning," reprinted in *Mind, Language, and Reality: Philosophical Papers II*. New York: Cambridge University Press.

Rawls, J. (1993) *Political Liberalism*. New York: Columbia University Press.

Scalia, A. (1997) *A Matter of Interpretation: Federal Courts and the Law*, in A. Gutman (ed.). Princeton: Princeton University Press.

Solum, L. (2010) "The Interpretation-Construction Distinction," *Constitutional Commentary* 27: 95–118.

Solum, L. (2013) "Originalism and Constitutional Construction," *Fordham Law Review* 82: 453–537.

Sunstein, C. (1996) *Legal Reasoning and Political Conflict*. New York: Oxford University Press.

Sunstein, C. (2005) *Radicals in Robes*. New York: Basic Books.

Waldron, J. (1999) *Law and Disagreement*. Oxford: Clarendon Press.

Waldron, J. (2006) "The Core of the Case Against Judicial Review," *Yale Law Journal* 115: 1346–406.

Waluchow, W. J. (2007) *A Common Law Theory of Judicial Review: The Living Tree*. New York: Cambridge University Press, 52–69.

Whittington, K. (2004) "The New Originalism," *The Georgetown Journal of Law and Public Policy* 2: 599–613.

13

Was Dworkin an Originalist?

by Lawrence A. Alexander

1. The Question, and a Tentative Answer

The question asked by my title will strike many readers as absurd, or if not absurd, at least rhetorical. Of course, Ronald Dworkin was not an originalist, they will respond. Dworkin wrote at great length and over his entire career about topics in American constitutional law—free speech, religious liberty, equality, autonomy—but nowhere in his writings can we find the telltale signs of an originalist outlook. There are no references to the debates at the constitutional convention or the state ratifying conventions. There are no citations to the *Congressional Globe* during the debates over the Thirteenth and Fourteenth Amendments of the Constitution of the United States (US Constitution or the Constitution). Nor is there any mention of the relevant case law, dictionary definitions, or public discussions contemporaneous with the adoption of the constitutional provisions of interest to Dworkin. So why in the world would anyone think Dworkin was an originalist?

The reason the question in my title is not absurd or rhetorical is that Dworkin, in his comment on Justice Antonin Scalia's theory of interpretation, endorses originalism.[1] In that essay, Dworkin both defends and criticizes Scalia's textualism with respect to constitutional interpretation. In so doing, Dworkin draws a distinction between what authors of a text intend to *say* and what they hope or expect will be the *consequences* of their saying it.[2] Dworkin calls the former the author's semantic intention; and he says—and this is the crucial statement—"Any

---

[1] Dworkin (1997a). My assertion that Dworkin endorses originalism in this essay echoes Jeffrey Goldsworthy, whose excellent article, published on the heels of Dworkin's Scalia essay, makes a persuasive case for Dworkin's originalism. Goldsworthy (2000). See also Whittington (2000) (reaching a similar conclusion). My case for Dworkin's originalism is no more than an abbreviated version of Goldsworthy's. My value added, if any, is in relating Dworkin's originalism to his jurisprudential theory and to show why it is simultaneously both necessary to his theory and destructive of it.

[2] Dworkin (1997a: 116–117).

reader of anything must attend to semantic intention, because the same sounds or even words can be used with the intention of saying different things."[3]

Although Dworkin equates semantic intention with what the speaker intends to *say*, he is really and properly equating it with what the speaker intends to *mean* by what he says—the meaning he is attempting to convey to his audience. In Gricean terms, Dworkin is equating semantic intention with utterer's meaning.[4] And Dworkin is endorsing Scalia's position that officials' semantic intentions are the proper quarry for judges in interpreting official directives—administrative rules, statutes, and, importantly, constitutional provisions. Although, he says, Scalia and he will not agree about what those semantic intentions are (in the case of constitutional rights),

> we do agree on the importance of the distinction I am emphasizing: between the question of what a legislature intended to say [intended to mean] in the laws it enacted, *which judges applying those laws must answer*, and the question of what the various legislators as individuals expected or hoped the consequences of those laws would be, which is a very different matter.[5]

So Dworkin endorses the primacy of authorial intended-meaning legal interpretation, including constitutional interpretation. Moreover, what he says in his Scalia essay is not inconsistent with what he says in his later works. It is less clear, however, whether it is inconsistent with what he says in his earlier ones. In chapter 4, "Hard Cases," of *Taking Rights Seriously*, Dworkin distinguishes between the enactment force of precedents and their gravitational force.[6] The enactment force is the force of the announced rule in the precedent case. It requires that subsequent courts apply that rule according to its terms. Gravitational force is the force in favor of extending the precedent beyond its announced rule to cases that are in principle morally similar. Morally infelicitous precedents have only enactment force and lack gravitational force.

What applies to precedent rules also applies to administrative, statutory, and constitutional rules. If they are morally infelicitous, they have enactment force but no gravitational force. They are confined to their terms.

But here is the crucial point: Morally infelicitous rules *do* have enactment force.[7] And what they mean is a matter of the semantic intentions—the authorially intended meaning—of their enactors.

Now Dworkin does not, in *Taking Rights Seriously*, overtly endorse the position he takes in his essay on Scalia, namely, that semantic intentions are the key to legal interpretation. He allows for the possibility of infelicitous legal rules that have only enactment force—how could he not?—but he does not offer a

---

[3] Dworkin (1997a: 117). See also Goldsworthy (2000: 65-67); Dworkin (1997b: 1815).
[4] Grice (1989: 117-137).
[5] Dworkin (1997a: 118). I have added the bracketed words.
[6] Dworkin (1977: 111-123).
[7] Dworkin (1977: 121-122).

developed theory of interpretation, one that would allow for the possibility that a rule, correctly interpreted, could nevertheless be infelicitous.[8]

In *Law's Empire*, published nine years after *Taking Rights Seriously*, Dworkin expressly eschews the semantic intentions approach to interpretation that he later endorses in favor of interpreting legal rules to be the morally best they can be.[9] On the other hand, Dworkin also says that interpretation must be consistent with "what the plain words of the statute plainly require."[10] Notice, then, the internal inconsistency in Dworkin's position, given what he correctly says in his comment on Scalia: "Any reader of anything must attend to semantic intention, *because the same sounds or even words can be used with the intention of saying different things.*"[11]

I noted this difficulty with Dworkin's statements about interpretation in *Law's Empire* in my critical review of the book:

> The third significant way in which *Law's Empire* differs from the earlier Dworkin is in its extensive treatment of the interpretation of canonical legal rules. Here, Dworkin has not so much changed his argument as he has developed an argument that was embryonic in *Taking Rights Seriously*. In brief, Dworkin argues that canonical legal rules—constitutions, statutes, regulations—should not be interpreted "conversationally," that is, as we would interpret ordinary communications from other persons. Rather, they should be interpreted in the same way we "interpret" political decisions other than canonical rules, that is, as the morally best they can be (336-47). We cannot interpret every canonical rule to be what we believe is morally ideal, for then our interpretation might not fit the data sufficiently well (352-53). But among meanings of the rule that do fit the data above the threshold level, we must choose that meaning which is morally best. (In order for Dworkin's overall approach to be internally consistent, the meaning given the rule through this method of interpretation must presumably fit not only with the words of the rule but also with the other political decisions, canonical and non-canonical.)... Dworkin's approach of abandoning conventional conversational standards of interpretation leads inevitably to "interpreting" each canonical rule as if it were the rule—or, indeed, the complete set of rules—that the interpreter regards as morally ideal (subject to the constraint of fit with other political decisions). Dworkin, of course, denies this because he argues that the interpretation

---

[8] See Dworkin (1977: 109). For a much more thorough analysis of Dworkin's approach to interpretation prior to *Law's Empire*, see Goldsworthy (2000: 50-56).

[9] Dworkin (1986: 336-347).

[10] Dworkin (1986: 338). Note that when Dworkin discusses and criticizes as unprincipled so-called "checkerboard statutes," he obviously accepts that "the best they can be" is nonetheless what their words prescribe, namely, an unprincipled and thus morally infelicitous checkerboard approach. See Dworkin (1986: 178-184).

[11] See Dworkin (1997a: 117) (emphasis added).

must fit reasonably well with the rule's words. But without the standards of conversational interpretation, what are words but sounds and shapes? And why can we not give those sounds and shapes the meaning we would morally prefer them to bear? Either a canonical rule comes to the interpreter already bearing a meaning that is independent of how well the rule fits with other political decisions and how morally agreeable it is, or it comes to the interpreter as formless material to be molded as the interpreter desires.

Abandoning conversational standards for interpreting the words of canonical rules is morally undesirable because it is morally desirable that legislative bodies have the ability to settle moral controversies through the enactment of canonical rules. They cannot have this ability if the rules they enact are "interpreted" to be the morally best they can be.

Thus, in a sense, making canonical rules "the best they can be" means interpreting them through methods that leave open the possibility that they will, when interpreted, turn out not to be the best they could have been. Put differently, the morally best standards to adopt for interpreting canonical rules are standards that do not guarantee (from the interpreter's perspective) the moral perfection of the rules so interpreted. If this is Dworkin's argument, then he is correct. But this victory of the moral over the conversational theory of interpretation is surely hollow, since it does not entail the rejection of conversational standards of interpretation; indeed, it relies on them for moral reasons. Moreover, as I understand Dworkin, he does not make this argument, so my criticism of this approach to interpreting canonical rules stands.[12]

---

[12] Alexander (1987: 423-425) (footnotes omitted). At the end of the quoted passage, I added the following textual footnote:

Indeed, in an article published after *Law's Empire*, Dworkin provides further evidence that interpreting canonical rules to be the morally best they can be really does entail the complete rejection of conversational standards of interpretation in favor of seeking the most abstract conception of the author's normative intentions. See Dworkin, "The Bork Nomination", *New York Review of Books*, Aug. 13, 1987, 3-10.

Of course, at the most abstract normative level, any author whose normative statements we would treat as authoritative intends what is (really) morally correct. (If a legal text's authors do not have that abstract intention—if they are not trying to do what is ultimately right, just, good—they should not be treated as authorities.) In interpreting legal texts by reference to the authors' intentions, we must choose a level of generality at which to characterize those intentions, since their abstract intentions and their concrete intentions, which for them were consistent, for us may not be consistent. If we are to treat the legal texts as sources of principles, and not as narrow rules that are restricted by the very concrete intentions of the authors, we are led inevitably to "interpreting" each legal text as the same injunction: "Do what correct political morality requires". Any principle that is not endorsed by correct political morality cannot really be applied as a principle, since incorrect principles lack weight. (See note 20.) And since the authors did really intend, at the most abstract level, correct political morality, we are honoring their intention as much by following what we believe is correct political morality as by following any more specific principle that they endorsed but that we believe correct political morality does not endorse. Thus one might conclude that in reading every legal provision as a warrant for applying what we believe is

I believe, then, that charity in interpreting Dworkin on interpretation demands that we take Dworkin's comment on Scalia to be Dworkin's actual position. I can find no place in his subsequent writings where he repudiates that position. I conclude that if Dworkin endorsed the primacy of semantic intention—speaker's intended meaning—in the interpretation of legal texts, then Dworkin was, after all, an originalist, despite the absence of originalist evidence in his constitutional arguments, and despite his opposition to the substantive positions taken by most self-declared originalists.

2. Dworkin's Originalism, and Its Flaws

That is the affirmative case for Dworkin's being an originalist. Why is this a surprising conclusion, if it is so? I have already given some reasons for this. Dworkin never cited to the kind of evidence originalists tend to adduce to support their constitutional and statutory interpretations. And with respect to constitutional interpretation in particular, Dworkin's interpretations do not track those of most

---

correct political morality, we are correctly interpreting that provision in accordance with the intentions of its authors....

The problem with "interpreting" legal texts in the way Dworkin advocates is that those legal texts can no longer serve what some view as the central function of law: the settling by authoritative human decision of what is morally controversial. See Raz, "Authority, Law and Morality", The Monist 68 (1985): 295. For if in order to "interpret" a legal text we must ask what correct political morality really requires, as opposed to what the authors thought it required, the legal text cannot itself settle the question of what political morality requires. No human decision can do so authoritatively, since every interpreter will have to take up anew the moral questions that prior decisions purported to settle in order to "interpret" those decisions....

Alexander (1987: 425-426 n. 14).

In the footnote 20 referred to the quoted footnote, I give the following reason why only morally correct principles, *whether or not they fit with the community's past and present coercive political decisions,* can have "weight":

I believe that it is impossible for one sensitively to construct and apply principles that one believes to be incorrect, that is, to engage in their complex weighing and to attend to their subtleties and nuances. Certain facts carry certain real weights in moral decisions, weights which are derived from the correct political morality. Those weights cannot be posited by human decisions, which means that real principles cannot be posited. Norms that function as (weightless) rules can be posited, and the fact of their being posited can bear real moral weight, which may even (paradoxically) dictate that the norms be treated as binding (infinite weight). And posited norms can dictate that one act as if consideration A "outweighs" consideration B, even if consideration A really does not. But real moral weight itself cannot be posited, and that means that the incorrect principles that fit with incorrect political decisions cannot really be weighed. Only real (correct) principles have weight and can be weighed. And if this abstract point is not convincing, the reader should try to imagine herself sensitively constructing, extending, and balancing, say, Nazi "principles."

Alexander (1987: 432 n. 20).

originalists.[13] Moreover in *Law's Empire*, Dworkin explicitly rejected the model of conversational interpretation, which, of course, rests on attempting to discern speaker's meaning.

Nonetheless, by the time of the Scalia essay, Dworkin was clearly endorsing interpretation by reference to the authors' semantic intentions, which is another way of saying the proper quarry in interpreting canonical legal texts is the author's intended meaning of those texts—which is exactly what some originalists assert.[14] Dworkin may have denied he was an originalist because he equated originalism with author-expected applications rather than with author-intended meanings. If so, he was constructing a straw-man version of originalism. Originalists do cite author-expected applications, but usually only as *evidence*—and frequently strong evidence—of author-intended meaning.

Dworkin squared his originalism with his quite heterodox (among original-ists) conclusions about the correct interpretation of constitutional rights by claiming that the constitutional authors' semantic intentions were to enact the best conceptions of the abstract concepts of freedom of speech, freedom of reli-gion, equal protection, due process, and cruel and unusual punishment. They did not intend, by these terms, to enact their own conceptions of these concepts. Those conceptions explain why, for example, they might have believed that cap-ital punishment is not cruel and unusual, or that racially segregated schools do not violate equal protection. To put this in the terms Dworkin used in his essay on Scalia, the constitutional authors might have expected these *consequences* from what they enacted—namely, that capital punishment and racially segre-gated public schools would be upheld against constitutional challenges; how-ever, what they *said* in proscribing cruel and unusual punishment and denials of equal protection of the laws might dictate otherwise. Their semantic inten-tions were to enact vague, abstract concepts, not concrete conceptions of those concepts. Originalists like Scalia err when they invoke the latter rather than the former.

This is why Dworkin could be an originalist and yet seem quite heterodox by originalist standards. Being heterodox does not mean that one is wrong. But, of course, neither does it mean one is correct.

Indeed, if, as I have asserted, Dworkin was an originalist, he was, in my opinion, a damn poor one by originalist standards. Dworkin proffered no evi-dence to support his claims that the constitutional authors intended to enact abstract concepts—no evidence, that is, other than the fact that there are no agreed-upon definitions of terms like equal protection, cruel and unusual

---

[13] Jack Balkin, who claims to be an originalist, is exceptional in this regard. See, e.g., Balkin (2011).

[14] I say "some" because some originalists take the original public meaning of the constitutional text as the proper target of constitutional interpretation rather than the meaning the constitutional authors intended. I believe the latter is the proper target and have so argued elsewhere. See, e.g., Alexander (2013); Alexander (2011: 87-98).

punishment, and the like. Indeed, from what we know about the framers and ratifiers of the relevant constitutional provisions, it seems highly unlikely that they would have given judges the quite awesome power to read their conceptions of abstract concepts into the Constitution as trumps of democratically enacted laws.[15]

Moreover, it is questionable whether there are abstract concepts that exist apart from people's conceptions of them. It is true that one can believe that the criteria by which one defines a term can differ from that to which one believes those criteria apply. One can have criteria for the term *poison* that dictate that arsenic is a poison even if one believes it is not (because one does not understand arsenic's effects), or criteria for the term *fish* that dictate that whales are not fish even if one believes they are (because one believes they have gills and lack mammary glands). Likewise, one can represent a concept in thought in ways that differ from the criteria one would offer as its definition. But it is doubtful that one can have a concept that lacks criteria for application and that differs from how one applies it.[16]

Beyond this skepticism about the reality of concepts about which everyone can be mistaken is another worry about Dworkin's concept-conception distinction. For why should we assume that specific terms, like freedom of speech or equality, refer to moral concepts that exist in morality's ontological cupboard?[17] If one were a Benthamite utilitarian, for example, there would be no joint in one's moral ontology corresponding to freedom of speech, freedom of religion, and so forth. There would only be the injunction to maximize the happiness of the greatest number, which could conceivably entail that speech and religion be suppressed. Rawlsians and libertarians would have more complex moral ontologies, but none would have distinctions that map neatly or at all onto the distinctions suggested by the terms in the US Constitution. Indeed, I have argued that there are no moral principles that correspond to freedom of speech or freedom of religion, so that a search for the best conception of those concepts will be bootless.[18]

---

[15] I realize that I have cited no evidence for this proposition after having accused Dworkin of citing no evidence for his interpretation.

[16] See, e.g., Marmor (2013: 209-229). David Brink, on the other hand, seems more receptive to Dworkin's concept-conception distinction. See Brink (forthcoming). Brink also notes that Dworkin distinguishes authors' concrete intentions from their abstract intentions and endorses following only the latter. The problem with this is that every author of norms has the same abstract intention: Do the right thing.

I should note that Dworkin's argument that constitutional authors constitutionalized concepts rather than their conceptions of them relies on W. B. Gallie's notion of essentially contested concepts. See Gallie (1956). I can only state but not buttress my skepticism regarding the existence of such concepts and the proposition that people arguing about their application are really arguing with rather than past each other. See Barauh (2014: 351-356).

[17] See Alexander and Schauer (2007: 1599-1601).

[18] See Alexander (2005: ch. 8).

3. Dworkin's Originalism and His Jurisprudence

So Dworkin was an originalist, but his originalism was flawed when he came to constitutional rights. Nonetheless, he was an originalist when it came to other constitutional provisions and to statutes and administrative rules. Semantic intentions have primacy there.

How does this originalist aspect of Dworkin fit with Dworkin's jurisprudential view, his interpretive, make it the "morally best it can be" view of law? For Dworkin, law, including constitutional law, consists of those principles that best justify most (but not necessarily all) of the community's past coercive political decisions.[19] But before I analyze how Dworkin's originalism fits with his jurisprudential views, I want to digress and situate the latter within jurisprudential debates more generally.

3.1. LEGAL POSITIVISM AND NATURAL LAW: A FALSE ANTAGONISM

As the readers know, traditionally, jurisprudents have been divided into two presumably warring camps: the legal positivists and the natural lawyers. Legal positivists seek to identify those criteria that distinguish the phenomena that most people call laws—statutes, constitutions, administrative rules, judicial decisions—from other normative systems, such as the rules of the Catholic Church, professional golf, morality, etiquette, and chess. Some legal positivists identify law with orders backed by threats of sanctions issued by those who are habitually obeyed.[20] Some identify law with those norms that purport to justify the imposition of sanctions.[21] Some identify law with the union of primary rules of obligation and secondary rules of change, all ultimately validated by a master rule of recognition.[22] Some identify law with rules that claim to settle authoritatively what morally ought to be done,[23] or with nested plans that do so.[24]

What unifies legal positivists and makes them positivists is that they all deny that law identified by their favored criteria necessarily has any actual normative force, even if it so claims. Many legal positivists deny, in fact, even a prima facie obligation to obey—or even to *comply with*—law as positivists identify it. They are, on their conception of their enterprise, philosophical sociologists. They identify a certain phenomenon, seek to define it, but withhold any evaluation of it.

If legal positivists seek to identify law but deny that law so identified has any necessary normative force, natural lawyers are primarily interested in law's

---

[19] See Dworkin (1986: chs. 6, 7); Alexander (1987: 420-421).

[20] Austin (1832/1965).

[21] Kelsen (1961: Part One).

[22] Hart (1961).

[23] Raz (1979).

[24] Shaprio (2011).

normativity. Natural lawyers typically do not disagree with legal positivists when the latter identify law with the stuff people usually identify when they speak of it—that is, constitutions, statutes, judicial orders, and the like. But whereas positivists seek to discover the criteria that identify this stuff as law, natural lawyers want to discuss the normativity of the positivists' law. Typically, natural lawyers argue that if law is wicked or morally obtuse, it is a degraded, noncentral form of LAW, which is truly law.[25] The function of LAW is to make vague moral principles determinate—to bring morality down to earth, so to speak.[26] If law fails to do this, then it is not truly LAW. Law is, for natural lawyers, an honorific term. Mere law—the positivists' law—does not merit the honor of that label unless it is LAW.

On this account, positivists and natural lawyers are not disagreeing, for they are each discussing the nature of a different thing. The positivists are discussing law, the natural lawyers, LAW. Neither need deny the others' claims.[27]

I realize I have painted the legal positivists and natural lawyers with a very broad brush, and I have glossed over the many fine distinctions and nuances that characterize the debates within and between these camps of jurisprudents. Moreover, by denying that legal positivists and natural lawyers are arguing with as opposed to past each other, and by claiming that they engage in different and somewhat complementary enterprises, I know I will have provoked the intellectual ire of a lot of very talented people who see things quite differently. Moreover, to vindicate fully these provocative claims would require much more argumentation than I am prepared to offer here. So I must content myself with firing these shots across the jurisprudential bow and then moving on to return to Dworkin. Before I return to Dworkin, however, I want to show why the proponents of legal positivism and natural law are not only arguing past each other but are also both facing a normativity problem, a normativity problem that Dworkin's own third-way jurisprudence might conceivably avoid.

3.2. WHY "IT'S THE LAW" CANNOT BE A REASON TO OBEY, AND THE BEARING OF THIS ON JURISPRUDENCE

If I ask why I shouldn't phi, and someone responds "Because it's the law," what kind of reason have they given me? Or have they given me any reason at all?[28]

Let me put my question this way. I *comply* with what the law tells me to do or not do most of the time. The law tells me not to kill or steal, and I do not. It

---

[25] Finnis (1980: 276-281); Murphy (2007: 43-45).

[26] Finnis (1980: 281-906).

[27] One may characterize the dispute between positivists and natural lawyers as, in David Plunkett's apt phrasing, a metalinguistic negotiation over the proper use of the term *law*. Plunkett (forthcoming).

[28] The discussion in this section is, I believe, consistent with the position of Hershovitz (2015) in his excellent article, "The End of Jurisprudence." I obtained Hershovitz's article after writing this section and so cannot discuss it here. But I do believe his eliminative approach parallels mine here. For what I believe to be an unsuccessful attack on Hershovitz's argument, see Schaus (2015).

tells me not to eat human flesh, and I do not. On the other hand, it tells me not to exceed the speed limits, but I frequently do—when I think it is safe for me and for others to do so, and when I cannot see any cops around. But even if I am complying with the law, am I *obeying* the law? Am I complying *because* "It's the law" that I must comply? Is "It's the law" my *reason* for complying?

Take those legal commands away, and I still would not kill or steal. For I have good reasons apart from the law to refrain from killing and stealing. Morality provides me with those reasons. Nor would I eat human flesh were it legal to do so. I have nonmoral reasons—prudential reasons—not to do so. But when I believe I have no moral, religious, or prudential reasons to do what the law tells me I must do—as, for example, in many of the instances in which I drive over the speed limit—does the fact that "It's the law" give me a reason that might tip the balance of my reasons in favor of doing what the law requires? When I lack other reasons to comply, do I nonetheless have a reason to *obey* and thereby comply?

Now it is surely true that "It's the law" can, in David Enoch's useful terminology, *trigger* pre-existing reasons[29]—moral reasons, prudential reasons, and, in some cases, religious reasons. Laws change the facts on the ground, facts that bear on what we are morally or religiously obligated to do, or that bear on what is in our self-interest to do. One way law does this is by informing us about that conduct we can expect of others.[30] If laws change how people act, and if how they will act bears on our practical reasoning—moral, religious, and prudential—then "It's the law" will be something our practical reasoning should take into account. Similarly, knowing that "It's the law" will frequently lead us to believe that we will be punished if we fail to comply, a fact that surely bears on our prudential reasoning and perhaps on our moral reasoning, too.

Another way law can trigger pre-existing reasons is by giving us information about the prohibited or mandated activity that is relevant to our practical deliberations. If the law bans the use of substance X, that may indicate to us that substance X is dangerous to handle, or is a pollutant, something we did not realize prior to the ban. Because we have moral and prudential reasons not to use dangerous or polluting substances, "It's the law" has triggered pre-existing reasons we had not to use substance X.

Finally, if we have moral and prudential reasons to encourage or at least not undermine others' law abidingness, then "It's the law" can trigger those reasons and lead us not to flout the law, at least when that flouting will likely be discovered and influence others.

Although "It's the law" can trigger these pre-existing practical reasons and lead us to comply with its commands, this fails to establish that "It's the law" is itself a reason. Reasons to comply are not reasons to obey.

---

[29] Enoch (2012); Enoch (2011: 1-38). See also Bertea (2014). For an argument that law can create and not just trigger pre-existing reasons, which I believe is unconvincing, see Reeves (2015).

[30] Claus (2012) on building a theory of law from mutual expectations. See also Morrison (2013).

This point can be stated a different way. Suppose in deciding whether to phi, we consult all of our moral, religious, and prudential reasons, including those reasons triggered by the law, "Don't phi"—that is, triggered by the information that law provides about how the legislators regard phi-ing, about whether others will be less likely to phi, and about whether we will be sanctioned if we phi. Let us call the conclusion of this deliberation our all-things-considered-but-law conclusion, or our ATCBL balance of reasons. And suppose our conclusion regarding our ATCBL balance of reasons is that we should go ahead and phi. Can "It's the law" that we not phi change this conclusion? Does "It's the law" provide us with a reason to put on the not-phi side of the balance? We have already taken into account the reasons the law triggered. Is "It's the law" a reason in itself?

I cannot see how it can be. Even our consenting or promising to obey—as when we take an oath to obey—would not make it a reason. If we believe the moral balance of ATCBL reasons favors phi-ing, then consenting or promising not to phi carries no moral weight.[31] I cannot obligate myself to commit murder by consenting or promising to do so. Nor can I alter the balance of reasons against murder even slightly by promising to murder or consenting to be ordered to murder. And as for prudential reasons, why would we ever consent or promise (for the benefit of the state) to act against our self-interest unless it was to comply with our moral or religious duties? The state is not our child or a friend, someone for whom we might sacrifice for their benefit. Nor does the state in any way benefit by our promising to obey in the face of our ATCBL reasons for disobedience.[32]

This last point also shows why fairness or gratitude cannot support a duty to obey. Whatever work fairness does is already accounted for in the ATCBL balance of reasons. And it is difficult to understand how gratitude to our compatriots is ever shown by acting against the ATCBL balance. Indeed, acting against the ATCBL by obeying law if anything seems like *in* gratitude.

Nor does the fact that the law is democratically enacted change matters. That John and Jane outvote Jean and ban phi-ing cannot be a reason for Jean not to phi if her ATCBL deliberations come out in favor of phi-ing. Democratically

---

[31] The inability of consent to obligate one to obey has been noted by others. See Greene (2012: 101).

[32] Here, an objection is foreseen. Can we not promise others to perform acts that are not morally infirm and that come within the ambit of our moral freedom? For example, if I am morally free both to go to the ballgame with you and to stay home, and I promise you that I will go the ballgame with you, then I have a duty to do so. That duty is typically not canceled by the balance of my prudential reasons. And can we not then derive a duty to obey the law from promises to do so, at least if the law is not morally infelicitous? Such a promise could be viewed as a promise we make, not to the state, but to each other.

I admit that if we all did promise to obey the law for each other's benefit in cases in which such a promise would not be a promise of immorality and hence invalid, then "It's the law" could be a reason to obey. But such promises by the entire citizenry are highly unlikely to exist. And they would make sense only if virtually everyone were so promising. Nor does this apply to officials' oaths to enforce law, as they have no moral freedom to enforce laws if ATCBL reasons militate against doing so.

enacted laws may be more likely to accord with ATCBL reasons than laws that have no democratic provenance. That, however, seems to exhaust the reason-giving force of democratic procedures.

Many people disagree with this point, however. Their strongest argument is that disobeying democratically enacted laws that contradict the ATCBL balance of reasons is to unfairly arrogate to oneself the authority to disregard what a majority of one's fellow citizens have determined should be done. It puts one above those who are his equals. It is a hierarchical view.[33]

I can concede that democracy has value as a decision-making process, including the value of institutionalizing a certain kind of equality among citizens. I also can concede that flouting laws can, if frequent and visible, undermine democratic institutions. Those are considerations of which ATCBL reasoning should take account. Moreover, one should be epistemically humble and think hard about cases in which ATCBL reasoning seems to contradict the conclusions of a democratic legislature. But if ATCBL reasoning, carefully done, concludes that one should disobey a democratically enacted law, the fact that the disobedient will, in a sense, be asserting his superiority to the majority of his fellow citizens, does not counsel disregarding the ATCBL conclusion. One's moral obligations to one's fellow citizens will already have been duly considered.

So I don't see how "It's the law" can ever be a reason in itself.[34] That is not deny that it might be a good thing—a morally good thing—were most citizens and officials to believe that "It's the law" *is* a reason, and a strong reason at that, capable of outweighing ATCBL practical reasons. But just as it might be very profitable to believe, contrary to fact, that the toxin in Kavka's Toxin Puzzle will taste really good, that it would be useful to believe something does not make it true.[35] If "It's the law" is not a reason, then that it would be advantageous to believe otherwise is beside the point.

If law cannot be itself a reason to do what it demands, then it becomes apparent why sanctions are so important in law. The prospect of sanctions can obviously change the prudential calculus and sometimes even the moral calculus. (Martyrdom may be immoral in many circumstances.) If people cannot believe that "It's the law" is a reason, then compliance with—not obedience to—the law may be more reliably assured if the law triggers the reasons to avoid sanctions. Of course, it is difficult for sanctions to play the role all the way up the hierarchy of officials, though sanctions need not take the form of criminal punishment to be effective. Officials, for example, even if not subject to formal sanctions such as punishment or loss of employment for not complying with the law, may suffer informal sanctions such as public obloquy.[36]

---

[33] Kolodny (2014); Viehoff (2014). See also Goldman (2006), expressing the view that those who disobey decent rules based on a belief that disobedience in the particular case is all-things-considered optimal are unfairly arrogating to themselves an authority that they do not possess.

[34] Crowe (2013: 95-102).

[35] Kavka (1983).

[36] Schauer (2015: 85-92); Morrison (2013: 10-12).

If having a legal system and having a high level of law compliance is a good thing—and it is surely a good thing, a morally good thing, at least if it is a morally decent legal system—then it may be helpful to have, in addition to sanctions, a widespread belief that "It's the law" is itself a reason, a reason to obey and thereby to comply even when one believes his or her ATCBL balance of reasons comes out the other way. Call such a belief law fetishism. If, however, as I have argued, "It's the law" is *not* a reason, then it will take deception to create law fetishism, the belief that "It's the law" *is* a reason. (Law fetishism is present to varying degrees in ours and other societies; Schauer notes that the Finns obey "Don't Walk" signs even if no moral or prudential reasons to do so are apparent.)[37] The inculcation of the false beliefs that produce law fetishism may thereby produce a morally good outcome, just as the punishment of those who act in accord with their ATCBL reasons, but not the law, may do so. (Many people are mistaken about their ATCBL reasons and would better comply with them by obeying the law.)

"It's the law," backed up by sanctions and an ideology of law fetishism, may turn out to play a role analogous to that of the evil demon in wrong-kind-of-reason scenarios. The demon tells us that he will destroy the world unless we believe that eating mud is delightful. The reason he gives us is the wrong kind of reason for believing something, the right kind of reason being its truth. Likewise, the efficacy of a good legal system, with a high level of law compliance, provides us with a reason—indeed, a moral reason—to punish the noncompliant and to inculcate the belief that "It's the law" is itself a reason to do what the law requires. But that moral reason is the wrong kind of reason for punishing those who act in accord with the ATCBL balance of reasons, and it is the wrong kind of reason for believing that "It's the law" is a reason to obey and thus comply.[38] The right kind of reason for punishing is that the one punished acted culpably wrongly—which is not true of one who acted in accord with his ATCBL reasons. And the right reason for believing is the truth of the proposition believed—and that "It's the law" is a reason to obey and thereby comply is, quite simply, false.

---

[37] Schauer (2015: 73).

[38] Some people of the indirect consequentialist persuasion believe "It's the law" *is* a reason because it would be conducive to good consequences were people socialized to *believe* that it is a reason. Of course, those who hold this view usually want to qualify it in various ways. Believing "It's the law" is a reason may not be conducive to good consequences if one is in Nazi Germany or Stalinist Soviet Union. And believing "It's the law" to be a reason leaves open the weight of that reason in which it would be good for people to believe. It is doubtful that it would be conducive to good consequences for people to believe "It's the law" is a weighty enough reason to override all other practical reasons. At least it would not be so in the legal systems of which I am aware—those with sometimes quite imperfect laws and quite imperfect lawmakers. Finally, one would think believing "It's the law" is a reason, and a reason with a particular weight, will be conducive to good consequences only if a sufficient number of other people, especially those in particular social positions, in fact believe "It's the law" to be a reason with that weight. Indeed, the weight of the reason "It's the law" in which it would be good for people to believe would likely vary with the number of people who in fact believe "It's the law" is a reason with that weight.

I conclude with these observations. Many have denied that there is an obligation to obey the law, even a prima facie obligation. Some have denied the prima
facie obligation because they deny that we have consented to obey, expressly or
tacitly. I believe, however, as I have argued, that the presence or absence of consent is immaterial.

So the position that I have argued for here, that "It's the law" cannot be a reason in itself to obey, is not a novel position among theorists. Indeed, it is almost
an orthodoxy. What I hope to have shown is why "It's the law" *cannot* be a reason
to obey, and why it can be, at most, a reason to comply by triggering our pre-
existing practical reasons.

Those who seek to show that law can make a practical difference must be satisfied by the ability of law to trigger these pre-existing practical reasons. But those
who seek an account of law's normativity *qua* law will come up dry. For "It's the
law" is itself normatively inert.

There is one final point I wish to make regarding legal positivism and natural
law more generally. If "It's the law" can never itself be a reason for conduct, but
at most can only trigger pre-existing reasons, then the natural lawyer's project is
doomed from the start, and the legal positivist is forced to see law as ultimately
based upon an illusion, coercion, or both. It is easy to see that if "It's the law"
cannot itself be a reason for conduct, then positive law can at most mimic but can
never *be* LAW, and the natural lawyer's quest is quixotic.[39] But the legal positivist
is also in trouble. If, like some, she wishes to base law on a claim of law's moral
authority, then law will rest on a necessarily false claim. If, like others, she wishes
to base law on the threat of sanctions, then those imposing the sanctions will either
believe falsely that law *qua* law should be obeyed, and thus that disobedience war-
rants sanctions, or, if she does not believe this, she ultimately is indistinguishable
from the gunman who threatens violence unless others bend to his will.[40] False
beliefs, false claims, and violence—those are the legal positivist's building blocks
once "It's the law" is defrocked and stripped of reason-giving power.

3.3. MARK GREENBERG: ACHIEVING THE NORMATIVITY
OF LAW BY REJECTING THE STANDARD PICTURE?

It is worthwhile to contrast Enoch's idea, which I endorse, that law can trigger
pre-existing reasons, including moral reasons, with Mark Greenberg's idea that
LAW consists of new moral obligations—improvements in our "moral profile"—
that are brought about in a "legally proper" way.[41] I find Greenberg's idea quite
opaque.

Enoch's idea fits well with what Greenberg calls the Standard Picture. The
Standard Picture goes roughly like this: We attribute to certain institutions and

---

[39] Some natural lawyers assert that the positivists' law is merely *evidence* of LAW. Hurd (1990).
[40] Schauer (2015: 159-161).
[41] Greenberg (2014: 1323).

individuals the power to choose, promulgate, and apply the norms that will govern us. The norms they choose are linguistically encoded and then communicated to us in the texts of constitutions, statutes, administrative rules, judicial decisions and orders, and so on. We interpret those texts to ascertain the norms that those who promulgated them intended to communicate. In other words, we seek the communicative intent behind the text because only by doing so can we discover what norms those who have authority to choose and promulgate our governing norms actually chose and promulgated.

The Standard Picture fits the positivists' view of law, but it also fits the natural lawyers' view of law, if not of LAW. And if, as I have argued, Dworkin's view, after *Law's Empire,* is originalist, then it fits Dworkin's view of law, if not of LAW. But Greenberg rejects the Standard Picture and argues that it is inconsistent with his view.

First, with respect to Greenberg's idea that LAW improves our moral profile, ultimate moral principles would seem to be impossible to change, much less improve, on most moral theories of which I am aware. How would improvement be measured, except by reference to ultimate moral principles? Changes in facts on the ground can improve the situation morally by producing states of affairs that are closer to the full realization of ultimate principles than the states of affairs that existed prior to those changes. That is consistent with the idea of triggering pre-existing moral reasons but not with the idea of changing them. So Greenberg must not be arguing that law improves the moral norms themselves.

Second, if Greenberg's idea is that LAW represents the improvement in the moral situation—the greater realization of pre-existing moral principles— through triggering pre-existing moral reasons, then how do we distinguish LAW from the many other things that can trigger those pre-existing reasons and improve our moral situation? Greenberg clearly does not want to endorse the view that statutes, executive actions, and judicial decisions are indistinguishable as sources of LAW from the many other things that can improve our moral situation by triggering pre-existing moral reasons. Greenberg wants to restrict LAW to those moral obligations brought about by legal institutions in the legally proper way.

Greenberg's qualifier, the "legally proper way," is supposed to rule out obligations triggered by bad laws, such as the obligation to strive for their repeal. Presumably, bad laws, which are clearly not LAW in Greenberg's scheme, can be identified and distinguished from other worsenings of our moral situation, by having been generated by legal institutions. But how do we identify legal institutions, which we ordinarily think are themselves products of laws? How, in other words, does Greenberg avoid the vicious circularity of defining LAW as the product of institutions created by, well, LAW?

Greenberg says that legal institutions are institutions meant to improve our moral situation.[42] Although that might work as a necessary condition, it is surely

---

[42] Greenberg (2014: 1324).

not a sufficient one. Churches, civic organizations, and courses in ethics are also arguably meant to improve things morally.

Greenberg lists various ways that law can improve our moral situation, assuming that we can identify law and legal institutions by some undisclosed method. First, law and legal institutions can replace self-help and thereby reduce violence.[43] So, however, can reliable vigilantes.

Second, law can specify and give advance notice of what punishment will be meted out for what crimes, making those punishments morally permissible.[44] The implication of Greenberg's point, that punishments for crimes would be morally impermissible without notice and specification, is, however, false, at least for *malum in se* crimes. The Nuremberg trials are a clear counterexample, at least if one accepts the justness of the punishments imposed there.

Third and sixth on Greenberg's list, law can make moral obligations more determinate.[45] This is true. Law can at least attempt to settle controversy and uncertainty over what more abstract moral principles require. Whether such settlement is possible, so that actors' moral obligations are to comply with the terms of the settlement even if the actors perceive their determinate moral obligations differently, is, as I have frequently argued, doubtful.[46]

Fourth, law can solve coordination problems.[47] So, however, can forceful personalities or other salient factors.

Fifth, Greenberg argues that law produced by democratic institutions can alter our moral obligations solely based on its democratic pedigree, and even if the content of the law is morally flawed.[48] I think this is seriously mistaken, for, as I argued in the previous section, I do not believe morally flawed prescriptions create obligations merely because they are endorsed by a majority.

Seventh, Greenberg argues that legal coercion can solve collective action problems, which is true, and eighth, that adjudication changes the moral profile by virtue of treating like cases alike and by inducing justifiable reliance.[49] Reliance is, of course, triggered by the linguistic content of judicial decisions, which is also true of many of the other ways that law improves the moral situation— particularly producing coordination and making moral obligations determinate. I shall have more to say about the linguistic content of laws momentarily, as Greenberg wishes to distinguish the linguistic content of laws from LAW. As for treating like cases alike, there is no value of equality that is advanced by extending the impact of an infelicitous precedent to future cases.[50] Nor is the model of precedent on which Greenberg relies, in which only the result reached, and not

---

[43] Greenberg (2014: 1311).
[44] Greenberg (2014: 1311).
[45] Greenberg (2014: 1311-1312, 1314-1315).
[46] Alexander and Sherwin (2001: ch. 4).
[47] Greenberg (2014: 1314).
[48] Greenberg (2014: 1313-1314).
[49] Greenberg (2014: 1315-1316).
[50] Alexander and Kress (1995: 279-327, 308-326); Alexander (1989: 9-12).

the norm used by the court to justify that result, carries the force of precedent, a coherent model of precedent.[51]

None of the ways Greenberg argues that law alters our moral situation differentiates Greenberg's view of law from the so-called Standard Picture, in which law consists primarily of norms intentionally posited by officials and enforced by other officials. Greenberg recognizes the significance of texts as instructions to officials and to the public. Officials, he believes, are morally obligated to obey their instructions by virtue of having consented to do so. But consent cannot obligate one to act immorally.[52] Therefore, if legal obligations are moral obligations, as Greenberg asserts, then officials could not be legally obligated to carry out instructions, such as enforcing statutes, unless the content of those statutes was LAW and not just law. And the content could be LAW only if it improved the moral profile, which, Greenberg argues, requires that the officials determine whether following the linguistic content of their instructions would produce that improvement.

That brings me finally to Greenberg's view of the linguistic content of laws and statutory interpretation. Greenberg believes that his foil, the Standard Picture, has it that statutory interpretation—and presumably, constitutional interpretation and the interpretation of administrative rules and orders—consists of extracting the linguistic content from the law's words.[53] But, he counters, the linguistic content could either be its semantic content or its communicative content—its utterance meaning or its speaker's meaning. On Greenberg's view, the law's meaning is determined by asking what impact on our moral obligations is effected by the fact that a majority of legislators (or administrators authorized by legislation) voted for the law's text.[54]

The first thing to note is that Greenberg fails to keep separate two distinct items: the norm that the legislators intended to enact and the fairness or unfairness of giving that norm effect. As for the first item, it is a mistake to argue, as Greenberg does, that the linguistic content of statutes does not itself adjudicate between the semantic meaning of the text and the communicative intent of those who authored the text. Recall Dworkin's correct point, namely, that texts divorced from the intended meanings of their authors are just marks (or sounds) that can mean anything. What Greenberg calls semantic meaning is just the meaning intended by most speakers using those marks at particular moment in history. But if democracy means anything, it means that the norms decided upon by a majority of elected representatives should govern. Statutes' texts are merely the legislators' vehicles for communicating those norms to the populace. Greenberg's semantic meanings are evidence of the intended meanings—the norms—but are not the norms themselves. (The reason we look at the semantic

---

[51] Alexander (1989: 34-44); Alexander and Sherwin (2008: 64-103).

[52] See n. 32.

[53] Greenberg (2014: 1292).

[54] Greenberg (2014: 1293).

meanings at the time of statutes' enactment rather than at the time of adjudication shows this. Allowing the mindless changes in semantic meanings to alter the legislatures' enacted norms would be obtuse. But fixing those meanings at the time of enactment makes sense if intended meanings are the real quarry.)

On the other hand, semantic meanings might create ambiguity about what norms were intended, or the intended meanings might be vague. So applying the intended norms might be unfair in certain situations. The doctrine of void for vagueness in criminal law and First Amendment law is a case in point. Other doctrines, such as lenity, avoidance of constitutional questions, and construction to accord with human rights, are more dubious because they appear to authorize substitution of judicially crafted norms for the norms enacted by the legislature. And likewise dubious are the various policies and canons that Greenberg says should affect the moral impact of statutes.[55]

The positivists' standard picture together with Enoch's notion of triggering pre-existing reasons can account for all the phenomena coherently. Greenberg's moral impact theory, to the extent it differs from this, only confuses rather than clarifies.[56]

4. Back to Dworkin

Where, then, does Dworkin fit in this picture of general jurisprudence? I think it is fair to say, as others have said, that Dworkin is a natural lawyer. He is interested in LAW, not law. He is different, however, from the other natural lawyers in one important respect. For most natural lawyers, if a community's law is morally deficient—if it fails to make moral norms determinate—then the community has law but not LAW.

For Dworkin, however, except in very evil legal regimes, there is always LAW. For Dworkin does not regard law's function to be making moral norms determinate. Rather, for Dworkin, LAW is what justifies the community's coercive political decisions. And that includes not only its current coercive political decisions but also its past coercive political decisions, even if those decisions were not morally optimal. For Dworkin, LAW is those principles that best justify (most) past and present coercive political decisions.[57] And unless those decisions are very wicked, there will be principles that justify them. Thus, there will practically always be LAW wherever there is law.

Dworkin believes that past morally nonoptimal decisions can be justified because he attaches moral value to diachronic and synchronic consistency—a value that he calls integrity in *Law's Empire* but which is best thought of as a

---

[55] Greenberg (2014: 1333).

[56] For an excellent critique of Greenberg's argument against the positivists' view that law consists only of social facts, see Levenbook (2013: 75-102, 75-88).

[57] Dworkin (1986: chs. 6, 7).

form of diachronic and synchronic equality of treatment.[58] I have argued at great length elsewhere that Dworkin's Integrity is a false value, and that his desire that communities make their coercive decisions over time as if they are following a consistent set of principles is wrong headed, indeterminate, and, indeed, morally obtuse. I shall not repeat those arguments here, for my aim is to locate Dworkin on the jurisprudential map, not to refute him.[59]

The oddity of this diachronic and synchronic notion of principle should be apparent. In the United States, for example, we had coercive decisions enslaving persons, followed by coercive decisions emancipating them, followed by coercive decisions segregating them, followed by coercive decisions desegregating them. What "principle" covers this history of coercive decisions? And why must we strive to justify the unjustifiable?[60] What possible reason is there for giving present force to past injustices?

One thing to note about Dworkin's view is that it is incorrect to say that Dworkin has a theory of adjudication but not of law. In fact, his theory applies not only to adjudication but also to legislation and other forms of lawmaking. For, logically, all participants in the project of political coercion and not just judges are bound by Integrity. (Recall Dworkin's rejection of checkerboard statutes.)[61]

Finally, I should mention that Dan Priel has recently argued that the orthodox picture of Dworkin that I have painted, in which LAW is the product of the most morally acceptable principles that fit the past and present coercive decisions, may be a misreading of Dworkin's view of moral acceptability.[62] On my orthodox account, morality and moral acceptability are external to law, and law becomes LAW by imitating morality. But Priel argues that on Dworkin's nonrealist but objective view of morality, morality is internal to law. We construct our political morality through our legal decisions and our attempts to justify them. The picture resembles that of reflective equilibrium in moral epistemology, except that the decisions from which the principles are derived cannot be revised, unlike the case specific intuitions in the standard account of reflective equilibrium.

I grant that Priel's view of Dworkin makes Dworkin's jurisprudence less morally obtuse than the orthodox view. That is because it makes morality internal to rather than external to law. But it helps Dworkin's jurisprudence at the severe cost of hurting his moral epistemology. For it relativizes political morality and deprives it of the resources to call wicked regimes wicked instead of "just not ours."

---

[58] Alexander and Kress (1995: 308-326).

[59] For those interested in those arguments, they are fully elaborated in Alexander and Kress (1995: 308-326). There, Kress and I argue that there is no value such as Dworkin's integrity that requires that correct moral principles be distorted to fit with past coercive decisions, and that there are no principles with weight other than correct moral principles.

[60] Alexander and Kress (1995: 294-295, 325).

[61] Dworkin (1986: 178-184).

[62] Priel (2015).

5. Fitting Dworkin's Originalism into His Jurisprudence

It is time now to circle back to the question raised by the title: Was Dworkin an originalist? I think the most accurate answer to it is yes and no. The *yes* points to Dworkin's claim (in the Scalia book) that the semantic intentions of legislators—which include constitutional authors—determine the meaning of the norms they enact. The crucial point, however, is that the norms they enact are law but not LAW. Those norms are, as Dworkin puts it, pre-interpretive or first-stage law. Whether they are LAW, however, turns on what emerges when the fit-acceptability engine of integrity is turned on them. Once that occurs, the law that corresponds to the original semantic intentions of the legislators may differ from the LAW that is the community's principles, displayed both diachronically and synchronically. In the case of the constitutional provisions Dworkin typically discusses, given his understanding of the framers' semantic intentions, the law will happily correspond to the LAW. But were the framers' semantic intentions more in line with Scalia's understanding of them, those constitutional provisions would be law but might not be LAW.

Now what happens when the semantic intentions of the law's authors constitute the content of law but not LAW—presumably because the law fails to conform to the most morally acceptable principles that fit with most of the rest of the law? There are passages, especially in *Law's Empire*, in which Dworkin can be read as claiming that judges should disregard law, which is only pre-interpretive LAW, in favor of LAW.[63] I believe, however, in light of what Dworkin says in *Taking Rights Seriously* about enactment force versus gravitational force,[64] and what he says after *Law's Empire* regarding authorial semantic intentions, that his position is that law has enactment force but not gravitational force unless it comports with LAW.

Indeed, this interpretation makes sense of Dworkin's criticism of checkerboard statutes in *Law's Empire*.[65] Such statutes are unprincipled and thus cannot be part of LAW. If because of that, however, they lack even enactment force, then there is no reason to worry about them. If, on the other hand, they do have enactment force, Dworkin's criticism of them makes sense, even if it is unconvincing.[66]

Even more basically, LAW cannot, through Dworkin's interpretive approach to it, make laws "the best they can be" unless there is a *there* there with respect to those laws. There has to be something that laws are for Dworkin's approach to make that something the best it can be. And that something cannot be the texts apart from the authorial semantic intentions that give those texts content. For as Dworkin recognizes, texts severed from authorial semantic intentions are just marks (or sounds) that can symbolize anything. They can be one's favored moral views merely by reading those views into them. The fit dimension has no work to

---

[63] Dworkin (1986: 90-93).
[64] Dworkin (1977: 111-123).
[65] Dworkin (1986: 178-184).
[66] Alexander and Kress (1995: 325).

do, then, because the entire corpus juris will mean whatever we want it to mean and cannot deviate from our moral views. And checkerboard statutes, if morally objectionable, will no longer exist because the symbols by which their authors intended a checkerboard meaning will be re-employed to mean something more principled and agreeable. So it is only sensible to conclude that laws given their originalist meanings will have enactment force.

The resulting picture of Dworkin's jurisprudence looks like this. There is law consisting of the constitutional, statutory, administrative, and judicially authored rules. Those rules are interpreted by reference to the semantic intentions of their authors—Dworkin's originalism. Those rules have enactment force. In addition, there is LAW, consisting of the most morally acceptable principles that can account for (most of) law past and present. Law that comports with LAW has gravitational force as well as enactment force because the principles that account for it—LAW—extend beyond the law.

Note the oddity of this picture. If laws are enacted that are inconsistent with LAW as it exists at the time, the dimension of fit may dictate that the principles that make up LAW change. For the existing principles may no longer fit with a sufficient number of laws or past legal decisions. LAW then, might be thought of as like a viscous liquid in which there are air bubbles. The liquid represents the principles that constitute LAW, and the air bubbles the coercive decisions that do not fit. The threshold of fit demanded by Dworkin's account is some ratio of the area of liquid to the area of the bubbles. Once that threshold is reached, any new bubble—a decision inconsistent with the principles that are LAW—will force the liquid to take a new shape, covering up old bubbles and producing new ones.

So here are my conclusions. In order to make the law the best it can be, there has to be a *there* there, something the law is that can be made better. Or, put differently, for the dimension of fit to do any work, there has to be something with which to fit. As Dworkin realizes, at least after *Law's Empire*, the mere marks of legal texts, when divorced from the intended meanings of the texts' authors, can mean anything. So legal texts must be given their author-intended meanings. Those meanings will have enactment force but not necessarily gravitational force. They will be law but may not be LAW. LAW consists of those principles that are the most morally attractive ones that pass some threshold of fit with laws, past and present. I do not believe this jurisprudential picture is either attractive or coherent, but I do believe it is the picture Dworkin painted for us.

References

Alexander, L. (1987). "Striking Back at the Empire: A Brief Survey of Problems in Dworkin's Theory of Law," *Law and Philosophy* 6:419–38.

Alexander, L. (1989). "Constrained by Precedent," *Southern California Law Review* 63:1–64.

Alexander, L. (2005). *Is There a Right of Freedom of Expression?* Cambridge: Cambridge University Press.

Alexander, L. (2011). "Simple-Minded Originalism." In *The Challenge of Originalism*, G. Huscroft and B.W. Miller (eds.). Cambridge: Cambridge University Press.

Alexander, L. (2013). "Originalism, the Why and the What," *Fordham Law Review* 82:539–544.

Alexander, L. and Kress, K. (1995). "Against Legal Principles." In *Law and Interpretation*, A. Marmor (ed.). Oxford: Oxford University Press.

Alexander, L. and Schauer, F. (2007). "Law's Limited Domain Confronts Morality's Universal Empire," *William & Mary Law Review* 48:1579–1603.

Alexander, L. and Sherwin, E. (2001). *The Rules of Rules: Morality, Rules, and the Dilemmas of Law*. Durham: Duke University Press.

Alexander, L. and Sherwin, E. (2008). *Demystifying Legal Reasoning*. Cambridge: Cambridge University Press.

Austin, J. (1832/1965). *The Province of Jurisprudence Determined*. Reprint ed. London: Weidenfeld & Nicolson.

Balkin, J. (2011). *Living Originalism*. Cambridge, MA: Harvard University Press.

Barauh, P. (2014). "Human Dignity in Adjudication: The Limits of Placeholding and Essential Contestability Accounts," *Canadian Journal of Law & Jurisprudence* 27:329–356.

Bertea, S. (2014). "Law, Shared Activities, and Obligation," *The Canadian Journal of Law & Jurisprudence* 27:357–381.

Brink, D. (forthcoming). "Originalism and Constructive Interpretation." In *The Legacy of Ronald Dworkin*, W. Waluchow and S. Sciaraffa (eds.). Oxford: Clarendon Press.

Claus, L. (2012). *Law's Evolution and Human Understanding*. Oxford: Oxford University Press.

Crowe, J. (2013). "Normativity, Coordination and Authority in Finnis's Philosophy of Law." In *Jurisprudence as Practical Reason: a Celebration of the Collected Essays of John Finnis*, M. Sayers and A. Rahemtula (eds.). Queensland: Supreme Court Library Queensland.

Dworkin, R. (1977). *Taking Rights Seriously*. Cambridge, MA: Harvard University Press.

Dworkin, R. (1986). *Law's Empire*. Cambridge, MA: Harvard University Press.

Dworkin, R. (1987). "The Bork Nomination," *New York Review of Books*, August.

Dworkin, R. (1997a). "Comment." In A. Scalia, *A Matter of Interpretation: Federal Courts and the Law*. Princeton: Princeton University Press, 115–127.

Dworkin, R. (1997b). "Reflections on Fidelity," *Fordham Law Review* 65:1799–1818.

Enoch, D. (2011). "Reason-Giving and the Law." In *Oxford Studies in the Philosophy of Law: Volume 1*. L Green and B. Leiter (eds.). Oxford: Oxford University Press.

Enoch, D. (2012). "Authority and Reason-Giving," *Philosophy and Phenomenological Research* 89:296–332.

Finnis, J. (1980). *Natural Law and Natural Rights*. Oxford: Oxford University Press.

Gallie, W. B. (1956). "Essentially Contested Concepts," *Proceedings of the Aristotelian Society* 56:167–198.

Goldman, A. H. (2006). "The Rationality of Complying with Rules: Paradox Resolved," *Ethics* 116:453–570.

Goldsworthy, J. (2000). "Dworkin as an Originalist," *Constitutional Commentary* 17:49–78.

Greenberg, M. (2014). "The Moral Impact Theory of Law," *The Yale Law Journal* 123:1288–1342.

Greene, A. (2012). *The Multiple Sources of Authority in a Liberal Democracy.* Cambridge, MA: Harvard University Press.

Grice, P. (1989). *Studies in the Way of Words.* Cambridge, MA: Harvard University Press.

Hart, H. L. A. (1961). *The Concept of Law.* Oxford: Oxford University Press.

Hershovitz, S. (2015). "The End of Jurisprudence," *The Yale Law Journal* 124:1160–1204.

Hurd, H. M. (1990). "Sovereignty in Silence," *The Yale Law Journal* 99:945–1028.

Kavka, G. S. (1983). "The Toxin Puzzle," *Analysis* 43:33–36.

Kelsen, H. (1961). *General Theory of Law and State.* New York: Russell & Russell.

Kolodny, N. (2014). "Rule Over None II: Social Equality and the Justification of Democracy," *Philosophy & Public Affairs* 42:287–336.

Levenbook, B. B. (2013). "How to Hold the Social Fact Thesis: A Reply to Greenberg and Toh." In *Oxford Studies in the Philosophy of Law: Volume 2.* L. Green and B. Leiter, (eds.). Oxford: Oxford University Press.

Marmor, A. (2013). "Farewell to Conceptual Analysis (in Jurisprudence)." In *Philosophical Foundations of the Nature of Law.* W. Waluchow and S. Sciaraffa (eds.). Oxford: Oxford University Press.

Morrison, A. S. (2013). "Yes, Law is the Command of the Sovereign" or "Eminent Legal Philosophers." University of Michigan Law School (unpublished).

Murphy, M. C. (2007). *Philosophy of Law: The Fundamentals.* Malden, MA: Blackwell Publishing.

Plunkett, D. "The Metalinguistic Dimension of the Dispute Over Legal Positivism" (to be published).

Priel, D. (2015). "Making (Some) Sense of Nonsense Jurisprudence." Osgoode Hall Law School (unpublished).

Raz, J. (1979). *The Authority of Law.* Oxford: Oxford University Press.

Raz, J. (1985). "Authority, Law and Morality," *The Monist* 68:295–324.

Reeves, A. R. (2015). "Practical Reason and Legality: Instrumental Political Authority Without Exclusion," *Law & Philosophy* 34:257–298.

Schauer, F. (2015). *The Force of Law.* Cambridge, MA: Harvard University Press.

Schaus, S. (2015). "How to Think About Law as Morality: A Comment on Greenberg and Hershovitz," *The Yale Law Journal Forum* 124:224–245.

Shapiro, S. J. (2011). *Legality.* Cambridge, MA: Harvard University Press.

Viehoff, D. (2014). "Democratic Equality and Political Authority," *Philosophy & Public Affairs* 42: 337–375.

Whittington, K. E. (2000). "Dworkin's 'Originalism': The Role of Intentions in Constitutional Interpretation," *The Review of Politics* 62:197–229.

14

The Moral Reading of Constitutions
by Connie S. Rosati*

Of the many ideas for which Ronald Dworkin is justly famous, perhaps the most striking is his idea that the Constitution should be read "morally."[1] Over the course of a long career, Dworkin advanced this idea, partly in his theoretical work, but also in the many essays in which he applied what he came to call "the moral reading" to some of our most pressing and divisive constitutional questions. Dworkin's critics commonly charged that his approach amounted to no more than appealing to moral principles he accepted in order to reach outcomes he favored.[2] The moral reading, critics claimed, leaves judges untethered from the Constitution, free to project onto it a constitutional world more to their own liking.

This criticism of Dworkin's approach to constitutional interpretation has considerable force. Yet we would do well to distinguish between Dworkin's *way* of reading a constitution morally and the general *idea* that a constitution should be read morally, for problems with the former need not tell against the latter. My interest in this essay lies with Dworkin's fundamental idea, and my aim is to

---

*An early version of this paper was presented to faculty at the University of San Diego Law School. I want to thank those in attendance for their helpful comments. I would also like to thank those in attendance at *The Legacy of Ronald Dworkin* (lawconf.mcmaster.ca), the McMaster University conference, which was sponsored by the Ontario Legal Philosophy Partnership, for much helpful discussion of the ideas presented in this article. Thanks also to Brian Bix, Sameer Bajaj, Ruth Chang, Miranda McGowan, Stefan Sciarffa, and Jerry Vildostegui for helpful comments and discussion of earlier drafts.

[1] Dworkin's idea applies not only to the United States Constitution, but also to relevantly similar constitutions. See Dworkin (1996). Throughout, though I talk in terms of "a constitution," I shall employ examples concerning the Constitution of the United States (US Constitution or the Constitution).

[2] For this and other criticisms of Dworkin's views, see, e.g., Alexander and Kress, (1995) and Berger (1997). See also Leiter (2004-2005) (arguing more generally that Dworkin's central ideas are deeply problematic). Dworkin has, of course, had his defenders, though they depart from his views in important ways. See, e.g., Greenberg (2009a), (2009b), and (2014); and Brink (1985), (1988), and (2001).

honor that idea by sketching an alternative approach to reading a constitution morally.[3] I shall begin by distinguishing between the idea of a moral reading of a constitution and Dworkin's own approach to reading a constitution morally. Next, I consider some of the well-known difficulties for Dworkin's approach, in order to make clear how an alternative would need to do better. I then present the basics of an alternative—what I call the *moral learning approach*. As I shall explain, the moral learning approach has a number of virtues: It can, in principle, be accepted by constitutional theorists of varying stripes, including constitutional originalists; it requires of judges only the exercise of skills that judges do possess—and must possess, if they are to be competent judges; it promises to preserve constitutional legitimacy; and it is consistent with constrained judicial decision-making, thereby preserving rule of law values and avoiding worries about what Justice Antonin Scalia has derisively called the "judge moralist."[4] The moral learning approach preserves and builds on Dworkin's key insight that constitutions should be read, insofar as the text allows, so as to reach results that show the law in its best moral light.

1. The Idea of a Moral Reading

It is important to distinguish between Dworkin's idea of reading a constitution morally and what he called *the* moral reading, for one could accept the basic idea that constitutions of a certain sort should be read morally, while disagreeing with Dworkin about precisely what this idea entails for how interpreters are to approach the task of interpretation. Natural law theorists of various sorts, for example, might agree with Dworkin's idea, but differ as to how to read a constitution morally.[5] I want to begin, then, by considering what we might glean about the basic idea of reading a constitution morally—the basic idea of *a* moral reading—from what Dworkin says about *the* moral reading of a constitution.

1.1 THE MORAL READING

In *Freedom's Law*, Dworkin describes the moral reading as "a particular way of reading and enforcing a political constitution," one that "brings political morality

---

[3]A different alternative can be found in Michael S. Moore, "A Natural Law Theory of Interpretation," 58 S. Cal. L. Rev. 277 (1985). Though their approaches differ markedly, Moore's alternative, in my view, suffers from the same principal difficulties as Dworkin's approach. There are, of course, other theorists who advocate interpreting a constitution in ways that invoke values or moral principles. See Fallon (1987).

[4]It thereby not only avoids the criticisms Dworkin's approach faces, but more general criticisms of the sort raised by Justice Scalia in his 2013 address to the North Carolina Bar Association. http:// www.huffingtonpost.com/2013/06/21/antonin-scalia-north-carolina-bar-association_n_3479874. html.

[5]See, e.g., Moore (1985).

into the heart of constitutional law."[6] As he explains it, the moral reading begins with the fact that the US Constitution—and most modern constitutions—have clauses that contain abstract moral terms, such as 'rights,' 'due process,' and 'equal protection.' The moral reading holds that constitutional clauses that are drafted in abstract moral language are "moral principles that must be applied through the exercise of moral judgment."[7] Clauses such as the free speech clause of the First Amendment of the Constitution, the due process clause of the Fifth Amendment, and the equal protection and due process clauses of the Fourteenth Amendment, "must be understood in the way their language most naturally suggests: They refer to abstract moral principles and incorporate these by reference, as limits on government's power."[8] The moral reading thus applies only to certain clauses of the Constitution and to like clauses in constitutions other than our own.

A constitution's abstract moral clauses stand in contrast to its concrete clauses. In comparing the clauses of the Constitution that are written in abstract normative language with those that are not, such as the Article II requirement that the president be at least thirty-five years old, or the Third Amendment restriction on the quartering of soldiers in citizens' homes in peacetime, Dworkin remarks that "given the words [the framers] used, we cannot sensibly interpret them as laying down any moral principle at all, even if we believe they were inspired by one."[9] They used these words to say what they would normally be used to say, which is something concrete rather than abstract and moral. In contrast, he contends, the "process of reasoning about what the framers presumably intended to say when they used the words they did," for example, in the Fourteenth Amendment Equal Protection Clause, "yields an opposite conclusion."[10]

As Laurence Tribe has observed, it is less clear than Dworkin seems to suppose which clauses of the Constitution should be understood as expressing concrete rules or requirements as opposed to abstract moral principles.[11] We might usefully distinguish between clauses that *explicitly* or *directly* express moral principles by employing normative language, and those that *implicitly* or *indirectly* reference them—that are framed in descriptive language but rest on underlying moral principles. The requirement that the president be at least thirty-five years

---

[6] Dworkin (1996: 2).

[7] Id., 6.

[8] See Id., 7, and see 8.

[9] Id., 8.

[10] Id., 8-9.

[11] In his comment on Justice Scalia's Tanner Lecture, Laurence Tribe, while agreeing with some of Dworkin's criticisms of Scalia's view, disagrees with both Scalia and Dworkin in being skeptical of the idea that we can "discover which provisions are of which sort [concrete or abstract] either by meditating about the language used or by ascertaining, through accurate use of the tools of history and psychology and biography, the empirical facts about what a finite set of actors at particular moments in our past meant to be saying. Nor do I agree that the level of abstraction or generality at which a constitutional clause or phrase is to be read is normally obvious to the astute reader...." See Tribe (1998: 68). And see Dworkin (1998).

old no doubt rests on the concern that the executive be sufficiently mature, the requirement itself, though, is pragmatic; it settles an issue that had to be settled but that could have been settled in any number of ways, consistently with its purpose. The Third Amendment restriction on the quartering of soldiers in citizens' homes in peacetime, in contrast, though framed in descriptive language, arguably references a moral principle of respect for property and privacy.[12] For present purposes, we can simply restrict our discussion to those clauses that, as Dworkin sees it, directly express moral principles by their use of normative language, but a full account of how to read a constitution morally would arguably need to address the reading of clauses that implicitly reference moral principles.

With regard to abstract moral clauses, Dworkin goes on to acknowledge that there might be disagreement about the best way to state the principles they refer to, so as to help us apply the clauses in deciding concrete cases. He indicates, though, that he himself favors stating these principles "at the most general level possible."[13] Dworkin does not make clear what favors specifying the moral principles expressed by constitutional clauses at the most general level possible, beyond the fact that the clauses contain abstract normative language. Nor does he make clear what the "most general level possible" comes to or how one would be confident that one had stated principles at that level. It may be no more clear what it means to state a principle at the most general level possible than what it means to state a principle (or a tradition) at the most specific level possible, the latter being roughly Justice Scalia's prescribed and much criticized approach to the "levels of generality problem," in footnote 6 of *Michael H. v. Gerald D.*[14] For present purposes, let us simply assume that we can identify the most general level at which to state a moral principle expressed by a constitutional clause.

Dworkin tells us that according to the moral reading, any interpreter of the Constitution, whether judge, citizen, legislator, or lawyer, ought to "interpret and apply these clauses on the understanding that they invoke moral principles about decency and justice."[15] These principles must then be applied to new issues raised

---

[12] Dworkin remarks about the Third Amendment that it "may have been inspired by a moral principle" concerned with "protecting citizen's rights to privacy"; but it "is not itself a moral principle: its content is not a general principle of privacy."(1996: 8.) He also suggests that it is a concrete application of a principle, rather than a principle. (Id.: 9) But see *Griswold v. Connecticut* (1965) (finding a right of privacy in the "penumbras" of the First, Third, Fourth, Fifth, and Ninth Amendments).

[13] Dworkin (1996: 7). Dworkin tells us, "I believe that the principles set out in the Bill of Rights, taken together, commit the United States to the following political and legal ideals: Government must treat all those subject to its dominion as having equal moral and political status; it must attempt, in good faith, to treat them all with equal concern; and it must respect whatever individual freedoms are indispensible to those ends, including but not limited to the freedoms more specifically designated in the document, such as the freedom of speech and religion."(1996: 7-8)

[14] 491 U.S. 110 (1989). More precisely, what Justice Scalia advocates is testing the claim of an asserted right against tradition at the "most specific level at which a relevant tradition protecting, or denying protection to, the asserted right can be identified." For criticism of Justice Scalia's favored approach, see Justice Brennan's dissent. See also Tribe and Dorf (1993: ch. 5).

[15] Dworkin (1996: 2).

in concrete cases in order to determine what the law is, and doing so involves making "fresh moral judgments."[16]

1.2 THE CORE IDEA

Pulling the foregoing points about the moral reading together, we might characterize the core idea that a constitution is to be read morally as follows:

> MR: When a constitution contains clauses that are framed in abstract moral terms, those clauses are to be understood as expressing general moral principles, and interpreters are to understand and apply those clauses accordingly.

This characterization of the core idea makes clear that a moral reading applies only to constitutions that contain clauses framed in abstract moral terms, and it applies only to those clauses. Because the clauses that are framed in abstract moral language would typically constitute only a small part of a written constitution, the scope of a moral reading is quite limited. As a consequence, an approach to reading a constitution morally would be but one part of a complete theory of constitutional interpretation.[17]

Different theorists may have different ideas about what is involved in applying a constitution's abstract moral clauses on the understanding that they express moral principles. But their approaches, while developing alternative ways of reading a constitution morally, would share the core idea. As a consequence, they would all aim in their differing ways to show a constitution in its best moral light.

2. Dworkin's Approach to Interpretation

Let us turn now to how Dworkin develops his core idea, that is, to his particular way of reading a constitution morally—of interpreting and applying a constitution's abstract moral clauses. I will not attempt in what follows to track whatever changes there might have been over the years to Dworkin's approach to interpretation. Instead, I shall present a reading of Dworkin that attempts to reflect later developments in his view, consistently with retaining what has been, throughout, most important in his treatment of constitutional interpretation. On this reading, there are two key components of Dworkin's approach to the moral reading of constitutions. The first component is a semantic view about the meaning of the constitutional text. The second component is an interpretive view about how to get from the semantic content of the text to the content of the law.

---

[16] Id., 3.

[17] And a theory of constitutional interpretation would be just one part of a theory of constitutional adjudication. See Moore (1985) (distinguishing a theory of interpretation from a theory of adjudication).

2.1 DWORKIN'S SEMANTIC ORIGINALISM

With regard to the first component, Dworkin appears, in some of his work, to subscribe to a version of originalism that is sometimes referred to as *original intended meaning originalism*, or at least a variant of it.[18] According to this version of originalism, interpreters should look to "speaker's meaning" to understand the meaning of constitutional clauses (perhaps together with whatever pragmatics may pertain to a written text).[19] We can see this in a passage cited earlier. The reason we should interpret certain clauses as expressing abstract moral principles is because this is what follows from the "process of reasoning about *what the framers presumably intended to say* when they used the words they did."[20] In his commentary on Justice Scalia's Tanner Lecture, Dworkin expresses a commitment to what he calls *semantic originalism*, which "insists that the rights-granting clauses be read to say what those who made them *intended to say*."[21] And he tells us that "any reader of anything must attend to *semantic intention*, because the same sounds or even words can be used with the *intention of saying different things*."[22]

Original intended meaning originalism contrasts with *original public meaning originalism*, according to which interpreters should look to what words would have been understood to mean at the time, or the *sentence meaning* of constitutional clauses. Original public meaning originalism appears to be the prevailing view at present. Theorists have largely abandoned original intended meaning originalism because of the insuperable difficulty, raised most famously by Paul Brest, of determining (possibly nonexistent) collective intent.[23] The difficulty, as

---

[18] Dworkin does say things at odds with a strict intended meaning originalism, which is why I suggest he holds a variant of the view. After the passages I quote in this paragraph from "Freedom's Law," Dworkin says this: "The framers meant, then, to enact a general principle. But which general principle? That further question must be answered by constructing different elaborations of the phrase 'equal protection of the law,' each of which we can recognize as a principle of political morality that might have won their respect, and then by asking which of these it makes most sense to attribute to them, given everything else we know." See (1998: 9). This passage is ambiguous as between at least two ways of understanding the notion of what it "makes most sense" to attribute to them. The notion could be understood as an idealization. See infra. note 27. See also Dworkin (2006: 120) (treating the effort to determine what the authors of a text intended to say as an exercise in constructive interpretation). Alternatively, it could be understood as an appeal to evidence, so that what it makes more sense to attribute to them is what we have most evidence for attributing to them. It is not clear, though, that the approach of constructing different elaborations of the phrase "equal protection of the law" makes sense if what we are looking for is evidence of their intended meaning.

[19] For a discussion of pragmatics and law, see Marmor (2011). See also Moore (1985: 290-291) (suggesting that a theory of law "has little need for a theory of pragmatics").

[20] Dworkin (1996: 8-9, emphasis added).

[21] Dworkin (1998: 119, emphasis added). The contrast Dworkin draws is with what he calls "expectation originalism," according to which these clauses must "be understood to have the consequences that those who made them expected them to have."

[22] Id., 117 (emphasis added).

[23] See Brest (1980). See Barnett (1999: 621) (explaining the shift to public meaning). See also Barnett (2005). For some defenders of original intended meaning originalism, see, e.g., Alexander (2011: 87-98) and Michael (2009).

he presents it, concerns not only how to ascertain the substantive and interpretive intentions of long dead framers and ratifiers, but also how to aggregate those intentions.[24]

Dworkin was alert to these difficulties, and this is reflected in his approach to identifying the original intended meaning. Committed originalists who favor a speaker's meaning view would ordinarily engage in historical inquiry to discover the framers' or ratifiers' intended meaning; and they would be critical of Dworkin for failing to produce historical evidence for his claims about the intended meaning of the Constitution's moral clauses.[25] On Dworkin's approach, although history is, he says, crucial, identifying intended meaning is not a matter of purely historical inquiry but, rather, involves a kind of idealization.[26] In his commentary on Scalia's Tanner Lecture, he explains,

> When we are trying to decide what someone meant to say, in circumstances like these, we are deciding which clarifying *translation* of his inscriptions is best. It is a matter of complex and subtle philosophical argument what such translations consist in, and how they are possible—how, for example, we weave assumptions about what the speaker believes and wants, and about what it would be rational for him to believe and want, into decisions about what he meant to say. The difficulties are greatly increased when we are translating not the utterances of a real person but those of an institution like a legislature. We rely on personification—we suppose that the institution has semantic intentions of its own—and it is difficult to understand what sense that makes, or what special standards we should use to discover or construct such intentions.[27]

We have to choose, he thinks, between clarifying translations in identifying the semantic intentions of the speaker, and the spelling out of such translations partly involves assessing complex counterfactuals that idealize the speaker's beliefs and wants.[28] Dworkin concludes, with respect to the Equal Protection Clause, that the "best understanding" of the framers' semantic intentions is that they intended to "lay down a general principle of political morality that condemns racial segregation."[29]

---

[24] Brest is not careful about treating originalism as a view about the semantics of legal texts. I use the term *substantive* because he often treats originalism as concerned with intentions in a broader sense.

[25] For such criticism of Dworkin, see Alexander (2016). See also Berger (1997: 1105).

[26] Dworkin (1996: 8).

[27] Dworkin (1998: 117-118). Dworkin underplays or perhaps misses a critical distinction between his view and Scalia's, because Scalia's textualism commits him to a public meaning version of originalism, which rejects Dworkin's semantic originalism. But, at least officially, Scalia does agree with Dworkin in rejecting expectation originalism.

[28] Id., 120. See also Dworkin (2006: 129, emphasis added): "we decide what propositions a text contains by *assigning* semantic intentions to those who made the text, and we do this by attempting to make the best sense we can of what they did when they did it."

[29] Dworkin (1998: 119. See Brink (2016), interpreting Dworkin as advancing an "originalism of principle."

Although these passages strike me as quite strong evidence for attributing to Dworkin a version of the semantic thesis of original intended meaning originalism—what we might call "ideal intended meaning originalism"—there is room for alternative interpretations. As noted earlier, Dworkin does say, for example, in explaining the moral reading, that the Constitution's abstract moral clauses "must be understood in the way their language most naturally suggests."[30] Or again, in talking about the Constitution's concrete clauses, he remarks, that the framers "said what the words would normally be used to say."[31] These passages might seem to suggest a public meaning view, or perhaps, the view that ordinary meaning is a defeasible best indicator of intended meaning. Because legal speakers presumably intend and aim to be understood, and the best way to ensure this is to use words with their ordinary meanings, the distinction between intended meaning and public meaning may, in the end, matter little to constitutional interpretation. What is clear is that Dworkin did not think that the framers either meant to enact or in fact enacted their own views about, say, what equal protection requires; rather they meant to enact and did enact what equal protection really requires, whatever that turns out to be.[32] So much is clear, he thinks, from the words they chose.

---

[30] Dworkin (1996: 7). Dworkin does, after all, rely on the types of words used—normative words—in identifying certain clauses as expressing moral principles.

[31] Dworkin (1996: 8). See also Dworkin (2006: 122).

[32] Dworkin (1998: 118, 119) and (2006: 122-124). See also Dworkin (1998: 120-124), criticizing Scalia for treating the abstract clauses of the Constitution as "dated." Was Dworkin's acceptance of semantic originalism enough to make him a constitutional originalist? That depends on what it takes for a theory to count as originalist. Originalism, of course, is not a single constitutional theory, but a family of theories. As I understand the interfamilial disputes, they chiefly concern two things. The first, which we have already considered, concerns the proper account of the meaning of the constitutional text: is it the framers' or ratifiers' intended meaning (speaker's meaning) or the public meaning (sentence meaning)? The second concerns how to get from the meaning of the constitutional text to the content of the law. In my view, merely to accept one or another semantic view is not to accept a constitutional theory; it is simply to accept a theory of meaning in the philosophy of language, a theory that might well be accepted by many non-originalists. In order to have an originalist constitutional theory, that is, a full theory of interpretation or adjudication, one has to have a distinctively originalist account of how interpreters are to get from the semantic content to the content of the law. The second dispute concerns exactly this. Among originalists, there seem to be four types of views about how to get from the semantic content of the Constitution to the content of the law. A first view says that the semantic content of the text itself gives us the content of the law. I have not seen a well-developed theory, however, of how that might be, and as many originalists would agree, although text may be sufficient to give the content of the law in which the meaning of the text is plain, text is unlikely to be sufficient to give the legal content of the constitutional clauses that chiefly concerned Dworkin. A second view would treat the content of the law as given by the semantic content of the text together with the original expected applications. Most, if not all, contemporary originalists disavow what is sometimes called "original expected applications originalism." (But see Berger (1997: 1106-1107).) They emphasize that what was enacted was the text, not what the framers or ratifiers expected would follow from the text. What the framers or ratifiers of a provision expected would follow from its enactment or fall within the extension of a clause is obviously not irrelevant to constitutional interpretation. But original expected applications cannot plausibly be treated either as providing the meaning of a constitutional provision or as setting the parameters of that provision's application. As some originalists correctly maintain,

2.2 FIT AND JUSTIFY

Dworkin tells us that because certain constitutional clauses express moral principles, they "must be applied through the exercise of moral judgment."[33] But what precisely does this moral judgment involve? Here we arrive at the second component of Dworkin's moral reading.

As Dworkin describes his approach to legal interpretation in *Law's Empire*, the interpreter is to engage in what he calls *constructive interpretation*, which involves "imposing purpose on an object or practice in order to make of it the best possible example of the form or genre to which it is taken to belong."[34] A participant interpreting a practice proposes a value for it by "describing some scheme of interests or goals or principles the practice can be taken to serve or express or exemplify."[35] The problem is that the raw behavioral data of the practice—what people do in different circumstances—may underdetermine ascriptions of value. When that is the case, each interpreter's view will reflect his or her idea as to "which interpretation proposes the most value for the practice—which one shows it in the better light, all things considered."[36]

There is also indeterminacy when it comes to the moral principles expressed by the abstract moral clauses of the Constitution. The semantic content of those clauses does not specify a particular conception of the concepts that they contain—a particular "conception of the principle," they express. As a consequence, interpreters must choose between competing conceptions in order to resolve the case at hand. Dworkin describes two dimensions to interpretation.

---

they might be *evidence* of original meaning. But what is needed to make use of expected applications as evidence of semantic content rather than as evidence of the content of the law is some account of how expected applications provide evidence of meaning. As far as I am aware, no originalist has yet offered such an account. In fact, originalists are often fairly criticized for slipping and invoking expected applications in determining the content of the law, rather than semantic content. In his commentary on Justice Scalia's Tanner Lecture, Dworkin criticized Scalia on just this score. See Dworkin (1998). The third and fourth types of view appeal, respectively, to "original interpretive methods" and to "constitutional construction," on one or another view of how such construction must take place. For one controversial example of the latter sort of view, see Barnett (2005, ch. 5). Each of these final two approaches has its strengths and weaknesses. The currently favored view among originalists appears to be constitutional construction, but there seems to be no widely shared view as to how it should proceed. Whether Dworkin's moral reading approach counts as a form of originalism depends not simply on his semantic originalism but on whether his approach to interpreting the Constitution or adjudicating constitutional questions—constructive interpretation—counts as a form of recognizably originalist constitutional construction. For related discussion, see Goldsworthy (2000). See also, Alexander (2016), and see Brink (2016). One bit of evidence against counting Dworkin as an originalist is his stated position that "precedent and practice over time can in principle supersede even so basic a piece of interpretive data as the Constitution's text when no way of reconciling both text and practice in an overall constructive interpretation can be found" (2006: 128-129).

[33] Dworkin (1996: 6).
[34] Dworkin (1986: 52).
[35] Id.
[36] Id.

First, there is the dimension of *fit*, which seems, in some of Dworkin's writing, to be a threshold condition for candidate conceptions of a principle.[37] Fit is a matter, roughly, of consistency with the extant legal materials, in particular, in the case of constitutional interpretation, with precedent. Dworkin offers a kind of counterfactual test of fit, namely, whether the outcome in precedent cases would have been the same had judges been applying the principle understood in a particular way.[38] The second dimension is that of *justification*. The interpreter must select from among those competing conceptions of a principle that pass the test of fit the one that shows the law in its best light from the standpoint of political morality.

As an illustration, Dworkin describes his ideal judge, Hercules, as trying to determine the "dimensions" of equal protection, and in particular, the "right not to be the victim of official state-imposed racial discrimination."[39] He imagines Hercules as constructing three accounts of this right, what he calls the *suspect classifications, banned categories*, and *banned sources* accounts. According to the suspect classifications account, the right against discrimination follows from the "more general right people have to be treated as equals according to whichever conception of equality their state pursues."[40] This standard requires only that groups that have historically been mistreated "receive the right consideration in the overall balance, and a state may meet that standard even though it treats them differently from others."[41] This account might, for example, allow for segregated schools. According to the banned categories account, which offers a principle of "color-blindness," "the Constitution does recognize a distinct right against discrimination as a trump over any state's conception of the general interests."[42] On this account, the right not to be the victim of official state-imposed racial discrimination is violated when the law makes distinctions among groups of citizens based on particular designated categories. Finally, the banned sources account advances a principle that "prohibits legislation that could be justified only by counting, within the overall calculation determining where the general interest lies, preferences directly or indirectly arising from prejudice."[43] The concern

---

[37] In some places, though, a natural reading of Dworkin suggests a tie-breaker rather than a threshold view. Whereas on a threshold view, once a certain threshold of fit has been satisfied, the dimension of justification takes over, on the tie-breaker view, justification functions as a tie-breaker between interpretations that equally satisfy the dimension of fit. For helpful discussion distinguishing these ways of reading Dworkin, see Shpall, "Dworkin's Literary Analogy" (manuscript).

[38] Id., 242. In discussing how his imaginary judge, Hercules, would approach deciding *McLoughlin v. O'Brian*, (1983) A.C. reversing (1981) Q.B. 599, he says that "Hercules begins testing each interpretation on his short list by asking whether a single political official could have given the verdicts of the precedent cases if that official were consciously and coherently enforcing the principles that form that interpretation."(242)

[39] Id., 382.

[40] Id., 382-383.

[41] Id., 383.

[42] Id., 383-384.

[43] Id., 385.

here is with governmental action that makes distinctions among groups based on "tainted preferences" or prejudice against certain groups.

Hercules must now consider how well each of these accounts "fits and justifies, and so provides an eligible interpretation of, American constitutional structure and practice."[44] He must determine, that is, which of these accounts gives the correct theory of the force of the Fourteenth Amendment's requirement of equal protection of the law. The question, as Dworkin puts it, is "Which is the Constitution's theory?"[45] He imagines Hercules looking at the extant legal materials, *Plessy v. Ferguson* and *Brown v. Board of Education*, moving on to *Regents of the University of California v. Bakke*, and selecting from among these accounts the one that shows the law in its best light.[46] Dworkin argues that Hercules would reject the suspect classifications account; it might have "been adequate under tests of fairness and fit" at the time *Plessy v. Ferguson* was decided, but it is not adequate by the time of *Brown v. Board of Education.*[47] If it is just a matter of deciding *Brown*, neither of the remaining two accounts fit the extant law better than the other, so Hercules need not decide between them. When it comes to *Bakke*, however, Hercules must choose between the banned categories and banned sources accounts. Ultimately, Dworkin argues, Hercules would choose the banned sources account, according to which preferences that are rooted in prejudice against one group cannot figure in a collective justification of a policy that disadvantages that group. Dworkin walks us through what Hercules' reasons would be for concluding that the banned sources account, which would permit some affirmative action programs, shows the law in its best light.

In his introduction to *Freedom's Law*, Dworkin offers the following example to clarify his view, with a rather different characterization of what the interpreter must do. The First Amendment, he tells us, expresses a moral principle against governmental censorship or control of individual speech.

> So when some novel or controversial constitutional issue arises—
> about whether, for instance, the First Amendment permits laws against
> pornography—people who form an opinion must decide how an abstract
> principle is best understood. They must decide whether the true ground of
> the moral principle that condemns censorship, in the form in which this
> principle has been incorporated into American law, extends to the case of
> pornography.[48]

---

[44] Id., 387.

[45] Id., 387.

[46] *Plessy v. Ferguson* (1896) (upholding segregated railway cars and announcing the doctrine of "separate but equal"); *Brown v. Board of Education* (1954) (holding that segregation in public schools violates the Equal Protection Clause and overturning the *Plessy* doctrine of separate but equal); *Regents of the University of California v. Bakke* (1978) (striking down as in violation of the Equal Protection Clause the UC Davis medical school's affirmative action program, which had adopted a quota system for admissions).

[47] Id. Dworkin, curiously, talks about "fitting attitudes in the community," which seems quite a different matter from fitting extant legal materials, and one which presents its own difficulties.

[48] Dworkin (1996: 2).

Dworkin says two different things in this passage: (1) that interpreters must decide on the best understanding of the moral principle expressed by a clause of the Constitution; (2) that they must decide "the true ground of the principle." It is not entirely clear what Dworkin means by deciding on the true ground of a principle. But in light of his earlier discussion of "constructive interpretation," he might have had in mind that interpreters must decide what values make sense of a principle and its importance. The idea that interpreters must decide on the best understanding of a moral principle expressed by a clause of the Constitution is not, I take it, part of the core idea that a constitution is to be read morally. Rather, it is a distinctive part of Dworkin's own way of reading a constitution morally. With regard to deciding on the best understanding of a moral principle, it is here that the interpreter must presumably exercise moral judgment. And it is here that concerns about what constrains the interpreter arise, a point to which I will return momentarily.

2.3 PROBLEMS FOR DWORKIN'S MORAL READING

The moral reading, according to Dworkin, is in fact widely used by judges, even if its use is not explicitly acknowledged. What is more, he contends, no viable alternative to the moral reading of the Constitution exists. Why then have so many dismissed it? According to Dworkin's diagnosis, opposition to the moral reading stems from a certain misconstrual of the core debate among constitutional theorists and interpreters, together with a certain inadequate conception of democracy. The misconstrual says that the debate concerns whether judges should alter the Constitution, imposing their own moral views on the people, or whether they should merely interpret and apply it. The moral reading supposedly commits one to the former view, and critics accordingly deem it anti-democratic. The inadequate conception of democracy that underlies their criticism rests on the majoritarian premise, according to which "political procedures should be designed so that, at least on important matters, the decision that is reached is the decision that a majority or plurality of citizens favors, or would favor if it had adequate information and enough time for reflection."[49]

Dworkin argues that the debate has always, instead, been about how to interpret the Constitution and that the moral reading of the Constitution is not opposed to democracy, correctly conceived. He goes on to defend what he calls the "constitutional conception of democracy," which abandons the majoritarian premise and takes as the defining aim of democracy that "collective decisions be made by political institutions whose structure, composition, and practices treat all members of the community, as individuals, with equal concern and respect."[50] Dworkin maintains that the "only substantial objection" to the moral reading is that it "offends democracy."[51] Because he believes that his arguments show

---

[49] Id., 15-16.
[50] Id., 17.
[51] Id., 15.

that objection to be mistaken, Dworkin would have us conclude that continuing opposition to the moral reading is unfounded.

I agree with Dworkin that appeals to morality in constitutional interpretation need not offend against democracy. For example, if Dworkin is right about the original meaning of the moral clauses of the Constitution,[52] and if he is right that interpreters must engage in moral reasoning to interpret the Constitution in light of its original meaning, then the real complaint would be not that his view offends against democracy, but that the Constitution places limits on majoritarian processes. This might be either because the Constitution's conception of democracy is a constitutional rather than a pure majoritarian conception, as Dworkin suggests, or alternatively, because democracy is just one among the values the Constitution serves. But Dworkin is mistaken to think that concerns about its alleged anti-democratic character provide the *only* substantial objection to the moral reading.

The more serious objections concern the defensibility of Dworkin's way of reading the Constitution morally, and these objections fall into two main categories. The first concerns whether the approach is sufficiently determinate, and so whether it preserves rule of law values and constitutional legitimacy. The second concerns whether judges are well equipped to employ that approach, notwithstanding Dworkin's claim that they already do.

To begin with, we might ask about the details of the "fit and justification" of constructive interpretation in an effort to pin down the exact decision procedure or process of practical reasoning the interpreter is supposed to follow. These include questions about what exactly principles are supposed to fit with, about the precise role of contemporary community attitudes and values in assessing fit, about how relative fit of principles is to be assessed, and about how the dimensions of fit and justification are to be weighed or balanced against each other.[53] These questions point us to fundamental problems with Dworkin's account.[54] The first concerns whether constructive interpretation is sufficiently determinate to constrain conscientious judges. Consider each dimension of "fit and justification." The notion of fit is rather metaphorical. Dworkin does not offer clear criteria of fit. Moreover, no specification of a constitutional principle will fit every bit of the relevant extant legal materials, so some bits will have to be treated

---

[52] As noted earlier, originalists have been critical of Dworkin on the grounds that he does not offer historical evidence for his semantic claims. See note 26.

[53] For some discussion of the latter problem, see Brink (2016).

[54] I began with Dworkin's account of the moral reading in *Freedom's Law* but have turned back to his account of interpretation in *Law's Empire*. One might wonder whether this is fair. Dworkin's discussion of the moral reading occurs in the introduction to a collection of essays written at various times and which Dworkin reports that he has not updated or substantively altered. What he says in the introduction suggests that he takes the various essays to exemplify the moral reading, and he does not indicate that he has altered his view of that approach, nor does he remark on any differences between the interpretive approach in *Law's Empire* and the moral reading approach in *Freedom's Law*. This leaves entirely open, of course, that the accounts of interpretation in these two works differ in important ways, even if this was unremarked on by Dworkin himself.

as outliers. But Dworkin offers us no account of how much in the way of fit is required or of when a precedent case is properly treated as an outlier.

Matters are, if anything, worse when it comes to the dimension of justification. Consider Hercules' choice between the banned categories and banned sources accounts. Given how contested the morality of affirmative action is, we should expect that conscientious judges will disagree about which of these accounts is more just. Generalizing, we can expect—as Dworkin himself acknowledges— that conscientious judges will disagree about which conception of a principle (or right) shows the law in its best moral light. Dworkin's account yields a certain picture of the nature of constitutional facts; they are, at least in the case of the Constitution's abstract moral clauses, facts about what would be required, for- bidden, or permitted by the conceptions of the principles those clauses express that best fit and justify the extant law. But the indeterminacy of constructive interpretation would seem to make it no more likely that judges who follow the approach faithfully would discover the constitutional facts, rather than simply enforce their preferred moral views.

Dworkin, of course, denies this. He remarks that

> Judges may not read their own convictions into the Constitution. They may not read the abstract moral clauses as expressing any particular moral judgment, no matter how much that judgment appeals to them, unless they find it consistent in principle with the structural design of the Constitution as a whole, and also with the dominant lines of past constitutional interpre- tation by other judges. They must regard themselves as partners with other officials, past and future, who together elaborate a coherent constitutional morality, and they must take care to see that what they contribute fits with the rest.[55]

But this fails to answer the worry, because it does not directly address the issue of what constrains justification beyond the criterion of fit. And insofar as it appeals to fit, it simply invites again the worries raised about that first dimension of interpretation.

Even if there were, in principle, determinate answers to be yielded by construc- tive interpretation, judges are arguably not well suited to engage in it. They are not trained in the requisite skills to discern competing specifications of abstract moral principles or to assess their relative merits. The fact that judges have some- times decided cases in ways that strike us as paradigms of justice, like *Brown*, does not show otherwise, for the best explanation of how they reached these outcomes is likely not that they were (perhaps unself-consciously) following Dworkin's

---

[55] Dworkin (1996: 10). Dworkin offers as an example that "a judge who believes that abstract justice requires economic equality cannot interpret the equal protection clause as making equal- ity of wealth or collective ownership of productive resources, a constitutional requirement, because that interpretation simply does not fit American history or practice, or the rest of the Constitution."

moral reading.[56] In any case, even if they had the requisite skills, we should expect that conscientious judges will differ in the constitutional morality they believe best fits and justifies the extant law. Finally, in a diverse society in which people have differing moral views, the role of judges interpreting a constitution is arguably not to decide among such constitutional moralities but, rather, consistently with text and history, to preserve the constitution as the basis of an "overlapping consensus."[57] For more than one reason, then, I think Dworkin's critics are right in their suspicions that Dworkin's *way* of reading the Constitution morally places too little in the way of constraints on constitutional interpretation.

3. Reading Constitutions Morally

Much more would need to be said to begin to do justice to Dworkin's rich theory of interpretation. My point in raising the foregoing difficulties is simply to put us in mind of how an alternative approach to reading constitutions morally would need to do better. Despite problems with Dworkin's moral reading, the idea that a constitution should be read morally seems correct. It would be helpful to begin by considering why: What would rationally motivate the idea of a moral reading in the first place? And why continue to look for a way to read a constitution morally, given the problems with Dworkin's approach to the moral reading?

Begin with the latter question. Suppose that one has concerns about judges engaging in the kind of philosophical inquiry into the best expression of abstract moral clauses of the Constitution in the way Dworkin's moral reading envisions. Suppose, to put it another way, one is skeptical of the idea that judges either can or should engage in efforts to select from among competing conceptions of equal protection the conception that shows the law in its best moral light. Suppose further, however, that one thinks it likely that certain clauses of the Constitution express abstract moral principles, that the Fourteenth Amendment guarantee of the equal protection of the laws, for example, expresses a moral principle of equal protection, and so a commitment to whatever equal protection really requires. Fidelity to those clauses would seem to require that we find an alternative way of reading the Constitution morally, that we read it in a way that does justice to the meaning of those clauses.

The motivation for a moral reading of constitutions runs yet deeper, to the normative supremacy of morality and the corresponding requirements of constitutional legitimacy. Although the assumption is not wholly uncontroversial,

---

[56] After all, judges commonly employ alternative approaches to constitutional interpretation or simply follow doctrinal tests and precedent.

[57] See Rawls (1993). As Rawls defines it, an overlapping consensus "consists of all the reasonable opposing religious, philosophical, and moral doctrines likely to persist over generations and to gain a sizable body of adherents in a more of less just constitutional regime, a regime in which the criterion of justice is that political conception itself."

morality is commonly assumed to have overriding authority. In conflicts between self-interest and morality, aesthetics and morality, and law and morality, morality trumps. The overriding authority of morality bears in turn on the legitimacy of a constitution. On one view about the legitimacy of constitutions, a view that I find appealing, a constitution is legitimate when its content and the processes of law-making that it specifies are such as to give rise to laws that one has pro tanto moral obligation to obey; and in order for those law-making processes to give rise to laws that one has *pro tanto* moral obligation to obey, the laws to which it gives rise must tend, as a consequence of its content and law-making processes, to comport with morality, at least over time.[58]

Of course, even if a constitution is legitimate in this way, specific laws can fail to comport with morality. We well know, based on painful experience, that we can be mistaken about what morality requires, forbids, or permits. This fact reinforces the importance of reading a constitution morally, but it directs efforts to read a constitution morally in a particular way. Respect for the overriding authority of morality and humility about our own limitations support an approach to interpreting a constitution that constrains interpretation, while allowing for *moral learning* to be reflected in the law.[59] One part of the law-making process is the part played by the courts, and to the extent that a court effectively interprets a constitution in a way that allows moral learning to be reflected in the law, the resultant law will be more likely to comport with morality.[60] Interpretation will thereby tend, at least over time, to be legitimacy enhancing.

The question now is whether there is an account of what it is to read a constitution morally that gets us this result. Is there a way to read a constitution morally that has greater determinacy than Dworkin's approach, and so preserves rule of law values and constitutional legitimacy? Is there a way to read a constitution morally that does not call on judges to exercise skills for which they have no special training or to settle on a constitutional morality? I want to offer some suggestions regarding how to think our way toward a more plausible version of the thesis that a constitution ought to be read morally. Before presenting these suggestions, though, I want to offer some general remarks that will help to make sense of my approach.

---

[58] This is roughly the view advanced by Randy Barnett, but one can take differing views as to what it takes to comport with morality. On Barnett's view, that means protecting and not violating negative rights. Anyone who believes there are also positive rights, will reject the specifics of Barnett's view, but we can here see how the general idea would help to motivate the moral reading of constitutions, without settling precisely what it takes to comport with morality. See Barnett (2005: Ch. 2).

[59] I take this to be true of any approach to reading a constitution morally, but some approaches may be more apt for making moral learning possible, without running into the problems faced by Dworkin's approach to the moral reading.

[60] What it is for moral learning to take place in the law is no different from what it is for moral learning to take place outside of the law. And whatever we say about *who* learns when moral learning takes place outside of the law, we should say comparable things about who learns when moral learning is reflected in the law.

3.1 EXTRA-CONSTITUTIONAL CONSTRAINTS
ON CONSTITUTIONAL INTERPRETATION

For purposes of sketching an alternative approach to reading a constitution morally, I will make certain assumptions. First, I will assume that Dworkin was correct when he claimed that certain clauses of our constitution—those framed in normative language—express abstract moral principles, whether this is true as a matter of what the framers intended to say in using the words they used, as a matter of the original public meaning of the clauses, or simply as a matter of long-standing constitutional practice. Second, I will also assume that the semantic content of these clauses does not alone determine the content of the law—that we must engage in a kind of specialized practical reasoning to adjudicate constitutional questions when it comes to these clauses in a way that we need not when it comes to many of the concrete clauses of a constitution.[61] My interest lies with certain elements of that practical reasoning. Finally, to simplify, I will talk in terms of the US Constitution, though my remarks are intended to apply to any constitution that contains clauses that express like moral principles, that is, clauses requiring equal protection, due process, and so on.

Let us start with what I take to be an obvious, if underappreciated, point: Persons who engage in constitutional interpretation and adjudication are bound by extra-constitutional norms and constraints simply in virtue of the fact that they are engaged in practical reasoning. Consider some examples.

Suppose that the framers had false beliefs about the correct theory of meaning in the philosophy of language. To make the hypothetical a bit more concrete, suppose that they accepted an intended meaning theory, whereas the public meaning theory is correct. Suppose further that they expected and intended that the constitution they had drafted would be understood in light of the intended meaning theory. Perhaps they had even included a little preamble to that effect: "All future interpreters of this Constitution shall construe its provisions according to the correct theory of meaning and, therefore, heed our intended meanings." Would we be bound in interpreting the Constitution to try to discover the intended meaning of its provisions? I take it that the answer is *no*.[62] If the correct theory of meaning is the public meaning theory, then if we want to understand the meaning of the Constitution, we had better not interpret it in the way the framers expected and intended. If interpreters are to understand the meaning of the text they are

---

[61] I call this *practical reasoning*, because at least in the case of judicial decision-making, it is reasoning that issues in an order. But it would be fair to say that judges interpreting a constitution are at the same time engaged in a specialized kind of theoretical reasoning that calls for attention to text, history, and practice and that issues in claims about the content of the law that provide the basis for the outcome in a given case.

[62] Unless, that is, there is a good case to be made that even the meaning of a prescriptive text is a normative issue that could be settled by practical reasoning. I suspect that there may, in fact, be a decent case to be made, but I won't explore the matter further here.

interpreting, they are constrained in their activity, other things equal, by how texts get their meaning.[63]

Constitutional interpreters and adjudicators engage in a special kind of practical reasoning and must draw inferences from the considerations before them. Indeed, if they are to engage successfully in practical reasoning, if they are to draw correct inferences, they are constrained by the rules of logical inference. Adherence to the rules of logical inference is not a legal requirement, it is a requirement of any practical reasoning whatsoever, and so it is a requirement of legal practical reasoning.

Practical reasoning must make use not only of logic, but also of relevant information. It is therefore constrained by the facts, and as a consequence, practical reasoners are bound by standards of empirical evidence. Legal practical reasoners are likewise bound by standards of empirical evidence. Practical reasoners, including legal practical reasoners, are rationally bound to make use of the best information currently available, as determined by the best science of the day.[64]

Now, as I have said, I take the claim that persons who engage in constitutional interpretation and adjudication are bound by extra-constitutional norms and constraints to be obviously true. But notice that although the particular norms and constraints I have discussed are extra-constitutional, it is doubtful that anyone would protest that they do not appear in the text of the Constitution. It is doubtful that anyone would protest that the interpreter who reads the Constitution understanding how texts get their meaning or who adheres to standards of empirical evidence and rules of logical inference in her reasoning is importing her personal preferences or values, or "taking sides in the culture wars."

3.2 TOWARD A MORAL READING OF CONSTITUTIONS

What is the importance of such extra-constitutional norms and constraints for a moral reading of constitutions? Consider that those of us who study moral philosophy and work as moral philosophers disagree as much as any group of people about what the correct moral principles are—about the best understanding of equal protection, for example. The work of moral philosophers is in large part the work of developing and defending competing conceptions of our moral concepts. Interestingly, though, theoretical disagreement in moral philosophy is arguably greater than disagreement about many more particular moral issues. A common way of explaining this would appeal to the fact that views about particular moral issues often depend critically on empirical claims and inferences from these claims, together with one or another moral principle. Given the tight connection between moral and nonmoral facts—the supervenience of moral facts

---

[63] This is, of course, not to say that a philosophical theory of meaning somehow settles the semantic content of constitutional clauses; it certainly does not settle their legal content.

[64] The idea of rational criticism as involving appeal to facts and logic plays a key role in a number of metaethical theories. See, e.g., Brandt (1979), and Railton (1986a) and (1986b).

on non-moral facts—this should be unsurprising. Even if we may disagree about moral principles, we can rationally agree that a factual claim in support of a moral conclusion is false or outstrips the evidence for it; we can agree that an inference to a moral conclusion is fallacious or displays poor inductive reasoning. Without agreeing in their theories, moral philosophers can agree on the facts and on the merits of particular arguments. As a consequence, particular moral views are subject to rational criticism even if we cannot settle our theoretical disagreements. When we subject particular moral views to such criticism, ruling out certain views and leaving others standing, we are engaged in a process of moral learning.

What it is important to notice is that subjecting moral views to rational criticism in these ways does not depend on any peculiarly philosophical skills. Students in introductory applied ethics courses are often quick to spot invalid or unsound arguments, even as they remain unable to sort out the claims of competing moral theories. Subjecting moral views to rational criticism based on logic, facts, and standards of evidence requires only good skills of practical reasoning and sensitivity to the standards that govern all practical reasoning. But as I have explained, these are standards that already place normative constraints on constitutional interpreters.

My suggestion regarding an alternative approach to reading a constitution morally comes to this: Interpreters should interpret a constitution or adjudicate constitutional questions involving abstract moral clauses of a constitution in a way that allows moral learning to take place by making use of such formal, extraconstitutional norms and constraints. A few examples may help to explain how standards of practical reasoning might allow moral learning to take place in the constitutional context.

Consider the move from *Plessy v. Ferguson*,[65] which embraced the doctrine of separate but equal, to *Brown v. Board of Education*,[66] which rejected that doctrine in the context of public education as in violation of the Equal Protection Clause of the Fourteenth Amendment. The rejection of *Plessy* arguably did not require choosing among competing conceptions of the moral principle expressed by the Equal Protection Clause of the Fourteenth Amendment. What it did require was the appreciation of facts about the effects of state-sponsored and enforced segregation, an appreciation sorely missing in *Plessy* but striking in *Brown*. Compare some of the language of the cases. Here is *Plessy*:

> We consider the underlying fallacy of the plaintiff's argument to consist in the assumption that the enforced separation of the two races stamps the colored race with a badge of inferiority. If this be so, it is not by reason of anything found in the act, but solely because the colored race chooses to put that construction upon it.[67]

---

[65] 163 U.S. 537 (1896).
[66] 347 U.S. 483 (1954).
[67] I63 U.S. 537, 551.

Now, the following is from *Brown:*

> To separate [students] from others of similar age and qualifications solely because of their race generates a feeling of inferiority as to their status in the community that may affect their hearts and minds in a way unlikely ever to be undone. The effect of this separation on their educational opportunities was well stated by a finding in the Kansas case by a court which nevertheless felt compelled to rule against the Negro plaintiffs:
>
> "Segregation of white and colored children in public schools has a detrimental effect upon the colored children. The impact is greater when it has the sanction of the law, for the policy of separating the races is usually interpreted as denoting the inferiority of the negro group. A sense of inferiority affects the motivation of a child to learn. Segregation with the sanction of law, therefore, has a tendency to [retard] the educational and mental development of negro children and to deprive them of some of the benefits they would receive in a racial[ly] integrated school system."
>
> *Whatever may have been the extent of psychological knowledge at the time of Plessy v. Ferguson, this finding is amply supported by modern authority.* Any language in *Plessy v. Ferguson* contrary to this finding is rejected.[68]

Consider next *Romer v. Evans*,[69] which struck down Colorado's Amendment 2 to the Colorado state constitution on the grounds that it violated the Equal Protection Clause, failing to pass even rational basis review. Again, reaching the outcome in *Romer* did not require generation of and choice among more specific principles under equal protection, nor from a doctrinal perspective, did it require finding that homosexuals constitute a suspect or quasi-suspect class. Justice Anthony Kennedy's arguments suggest two formal reasons of the sort we have been considering for striking down the amendment on the grounds that it does not pass even the lowest level of review. He first explains the contours of the Court's doctrinal tests.

> The Fourteenth Amendment's promise that no person shall be denied the equal protection of the laws must coexist with the practical necessity that most legislation classifies for one purpose or another, with resulting disadvantage to various groups or persons...We have attempted to reconcile the principle with the reality by stating that, if a law neither burdens a fundamental right nor targets a suspect class, we will uphold the legislative classification so long as it bears a rational relation to some legitimate end.[70]

Amendment 2, Justice Kennedy remarks, "fails, indeed defies, even this conventional inquiry."[71]

---

[68] 347 U.S. 483, 494-495 (emphasis added).
[69] 517 U.S. 620 (1996).
[70] 517 U.S. 620, 631.
[71] Id.

The first of the reasons for striking down the amendment that is of interest for present purposes is that its extraordinary breadth was "*so discontinuous with the reasons offered for it* that the amendment seems inexplicable by anything but animus toward the class that it affects; it lacks a rational relationship to legitimate state interests."[72] Here, Justice Kennedy treats the gap between the reasons offered in support of the amendment and the disability the amendment imposed on homosexuals—a problem with the logic of the state's position—as showing a lack of rational relationship that suggested an illegitimate purpose.

The second problem with Amendment 2 that is of interest for present purposes concerned its scope, which denied to persons identified by a "single trait . . . protection across the board."[73] Justice Kennedy explains,

> The resulting disqualification of a class of persons from the right to seek specific protection from the law is unprecedented in our jurisprudence. The absence of precedent for Amendment 2 is itself instructive; "[d]iscriminations of an unusual character especially suggest careful consideration to determine whether they are obnoxious to the constitutional provision."
>
> Central both to the idea of the rule of law and to our own Constitution's guarantee of equal protection is the principle that government and each of its parts remain open on impartial terms to all who seek its assistance . . . Respect for this principle explains why laws singling out a certain class of citizens for disfavored legal status or general hardships are rare. *A law declaring that in general it shall be more difficult for one group of citizens than for all others to seek aid from the government is itself a denial of equal protection of the laws in the most literal sense.*[74]

Here, we see an additional and unusual move, but another formal move. For Justice Kennedy makes a kind of conceptual point. If anything constitutes a denial of equal protection, it is a blanket denial, to one group, of the ability to seek equal protection.[75]

Lawrence v. Texas,[76] which overturned the Supreme Court's decision in *Bowers v. Hardwick*[77] on due process grounds, provides another illustration. The crucial difference between these cases, for present purposes, is the Court's rejection in *Lawrence* of the Court's position in *Bowers* that the bare fact that the majority of a state thinks conduct immoral is a sufficient basis for a criminal law. Justice Kennedy's arguments in *Lawrence* are less clear than would be optimal, but what

---

[72] 517 U.S. 620, 632 (emphasis added).

[73] 517 U.S. 620, 633.

[74] 517 U.S. 620, 633 (emphasis added).

[75] Much more needs to be said to understand precisely the move that Justice Kennedy is making, of course. But what is important to see is that there is no importation of controversial moral principles at work.

[76] 539 U.S. 558 (2003).

[77] 478 U.S. 186 (1986).

is critical to recognize is the work that can be done simply by appeal to facts and logic. As anyone who has considered the standard arguments offered for the immorality of homosexual conduct knows, the arguments are all fallacious; they all depend either on false factual claims or on invalid reasoning. Justice Kennedy's opinion appeals to the liberty protected by the due process clause, but what arguably does much of the work is an appreciation of the facts about the role of sex and intimacy in the lives of homosexuals and the parity with their role in the lives of heterosexuals. He emphasizes that the case did not involve minors, or persons who might be injured or coerced; it did not involve public conduct or prostitution; and it did not concern whether "the government must give formal recognition to any relationship that homosexual persons seek to enter."[78] At issue was only the private, noncommercial conduct of consenting adults. Kennedy's argument amounts to an appeal to rational consistency in determining the scope of fundamental rights. Now, there are steps that would no doubt require filling in, but however we understand the rights guaranteed by the Due Process Clause of the Fourteenth Amendment, surely a free state is not one in which some members of society can be subject to criminal penalties for conduct that is believed to be wrong for no good reason.[79]

As a final example, a string of recent federal cases striking down state laws barring marriage between same-sex partners exhibit a similar appeal to formal norms; in particular, they appeal to logic and to empirical evidence relevant to claims made by parties to the cases.[80] Consider just one example. In *Baskin v. Bogan*, discussing cases involving both Wisconsin's and Indiana's laws, Judge Richard Posner cites psychological evidence of the immutability of homosexuality.[81] He discusses evidence of the harm to homosexuals and their adopted children of being unable to marry.[82] And he cites evidence finding that permitting same-sex marriage has no effect on the rate of heterosexual marriage.[83]

Regarding the arguments advanced by Indiana and Wisconsin, Judge Posner writes,

> Our pair of cases is rich in detail but ultimately straight-forward to decide. The challenged laws discriminate against a minority defined by an immutable characteristic, and the only rationale that the states put forth with any conviction—that same-sex couples and their children don't *need* marriage because same-sex couples can't *produce* children, intended or unintended—is so full of holes that it cannot be taken seriously. To the

---

[78] 539 U.S. 558, 567.

[79] Of course, opposition to homosexual conduct, as Justice Kennedy observes, may rest on heartfelt religious convictions. But under our Constitution, the fact that some people's religions find something abhorrent is insufficient grounds for a criminal law.

[80] See, e.g., *Deboer v. Snyder* (2014); *Geiger v. Kitzhaber* (2014); *Baskin v. Bogan* (2014); and *Kitchen v. Herbert* (2013).

[81] *Baskin*, 9-10.

[82] Id., 10-13.

[83] Id., 32.

extent that children are better off in families in which the parents are married, they are better off whether they are raised by their biological parents or by adoptive parents. The discrimination against same-sex couples is irrational, and therefore unconstitutional even if the discrimination is not subjected to heightened scrutiny . . .[84]

Among the many holes in Indiana's arguments, Judge Posner notes, first, the inconsistency between the state's claim that the only reason Indiana recognizes marriage is to channel procreative sex into marriage and the fact that it allows infertile persons to marry.[85] Second, while denying homosexuals the right to marry because their sexual activity is not procreative, Indiana specifically exempts first cousins from the bar on intermarriage, if they are at or beyond the age of sixty-five, *because* they are then infertile. What is more, Indiana will not recognize same-sex marriages validly performed in other states but will recognize marriages validly performed in other states of first cousins *below* the age of sixty-five.

Finally, Judge Posner recalls that at oral argument, the lawyer for Indiana was asked why the ban on marriage of same-sex couples should not be lifted, given that Indiana's law is supposedly about raising children successfully, and the lawyer had agreed that same-sex couples can raise children successfully.

> The lawyer answered that "the assumption is that with opposite-sex couples there is very little thought given during the sexual act, sometimes, to whether babies may be a consequence." In other words, Indiana's government thinks that straight couples tend to be sexually irresponsible, producing unwanted children by the carload, and so must be pressured . . . to marry, but that gay couples, unable as they are to produce children wanted or unwanted, are model parents—model citizens really—so have no need for marriage. Heterosexuals get drunk and pregnant, producing unwanted children; their reward is to be allowed to marry. Homosexual couples do not produce unwanted children; their reward is to be denied the right to marry. Go figure.[86]

In substance, if not in tone, Posner's critique of the irrationality of Indiana's and Wisconsin's laws is typical of the cases striking down state marriage laws barring marriage between same-sex partners. The courts have consistently argued that the laws at issue do not even satisfy rational basis review—that the reasoning offered in support of them is so weak as to strain credulity.

---

[84] Id., 7-8. Posner goes on to explain why the possible responses to this difficulty are inadequate.

[85] Posner remarks, "if channeling procreative sex into marriage were the only reason that Indiana recognizes marriage. . .it would make marriage licenses expire when one of the spouses (fertile upon marriage) became infertile because of age or disease."(Id., 17).

[86] Id., 19-20.

4. Objections

I have offered only a bare sketch of the moral learning approach. As the examples should suggest, something like this approach may already be at work in important court decisions. Still, one might have doubts about whether a moral learning approach merits further exploration. Here, I want to address briefly two worries about the approach.

A first concern is that whatever benefits its appeal to formal, extra-constitutional norms gives to the moral learning approach, its formality comes at a cost.[87] Consider again the first illustration involving the transition from *Plessy* to *Brown*. Insofar as the Court based its conclusion on factual information about the effects of segregated schools would not the effect have been to leave open the possibility that segregation *might* be constitutionally permissible in cases in which the facts do not indicate harmful effects from segregation? Appeal to substantive moral principles, such as in the way that Dworkin envisioned, is necessary to avoid this kind of result.

Appealing to formal criteria might sometimes be insufficient to enable moral learning if constitutions did not already contain the moral principles expressed by their abstract moral clauses. But I have assumed that the moral learning approach applies only to constitutions like our own. Still, one might worry that without engaging in something like the kind of moral reasoning Dworkin described, courts would not be able to reach morally desirable constitutional conclusions. I doubt this, in part, because it overlooks the work done by precedent and the Supreme Court's doctrinal tests, tests that do not require for their development or application that judges engage in picking from among competing conceptions of the moral principles expressed by the Constitution's abstract moral clauses.[88] With regard to *Brown*, by its express terms, the case struck down the doctrine of separate but equal only in the context of public education. But consideration of the effects of state sanctioned and enforced segregation would

---

[87] Thanks to David Brink for pressing this worry.

[88] See Fallon (1997) (discussing how the Court implements the Constitution through the development of doctrine). One might argue that the abstract moral clauses will require interpretation, which would seem to bring Dworkin's approach back into play. But even if, ultimately, some interpretation of these clauses is necessary beyond what is provided by doctrinal tests and precedent, there is more than one way of approaching the task of interpretation. For example, an alternative to identifying a favored reading of an abstract moral clause would be to proceed on the basis of an overlapping consensus of readings; another would be to simply exclude implausible readings. These and other alternatives would, of course, require development; the point is simply that more than one interpretive approach would be available. One might nevertheless stress that whichever alternative was adopted, it would add to a moral reading approach something non-formal. As I said earlier, until we have a fully developed moral learning approach, we cannot be certain how far formal norms will carry us in constitutional interpretation. In any case, if an adequate moral learning approach required something beyond the kinds of formal norms I have described, I would be prepared to embrace it. What is important for my purposes is recognizing the work that can be done by formal, extra-constitutional norms. Thanks to Sameer Bajaj for pressing this objection.

no doubt, together with the Court's test of strict scrutiny, support the general unconstitutionality of the doctrine of separate but equal.

Two final points in response to this first objection. As I have tried to make clear, the moral learning approach would be just one part of a theory of constitutional interpretation. Resources relevant to alleviating the worry might be found in other norms that would make up a complete theory of constitutional interpretation. In addition, we do not yet have a fully developed version of the moral learning approach. Without a fully developed version, with the full array of formal norms at hand, we have insufficient grounds for concluding that the approach wouldn't have adequate resources to succeed in its aim of enabling moral learning to be reflected in the law.

A second objection concerns whether judges are any more adept at deploying empirical evidence than they are at engaging in the kind of moral reasoning that Dworkin envisioned.[89] Some evidence that judges are not better suited to deal with the facts than to sort out moral principles might be thought to be suggested by *Brown* itself. In *Stell v. Savannah-Chatham County Board of Education*, the District Court opinion noted the paucity of evidence supporting the factual claims made in *Brown*, and it discussed problems with the study that was therein cited.[90] Whatever one thinks of the *Stell* decision, one might think it illustrates how judges can be unable to assess the quality of empirical evidence offered to the courts. A recent article in the *New York Times* might seem to suggest that the problem is quite severe.[91] According to the article, Justices on the Supreme Court not only cherry-pick from among the studies and empirical claims presented in a case by the parties or in amicus briefs, but seem unable to distinguish between briefs that back up their factual claims with credible studies and those that do not. "Some of the factual assertions in recent amicus briefs would not pass muster in a high school research paper. But that has not stopped the Supreme Court from relying on them. Recent opinions have cited 'facts' from amicus briefs that were backed up by blog posts, emails or nothing at all."[92]

But these considerations are insufficient to show that justices are as ill-suited to dealing with the facts as with Dworkinian moral reasoning. First, the article suggests something far more worrisome, namely, a tendency on the part of some justices to look for facts that will support their views, rather than an effort to work fairly with the evidence presented. Such a tendency, however, does not support the contention that judges are ill-suited to deal with empirical evidence. Second, appellate courts are supposed to rely on the factual record produced at

---

[89] Thanks to Jerry Vildostegui and Christoforos Ioannidis for pressing this line of objection.

[90] *Stell v. Savannah-Chatham County Board of Education*, United States District Court Southern District of Georgia, Savannah Division, June 28, 1963.

[91] Adam Liptak, "Seeking Facts, Justices Settle for What Briefs Tell Them," *The New York Times*, September 1, 2014, http://www.nytimes.com/2014/09/02/us/politics/the-dubious-sources-of-some-supreme-court-facts.html?module=Search&mabReward=relbias%3As%2C{%221%22%3A%22RI%3A8%22.

[92] Id.

trial, and so at least appeals courts will be limited by the record, which may be deficient; but a deficiency in the record is different from a deficiency in skills and training. It is a regular part of the trial process that judges determine, in their interchange with attorneys, who will be accepted as an expert witness and what testimony will be treated as credible. No doubt some judges are better at this than others, just as some judges are better than others at reasoning logically. It is nevertheless an ordinary part of what judges do, something for which the practice of law trains them, and something that the law itself provides for and guides.

5. Conclusion

I have offered just the basics of an alternative approach to reading a constitution morally. Developing an alternative along these lines would require arriving at a fuller understanding of the extra-constitutional constraints and norms that apply to all practical reasoners, and so to constitutional interpreters. Because interpretation and adjudication take place within a constitutional system with developed doctrines and practices, it would also require working out the relationships among these constraints and relevant doctrine and practice. The examples I have given of formal, extra-constitutional constraints and norms have their clearest bearing on equal protection analysis, though we also see them at work in due process cases, like *Lawrence*. It would be important to understand more systematically any differences in how formal constraints figure in equal protection as opposed to due process analysis and how they bear on the determination of fundamental rights.[93] Developing the moral learning approach in these ways would amount to developing a key part of a theory of constitutional practical reasoning.

Along the way, I have indicated what I take to be some strengths of the suggested approach, but I want to say a bit more in closing. A virtue of the approach sketched herein is, as I indicated at the outset, that it can, in principle, be accepted by constitutional theorists of varying stripes—including constitutional originalists. Originalists, like all constitutional theorists, are in need of more well-developed theories of how to get from the semantic content of the Constitution to the content of the law. A moral reading, as I have sketched it, need not be in conflict with core originalist or core nonoriginalist ideas, and so might form one part of such theories.

The reasons for accepting some such view about reading constitutions morally go beyond its general availability to theorists. Suppose we accept as a criterion of adequacy on a constitutional theory that it make sense of how constitutions could be normative, of how they could give practical reasons, and not only to their adherents. Suppose that we accept as a criterion of adequacy on a constitutional theory that it allow for interpretation that promotes stability, and not

---

[93] Thanks to Miranda McGowen for raising the importance of extending the approach beyond equal protection analysis.

by sanctioning strong arming, but, rather, by enlisting people's sense that constitutional government is reasonable and apt for achieving justice. I conjecture that on both counts a theory that prescribes, in part, that constitutions be read morally, in the limited sense I have sketched, will do better by both criteria. That is because a moral learning approach to reading a constitution has at its core the prescription that where a constitutional text allows it—where the semantic content of a constitution is sufficiently normatively rich—interpreters employ extra-constitutional constraints and norms so as to reach more morally compelling, and, therefore, more constitutionally compelling results.[94]

References

Alexander, L. (2011). "Simple-Minded Originalism." In *The Challenge of Originalism: Essays in Constitutional Theory,* Grant Huscroft & Bradley W. Miller (eds.). Cambridge: Cambridge University Press, 87–98.

Alexander, L. "Was Dworkin an Originalist?" (2016). In *The Legacy of Ronald Dworkin,* Wil Waluchow and Stefan Sciaraffa (eds.). Oxford: Oxford University Press, 299–322.

Alexander, L., and Kress, K. (1995). "Against Legal Principles." In *Law and Interpretation,* A. Marmor (ed.). Oxford: Clarendon Press, 279–327.

Alexander, L. and Sherwin, E. (2008). *Demystifying Legal Reasoning.* Cambridge: Cambridge University Press.

Bakke v. Regents of the University of California. (1978). 435 U.S. 265.

Barnett, R. (1999). "An Originalism for Nonoriginalists," 45 Loy. L. Rev. 611.

Barnett, R. (2005). *Restoring the Lost Constitution.* Princeton: Princeton University Press.

Baskin v. Bogan, United States Court of Appeals, Seventh Circuit, decided September 4, 2014.

Berger, R. (1997) "Ronald Dworkin's The Moral Reading of the Constitution: A Critique," 72 *Indiana Law Journal* 1097.

Bowers v. Hardwick. (1986). 478 U.S. 186.

Brown v. Board of Education. (1954). 347 U.S. 483.

Brandt, R. (1979). *A Theory of the Good and the Right.* Oxford: Clarendon Press.

Brest, P. (1980). "The Misconceived Quest for the Original Understanding," 60 B.U. L. Rev. 204.

Brink, D. (1985). "Legal Positivism and Natural Law Reconsidered," *The Monist* 68:364–387.

Brink, O. (1998). "Legal Theory, Legal Interpretation, and Judicial Review," *Philosophy & Public Affairs,* 17:105–148.

Brink, O. (2001). "Legal Interpretation, Objectivity, and Morality." In *Objectivity in Law and Morals.* Brian Leiter (ed.). New York: Cambridge University Press.

---

[94] As I see it, the brilliance of our own constitution lies partly in the fact that it includes provisions that, given the proper interpretive approach, allow moral learning to take place—and, most important, allow for that moral learning to be reflected in the law. It is this, in large measure, I believe, that accounts for both the normative force of our own constitution and the resilience of the government and society adherence to it enables.

Brink, O. "Originalism and Constructive Interpretation" (2016). In *The Legacy of Ronald Dworkin*, Wil Waluchow and Stefan Sciaraffa (eds.). Oxford: Oxford University Press, 273–298.

Deboer v. Snyder. (2014). United States District Court, Eastern District of Michigan, Southern Division, Civil Action No. 12-CV-10285.

Dworkin, R. (1986). *Law's Empire.* Cambridge: Harvard University Press.

Dworkin, R. (1996). "Introduction: The Moral Reading and the Majoritarian Premise." In *Freedom's Law.* Cambridge: Harvard University Press.

Dworkin, R. (1998). "Comment." In Antonin Scalia, *A Matter of Interpretation.* Princeton: Princeton University Press, 115–127.

Dworkin, R. (2006). "Originalism and Fidelity," in *Justice in Robes.* Harvard: Belknap Press, 117–139.

Dworkin, R. (2011). *Justice for Hedgehogs.* Cambridge: Harvard University Press.

Fallon, R. (1987). "A Constructivist Coherence Theory of Constitutional Interpretation," *Harv. L. Rev.* 100:1189.

Fallon, R. (1997). "Foreword: Implementing the Constitution," *Harv. L. Rev.* 111:54.

Geiger v. Kitzhaber, United States District Court, D. Oregon, May 19, 2014.

Goldsworthy, J. (2000). "Dworkin as an Originalist," *Const. Comment* 17:49.

Greenberg, M. (2009a). "How Facts Make Law I." In *Exploring Law's Empire, the Jurisprudence of Ronald Dworkin,* Scott Hershovitz (ed.). Oxford: Oxford University Press, 225–265.

Greenberg, M. (2009b). "How Facts Make Law II." In *Exploring Law's Empire, the Jurisprudence of Ronald Dworkin,* Scott Hershovitz (ed.). Oxford: Oxford University Press, 265–290.

Greenberg, M. (2014). "The Moral Impact Theory of Law," *Yale Law Journal* 123:1288.

Griswold v. Connecticut (1965). 381 U.S. 479.

Hart, H. L. A. (1994). *The Concept of Law,* second ed. Oxford: Oxford University Press.

Kitchen v. Herbert, United States District Court, District of Utah, Central Division, December 12, 2013.

Lawrence v. Texas. (2003). 539 U.S. 558.

Leiter, B. (2004-2005). "End of Empire: Dworkin and Jurisprudence in the 21st Century," *Rutgers L.J.* 36:165.

Liptak, A. (2014). "Seeking Facts, Justices Settle for What Briefs Tell Them," *The New York Times* online, September 1, http://www.nytimes.com/2014/09/02/us/politics/the-dubious-sources-of-some-supreme-court-facts.html.

Marmor, A. (2011). "Can the Law Imply More Than It Says? On Some Pragmatic Aspects of Strategic Speech." In *Language in the Law.* A. Marmor and S. Soames, S. (eds.). Oxford: Oxford University Press.

McGinnis, J., and Rappaport, M. (2007). "Original Interpretive Principles as the Core of Originalism," *Const. Comment.* 24:371.

McGinnis, J., and Rappaport, M. (2009). "Original Methods Originalism: A New Theory of Interpretation and the Case Against Construction," *NW.U.L. REV.* 103:751.

Michael H. v. Gerald D. (1989). 491 U.S. 110.

Michael, W. (2009). "A Defense of Old Originalism," *W. New Eng. L. Rev.* 31:21.

Moore, M. (1985). "A Natural Law Theory of Interpretation," *S. Cal. L. Rev.* 58:277.

Plessy v. Ferguson. (1896). 163 U.S. 537.

Railton, P. (1986a). "Facts and Values," *Philosophical Topics* 14: 5–31.

Railton, P. (1986b). "Moral Realism," *Philosophical Review*, 95:163–207.

Rawls, J. (1993). *Political Liberalism*. New York: Columbia University Press.

Romer v. Evans. (1996). 517 U.S. 620.

Scalia, A. (1998). *A Matter of Interpretation*. Princeton: Princeton University Press.

Scalia, A. (2013). Address to the North Carolina Bar Association. http://www.huffing-tonpost.com/2013/06/21/antonin-scalia-north-carolina-bar-association_n_3479874.html

Shpall, S. "Dworkin's Literary Analogy" (manuscript).

Stell v. Savannah-Chatham County Board of Education, United States District Court Southern District of Georgia, Savannah Division, June 28, 1963.

Tribe, L. (1998). "Comment." In Antonin Scalia, *A Matter of Interpretation*. Princeton: Princeton University Press, 65–94.

Tribe, L., and Dorf, M. (1993). *On Reading the Constitution*. Cambridge: Harvard University Press.

15

Authority, Intention, and Interpretation
by Aditi Bagchi*

This essay explores and builds on the link between authority and interpretation in Ronald Dworkin's *Law's Empire*. Dworkin argued that legal rules should be interpreted as consistent with the moral principles that define a political community. By ensuring fidelity to those principles, rather than the intentions behind rules, constructive interpretation preserves legitimate authority. By contrast, traditional methods of interpretation would endeavor to respect authority by interpreting texts in line with authorial intent. Dworkin highlights the contingent and dynamic character of legitimate authority and shows how those features require a practice of interpretation that continuously justifies authority.

Part I shows how Dworkin's combined theories of interpretation and authority operate in the context of statutes and case law. Part II extends his insights to contract. Because private parties have contingent authority over the terms of their transactions, their intent cannot be the sole fountain of meaning in contract interpretation. Instead, ambiguous terms should be construed to render them reasonable in light of background legal duties.

A foundational question with respect to interpretation of any text is the deference due its author. Does it matter what she intended the text to mean? Questions of interpretation arise in a wide variety of contexts, from ordinary speech to literature. I focus here on three kinds of legal text: case law, statutes, and contracts. These legal texts differ from most non-normative texts in that each asserts its own authority. Legal instruments claim to bind the judges who enforce them.

The first two types, cases and statutes, raise common questions regarding the nature of political authority but distinct concerns about the nature of judicial and legislative authority, respectively. The last category of text, contract, raises parallel questions about the authority of private parties over the terms of their transactions. Drawing on Ronald Dworkin's work on authority and interpretation, I will

---

*This chapter benefited from comments received at a Fordham Law School faculty workshop and at the McMaster Philosophy of Law conference.

argue that the centrality of an author's intention to interpretation of her text depends on the nature of her authority.

Dworkin's work on constructive interpretation offers a theory about the relationship between authority, intention, and the activity of interpretation. Dworkin argues that law as a practice involves constructive interpretation of legal rules to cast them in their best light, or to exemplify the values in law. His theory of interpretation follows from his theory of law's authority. On his view, the legitimacy of political authority derives from the status of the jurisdiction as a community of principle. We secure that legitimacy by interpreting laws as consistent with the set of principles that define our political community.

My aim is not to study his claim about the nature of political authority but only its relationship to the mode of interpretation he recommends, i.e., reading legal rules in light of normative commitments exogenous to the immediate legal source for the rules. Dworkin inverts the presumptive conceptual chronology by asking how interpretation might serve authority—not yet secured—instead of assuming that we interpret only those texts that are backed by authority. He construes the constraints of intention in line with the political-moral function of interpretation instead of taking interpretation to revolve around some natural idea of authorial intent. Dworkin recognizes that interpretation and intention are both functional concepts and, in the context of law, their function is moral.

I argue that contracts should be read in a similar manner, i.e., courts should read contract terms to render them reasonable, or consistent with exogenous legal norms, where possible. Just as we should read public rules (according to Dworkin) in a manner that justifies deference to political authority, so too, should we read contract terms in a manner that justifies deference to the authority of contracting parties over their terms of exchange. The general principle might be stated: Where authority is content-dependent, intention is to that extent displaced in interpretation. I aim to show that this principle is generally true so that we can extend or adapt Dworkin's method of interpretation to other contexts.

Dworkin's argument depends on rejecting the presumptive authority of governments and courts; their authority depends on how they use it. Such contingent authority is never conclusively established; it is continuously justified over time. Judges read legal texts authored by government officials who had procedural authority at the time of authorship but may have no present democratic credentials. In the process of interpretation, we presume that lawmakers have exercised authority consistent with the principles to which the polity is committed over time; we presume this without necessarily believing that lawmakers intended to exercise it in this way. Inasmuch as we traditionally regard interpretation as a reconstruction of rules as intended by those who drafted earlier articulations of those rules, Dworkin would have us engage in a regulative fiction about their allegiance to foundational principles.

An argument of remarkably similar form applies to contract interpretation. Post-*Lochner* (in the United States), individuals have no inherent claim of authority over the terms on which we deal with others. Our *interest* in moral agency is among the reasons for leaving it to us to decide how we deal with others and that interest may be advanced irrespective of the content of our choices. But our interest in agency is not the only relevant interest. The interests of others must also be well-served by our contribution to a system of private ordering. Whether these interests are well served is content-dependent. That is, the force of public reasons for deferring to private terms of exchange depends in part on the terms that contracting parties choose. When we read contracts, we should engage in another regulative fiction, i.e., that contracting parties intended to comply with background duties. This fiction is justified because courts should defer to parties' intentions only inasmuch as parties intended to comply with background duties.

Those who reject the content-dependent character of authority are more wedded to the intentions behind a rule or text. Consider an (exclusive) positivist account of law, in which the sources of legal obligation do not depend directly on the moral attributes of law.[1] On such a view, political authority is content-independent in that our reasons for respecting political authority do not depend on the substance of particular laws. For that reason, depending on how we construe the scope of authority and the process of law-making, courts might care whether the legal authority that passed a law intended it to prohibit or permit some conduct.[2] Although exclusive legal positivists might expect law to take into account certain moral values, they would not have judges reference those values directly in interpretation.

Similarly, those who view contract as inherently self-justifying by virtue of the process by which it comes to be will reject the content-dependent mode of interpretation I recommend. They accept that an unconscionable contract, or a contract against public policy, should not be enforced; but they would not construe ambiguous terms to avoid the specter of unconscionability or in a manner that promotes public policy. As long as a contract is enforceable, classical theorists would hold that parties' intentions are the primary benchmark by which ambiguity is resolved. Although we expect freely negotiated contracts to advance values related to reciprocity and fair exchange, traditional contract theory would hold that those values do not directly inform contract interpretation.

This essay develops the relationship between attributions of authority and appropriate norms of interpretation. The intuitive proposition is that where

---

[1] See Raz (1979: 37-52); Waluchow (1994: 3) (Raz "excludes morality from the logically or conceptually possible grounds for determining the existence or content of valid law").

Dworkin's views on interpretation are mostly starkly different from those of exclusive legal positivists but others endorse aspects of his interpretive view. Inclusive legal positivism similarly allows that legal meaning will turn on secondary interpretive rules and is not controlled by the intentions of lawmakers. Id. at 250.

Even exclusive legal positivism need not claim a radical separation of law and morality, or that legal reasons replace moral ones. Legal reasons may reflect moral considerations. Raz (2009: 192) ("It is time to abandon the dramatic metaphor of the law excluding morality... [L]aw modifies the way morality applies to people."). However, when legitimate law specifies the demands of morality, on an exclusive positivist view, those whom it addresses are no longer free to process the underlying moral considerations directly. At the least, Dworkin's emphasis is the opposite of Raz: Morality modifies the way laws apply to people.

[2] Andrei Marmor endorses intentionalism conditionally for this kind of reason: "[I]f, and only if, a certain law is justified on the basis of the expertise branch of the normal justification thesis, would it make sense to defer to the legislature's intentions in the interpretation of the law." Marmor (2005: 139).

authority depends on content, interpretation aims to read rules or terms as compliant with content-based constraints on authority. Part I identifies this principle in Dworkin's theory of interpretation as applied to cases and statutes. Part II will elaborate it in the context of contract, as an approach I call "normative triangulation." Part III concludes.

1. Content-Based Interpretation of Legal Rules

1.1 CONSTRUCTIVE INTERPRETATION AND POLITICAL AUTHORITY

Dworkin's idea of constructive interpretation offers a theory about the relationship between authority, intention, and the activity of interpretation.[3] He argues that law—whether in case law or in statutes—should be read in their best light from the standpoint of political morality. This theory of interpretation follows from his theory of legal authority. On Dworkin's view, the legitimacy of political authority derives from the status of the jurisdiction as a community of principle:

> A community of principle, faithful to [the promise that law will be chosen, changed developed and interpreted in an overall principled way] can claim the authority of a genuine associative community and can therefore claim moral legitimacy—that its collective decisions are matters of obligation and not bare power—in the name of fraternity.[4]

On this view, law obligates us *to the extent* it reflects and reinforces the community's constitutive principles. Courts help secure the legitimacy of law and its claims of authority by interpreting laws as consistent with that set of principles that define their political community.

At first blush, one might think Dworkin moves too seamlessly here from a claim about the legitimacy of law to a claim about its ability to obligate citizens. Law might obligate us so long as it is valid; the question of legitimacy is one of moral and sociological significance that rests on moral and sociological inquiries—questions of the sort that cannot drive general principles of interpretation. Dworkin does not offer a detailed account of the distinction between validity and legitimacy, though he is clearly more interested in the latter. Fortunately, the relationship between legal validity and legitimacy need not be settled in order to prefer interpretive principles that promote *at least* legitimacy, even if they are not necessary to secure validity.

The question on the table in matters of interpretation is whether courts should read statutes and cases one way or another. Even if Dworkin's argument speaks only to legitimacy, arguing that law is *valid* irrespective of the method chosen does not guide an answer to the question at hand. One need only agree with

---

[3] All related references are to Dworkin (1986).
[4] Id. at 214.

Dworkin that legitimacy is preferable to illegitimacy, and that therefore a method of interpretation that promotes legitimacy is preferable to one that does not (or that potentially undermines it) for his argument about the relationship between authority and interpretation to work. Once we see that the authority of law falls on a spectrum, we can locate the role of interpretation in moving it along that spectrum, toward greater legitimacy.

Dworkin was uniquely focused on the feedback effect of interpretation on authority. Some discussions of authority proceed without attention to interpretation. Theories of authority may be entirely stagnant, i.e., focused on the content of laws or institutional conditions at the moment of enactment, or only backward-looking, i.e., focused on procedural pedigree. Likewise, theories of interpretation do not always systematically address the question of authority. Dworkin was unusual in highlighting the manner in which a mode of interpretation helps secure authority. Although he departs from positivism, he is not a natural lawyer either: The authority of any given law on his view does not depend simply on *its* being just. Authority is ultimately a feature of legal systems, and only derivatively a property of laws. Authority of individual laws depends on both origination *and* *application* in the way that the volume of a sound turns on perception. Because authority depends in part on the practices by which law is administered, it turns in part on the ways in which laws are interpreted. The best interpretation will *make* a law authoritative—it will realize its potential for authority, redeem its claim of authority. Substantively, in Dworkin's account, the best interpretation depends on the contingent set of principles that define a given community; these are not universal in the way we might expect a natural law theory to claim.

In Dworkin's account, the question of how to interpret a law does not presuppose its authority. By contrast, one might think that we only undertake to interpret laws that are authoritative, i.e., that authority is a prior question before a law presents itself for interpretation. But in constructive interpretation, the question of laws' authority depends on the manner in which those laws are interpreted. Although laws must meet some threshold conditions that make it possible for interpretation to render them and the system of which they are apart authoritative, there is a symbiotic relation between norms of interpretation and the criteria of authority. Courts are bound to read public rules in a manner that justifies deference to political authority.

1.2 MORAL MOTIVATION IN INTERPRETATION

One might worry that interpretation motivated by the demands of political legitimacy veers us away from interpretation as such.[5] But Dworkin recognizes that interpretation is essentially a functional concept, just like intention. We might in

---

[5] Larry Solum argues, for example, that the practice Dworkin recommends for statutes and constitutions is better regarded as construction than interpretation. Solum (2010). The distinction between construction and interpretation is analytically important in some contexts. But because

principle conclude that intention describes some cognitive state, even a neuro-chemical one. But in law, the concept of intention adapts to the various purposes for which it is deployed. Its moral significance, and therefore its legal criteria, var-ies from one subject to the next. The concept of intention is subjective in one area, like criminal law, objective in tort. It is adapted to corporations and legislatures. There is always something there that justifies our referring to the phenomenon in question as a sort of intention but we do not expect the concept to operate uni-formly, or the related legal inquiry to be consistent, across contexts.

So it is with interpretation. Dworkin does discuss interpretation across a range of contexts. But his constructive interpretation is ultimately a practice justified by a theory of political authority and it applies outside of law only where parallel motivations arise. His discussion in *Law's Empire* seems to aspire simultaneously to demonstrate that the practice is indeed interpretation—and has important fea-tures elucidated by comparison with interpretation of other texts—and to justify itself as a method by virtue of the particular moral function it serves in a political community.

Dworkin elaborates constructive interpretation by way of a lengthy discussion of artistic interpretation. That context highlights that interpretation of the sort he has in mind is essentially creative, that is, the aim is to "interpret something created by people as an entity distinct from them."[6] But he emphasizes that con-structive interpretation is also purposive in that it aims to "assign meaning in light of the motives and purposes and concerns it supposes the speak to have, and it reports its conclusions as statements about his 'intentions' in saying what he did."[7]

There is apparent tension between the goal of acknowledging the intention-ality of a work and taking interest in the work product as independent of those intentions. Dworkin's solution is to regard interpretation as "essentially con-cerned with purpose" but "the purposes in play are not (fundamentally) those of some author but of the interpreter. Roughly, constructive interpretation is a matter of imposing purpose on an object or practice in order to make of it the best possible example of the form or genre to which it is taken to belong."[8] We see here a morally motivated reconstruction of the idea of intention to suit the task of legal interpretation.

The idea of "making the best" of a work of art invites debate about the appro-priate criteria for judging art. Making the best of law invokes contested princi-ples of political morality. Dworkin admits that a judge will need "convictions

---

the question before courts is usually what meaning to ascribe a legal text, and because that choice is normally framed as one of *how* to interpret the text rather than *whether* to interpret the text (or instead construct it), it makes sense as a functional matter to characterize both constructive inter-pretation and normative triangulation as methods of interpretation when advocating a method by which courts should ascribe meaning to legal texts.

[6] Id. at 50.
[7] Id.
[8] Id. at 52.

about how far the justification he proposes at the interpretive stage must fit the standing features of the practice to count as an interpretation of it rather than the invention of something new" as well as "substantive convictions about what kinds of justification really would show the practice in the best light."[9] Although Dworkin separately propounds the principles that he views as constitutive of the American political community, the point that interpretation relies on some conception of political morality, or at least, the principles that define a political community, does not require agreement on the principles themselves.

It is controversial enough to admit that judges should invoke substantive values in interpretation, even if those values are those ostensibly constitutive of the community and not only principles to which judges are variously and personally committed. In fact, the proposition that judges should invoke substantive considerations in interpretations is probably more contestable than the kinds of values that Dworkin would identify as controlling. Disagreement will lie in the application of high-level commitments like equality to particular cases.

Anticipating that disagreement, critics will regard constructive interpretation as allowing judges more authority than they are properly assigned in a democratic system. The principles that define community might in the end be more procedural than substantive—or at least, procedural tenets of political morality might vie with substantive ones in our collective self-understanding. This line of challenge shows that highlighting the centrality of authority to interpretation does not resolve much—but it focuses the question of authority: What authority do we attribute to the authors of a case or statute? How does their authority compare to that of the interpreter?

Dworkin implies that we cannot adopt maxims of interpretation without answering these questions about the nature and distribution of authority. In so doing, Dworkin clarifies the moral dimension of interpretation. Even those who reject constructive interpretation must engage the question of authority. It is hardly responsive to insist on interpretation as conceptually requiring a certain methodology. By outlining a method of interpretation that is morally motivated, Dworkin makes the debate about interpretation a debate about political morality, and in particular, a debate about the authority of law and how it is best preserved at the moment of interpretation.

1.3 INSTITUTIONAL CONTINGENCIES AND CONSTRAINTS

"The adjudicative principle of integrity instructs judges to identify legal rights and duties, so far as possible, on the assumption that they were all created by a single author—the community personified—expressing a coherent conception of justice and fairness."[10] The presumption of coherence and fairness imposes a soft but substantive constraint on lawmaking. That constraint appears to apply to all

---

[9] Id. at 67.
[10] Id. at 225.

law. Elsewhere, Dworkin distinguishes between the task of interpreting common law cases, on the one hand, and statutes, on the other.

The distinction should interest Dworkin (perhaps even more than it apparently did), given the centrality of authority to his theory of interpretation, and the contingent and dynamic conception of authority he proposes. Dworkin observes that judges do not have the authority to hold people liable for damages for not acting where they had no pre-existing legal duty to act. Judges must cite principle, not policy, for their decisions.[11] Judges should therefore seek "an interpretation of what judges did" in earlier cases "that shows them acting in the [right] way, not in the way...judges must decline to act."[12] The line Dworkin draws between principle and policy seems dubious: It seems like that most policy considerations can be cast as in the service of some principle, stated at a sufficient level of generality. For example, the kind of welfare analysis he seems to wish to exclude might be regarded as an extension of some utilitarian strands already present in common law reasoning, and therefore consistent with existing political commitments and not sui generis to the adjudication of a particular dispute. That said, the appropriate mode of interpretation he would assign common law judges in principle takes into account not only their own authority but also the authority of those who authored the text to be interpreted. The fact that author and reader are both judges empowers the reader (interpreter) in some respects; the author did not have the power to constrain the reader with respect to question of policy. But the fact that the interpreter too is a mere judge—even if Herculean—limits what she is entitled to extract and extrapolate from prior decisions.

The principles of interpretation appropriate to case law must be designed to solve the problem of authority over time, or relative authority among judges *qua* authors and interpreters. We might attempt to resolve that problem by balancing—and implicitly accepting a trade-off between—the benefits of continuity and responsiveness. Similarly, we might compare the advantages of fidelity to rules developed *ex ante* and without the benefit of particular facts, to the advantages of adapting rules to each case with the benefit of *ex post* knowledge. Dworkin approaches the problem of authority over time differently: The interpreter is to read the earlier text as if it were authored by a single actor over time, a figurative character perfectly committed to the best reading of the community's political commitments. Constructive interpretation recognizes the substantive boundaries on earlier authority and solves the intertemporal problem by crediting that authority only to the extent it embodies enduring principles not traceable to any single authoritative legal officer. The interpreter respects authority by depersonalizing it and limiting its scope just to that extent it was exercised on behalf of common principles.

In the context of statutory interpretation, the ideal common law judge will "treat Congress as an author earlier than himself in the chain of law . . . an author

---

[11] Id. at 244.
[12] Id.

with special powers and responsibilities different from his own, and he will see his own role as fundamentally the creative one of a partner continuing to develop, in what he belies is the best way, the statutory scheme Congress began."[13] In some respects, this is not so different from the interpretation of case law. Here too, constructive interpretation "aims to enforce the most abstract and general political convictions from which legislators act rather than the hopes or expectations or more detailed political opinions they have in mind when voting."[14] But though a judge will ask a familiar question—which reading of the statute shows it in its best light—the object that she optimizes is different here: The judge will try to cast the political history surrounding the statute in a positive light, taking into account the best answer to several political questions, including "how far Congress should defer to public opinion in matters of this sort, for example, and whether [a given result] would be absurd as a matter of policy."[15] Making the best of the statute is not just a matter of making the best law but of making the law that best reflects an appropriate exercise of the authority that legislatures have. The authority of a legislature, its ideal procedural foundations as well as the ideal process by which it exercised, differ from those of common law cases. Therefore, a judge interpreting a statute undertakes interpretation with somewhat different purposes, even if with the constant purpose of upholding the moral authority of law.

The interesting move is to tie the mode of interpretation to the respective institutional roles of the person engaged in interpretation and the author of the legal text. Extending his reasoning, we should expect other actors who might be placed to interpret cases to be subject to different principles—for example, citizens, attorneys, law-makers, and judges of other jurisdictions. The connecting line between institutionally defined authority and the proper mode of interpretation implies some contingency to the details of interpretive choice. One might have associated morally charged interpretation with a more blunt approach, insensitive to institutional design. But because the political morality with which Dworkin is ultimately concerned is not substantive justice but the *justice of political obligation*, i.e., authority, constructive interpretation does take into account the institutional role of judges relative to the authors of the texts they are charged with interpreting.

2. Content-Based Interpretation of Contract

2.1 THE DISTRIBUTION OF AUTHORITY, POST-*LOCHNER*

Contract interpretation differs from legal interpretation in several respects, including the nature and basis of the authority we recognize in those whose words are subject to interpretation. But contract interpretation is similar to Dworkin's constructive interpretation in a deep sense: The best rules of interpretation

---

[13] Id. at 313.
[14] Id. at 317.
[15] Id. at 313.

depend on our conception of the practice and its purposes, and in particular on the nature of authority we ascribe to authors of legal text. The practice of contract as a method of regulating exchange depends for its legitimacy or at least its appeal on the theory of interpretation it presupposes. A silly theory of interpretation will result in a contract regime that no one would endorse. A better interpretive practice will deliver a better practice of contract and makes it a more attractive alternative to mandatory regulation than it would otherwise be.

Courts have interpretive choices in contract much like those in the context of interpreting cases or statutes. Black-letter law is that courts will enforce the most reasonable interpretation of an ambiguous contract term.[16]

What is the most reasonable interpretation? Probably more frequently and adamantly than is advocated in the context of interpreting laws, courts sometimes suggest that the most reasonable understanding of a contractual obligation turns only on intent, i.e., as it expressed in the parties' words and acts.[17] But reasonableness has a reference that is not reducible to party intent, and courts already, if inconsistently, read ambiguous contracts to impose substantively reasonable obligations.[18] For reasons akin to those that recommend constructive interpretation, these courts are right to employ a more expansive understanding of reasonableness than most contract scholars allow.[19] Although courts are

---

[16] "Our goal must be to accord the words of the contract their 'fair and reasonable meaning.'" *Sutton v. East River Sav. Bank*, 55 N.Y.2d 550, 555 (1982). This Essay concerns the interpretation of ambiguous terms. In line with existing law, it presumes that unambiguous terms are either enforced in a manner consistent with their unavoidable meaning, or rejected altogether.

[17] *See, e.g., Stolt-Nielsen S.A. v. AnimalFeeds In'l Corp.*, 559 U.S. 662, 682 (2010) ("the parties' intentions control"); *ACE Am. Ins. Co. v. Freeport Welding & Fabricating, Inc.*, 699 F.3d 832, 842 (5th Cir. 2012) ("The primary concern of a court construing a written contract is to ascertain the true intent of the parties as expressed in the instrument."); *Walker v. Martin*, 887 N.E.2d 125, 135 (Ind. Ct. App. 2008) ("[I]t is the court's duty to ascertain the intent of the parties at the time the contract was executed as disclosed by the language used to express their rights and duties.").

[18] *See, e.g., Columbia Propane, L.P. v. Wisconsin Gas Co.*, 661 N.W.2d 776, 787 (Wis. 2003) ("In ascertaining the meaning of a contract that is ambiguous, the more reasonable meaning should be given effect on the probability that persons situated as the parties were would be expected to contract in that way as opposed to a way which works an unreasonable result."); *Glenn Distributors Corp. v. Carlisle Plastics, Inc.*, 297 F.3d 294, 301 (3d Cir. 2002) ("Courts must be mindful to adopt an interpretation of ambiguous language which under all circumstances ascribes the most reasonable, probable, and natural conduct of the parties, bearing in mind the objects manifestly to be accomplished.") (internal citations omitted); *Tessmar v. Grosner*, 23 N.J. 193, 201 (1957) ("Where the common intention of the parties is ambiguous, the fairest and most reasonable construction imposing the least hardship on either of the contracting parties should be adopted so that neither will have an unfair or unreasonable advantage over the other.").

Restatement (Second) of Contracts §207 expressly allows that "in choosing among the reasonable meanings of a promise or agreement or a term thereof, a meaning that serves the public interest is generally preferred." Unfortunately, the principle has not caught on outside of limited contexts, such as those involving the provision of public services. See Zamir (1997: 1723-1724) (describing situations in which the rule has been applied). Zamir is among the few scholars to argue that substantive reasonableness is given inadequate weight in orthodox theories of interpretation.

[19] Scholarly debate regarding contract interpretation primarily concerns the question of whether interpretation should be formalist or contextualist—but scholars on both sides of this debate defend their position on the grounds that it is most likely to capture party intent. See Schwartz and Scott

appropriately focused on parties' objective intent, their inquiry into the most reasonable construction of that intent is *in part* an inquiry into how we can understand an agreement such that the agreement is reasonable, i.e., how we can read it as compliant with background duties that parties in contract have toward one another.

Some contract scholars begin from an implicit premise that parties to contract owe each other nothing prior to contract. But since the infamous *Lochner v. New York*[20] was reversed,[21] private parties do not have full autonomy—that is, authority—over the terms on which they transact with each other. The state now has the authority to override their choice of terms with mandatory regulation. Indeed, it does so by way of a wide variety of statutory schemes and common law doctrines. Private contract, or at least its voluntary dimension, is an *alternative* to those mandatory regimes.

Contrary to occasional rhetoric, parties in contract are not inevitably "free" to contract as they see fit.[22] The post-*Lochner* era is characterized by a broad, if imperfect, consensus that the state has a legitimate interest in regulating exchange for purposes other than policing consent. We regard contract as voluntary because contracting parties exercise normative power over their relations with contracting partners; they are the source of their own obligations. But in fact the power of contracting parties rivals the regulatory power of the state; individuals and state *both* have say over how transactions proceed. Because the state has a range of regulatory interests in contract outside of promise, even if parties' intentions control their promissory obligations in contract, they do not similarly control the scope of legally binding agreement.

Background duties that the law leaves individuals to navigate on their own persist in a regime of contract—not only morally, but legally. Duties of reciprocity, fair play, and nonexploitation are manifest in legal duties inside and outside of contract; those duties are not suspended but apply precisely in the context of private exchange. The background duties I refer to throughout this discussion are thus immanent in existing legal norms. Courts glean these background duties from existing law—in much the same way they already extract principles of public policy from statutes, case law, and common law history.[23] Voluntary commitments in contract are undertaken in the shadow of these background duties.

Individuals possess no inherent *authority* to dictate the terms on which we will discharge our involuntary duties. If private contract is to govern the terms of an

---

(2010) (advocating formalism); Burton (2009) (advocating middle course of "objectivism"); Bayern (2009) (advocating contextualism).

[20] 198 U.S. 45 (1905).

[21] *West Coast Hotel Co. v. Parrish*, 300 U.S. 379 (1937).

[22] See *Printing and Numerical Registering Co v. Sampson L R.*, 19 Eq. 462, 465 (1875) ("if there is one thing which more than another public policy requires it is that men of full age and competent understanding shall have the utmost liberty of contracting, and that their contracts when entered into freely and voluntarily shall be held sacred and shall be enforced by the Courts of justice").

[23] *Restatement (Second) of Contracts* § 179 (1981).

exchange, it must actually function as an alternative to mandatory regulation. That is, it must reasonably specify the duties implicated in exchange—which is to say, it *must be read* to reasonably specify the relevant duties. There are many reasons to harness the practice of promise for purpose of specifying duties in exchange; it allows individuals to set our own prices, choose our own products and providers, ratchet our warranty protections up and down based on our particular levels of risk aversion and productive capacities. Private individuals are usually better at setting the terms of exchange than is a third party like the state. But courts' reasons for deferring to our terms are instrumental; contract expands individual agency while regulating conduct in the course of exchange. Although individuals' authority on the terms of exchange is not entirely epistemic— grounded in their superior information—it is not fully jurisdictional either. We are authoritative only inasmuch as the terms we choose are consistent with the regulatory functions served by contract. Thus even if, by virtue of state's commitment to private ordering, our promises generate some content-independent reasons for state enforcement, our terms are effective substitutes for the background legal scheme only where they fall within certain bounds—and that inquiry is content-dependent.[24] The force of public reasons for deferring to private terms of exchange depends in part on the terms that contracting parties choose.

2.2 MORAL MOTIVATION IN INTERPRETATION

I label the above method of contract interpretation *normative triangulation*. (As discussed further below, it is sufficiently distinct from Dworkin's constructive interpretation to warrant a different label.) Drawing on Donald Davidson's concept of triangulation, Brian Langille and Arthur Ripstein have suggested that contracts are and should be interpreted by incorporating facts about the world into party intent, irrespective of whether parties actually thought about those facts.[25] We cannot know what others mean directly. We rely on language, and language has no meaning except in the common space shared by speaker and listener. Ripstein and Langille argue that in contract as in ordinary speech, in light of the inherent limitations on the intelligibility of others we "must take his or her beliefs to be largely true" and figure out what people are saying "by finding a way to make most of what a speaker says come out true."[26] The factual world thus serves as a reference point for filling in apparent gaps in the meaning of words in contract.

The practice that I describe and defend here extends this method to reference shared *norms* (in a way Langille and Ripstein would probably reject). Normative

---

[24] Even Joseph Raz allows, though he does not pursue, the possibility that promissory norms may be justified on grounds which "combine content-independent and content-dependent arguments." Raz (1977:96).

[25] Langille and Ripstein (1996:63-64).

[26] Id. at 73-74.

triangulation is doubly normative. First, the facts at which it is directed, i.e., the objects of interpretation, are normative. What are the parties' obligations toward one another? Second, normative triangulation is normative in motivation. Unlike interpretation of ordinary descriptive speech ("the cat is on the mat"), courts interpreting contracts bring normative criteria to bear on the choice of interpretative rules *and* on their interpretation of ambiguous terms.[27] Courts try to find a way to make most of what contracting parties are saying come out right—that is, compliant with hard and soft legal norms.

This is in many ways an extension of Dworkin's rule of charity with respect to legal texts, which he argues should be interpreted as consistent with the principles that define a political community. However, normative triangulation in the context of contract is narrower, and the exercise of fit less ambitious. Contracts do not need to extend the fabric of communal life; but they do need to be consistent with the existing outlines of that common life as expressed in existing law. The principle of charity in contract requires that courts reads contractual obligations as compliant with those background duties that apply to private exchange. The basic triangle in Davidson triangulation runs between a speaker and her object, between object and interpreter, and between speaker and interpreter. Davidson's principle of charity holds that the interpreter should maximize agreement with the speaker, or interpret the speaker so as to make as much as possible of what she says true. The principle follows from the relation between speaker and interpreter, and in particular, the interpreter's belief that they will respond similarly to stimuli.[28] In the context of contract interpretation, a court charitably reading an agreement will read it as "in agreement with" or just compliant with background duties that attend exchange.

Courts' reasons for applying a principle of charity are very different than those which motivate Davidson's interpreter. Like Dworkin's constructive interpretation, normative triangulation is morally motivated. Because contract is a method of regulating private exchange, courts do not have to interpret agreements as if indifferent to their content.

Notably, in contrast to Dworkin's theory of legal interpretation, I am not proposing that we read contracts to be the *most* reasonable terms of exchange possible. Contract enforcement is content-dependent but not content-determined. First, normative triangulation kicks in only where ambiguity is present. Second, normative triangulation aims to bring terms within the bounds of reasonableness while remaining agnostic about the most reasonable term. That is because a regulatory regime must make a decision about the bounds of reasonableness but it is characteristic of a regime of contract (as opposed to mandatory regulation) that it is agnostic as to the best term.

---

[27] Cf. Myers (2004) (arguing that we must make assume that others' values and desires, not just their reactions/perceptions, are the same as our own, but on epistemic grounds).

[28] See Davidson (2001:119).

The committed agnosticism of the state as to the ideal terms of exchange might at first appear to render the analogy to Davidson's triangulation inapt. Davidon's concept of triangulation is bound up with objectivity, that is, an awareness that thoughts are true or false. Only beings that possess this concept and thus see their own perceptions and those of others as capable of falsity will use triangulation to prefer interpretations that render utterances largely true. One might think that triangulation is never possible with respect to normative facts such as the obligations of parties in exchange toward each other if one is a skeptical about the existence of any objective obligation. However, judges at least must adopt the perspective that legal norms are objectively binding and constitute a shared normative framework for contracting parties, who after all seek to invoke some of those norms.

More problematic for our purposes, one might doubt that the state can triangulate to impute meaning to contracting parties' utterances if we see the state as committed to neutrality with respect to those terms, i.e., not committed even to the existence of any optimal terms. While we have reason to believe that we should be responding to a cat on the mat in the same way as others (or at least, observing the same phenomenon), a liberal state should not expect contracting parties to perceive normative facts similarly, and judges should not expect parties to see their obligations in exchange as judges might themselves construe them.

A liberal state is in a bit of bind on this question. On the one hand, I have just described it as committed to a certain agnosticism about the correctness of normative perception, i.e., whether the obligations parties choose to assume are the right ones. On the other hand, a liberal state is committed to regulating exchange and its aggregate outcomes, and this means having some preferences about precisely those terms it delegates to private parties.

We can reconcile the tension by characterizing obligations as only partially indeterminate to the state. The state can be committed to certain boundaries— e.g., a maximum price or a minimum duty of care—without ranking terms within the acceptable range. The result is that the state is not committed to maximizing agreement, as an interpreter in Davidson's triangulation would be; instead, it is committed to a presumption of reasonableness. Courts attribute reasonableness to the obligations parties have selected by reading obligations as falling within the range of reasonableness.

To put it another way, courts should read ambiguous contract terms as if they were uttered by a reasonable person. Whereas Dworkin would have courts read laws as if written by lawmakers loyal to the community's defining principles, courts need only suppose that contracting parties aim to comply with background duties that apply to voluntary exchange. The resulting constraint is weaker than that in constructive interpretation in two senses: The set of binding norms is narrower, and they do not optimize the result. As discussed further below, the difference follows from the wider authority allowed contracting parties within the domain of permissible contract.

Andrei Marmor describes interpretative statements as counterfactuals about the communicative intent of a hypothetical speaker.[29] In contract, the hypothetical speaker is one committed to successfully navigating background duties in contract. Thus, a court interpreting an ambiguous term must answer the question: What would a reasonable person (intending to comply with her background duties) mean by these words? In this way, courts are properly constrained by the words actually chosen and are not merely asking what a reasonable person would do. They can give proper weight to background constraints while respecting the underlying policy choice to regulate a given transactional space by way of contract rather than mandatory rules.

2.3 POSITIVE CONTINGENCIES AND CONSTRAINTS

The substantive constraints on contract are narrower than the community principles at work in constructive interpretation. Even if, as I argue here, courts should read contract with the aim of bringing them in line with substantive policy preferences, those preference cannot be as free-ranging as Dworkin would allow in the interpretation of cases and statutes. The authority of judges interpreting laws rivals those of earlier judges who authored cases. And judges have an assigned, arguably co-equal institutional role in democracies that legislatures anticipate in drafting laws. But contract is a private law institution. The status of any private agreement as an enforceable legal instrument is wholly contingent on the state's choice not to regulate that space directly. But once the state leaves some transactional space to contract, its choice is best understood as one that allows an expansive role for private discretion. Although contracting parties have no natural authority over the terms of their transactions, they have been delegated substantial authority by the state.

We should read contracts in light of background duties if and only if those duties have a legal character, broadly understood. Contracts are not like cases or statutes, thoroughly political texts that presumptively and thoroughly implicate political morality. Part of the idea of contract is to create some separate space for private interaction. To the extent courts undertook to maximize fit with the principles of justice generally espoused by the political community, contracts would cease to be private agreements. Because contracts are governed by law without being law, moral constraints in contract are not relevant to contract interpretation unless they arise from duties that support state functions. But inasmuch as contracts support legitimate state interests—that is, inasmuch as we defer to parties to regulate themselves *instead of regulating them directly*—courts should construct contractual intent to ensure private exchange occurs on acceptable terms.

Some of the background duties discharged in contract are subject to state enforcement while others are not.[30] Courts should read contractual promises in a

---

[29] Marmor (2005: 23).

[30] The idea herein is not really to delineate the border between enforceable and nonenforceable obligations but to identify the role of that boundary, whatever it may be. Cf. Sheinman (2000)

manner that allows them to effectively discharge background duties, even those emanating from soft legal norms. However, courts should not go further and read contracts to comply with moral duties that are not properly subject to legal enforcement in a liberal state. When entirely private duties motivate contractual promise, those duties ought not to inform how they are read. For example, a court charged with enforcing a contractual promise made to carry out the duties of friendship should not import the duties of friendship into its adjudication of rights and obligations under the contract between friends.

Courts have a different role when the background duty at issue is one that is the ordinary subject of legal regulation. For example, a contractual promise made by an employer to an employee in order to discharge obligations emanating from, if not strictly speaking arising under, a civil rights or employment statute should be interpreted in light of those background duties.

Not all duties of legal character are legal duties, in the way that not all principles of public policy recognized by common law courts are specifically set forth by statute. Duties that govern voluntary exchange are the private counterpart to principles of public policy. They can be extracted from statutes, gleaned from case law, or otherwise gathered from the history and state of the law with respect to some issue.[31] They are subject to controversy but their scope of application is relatively narrow. They are incorporated into the decision that courts make about whether it is appropriate to bring the coercive powers of the state to bear on the enforcement of a private agreement.

What are the duties that contract implicates? Some are perfect legal duties. For example, duties not to discriminate and duties not to impair competitive markets both constrain the terms on which we contract. Duties not to recklessly induce reliance that has no payoff, or not to induce another person to confer a benefit on you with the false expectation of compensation are also already subject to enforcement through contract principles like promissory estoppel and unjust enrichment.[32] Even the duty to compensate for a benefit already received has limited enforcement through the contract doctrine of moral obligation as substitute for consideration.[33] Thus, promises that make good on any of these background duties should be interpreted in their light.

Although the formulation is foreign to the prevailing rhetoric of contract scholarship, courts already interpret promises in the light of background duties

---

("Only those morally legitimate expectations that clear the moral-political and institutions limitations upon legal intervention are protected by the imposition of contractual liability.").

[31] For the amorphous boundaries of public policy, see *Maryland-Nat'l, etc v. Wash Nat'l Arena*, 282 Md. 588, 605-07 (1978) (noting public policy is extracted from constitutions, statutes, and judicial decisions, but not limited to express statements in those sources).

[32] See Restatement (Second) of Contracts § 90 (promissory estoppel); Restatement of Restitution § 1 ("A person who has been unjustly enriched at the expense of another is required to make restitution to the other.").

[33] See *Webb v. McGowin*, 27 Ala. App. 82 (1935) (promise made to employee who saved promisor's life enforceable against estate of promisor).

of the appropriate sort. In particular, courts regularly set defaults in light of prevailing expectations and norms, including those deriving from intuitions of equity. The interpretation of contracts so as to render them reasonable similarly incorporates norms exogenous to party intent into the exercise of deciphering and constructing contractual intent.

Such angled interpretation not only resembles constructive interpretation in theory, it is already familiar to us as a practice in the way American courts read statutes to conform to constitutional principles. A court interpreting a statute will prefer a reading that saves it; indeed, it will prefer a reading that avoids the constitutional question altogether.[34]

One way to understand this rule is that courts are simply trying to respect the separation of powers and avoid stepping on the toes of the legislature any more than necessary, instead prompting the legislature to act if necessary.[35] In that case, the court has reasons to strike down the law but it is outweighed by general reasons not to strike down any law. But we might go further: A reading of a statute under which it is not only constitutional but robustly constitutional delivers a better interpretation—because as a general matter, a statute that is clearly constitutional is preferable to a statute that only barely survives scrutiny. Although reasons to strike down the law are outweighed by structural considerations, those reasons do not disappear. They cut in favor of the more constitutional reading.

As with legislative deference, a court has many reasons to respect private ordering and the voluntary dimensions of contract by declining to substitute its own preferred terms for those selected by the parties.[36] These general reasons cut in favor of delegating to parties the terms of their own exchange and respecting those terms with narrow exceptions. But the political interest in the terms of exchange is not extinguished by the virtues of private ordering and a legal culture that recognizes promise; they are merely outweighed by them. Thus, the residual interest in fair exchange, or in exchange that does not undermine background justice, still appropriately shapes interpretation of private agreement. For example, if we have pragmatic and moral reasons for limiting direct invocation of considerations of distributive justice in the regulation of particular transactions, we can avoid the distributive question by interpreting agreements in a manner that neutralizes it.

Normative triangulation is more familiar than my argument for it. Like Davidson's triangulation, it describes an interpretive strategy we continuously

---

[34] See *Solid Waste Agency of N. Cook County v. Army Corps of Eng'rs*, 531 U.S. 159, 74 (2001) ("We thus read the statute as written to avoid the significant constitutional and federalism questions raised by respondents' interpretation."); *Edward J DeBartolo Corp. v. Florida Gulf Coast Bldg & Constr Trades Council*, 485 U.S. 568, 575 (1988) ("where an otherwise acceptable construction of a statute would raise serious constitutional problems, the Court will construe the statute to avoid such problems unless such construction is plainly contrary to the intent of Congress").

[35] Ginsburg (1992:1204-1206).

[36] Unlike legislative lawmaking, however, private ordering in the broad terms conceived here is not constitutionally mandated.

deploy. Facts about duty describe a common moral space inhabited by promisor and promisee (and court). Duties of all sorts make up our moral world in the way that hard facts make up our physical world. People speak—and communicate intentions to assume obligations—in a shared context. When a cashier says that she "will go get five," we may take her to mean that she will go get five dollars, and not five cents, because we know that she owes us five dollars. We interpret her words in light of existing obligation.

Courts interpret contracts in the same way. Consider the case of *Embry v. Hagardine, McKittrick Dry Goods Co.*, in which an employee threatened to quit unless his contract was renewed. His employer replied: "Go ahead, you're all right; get your men out and don't let that worry you."[37] The court held that it was reasonable for Embry to conclude that McKittrick had thereby renewed the employment contract. One might take the court to mean just that most people in Embry's shoes would understand McKittrick to have intended renewal. But this empirical question depends on a variety of factors, including the perceived attitude and perceived practices of most employers, and of McKittrick in particular. Probably more important in this case was the fact that it is *right* or simply *better* to hold McKittrick to the agreement that he may or may not have intended to make. Labor markets operate more fairly and efficiently if employees are able to extract reliable information from their employer prior to taking steps that will limit their mobility going forward. Embry's proposed interpretation of McKittrick's statement is most reasonable from this normative standpoint.

3. Conclusion

Constructive interpretation of law and normative triangulation in contract both rest on the theory that authority matters to the weight of intention in interpretation. If authority is content-dependent, the intention of an author is to that extent displaced. That displacement does not disrespect the author's authority; it preserves it. For whereas the authority of the author depends on how it is exercised, interpreting a text in a way that is faithful to intention but inconsistent with background constraints actually undermines the author's authority, if not in a single case, then over time.

One might argue that the idea that content-dependent authority justifies the displacement of intention in interpretation rests on confused notions of both authority and interpretation. The very concept of authority entails that it provides content-independent reasons for action.[38] But constructive interpretation and normative triangulation alike are proposed as interpretive methods for judges; they would need to be modified for citizens interpreting laws directly, taking into account their own relative authority. In any case, nothing in the idea

---

[37] 127 Mo. App. 383 (1907).
[38] Raz (1988: 35).

of authority that Dworkin attributes to law nor that I attribute to private parties denies that laws create reasons for judges to act in particular ways (reasons not reducible to content), and that contracts give parties and courts reason to act in ways not reducible to the merits of contract terms.

The mistake would be to regard authority as a binary property, which persons either have completely or lack altogether. Authority is never categorical; it is always conditioned in myriad ways. Even the idea of absolute authority (over one's thoughts, for example) is constrained by scope (limited to thoughts), and thus requires some investigation into how it has been exercised to determine whether the bounds of authority have been respected. No one denies that some laws are unconstitutional or that some contracts are invalid. The question is whether the boundaries of authority operate only as a cliff over which a few laws or agreements fall, or whether they instead inform how we read law and contracts that sit safely on the side of validity. Both constructive interpretation and normative triangulation make the character of authority central not peripheral to interpretation. This may be because both are animated by a concern to avoid the threat of a particular injustice—wrongful exercise of power. They thus share something more than either does with artistic or literary interpretation; they are morally motivated.

Nor are these content-dependent modes of interpretation confused about the concept of interpretation itself. Dworkin does not deny that "an interpretation is by nature the report of a purpose."[39] My own account of contract interpretation may sharply limit but does not dethrone party intent as the primary anchor for interpretation of private agreements. It would again be an error to frame the question in binary terms: Interpretation is not either about intention alone or not about intention at all. The smaller, better question is how much weight authorial intention should have. That is still a big question. The political-moral imperative to recognize the appropriate boundaries of authority offers some guidance.

References

Bayern, S. J. (2009). "Rational Ignorance, Rational Closed-Mindedness, and Modern Economic Formalism in Contract Law," *California Law Review* 97:943–73.

Burton, S. (2008). *Elements of Contract Interpretation.* Oxford: Oxford University Press.

Davidson, D. (2001). *Subjective, Intersubjective, Objective.* Oxford: Oxford University Press.

Dworkin, R. (1986). *Law's Empire.* Cambridge: Harvard University Press.

Ginsburg, R. B. (1992). "Speaking in a Judicial Voice," *New York University Law Review* 67:1185–1209.

---

[39] Dworkin (1986: 58).

Langille, B., and A. Ripstein. (1996). "Strictly Speaking—It Went without Saying," *Legal Theory* 2:63–81.

Marmor, A. (2005). *Interpretation and Legal Theory.* Portland: Hart Publishing.

Myers, R. (2004). "Finding Value in Davidson," *Canadian Journal of Philosophy* 34: 107–136.

Raz, J. (2009). *Between Authority and Interpretation.* Oxford: Oxford University Press.

Raz, J. (1988). *The Morality of Freedom.* Oxford: Oxford University Press.

Raz, J. (1979). *The Authority of Law.* Oxford: Oxford University Press.

Raz, J. (1977). "Promises and Obligations." In *Law, Morality, and Society: Essays in Honour of H. L. A. Hart*, P. M. S. Hacker and J. Raz (eds.). Oxford: Oxford University Press, 210–228.

Sheinman, H. (2000). "Contractual Liability and Voluntary Undertakings," *Oxford Journal of Legal Studies* 20:205–220.

Schwartz, A., and R. E. Scott. (2010). "Contract Interpretation Redux," *Yale Law Journal* 119:926–64.

Solum, L. (2010). "The Unity of Interpretation," *Boston University Law Review* 90:551–578.

Waluchow, W. (1994). *Inclusive Legal Positivism.* Oxford: Oxford University Press.

Zamir, E. (1997). "The Inverted Hierarchy of Contract Interpretation and Supplementation," *Columbia Law Review* 97: 1710–1803.

16

Concern and Respect in Procedural Law
by Hamish Stewart[*]

1. Introduction

In "Principle, Policy, Procedure,", his only extended essay on procedural law, Ronald Dworkin considered the question whether the procedural entitlements of the parties to litigation could properly be called "rights" in his sense.[1] That is, are a party's procedural entitlements "trumps" that defeat an opposing party's procedural and substantive claims even if the general public interest would be promoted by recognizing those claims? The difficulty in understanding procedural entitlements as rights is that procedural law so often seems motivated by some kind of willingness to compromise accurate fact-finding in the interest of general welfare: The legal system limits the amount of social resources devoted to fact-determination in a way that is plainly inconsistent with the assertion that the parties have a right, in the sense of trumping other social values, to the highest degree of accuracy in fact-finding. Dworkin tried to solve this problem by understanding procedural law as fixing the degree of accuracy in fact-finding through a political decision that more or less equalized across citizens the risk of the moral harm generated by inaccurate fact-finding, and as requiring consistent application of the procedures so determined even when the general interest would favor a departure from them. In this way, Dworkin argued, procedural law could be understood as consistent with his foundational principle of equal concern and respect without demanding that the state devote infinite resources to fact-finding. In this paper, I question whether this argument fits certain features of procedural law and whether it succeeds in showing that procedural entitlements are rights in

[*] I am very grateful to Roger Shiner, David Dyzenhaus, Vincent Chiao, Diana Berbece, and several participants in *The Legacy of Ronald Dworkin* (lawconf.mcmaster.ca), the McMaster University conference, which was sponsored by the Ontario Legal Philosophy Partnership, for comments on drafts of this paper.
[1] Dworkin (1986: ch. 3). For the original version of the paper, see Dworkin (1981).

Dworkin's sense. On the one hand, some features of procedural law are designed with little regard to the fair distribution of error; on the other hand, Dworkin's account of how one should arrive at a fair distribution of error is potentially threatening to core doctrines of procedural law, particularly in criminal proceedings. These tensions between Dworkin's account and the law suggest that some procedural entitlements are generated not by the need to distribute the risk of error fairly but by the more basic need to recognize that the parties to litigation are persons, and, moreover, that those procedural entitlements are rights in a strong sense akin to Dworkin's.

2. Equal Concern and Respect

Dworkin builds his account of law and justice on two principles of ethical individualism. The principle of equal importance tells us that "it is important, from an objective point of view, that human lives be successful rather than wasted, and this is equally important . . . for each human life." The principle of special responsibility tells us that "one person has a special responsibility for that success— the person whose life it is."[2] These two principles place abstract but important demands on a liberal political order: The first requires the state to treat every person as "a human being whose dignity fundamentally matters;"[3] the second requires the state to recognize each person's responsibility for making his or her own choices, for defining and pursuing his or her own conception of a successful life.[4] The first is a principle of equality, the second a principle of liberty; in Dworkin's view, they work together to define and constrain the role of the liberal state. In short, as Dworkin often puts it, the state must treat individuals with equal concern and respect.[5]

Dworkin used his conception of equal concern and respect as a standard against which to measure the justice or rightness of substantive law, particularly of the law concerning constitutional rights. The standard ought to apply also, perhaps especially, to procedural law. If there is one practical skill in which lawyers arguably have both absolute and comparative advantage over other citizens, it is not in determining the principles of political morality that should be embodied in substantive law; Dworkin believed that these should be everyone's concern and that they were not sharply distinct from other moral principles. Rather, as Dworkin recognized in the opening paragraphs of "Principle, Policy, Procedure," the lawyer's distinctive practical skill is in procedure. The basic elements of procedural fairness—do not prejudge, hear both parties, allow each party to present

---

[2] Dworkin (2006: 6).

[3] Dworkin (2011: 331).

[4] Dworkin (2011: 336).

[5] The details of Dworkin's presentation of this idea changed over his long career, but its core did not; compare Dworkin (1977: 272-278) with Dworkin (2011: 331-348).

its own case and to challenge the other's, decide according to the evidence and the law—are called principles of *natural justice* because they are obvious and come naturally to properly trained lawyers (whether or not they are obvious to everyone else). Moreover, procedural rules often have a much greater impact than substantive law on the outcome of litigation, and differences in procedure over time or across jurisdictions can often explain patterns in litigation that are nearly invisible from the point of view of substantive law.[6] But Dworkin wrote almost nothing about procedure. "Principle, Policy, Procedure," his one major essay on point, is occasionally cited but rarely analyzed in detail.[7] Perhaps commentators, and Dworkin himself, thought of it as a relatively straightforward application of the principles of equal concern and respect to a topic much less exciting than freedom of expression or euthanasia. But, as I will show, the application is not so straightforward after all.

3. What Is Procedure for?

The purpose of a legal proceeding is to provide a reasoned, final, and binding determination of a dispute about legal rights. The plaintiff says that the defendant breached his contract; the defendant denies it. The prosecution says the accused committed a crime; the accused says he did not. The constitutional litigant says the government violated her constitutional rights; the government says it respected them. A legal procedure does not merely give an answer to the question in dispute—anyone or any procedure could do that; nor does it merely give a good reason to answer the question in one way rather than another—many people could do that too. The legal procedure gives a reasoned answer that is final and enforceable.

There are at least three types of disputes that are resolved through the legal process: disagreements about the law, disagreements about the facts, and disagreements about the application of the law to the facts.[8] The parties may disagree about the content of the applicable law; the court tells them what it is. The parties may disagree about the facts; the court's job is then to decide what the facts are. And, surprisingly often, even if there is no disagreement about the applicable law or the facts, there may be disagreement about the legally correct outcome, particularly if the law in question requires the application of a vague or

---

[6] As emphasized by Stuntz (2011: ch. 1), though Stuntz also recognizes the effect of changes in substantive law.

[7] The major exception is Bone (2010), an important and stimulating analysis of Dworkin's arguments about procedure. More characteristic is Joseph Raz's review of *A Matter of Principle*, which devotes only one sentence to "Principle, Policy, Procedure": Raz (1986).

[8] When a claim succeeds, there are also disagreements about the determination of an appropriate remedy, but those disagreements replicate these three questions at a later stage in the proceedings, since there are often legal standards and facts that are not relevant to liability but are relevant to remedies.

multifaceted standard.[9] The court's task is then to provide an authoritative application of the law to the facts. Much of Dworkin's work is an attempt to explain how judges should answer the first question, to give an account of the Herculean task of determining the content of the applicable law. In contrast, the great bulk of ordinary litigation is about the second question: What are the facts?

Dworkin, like most legal scholars, takes the purpose of procedures for fact-determination to be accuracy.[10] Speaking of accuracy in fact-finding can be misleading because it may suggest a single-valued approach in which the only question is how close the court came to determining the facts as they really were, as if fact-finding was analogous to a problem like measuring an imperfectly known but presumably stable quantity like the gravitational constant. But the purpose of fact-finding in litigation is not to find facts for their own sake but to use the facts found to grant or deny a legal claim. So it is helpful to distinguish between two kinds of error: false positives and false negatives, or Type I and Type II errors. For the purposes of this paper, I take a false positive or Type I error in adjudication to be a factual error in favor of the party having the burden of proof in the litigation: a wrongful conviction, judgment against a defendant who did not in fact commit the wrong alleged by the plaintiff, judgment for a constitutional claimant where the state did not in fact violate the claimant's constitutional rights. I take a false negative or Type II error to be a factual error against the party having the burden of proof: the acquittal of the factually guilty, the dismissal of an action against a tortfeasor or contract-breaker.[11]

The effect of any given rule of procedure and evidence on these two types of error is evidently an empirical question, and one very difficult to assess at that. But it is plausible to suppose that a rule requiring the prosecution or plaintiff to meet a high burden of proof would tend to reduce the likelihood of Type I errors and increase the likelihood of Type II errors, when compared with a rule placing a lower burden of proof on those parties. Similarly, it is plausible to suppose that a rule preventing an accused or defendant from leading a particular kind of probative evidence would tend to increase the likelihood of Type I errors and decrease the likelihood of Type II errors. So any measure of the accuracy of the fact-finding process must be a function of the likelihood of both

---

[9] Consider, for example, the Supreme Court of Canada's approach to determining whether an individual has a "reasonable expectation of privacy" for the purpose of search and seizure law. In cases such as *R v. Tessling*, 2004 SCC 67, and *R v. Patrick*, 2009 SCC 17, there was little disagreement about the facts or the governing legal test but great uncertainty about the outcome.

[10] Dworkin (1986: 72-73).

[11] Type I and Type II errors are, strictly speaking, defined in relation to a null hypothesis that is assumed to be true, usually for the purpose of testing the proposition that it is false. For a presentation designed for legal decision-makers, see *Science Manual for Canadian Judges* (National Judicial Institute, 2013), ch. 2 (online: http://www.nji-inm.ca/nji/inm/nouvelles-news/Manuel_scientifique_Science_Manual.cfm?lang=en&). By analogy, the presumption of innocence means that the null hypothesis of the criminal trial is that the accused is innocent, and placing the burden of proof on the plaintiff means that the null hypothesis of the civil trial is that the defendant is not liable.

types of errors. Moreover, what is of real concern to Dworkin is not the wrong outcome for its own sake but the moral harm caused when a rightful claim is not vindicated or a wrongful claim is accepted.[12] Dworkin recognized that erroneous imposition of liability on civil defendants caused moral harm,[13] but it might be thought that in criminal proceedings he would only be concerned about the moral harm generated by Type I errors, i.e., wrongful convictions. But that was not so: He recognized that both improper acquittals and erroneous dismissals of civil actions caused some moral harm.[14] And it makes sense to recognize that Type II errors generate moral harm. If there was no moral harm generated by incorrect acquittals, one could avoid moral harm entirely in criminal proceedings by not prosecuting anyone. And Dworkin would not have been so concerned about the correct adjudication of civil disputes if he had thought no rights, and therefore no moral harms, were at stake in civil litigation.

So, any set of procedures generates likelihoods of Type I and Type II errors. Comparing different procedures, or considering the desirability of a change in procedures, requires some way of combining these two likelihoods; and, since what is ultimately of concern is not the errors themselves but the moral harms they cause, the method of combining them must take into account the significance of different kinds of moral harms. For example, a 5-percent likelihood of wrongful conviction will probably deserve more weight than a 5-percent likelihood of incorrect acquittal. I will refer to such a combination of the likelihoods of Type I and Type II errors as a *moral loss function*. Its inputs (independent variables) are the likelihoods of error associated with a given set of procedures; its form depends on how those likelihoods are valued; and its output (dependent variable) is a measure of the degree of moral harm generated by the procedures in question. Assuming the form of the function is stable because dependent on a considered assessment of the importance of different types of moral harms, the value of the function depends on the procedures chosen.

Dworkin does not use the mathematical metaphor of a moral loss function. Instead, he speaks of "the design of criminal and civil procedures as a fabric woven from the community's convictions about the relative weight of different forms of moral harms, compared with each other, and against ordinary sacrifices and injuries."[15] The fabric metaphor reminds us that construction of a moral loss function is as much an exercise in political morality as determining the content of substantive law. Nevertheless, the mathematical metaphor is helpful because it reminds us that any change in procedural rules is likely to involve some sort of trade-off between the two types of error and therefore between different moral harms. All references in this paper to the degree of accuracy of the fact-finding

---

[12] Dworkin (1986: 79-80), and see Section 4 below.

[13] Dworkin (1986: 92); Dworkin (2010: 1084-1085). See also Bone (2010: 1021-1022).

[14] See Dworkin (1986: 89) (accepting that an error either way in criminal proceedings causes some moral harm).

[15] Dworkin (1986: 86).

process are to a moral loss function, which is consistent with Dworkin's understanding of procedure, even if he did not express it that way.

The value of the moral loss function matters because legal proceedings determine facts not for their own sake but for the contribution that factual findings make to the reasoned, final, and binding determination of disputes about legal rights. The rights in question are the rights of persons, those whom the state must treat with equal concern and respect. Accordingly, the procedural entitlements of the parties to litigation should in some way connect to the requirements of equal concern and respect. In the next section, I argue that Dworkin's own way of making that connection is inadequate.

4. "Principle, Policy, Procedure"

In "Principle, Policy, Procedure," Dworkin poses the following conundrum. Dworkin holds that in every substantive legal dispute, the party that can point to a correct argument of political morality entitling him or her to judgment has the right to win.[16] The correct argument is founded immediately on the legal rules and principles that are applicable to the dispute, and ultimately on the political value of equal concern and respect that provides the best justification for those rules and principles. But the argument that one party always has the right to win was constructed with reference to the problem of determining the applicable law. When we turn to the problem of fact-determination, the question of who has the right to win seems to be in one sense easy but in another sense impossible to answer. It is easy because the right answer in fact determination is a matter of fact, not of contested questions of political morality: If the prosecution says that the accused shot the victim, and the accused says he did not, then the right answer at trial depends on whether the accused shot the victim. But it is impossible because there is no known procedure that will determine disputed facts with perfect accuracy, i.e., with zero likelihood of both Type I and Type II errors (when the value of the moral loss function would be zero). Regardless of the procedure adopted, and regardless of the success of the Herculean judge in correctly answering questions of law, errors in fact determination—and therefore wrong answers and associated moral harms—are unavoidable.

---

[16] Dworkin (1977: 279-290). The *right answer thesis* is an important and controversial part of Dworkin's argument about the nature of law. Despite what might seem to be moments of equivocation, Dworkin remained strongly committed to it throughout his career, including in his late work: see, for instance, Dworkin (2011: 88ff, 151-152, 377-378). I share the doubts of many commentators about the viability of the right answer thesis, but that is not the subject of this paper. Whether or not it applies to the deeply contested questions of political morality that were so important to Dworkin, it does apply to factual determinations. When a trial court convicts the innocent or acquits the guilty, it has to that extent given the wrong answer to the dispute before it. That is all that is required to generate the conundrum of "Principle, Policy, Procedure."

To resolve this problem, it seems that courts routinely engage in a kind of rough cost-benefit analysis. No one suggests that there is a right to "the most accurate trials possible"[17] because that would, implausibly, require society to devote resources to fact-finding and nothing else until the marginal improvement in accuracy was zero (the moral loss function was minimized). Moreover, procedural rules seem readily to be understood as striking a utilitarian type of balance between the benefits to be achieved by accurate fact-finding and the costs of engaging in that fact-finding.[18] The rule requiring judges to balance probative value and prejudicial effect is a good example. A trial judge should exclude prosecution evidence if the prejudicial effect of that evidence—its anticipated detrimental effect on the trial process, including improper use and undue consumption of time—outweighs its probative value—its anticipated weight if used correctly.[19] When applied to evidence tendered by the prosecution in a criminal case, this exclusionary rule probably increases the likelihood of Type II errors, but this increase is thought to be justified not only by decreases in the likelihood of Type I errors but also by the reduction in the length and complexity of trials and therefore their overall social costs. Other procedural and exclusionary rules might be explained similarly.

But if this picture of procedural law is correct, the picture of the court as a forum of principle is threatened by the utilitarian justification of its procedures. If courts routinely give up on minimizing the moral loss function so as to save society from the expense of the procedures that would do so, then procedure is inconsistent with substance.[20] Hercules may be able to assure the parties that he has the right answer to any disputed questions of political morality that apply to their dispute, but even so he cannot assure them that his procedures for determining their disputed questions of fact will deliver a verdict in favor of the party who in fact has the right to win. And if that party loses because of the application of a procedural rule that is justified by the general interest, then the wrong answer has been delivered and moral harms have been caused so as to promote overall welfare. Moreover, if that is the correct understanding of procedure, then what lawyers usually call rights in procedure are not rights at all, in Dworkin's sense. Must we choose between ensuring "the most accurate trials possible," i.e., minimizing the moral loss function regardless of the cost to other legitimate governmental objectives, and holding that there are no procedural rights?[21]

Dworkin's solution to this conundrum is to apply the two principles of political morality to procedure. He distinguishes between two kinds of harms associated with inaccurate fact-finding in the criminal process: the bare or utilitarian

---

[17] Dworkin (1986: 72).

[18] For a systematic attempt to do this, see Laudan (2006).

[19] For a classic presentation of these principles, see McCormick (1954: 319-320). See also Stewart (2012: 183-192).

[20] Compare Bone (2010: 1014-1015).

[21] Dworkin (1986: 72-73).

harm of being punished and the moral harm of being inadvertently but *wrongly* punished.[22] First, political decisions must treat everyone with equal concern and respect, and in particular may not "deliberately impose on any citizen a much greater risk of moral harm than it imposes on any other." Second, a subsequent political decision applying the principles so chosen must not be "a fresh political decision."[23] Applying the first principle in the procedural context, the legislature should pick a particular level of accuracy in fact-finding, i.e., choose procedures that will generate a particular value for the moral loss function, without any bias "against some independently distinct group."[24] Applying the second principle, a court should not later depart from the chosen level of accuracy for utilitarian reasons. So the parties to litigation then have the following rights: "a right that criminal procedures attach the correct importance to the risk of moral harm," and a right to "procedures consistent with the community's own evaluation of moral harm embedded in the law as a whole."[25] These rights do not, however, require the community "to sacrifice the general welfare altogether" to achieve maximal accuracy in fact-finding. In choosing the appropriate level of accuracy, it is legitimate for the legislature to make political decisions that take both bare harm and moral harm into account, as long as the decision "is equally in or against the antecedent whole interest of each person, [that is] the combination of his or her moral and bare interests."[26]

But Dworkin's solution to the conundrum is not a very powerful argument for the proposition that a litigant's procedural entitlements are rights in Dworkin's own sense because it imposes no particular constraint on the degree of accuracy in fact-finding that the legislature should choose; it insists only that whatever procedural rules are chosen should not be very unequal in their likelihood of generating moral harm and should not be reconsidered on each occasion when they are applied. These constraints can explain why it is wrong to frame someone— a straightforward violation of the second principle[27]—but not why the burden of proof in criminal proceedings should be on the prosecution rather than the defense, or why it is wrong to compel someone to incriminate himself or herself. Indeed, Dworkin adopts a fairly conventional consequentialist understanding of these rules: The requirement that the prosecution prove guilt beyond a reasonable doubt is a way of "pay[ing] a price *in* accuracy to guard against a mistake

---

[22] Dworkin (1986: 80). Dworkin has, of course, no time for the proposition that it might be legally or morally permissible to intentionally convict a particular innocent person: "there is a special injustice in knowingly and falsely claiming that someone has committed a crime:" Dworkin (1986: 79).

[23] Dworkin (1986: 85).

[24] Dworkin (1986: 88).

[25] Dworkin (1986: 89).

[26] Dworkin (1986: 87). The idea of a person's "whole interest" somewhat obscure; Dworkin does not provide an account of how to combine these two different types of interests to arrive at a measure of a person's "whole interest."

[27] Dworkin (1986: 85).

that involves greater moral harm than a mistake in the other direction;" and one consideration supporting the right against self-incrimination is "weighing the scales in favor of the accused, at the cost of accuracy."[28] But all Dworkin appears to require of the legislative process is that it recognize the distinctness of moral harm, not that it value moral harm in a particular way or trade it off against bare harm at a particular rate. He does not seem to mean that the legislature wrongs us all if it chooses an incorrect moral loss function, but that the legislature must construct the moral loss function in a way that is fair to everyone. It would be wrong for the legislature to disregard moral harm altogether, but it is not wrong for the legislature to choose procedures to achieve a certain level of accuracy in adjudication, and so to impose a certain risk of moral harm, as long as everyone is treated equally by the legislature's choice.[29] So there would be no wrong in the legislature's departing from the classical requirement that the prosecution prove guilt beyond a reasonable doubt, in general or in particular cases (e.g., for certain offenses or offense elements, or by requiring the accused to prove a defense). Nor would it be wrong to specify the rules relating to self-incrimination so as to give the police considerable freedom of action in obtaining statements from suspects.[30] For these reasons, one wonders whether Dworkin's account of procedure is a variety of consequentialism, or even utilitarianism.[31]

Moreover, Dworkin's account of procedure is hard to square with certain pervasive features of litigation. As Bone puts it, Dworkin's approach to procedure is "outcome-based,"[32] that is, concerned with accuracy in fact-finding (subject to avoiding moral harm in the form of inaccurate outcomes); yet many rules of civil procedure give the litigants entitlements that seem to have little to do with accuracy. For example, litigants have strongly protected entitlements to participate in their own litigation, but this entitlement is hard to reconcile with the idea that the only thing that matters in procedure is protecting the degree of accuracy chosen by the legislature. To take an example from Bone, the structural features of class action litigation are in some tension with every individual's entitlement to participate in his or her own litigation;[33] but if all the legal system cared about was the accurate adjudication of the kinds of claims that are typically litigated through class actions, this tension would not matter. Analogously, criminal proceedings have a strong aversion to proceeding in the absence of the accused, no matter how strong the case against him or her; in Canada, this aversion is so strong as to have

---

[28] Dworkin (1986: 89).

[29] Dworkin (1986: 87).

[30] See *R v. Singh*, 2007 SCC 48, para. 28, noting the usefulness of a suspect as a source of information and calibrating the constitutional right to silence accordingly.

[31] Compare Raz (1986: 1103); Plaxton (2008: 364-366). In response to Bone, "Procedure, Participation, Rights," Dworkin conceded that in some civil cases "when the best interpretation attributes an entirely instrumental purpose to legislation, a . . . thorough cost-benefit analysis might be appropriate": Dworkin (2010: 1085).

[32] Bone (2010: 1015).

[33] Bone (2010: 1012-1013).

led to a substantial body of case law concerning which parts of the criminal trial may and may not be conducted in the absence of the accused.[34]

To take another of Bone's examples from civil procedure, civil litigants have a surprisingly strong entitlement to pursue claims that are certain to fail.[35] And there are at least two analogous entitlements in criminal procedure. First, the accused always has a right to take his or her case to the jury, not only if the defense case is factually weak but even if, taken at its highest, it discloses no legally viable defenses.[36] It may be tempting to explain this rule as allowing for jury nullification, as indeed it does, but that merely displaces the puzzle. Jury nullification is the intentional acquittal of a person known (or at least proved beyond a reasonable doubt) to be guilty, for reasons extrinsic to the legal process. It is the mirror image of framing a person known to be innocent and should have no place in a legal system dedicated to accuracy in fact-finding and to reducing the moral harm caused by incorrect verdicts.[37]

Second, consider the doctrine of issue estoppel in criminal proceedings. Issue estoppel prevents a party from retrying a factual issue that has been determined against him or her in previous proceedings against the same opposing party. In Canada, issue estoppel applies to the prosecution: the Crown may not lead evidence on a factual issue that was decided in the accused's favor in a previous trial.[38] For example, if the accused was acquitted of an offense, the Crown cannot in a later trial for a different offense allege that he committed that offense, e.g., as similar fact evidence to establish his identity. But Canadian courts are extremely reluctant to apply issue estoppel to accused persons. One might think that a person who has been convicted of a crime and who has exhausted his or her appeals should not be allowed to contest the conviction in subsequent proceedings, perhaps because of issue estoppel, perhaps because the subsequent assertion of innocence would be an abuse of process. Nevertheless, an accused always permitted to assert his or her innocence in subsequent proceedings, as unlikely as it may be that the assertion will succeed. This principle was recently reinforced in *Jesse*, which on its facts provided an ideal opportunity to revisit it.[39] The accused had been convicted of a very serious sexual assault that occurred in 1993. In a subsequent prosecution for a sexual assault on a different complainant in 2005, the Crown sought to lead evidence relating to the 1993 assault as similar fact evidence. The accused consistently denied that he had committed either of these two assaults. In the *voir dire* to determine the admissibility of the evidence concerning

---

[34] See especially *R v. Vezina*, [1986] 1 SCR 2.

[35] Bone (2010: 1014); see also Bone (1992).

[36] *R v. Krieger*, 2006 SCC 47.

[37] For a reflection on the difficulty of eliminating jury nullification from the system of criminal justice, see Berger (2011: 596-603). Stuntz suggests that what we now think of as jury nullification was once a pervasive feature of American criminal justice, owing to what he sees as the salutary vagueness of traditional *mens rea* standards: Stuntz (2011: 260-267, 303-305).

[38] See *R v. Mahalingan*, 2008 SCC 63 at para. 26; see also Stewart (2012: 181-183).

[39] *R v. Jesse*, 2012 SCC 21.

the 1993 assault as similar fact evidence going to his identity as the 2005 assailant, he sought to argue that he had not committed the 1993 assault—that is, to retry the very issue that had been determined against him in the previous trial. The trial judge held that he was estopped from contesting his prior conviction in the *voir dire*.[40] But the Supreme Court of Canada held that this holding was erroneous: neither *res judicata* nor abuse of process could prevent the accused from contesting his conviction in the *voir dire*.[41] Moreover, even if the Crown succeeded in the *voir dire*, neither the trial judge nor the Supreme Court of Canada had any doubt that the accused could, if he wished, continue to deny in the main trial that he had committed the 1993 assault.[42]

Doctrines like the presumption of innocence do not seem to be well explained merely as fair distributions of the risk of moral harm, as other doctrines that attached different values to various kinds of moral harms could also distribute the risk fairly. On the other hand, doctrines concerning the parties' rights to participate in litigation about their own rights do not seem to be well explained by their role in reducing the value of the moral loss function or as fairly trading off increases in moral losses against other social values; from either perspective, they seem perverse. So how might such doctrines be understood?

4. Equal Concern and Respect, Again

Dworkin was right to say that the risk of moral harm should be fairly distributed, but he was mistaken in thinking that developing this thought could provide a complete solution to the conundrum of procedure. He must be right to say that the legislature does not wrong each of us when, having due regard for moral harm and for other demands on public resources, it establishes procedures that do not minimize the moral loss function. But this exercise properly belongs at a second stage of an argument for procedural rights. There is a normatively prior first stage, based on the same liberal principles that animate the concern for fair distribution of risk, that requires persons to have certain rights just because they are persons. Among those rights are certain procedural entitlements that are not justified as part of a mechanism for distributing the risk of moral harm but as procedural rights that everyone has just because they are persons. This first stage is implicit in Dworkin's early summary of his two principles of political morality:

> Government must treat those whom it governs with concern, that is, as human beings who are capable of suffering and frustration, and with

---

[40] She went on to hold that the conviction was some evidence that he had committed the 1993 assault, and that the evidence relating to it was admissible in the main trial.

[41] *Jesse* (n 39) para 59. The trial judge's decision to prevent the accused from contesting his conviction in the *voir dire* was nonetheless upheld as a proper exercise of the trial judge's trial management power: id paras 60-63.

[42] Id. para 21 (summarizing the trial judge's reasons) and para 64.

respect, that is, as human beings who are capable of forming and acting on intelligent conceptions of how their lives should be lived. Government must not only treat people with concern and respect, but with equal concern and respect.[43]

Dworkin moves immediately in the next sentence to speak of the distribution of "goods or opportunities," just as in "Principle, Policy, Procedure," he moves directly from the principle of equal concern and respect to speak of the fair distribution of the risk of moral harm. But the core idea of concern and respect must include some entitlements that everyone is equally entitled to not because they are a fair distribution of something but because everyone gets them simply in virtue of being a person. The point of procedural law is to resolve disputes between persons about their rights, so even before any question of procedural law appropriately distributes something (the likelihood of moral harm generated by various types of errors), there is a question whether procedural law gives the parties certain entitlements just in virtue of being persons. It would be correct to say that such entitlements constrained accuracy in adjudication, but it would not be right to say that these constraints were alien to the process or could readily be given up if doing so might make the process more accurate. Rather, they would be constraints required by the kind of process it is: determining disputes about the rights of persons. And they would be rights in a sense akin to Dworkin's because they would be, if not immune, at least highly resistant to being compromised on grounds of other social values such as overall welfare.

So, are there any such entitlements? Could Dworkin recognize them as requirements of his conception of equal concern and respect? Do they explain some of those pervasive features of procedural law that seem at odds with Dworkin's outcome-based understanding? I suggest that there are at least four such entitlements: the presumption of innocence, the placing of the burden of proof on the plaintiff in civil proceedings, the testimonial core of the privilege against self-incrimination, and a party's entitlement to participate in litigation about his or her rights. Moreover, these entitlements, if not rights in Dworkin's precise sense, are closely akin to Dworkinian rights.

The first two of these entitlements have a common theme: Every criminal prosecution and every civil cause of action is an allegation that a person has done something wrong. Merely being a person whose conduct has effects on the world is not a basis for liability; rather, we are liable for the effects of our wrongful conduct. As Kant put it, among the rights that everyone enjoys merely because he or she is a person is "the quality of being . . . a human being *beyond reproach* . . . since before he performs any act affecting rights he has done no wrong to anyone."[44]

---

[43] Dworkin (1977: 272-273).

[44] Kant (1996: 30). Or, as Ripstein has more recently put it in an account of the law of defamation, since "human beings are responsible agents to whom particular acts can be attributed . . . nobody can ever require you to clear your name" because your reputation in the community can only be rightly determined by your deeds: Ripstein (2013: 4).

So if there is a dispute about whether someone has done something wrong, the procedural starting point must always be that he or she has not. The right to be without reproach would mean little if it could be displaced by a mere allegation of wrongdoing, without proof of the facts that constitute the wrongdoing. And there is always the possibility that without this kind of procedural guarantee, there would be a temptation to allow the state (or the plaintiff) to interfere with the accused's liberty (or the defendant's assets) before liability was established. The presumption of innocence, and the placement of the burden of proof on the plaintiff, are procedural rules that are required only because criminal and civil trials are disputes between persons about rights, not because they are part of an apparatus for fairly distributing the likelihood of inaccuracy.[45] Everyone is equally entitled not to be found liable without proof of wrongdoing.

The core of the privilege against self-incrimination prevents the police or the prosecution from requiring the accused to provide testimonial evidence for use in the proceedings against him.[46] This privilege is closely related to the presumption of innocence and so similarly explained as a right everyone has just in virtue of being a person. A legally innocent person does not have anything to answer for. A person whose guilt has not been determined through the legal process is innocent. Forcing legally innocent persons, including suspects and accused persons, to respond to questions about their activities with a view to establishing their wrongdoing, is therefore inconsistent with the presumption of innocence. It may well be the case that the privilege against self-incrimination helps the guilty, as Bentham thought,[47] or helps the innocent, as Seidmann and Stein have argued.[48] But even if Bentham was right and Seidmann and Stein wrong, and even if their arguments could justify different ways of specifying or spelling out some aspects of the privilege, the testimonial core of the privilege against self-incrimination would survive as an essential adjunct of the right to be presumed innocent.

The right of the litigant to participate meaningfully in the process of determining his or her own rights and liabilities, similarly, cannot be fully explained as part of a complex of rules designed to fairly distribute the risk of error in fact-determination. No doubt the accuracy of fact-determination is generally much better when the people whose conduct is in issue participate in the process; but, as we saw above, the law recognizes procedural entitlements that cannot be plausibly explained this way. Again, I suggest that the entitlement of a litigant to participate in the process is straightforwardly explained by the fact of the litigant's personhood. His or her deeds and the legal consequences to him or her for these deeds are at issue. To determine what those deeds were, whether they were rightful

---

[45] Stewart (2014).

[46] There is considerable controversy about whether and how far the privilege extends beyond forced testimony, e.g., whether it protects the accused against having to produce documents (*U.S. v. Hubbell*, 530 US 27) or from being forced to provide bodily samples (*R v SAB*, 2003 SCC 60). For a recent doctrinal overview, see Choo (2013). I do not attempt to resolve this controversy here.

[47] Bentham (1825: 240-245).

[48] Seidmann and Stein (2000).

or wrongful, and what the consequences for the litigant would be, without the litigant's participation would be to treat the litigant without respect in Dworkin's sense, that is, as someone who has no responsibility for how his or her life goes. A litigant may decide to admit allegations of wrongdoing, and there may be good reasons for that; or a litigant may decide that his or her conception of himself or herself precludes any such admission. The legal process respects those decisions by affording the litigants significant rights of participation. Again, this is not a matter of distributing the likelihood of error across potential litigants, but of recognizing the special responsibility of each actual litigant for his or her fate.

As a criticism of Dworkin, this argument may seem to miss its target. Surely Dworkin would accept that everyone has rights, including procedural rights, that are justified not because they are a fair distribution of something but because they are direct requirements of the principles of equal concern and respect. My argument for the right of a litigant to participate in litigation about his or her own rights might be one that Dworkin could accept; like Dworkin's arguments for a robust right to freedom of expression,[49] that argument is connected to the requirement that government treat each person as a responsible moral agent. And surely Dworkin would reject my suggestion that his account permits the legislature to abandon such core requirements as the presumption of innocence as long as it does so in a way that fairly distributes the risk of moral harm (wrongful convictions and incorrect acquittals). In rejecting that suggestion, Dworkin might say that a fair distribution of the risk of moral harm require "criminal procedures [that] attach the *correct* importance to the risk of moral harm"[50] and that the presumption of innocence is the only doctrine that would do so. Once the correct assessment of moral harm was made, there would be no room to change the moral loss function by, for example, adopting procedures that would shorten trials for the purpose of promoting overall welfare.

I think it is indeed likely that Dworkin would have been very resistant to the idea that the legislature could justly jettison the presumption of innocence or systematically prevent litigants from participating in their own litigation, provided that the risk of moral harm was fairly distributed. But his arguments in "Principle, Policy, Procedure" do not show why because they depend solely on the idea of a fair distribution of moral harm rather than on the idea that some procedural entitlements are direct requirements of the principle of equal concern and respect. In this vein, he explicitly rejects the claim that the avoidance of moral harm—that is, choosing procedures that would minimize the value of the moral loss function—is "lexically prior to all other needs."[51] And his account of the legislative procedure for setting the level of accuracy (choosing a moral loss function) depends solely on considerations about the fair distribution of the risk of moral harm. He requires a "consistent and unbiased," not a correct,

---

[49] See, for example, Dworkin (1996: 195-213).

[50] Dworkin (1986: 89 emphasis added).

[51] Dworkin (1986: 84).

assessment of moral harm; consistent with this approach, his brief reference to the presumption of innocence speaks only of the need to avoid moral harm,[52] not of the relationship between the presumption and the personhood of the accused.

In making these claims, I do not mean to say that Dworkin is wrong to understand some procedural entitlements as a way of fixing the level of accuracy in fact-determination, and therefore of distributing the risk of moral harm, in a way that is fair to all potential litigants. But that kind of entitlement is subsequent to the more basic demands that the fact of each litigant's personhood places on the process. So, for example, while the right to be presumed innocent is not a mechanism for distributing the risk of error, it may be that the requirement of proof beyond a reasonable doubt is part of such a mechanism. To say that the presumption of innocence could be displaced on a low standard, e.g., "reasonable suspicion" or "evidence capable of supporting guilt," would not give it any meaningful substance because such a low standard can probably always be met with the application of sufficient prosecutorial ingenuity. But the choice between more substantial standards, such as clear and convincing evidence, or beyond a reasonable doubt, or to a moral certainty, or to the point of producing "*intime conviction*" in the mind of the fact-finder, might well be influenced by concerns about fair distribution of the risk of moral harm.

Similarly, although the testimonial core of the privilege against self-incrimination is a right that every accused person has, it may be that some of the doctrinal details have to do with distributing risks of error. Consider, for example, the Canadian law relating to one aspect of self-incrimination, the taking of statements from accused persons in detention. The Supreme Court of Canada has repeatedly held that an accused person in detention should have a meaningful choice about whether to make a statement to the police; the court has interpreted both the common law voluntariness rule and the constitutional right to silence in light of this idea.[53] But in specifying the doctrines that give practical effect to this meaningful choice, the court has not hesitated to recognize the empirical reality that the accused, whether guilty or innocent, is often a useful source of information about the crime; the court has therefore been reluctant to place too many procedural obstacles in the path of a police officer who is determined to interrogate the detained accused.[54] My view is that the Supreme Court of Canada, like the Supreme Court of the United States before it, has been insufficiently protective of the detained accused's right to choose to speak, particularly in being too ready to recognize waivers of the right to silence. But that is a judgment that cannot be made solely on the basis of the relationship between the privilege against self-incrimination and the presumption of innocence. The arsenal of interrogation techniques licensed by the Supreme Court of Canada might

---

[52] Dworkin (1986: 89).

[53] *R v. Hebert*, [1990] 2 SCR 151; *Singh* (n 30).

[54] See especially *Singh* (n 30) para 28, but also *R v. Sinclair*, 2010 SCC 35 (detained accused has no right to the presence of counsel during an interrogation).

be objectionable in (at least) two ways. It might create situations in which, contrary to the court's stated view, the detainee does not have a realistic choice about whether to speak. If so, the law could be criticized as inadequate to the right it is supposed to define. Or it might create situations in which detainees frequently give false confessions. If so, the law could be criticized as unfairly distributing the risk of Type I error, especially if it was possible to identify categories of detainees who were more likely to confess falsely. Both kinds of criticism are relevant; but the first is logically prior to the second and does not fully determine the scope of the right in question.

5. Conclusion

If procedural rules routinely compromise accurate fact-determination, then procedure may undermine the substantive rights of the parties to litigation; but it would be fanatical to insist that public resources be devoted to minimizing the moral losses occasioned by errors in fact-determination before being used for any other valid public purpose. Dworkin's solution to this conundrum is to argue that the principles of equal concern and respect require procedural law to fairly distribute the risk of moral harm—the injustice of incorrect verdicts—among potential litigants, which is to say, among all of us. In this paper I have argued that equal concern and respect make more direct demands on the legal process, prior to its demand that the risk of error be distributed fairly. These procedural demands are the rights of parties to litigation because they are prior to and cannot be defeated by appeals to the fairness of the distribution of moral harm, much less but appeals to utilitarian concerns. If this is right, then the argument of "Principle, Policy, Procedure" is not wrong but needs to be supplemented by a consideration of the rights that the parties to litigation have simply in virtue of being persons.

References

Bentham, J. (1825). *A Treatise on Judicial Evidence*. Baldwin, Craddock and Jay.

Berger, B. (2011). "The Abiding Presence of Conscience: Criminal Justice Against the Law and the Modern Constitutional Imagination," *University of Toronto Law Journal* 61:579.

Bone, R. G. (1992). "Rethinking the 'Day in Court' Ideal and Nonparty Preclusion," *New York University Law Review* 67:193.

Bone, R. G. (2010). "Procedure, Participation, Rights," *Boston University Law Review* 90:1011.

Choo, A. T-L. (2013). *The Privilege Against Self-Incrimination and Criminal Justice*. Hart: 2013.

Dworkin, R. (1977). *Taking Rights Seriously*. Cambridge, MA: Harvard University Press.

Dwrokin, R. (1981). "Principle, Policy, Procedure" In *Crime, Proof and Punishment: Essays in Memory of Sir Rupert Cross*, Colin Tapper (ed). Buttterworths: 193.

Dworkin, R. (1986). *A Matter of Principle*. Cambridge, MA: Harvard University Press.

Dworkin, R. (1996). *Freedom's Law*. Cambridge, MA: Harvard University Press.

Dworkin, R. (2000). *Sovereign Virtue*. Cambridge, MA: Harvard University Press.

Dworkin, R. (2010). "Response," *Boston University Law Review* 1059.

Dworkin, R. (2011). *Justice for Hedgehogs*. Cambridge, MA: Harvard University Press.

Kant, I. (1996). *The Metaphysics of Morals*. Mary Gregor (ed. and trans.), Cambridge University Press.

Laudan, L. (2006). *Truth, Error and Criminal Law*. Cambridge University Press.

McCormick, C. T. (1954). *Evidence*. West.

Plaxton, M. (2008). "Arguments of Virtue and Constitutional Criminal Procedure," *University of Toronto Law Journal* 57:355.

Raz, J. (1986). "Dworkin: A New Link in the Chain," *California Law Review* 74:1103.

Ripstein, A. (2013). "Your Own Good Name" (unpublished, December 2013).

Seidmann, D. J. and Stein, A. (2000). "The Right to Silence Helps the Innocent: A Game-Theoretic Analysis of the Fifth Amendment Privilege," *Harvard Law Review* 114:431.

Stewart, H. (2012). "The Law of Evidence and the Protection of Rights." In *Rethinking Criminal Law Theory,* F. Tanguay-Renaud and J. Stribopoulos (eds.). Hart:177.

Stewart, H. (2014). "The Right to be Presumed Innocent," *Criminal Law and Philosophy* 8:407.

Stuntz, W. (2011). *The Collapse of American Criminal Justice*. Cambridge, MA: Harvard University Press.

INDEX

Figures are indicated by "f" following the page number. Dworkin's writings are by title; all other titles are under the names of the authors.